JUVENILE DELINQUENCY

JUVENILE DELINQUENCY

Mainstream and Crosscurrents

SECOND EDITION

John Randolph Fuller
University of West Georgia

Oxford   New York
OXFORD UNIVERSITY PRESS

Oxford University Press publishes works that further Oxford University's objective of excellence in research, scholarship, and education.

Oxford   New York
Auckland   Cape Town   Dar es Salaam   Hong Kong   Karachi
Kuala Lumpur   Madrid   Melbourne   Mexico City   Nairobi
New Delhi   Shanghai   Taipei   Toronto

With offices in
Argentina   Austria   Brazil   Chile   Czech Republic   France   Greece
Guatemala   Hungary   Italy   Japan   Poland   Portugal   Singapore
South Korea   Switzerland   Thailand   Turkey   Ukraine   Vietnam

For titles covered by Section 112 of the US Higher Education Opportunity Act, please visit www.oup.com/us/he for the latest information about pricing and alternate formats.

Published by Oxford University Press
198 Madison Avenue, New York, New York 10016
http://www.oup.com

Library of Congress Cataloging-in-Publication Data

Fuller, John R.
    Juvenile delinquency : mainstream and crosscurrents / by John Randolph Fuller.—2nd ed.
        pages cm.
    ISBN 978-0-19-985974-0 (alk. paper)
    1. Juvenile delinquency.   2. Juvenile justice, Administration of.   I. Title.
    HV9069.F85 2013
    364.36—dc23
                                    2012018456

9 8 7 6 5 4 3 2 1

Printed in the United States of America

on acid-free paper.

The book is dedicated to the memory of my parents

Clark B. Fuller
Carol J. Fuller

And to my siblings

Thomas
Susan
Bonnie
Randy

I am happy to say there is not a juvenile delinquent in the family.

(Unless, of course, if you count who Bonnie married.)

Brief Table of Contents

Contents

PART III Delinquency in Society

CHAPTER 7 〉 **Female Delinquency** *215*

CHAPTER 8 〉 **The Family and Delinquency** *247*

PART IV Juvenile Justice System and Cultural Comparisons

Preface

Who is responsible for a child's actions? If the child is intelligent, kind, creative, talented, or industrious, then there is a long line of adults ready to own up to having a hand in the child's development, including parents, teachers, coaches, religious leaders, friends, relatives, and siblings. And this is likely true. As the saying goes, "It takes a village to raise a child."

But what about the "bad kids"? Who claims the responsibility for a child who has broken the law? Often, too often maybe, the child bears the responsibility alone. If the offense is serious enough, or even heinous, the legal system may treat a youth as an adult. If the offense is less serious, then the youth, who may be a child or an adolescent, is treated as a juvenile delinquent. It might take a village to raise a child, but who raises a juvenile delinquent?

The current attitude toward delinquency is both harsh and sympathetic, often depending on the crime rate and the political climate. The very use of the word "delinquent" reflects this. Its usage to describe lawbreaking youths was coined early in the 20th century, a time of vigorous social reform.

The *Oxford English Dictionary* defines delinquency as "Failing in, or neglectful of, a duty or obligation... guilty of a misdeed or offense." This is an interesting way to describe youths who break the law. Why didn't the founders of the juvenile court simply call wayward youths "juvenile criminals" or "juvenile offenders?" Instead, youths who broke the law got their own designation of "delinquent." This isn't the same as "criminal," which has far more serious connotations. "Criminal" is "having the nature of a grave offense," and a "crime" is "an act punishable by law." Why did lawbreaking youths get a much more lenient term than lawbreaking adults?

This discussion is at the heart of the study of juvenile delinquency. That is, youths who stray out of society's legal boundaries, whether they participate in something as minor as spray painting graffiti or as heinous as homicide, are considered to be less morally responsible than adults. In the process of growing and learning, young people make mistakes. They aren't considered to have the life experience to know the consequences of their behaviors as well as an adult. A young child who deliberately touches a hot stove will get far more sympathy (and probably a lecture from mom or dad) than an adult, who will get little or none at all.

In our society, life experience is key. Another issue is control. Youths aren't allowed much control in our society, and often for good reason: they have little life experience with which to make wise decisions. Adults have the task of controlling children's experiences and environments in the way that will benefit the children most. Unfortunately, adults sometimes fail in this responsibility and not only neglect youths, but also victimize them, using the naïveté of youngsters to their own advantage. This is when the state steps in.

The purpose of this book is to explore the nature of delinquency, as well as the closely related issue of youth victimization. The text does this in two ways. First, the mainstream approach helps the student understand what issues are currently thought to be at the basis of juvenile delinquency, as well as the mechanisms society has created to deal with delinquency. Second, the crosscurrents approach takes an analytical point of view of what we currently believe to be true of juvenile delinquency and how society should deal with it.

Juvenile Delinquency: Mainstream and Crosscurrents is intended to give students a fresh look at the behavior of young people and why that behavior is classified as delinquent when it runs afoul of the law or simply what society believes is acceptable for a youth.

Outline of the Book

Part One defines what a juvenile delinquent is and how the definition was developed. Chapter 1 explores how we define and measure juvenile delinquency. Chapter 2 discusses social control and how we apply it to youths. Social phenomena must be measured in order to be understood. In Part Two, we'll turn to theories of juvenile delinquency, including ideas about what makes youths break the law. Chapter 3 examines the theoretical foundations of crime and delinquency, while Chapters 4, 5, and 6 delve into specific theories, including biological, psychological, sociological, as well as social reaction and conflict theories.

Part Three analyzes the place of delinquency in society. Chapter 7 discusses delinquency in girls, while Chapters 8 and 9 look at delinquency within the family and schools. Chapter 10 examines the role youth gangs play in juvenile delinquency. Chapter 11 looks at the contribution of drugs to delinquency.

Part Four examines the juvenile justice system, with coverage of the roles of the police, the juvenile court, and juvenile corrections in Chapters 12, 13, and 14. Chapter 15 is a look at the legal control of youths in other nations and how their systems compare with the United States.

New to This Edition

- » Chapter 11, on substance abuse, is completely new, and covers the problems associated with drugs and alcohol and their effects on youths. This chapter is particularly concerned with the types of drugs used by teens and children, as well as prevention and treatment issues.

- » "Focus on Diversity" is a new feature that highlights issues affecting juvenile delinquency and society's response.

- » Review questions have been added to all figures and tables, as well as at the end of each major section.

- » Learning objectives have been integrated throughout each chapter at major headings and are keyed to the summary.

- » "Programs for Children" is completely updated, and now highlights new and innovative programs that have been introduced to deal with juvenile justice and related social welfare issues. New programs include those from the federal, public, local, and private spheres.

- » "Crosscurrents" features present unusual, alternative, or provocative ideas and require students to think critically about juvenile justice issues.

Acknowledgments

Many people have contributed to the success of this book. I would first like to thank the following reviewers, who made many wonderful and substantive suggestions for improving the scope and focus of the text: Kathryn A. Branch, University of Tampa; Hogan N. Bui, University of Tennessee; Shaheen Chowdhury, College of DuPage; Theodore Darden, College of DuPage; Doris L. Edmonds, Norfolk State University; Jean Surratt Humphreys, Dallas Baptist

University; Lisa A. Kort-Butler, University of Nebraska–Lincoln; Leona Lee, John Jay College of Criminal Justice; Eric Madfis, Northeastern University; J. Mitchell Miller, University of Texas–San Antonio; Michael F. Raymond, NHTI–Concord's Community College; Caroletta Shuler, Claflin University; Rachel E. Stein, West Virginia University; Rebecca A. Stevens, University of Akron; Richard Tardanico, Florida International University; and Martine Wehr, Saddleback College. Any remaining shortcomings should be attributed to me alone.

Several other individuals have greatly assisted me in the writing of this text. At Oxford University Press I am indebted to Sarah Calabi, John Challice, Frank Mortimer, Richard Beck, and Tierra Morgan. They have been instrumental in helping redesign this text to make it more responsive to the needs of professors and students. My colleagues at the University of West Georgia have been generous with their advice and in letting me borrow books from their shelves. I hope I have returned them all. Specifically, I acknowledge Jane McCandless, Catherine Jenks, David Jenks, Mike Johnson, Richard Lemke, Kelly Christopher, and Laura Lutgen.

The person most responsible for this text, however, is Amy Hembree. She is my first editor, constant critic, best friend, brightest inspiration, and loving wife. Her contributions to this book cannot be overstated.

About the Author

John Randolph Fuller has been a professor at the University of West Georgia for over 30 years. He also serves as the university faculty ombudsman and helps resolve conflicts that arise among faculty, administrators, and staff.

Dr. Fuller brings both an applied and a theoretical background to his scholarship. He served as a probation and parole officer for the Florida Probation and Parole Commission in Broward County, Florida, where he managed a caseload of more than 100 felons. In addition, he served as a criminal justice planner for the Palm Beach Metropolitan Criminal Justice Planning Unit. In this capacity, he worked with every criminal justice agency in a three-county area, writing and supervising grants for the Law Enforcement Assistance Administration.

Dr. Fuller has received awards for both his scholarship and his teaching. The Textbook and Academic Authors Association bestowed on him its prestigious TEXTY Award for his book *Criminal Justice: Mainstream and Crosscurrents*. Additionally, he was given the first "Distinguished Scholar Award" by the University of West Georgia College of Arts and Sciences. He has also published *Think Criminology*, an introductory text based on a critical-thinking perspective.

In 2006, the Institute of Higher Education and the Center for Teaching and Learning at the University of Georgia named Dr. Fuller a Governor's Teaching Fellow. Additionally, he was chosen as Honors Professor of the Year, 2000–2001, by the students of the University of West Georgia's Honors College.

Recognized as an accomplished scholar, teacher, adviser, and mentor, Dr. Fuller is committed to the ideals of fairness and justice for all for victims, offenders, and practitioners in the juvenile and criminal justice systems.

In addition to reading widely, Dr. Fuller enjoys playing golf and painting.

JUVENILE DELINQUENCY

Juvenile Delinquency:
Definitions, History, and Measurement

What Is a Juvenile Delinquent?

Making the transition from child to adult is difficult in any society. It involves a change in status, rights, responsibilities, and self-concept. It isn't done overnight, and it isn't done easily. The road from childhood to adulthood passes through the exciting and dangerous landscape of **adolescence**, a relatively short transition of a few years that can completely alter a young person's social and psychological outlook. The fact that this journey is often precarious and that many young people lose their way makes the study of **juvenile delinquency** necessary.

The journey from childhood to adulthood not only varies across cultures, but is also different from one **generation** to the next.[1] A single body of knowledge about growing up that could be applied to all youths at all times throughout the world would be useful in predicting trends and controlling antisocial behavior. However, societies are different, and even within societies there are such vast variations that no single body of knowledge can comprehensively explain and control the behavior of young people. Each society has its own set of problems, ranging from the trivial to the deadly, yet the problems of gaining acceptance and identity are present in each and must be solved in different ways.[2]

The problems of growing up also differ across time. Each generation faces new problems and obstacles. Although many issues are similar, the resources to deal with these issues and the pressures and temptations to deviate can be quite different. When parents say, "My dad wouldn't let me have a car until I was 21, and I learned to deal with it and so will you," they fail to realize that this universal issue affects youths of different generations in different ways. How far is it from home to school? Where do their friends live? Is public transportation available? Does the youth need a car to get to a job, a sports practice, a religious study group, or a probation officer? Modern society makes demands on youths that might not have been as acute in the parent's younger years, and it can be difficult for older generations to appreciate the stresses under which young people operate.

This struggle between generations is nothing new. The conditions have changed, and one might argue that the consequences are more serious because, in some places, the public arena has become more dangerous. However, the conflict between youngsters and their elders has been a consistent feature of society for many generations. Some issues might have changed in their details, but the central problem remains: How does one pass from the status of child to adult? The

Growing up isn't an event but a process, and each generation faces different challenges. Often, one of these is learning to drive. Here, a driver-education teacher speaks with two teen students about safety. Car accidents are the leading cause of death for American teenagers.

answer to this question is "slowly." Growing up isn't an event, but a process. It involves trial and error, fights and disagreements, mistakes and great accomplishments, but most of all it involves gaining trust and respect. Sometimes the passage is never completed, and the youth ends up without the respect of parents and teachers, working at a low-wage job with no future, in prison, or dead. To understand why, we must understand how the concept of childhood is developed and defined and also what the term *delinquency* means in the juvenile justice system.

The Social Construction of Childhood

Sociologists talk about social status as being either achieved or ascribed. By this, they mean that people either earn their place in society, or it's given to them. For instance, one is either male or female, and social status is ascribed accordingly. There is little one can do about this ascribed status, as people are assumed to have certain characteristics, orientations, or abilities based on **sex**. Often these assumptions are wrong, but society will still act on the ascribed status. In contrast, achieved statuses are given according to accomplishment. For example, wealth, physical fitness, grade-point average, or number of children are subject to the individual's intentional behavior.

Because we consider ascribed statuses as basically uncontrollable, we believe we shouldn't discriminate against people because of their race, sex, or religion. However, achieved characteristics such as test scores and grade-point averages are used to make decisions about what university a student can attend; education and training decide what occupation one can pursue; and the speed of a pitcher's fastball determines whether he can pitch for the New York Yankees. Therefore, what people do seems like a perfectly valid reason to allocate rewards and punishments.

But what about age? Is age an achieved or ascribed status? It's certainly something that can't be controlled. As much as we would like to look older or younger depending on whether we are an adolescent trying to buy beer or a middle-aged actor trying to win a part in a movie, we are pretty much stuck with our age. Therefore, we can safely say that age is an ascribed status. The trouble is, however, that society discriminates according to age. Americans can't vote until age 18, drink alcohol until age 21, become president until age 35, or receive Social Security until age 62. Certain 16-year-olds might be better educated about political matters and be exactly the type of informed voters we would want to trust the future of the country to, but they aren't allowed to cast a ballot. Some 60-year-olds might routinely drink too much beer and pose a threat to society when they drive, but we still allow them to buy alcohol. Discrimination according to age is socially constructed. So, in some ways, some aspects of age constitute an achieved status. We agree through the legislative process to accord certain rights and privileges based on age because we believe that there are appropriate points to set restrictions based on developmental maturity.

Several criteria are used by various institutions and agencies, as well as families and schools, as a basis for treating youths differently than adults. It's useful to consider how and why this differential treatment is justified:

» **Physical development.** Children don't spring into the world fully developed. They start out as about 7 pounds of dependent and needy darlings and develop into adults with their own needs, wants, and ideas. As children grow, they are able to perform increasingly complicated tasks, lift more weight, and better defend themselves from harm. As they increase in size, strength, and knowledge, they receive more opportunities. For instance, some amusement parks post signs by the particularly exciting rides stating that customers must be a certain height to ride. This is a clear case of discrimination based on physical maturity. For safety reasons, based on the engineering of the ride, those who don't measure up to the standard aren't allowed to participate. Although age-graded divisions are used often (schools are the best example), there aren't that many divisions based on height. Occasionally, youth football leagues will compose teams based on weight to give smaller youths an opportunity to play against those of their own size. This difference in physical maturity is important when considering the separation of juveniles from adults in the penal system. Larger adults could take advantage of smaller, weaker juveniles. Therefore, a separate corrections system has been designed to keep youths from the clutches of predatory adults.[3]

» **Intellectual development.** From the earliest age, children are tracked into classes and programs based on their intellectual capacities. Some children are fast-tracked to allow them to master material without having to wait for the teacher to explain concepts to other children who don't grasp new concepts as quickly. Conversely, other children are placed in special classes or schools that present the material at a much slower rate than in traditional classes. Each of these strategies is designed to group children based on intellectual ability.[4] Although age is a rough indicator of intelligence, a percentage of youths at either end of the continuum require differential experiences if they're to progress. Similarly, the juvenile justice system takes extra precautions to protect juveniles because they don't have the knowledge or maturity to comprehend what is happening to them in court.[5] Although it could be argued that adults also don't understand the workings of the criminal justice system and therefore need attorneys, the problem is more acute with juveniles, because, not only do they not understand the system, but they also often have little idea that they did anything wrong.

» **Emotional development.** Individuals require adequate time to develop emotional maturity. Youths, especially adolescents, constantly struggle to deal with life's challenges and to find their emotional equilibrium. This struggle is complicated by biological changes resulting from the onset of puberty. Children aren't permitted to engage in a wide variety of functions because they lack the emotional maturity to make good decisions.[6] A good example of this is driving laws. Although 14-year-olds might have excellent hand-eye coordination and can score astronomically high on video games, they lack the emotional maturity to make responsible decisions while driving an automobile. Young people are more likely to drive at excessive speeds, take risks, and not anticipate what other drivers may do. Although they might make better race-car drivers than the average 70-year-old, motorists would much rather deal with the slow-driving, but more predictable, elderly motorist than with the adventurous adolescent.

Is it really fair to discriminate against individuals based on age? We certainly don't make such legal decisions based on gender or race. The best answer to this question is yes, under certain circumstances. The intent isn't to punish children, but to protect them from the risks and dangers of the adult world, both for their own sakes and the protection of society.

Defining the Terms

It's time to develop a couple of concrete definitions to guide our understanding of the legal and social implications of juvenile delinquency. The word **juvenile** refers to an age-related status that has legal ramifications. *Juvenile* is applied to those who aren't yet adults. In the United States, we generally draw this line at age 18. This is the age at which one can vote; however, for other privileges, such as drinking alcohol, the line is drawn at age 21. Some credit card companies won't extend unsecured credit until the individual is 25.

Although this distinction might appear to be a moving target, we will use the legal definition of a juvenile as being someone under age 18. We select this age because, for the most part, this is where the juvenile justice system has decided it should be drawn. In most states, those under 18 are processed by the juvenile justice system, and those over 18 are processed by the criminal justice system. Although there are many exceptions to this rule, including juvenile waiver, which we discuss in Chapter 14, it's a useful distinction for our discussions.

A **juvenile delinquent** is a juvenile who has broken the law. However, we must be careful when we employ this term because it has a specific meaning in the juvenile justice system. When the court determines that a youth has violated a law, the youth isn't "found guilty," but rather is "adjudicated a delinquent." This definition is more restrictive than that used in general conversation and is therefore a bit misleading. For our purposes, we will use a less restrictive meaning of the term *delinquent* to include those who have broken the law but might not have been caught and adjudicated.

The study of delinquency involves more than identifying and controlling those who break the law. Within the field are youths with other issues that must be considered. We will deal with these complexities in greater detail later, but they are worth mentioning now so the reader can put the following chapters in context. In addition to youths who cause trouble by breaking the law, the study of delinquency includes youths as victims. The term *victim* is used here in an inclusive sense. Youths aren't simply victims of other youths who might beat them up or steal their property. They are also victims of the various entities that are supposed to be working on their behalf. Parents, teachers, scoutmasters, clergy, and babysitters have victimized children. Schools that leave children behind, communities that don't provide safe parks and programs, states that fail to provide adequate health care for children in poverty all in some way victimize youths who are largely powerless to control their own fate.

Delinquency also includes youths who violate rules that pertain only to youths and wouldn't be considered an offense if committed by an adult. These **status offenses** include drinking under age, running away from home, truancy, and being **incorrigible**. There are no corresponding rules for adults, and youths who engage in these actions can find themselves before a judge. Finally, the study of delinquency includes children who are neglected, **dependent**, physically or psychologically abused, or caught between warring parents. The juvenile justice system looks out for the welfare of youths regardless of whether they are perpetrators or victims. The juvenile delinquency field considers a wide range of problems encountered by youths and offers a variety of theories, programs, and options.

Transition or Rebellion

One doesn't obtain adulthood overnight. It isn't a status that can be easily granted with a ceremony. Adulthood is earned through accomplishments, financial independence, and the exhibiting of mature judgment. It's a process that requires years and happens gradually without clear indicators. It requires some false starts, partial victories, and practice behavior. There is tremendous pressure from peers, family, and self to demonstrate the attainment of adulthood. To do this, juveniles occasionally engage in **deviant** behaviors. These behaviors can range from smoking tobacco, using illicit drugs, experimenting with sexuality, and skipping school to more dangerous actions, such as robbing liquor stores, selling drugs, engaging in prostitution, or joining a gang.

It would be inaccurate to argue that all delinquency is the direct result of children attempting to shortcut the route to adulthood, but there is ample evidence that this issue is at least a contributing factor in a great deal of youthful indiscretion. When considering the types of youths who wind up in trouble with the law, some social and psychological themes can be linked to their attempts to display adulthood:

>> **Autonomy from adult control.** Young people desire to depart from the control of their parents as soon as possible. They see their peers as their new primary group and are eager to adopt the norms and values of adolescents, while struggling to be free from the traditional sources of **social control**, such as the family and religion.[7] For many, this is a necessary, if not exactly desirable, process. The power over the child that is lost by the parents is often found by the clique, the group, or the gang. Young people have an intense desire to fit in somewhere and will go to great lengths to be accepted by their peers. Shoplifting, drug use, and gang violence are often nothing more youths' adaptations to their desire to be free of parental influence. What could be more liberating to the middle-class honor student than drinking alcohol or having sex? Although these activities are considered status offenses, they serve to demonstrate to parents and authorities that a certain level of autonomy has been obtained. For example, there is a generations-old struggle between parents and children in deciding the limits of a curfew. The controversy has gotten so beyond the control of parents that many communities have had to enact curfew laws that place the state in the role of parent to ensure that children return home at a reasonable time.[8]

>> **Displays of masculinity.** Many young men (and sometimes young women) believe they must display hypermasculine qualities to be taken seriously as emerging adults. These qualities can be observed in the aggressive demeanor that some youths employ on the street to keep from feeling or being disrespected. This demeanor has been deemed is called the "code of the street" by sociologist Elijah Anderson.[9] Under this code, a male youth must challenge those who look at him too intensely and be willing to fight to save his honor, even when no words have been exchanged or aggressive behavior exhibited. In other contexts, young men act aggressively toward females as a way of getting attention or get large tattoos as evidence of their ability to withstand pain. The list of ways in which young men display their masculinity can go on and on, but the important point is that these displays are often associated with unlawful behavior.

>> **Female adaptations.** The way that young people construct their identities varies greatly according to a number of factors, including gender. For example, some observers contend that promiscuity is a way for some girls to assert control over their bodies and lives, as well as demonstrate rebellion against parents and equality with young men.[10]

>> **Economic independence.** It can be embarrassing and even humiliating to have to ask parents for money. Many families have little or no money for

Children and teenagers often believe they must display hypermasculine qualities to be taken seriously as emerging adults.

the discretionary spending habits of their teenagers. Yet the economy is geared toward wringing every last dollar out of those who have the least to spend. The costs of clothes, shoes, cars, dating, and fast food can quickly exhaust the savings of teenagers working entry-level jobs. This peer pressure to spend lavishly is evidence of Thorstein Veblen's sociological idea of "conspicuous consumption."[11] It takes little imagination to see how this temptation to acquire beyond one's actual needs can inspire deviant behavior. Shoplifting is epidemic among some adolescents, and theft from automobiles, homes, and businesses is how some youths afford to keep pace with their peers.

》 **Willingness to take risks.** Finally, the willingness to take risks is ever-present in youth culture. We need only to look at the extreme sports that some youths engage in to see how status is allocated to those who perform feats of daring that have little utility other than showing the youth isn't afraid of injury or death. One wonders how the first guy to ride his skateboard on a metal railing came up with the idea and might be flabbergasted that kids continue to try this stunt after so many painful failures have been recorded and shown repeatedly on television and the Internet. Adults question why their children would attempt such feats when the result is broken ankles, wrists, legs, skulls, and worse.

This list of themes isn't exhaustive, merely illustrative. Other themes apply, and certainly some could also be attributed to adult offenders. These themes are presented here, however, as a method of alerting the reader to the problems of dealing with young people who don't always act in their own best interests. Juvenile delinquents are seldom rational beings who calculate the consequences

Among youths, status is often allocated to those who perform feats of daring that show the youth isn't afraid of injury or death. Here, a young man practices the extreme sport of parkour.

of their actions against the possible benefits. The juvenile justice system is charged with handling these often irrational youths. To make matters worse, the system must do this without sufficient resources or, all too often, supportive parents. Let's begin by looking at the state's legal authority to deal with the problems of delinquency.

Parens Patriae and the Law

The concept of ***parens patriae*** can be traced to medieval England, where, under the auspices of the chancery court, the state could care for and protect a child in place of the parent. This concern for children's welfare was primarily directed at the upper class, which had complicated issues of position and property to be resolved. The chancery courts weren't concerned with children's lawbreaking, which was handled in the same manner as adults', but rather with protecting the economic interests of wealthy children so that they weren't victimized by greedy relatives and advisers. The concept of *parens patriae* provided the legal foundation for the state to intervene in the lives of families for the protection of children and gradually grew to concerns other than financial ones. Today, the courts rule on a wide range of issues dealing with children's welfare.[12] (See Case in Point.)

The US justice system extended *parens patriae* to deal with juveniles of more modest means for two primary reasons. Not all parents adequately controlled their children, and the state needed to remove some youths from their homes to preserve community order. A second reason the state intervened was to protect children from abusive and neglectful parents. Although the idea that parents are

1.1 CASE IN POINT

THE CASE

Commonwealth v. Fisher (1905)

THE POINT

This case, which affirmed the philosophy of *parens patriae*, was used against similar challenges to the state's power to act as a parent until the 1960s.

Frank Fisher, age 14, was indicted for larceny and pleaded not guilty. The juvenile court committed Fisher to a house of refuge. Fisher appealed, contending that the law was unconstitutional because he wasn't taken to court with due process; he was denied a jury trial; the court was an unconstitutional body and without jurisdiction; similar offenses received different punishments according to the offender's age; and the law contained more than one subject.

The Pennsylvania Supreme Court affirmed the lower court's decision, holding that that law's purpose wasn't to punish children but to protect them. The protections that applied to adults in criminal proceedings didn't apply to informal juvenile proceedings because the state's intent was to act as a parent in preventing the child from further lawbreaking and possibly becoming an adult offender.

responsible for their children still resonates, it's long been observed that some families are so dysfunctional that youths must be removed from their homes to keep them safe. (Unfortunately, the state often doesn't have viable substitutes for the home, and children go to institutions that do little to ensure their welfare and are sometimes so deleterious to their safety and development that leaving them with abusive parents looks like a good idea.) The courts also intervened in family affairs by holding fathers responsible for the offenses their children committed. Today, states have juvenile and family courts that handle a wide range of problems and deal with children and families in an attempt to provide systematic and comprehensive solutions to delinquency, abuse, abandonment, child support, and divorce.[13]

Adolescents and Juvenile Delinquency

Delinquency isn't a new problem. However, in the United States, particularly in the late 20th and early 21st centuries, the problem seems particularly acute. The transition to adulthood can be difficult for both parents and children. We can use the sociological concept of the *generation*, that is, the total number of people born and living at about the same time, as a tool to better understand why the age range of 13 to 19 can be so problematic. Two aspects must be considered separately when considering the idea of generation.

» Adolescence is a period in the life course. Everyone is allocated one lifetime, and, as we pass through the life course, certain events, pressures, opportunities, and occurrences affect everyone and represent a shared experience. Parents talk about their children going through the "terrible twos," where they first began to challenge authority and develop a sense of self. This is a predictable stage, and it's necessary for the healthy development of the child's self-concept. The onset of puberty can bring a different set of predictable issues. Leaving home for the first time represents another life event that almost everyone must face. Adults must negotiate their adolescent years, and much of what happens in that important time are universal experiences shared by parents, grandparents, and eventually by their own children. Although each youth might think his or her problems are unique, youths learn later when they have children of their own that the first date, first sexual experience, and first run-in with the law are events common to virtually everyone.

» A generation is a cohort. Although each generation must endure adolescent years, each does so at a different time in history, which can make a big difference. The sociologist C. Wright Mills encourages students to develop an appreciation for the difference between public issues and personal troubles. Mills argues that individuals must understand how they live out their lives within a historical context that exerts unique social forces on their generation. Although people have a great deal of control over their life decisions, political, economic, and social forces affect people based on where they are in their life course. This **cohort** aspect of generations causes much tension between parents and children. Parents believe that their children's adolescent years are similar to their own and want to use their acquired wisdom to help make their children's situation safer and more productive. Children, on the other hand, see the historical forces affecting their generation as distinctly different from what their parents experienced and feel frustrated by their parents' lack of understanding. Of course, what makes this tension particularly acute is that adolescents are struggling for more control and responsibility over their affairs, while parents are reluctant to let go too soon.

Unraveling the differences between the relative effects of life-course events and historical-cohort events in one's particular situation is difficult. Consequently, if we are to appreciate what childhood means for today's youngsters, we must use what C. Wright Mills calls **sociological imagination** to take ourselves out of our own social location and view young people from a more open and objective paradigm.[14]

Each generation goes through adolescence at a different time in history, which can greatly affect how each develops. These boys stand before a booking officer at a New York City police station in July 1954. They were among about 90 picked up by police in a "drive" on juvenile delinquents and "generally undesirable characters" in the Times Square area. Their similar attire, including their identical shirts, marks them as possible members of a gang.

Life-course events that almost every teenager confronts include wresting control of his or her affairs from parents. This includes determining what classes to take in school, whether to work part-time, whom to date, dealing with money, dealing with transportation issues by borrowing the family car or owning an automobile, and deciding what religion to practice or whether to follow a religion at all. Teenagers and parents resolve these issues to varying degrees depending on the strength of their bond, the trust the teenager has been able to build, and, sometimes, the family's experience with older siblings who previously negotiated these issues.

Cohort events are unique to each generation. The "Greatest Generation" that came of age during the Great Depression of the 1930s and fought in World War II had a different outlook on life than did the baby boom generation that came of age in the 1960s with the civil rights movement, war in Vietnam, and the assassinations of Martin Luther King Jr. and the Kennedy brothers. Although it's easy to look back and identify the historical events that shaped a generation, it's more difficult to determine which events and historical forces shape today's teenagers. More particularly, how are these events going to affect the chances of today's teenagers in getting involved in the juvenile and criminal justice systems? What is offered next is speculation. Students should revisit this exercise and add to or delete from this list depending on how they see history unfolding.

» **War.** The threat of continued international terrorism and the commitments we have made to many nations will likely require the continued use of troops overseas for the foreseeable future. For adolescents today, this could mean the possibility of military service. It will mean that tax money for social services that might benefit them will be hard to wrest from military demands, and it will mean the economy will remain in a state of flux. This could affect the juvenile and criminal justice systems as more resources are devoted to security at home and abroad.[15]

» **Technology.** The economic engine of the United States is now greatly based on technology. As consumers, adolescents will have more and cheaper computers, video games, and electronic gadgets, but it will also mean that they will need to continually refine their skills to accommodate technological change. Finding a high-paying, stable job will continue to be problematic, and workers will need to continually retool to remain competitive. Also, technology has already changed many of the ways that offenses are committed and the ways in which the criminal justice system responds.

» **Economic shifts.** The old saying "The rich get richer and the poor get poorer" is all too true, and we can speculate that it will continue to be true. Although political parties will debate which has the best prescription for what ails the economy, it's likely that adolescents will be among the last to experience any improvement. Those who have entry-level jobs will continue to find themselves struggling to make ends meet. The US health-care system is among the best of the industrialized nations for the wealthy, but among the worst for the impoverished. Over 40 million citizens, about a quarter of them children, lack health insurance.[16] One need not have much imagination to speculate how a continued weak economy will affect young people and their likelihood to break the law.

Such issues will certainly affect American teenagers to some degree. These historical circumstances aren't the worst any generation has had to face, but they do promise to be challenging and will require adjustments by government, schools, parents, and adolescents themselves. For those interested in delinquency and the welfare of children and families, these concerns promise to challenge our ability to suggest new and innovative ways to prevent crime and reduce the suffering of victims.

Questions

1. Is there an adult version of the status offense?
2. What is achieved social status? Ascribed social status?
3. What social and psychological themes are linked to juveniles' attempts to display adulthood?
4. What is *parens patriae*?

Measuring Delinquency

Learning Objective 4.

Describe the dark figure of crime.

How do we know how much crime there is in our communities? Do all communities define and measure crime in the same way? Is delinquency measured in the same way as adult offenses? These and other stubborn questions have long concerned those who try to accurately assess the amount of crime in society. Despite a falling crime rate, the media continue to present stories about crime epidemics and juveniles who appear to be committing more serious offenses at younger ages.[17]

Crime is certainly a major social problem, but getting a handle on its actual prevalence (how many people it affects) and seriousness is an ongoing challenge.[18] Scholars and researchers have developed numerous techniques to try to accurately measure the incidence and effects of crime and delinquency. In this section, we will review some of the major issues in assessing the level of crime and explain the strengths and shortcomings of some of the popular measurement tools.

Defining Crime and Delinquency

Not all undesirable behaviors are offenses of the criminal law. Many transgressions of manners, etiquette, good taste, and civil demeanor might be offensive to some of us and yet aren't considered criminal offenses. The reason is that criminal offenses are violations of the criminal law. In a democracy, laws are made by representatives of citizens who are concerned about specific behaviors they believe should be prohibited. Often, there isn't a complete consensus on what behaviors should be considered criminal offenses, but once the legislature passes a law, we are all obliged to obey it. We can't pick and choose which laws to obey and which to violate.

On a continuum of social control, crime occupies an extreme position at the serious end. Other behaviors are arranged on the continuum based on their perceived seriousness.

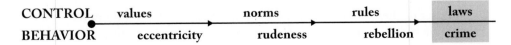

| CONTROL | values | | norms | | rules | | laws |
| BEHAVIOR | eccentricity | | rudeness | | rebellion | | crime |

There might be ramifications to violating a norm or rule, but these ramifications aren't supported by the criminal justice system. Spitting in the classroom will almost certainly draw a rebuke from your professor and the disgust of other students, but it won't get you arrested by the police and brought before a judge.

Your grade might suffer, and your classmates might ostracize you, but your liberty won't be curtailed. Informal means of social control are usually enough to keep us from committing undesirable acts. Laws are used when the acts are dangerous, when certain groups have the political muscle to get their values codified, or when there is a strong consensus that informal means don't effectively control the undesired behavior.

Once the government's legislative branch has defined the offenses, the executive branch is charged with enforcing the laws, and the judicial branch with trying the accused, as well as punishing the convicted. The actions of each of these branches of government are crucial to the measurement of crime because each plays a role in mediating how antisocial behavior is answered by the criminal and juvenile justice systems.

THE DARK FIGURE OF CRIME

When measuring crime and allocating resources to control it, the differences between reported and unreported crime have substantial significance. We can make educated guesses about the amount of unreported crime that exists in any jurisdiction, but we can't know for sure its actual incidence.[19] This is called the **dark figure of crime** (see Figure 1.1).

For example, if a 16-year-old hits a 14-year-old because of a disagreement over a call in a flag football game, is it a criminal offense? If the game went on and the two youths maintained their friendship, was any social harm done? Should this assault be considered a criminal offense or even an assault? If a 16-year-old punches a 14-year-old in the mouth while waiting at the bus stop, should that be considered a criminal offense? If the parents of the 14-year-old called the police, reported the incident to the school, and obtained a lawyer, should the case be treated differently than the flag football example?

By examining these two types of physical violence, we can see how a behavior's context can determine whether it's defined and measured as a criminal offense. Many behaviors (presumably very many) don't make it into the official crime statistics for many reasons. This dark figure of crime isn't quantifiable but must be considered when making criminal and juvenile justice policy. One

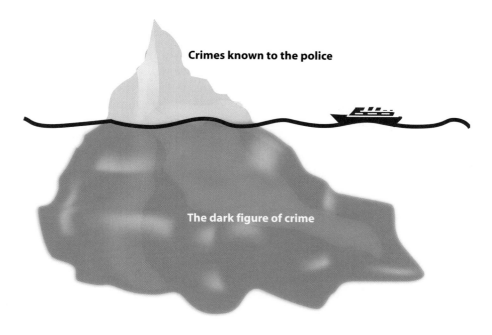

Crimes known to the police

The dark figure of crime

Figure 1.1

When children get into a fight, is a crime being committed? Or should children be allowed to learn and test the rules of society without intervention by legal authorities?

element of the dark figure of crime is unreported crime. A victim might not report an offense for several reasons.

>> The victim might not understand or believe an offense has been committed. Like the example of the boys' fight in the flag football game, some victims might not define a behavior as a criminal offense. A child who's being abused by his or her parents probably doesn't know that the parents' behavior is illegal and thinks that the beatings are because he or she is "bad."

>> The victim might lack faith in the system. Many victims don't report an offense because they don't believe the police will successfully apprehend the offenders. Many thefts go unreported because the value of the stolen goods is not significant enough to deal with the criminal justice system. A child's parents might not consider the child's stolen item valuable enough to bother reporting the theft to law enforcement. Some parents might even consider the theft to be a valuable lesson to the child, saying, for example, "If you hadn't left your bicycle so close to the road, it wouldn't have gotten stolen!"

>> The victim might wish to protect the offender. Many violent offenses happen at home. Usually, it's cases of spouses assaulting one another and parents abusing their children. In each of these examples, the victims have an interest in keeping the offense a secret. If the unlawful behavior were fully prosecuted, the victim, especially a child, could suffer as much as, or more than, the offender.

》 The victim might be guilty. When a drug deal goes bad, what can the victim do? The victim, maybe a teenager, paid good money for a pound of marijuana only to discover later that it's the herb oregano. Police officers aren't sympathetic to the victims of such fraudulent transactions, so they largely go unreported.[20]

》 Some offenses reported to the police don't get recorded as offenses. Police officers have discretion in deciding if a behavior constitutes a criminal offense or is a serious enough offense to record.

These are but a few examples of why many offenses go unreported. The important thing to keep in mind, however, is that unreported crime still has negative consequences for society and that crime-control policy must fashion solutions that address unreported crime. Those who observe criminal offenses sometimes decline to report the offense, often because they don't want to go to the trouble of reporting it to police. Other reasons include the following:

》 Distrust of the police

》 Recognition of a cultural code that demands that honorable people don't snitch or report criminal offenses

》 Fear of reprisals from the offender

》 Involvement in an offense while observing the commission of another, possibly unrelated, offense

Although the actual dark figure of crime is unknowable, the criminal justice system has attempted to make reporting crime easier, less intrusive, and even patriotic. Many agencies have anonymous tip lines that allow callers to report offenses.[21] Further, researchers use a variety of methodologies that attempt to measure crime in different ways to correct for underreporting. Let's examine the primary methods of measuring crime and delinquency.

Questions

1. What are criminal offenses?
2. What are the criminal justice functions of the legislative branch, the executive branch, and the judicial branch.
3. What is one element of the dark figure of crime?

Measurement Tools

Crime can be measured in a number of ways, and each has its strengths and weaknesses. Although no single method is perfect, together they can provide a reasonable picture of crime in a jurisdiction. What is most interesting, however, is the variety of methods that have been developed. These methods include efforts by law enforcement to measure the amount of crime reported to police, government studies that ask individuals if they have been a crime victim, and academic research that asks individuals if they have ever committed a criminal offense. Each measure looks at a different aspect of the crime picture.

Over the years, these techniques have been developed to the point that their discrepancies are probably due to variations in offending and not measurement error. However, it's prudent to remember that factors such as political influence, funding, and human error can all affect measurement. Now let's discuss the

Learning Objective 5.

Compare and contrast the Uniform Crime Reports, the National Incident-based Reporting System, and the National Crime Victimization Survey.

Learning Objective 6.

Explain the hierarchy rule.

Learning Objective 7.

Discuss the purpose of self-report studies.

Learning Objective 8.

Summarize how children can suffer from crime in different ways from adults.

various ways of measuring crime with the goal of appreciating just how difficult this task is.

The Uniform Crime Reports

The best-known method for reporting crime and delinquency in the United States is the **Uniform Crime Reports** (UCR). This is a highly coordinated effort in which almost every legal jurisdiction (over 17,000) reports the number of offenses, arrest statistics, and the characteristics of its agency to the Federal Bureau of Investigation. This system of reporting crime was designed to provide a comparative picture of the level of crime across jurisdictions, cities, and states. Collecting crime data in a consistent and uniform manner is a big step in providing lawmakers and criminal justice officials with the information they need to assess the nature and prevalence of crime.[22]

The strength of the UCR data is that each jurisdiction reports offenses according to a uniform set of parameters and definitions. The UCR collects data on four violent offenses

>> murder and nonnegligent manslaughter

>> forcible rape

>> robbery

>> aggravated assault

and four property offenses

>> burglary

>> larceny-theft

>> motor vehicle theft

>> arson.

The FBI defines violent offenses as those that involve force or threat of force and property offenses as those involving the taking of money or property without force or threat of force. One way in which the UCR displays crime data is by the raw number of incidents of each offense. In this collection, cities with large populations will appear more dangerous than sparsely populated small towns or rural areas simply because more offenses are happening there. Therefore, to correct for population size, another measure is presented: the crime rate. Here the population is divided into a constant number (100,000) to come up with a comparative rate of crime (see Figure 1.2). There are concerns, however, about how accurately the numbers reflect the true incidence and rate of crime.

How to Calculate a Crime Rate

$$\frac{\text{Number of crimes}}{\text{Population}} \times 100{,}000$$

For example, in the U.S. in 2009 . . .

$$\frac{10{,}639{,}369 \text{ Reported violent \& property offenses}}{311{,}387{,}118 \text{ Total U.S. population}} \times 100{,}000 = 3{,}417 \text{ Offenses per 100,000 people}$$

Figure 1.2

Sources: Federal Bureau of Investigation, Uniform Crime Reports, *Crime in the United States, 2009*, www2.fbi.gov/ucr/cius2009/index.html.

US Census Bureau, US Population Clock, www.census.gov/population/www/popclockus.html.

» **The hierarchy rule.** The UCR records only the most serious incident in a set of incidents. This means that if someone breaks into your home, murders your husband, beats your son, and steals your car, the UCR records only the murder. The exception to the hierarchy rule is arson. For example, if one offense is arson in a set of offenses that also includes murder, the arson is recorded along with the murder.[23]

» **Follow-up procedures.** The nature of an offense might change over time, and it's important that all jurisdictions adjust their crime figures according to the same procedures. For instance, an aggravated assault might turn into a murder if the victim dies from the injuries a month or two later. There is no way of knowing how diligently each reporting agency follows up on such cases. Although one agency might change the crime to a murder, another might leave it as an aggravated assault.[24]

» **Variations in definition.** Although the UCR attempts to get every agency on the same page when it comes to defining crime, there's a substantial amount of variation in local statutes. For instance, there might be ambiguity in how "carnal knowledge" is defined when dealing with rape cases. Some jurisdictions limit it to actual sexual intercourse, while others might use a more inclusive definition that covers other types of intimate behavior. Additionally, the definition of rape might vary across jurisdictions depending on whether the victim-offender relationship is restricted to strangers, whether they are acquaintances, or whether they are married.

» **Attempted offenses.** How do various jurisdictions code offenses that aren't completed? For example, an offense in which a teenager breaks into a building and runs away when an alarm goes off before committing any other offenses may be coded differently in different jurisdictions. Some may code it as a simple breaking-and-entering or as a case of vandalism, while others may code it as a burglary.

As we can see from these examples, the UCR is subject to some variation. Given these qualifications, the UCR is a wonderful tool for criminal justice practitioners, researchers, and the public in understanding crime and the workings of the criminal justice system. No other entity has been able to launch such an effort, and, as imperfect as it is, the UCR is instrumental in the nation's efforts to understand and control crime.

Juvenile Delinquency and the UCR. For recording purposes, the UCR considers all people under age 18 as juveniles regardless of state definitions. The program doesn't collect data on police contact with juveniles who haven't broken the law or in situations in which a juvenile is taken into protective custody, as in cases of abuse or neglect.[25]

It's impossible to know exactly how many offenses juveniles commit. Often, no perpetrator can be identified, so no one is arrested. We must also recognize that police departments are more likely to handle juvenile suspects informally than adult suspects. Also, juveniles are more likely than adults to be caught, as they tend to commit their offenses publicly, in sight of patrolling police officers, and are less accomplished than adults. These differences between adults and juveniles help to skew delinquency statistics.

It isn't always possible to know the ages of those who break the law, but it's possible to know the ages of those who are arrested. UCR data capture the age

It isn't always possible to know the ages of those who break the law, and many delinquents are never caught.

of arrestees and make it possible to talk with a small degree of confidence about delinquency. Although many delinquents are never caught, and some delinquents get arrested repeatedly for multiple violations, we can be fairly confident in the delinquency figures. Basically, the rates of delinquency remain fairly constant from year to year. A big swing in delinquency rates from year to year would raise concern about measurement errors. Because they seem fairly stable, we have some faith that changes in the rate of delinquency are what is actually being measured.

The information the UCR captures on juveniles does have some limitations. In many ways, the UCR is an excellent measure of what our criminal justice agencies do and a less reliable measure of the actual nature and frequency of crime. Some offenses are reported at a much greater rate than others. For instance, murder is reported at a high rate. Why? First, there is usually a body lying around somewhere, and people tend to notice a dead body after a while. Although perpetrators might attempt to hide the body, there is still the likelihood of a great deal of physical evidence, such as bloodstains, hair, fibers, and odors, which can bring inquiry. Second, the dead person is likely to be missed by family members, co-workers, or bill collectors. People can vanish into thin air, but someone usually notices the absence and notifies the authorities of the possibility of foul play. Other offenses, such as vandalism and drug sales, can go virtually undetected. Vandalism, such as spray-painting a wall, can be fairly easy for youths to commit without getting caught. Offenses in which there is no direct victim, such as drug sales, are underreported because, when both seller and customer are satisfied with a transaction, neither has any incentive to report anything to the police.[26]

Finally, UCR data can't give a comprehensive picture of crime because the data are heavily skewed toward **street crime**, which is what delinquents are most often involved in. The types of serious crime that the UCR doesn't adequately capture—such as white-collar crime, environmental crime, corporate crime, and organized crime—are less likely to involve juveniles. Many of these types of crime never become known to the police and therefore never show up in the UCR figures. For what it's designed to do, the UCR does a commendable job.

However, as students of the criminal and juvenile justice systems, we must be cognizant of the flawed and biased picture presented by the UCR. To this end, we now turn to other ways of measuring crime and delinquency that supplement the UCR.

The National Incident-Based Reporting System

In the Uniform Crime Reports, law enforcement agencies report what they know about the amount and seriousness of crime and delinquency. The major weakness of the UCR, however, is that many offenses aren't counted. The relatively new **National Incident-Based Reporting System** (NIBRS) is part of the FBI's Uniform Crime Reports system, but includes more information about offenses reported to police. The NIBRS doesn't use the hierarchy rule and records each offense in a multioffense incident. Because the two studies collect data so differently, NIBRS and UCR statistics can't be compared to one another. The NIBRS collects data on each incident and arrest on 46 Group A offenses and arrest data on 11 Group B offenses (see Table 1.1), including information on the location, date, and time of the offense, and the weapons used.[27] The NIBRS also collects information about victims, such as demographics; the level of injury; victims' perceptions of offenders' ages, sex, and race; and victim-offender relationships.

Relatively few law enforcement agencies participate in the NIBRS, so although it provides a more detailed picture of crime, it can't provide a comprehensive one. In 2007, 6,444 law enforcement agencies contributed NIBRS data, with the data representing 25 percent of the US population and 25 percent of the crime statistics collected by the UCR. However, according to the FBI, the NIBRS—which represents less than 10 percent of the US population—still has too little data to make useful generalizations about crime and delinquency in the United States.[28]

The NIBRS provides an alternative look at the crime picture. It shouldn't be thought of as a replacement for other types of reporting efforts, but rather as a

TABLE 1.1 ⟩ Offenses Recorded by the National Incident-Based Reporting System

GROUP A OFFENSES		GROUP B OFFENSES
Arson	Kidnapping/abduction	Bad checks
Assault	Larceny/theft offenses	Curfew/loitering/vagrancy violations
Bribery	Motor vehicle theft	Disorderly conduct
Burglary/breaking and entering	Pornography/obscene material	Driving under the influence
Counterfeiting/forgery	Prostitution	Drunkenness
Vandalism	Robbery	Family offenses, nonviolent
Drug/narcotic offenses	Sex offenses, forcible	Liquor law violations
Embezzlement	Sex offenses, nonforcible: incest,	Peeping Tom
Extortion/blackmail	statutory rape	Runaway
Fraud	Stolen property offenses	Trespass of real property
Gambling offenses	Weapon law violations	All other offenses
Homicide: Murder and nonnegligent manslaughter, negligent manslaughter, justifiable homicide		

Think About It

1. *In your opinion, are there any Group B offenses that should be Group A offenses?*

Source: Federal Bureau of Investigation, NIBRS General FAQs, www.fbi.gov/about-us/cjis/ucr/frequently-asked-questions/nibrs_faqs.

supplement. Because it's costlier and more labor intensive, it's unlikely that it will ever obtain the status and funding of the UCR. However, it's still a useful tool. Even though it has limitations—it gathers samples that aren't representative of the nation—it does help to shine a light on the dark figure of crime, because it includes all the offenses that occur in any single criminal event, rather than simply the most serious offense, as is the case with the UCR.

National Crime Victimization Survey

In addition to law enforcement agencies and offenders, crime victims can also shed light on the amount and seriousness of crime and delinquency while providing an entirely different picture. This picture is valuable because it taps into important dimensions the other two groups miss.

The primary source of criminal victimization data in the United States is the National Crime Victimization Survey (NCVS). Conducted annually by the Bureau of Justice Statistics and the Census Bureau, the NCVS collects information about the frequency, characteristics, and consequences of crime from individuals age 12 and older in 38,728 households, representing over 68,000 people.[29] Researchers use this data to estimate the likelihood of rape, sexual assault, robbery, assault, theft, household burglary, and motor vehicle theft.[30] Because it depends on self-reporting, the NCVS excludes data from victims who can't report or can't reliably report their experiences. This includes data on homicide, arson, commercial criminal offenses, and offenses against children under age 12.[31] The NCVS captures valuable information about the dark figure of crime because it gathers data about offenses regardless of whether they are reported to the police. For example, according to victims interviewed in 2009, only 49 percent of violent offenses and 39 percent of property offenses were reported to the police.[32]

Perhaps the most interesting finding of the NCVS regarding age is that adolescents and young adults experience the most violent crime (see Figure 1.3).[33] Crime victims also reported that juveniles committed up to a fourth of violent offenses, although this number has been declining.[34] We'll discuss youths as victims in greater detail later in this chapter.

Figure 1.3 Rates of violent crime by age of victim, 2010

Younger victims experience higher rates of violent crime. For example, nearly 28 percent of 12-14 year olds experienced violent crime in 2010.

Think About It
1. Discuss reasons that the crime victimization rate drops as people age.

Source: Jennifer L. Truman, *Criminal Victimization, 2010*, Table 9, (Washington, DC: Bureau of Justice Statistics, 2010), 11. Online at bjs. ojp.usdoj.gov/content/pub/pdf/cv10.pdf.

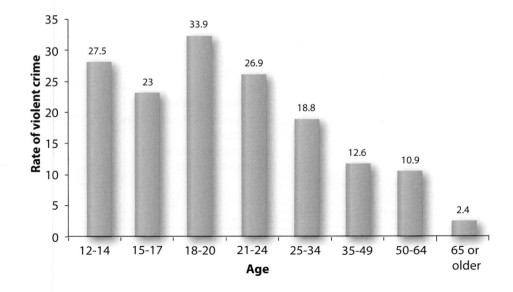

Self-Report Studies

Self-report studies ask participants to tell researchers what offenses they have committed. These can be offenses for which the participants were caught and punished or offenses in which they escaped detection.[35] Immediately, we can see some concerns of self-report studies. Why should respondents admit to offenses they have gotten away with? Presumably, offenders reporting their own offenses would be worried about giving away enough information so that they could be caught.[36] The reason that researchers can be fairly confident that respondents will report their own offenses is because the studies are anonymous. That is, respondents answer written questions without having to put their names on the answer sheet. The researchers, who are only interested in the types and levels of offenses committed, are then left with a hundred answer sheets and no way to link them to the respondents. Respondents are assured that the information they give won't be made available to law enforcement and that the police won't come knocking.

Self-report studies give criminal justice researchers a different angle on the measurement of crime. Rather than having data filtered through law enforcement agencies, researchers are able to go directly to offenders and delinquents. The major presumed advantage is that these self-report studies will reveal offenses that aren't known to the police. However, the researchers can never know if the offenses they are capturing with self-report studies were ever reported to the police.

The primary problems with self-report studies are the same as with any form of survey research. Two basic questions must be asked about survey research to determine its validity—which describes how well a study is measuring what it's designed to measure—and reliability—which refers to how successfully research can be repeated and provide similar results.[37]

1. Were the right people asked the right questions?
2. Did they answer truthfully?

The first question is difficult to deal with when measuring crime because of the issue of generalization. If the researcher were interested in drug use in a particular high school, taking a random sample of students from that school and asking them questions would be sufficient. However, if the researcher were interested in drug use in high schools in the United States, taking a sample from a single school wouldn't be adequate.

There are untold sources of possible measurement errors when a researcher collects information from a single school and tries to use the limited data to make statements about all the schools in the nation. Schools vary by racial and ethnic composition, by the school district's social and economic composition, by the availability of drugs and alcohol in the community, and by the rules and cultures of each particular school.[38] It's unfair and inaccurate to say that schools in New York, California, and Texas have a drug problem just because a researcher found a high degree of self-reported drug use at a high school in Bremen, Georgia.

Often the sample for a research project is obtained because it's convenient. Students in a research methods class developing questionnaires will often use their classmates to field-test the adequacy and clarity of the questions. However, classmates won't provide an adequate test of the questions, because often they aren't competent to evaluate the underlying logic and structure of the questionnaire. They often know even less than the researcher about what questions to ask.

For instance, suppose students in a criminal justice research methods class are required to develop a self-report questionnaire on some aspect of crime, and one of them decides to study juvenile gangs. This student reviews the literature and comes up with 20 questions that ask gang members about their motivations for joining a gang, then asks classmates to fill out the questionnaire. It's possible that none of the classmates is, or ever was, a gang member, therefore rendering all of them incompetent to provide feedback on the questionnaire's validity. The trick is to get the questionnaire to people who are likely to provide good information. Doing a drug survey in an elite prep school will provide a certain type of information, maybe even a high level of drug use, but this information can't be generalized to all schools in the United States because the elite prep school isn't representative.

How does one go about finding a representative sample? First, the researcher must be clear about how far the results will be extended in terms of generalizability. If one wants to claim that the results are particular to a single school, it's permissible to sample within that school. However, if one wants to generalize to the city, state, or nation, one must have a representative sample drawn from that population. The problem quickly becomes one of time and resources, and trying to get a nationwide picture of delinquency can be cumbersome and expensive. Often researchers will select specific cities and say that, for the purposes of the research, they will assume no large systematic differences exist between the chosen cities and other cities. Survey research involves compromises. The goal is to get as representative a sample as possible within the budget and resources available. Additionally, the researchers should specify how their sample was chosen and resist making claims that the data can't support.

Asking the right people the right questions can be challenging. However, the problem of getting respondents to tell the truth can be even more difficult. This is especially true when dealing with questionnaires that request information about crime and delinquency. The problems of truth-telling on self-report studies can be of two varieties.

1. **Underreporting of crime.** Individuals have many reasons to underreport.
   - *Fear of arrest.* If youths believe they may be arrested for admitting to unlawful behaviors, they won't report them in self-report studies. Although researchers might go to great lengths to assure confidentiality, some youths will suspect a law-enforcement trick and underreport their delinquent activities.
   - *Embarrassment.* Some youths have committed unlawful behaviors and are reluctant to acknowledge their acts to anyone, including themselves. They are embarrassed and ashamed of their behavior and are unwilling to have it recorded anywhere.
   - *Fear of action.* Someone who has a thriving business dealing drugs at school is unlikely to report that the school has a problem. If the truth were known, all kinds of bad things could happen, including police officers working undercover and drug dogs brought in to sniff lockers and students. Some students, therefore, don't want the truth to be known.

2. **Overreporting of crime.** Some students will purposely overreport deviant acts.
   - *As a joke.* Students might think it funny to make the school look like a haven for drug addicts. They decide to have fun with the researchers by giving wild and unsubstantiated claims. Unfortunately, the researchers

have little way of knowing the students are being playful and might report the exaggerated responses as evidence of a drug problem in the school.

❭ *As posturing.* Some students will use the self-report study to give class-mates the impression that they are much more involved in a criminal lifestyle than is actually true. Although these studies are anonymous to researchers, these "wannabe criminals" may try to earn a reputation among their friends by telling them they reported several offenses on the self-report study.

These sources of measurement error based on under- or overreporting of crime on self-report studies are difficult to gauge. Researchers will try to prevent them as much as possible by using tactics such as internal consistency checks, in which the same question is asked in several slightly different ways to see if the respondent provides the same answer. Sources of error other than purposeful lying are difficult to evaluate. Perhaps the greatest is the reliance on the respondent's memory. When asked questions such as "How many offenses have you committed in the past six months?" respondents might have difficulty remembering exactly when an offense was committed. It's hard for anyone to remember the exact date of conversations, events, or disputes. Other problems relating to the respondent's quality of recall depend on the gravity of the offense. A respondent might describe an aggravated assault in which a weapon was used and the victim suffered substantial injury as nothing more than a minor fight.

Self-report studies are valuable because they give us insight into crime that isn't captured by UCR data. For the most part, self-report studies verify some of the conclusions that researchers have already drawn. For instance, boys report a substantially greater number and variety of offenses than do girls. Additionally, and not surprisingly, older adolescents report more offenses than younger adolescents. This isn't simply because the older adolescents have had more time to commit the acts, because that issue is controlled for by asking only about recent behavior. Rather, it appears that older youths commit more offenses because they are willing to take more risks.

Perhaps the most significant finding from self-report studies is that delinquency is more evenly spread throughout the socioeconomic classes than it appears from UCR data alone.[39] Because self-report studies focus on more types of crime than the UCR, they are able to tap into a greater variety of antisocial behavior. Much of the crime reported by self-report studies is trivial. Rapes and armed robberies aren't generally found, but this is because these events are rare, especially among the types of school-age populations that are generally selected to participate in self-report studies. This type of research is especially effective in measuring offenses without direct victims, such as drug use and underage drinking. By doing youth self-report studies annually, researchers can follow trends in antisocial behavior. By sampling high school seniors over decades, it's possible to detect the ebb and flow of drinking and drug-use patterns.

Measures of Youths as Victims and Offenders

Adults commit more offenses than youths because there are so many more adults to get into trouble. Also, youths, especially the younger ones, are subject to a great deal more supervision than adults and don't have the opportunity to get into trouble at the same rate. What is apparent is that the adults who do violate the law are clustered around the lower end of the age scale, and their offenses seem to be an extension of delinquency. As Figure 1.4 shows, crime is still

Figure 1.4 Number of Arrests by Age, 2010

These data represent the number of people arrested. It's important to remember that some people may be arrested more than once in a year, so some of the statistics represent multiple arrests of the same person.

Think About It

1. Between which two age groups does the arrest rate drop most drastically? Discuss possible reasons why.

Source: Federal Bureau of Investigation, *Crime in the United States, 2010: Uniform Crime Reports*, Table 38: Arrests by Age, 2010, www.fbi.gov/about-us/cjis/ucr/crime-in-the-u.s/2010/crime-in-the-u.s.-2010/tables/10tbl38.xls.

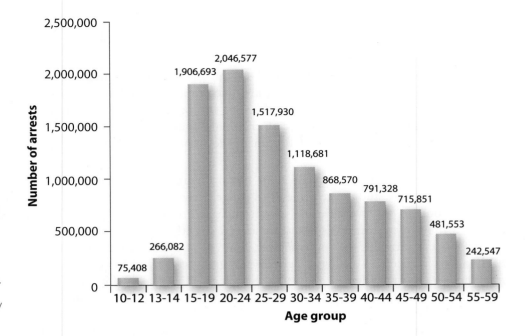

a young person's game, peaking in the late teens and early twenties and dropping off steeply after that. However, what needs to be kept in mind is that, for many offenders, crime is cumulative. The earlier youths start to participate in crime, the more likely they are to become heavily involved.

When discussing delinquency, we must remember that all offenses aren't equal. When raw statistics are considered, it isn't apparent that most delinquency consists of property offenses rather than violent offenses. In 2009, for example, juveniles accounted for 14.9 percent of all arrests for violent offenses, but 24.4 percent of arrests for property offenses.[40] Homicide, forcible rape, and aggravated assault rank among the lowest incidences of delinquency. The offenses most often committed by juveniles that aren't status offenses are arson and vandalism. In 2009, juveniles accounted for 44.3 percent of those arrested for arson (with half of those being under age 15) and 33.6 percent of those arrested for vandalism. Offenses for which juveniles represent the lowest proportion of arrests are driving under the influence (less than 1 percent), prostitution (1.9 percent), fraud (3.1 percent), and drunkenness (2.35 percent).[41] These figures aren't unusual when we consider the limited opportunities youths have to participate in these activities. For instance, an offender must be financially sophisticated to commit fraud. Youths are unlikely to enter positions in which they are given the responsibility to safeguard large amounts of money, so they have few occasions to commit fraud. By contrast, youths have ample time and opportunity to engage in vandalism.

What the statistics don't show us, however, is that these offenses aren't evenly distributed over age, sex, and geographic location. For instance, boys commit more offenses than girls, older teens more offenses than younger teens, and urban neighborhoods experience more crime than small towns or rural areas. We can see an example of this uneven distribution of crime in the arrests of juveniles for murder. Figure 1.5 shows how arrests of juveniles accused of murder rises from ages 10 to 18. The rate of increase from ages 15 to 16, which nearly doubles, is especially dramatic.

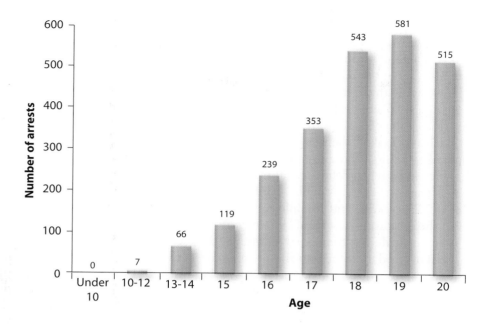

Figure 1.5 Arrests of Juveniles for Murder by Age, 2010

Note how the number of arrests increases with age and doesn't begin to decrease until age 20. The arrest rate for murder decreases steadily throughout adulthood.

Think About It

1. Why isn't the rate of increase of arrests for murder from ages 13-14 to age 15 as dramatic as that from ages 15 to 16?

Source: Federal Bureau of Investigation, *Crime in the United States, 2010*, Arrests by Age 2010, Table 38, www.fbi.gov/about-us/cjis/ucr/crime-in-the-u.s/2010/crime-in-the-u.s.-2010/tables/10tbl38.xls.

YOUTHS AS VICTIMS

When discussing victimization rates and numbers, it's easy to forget the tragedy of youth victimization. Children are truly victims because they don't participate in creating the conditions or environment that encourages crime. Children are under the control of parents, teachers, older siblings, or others who are charged with protecting them. Children can get into trouble and engage in dangerous behaviors, but society's attitude is that it's the responsible adult who is problematic, not the wayward child.[42]

Youths are a highly victimized segment of the population. According to the NCVS, from 1993 to 2003, youths between the ages of 12 and 17 were two and half times more likely than adults to be victims of violent crime. Still, research on the scope of juvenile victimization has been limited, and few theories address it. Although some research narrowly focuses on specific victimizations, such as family violence and sexual abuse, little research takes into account the full spectrum of abuse that may occur throughout childhood and adolescence. This is an important issue because youths are vulnerable to several forms of victimization from both adults and other youths.[43] Victimizers may be strangers, family members, adults in protective positions (such as teachers and religious authorities), adult acquaintances, or youth acquaintances. Victimization may occur anywhere, including the home, the school, and the street. Perhaps the reason that youths report more victimization than adults is that there are more opportunities in which victimization can occur and more potential victimizers.

Sexual Victimization. The sexual victimization of children is a major concern for parents, police, school administrators, and the media. Children are powerless to prevent their victimization when the offender is older, stronger, more worldly, or in a position of responsibility. Although we suspect the number of sexual assaults on children is substantial, official records don't clearly represent the problem. The UCR is reasonably good at reporting rapes known to the police, but it doesn't gather information about other types of sexual assaults, such as forcible sodomy, sexual assault with an object, and forcible fondling. Victimization surveys reveal a good bit more about how children are sexually victimized, but they reflect little about the relationship between the child and the offender.

However, with these qualifications clearly stated and understood, the NIBRS can provide a valuable angle from which to view the problem of child sexual victimization. Table 1.2 shows the age profile of sexual assault victims. It's most informative to look at the percentage of youths who are victims of forcible rape compared to adults. Those under 18 years of age account for 45.8 percent of the rapes. However, when other sexual offenses are considered, the percent of juvenile victims skyrockets: forcible sodomy (78.8 percent), sexual assault with an object (75.2 percent), and forcible fondling (83.8 percent). The single age that showed the greatest risk of sexual victimization was 14.

When considering the sexual victimization of children, another feature that jumps out of the data is the prevalence of female victims. At every level of the age profile, young females stand a greater risk of victimization than do young males. Figure 1.6 shows that although both males and females show a heightened risk of sexual victimization at about age 4, females are always at greater risk of sexual victimization than males throughout childhood and adolescence, and for females age 14 there is a substantially greater incidence of sexual assault.

Effects of Youth Victimization. The victimization of young people is a major concern for several reasons. Although adults significantly suffer from crime, it's worth noting that youths, especially children, can suffer in unanticipated ways. Here are some other ways that youths may be affected by victimization:

)) **Ignorance of victimization.** Children, especially young children, might unknowingly be crime victims. They don't know what constitutes criminal victimization, so they don't know that it should be reported. When friends or family members sexually or emotionally abuse them, children might mistake the attention for nurturing and love. Often, it's only after children become adults that they are able to identify and label the actions as abuse.

TABLE 1.2   Age Profile of the Victims of Sexual Assault

VICTIM AGE	ALL SEXUAL ASSAULT	FORCIBLE RAPE	FORCIBLE SODOMY	SEXUAL ASSAULT WITH OBJECT	FORCIBLE FONDLING
Total	100.0%	100.0%	100.0%	100.0%	100.0%
0 to 5	14.0%	4.3%	24.0%	26.5%	20.2%
6 to 11	20.1%	8.0%	30.8%	23.2%	29.3%
12 to 17	32.8%	33.5%	24.0%	25.5%	34.3%
18 to 24	14.2%	22.6%	8.7%	9.7%	7.7%
25 to 34	11.5%	19.6%	7.5%	8.3%	5.0%
Above 34	7.4%	12.0%	5.1%	6.8%	3.5%

Think About It
1. At what range of ages are youths most at risk of sexual assault?

Source: Howard N. Snyder, Sexual Assault of Young Children as Reported to Law Enforcement: Victim, Incident, and Offender Characteristics (Washington, DC: Bureau of Justice Statistics, July 2000), 2. Online at www.ojp.usdoj.gov/bjs/pub/pdf/saycrle.pdf.

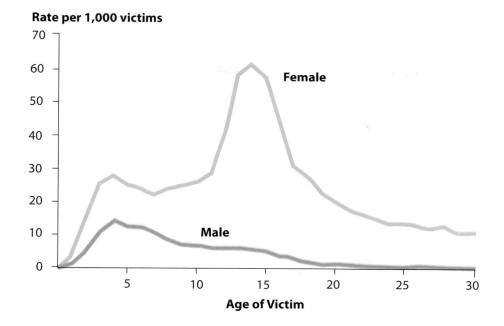

Rate per 1,000 victims

Figure 1.6 Age Distribution of Sexual Assault Victims by Sex, 2009

Think About It
1. Discuss possible reasons for the greater rate of female sexual assault.

Source: Howard N. Snyder, *Sexual Assault of Young Children as Reported to Law Enforcement: Victim, Incident, and Offender Characteristics* (Washington, DC: Bureau of Justice Statistics, July 2000), 4. Online at www.bjs.ojp.usdoj.gov/content/pub/pdf/saycrle.pdf.

» **Long-lasting harm.** The violation of trust in those who are supposed to be responsible for their welfare can have a deep and long-lasting effect on child victims. Often, the criminal behavior of adults can be traced back to the abuse and neglect they experienced as children. Trauma resulting from childhood victimization can lie dormant in a child's psyche and not be manifested for years until it emerges in one of a variety of forms, ranging from aggression and violence to being submissive and withdrawn.

» **Guilt.** Children can be convinced that the offenses committed against them are actually their own fault. For example, when a father is incarcerated for sexual abuse, the child might interpret, sometimes with the help of the mother, the event as the child's fault for reporting the offense.

» **Permanent physical injuries.** Because children's bodies aren't fully developed, any physical injury can become permanent. Some parents might slap their child's hand as opposed to spanking in the belief that it's less harmful. However, the carpal bones in a child's hand aren't fully developed, and the punishment can cause arrested development. Children who are spanked violently on the buttocks might suffer damage to nerve endings, bladders, and pelvic bones. While perhaps well meaning, this type of punishment can have greater ramifications than envisioned by parents.[44]

» **Family devastation.** When a child is a homicide victim, the effect on the family can be more severe than the loss of another family member. Parents invest hopes and dreams in their children and may feel particularly guilty when the child is lost as the result of crime.

» **Bullying.** Juvenile victimization research often focuses on maltreatment by caregivers, which significantly affects victims. However, regular maltreatment by peers—such as bullying, sexual harassment, and hazing— although often overlooked, can produce deep social and emotional problems, such as depression, anxiety, low self-esteem, and low academic achievement.[45]

These are but a few reasons why the victimization of children is detrimental to their development; however, these harms are all at the individual level. There

Status offenders are youths who have done things that aren't criminal offenses but are considered undesirable for young people to do, such as drinking alcohol.

is another factor in how crime affects children that isn't on the list. To some extent, the nature of how children interact with their environment has changed. Many parents are so concerned about their children's safety that they seldom let them out of the sight of responsible adults. A couple of generations ago, children would freely roam their neighborhoods or play unsupervised with other children. Today, many parents, who are often criticized as "helicopter parents," schedule their children's play dates and send them to supervised after-school programs or day care instead of letting them freely play and explore.[46] The nature of childhood might be undergoing subtle but fundamental changes because of parental perceptions of juvenile crime and victimization.

A Typology of Juvenile Delinquents

All delinquency isn't caused by the same factors and isn't equally serious. A **typology** of delinquents is useful in understanding the differences in types of delinquency. A typology is simply a conceptual grouping of items into categories so they can be considered separately and compared. The creating of typologies is one of the first steps in the scientific method, and an ideal typology should be mutually exclusive and exhaustive. *Mutually exclusive* means an item should fit into one and only one category. *Exhaustive* means that every item fits into a category.

Our typology of delinquents is neither mutually exclusive nor exhaustive. Many delinquents could fit into more than one category, and some delinquents wouldn't fit anywhere. However, this doesn't mean that our typology isn't useful in differentiating among the types and seriousness of delinquency. On the contrary, it provides a starting point from which to evaluate the seriousness of delinquent behavior and can point the way toward appropriate treatment or punishment. The typology presented here is designed to illustrate the major categories of delinquents.

Status Offenders. Status offenders are youths who have done things that aren't criminal offenses but are considered undesirable for young people to do. If these behaviors were committed by an adult, the state wouldn't intervene. Therefore, status offenses are activities that are specified as offenses strictly because of the

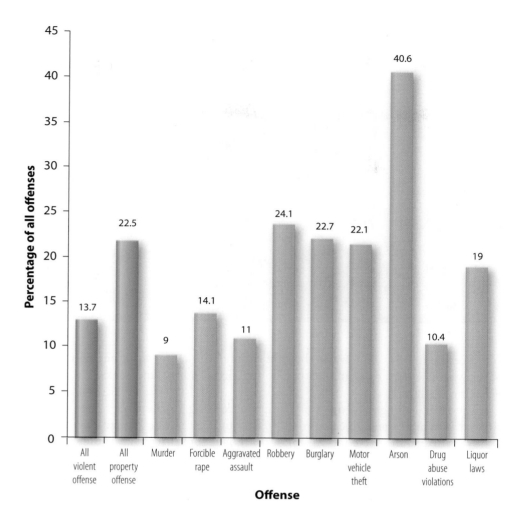

Figure 1.7 Juvenile Percentage of Arrests by Offense, 2010

The first two bars show the percentage of juveniles arrested in all violent crime and property crime. The remaining bars show the percentage of juveniles arrested in each offense. For example, juveniles represented 9 percent of all murder arrests.

Think About It

1. For which offense did juveniles represent the most arrests? Discuss possible reasons for this.

Source: Federal Bureau of Investigation, *Crime in the United States, 2010*, Arrests by Age, 2010, Table 38, www.fbi.gov/about-us/cjis/ucr/crime-in-the-u.s/2010/crime-in-the-u.s.-2010/tables/10tabl38.xls.

offender's age. Status offenses include underage drinking, curfew violations, underage smoking, running away, truancy, and being incorrigible. How serious are these offenses? Considered individually, each offense might appear to be trivial. However, when they occur in combination over a long period of time, they can signal the onset of more serious delinquency.

Although a juvenile might have a legitimate reason to run away from home, such as an abusive parent, where the juvenile goes is important. Juveniles whose destination is the street are in danger of becoming involved in more serious offenses. Status offenses are enacted for the welfare of the child, rather than for the protection of society. Although considered the least-serious offenses, they may indicate future criminality. There is a legitimate debate about what to do with status offenders so they aren't drawn into the juvenile justice system.

Property Offenders. Juveniles are responsible for a significant percentage of property offenses, including arson, burglary, and motor vehicle theft (see Figure 1.7). This is because these are the offenses that juveniles have the opportunity to commit. For instance, it's easier for them to break into cars and steal audio equipment than to embezzle money from a bank.

Drug Users and Abusers. Drug and alcohol use by juveniles is a concern that has plagued parents, teachers, and juvenile justice officials for decades. Youths typically begin to test the boundaries of appropriate behavior during the

Juveniles are responsible for a significant percentage of property offenses, including arson, because these are offenses juveniles have the opportunity to commit. Many juvenile arsons occur not because a youth was trying to destroy property but because the youth only wanted to "play with fire."

adolescent years. In some ways, they are simply mimicking adult behavior, and in other ways they are rebelling against conventional norms and seeking a thrill by breaking the law.

The actual danger of drug use varies according to the drugs used and the context in which they are consumed.[47] Although it can't be argued that any recreational drugs are good for children, there is a consensus that some drugs are worse than others. For instance, beer, wine, and marijuana aren't considered to be as harmful as vodka, crack cocaine, and heroin. Parents have real concerns, however, if their child drinks a six-pack of beer and gets behind the wheel of an automobile. The dangerousness of drugs and alcohol is difficult to define without considering the context. Many young people have violated these laws and gone on to lead productive lives as college professors, doctors, business executives, and politicians, including presidents. We will take a closer look at drug usage in Chapter 11.

Gang Members. Gang membership is highly correlated with delinquent behavior. This isn't surprising, since involvement with illegal activity gives gang identity much of its meaning. Whether it's a traditional street gang that struggles to define and protect its turf from other gangs, or a gang that deals in drugs, prostitution, and gambling, gangs are almost by definition criminal organizations. Joining a gang often requires breaking the law as an initiation rite, and in some neighborhoods, gang membership is inevitable, because being unaffiliated leaves one open to exploitation from every gang. Gangs are involved in a wide range of illegal activity. Although some specialize in particular offenses such as motor vehicle theft or drug sales, many others engage in opportunistic crime ranging from assault to drug dealing to larceny.[48] Some scholars have argued that most delinquency is committed by gang members. We will go into more detail on gangs in Chapter 10.

Chronic and Violent Juvenile Delinquents. The final category is that of chronic and violent delinquents. Some youths commit an inordinate number of offenses and are continually in and out of juvenile institutions. Some of these youths are violent delinquents who start as school bullies and graduate to assault and robbery.[49] Some are disturbed children who commit specialized offenses such as arson. Finally, some are extremely violent youths who kill others for a variety of reasons, such as revenge against parents, hatred of schoolmates, or terrorizing minority groups. These youths might have long criminal histories or commit heinous offenses with little or no warning. It's these delinquents who have their cases waived to the adult court system. The juvenile justice system, which is designed to work in the best interests of the child, is ill equipped to deal with serious delinquents who commit high-profile offenses that the public wants to see punished. This is the type of offender who draws negative publicity to the shortcomings of the juvenile justice system and has politicians calling for get-tough-on-crime legislation.

It should be clear by now that measuring crime, especially delinquency, is an inexact science. Because of the dark figure of crime, which can only be estimated, and the way the UCR documents only the most serious offense in a lawbreaking incident, official statistics must be used carefully. Although various attempts to measure crime require a great deal of effort and expense, they can only approximate the actual level of crime.

If measuring crime is so difficult, what about predicting it? Law enforcement policy makers are charged not only with responding to crime but also with trying to prevent it. How successful are they in forecasting illegal behavior? The short answer to this question is, they aren't that successful. So many variables influence predictions of delinquency that it's almost impossible to be accurate in the long term. Changes in school policies, parental involvement, economic conditions, and numerous other unforeseen factors will confound any forecast. Although it's useful and desirable to try to anticipate how the factors that appear now might influence future crime rates, policy makers can't continually look in the rearview mirror when allocating resources.

Questions

1. Why would a victim choose not to report an offense?
2. Why are the Uniform Crime Reports useful? What are their drawbacks?
3. What is the National Crime Victimization survey?
4. How do scholars determine the validity and reliability of self-report studies?
5. In what ways might crime affect youths differently than adults?

The System of Last Resort

Critics of the juvenile justice system who say it fails to keep children from breaking the law might not consider just how difficult this task is for a system that has little control over who enters it and how much money it has. Many programs and agencies have substantial control over whom they serve. For instance, universities set standards for admission and for graduation. Schools exclude those most likely to fail by setting standards for entry. Those who do get admitted and then asked to leave because of poor performance are considered to have failed personally; the institution is not considered to be at fault.

The juvenile justice system doesn't have this type of control over its charges. Police, parents, and schools all have a hand in deciding who enters the juvenile justice system. Although schools can flunk their lowest-achieving students, the juvenile justice system must keep its most recalcitrant and difficult clients. This

Learning Objective 9.

Explain why the juvenile justice system can't control who enters it.

Learning Objective 10.

Criticize the idea that some deviant behavior might actually benefit youths and society.

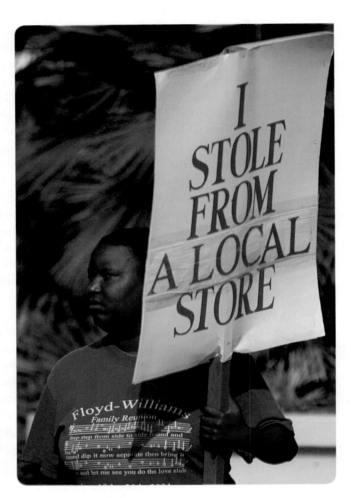

The public's perception of the dangerousness of delinquents has led to laws that treat delinquency more seriously. This youth was given an unusual sentence that required him to hold a sign announcing that he shoplifted from a store.

is what is meant by "the system of last resort." It can't pass its failures on to other institutions. Therefore, we should be tolerant of a certain amount of ineffectiveness in the juvenile justice system. Unless we are willing to provide a great deal more funding, we shouldn't expect the system to succeed where others have failed. If the schools, whose mission is teaching, can't get a child up to the desired reading level, why do we expect the juvenile justice system, whose mission is social control, to be successful? If a child's family can't provide the love and support that allows a child to feel wanted and valued, how can we expect the juvenile justice system to do the job with foster homes and detention centers?

Growing Up Too Soon

Are childhood and adolescence more precarious today than in the past? Are families more fragile, and are children more violent? Is it tougher to be a child today? The answers to these questions are important. The public's perception of the dangerousness of juvenile delinquents has led us to enact laws that treat delinquency more seriously than in the recent past. Our study of delinquency must consider the changing context of our perceptions of crime. When we take an absolutist view of delinquency, we fail to appreciate the nature and history of growing up in the United States.

Some deviant behavior might actually be beneficial for both the individual youth and society. The line between deviance and acceptable behavior is often fuzzy, and sometimes its crossing is rewarded. Social change requires that individuals test the boundaries of approved behavior, and laws that were enacted for the benefit of certain individuals may need to be challenged. For instance, the leaders of the civil rights movement purposefully violated laws that preserved the privileges of those in power. Further, nonviolent social protest exposed differences of opinion concerning wars, women's rights, and trade policies. For instance, in the 1960s, youths protested the government's ability to draft young men to fight in a war but not allow young people of that same age to drink alcohol or to vote. What future delinquency issues may signal possible change?

Are We Waging a War on Children?

Few people will dispute the goal of making the world safer for children. Adults can look back at their formative years and see points of conflict, missed opportunities, and outright mistakes in judgment and say to themselves that if only someone had alerted them to the problems, they might have made better choices. Although this is undoubtedly true, it misses a vital point. To learn, people sometimes must make their own mistakes. There's a fine line between parents cutting the apron strings and shirking their responsibilities to provide guidance and support.

When families, churches, schools, and recreational programs fall short of socializing youths to become productive citizens, there is a tendency to look to the government, particularly the juvenile justice system, to fill the gap. There are some things, however, that the juvenile justice system is ill equipped to do. The state-raised youth has never been a particularly successful one. Delinquents, it has been determined, generally do better when kept in families, traditional schools, and the juvenile justice system as opposed to the criminal justice system. Yet, as we enter the 21st century, there is a movement to "get tough on crime" that is affecting youth in negative ways.

Much of what has been and is being attempted in forging a productive life for youth has been remarkably successful. However, society continues to make mistakes which are, to a great extent, perpetuated by the war on crime. This book, then, can be considered not simply as a rote rendition of facts about delinquency and the juvenile justice system but rather as an occasion for students to think about why the system functions as it does and how it may be improved. The crosscurrent subtheme, along with the cross-cultural and critical focus, will provide the reader with much to ponder and discuss.

Question

1. Why is the juvenile justice system a "system of last resort?"

>> FOCUS ON ETHICS

The Dope on School

You're finishing your master's degree in criminal justice and suddenly find yourself in a pickle. You're ready to collect the data for your project comparing drug use by high school freshmen to that of high school seniors. You plan to track the temptations, opportunities, and attitudes of students as they progress through their high school years. However, your major professor has resigned from your thesis committee because she has accepted another job. The person she has recommended to replace her is an untenured assistant professor who has been at the university only four years.

Your research has been approved by the university's institutional review board; you've secured funding from a prestigious foundation; and you have the school board's blessing. You're the star of the graduate program, and your former major professor who helped you design the research project wants you to follow her to her new university, which has a top-flight doctoral program. Everything seems to be on the fast track until you get a call from the university president.

"I've heard about this research project you plan to do for your master's thesis," the president says to you, "and I want you to reconsider. I don't think this project fits with the best interests of the university so I'm asking you not to do it."

"Excuse me?" you say. "Why would I want to shut it down now?"

The president explains that she has received a phone call from the mayor. Apparently, the state has recently declared the high school to be a model high school, and it's now part of a statewide project that channels funds to schools that receive the distinction. The high school in your study has already earmarked the funds for a study-abroad student exchange program. Next year's seniors will go to Spain, and some Spanish students are ready to visit the town's high school. The mayor tells the university president that if any drug use is exposed at the school for any reason, the school is certain to lose its funding, and no students will go anywhere.

"I'm asking you to voluntarily discontinue this project," the president says.

"And if I don't?"

"You don't want to put me in that position. I'm asking you politely to do something for the good of the high school and this town. If you want to put your own agenda first, then we will have to see what happens."

You go to your new major professor. When you tell him what the president demanded, he informs you he has already spoken with the president and will resign from your committee if you continue your research. He says he's going up for promotion next year and that the president hinted that your project could be a factor in the school's decision. Because your professor has a wife and three children to consider, he claims that he doesn't want to get involved in a political firestorm.

Your former major professor is outraged by the president's behavior and promises to help you fight the decision. However, as she is leaving the school when the term is over next month and moving across the country to her new school, she warns you that her clout is negligible. She says the best thing she can do for you is to help you get into the master's program at her new school, where you would need to take several classes before you could do a thesis.

WHAT DO YOU DO?

1. Stay and do the project although your research may possibly hurt the high school kids.
2. Negotiate with the president and your new major professor for resources to do another research project.
3. Follow your former major professor to her new university although it will cost you an extra year of graduate work.

Summary

Summary

Learning Objective 1. Understand the difference between achieved social status and ascribed social status.	Ascribed statuses, like gender, are assigned by society. Achieved statuses are earned according to accomplishment.
Learning Objective 2. Define status offenses.	A status offense is considered to be a legal offense only when committed by a juvenile, and it can be adjudicated only in a juvenile court. Status offenses include drinking under age, running away from home, truancy, and being incorrigible. There are no corresponding rules for adults.

Learning Objective 3. Discuss the use of *parens patriae* in the modern juvenile justice system.	The US justice system extended *parens patriae* for two primary reasons: 1) not all parents adequately controlled their children, and the state needed to remove some youths from their homes to preserve order; 2) to protect children from abusive and neglectful parents. Today, state juvenile and family courts handle a range of problems in an attempt to provide systematic and comprehensive solutions to delinquency, abuse, abandonment, child support, and divorce.
Learning Objective 4. Describe the dark figure of crime.	When measuring crime and allocating resources to control it, the differences between reported and unreported crime have substantial significance. We can make educated guesses about the amount of unreported crime that exists in any jurisdiction, but we don't know its actual incidence. This is called the dark figure of crime.
Learning Objective 5. Compare and contrast the Uniform Crime Reports, the National Incident-Based Reporting System, and the National Crime Victimization Survey.	The Uniform Crime Reports is designed to provide a comparative picture of the level of crime across jurisdictions, cities, and states. The strength of UCR data is that each jurisdiction reports offenses according to a uniform set of parameters and definitions; its main weakness is the hierarchy rule. The National Incident-Based Reporting System is part of the FBI's Uniform Crime Reports system but includes more information about offenses reported to police. The NIBRS doesn't use the hierarchy rule and records each offense in a multioffense incident. The primary source of criminal victimization data in the United States is the National Crime Victimization Survey. The NCVS collects information about the frequency, characteristics, and consequences of crime from individuals age 12 and older in a sample size of about 68,000 people. The NCVS depends on self-reporting and excludes data from victims who can't report or can't reliably report their experiences, but captures valuable information about the dark figure of crime because it gathers data about offenses regardless of whether they are reported to the police.
Learning Objective 6. Explain the hierarchy rule.	The UCR records only the most serious incident in a set of incidents. The exception to the hierarchy rule is arson.
Learning Objective 7. Discuss the purpose of self-report studies.	Self-report studies give researchers a different angle on the measurement of crime. Rather than receiving data that has been filtered through law enforcement agencies, researchers can go directly to offenders and delinquents and try to discover offenses that aren't known to the police.
Learning Objective 8. Summarize how children can suffer from crime in different ways from adults.	Children don't participate in creating the conditions or environment that encourages crime. Children are under the control of parents, teachers, older siblings, or others who are charged with protecting them. Youths are a highly victimized segment of the population. Victimizers may be strangers, family members, adults in protective positions, or adult or youth acquaintances. Victimization may occur in the home, the school, and the street. Youths, especially children, can suffer in unanticipated ways, such as ignorance of victimization, long-lasting harm, guilt, permanent physical injuries, family devastation, and bullying.
Learning Objective 9. Explain why the juvenile justice system can't control who enters it.	Police, parents, and schools all participate in deciding who enters the juvenile justice system. The juvenile justice system can't reject anyone and must keep its most recalcitrant and difficult clients. It can't pass its failures on to other institutions. The juvenile justice system is "the system of last resort."
Learning Objective 10. Criticize the idea that some deviant behavior may actually benefit youths and society.	Some deviant behavior may benefit youths and society. Sometimes crossing the line between deviance and acceptable behavior is rewarded. Social change requires that individuals test the boundaries of approved behavior, and some laws may need to be challenged. Future delinquency issues may signal possible cultural changes.

Summary

Chapter Review Questions

1. In what ways is childhood socially constructed?

2. What is the reasoning for giving the government authority over juveniles in place of their parents?

3. What is the "dark figure of crime" and why is this important to understanding delinquency?

4. Why might a victim not report an offense?

5. What are the three major ways of measuring crime?

6. What are the differences between the Uniform Crime Reports and the National Incident-Based Reporting System?

7. In what ways are juveniles a highly victimized segment of the population?

8. What is a typology and how can juvenile delinquents be categorized into one?

9. In what ways can delinquency be considered a positive stage in the development of a youth?

10. Is the juvenile justice system waging war on children?

Key Terms

adolescence—The period between puberty and adulthood in human development that typically falls between the ages of 13 and 19.

cohort—A set of people who share a particular statistical or demographic characteristic.

dark figure of crime—Crime that goes unreported to police and criminal justice officials and is never quantified.

dependent—A term describing the status of a child who needs court protection and assistance because his or her health or welfare is endangered due to the parent's or guardian's inability to provide proper care and supervision.

deviant—Differing from a norm or from the standards of a society.

generation—All of the children in a society who are at about the same stage in their lives. Generations are about 20 years apart.

incorrigible—Unruly. Resisting correction, rehabilitation, or punishment.

juvenile—An age-related status that has legal ramifications. The US legal system generally considers anyone under 18 years of age a juvenile.

juvenile delinquency—A legal term used to describe the behavior of a youth that is marked by violation of the law and antisocial behavior.

juvenile delinquent—A person, usually under the age of 18, who is determined to have broken the law or committed a status offense in states in which a minor is declared to lack responsibility and who may not be sentenced as an adult.

National Incident-Based Reporting System—A crime reporting system in which each separate offense in a crime is described, including data describing the offender(s), victim(s), and property.

parens patriae—Latin for "father of his country," the philosophy that the government is the ultimate guardian of all children and disabled adults.

sex—The biological designation of male or female.

status offense—An act considered to be a legal offense only when committed by a juvenile, and one that can be adjudicated only in a juvenile court.

social control—The framework of rules and customs that a society collectively applies to the individuals within it to maintain order.

sociological imagination—The idea that one must look beyond the obvious to evaluate how social location influences the way one considers society.

street crime—Common violent and property offenses.

typology—A systematic classification of types.

Uniform Crime Reports—An annual publication from the Federal Bureau of Investigation that uses data from all participating US law enforcement agencies to summarize the incidence and rate of reported crime.

Endnotes

1 William Strauss and Neil Howe, *Generations: The History of America's Future, 1584 to 2069* (New York: William Morrow, 1991). The book gives an excellent analysis of the concept of generations. It's filled with research and is theoretically sophisticated.

2 See Chapter 4 for an analysis of how each country has different youth crime issues and different systems for dealing with them.

3 Anthony Platt, *The Child Savers: The Invention of Delinquency* (Chicago: University of Chicago Press, 1969).

4 Joel Spring, *American Education*, 11th ed. (New York: McGraw-Hill, 2004).

5 *In re Gault*, 387 U.S. 1, 87 S.Ct. 1428 (1967).

6 James M. Kauffman, *Characteristics of Emotional and Behavioral Disorders of Children and Youth*, 8th ed. (Upper Saddle River, NJ: Prentice Hall, 2005). See especially Chapter 3, "The History of the Problem: Development of the Field and Current Issues."

7 Strauss and Howe, *Generations: The History of America's Future*, 433–454.

8 David McDowall and Colin Loftin, "The Impact of Youth Curfew Laws on Juvenile Crime Rates," *Crime and Delinquency* 46 (2000): 76–92.

9 Elijah Anderson, *Code of the Street: Decency, Violence, and Moral Life of the Inner City* (New York: Norton, 1999).

10 Leora Tanebaum, *Slut!: Growing Up Female with a Bad Reputation* (New York: Seven Stories Press, 1999). See especially pp. 129–130.

11 Thorstein Veblen, *The Theory of the Leisure Class* (New York: Penguin, 1994).

12 Douglas S. Rendleman, "Parens Patriae: From Chancery to the Juvenile Court," *South Carolina Law Review* 23 (1971): 205.

13 Elizabeth Pleck, *Domestic Tyranny: The Making of Social Policy Against Family Violence from Colonial Times to the Present* (New York: Oxford University Press, 1987).

14 C. Wright Mills, *The Sociological Imagination* (New York: Oxford University Press, 1959), 11.

15 Russell D. Howard and Reid L. Sawyer, *Defeating Terrorism: Shaping the New Security Environment* (Guilford, CT: McGraw-Hill, 2004), 42. See "Prospects for the Future," in which the authors warn that the war on terrorism will be with the United States for a long time.

16 Joshua Norman, "Report: 59 Million Americans Lack Health Care," *CBS News*, November 10, 2010. Online at www.cbsnews.com/stories/2010/11/10/health/main7040408.shtml.

17 Vincent F. Sacco, *When Crime Waves* (Thousand Oaks, CA: Sage, 2005), 92–93.

18 James C. Howell, *Preventing and Reducing Juvenile Delinquency: A Comprehensive Framework* (Thousand Oaks, CA: Sage, 2003), 15–19.

19 Paul Tappan, "Who Is the Criminal," *American Sociological Review* 12 (1947): 96–102.

20 Paul Brantingham and Patricia Brantingham, *Patterns in Crime* (New York: Macmillan, 1984), 49.

21 Greenwich Police Department, Greenwich, CT, www.greenwichpolice.com/tips.htm.

22 Federal Bureau of Investigation, www.fbi.gov.

23 US Department of Justice, Federal Bureau of Investigation, *Uniform Crime Reporting Handbook*, www.fbi.gov/ucr/handbook/ucrhandbook04.pdf.

24 Clayton J. Mosher, Terance D. Miethe, and Dretha M. Phillips, *The Mismeasure of Crime* (Thousand Oaks, CA: Sage, 2002), 65–69.

25 Federal Bureau of Investigation, Uniform Crime Reports,[0] *Crime in the United States, 2009*, Arrests, www2.fbi.gov/ucr/cius2009/arrests/index.html.

26 Robert Meier and Gilbert Geis, *Victimless Crimes: Prostitution, Drugs, Homosexuality, Abortion* (Los Angeles: Roxbury, 1997).

27 Michael Maxfield, "The National Incident-Based Reporting System: Research and Policy Implications," *Journal of Quantitative Criminology* 15 (1999): 119–149.

28 Federal Bureau of Investigation, NIBRS General FAQs, www.fbi.gov/about-us/cjis/ucr/frequently-asked-questions/nibrs_faqs. David J. Roberts, *Implementing the National Incident-Based Reporting System: A Project Status Report* (Washington, DC: US Department of Justice, 1997).

29 Jennifer L. Truman and Michael R. Rand, *Criminal Victimization, 2009* (Washington, DC: Bureau of Justice Statistics, 2010), 1.

Online at bjs.ojp.usdoj.gov/content/pub/pdf/cv09.pdf.

30 Janet L. Lauritsen, "Social and Scientific Influences on the Measurement of Criminal Victimization," *Journal of Quantitative Criminology* 21, no. 3 (September 2005): 245–266.

31 Michael Rand, "The National Crime Victimization Survey: 34 Years of Measuring Crime in the United States," *Statistical Journal of the UN Economic Commission for Europe* 23, no. 4 (December 2006): 289–301.

32 Jennifer L. Truman and Michael R. Rand, *Criminal Victimization, 2009* (Washington, DC: Bureau of Justice Statistics, 2010), 2. Online at bjs.ojp.usdoj.gov/content/pub/pdf/cv09.pdf.

33 Bureau of Justice Statistics, *Victim Characteristics*, bjs.ojp.usdoj.gov/index.cfm?ty=tp&tid=92.

34 Bureau of Justice Statistics, *Key Facts at a Glance*, bjs.ojp.usdoj.gov/content/glance/offage.cfm.

35 Terence Thornberry and Marvin D. Krohn, "The Self-Report Method for Measuring Delinquency and Crime," in *Criminal Justice 2000: Measurement and Analysis of Crime and Justice* (Washington, DC: US Department of Justice, 2000), 33–83.

36 Gordon Waldo and Theodore G. Chiricos, "Perceived Penal Sanction and Self-Reported Criminality, a Neglected Approach to Deterrence Research," *Social Problems* 19 (1972): 522–540.

37 See Mosher, Miethe, and Phillips, *The Mismeasure of Crime*, pp. 102–106.

38 Gary Kleck, "On the Use of Self-Report Data to Determine the Class Distribution of Criminal and Delinquent Behavior," *American Sociological Review* 47 (1982): 427–433.

39 Charles R. Tittle, Wayne J. Villemez, and Douglas A. Smith, "The Myth of Social Class and Criminality: An Empirical Examination of the Empirical Evidence," *American Sociological Review* 43 (1978): 643–656. It should be noted, however, that this finding is disputed. See John Braithwaite, "The Myth of Social Class and Criminality Revisited," *American Sociological Review* 46 (1981): 36–57.

40 Federal Bureau of Investigation, Uniform Crime Reports, *Crime in the United States, 2009*, Table 32: Ten-Year Arrest Trends, www2.fbi.gov/ucr/cius2009/data/table_32.html.

41 Federal Bureau of Investigation, Uniform Crime Reports, *Crime in the United States, 2009*, Table 38: Arrests by Age, 2009, www2.fbi.gov/ucr/cius2009/data/table_38.html.

42 John Wright and Frank Cullen, "Parental Efficacy and Delinquent Behavior: Do Control and Support Matter?" *Criminology* 39 (2001): 691–693.

43 Joan A. Reid and Christopher J. Sullivan, "A Latent Class Typology of Juvenile Victims and Exploration of Risk Factors and Outcomes of Victimization," *Criminal Justice and Behavior* 36, no. 10 (2009): 1001–1024.

44 Murray A. Straus, *Beating the Devil Out of Them: Corporal Punishment in American Families and Its Effects on Children* (New Brunswick, NJ: Transaction, 2001).

45 Joan A. Reid and Christopher J. Sullivan, "A Latent Class Typology of Juvenile Victims and Exploration of Risk Factors and Outcomes of Victimization," *Criminal Justice and Behavior* 36, no. 10 (2009): 1001–1024.

46 Valerie Strauss, "Putting Parents in Their Place: Outside Class," *Washington Post*, March 21, 2006, p. A08. Online at www.washingtonpost.com/wp-dyn/content/article/2006/03/20/AR2006032001167.html.

47 Erich Goode, *Drugs in American Society* (New York: McGraw-Hill, 2004).

48 Randall Shelden, Sharon Tracy, and William Brown, *Youth Gangs in American Society* (Belmont, CA: Wadsworth, 2004).

49 Tonja Nansel et al., "Bullying Behaviors among U.S. Youth," *Journal of the American Medical Association* 289 (2001): 2094–2100.

The Development of Social Control

Because children require many years to mature into adults, society accords rights and responsibilities to them slowly. Parents, teachers, court officials, and legislators believe children must be protected not only from others but also from their own impulsive and immature behaviors. Although we may legitimately argue about the exact age at which adult rights and responsibilities should be granted, there is general agreement that children need socialization, protection, and time to develop a mature perspective. Societies grant adult status based on history, customs, and economic needs. Despite the fact that children (including teenagers) mature gradually, laws, by their nature, set cutoff points at which rights and responsibilities change suddenly. In most states in the modern United States, this age is 18.

Development of the Concept of Childhood

Learning Objective 1.

List why youths of past generations assumed adult responsibilities sooner than do today's youths.

Learning Objective 2.

Compare and contrast the experience of children today with the experiences of children in centuries past.

All societies have the task of socializing their young members to become functioning and productive adults. The rhythms of life demand that the young eventually come into their own and assume the roles that enable a society to survive from one generation to the next. We would be mistaken, however, to assume that past societies accomplished socialization as we currently do in the Western world. For many reasons, the long period of youth dependency, which ranges up to age 21, is relatively recent in human evolution. Modern, industrialized societies protect, nurture, help, or discriminate against the young to such a degree that many still live in a state of financial dependency long after their forebears would have been fully functioning members of society. Youths of past generations assumed adult responsibilities sooner than youths today for three important reasons.

» **Longevity.** Because people live longer today, we can afford to invest more time in preparing children for adulthood. Back when one's life expectancy was 30 to 50 years, it was impractical to devote half of it to preparation for adult roles and responsibilities (see Figures 2.1 and 2.2).

» **Economic pressure.** At a time when most of the population was engaged in working the land, the labor of young people was vital to a family's economic survival. Young children were assigned chores that increased in skill and sophistication as they grew older. Young boys were trained in hunting and/or agriculture and were expected to do a man's work by the time they were in their middle teens. As the division of labor became more sophisticated and the work required more skill, older and more mature craftspeople became necessary. Consequently, the workforce became older, and young people remained in states of economic dependency for longer periods. However, we should note that not all societies develop at the same rate. In many developing nations today, children work long hours in lieu of having what we would consider a normal childhood.

» **Cultural pressure.** Western civilization has changed so radically over the centuries that young people need a great deal more training, education, guidance, and support to function in society. In early agrarian societies, when life revolved around the land and the seasons, young people had only to learn a finite skill set before cultivating their own homesteads. The primary requirement was physical strength, which meant that older adolescents were encouraged to strike out on their own and start families. However, in mature societies in which land was at a premium, it became dysfunctional for all the

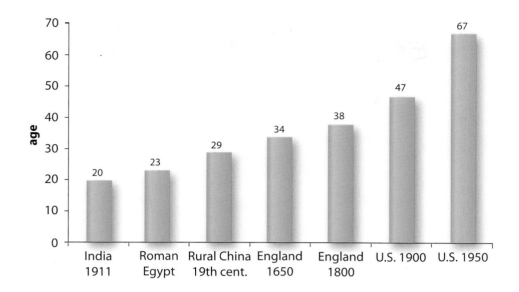

Figure 2.1 Life Expectancy at Birth in Various Societies Throughout History

Historically, life expectancy has been low relative to today's life expectancies.

Think About It

1. Note that life expectancies don't necessarily lengthen in more modern eras. For example, a child born in England in 1650 could expect to live longer than a child born in India in 1911. Discuss possible reasons for this.

Sources: James Z. Lee and Cameron Campbell, *Fate and Fortune in Rural China: Social Organization and Population Behavior in Liaoning, 1774–1873* (Cambridge: Cambridge University Press, 1996), 62. John Landers, *Death and the Metropolis: Studies in the Demographic History of London, 1670–1830* (Cambridge: Cambridge University Press, 1993), 158. Kingsley Davis, *The Population of India and Pakistan* (New York: Russell & Russell, 1968), 36. National Center for Health Statistics, *Health, United States, 2004: With Chartbook on Trends in the Health of Americans* (Hyattsville, Maryland: US Department of Health and Human Services Centers for Disease Control and Prevention, 2004), 143. http://www.cdc.gov/nchs/data/hus/hus04trend.pdf#027. Roger S. Bagnall and Bruce W. Frier, *The Demography of Roman Egypt* (Cambridge: Cambridge University Press, 1994), 109.

sons to receive a piece of the family estate. Therefore, a system of **primogeniture** was established in which the eldest son received the entire estate, and the younger ones were forced to move or join the military or church. Given this lack of land, many young men couldn't afford to start families until their parents died. Consequently, boys stayed home for longer periods to put off the hardships of starting out on their own.

The period of children's dependency has lengthened throughout history for several reasons. What is most fascinating about this process, however, is how Western concepts of childhood have evolved. Despite the fact that the economic and cultural landscape has changed, the concept of childhood has undergone such a radical transformation that it deserves special treatment if we're to fully comprehend the development of the **social control** of youth.

When we consider childhood, we think of innocent and dependent children who must be protected from the forces of nature, predatory adults, and their own curiosity. However, some past cultures didn't consider children as a distinct class in need of special protection and nurturing. For example, according to Neil Postman, there is little evidence that the ancient Greeks considered children special.[1] They practiced infanticide and, except for emphasizing education, showed little interest in the specialized care of children.

This isn't to say that parents had no concern for children; rather, the state didn't accord children particular rights or protections. In fact, much of the treatment of children during the time of the ancient Greeks would be considered child abuse today.[2] Postman emphasizes the effect of the collapse of the Roman Empire on Europe. He states that the Romans developed an idea of childhood that surpassed that of the Greeks. However, along with literacy and education, the concept of childhood disappeared from Europe during the period after the Roman Empire disintegrated.[3]

What is especially interesting about Postman's analysis is the role of education in the development of childhood. Without education, the socialization process is informal, haphazard, and nonsequential, and the line of demarcation in the transformation from child to adult is vague or even nonexistent. Without a period of formal education to differentiate children from adults, there is little need for the concept of childhood.

INSTANT RECALL
FROM CHAPTER 1

social control

The framework of rules and customs that a society collectively applies to the individuals within it to maintain order.

Figure 2.2 Life Expectancy at Birth in Various Nations, 2008

The nation with the highest life expectancy at birth in 2008 was the Republic of San Marino, a European microstate located within Italy, with 82.9 years. This life expectancy was closely followed by Japan, with 82.8 years. The nation with the lowest life expectancy was Afghanistan, at 41.9 years. The United States ranked 35th in life expectancy.

The average life expectancy of the global population in 2008 was 68 years.

Think About It

1. Discuss how a high life expectancy may change how a youth prepares for adulthood.

Source: World Health Organization, Life Expectancy at Birth, www.who .int/gho/mortality_burden_disease/ life_tables/situation_trends/en/ index.html.

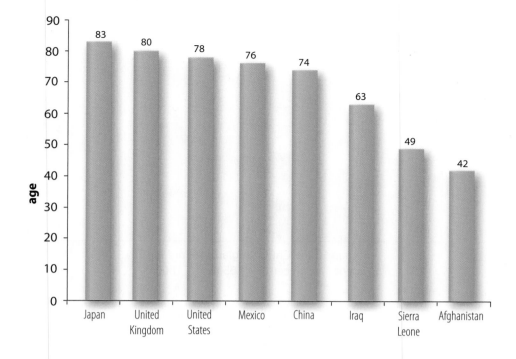

As we move to medieval times, we find that the English thought of child-hood as a special time by at least the 12th century, and the Church and common law clearly distinguished between adults and children. Scholar Nicholas Orme writes that by 1250, most of the English had at least had contact with literacy, and literate parents taught those skills to their children.[4] Children also received special foods and living accommodations, as well as clothes designed specifically for them. In some cases, however, medieval children were treated more like adults than they are now. For instance, it was possible for those under the age of 12 to marry or enter a religious order.

In the late 1700s, German parents began recording systematic observations of their children's physical and linguistic milestones.[5] These "baby biographies" encouraged observers of children, experts who might now be called pediatricians and child psychologists, to quantify the age at which children developed motor and cognitive skills. This information helped to establish the norms that we now use to gauge the development of biological, psychological, and social maturity.

Acquiring Adulthood

One issue that affects the granting of adulthood is that of **patriarchy**. Patriarchy can be defined as situations in which men hold power and authority in political, religious, legal, educational, military, and domestic areas.[6] Patriarchy is exerted over children, not only in the families in which the father seeks final authority over decisions concerning the children (often with mixed success), but also in the child-serving institutions of society, such as religion, school, and the juvenile justice system.

Another issue that affects the granting of adulthood is self-discipline. Self-discipline is pervasive in society and exerts a surveillance and conforming function on all of us, especially children.[7] One indication of successful **socialization** is the self-discipline that compels members of a society to believe in and conform to that society's rules. The better that children acquire self-discipline, the more they are allowed discretion, flexibility, control, and self-direction.

Some past cultures didn't consider children as a distinct class that needed special protection and nurturing. This ancient Minoan fresco depicts boys boxing.

But what happens when a youth doesn't demonstrate the acquisition of self-discipline and defies the rules of parents and society? This is a central question in the development of juvenile justice systems. In the early North American colonies, the General Court of Massachusetts Bay created a law that provided for the execution of children who disobeyed their parents. Derived from biblical language, the "stubborn child law" developed two features that are currently utilized in juvenile justice. First, it directed families to control their children in the interests of society. Second, it sought to limit conflicts and maintain established authority. Although deviance was regarded by the Puritans as an innate flaw in the individual, this law extended the problem to everyone. Temptation was everywhere, and a systematic external discipline, such as the stubborn child law, was required to ensure that the state augmented and supported the family in the social control of children.

Leaving Home at an Early Age

How do children gain control over their affairs? Ideally, they gradually earn the trust and confidence of the adults responsible for them. As children take on more responsibility and ever more complex duties, they are given more freedoms, more opportunities to use their judgment, and more chances to make mistakes. Parents hope that their children learn from many little mistakes and seldom make big ones. There are times, however, when this graduated sense of responsibility isn't instilled in children. Sometimes children must grow up fast and assume roles for which they have not been prepared. Although this might seem to be a recipe for disaster, for many youths, there are countless cases in which young people who were thrust into adult roles at an early age not only survived but also prospered.

An important example of this phenomenon, from US history, is Benjamin Franklin. Although Franklin is generally recalled as a scientist and icon of the American Revolution, his early life is informative to the study of juvenile delinquency. His childhood wasn't easy, yet it shows how a bright, determined youth could negotiate the perils of becoming an adult without the benefit of much parental authority. At the age of 12, Franklin was apprenticed to his older brother's Boston printing shop. Franklin chafed under his brother's poor treatment and, at the age of 15, ran away to Philadelphia. Amazingly self-reliant, he sought to better himself by self-education and hard work and became one of the most accomplished men of his era.[8]

Franklin is but one example of someone who was successful despite leaving home at an early age. There are many more examples, but the fact remains that they aren't the norm. In fact, history is replete with stories of individuals who failed because they didn't have the proper guidance. Poverty, crime, prostitution, and destitution have been the fates of many children who found themselves without supportive and nurturing families.

Is society obligated to care for those youths who for one reason or another are without a support network? Regardless of how we answer this question, it's in society's interest to ensure that its children have an opportunity to thrive. In a highly competitive world in which the losers are left without the means to survive, only bad results can be expected. People don't suffer the pains of poverty and desolation alone, and sometimes they attempt to compete, or even survive, through illegitimate means such as robbery, extortion, burglary, or worse.

Questions

1. If you were forced to leave home now, where would you go? What social support agencies are there today that were absent in the past?
2. How is childhood different today than in past centuries?

The Child Reform Movement

American society has evolved quickly since its inception and, as a result, has seen many major and minor social upheavals brought on by social catalysts such as repeated waves of immigration, industrialization, technology, economic collapse, war, and the expansion of civil rights. The era of social upheaval that extended from the late 19th to the early 20th centuries was marked by lucrative economic opportunities, urban expansion, extensive European immigration, industrialization, and the movement of large clusters of the population from farms to cities.

This turmoil left many people better off as they pursued new opportunities, but it also left many people in worse straits. Impoverished and disoriented, immigrant parents began to lose control of their Americanized children, and rural American parents who had moved to the cities to look for work began to lose control of their urbanized children. With child-labor laws still developing, many children spent long days in factories doing hard labor. The general result of this disarray was crime, delinquency, and the large-scale abuse and neglect of youths. During this time, several social reform movements arose in an attempt to improve social conditions for children.

One example of how society attempted to ease the burdens of impoverished youth is the **orphan train** of the late 19th century.[9] Large eastern cities such as

In the early 20th century, many children spent long days doing hard labor. These boys worked as miners in Pennsylvania.

New York and Boston found themselves with an influx of population from both rural areas and overseas, particularly Europe. Although these teeming cities profited from the supply of cheap labor, they also found themselves with many social problems, including large numbers of orphaned, abandoned, and poverty-stricken children from large families. Social service agencies were stretched thin to provide shelter and food for these children. From 1850 well into the 20th century, over 200,000 children were sent west on orphan trains. This "placing-out" served two key purposes.

» **Removing impoverished children from big cities.** By taking unconnected or loosely connected youth from the cities and resettling them in rural areas, social service workers kept their caseloads manageable. Financial resources, institutional bed space, and low-wage jobs didn't exist for the vast numbers of poor youth. By placing them out, it was believed that the social problems of crime, poor education, and health issues were, if not overcome, then at least pushed so far away that they became someone else's problem.

» **Labor.** The expanding West constantly needed labor to work the farms and ranches, as well as the small businesses in the towns. The chores were endless, and farmers whose children had grown to adulthood and started farms of their own required young people as replacements. It was considered good, honest, healthy outdoor work that was suitable for the children of the cities. By being sent to work on farms, children got a chance to escape the social problems of the cities and learn skills. Although the process was somewhat similar to indentured servitude, for the most part, it allowed many children to be placed with kind families who took a sincere interest in their welfare and didn't exploit their labor.

The practice of placing-out ended at the close of the 1920s, when two major societies, the New York Children's Aid Society and the New York Foundling

Hospital through the Sisters of Charity, halted their programs and directed their resources toward local foster homes and children's aid programs. There were also allegations that placing-out was not the panacea it was thought to be. Inevitably, some children ended up in bad homes and others with employers who wanted only to exploit their labor and provided no education or family life. Some children lost contact with their biological families, while others behaved just as badly in their new homes as in their old. Although these things occasionally happened, the most likely reason the brake was put on the orphan trains was that the West no longer needed people. In fact, some urbanized western areas were being quickly introduced to the very problems in the East that had created the orphan trains.[10]

What happened to those who were not placed out? Only a relatively small percentage of youths were sent west to serve as labor on the developing frontier. **Houses of refuge** were created in the larger cities such as New York, Philadelphia, and Boston. These institutions were started by wealthy philanthropists who financed them as vehicles for rescuing and reforming youths from squalid slums. Further, these houses of refuge, in the philanthropists' view, got children off the streets and helped to curb social disorder among the poor and recently arrived immigrants.[11]

The stated intent of houses of refuge was to provide a safe environment where youths could be trained and educated in a trade. The legal authority for placing youths in such institutions came from the principle of *parens patriae*.

In 1839, *Ex parte Crouse* (see Case in Point) established the justification of the state's intervention in the life of a young girl placed in a Philadelphia house of refuge.

The Child Savers

An important step in the development of social control of youth came about at the end of the 19th century with the work of the **child savers**, whose activities coincided with and were partly responsible for the eventual development of the juvenile justice system. The term "child savers," according to sociologist Anthony Platt, describes the loose coalition of philanthropists, feminists, and social reformers who "helped create special judicial and correctional institutions for the

INSTANT RECALL
FROM CHAPTER 1

parens patriae

Latin for "father of his country." Refers to the philosophy that the government is the ultimate guardian of all children or disabled adults.

2.1 CASE IN POINT

THE CASE

Ex parte Crouse (1839)

THE POINT

This case reinforced the doctrine of *parens patriae* and the increasing power of the juvenile court.

At age 16, Mary Ann Crouse was committed to a Philadelphia County, Pennsylvania, house of refuge by her mother. The county justice of the peace stated that Mary Ann's mother had proved to him "that the said infant by reason of vicious conduct, has rendered her control beyond the power of the said complainant. ("By writ of habeas corpus, Mary Ann's father tried to reclaim her from the house of refuge, contending that she was under detention without a jury trial, which was unconstitutional. In denying the motion, the state Supreme Court responded that the house of refuge was a school, not a prison. The court also stated that "the right of parental control is a natural, but not an unalienable one," and that the community's need for productive members superseded a parent's right to raise a child "when unequal to the task of education, or unworthy of it."

labeling, processing, and management of 'troublesome' youth."[12] For the past century, the juvenile justice system has labored under the philosophy of child saving that was established by reformers who sought to make the world a better place for unfortunate children. However, the ambiguity in these reformers' motivations is inherent in the development of the juvenile justice system.

Despite their humanitarian aims, Platt faults the child savers for being naïve and even disingenuous. For instance, although they professed to represent the best interests of children, their criteria for what was good for children were embedded in their own value systems. The child savers wanted to save troubled youngsters by ensuring that they adopted middle-class values. Given the child savers' rural, Protestant values, it isn't surprising that, because of their different cultural backgrounds, immigrant, Catholic, and urban children often found it difficult to accept the standards set by the state. When snared in legal difficulties, children were subjected to treatment that the juvenile court, not the children or their parents, determined was in the best interests of both society and the child. Let's look at the court's philosophy in terms of reformatories.

» Young offenders must be segregated from the corrupting influences of adult offenders.

» "Delinquents" must be removed from their environment and imprisoned for their own good and protection. Reformatories should be guarded sanctuaries, combining love and guidance with firmness and restraint.

» "Delinquents" should be assigned to reformatories without trial and with minimal legal requirements. Due process is not required because reformatories are intended to reform and not to punish.

» Sentences should be indeterminate so that inmates are encouraged to cooperate in their own reform and recalcitrant delinquents are not allowed to resume their criminal careers.

» Reformations should not be confused with sentimentality. Punishment is required only insofar as it's good for the punished person and only when other methods have been exhausted.

» Inmates must be protected from idleness, indulgence, and luxuries through military drill, physical exercise, and constant supervision.

» Reformatories should be built in the countryside and designed according to the "cottage plan."

» Labor, education, and religion constitute the essential program for reform. Inmates should not be given more than an elementary education.

» The value of sobriety, thrift, industry, prudence, "realistic" ambition, and adjustment must be taught.[13]

It's easy to see how these principles were designed to serve society's interests far more than the interests of children. An elementary education prepared the youths for little more than menial occupations, and they were encouraged to develop only "realistic" ambitions. The program was designed around the assumption that delinquent behavior could be changed by placing children in their proper place as defined by the values of the dominant society. This plan didn't attempt to elevate wayward children above their predetermined place on the social continuum.

The institution of the juvenile justice system formalized the practice of treating children differently, but it also did much more. It brought a wide range of

INSTANT RECALL
FROM CHAPTER 1

status offense

An act considered to
be a legal offense only
when committed by a
juvenile and which can
be adjudicated only in a
juvenile court.

behaviors that weren't considered criminal offenses under the state's control. By
acting in the best interests of the child, the juvenile court didn't have to wait until
the child actually broke the law but could intervene whenever it was suspected
that a problem was brewing. Many behaviors for which a juvenile could be placed
under court supervision were (and are) called **status offenses**, because it's only
the child's age that renders such behaviors illegal. Adults who commit the same
acts are not subject to sanctions.

The problems of children in the early United States were substantial and of
concern to individuals who saw the debilitating effects of poverty and rapid social
change. Because the urban poor couldn't or wouldn't care for their children according to middle-class standards, a number of institutions, charities, and phi-
lanthropies were established to partially fill the gaps. Families of immigrants and
the poor allowed their children to roam the streets, avoid school, and work in
dangerous occupations. Although these conditions were business as usual for the
impoverished, those in the established, and often wealthy, social classes considered impoverished children to be neglected, abused, and out of control.

Just how bad was this situation? By today's standards we would be appalled
by the lack of health care, education, and family support, and by the level of delinquency. Children were unsupervised and often found themselves abandoned
or forced out of their large families at an early age to make their own way in the
world. This situation alarmed those who saw the ills of urbanization as harmful
to society and children. What we must realize is that these concerned individuals
viewed the world through their own class-based perspective and failed to understand that much of what they considered deviant was, in fact, normal behavior for
those in desperate circumstances.

According to C. Wright Mills, many early sociologists considered the process of urbanization to be evil and judged it against the values they brought from
their small, rural societies, where life was ordered and predictable and children
were taught a strict moral code.[14] They saw social disorganization in the city and
worked with philanthropists to develop charities and child-saving agencies that
would apply their own sense of order and control to the lives of those they considered to be less fortunate. It was in this environment that the idea for the juvenile court and ultimately the juvenile justice system was envisioned.[15]

Question

1. Who were the "child savers?" What were their motivations for helping children? Was there any downside to their help?

Learning Objective 4.

Show how social-class
bias was part of the
philosophical foundation
of the first juvenile court.

Learning Objective 5.

Analyze how the first
juvenile court evolved in
its early history.

Learning Objective 6.

Explain how the
philosophy of what is
good for the child is often
combined with other
concerns.

Learning Objective 7.

Compare and contrast
the terminology of the
adult criminal justice
system with that of the
juvenile justice system.

The Juvenile Court

The juvenile court is an important step in the development of the social control of
American youths. Although we will discuss the juvenile justice system in detail
later, we need to become familiar with the juvenile court now because it's critical
to the way that we control and protect youngsters.

Before the juvenile court, children and adolescents were treated much like
adult offenders. The juvenile court, which is just one aspect of the larger social
reform movement of the late 19th and early 20th centuries, changed all that.
Youths now had a legal system of their own designed to protect them from
predatory adults, abusive parents, and social and economic hardships, as well as
from themselves and each other. This same legal system also established formal
civil control over youths, and to a limited extent over their parents, simply by

designing laws that pertained especially to them. At the time, this dual endeavor of protection and control was something new in legal history because it came from the government. Throughout history, the protection and control of youths came from parents and to a lesser and informal extent from religion and social networks. The establishment of the juvenile court represented the first time that a political government utilized a separate legal system to insert itself on a regular basis between youths and their parents, their religious institutions, and their social networks in order to deal with youths for their own good.

History of the Juvenile Court

The first juvenile court was established in Chicago, Illinois, in 1899. Reformers and child activists had struggled for a decade to create a court to separate the cases of children from those of adults. The new court ushered in a philosophy of helping children instead of punishing them, but the child savers didn't get all they wanted in the new juvenile court because several entrenched interests were working against them to preserve the status quo. For example, the law that created the juvenile court, "An Act to Regulate the Treatment and Control of Dependent, Neglected and Delinquent Children," applied only to Cook County, Illinois, leaving the rest of the state to deal with delinquent children in the usual manner.[16] Urban Chicago and the rest of Illinois were different in two significant ways. First, the city was swamped with the problems of a rapidly changing environment. Immigration, poverty, crime, and unemployment made Chicago a vastly different place from the agricultural rural areas and small towns. The second significant difference was the presence of activist, mainly female, reformers who saw it as their civic duty to rescue children from the problems of the city.[17] In a backlash to curtail the range and scope of the proposed legislation, opponents inserted several items that blunted the full reforming effect sought by the child savers.

» **Secret hearings.** The reformers wanted the hearings of the new juvenile court to be closed to the public and the press. The bill's opponents contended that this would rob the public of its right to appreciate how the new institution operated. Although modern juvenile hearings have restrictions about revealing youths' names, the original legislation provided for a more open court.

» **Foster homes.** The legislation prevented the court from paying adults to take children into their homes under foster-care agreements. This legislation resulted from the influence of the industrial (reform) school lobby that lost the labor of children who went into foster care. As a result, Illinois continued to institutionalize dependent children at a high rate.

» **Jurisdiction.** The bill prevented the juvenile court from controlling those who were committed to a state industrial or training school. Additionally, the court lost jurisdiction over children committed to private institutions. This was done primarily to prevent Protestant state officials from influencing Catholic institutions. The bill went so far as to recommend that children be placed with custodians who were of the same faith. Catholic and Jewish supporters of the bill used this provision to ensure that the new court didn't use the legislation to steal the child's faith.[18]

Further reforms chipped away at the original structure and scope of the first court. In spite of these limitations, the first juvenile court went a long way toward ensuring that the welfare of juvenile and delinquent children was considered and that punishing them wasn't the state's first goal. The history of the bill's passage demonstrates that it was a highly political process and that the vested interests that had profited from the plight of neglected or delinquent children were quick to protect their turf.

The juvenile court heard its first case on July 3, 1899. Henry Campbell, an 11-year-old boy accused of larceny, appeared before Judge Richard Tuthill. It was a public event, and spectators and the press packed the courtroom to hear Campbell's mother plead for his freedom. She contended that Henry wasn't a bad boy but that he had been led into trouble by others and that she and her husband didn't want Henry institutionalized. They offered an alternative plan in which Henry would be sent to Rome, New York, to live with his grandmother, away from the corrupting influences of Chicago city life.[19] The disposition handed down by the court, which sent Henry to his grandmother, was consistent with the philosophy of the new institution as articulated by its first chief probation officer, Timothy Hurley:

> Instead of reformation, the thought and idea in the judge's mind should be formation. No child should be punished for the purpose of making an example of him, and he certainly cannot be reformed by punishing him. The parental authority of the State should be exercised instead of the criminal power.[20]

The juvenile court took over a decade to mature into the institution envisioned by its proponents. Several intractable issues had to be considered and solved before the court could provide the type of justice its designers envisioned. We will see in later chapters how some of these issues continue to be problematic:

» **Probation officers.** Although the judge is the head of the juvenile court and exercises great discretion in the disposition of cases, the probation officer is in a more pivotal position. The court has always struggled with defining how probation officers should be trained and what their role should be. At its inception, the juvenile court was concerned with the religion of probation officers. Within a decade, probation officers were evenly divided between the Protestant and Catholic faiths, and there was tension concerning how far the court should intervene into families' lives. Catholic supporters of the juvenile court were suspicious of the court's interventionist tactics and feared that a Protestant, middle-class standard was being applied to all cases.

» **Minority children.** Chicago was undergoing a radical transformation in the early part of the 20th century with unprecedented immigration from Europe and the southern United States. Like many American institutions, the juvenile court struggled to integrate these new arrivals into mainstream society. This problem became particularly acute for black people who were moving into cities like Chicago. Many social institutions, primarily private ones that had discriminated mostly based on religion, started to discriminate by race, as well. Consequently, probation officers soon found that they had few treatment options available for black children who were neglected, dependent, or delinquent. The court was forced to keep minority children under much more severe constraints than youths who could be placed in alternative situations because they were white.[21]

» **Girls.** Young women also presented challenges to the new juvenile court. The first was that parents used the courts to help them control sexually adventurous daughters who were demanding more control over their lives.

Fearing that these girls would turn into promiscuous women who would become prostitutes, the courts tended to incarcerate girls at a higher rate than boys.[22]

» **Private hearings.** One problem of having public juvenile court hearings is the frequent exchange of sensitive personal information that is embarrassing to the youth. This was particularly true of cases concerning the sexual behavior of young women. Having a male judge questioning a young girl about her sexual experiences, however necessary to determine an appropriate outcome for the case, was problematic in an open court. In fact, at the time, having a middle-aged man exploring the sex life of girls under any circumstances was deemed questionable. In 1913, the Chicago Juvenile Court hired attorney Mary Bartelme to act as a "referee" on behalf of female defendants. By 1920, many of the hearings involving sensitive female sexual information were closed to the public.[23]

The juvenile court reforms took place over a period of time. As with any new enterprise, it took time to develop the court's new procedures and to overcome vested interests and inappropriate, counterproductive policies. Such a major reorientation of the philosophy of handling problem children required experimentation with policies and procedures in light of the prevailing political environment.

Boys, Girls, and Bias: The Double Standard

There has always been a double standard in how males and females are accorded rights, responsibilities, and protections. This double standard is an especially sensitive issue in both the juvenile and criminal justice systems, because many of our principles and methods of social control are based on it.

Across a broad range of concerns, including the right to vote, to own property, to file for divorce, to choose one's marriage partner, and to work in certain occupations, men have, until relatively recently, enjoyed discretion, whereas women's choices were restricted. This double standard also applied to boys and girls. Boys were prepared for positions of leadership in society and families, whereas girls were prepared to raise children and take care of the home. The early juvenile justice system applied this same double standard to the rehabilitation and protection of youths. Delinquent and needy boys were prepared for trades, and delinquent and needy girls were instructed in home arts and trades based on these skills, such as cooking, sewing, and child care. Let's look at some of the common reasons for differential treatment of males and females throughout history.

» **Biological.** Because females bear children, human societies tend to divide labor between males and females so that males ensure the livelihood of the family while females care for the children and attend to domestic duties. It seems obvious to many that this arrangement grows naturally out of the biological differences between males and females and that one has only to observe patterns in the animal kingdom to conclude that this is a naturally occurring arrangement. This is a contested argument, but it's still used to account for this disparity.

» **Physical.** Related to the biological argument is the physical justification for treating males and females differently. Because males are typically bigger and stronger than females, females have been considered to need protection. Because of the aggressive nature of males, females are often the victims of rape, assault, and intimidation. Therefore, females have often been constrained in the activities in which they engaged. (In some cultures, they still are.)

» **Religious.** Many religions prescribe that rigid social roles for males and females are supernaturally ordained. Religious texts specify a broad range of behaviors appropriate for one sex, but not for the other. These are particularly persuasive arguments for many people. Religious doctrine provides people with what Alvin Gouldner calls "domain assumptions."[24] Domain assumptions are those ideas that seem so obvious to us that we don't question whether they're true; we simply assume they're true. Many individuals follow religious teachings that specify rigid, precise roles for males and females.

» **Economic power.** Because males have dominated societies for so long, they have been able to control the educational, religious, and social systems that provide what can be called "conventional wisdom." Much conventional wisdom places males in a privileged position, and many critics point out that this state of affairs between the sexes is self-serving. Power is seldom given up lightly, and it's interesting to observe the intense struggle of women who want to be treated equally in societies in which men are unwilling to give up power and share decision-making authority with women.

Because of the successes of the women's movement, numerous laws have been rescinded and new legal protections for women have been enacted, and, most significantly, there have been changes in the collective way that women consider themselves and the way that girls are treated.

However, despite advances in equal treatment under the law, males and females, as well as boys and girls, are still treated differently by the justice system, which is often necessary. This brings us to a controversial issue that is made even more sensitive because we live in a society that seeks to equalize opportunity and social treatment between males and females. For a variety of biological, political, and social reasons, many of which are unknown, males break the law more than females. There are more men in prison than women, and more boys enter the juvenile justice system than girls. Let's look at some statistics.

» In 2009, just 7 percent of all prison inmates were women.[25]

» According to the FBI Uniform Crime Reports, in 2009, males represented 75 percent of all arrestees (both adult and juvenile), 81 percent of violent-crime arrestees, and 63 percent of property-crime arrestees.[26]

» In 2009, 1,054,659 males under 18 were arrested, as opposed to 460,927 females under 18. To be fair, the 10-year arrest trend, 2000–2009, shows that the number of male arrestees decreased 4.9 percent, while the number of female arrestees increased 11.4 percent. However, the gulf between the number of males and females within the justice system is still quite wide (see Focus on Diversity for more on this).[27]

This disparity between male and female offenders of all ages means that both the juvenile and criminal justice systems process more males than females and more boys than girls. This is both good news and bad news for females. They aren't involved in crime as much as males, nor are they processed by the justice system in high numbers. However, because females are such a minority in criminal and juvenile justice systems, the facilities to handle them aren't always adequate. Consequently, like male facilities, they're often crowded.

The Crime Wave That Wasn't

⟨ **FOCUS** ON
DIVERSITY

It's true that girls are being arrested more than ever. Although juvenile arrests have been falling the past few years, girls represent a greater percentage of those arrests since the 1980s. Even more disturbing, girls have also claimed a greater percentage of violent arrests. As of 2009, girls comprised 30 percent of juvenile arrests, up from 22 percent in 1986 (see Figure 2.a).

These statistics—along with the increased visibility of female violence in the media and on the Internet—have raised concerns of a "crime wave" amongst girls, but researchers say this just isn't so. Girls still represent a low percentage of juvenile arrests, and this number has been dropping along with the general juvenile arrest rate (see Figure 2.b). Rather than "girls gone wild," it's far more likely that the increase in the arrests of girls is more about policy than it is about female deviance.

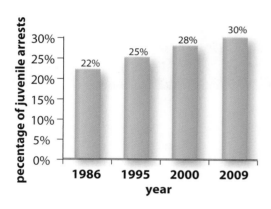

Figure 2.a Girls' Arrests

The percentage of girls who have been arrested has steadily risen since 1986. In 2009, girls represented 30 percent of juvenile arrests.

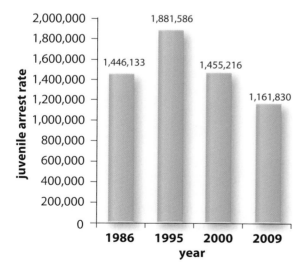

Figure 2.b Juvenile Arrest Rate, 1986–2009

The juvenile arrest rate spiked in 1995 but has dropped steadily since.

---

[1]Margaret A. Zahn et al., *Girls Study Group Understanding and Responding to Girls' Delinquency* (Washington, DC: US Department of Justice, Office of Justice Programs, Office of Juvenile Justice and Delinquency Prevention, 2008). Online at girlsstudygroup.rti.org/docs/OJJDP_GSG_Violence_Bulletin.pdf.

This image taken from video shows a 13-year-old girl being beaten by one of three teenage girls who attacked her in a school yard in North Babylon, NY. The victim was lured to the school yard to meet another teen to resolve a love triangle. After the video was posted on the Internet and broadcast on television, the three attackers—two 14-year-olds and a 13-year-old—were arrested and charged with juvenile delinquency.

Police officers are simply more apt to arrest girls than they were decades ago. This may be because of general changes in law enforcement policy regarding domestic violence: police are more likely to arrest perpetrators of domestic violence than they were in decades past, even if the perpetrator is a juvenile. Girls are more likely to fight at home with parents—typically their mothers—whereas boys tend to fight outside the home. Therefore, if police are called, a girl engaged in a violent conflict with her mother is more likely to be arrested today than in the 1980s or 1990s.[1]

THINK ABOUT IT

1. Why are more girls being arrested today than in the past?
2. Why do girls typically represent a greater percentage of arrest for property offenses than for violent offenses? Discuss.

For Their Own Good

Protecting neglected, dependent, and delinquent children is a delicate task that requires constant evaluation. Because there's no consensus on what is in the best interests of children, the court must tread lightly in developing policies that incarcerate, treat, and divert those who fall under its purview. Although the court is philosophically committed to acting in the best interests of children, it must still observe a fine line in balancing these interests with the protection of society and the expectations and demands of parents, schools, and community standards. The historic pressures under which the early juvenile courts operated reflected the political, social, economic, and religious sensibilities of the time. It's important to understand some of the issues that shaped the evolution of the juvenile justice system. When discussing designing programs for the benefit of children, it's important to remember that this task is always accomplished according to the values of powerful adults. Although well meaning, some of these programs, reforms, or initiatives might have detrimental consequences for problem children.

The invention of the juvenile court was accompanied by a new philosophy of helping, rather than punishing, young lawbreakers. Because the court had the best interests of children in mind, there was no need to protect the children from court processes and decisions. Children didn't need legal protection because the court was helping them, not punishing them. This was the underlying philosophy, but several problems emerged in practice. First, a person who's confined might have trouble telling the difference between treatment and punishment. Confinement can be harsh, restrictive, perceived as unfair, and lacking in rehabilitation. Calling the confinement "treatment" is a semantic sleight of hand that doesn't alter the hardships of detention. Today, delinquents are accorded more due process rights than they were at the inception of the juvenile court. Joseph Sanborn and Anthony Salerno list five reasons for the denial of juveniles' rights at the court's inception:

» Juvenile rights were deemed unnecessary. Because the juvenile court was benevolent and rehabilitative, young lawbreakers didn't need due process rights as found in the adversarial criminal justice system. This philosophy was exemplified in the 1905 case *Commonwealth v. Fisher* (see Case in Point, Chapter 1). The state was viewed as a friend of the youth, not the enemy.

» Juvenile rights were deemed inappropriate. The juvenile justice system's goal was to correct the underlying problem that caused the delinquency, not to punish the youth. A partisan defense attorney or a jury that knew little about childhood development or youth culture was ill equipped to diagnose the problem and prescribe adequate treatment.

Protecting neglected, dependent, and delinquent children is a delicate task that requires constant evaluation.

» Juvenile rights were deemed harmful. In addition to being costly and time consuming, providing due process rights to delinquents might enable them to escape treatment. If the police's case was flawed or the juvenile court process was faulty, the youth might be able to use due process rights to challenge the legality of the proceedings and have the charges dismissed. By not allowing due process rights, the court could intervene when it saw a problem regardless of evidence that an offense had been committed.

» Juvenile rights were undeserved. Adults had full constitutional rights. Juveniles were considered too immature to exercise these rights and were kept under the control of their parents and the state. Only when they reached the age when they could become productive members of society were they entitled to constitutional rights.

» Juvenile rights were inapplicable. Theoretically, what happened in juvenile court was so different from what happened in criminal court that giving rights to juveniles was considered a bad idea. Juveniles weren't "arrested," "tried," or "punished." The vocabulary of the juvenile court process facilitated helping children, so due process rights weren't considered to apply to the juvenile court experience.[28]

As can be determined from this list, those who developed the concept of the juvenile court didn't see the necessity or desirability of providing legal rights to juveniles. This philosophy guided the juvenile court until the 1960s, when a series of groundbreaking cases affected not only the juvenile court but also a vast number of criminal justice issues, ranging from offenders' protections from police searches and seizures to the rights of prison inmates.

The Modern System

In an effort to improve crime response, the United States has a separate juvenile justice system. Although this system shares many features and resources with the criminal justice system, it has a different philosophy, terminology, process, personnel, and organizational structure. Later, we'll discuss moves to combine the juvenile justice system with the criminal justice system, but for now we will talk about the differences between the two systems and specify how they affect the quality of assistance and justice received by juveniles. However, a caveat is necessary. The juvenile justice system is even more fragmented than the criminal

Although the United States has a separate juvenile justice system, there's no typical system because the states' juvenile justice systems vary so greatly.

justice system. Because the states' juvenile justice systems vary so greatly, there's no typical system. Therefore, what we present may be somewhat imprecise when compared to the juvenile justice system in any particular state. Status offenses, however, tend to be largely similar across state and federal jurisdictions. Let's take a look at these first.

STATUS OFFENSES

Status laws exist out of a legitimate concern for youth welfare. Young people can be neglected and exploited by adults, and these statutes are designed to protect youths until they are mature enough to make their own decisions.

» **Running away.** Regardless of the home's suitability, children aren't free to leave. They are legally under the control of their parents and must submit to legal restrictions. Although some children may have legitimate reasons for wanting to leave home, such as abuse and neglect, they are required to get official court approval for leaving and for making sure their new living conditions are satisfactory. Running away and living on the streets or at friends' homes isn't permitted without court investigation and approval.

» **Curfew violations.** Some jurisdictions require adolescents to be off the streets at certain times of the night. Communities don't want youths roaming the streets after businesses have closed, and there are few legitimate activities for young people. Although the children may simply wish to hang out with their friends, many communities believe that wandering youths pose significant public safety concerns. Some jurisdictions relax the curfews for youths who have a reason for being out late, such as employment.

» **Sexual behavior.** Young people are restricted from engaging in certain sexual conduct. Depending on the jurisdiction, the age at which someone may engage in sexual relations differs, but as a general rule, children are prohibited from having sex. (See Prevention and Intervention, about one state's efforts to control juvenile prostitution.)

In most states, smoking tobacco under the age of 18 is a status offense.

» **Alcohol and tobacco consumption.** Children may not drink alcohol or use tobacco products until a certain age. The typical age for legal alcohol consumption is 21 and for legal tobacco consumption, 18, but this can vary by state law. Protecting youths from these addictive substances is considered appropriate until they attain the necessary maturity to make an informed decision about their consumption.

» **Incorrigibility.** Children are supposed to obey their parents. Although there are always conflicts when parents draw boundaries, children sometimes refuse to adhere to these limits, and the court is forced to intervene to protect the child and society.

» **Truancy.** Children must attend school. In most states they can't drop out until age 16.

Although these status laws are intended to protect youths, they may have the unintended consequence of stigmatizing juvenile delinquents or making prohibited behaviors appear more desirable. For instance, smoking cigarettes can appear to be the mark of adulthood to children, so the age-based restriction may make smoking even more attractive. More problematic, however, is what happens to those who are caught up in the system after being caught in a status offense. A youth who is discovered engaging in an illegal activity and is processed by the court may end up with a stigma that could make later life difficult. Schools, families, and the juvenile justice system may treat the youth more harshly because of the status offense. The Juvenile Justice and Delinquency Prevention Act of 2002 doesn't allow status offenders to be confined in secure facilities, but accused

2.2 PREVENTION AND INTERVENTION

Outlawing Youth Prostitution

A major source of profit for human traffickers is the prostitution of youths under age 18. States have status offense laws prohibiting youths of a certain age from having sexual intercourse. Prostitution is a criminal offense in 49 states (except Nevada), and prostitution with youths under a specified age is an offense in all states. In Georgia, the specified age is 16.

In July 2007, Georgia passed tough laws against human trafficking. However, the Georgia law also specified punishment for youths who had been trafficked. House Bill 200, which became law in July 2011, proposed to treat trafficked youths as victims.[1]

"The measure includes protections that allow a prostituted child or adult to avoid criminal charges if they can prove they were coerced into it. Under the measure, coercion doesn't mean just physical abuse but also financial harm, destruction of immigration documents and drug use. The bill allows access to the state's victim fund for medical treatment, provided they cooperate with law enforcement."[2]

Critics say without the threat of sanctions against youths arrested for prostitution, the state wouldn't be able to convince arrested youths to identify their pimps and traffickers. The bill's supporters, who assert that youth prostitution is simply part of a larger human trafficking problem, say youths arrested for prostitution should be treated as victims.

THINK ABOUT IT

1. Should children and adolescents arrested for prostitution face charges of delinquency or even criminal charges? Why or why not?
2. Why is sexual intercourse a status offense? Discuss your answers.

[1]Georgia General Assembly, 2011–2012 Regular Session, HB 200, www.legis.ga.gov/legislation/en-US/display.aspx?BillType=HB&Legislation=200.

[2]Errin Haines and Greg Bluestein, "Ga. Senate Votes for Tougher Sex Trafficking Rules," Associated Press, April 1, 2011.

status offenders may be held in secure juvenile facilities for up to 24 hours following initial contact with law enforcement or the court.[29]

Some critics believe that because children usually outgrow deviant behavior, the best thing to do is to ignore many of their transgressions. The three primary models for dealing with status offenders have been the treatment model, the deterrence model, and the normalization model.

» **The treatment model.** In the early decades of the 20th century, status offenders were thought to have learned their behaviors in response to social and family issues. Therefore, status offenses were considered less as illegal acts than as behaviors that signaled emotional problems that needed treatment to prevent even deeper deviant and antisocial behavior in adulthood. However, by the 1960s, the treatment model was considered to be ineffective, and the deterrence and normalization models were given more attention.

» **The deterrence model.** This model treats status offending from a legal standpoint and asserts that failure to legally sanction and negatively label status offenders will likely result in dire consequences for society as well as the status offender. Some researchers point out that the results of this harsh approach to status offending are about as mixed as those of the treatment model.

» **The normalization model.** Almost an opposite approach to the deterrence model, the normalization model suggests that status offending is normal and doesn't really indicate serious behavioral problems or predict an adult life of crime. As such, medical-style treatment won't make much difference in the youth's behavior, he or she will probably grow out of it anyway, and submitting a youth to harsh legal sanctions may worsen the youth's problems by inserting him or her more deeply into the juvenile justice system.

Some research has suggested that both the deterrence and normalization models are far more effective than the treatment model, and that the normalization model is at least twice as effective as the deterrence model. In a way, this recalls the early, pre-juvenile-justice-system manner of considering youth deviance as just "kids being kids."[30]

LANGUAGE AND TERMINOLOGY

When police officers respond to an incident, they don't know in advance if the suspect they will be dealing with is an adult or a juvenile. Consequently, the police are the first agency confronted with differentiating between delinquency and criminality. The police arrest an adult suspect but "take into custody" a juvenile. The action may look similar, but the terminology is important. To avoid imposing the stigma of "criminal" on a juvenile, the juvenile justice system uses an alternative vocabulary.

» A convicted adult is an "offender," but a young offender is considered a **juvenile delinquent**.

» The adult is served with an **indictment**; the youth, with a **petition**.

» The adult has a trial; the youth, a fact-finding **hearing**.

» The adult is convicted of a criminal offense; the youth is **adjudicated**.

» The adult is sentenced; the youth receives a **disposition**.

The list of different terms for similar actions goes on, but the point has been made here for our purposes. The terms are different because language is

INSTANT RECALL
FROM CHAPTER 1

juvenile delinquent
A person, usually under the age of 18, who is determined to have broken the law or committed a status offense in states in which a minor is declared to lack responsibility, and who may not be sentenced as an adult.

important, and softer, less stigmatizing terms are employed to limit the negative connotations of juvenile proceedings.

PROCESS

Although police officers who arrive at a crime scene may detain youths, adults, or both, once it's determined that a suspect is a youth, a separate process is initiated. Often, officers who specialize in juvenile delinquents will assume the case. At the very least, the case will be referred to juvenile intake at a detention center. Every effort is made to separate youths from adults and to ensure that youths are treated according to the juvenile law. However, in serious cases, juvenile suspects might be bound over to criminal court for trial, as most states have several provisions for doing this.

In addition to referral by the police, a youth may enter the juvenile justice system by other avenues. Parents who are unable to control a child may petition the court to intervene and impose restrictions. A youth doesn't have to break the law before the court can specify a treatment plan and limit the youth's freedom and autonomy. Likewise, a school can alert the court to problems, including truancy, that will allow the court to take action. Abused or neglected children can also enter the court's protection. Individuals in some positions, such as a nurse or teacher, who suspect child abuse are required by law to report it to the proper authorities even if there is no complaint by the child.

Questions

1. The juvenile justice system treats boys and girls differently. Is this fair?
2. What is the difference between criminal offenses and status offenses?
3. What are the differences between the juvenile justice system and the criminal justice system? How are these differences reflected in the language of each?

The Changing Nature of Childhood

Learning Objective 8.

Describe how technology and rapid social change have altered our view of childhood.

Learning Objective 9.

Evaluate the idea that modern youths have more freedom to express themselves but are also growing up in a more dangerous world.

The way that we have responded to the concept of childhood over the centuries reveals much about the progress of Western civilization. As adults took more care to nurture and develop the children's capabilities and protect them from the social and economic realities of adulthood, children were able to develop better skill sets with which to finally take their place in society. One way to trace the development of the concept of childhood is to consider the media. Typically, throughout early history, learning and knowledge were controlled by a child's parents and, to a somewhat lesser extent, by the child's extended family and community. Parents taught their children in a personal manner, for example, "at father's knee," and the child's exposure to knowledge was tightly controlled. The media, which began in earnest with the invention of the printing press, changed that.

Neil Postman argues that children benefited from the invention of the printing press because, for the first time, the masses could learn exactly what the elites learned.[31] The printing press was responsible for transmitting religion, politics, social etiquette, child-rearing advice, and education. The first schools divided students according to ability, but as more children started going to school, they were separated into classes according to age. This age gradation facilitated the development of different rules and responsibilities for children.[32] With the development of the idea of childhood came the demand to explain how children were different from adults and how they should be treated in order to maximize their potential to learn and become productive members of society. According to Postman, Sigmund Freud and John Dewey were especially influential in how we have come to think about children, with the publication of Freud's *The Interpretation of Dreams* and Dewey's *The School and Society*, both of which appeared in 1900.[33]

The contribution Freud made to understanding children's minds was the dismissal of John Locke's notion that children's brains were a *tabula rasa*, or blank slate.[34] Freud argued that children possessed psychological drives and sexuality and that they needed to overcome their instinctive passions and learn to control their behavior. If they didn't repress and sublimate these passions, according to Freud, they couldn't conform to the civilized world. John Dewey considered the development of children and asked, "What is it that the child needs now?" By addressing what the child is, rather than what the child will become, he determined that it was easier to meet children's mental needs and enable them to become constructive participants in the community.

Modern Childhood

The existence of a generation gap has long been taken for granted, but the pace of social change has accelerated to such a degree that many parents' adolescent experiences are irrelevant for today's youngsters.[35] Although each generation goes through a somewhat predictable cycle of life crises (puberty, first love, first car, first pregnancy), each generation experiences these crises differently because of the broad social forces that affect individuals based on their age location. For instance, September 11, 2001, and the wars in Afghanistan and Iraq have different effects on those of fighting age than those of retirement age, just as the latter generation was affected differently by the war in Vietnam than their parents, who were affected by World War II.

It's important to remember that one's age at which major events happen is an important filter by which these events are interpreted. Therefore, although parents and teachers were once teenagers themselves, they had different pressures and temptations, as well as different guidance, support, and nurturing to prepare them. It's worthwhile to use Mills's **sociological imagination** to illustrate how complicated it can be to appreciate one's own circumstances. This challenge to view the young people of today from an objective and neutral appreciation of their social world brings us to the task of describing the historical forces and social pressures that today's children are forced to confront.

It's in this new reality that the juvenile justice system, as well as other institutions in society such as religion, school, and family, must attempt to control and socialize children. Because of the rapid rate of social change, especially in technology, much of the fabric of society is being challenged anew. As technology progresses and societies change to accommodate and take advantage of this progression, the parents of each generation will have to struggle to understand the pressures and temptations that their children are experiencing.

Trends in Thinking About Delinquency and Juvenile Justice

The nature of childhood (the period before puberty) and adolescence (the period after puberty and before adulthood) in the United States has changed in the past century. This is especially true in small towns and rural areas. Schools, day care centers, and recreational facilities are no longer considered the safe havens they once were. Children have cell phones so parents can keep track of them, and many homes have security systems. It's less common these days for children to roam their neighborhoods looking for fun and to organize their own games. Parents schedule their children's play dates and enroll them in structured

INSTANT RECALL FROM CHAPTER 1

sociological imagination
The idea that one must look beyond the obvious to evaluate how social location influences how one considers society.

activities and sports to fill the hours they aren't at school.[36] What do these features of contemporary American life mean for the nature of childhood?

At the very least, changes in American society mean that the social control exerted on children has drastically changed. Paradoxically, a great deal more control is placed on youngsters' freedom, although there are now many areas in which they have considerably more freedom. How can this be? One explanation is that social control in the United States has, in many ways, shifted from social accountability to personal accountability. Let's consider this important phenomenon in detail.

In the past, social expectations of individuals' actions and appearances were far more regimented than they are today. Throughout history, up until the 1950s, males and females were expected to dress a certain way, obey a specified etiquette, engage in a specific set of activities, and meet social expectations. For example, until the early 1960s, American men generally didn't appear in public without a hat, and many American women wore gloves to go out on even minor errands. Men went to work and earned money, while women took care of the home and children. The place of children was equally regimented: they went to school and dressed and acted in a manner specified by their parents. A common scenario in impoverished families was that the children quit school, often before their middle school years, and went to work. Divorce (considered socially improper) was relatively rare, and single parents, latchkey children, and blended families were unheard of as demographic classes. Consider, for example, pre-1970s movies and television shows about families in which one parent is missing. The absent parent is almost always dead, not divorced.

Until the mid-20th century, American society expected its citizens, including children, to act and appear in certain ways, and they generally did so or risked censure or even ostracism.

Because of the level of social accountability, the level of personal accountability was somewhat less, especially for youths. Children were treated less as individuals and more as extensions of their parents and of society. For example, much of the work of the child savers involved separating children from their families, religions, and neighborhoods. They weren't considered to be individuals who needed these institutions; children, it was expected, could grow wherever they were planted.

This changed during the 1960s, when many of these informal, but strict, social rules were dismantled. Women and minorities were no longer restricted to specific

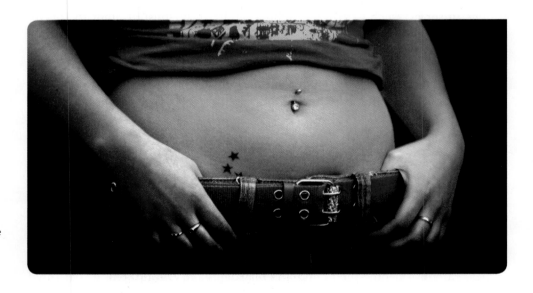

Until the mid-20th century, American children were expected to act and appear in certain ways or else risk censure or ostracism. Today's children and teens have greater latitude in grooming and appearance.

roles and social levels, and people were not only allowed to express more individuality and flout social conventions, but expected to. After the 1960s, divorce rates went up, as did the crime rate (although it has dropped since the 1990s), with the nuclear family being considered endangered, if not already extinct.[37]

Since the 1960s, personal expression has expanded in all directions for all ages. This can be observed, for example, in the form of tattoos, piercings, plastic surgery, extreme sports, consumer-product choice, music, and cars, as well as in blogs and social networking websites.[38]

The expectation of strict obedience to a set of social standards encompassing all aspects of life and allotted according to age, race, and socioeconomic status has withered. To replace it, it can be argued, is a greater expectation of personal accountability, not only for adults, but also for youths. A person might have as many tattoos as he or she wishes, but if he or she breaks the law (the ultimate set of social standards), then, increasingly, the blame isn't placed on society or family, but on the individual. The individual, unless a very young child, is expected to be responsible for his or her actions and to bear the consequences. This isn't to say that individuals were not held accountable and punished for lawbreaking before the 1950s—they most certainly were—only that now the offenses of youths (and adults) are considered to be more a product of individual choice, rather than family, religion, or society.

What does this have to do with delinquency and juvenile justice? Basically, youths are now considered less a subset of society and more as individuals who are expected to be responsible for their own actions, almost regardless of age. A product of this philosophy can be observed in the increased waiver of juvenile cases to criminal (adult) court. Oddly, this move toward greater juvenile accountability can be considered to stem from the juvenile justice system. The US juvenile justice system was the first organ of civil government that came between youths and their parents (and other social institutions) for the youth's sake. Even in the midst of the child-saving movement, which, as you will recall, shipped whole classes of children off to the West, the government began the practice of treating problematic youths as individuals who needed individualized treatments. In its treatment of individuals, then, the juvenile justice system diverged from its child-saving roots, giving rise to many of our current ideas about youth.

Currently, youngsters are freer than ever to express themselves. However, in many ways it's this individualized focus and expectation of personal accountability that has abbreviated the tolerance of their growing pains as they experiment with the boundaries of appropriate behavior. Some parents drug-test their children; schools adhere to **zero-tolerance** policies for trivial behaviors, sometimes calling the police instead of the parents if there's a problem; and communities demand curfews to keep children home at night.

Some teenagers work minimum-wage jobs that require them to drive and stay out late. Younger children are home alone in the afternoon with only the television, Internet, and video games for entertainment and guidance, and young children must negotiate the politics of preschool with other children. In these examples, youngsters are moving toward some aspects of adulthood at a much faster pace than they have for a couple of generations. This illustrates the paradox: youngsters are freer to express themselves, but they must often make difficult personal decisions concerning drugs, violence, and values that their grandparents didn't have to make until they were adults. Prior generations typically assumed the adult responsibilities of their respective eras sooner, but social regimentation left fewer personal choices and, in many ways, made these responsibilities simpler to assume.

Often, young children are left home alone with only the television, Internet, and video games for entertainment and guidance.

For instance, a young rural man in 1900, having little formal education, might have left his father's home to get married and start his own farm and family. So, although he assumed adult responsibilities, he had few decisions to make concerning lifestyle, values, and self-expression, and he had already learned all the skills he needed to run a farm. Now imagine a young rural man of 17 today. He will probably finish high school having already negotiated decisions on whom to hang out with, how to dress, what music to listen to, what drugs to try (or not to try), how to deal with his parents' divorce, how to get along with his stepparents, whether he should stick to the religion in which he was raised (if any) or seek out a new one, and what career he wants to pursue. This is the short list. He must also decide if he wants to attend college and, if so, where. Should he get an apartment? A career? A significant other? Should he instead join the military? Or should he pursue none of the above and remain in his parents' basement working a minimum-wage job?

As you can see (and have probably experienced for yourselves), the young man's personal options are various and complicated, far more than those of the young farmer of a century before. The modern teenager has to make many life-altering decisions but gets a long, graduated transition into adulthood. This long transition allows more chances for contact with the juvenile justice system simply because of the number of critical decisions that must be made so early.

Finally, we tend to forget that in many ways American youngsters are better off now than ever in terms of longevity, justice, medical care, social mobility, and the chance to get an education. In the United States, it's no longer typical for poor children to be pulled out of school to go work in the fields, and no American child today would be placed on an orphan train. Thanks to improvements in medicine, the rate of infant deaths has dropped from 58.2 per 1,000 live births in 1933 to less than 7 in 2009.[39] The chance for a child born today in the United States to live to see adulthood is greater than it has ever been.

Questions

1. In what ways do young people have more freedom than they did in the past? In what ways do they have less?

2. How has technology changed the way we think about childhood?

>> FOCUS ON ETHICS

Boys Will Be Boys. Girls Will Be Home by 11.

You're a parent with 16-year-old twins. Your daughter, Eve, has been dating the captain of the basketball team for several months and thinks she's in love. This young man, a high school senior, has a reputation as a great basketball player and a good student. He's been accepted at a university with a major basketball program and seems to have a bright future as either a professional athlete or a medical doctor.

Recently, you and your spouse have had concerns about how late Eve stays out with this boy. You both believe it necessary to lay down the law and establish an 11:00 PM curfew on weeknights and a midnight curfew on weekends. Eve is furious with you because she says the seniors' parties last much later and that her boyfriend will ensure that nothing bad will happen.

Eve's twin, Riley, just got his driver's license and is constantly out with his friends. Riley is responsible, and you haven't yet thought it necessary to establish a curfew for him. He has recently started dating a girl in his math class, and they stay up late studying for tests at her house. He is getting his best grades ever, and you believe his girlfriend is having a positive influence on him.

Eve says that you treat her differently because she is, as she says, "a girl." Because she and Riley are exactly the same age—actually she's older by five minutes, a fact she never lets you forget—she demands equal treatment. You say that because Riley is male, and therefore bigger and stronger, he can better take care of himself in dangerous situations and that, for the most part, his late nights have been devoted to studying rather than partying. You tell Eve that, although you trust her, her boyfriend is two years older and, although he seems nice, he's at a stage in life when he can take more risks than you are prepared to let her take. You tell her if she were dating someone her own age and not partying so much, you might consider treating her like Riley. This conflict is causing a lot of friction in the family, and you wonder if you're doing the right thing.

WHAT DO YOU DO?

1. Should age determine how late teenagers stay out?
2. Are boys really better able to physically protect themselves than girls?
3. As long as you believe your children are safe, do you care what they think of your rules?

Summary

Summary

Learning Objective 1. List why youths of past generations assumed adult responsibilities sooner than do today's youths.	Youths of past generations assumed adult responsibilities sooner than youths do today for three important reasons: longevity, economic pressure, and cultural pressure. All societies socialize their young members into functioning and productive adults.
Learning Objective 2. Compare and contrast the experience of children today with the experiences of children in centuries past.	Children require many years to mature into adults, and societies grant adult status based on history, customs, and economic needs. The period of children's dependency has increased throughout history, and young people even as recently as 50 years ago became adults sooner than today's children due to longevity, and economic and cultural pressures. In the early American colonies, the General Court of Massachusetts Bay legislated the execution of children who disobeyed their parents. The stubborn child law directed families to control their children for society's sake and sought to limit conflicts and maintain authority.

Summary

Learning Objective 3. Discuss how the child savers of the 19th century wanted to save troubled youngsters by ensuring that they adopted middle-class values.	During the 19th century, juvenile authorities attempted to ease the burdens of impoverished youths by "placing out" children on orphan trains. Others were placed in state and local houses of refuge where they could be educated and trained to work. The legal authority for placing them in such an institution came from the *parens patriae* principle. Anthony Platt credits the child savers with establishing the modern juvenile justice system. Although the child savers had good intentions, those intentions stemmed from their own value systems. The child savers sought to ensure that the juveniles acted in accordance with the values of the dominant society.
Learning Objective 4. Show how social-class bias was part of the philosophical foundation of the first juvenile court.	Probation officers were divided between the Protestant and Catholic faiths. Catholic supporters of the juvenile court were suspicious of the court's interventionist tactics and feared that a Protestant, middle-class standard was being applied to all cases.
Learning Objective 5. Analyze how the first juvenile court evolved in its early history.	The early juvenile justice system formalized the practices of treating children differently and brought a wide range of behaviors that weren't considered criminal offenses under the state's control (status offenses). The first juvenile court was established in Chicago, Illinois, in 1899, with the philosophy of helping children instead of punishing them. Some of the court's problems included probation officers, minority children, and girls. The early court disregarded juveniles' due process rights.
Learning Objective 6. Explain how the philosophy of what is good for the child is often combined with other concerns.	Although the juvenile court seeks to act in the best interests of children, it must still balance these interests with the protection of society and the expectations and demands of parents, schools, and community standards.
Learning Objective 7. Compare and contrast the terminology of the adult criminal justice system with that of the juvenile justice system.	The police arrest an adult suspect but take into custody a juvenile. A convicted adult is an offender, but a young offender is a juvenile delinquent. The adult is served with an indictment; the youth, with a petition. The adult has a trial; the youth, a fact-finding hearing. The adult is convicted of a crime; the youth is adjudicated. The adult is sentenced; the youth receives a disposition.
Learning Objective 8. Describe how technology and the rapid pace of social change have altered our view of childhood.	The rapid rate of social and technological change challenges the fabric of society. As technology progresses, societies must change to accommodate and take advantage of this progression.
Learning Objective 9. Evaluate the idea that modern youths have more freedom to express themselves, but are also growing up in a more dangerous world.	Changes in American society mean that the social control of children has changed. Social control in the United States has shifted from social accountability to personal accountability. Youths are now considered less a subset of society and more as individuals who are expected to be responsible for their own actions, almost regardless of age.

Chapter Review Questions

1. Why do today's youth take longer to assume adult responsibilities than past generations of young people?

2. At what age do you think it's appropriate for a child to leave home?

3. When did the child reform movement first become influential in the United States?

4. Who were the "child savers" and who were they protecting children from?

5. Why did government officials develop a juvenile court instead of handling the cases in a regular criminal court?

6. Are young boys treated differently by the juvenile justice system than young girls? Why or why not?

7. Why do juveniles have fewer legal rights than adults?

8. How are status offenses different from other types of offenses?

9. How has the status of children in the United States changed as we have moved from a philosophy of social responsibility to one of personal responsibility?

10. Has the increase of freedom enjoyed by today's young people been a positive feature for their overall development?

Key Terms

adjudicate—To arrive at a judicial decision. To pass judgment.

child savers—People at the end of the 19th century who were instrumental in creating special justice institutions to deal with juvenile delinquents and troubled youths.

disposition—The final determination of a case or other matters by a court or other judicial entity.

hearing—A session that takes place without a jury before a judge or magistrate in which evidence and/or argument is presented to determine some factual or legal issue.

house of refuge—An early form of the reformatory during the mid- to late 19th century that housed impoverished children, juvenile delinquents, and status offenders.

indictment—A formal written statement that charges a person or persons with a serious offense, usually a felony.

orphan train—A term that encompasses the practice of 19th- and early 20th-century child-welfare societies of placing many orphans, impoverished children, and young adults on trains to less populated parts of the United States, usually the West.

patriarchy—A social system in which males have authority and fathers are considered the absolute head of the family.

petition—In juvenile court, a document that alleges that a juvenile is delinquent and that asks the court to assume jurisdiction over the juvenile or asks that an alleged delinquent be waived to criminal court to be prosecuted as an adult.

primogeniture—A system of inheritance in which the oldest son receives the entire estate.

socialization—The process by which people learn the norms, values, and culture of their society.

zero-tolerance policies—School regulations that give teachers and administrators little to no discretion in dealing with rule infractions.

Endnotes

1 Neil Postman, *The Disappearance of Childhood* (New York: Random House, 1982), 5–8. See especially Chapter 1.

2 Lloyd deMause, "The Evolution of Childhood," in Lloyd deMause, ed., *The History of Childhood* (New York: Psychohistory Press, 1974).

3 Postman, *The Disappearance of Childhood*, p. 10.

4 Nicholas Orme, *Medieval Children* (New Haven, CT: Yale University Press, 2001), 5–9, 238.

5 Robert S. Feldman, *Child Development*, 3rd ed. (Upper Saddle River, NJ: Prentice Hall, 2004), 11.

6 Nijole V. Benokraitis, *Marriages and Families: Changes, Choices, and Constraints*, 5th ed. (Upper Saddle River, NJ: Prentice Hall, 2005), 114.

7 Michel Foucault, *Discipline and Punish: The Birth of the Prison* (New York: Random House, 1979).

8 H. W. Brands, *The First American* (Garden City, NY: Doubleday, 2000).

9   Marilyn Irvin Holt, *The Orphan Trains: Placing Out in America* (Lincoln: University of Nebraska Press, 1992).

10   Ibid., 162–163.

11   Barry Krisberg and James F. Austin, *Reinventing Juvenile Justice* (Newbury Park, CA: Sage, 1993), 14.

12   Anthony M. Platt, *The Child Savers: The Invention of Delinquency* (Chicago: University of Chicago Press, 1969), 3.

13   Ibid., 54–55.

14   C. Wright Mills, "The Professional Ideology of Social Pathologists," *American Journal of Sociology* 49 (1943): 165–180.

15   Maureen A. Flanagan, *Seeing with Their Hearts: Chicago Women and the Vision of the Good City* (Princeton, NJ: Princeton University Press, 2002). See Chapter 1.

16   David S. Tanenhaus, *Juvenile Justice in the Making* (New York: Oxford University Press, 2004), 16.

17   Victoria Getis, *The Juvenile Court and the Progressives* (Urbana: University of Illinois Press, 2000), 10–22.

18   Tanenhaus, *Juvenile Justice in the Making*, 33–54.

19   Ibid., 23–24.

20   Ibid., 23.

21   Barry C. Feld, *Bad Kids: Race and the Transformation of the Juvenile Court* (New York: Oxford University Press, 1999), 23–28.

22   Anne Meis Knupfer, *Reform and Resistance: Gender, Delinquency, and America's First Juvenile Court* (New York: Routledge, 2001). See Chapter 6.

23   Tanenhaus, *Juvenile Justice in the Making*, pp. 51–52.

24   Alvin W. Gouldner, *The Coming Crisis of Western Sociology* (New York: Basic Books, 1970), 29.

25   Heather C. West and William J. Sabol, *Prisoners in 2009* (Washington, DC: US Department of Justice, Bureau of Justice Statistics, 2010), Table 1. Online at bjs.ojp.usdoj.gov/content/pub/pdf/p09.pdf.

26   Federal Bureau of Investigation, Uniform Crime Reports, *Crime in the United States, 2009*, Table 42: Arrests by Sex, 2009, www2.fbi.gov/ucr/cius2009/data/table_42.html.

27   Ibid., Table 33: Ten-Year Arrest Trends, 2009, www2.fbi.gov/ucr/cius2009/data/table_33.html.

28   Joseph B. Sanborn Jr. and Anthony W. Salerno, *The Juvenile Justice System: Law and Process* (Los Angeles: Roxbury, 2005), 24–25.

29   Melissa Sickmund, *Juvenile Offenders and Victims National Report Series: Juveniles in Corrections* (Washington, DC: US Department of Justice, 2004), 17. Online at www.ncjrs.gov/pdffiles1/ojjdp/202885.pdf.

30   Wesley G. Jennings, Chris Gibson, and Lonn Lanza-Kaduce, "Why Not Let Kids Be Kids? An Exploratory Analysis of the Relationship Between Alternative Rationales for Managing Status Offending and Youths' Self-Concepts," *American Journal of Criminal Justice* 34, nos. 3–4 (December 2009): 198–212.

31   Postman, *The Disappearance of Childhood*, pp. 24–27.

32   Philippe Ariès, *Centuries of Childhood: A Social History of Family Life*, trans. Robert Baldick (New York: Random House, 1962), 57.

33   Postman, *The Disappearance of Childhood*, p. 62.

34   Locke forwarded this idea in his 1693 book *Some Thoughts Concerning Education*.

35   William Strauss and Neil Howe, *Generations: The History of America's Future, 1584–2069* (New York: Morrow, 1991), 43–58.

36   C. Wright Mills, *The Sociological Imagination* (New York: Oxford University Press, 1959), 11.

37   Ann Hulbert, "The Paradox of Play: Are Kids Today Having Enough Fun?" *Slate*, June 20, 2007, www.slate.com/id/2168764.

38   Claudia Wallis, "The Nuclear Family Goes Boom!" *Time*, Oct. 15, 1992, www.time.com/time/magazine/article/0,9171,976754,00.html.

39   As of 2011, the most popular of these sites included Facebook, YouTube, Flickr, and Twitter.

40   National Vital Statistics System, National Center for Health Statistics, Centers for Disease Control and Prevention, Provisional Monthly and 12-Month Ending Number of Live Births, Deaths, and Infant Deaths and Rates: United States, January 2009–June 2010, www.cdc.gov/nchs/data/dvs/provisional_tables/Provisional_Table01_2010Jun.pdf.

Theories of Delinquency

CHAPTER 3

Theoretical Foundations of Crime and Delinquency

One of the most fascinating features of juvenile delinquency that students quickly discover is that whatever they think the solution to delinquency is, someone else has thought of it already. Students are sometimes surprised to discover that their original ideas are actually well-established explanations for delinquency and have been used to develop laws, policies, and programs in the juvenile justice system. These established explanations are generally situated within one of two schools of criminological thought: the classical school and the positivist school.

What Good Is Theory and What Is Good Theory?

Learning Objective 1.

List three ways of explaining crime and delinquency.

Learning Objective 2.

Compare and contrast theories and hypotheses.

Learning Objective 3.

Recall the criteria that must be addressed when evaluating theories.

The classical and positivist schools were developed by scholars, researchers, thinkers, philosophers, sociologists, and early criminologists who were looking for rational explanations for crime and delinquency. A third way of thinking about crime and delinquency, **spiritual explanations**, is one that's been developed by everyone who has ever wondered why another person breaks the law or violates society's rules and norms. The classical and positivist schools go back to the 18th and 19th centuries; spiritual explanations probably reach back to the dawn of humanity.

This chapter will explore these three ways of thinking about crime and deviance because they are the most important to the creation of the criminal and juvenile justice systems. Although developed in the past, these systems of thought still influence our current system and ideas of justice, and none have truly fallen out of favor.

》 Many people still suggest spiritual explanations for deviant behavior and lawbreaking. As a social institution, religion continues to influence social control in the United States.[1] Spiritual ideas are embedded in our popular culture and are at the foundation of the modern criminal justice system.

》 The **classical school of criminology** is fundamental to our understanding of crime. Although classical criminology was developed during the

The established explanations of juvenile delinquency are generally situated within the classical school and the positivist school of criminological thought.

Enlightenment, it's still an important part of our laws and criminal justice system.

>> The **positivist school of criminology** focuses on the offender, rather than on the offense. The positivist school seeks the truth about human nature through science, rather than religion or philosophy.

The important work of the juvenile justice system is based on theory, and the study of theory is crucial to all academic enterprise, including the study of juvenile delinquency.[2] We will devote the next four chapters to considering many of the theories that seek to explain why some youths break the law and how the juvenile justice system responds. First, however, we must understand why theories are important, how they are constructed, and how to evaluate them so that we can compare and contrast the various explanations of juvenile delinquency.

At the bases of the classical and positivist schools are theories, and to understand these two schools, we first have to know what a **theory** is. Contrary to popular belief, a scientific theory isn't an educated guess. That would be a **hypothesis**, an early step in the **scientific method** that is a tentative explanation for an observation or phenomenon. In science, a theory is a way to organize facts and explain data, offering a framework for discussion and investigation. If another theory comes along that offers a better explanation for a problem, the old theory may be discarded. In the social sciences, theories use facts and data to explain human behavior; in criminology, theories seek to explain human deviance.

Theories are based on real-life observations and data and are important tools for understanding the world.[3] We use theories and hypotheses every day whether we realize it or not. For example, say you're driving your car and following a loaded pickup truck from a construction site. After a few miles, you hear a loud bang and begin to have trouble controlling the car. You develop a quick hypothesis that you have a flat tire. Upon halting the car and seeing the nails sticking out of the flat tire, you develop a theory that some nails fell out of the pickup truck; you ran over them, and they punctured your tire. You don't know this for sure, but based on the evidence, you theorize it to be true.

Some theories are simple, such as our flat-tire theory, and some are complicated, such as Albert Einstein's theory of general relativity. Although textbook definitions of theory might differ slightly, they consistently address similar issues. In this text, we will use the definition developed by sociologists Daniel Curran and Claire Renzetti: "A theory is a set of interconnected statements or propositions that explain how two or more events or factors are related to one another."[4]

For example, if we say that the crime rate decreases as educational level increases, we're considering two factors, crime rate and educational level, and specifying their inverse relationship. By specifying the direction of the relationship, we can then conduct observations to determine the theory's validity. Within Curran and Renzetti's simple definition is the potential to specify how any two clearly stated factors are related to each other. According to criminologists Ronald Akers and Christine Sellers, some criteria must be addressed when evaluating theories.[5]

>> **Logical consistency.** Does the theory make sense? For example, Akers and Sellers state that the theory must have propositions that are logically stated and internally consistent. They contend that if a theory argues that offenders have biological reasons for what they do, then it makes no sense to claim that family socialization is a basic cause of criminal behavior. It would make more sense to claim that the cause of criminal behavior is a gene that is passed from the parents to the children.

》 **Scope.** The amount of deviant behavior that a theory can explain depends on its scope. A theory that addresses only shoplifting is useless for explaining violent offenses. Although good theories attempt to explain a broad range of behavior, some theories overreach. There can be a trade-off between the broad scope of a theory and its ability to produce strong and consistent results.

》 **Parsimony.** In terms of theory, parsimony refers to the economy of an explanation. Parsimonious theories explain a good deal of behavior using straightforward language. Parsimony and scope are related, and some of the best theories carry a great deal of meaning with carefully selected words.

》 **Testability.** A good theory should be stated in such a way that the propositions and their relationships can be scientifically tested. According to Akers and Sellers, a theory might not be testable for a number of reasons. First, it might be based on a tautology, or circular reasoning.[6] If we say that low self-control is measured by a failure to refrain from crime and then say that crime is caused by low self-control, we haven't offered a testable theory.[7] The key to developing testable theories is to start with observable criteria. If we say, "The devil made me do it," we must then find some way to observe the actions of an individual called the devil. Because belief in the devil, like the belief in a supreme being, is considered a matter of faith, it's difficult to observe such factors with any scientific certainty. Finally, Akers and Sellers point out that it's not sufficient to simply construct theories that can be supported, but that a good theory can also be rejected or falsified.[8] If the facts of a case are continually reinterpreted to support a theory, the theory can never be rejected.

》 **Empirical validity.** Empirical validity is evidence that an instrument is measuring what it has been designed to measure. By repeatedly testing a theory with different populations or in different geographic locations, researchers can collect data about a theory's reliability and empirical validity. For example, several small-scale treatment programs that appeared to be successful didn't succeed when tried on a larger scale or in different locations. It became evident that the earlier positive results stemmed from the determination of a staff who was dedicated to a new and innovative program.[9] Once the program became routine and subject to staff who considered the program as just a job, the positive results vanished. So, in this case, it was repeated testing of a program's features in other locations that helped researchers determine if the program worked.[10]

》 **Usefulness and policy implications.** The thing that keeps criminological theory from being just an academic exercise is the degree to which it can guide policy. Crime and crime control are pressing concerns, and academic theories can have far-reaching ramifications. For instance, a theory that demonstrates that youths who are exposed to alcohol at an early age are more prone to drinking problems as adults would suggest that parents should protect their children from alcohol for as long as possible. However, some theories suggest policy changes that are unreasonable, impossible, or unethical. Imagine that a researcher develops a theory that left-handed children are at a greater risk of becoming delinquent than right-handed children. Should we force all left-handed children to use their right hand? What would be the unintended consequences of such a policy? Policies suggested by theory must be considered in the light of ethical and professional guidelines to ensure responsible implementation.

>> **Ideology.** Finally, Akers and Sellers suggest that a theory must be considered based on its ideological underpinnings.[11] Theories can be derived from the agendas of reformers or the worldviews of those in charge, with the explicit purpose of forwarding a particular political or social purpose. For instance, those concerned with the modern, Western-style nuclear family will most likely reject theories that suggest that an intact nuclear family isn't absolutely required for the development of healthy children. Regardless of the veracity of theories, it's useful to know the ideology of those responsible for them. Although it's possible for someone to have a slanted ideological perspective and still develop an objective theory, it's intellectually honest to reveal ideological bias.[12]

It's easy to see from these criteria for evaluating theory that a lot of thought and research goes into constructing explanations of crime and society's response to it. Few theories fall out of favor in criminology. Like flotsam and jetsam on a beach, theories wash ashore and are added to the theories that came before them. Some remain in use, while others are only half-used or occasionally considered.

One of the first concerns we will observe in our study of theory is that no single theory completely explains all the issues that are important to the study of juvenile delinquency. Many theories might reveal some truth but still fail to capture the whole truth. This is because crime is complicated and multifaceted. For now, we must be satisfied with partial explanations, conflicting theories, and an incomplete understanding of why people, including juveniles, break the law.

The Scientific Method and Social Science

Science is a methodical way to acquire knowledge, not the knowledge itself. The scientific method is based not on belief, but on evidence. The exact steps in the scientific method may vary somewhat from one scientist to the next, but scientists generally follow these steps:

1. Identify a problem or ask a question.
2. Develop a hypothesis.
3. Formulate a procedure to test the hypothesis.
4. Collect and analyze data through experimentation or observation.
5. Arrive at a conclusion and communicate the results.

The questions that scientists ask must be answerable. This might require narrowing the terms. For instance, the question "Why are all juvenile delinquents bad?" is unanswerable. What is bad? Does bad mean evil? What does evil mean? Does bad mean criminal? Does bad refer to an action or a state of mind? The wording also poses a chicken-and-egg problem. Are some juveniles delinquent because they're bad, or are they bad because they're delinquent? It also supposes that all juvenile delinquents are "bad." This question is highly subjective, so the scientific method can't answer it.

A better question is, "What causes some youths to break the criminal law?" First of all, the terms are easily defined. In the United States, juveniles are typically defined as people under the age of 18. Unlike the prior question, it doesn't frame juveniles as delinquents. The criminal law is the criminal code of the United States. It's known that some people under the age of 18 break the criminal law. Asking "What causes?" and not "Why" refines the question even further.

"Why?" is a philosophical question that might muddle the issue. "What causes?" looks for measurable, quantifiable concerns that may cause a juvenile to break the criminal law.

Next, a scientist forms a hypothesis. This means gathering as much information as possible, which usually means reading the literature. Hypotheses don't have to be correct; a good hypothesis is also one that can be rejected. There must be a way to test the answers to try to make the hypothesis fail. Also, a hypothesis is never proven. It's either confirmed or not confirmed.

The scientist must then come up with a way to test the hypothesis. In the natural sciences, this usually involves both experimentation and observation. In the social sciences, such as the study of criminology and criminal justice, testing a hypothesis is a little more problematic. A chemist can mix some substances in a flask and place them over a Bunsen burner, and space scientists can crash as many probes into comets as their budget allows. But social scientists can't just dream up a social situation and inject some human beings into it. Good science depends on observation and experimentation; however, there are moral, legal, and ethical issues when dealing with human subjects.

Although in the past, some social scientists used humans in experiments—the most famous (or infamous) being Philip G. Zimbardo's 1971 Stanford Prison Experiment—social science typically relies on observation and statistical analysis to gather information (see Crosscurrents for more on human experimentation). Social science issues, even those involving criminal and juvenile justice, don't involve immediate life-and-death problems, and the legal and ethical issues of human experimentation are often too great to justify the knowledge that could be gained.

Another problem with human experimentation is that, because of human psychology, it's best to observe people who don't know they're being observed. This is difficult enough to do with simple observation. It's nearly impossible to set up social experiments on people so that they don't know they're participating in an experiment.

Therefore, testing a criminal justice hypothesis involves gathering data on real-life scenes that already exist and events that have already happened, such as the number of arrests or offenses or inmates. It also involves the use of demographic information, such as that gathered by the US Census. Offenders and victims can report their experiences and perceptions in self-report studies, and a good study can refine this information into useful, consistent data. Social scientists use statistical analysis to measure the probability of an answer, not to provide an answer. In the end, there are only two options: reject the hypothesis or don't reject the hypothesis. Proof only exists when the chance for error is zero, and there's always some chance for error.

The conclusion and the communication of the results state how the results relate to the hypothesis, the results that were contrary to the hypothesis, and ideas for further testing. Good scientific method doesn't change the hypothesis or omit results that don't support the hypothesis; it also presents reasons for the difference between the hypothesis and the results of the analysis.

Questions

1. What is a theory?
2. What is a hypothesis?
3. What is focus of the positivist school of criminology?
4. When was the classical school of criminology developed?

3.1 **crosscurrents**

Human Experimentation

The following two criminological studies are among the most controversial in the literature. In the first, the Concord Prison Experiment, Harvard University researchers gave psychoactive drugs to prison inmates. In the second, a group of young men participated in an experiment that sought to replicate the conditions of a prison and its effects on human beings.

THE CONCORD PRISON EXPERIMENT

The Concord Prison Experiment was conducted from 1961 to 1963 by Harvard University researchers led by Timothy Leary. It involved the administration of psilocybin, a hallucinogen obtained from some types of mushrooms, to 32 prison inmates in an effort to reduce recidivism. The subjects, who were incarcerated in Massachusetts Correctional Institute–Concord near Boston, all volunteered to participate in the study. Administration of the drug was combined with group therapy and psychological tests.

Although the researchers claimed the psilocybin positively affected recidivism rates, a follow-up study published in 1998 contradicted this claim.[1] Leary wrote in his autobiography, "We had kept twice as many convicts out on the street as the expected number."[2] However, in 1969, he admitted that drugs alone weren't enough to rehabilitate offenders: "The main conclusion of our two year pilot study is that institutional programs, however effective, count for little after the ex-convict reaches the street. The social pressures faced are so overwhelming as to make change very difficult."[3]

THE STANFORD PRISON EXPERIMENT

In 1971, Stanford University psychology professor Philip Zimbardo created an experiment to test the effects of prison life on inmates and staff by recruiting 24 young men to act as inmates and guards. The college-age men, who had answered a newspaper ad, were randomly split into guards and inmates and taken to a makeshift prison in the basement of a university building. The researchers tried to run the experiment as much like a prison as possible—which included strip-searching and delousing the inmates—and the guards had almost complete control over the inmates.[4]

The staff and guards came to treat the inmates so cruelly that, according to Zimbardo, "There was no longer any group unity; just a bunch of isolated individuals hanging on, much like prisoners of war or hospitalized mental patients. The guards had won total control of the prison, and they commanded the blind obedience of each inmate. At this point it became

In 1971, Stanford University psychology professor Philip Zimbardo created an experiment to explore the effects of prison life by recruiting 24 young men to act as inmates and guards. Here, Zimbardo gives a lecture at Stanford University on Abu Ghraib prison in Baghdad, Iraq.

clear that we had to end the study. We had created an overwhelmingly powerful situation—a situation in which inmates were withdrawing and behaving in pathological ways, and in which some of the guards were behaving sadistically."[5] The experiment, slated to last two weeks, ended in six days.

In 2002, the United Kingdom's BBC repeated the experiment and broadcast the resulting show, called *The Experiment*. Although closely monitored by researchers, the BBC Prison Study, like the Stanford Prison Experiment, was terminated early. Zimbardo criticized the experiment, saying that the original is considered unethical by today's standards and didn't need to be repeated.[6]

THINK ABOUT IT

1. Why is such human experimentation considered unethical today?
2. Can anything useful be learned from human social experimentation?
3. Discuss how the young age of the men in the Stanford Prison Experiment may have affected the study.

[1]Rick Doblin, "Dr. Leary's Concord Prison Experiment: A 34-Year Follow-Up Study," *Journal of Psychoactive Drugs* 30, no. 4, Criminal Justice Periodicals (Oct–Dec 1998): 419–426.

[2]Timothy Leary, *High Priest* (Berkeley: Ronin Press, 1995).

[3]Timothy Leary, "The Effects of Consciousness-expanding Drugs on Prisoner Rehabilitation," *Psychedelic Review* 10 (1969): 20–44.

[4]Kathleen O'Toole, "The Stanford Prison Experiment: Still Powerful after All These Years," Stanford University News Service, January 8, 1997, news.stanford.edu/pr/97/970108prisonexp.html.

[5]Philip G. Zimbardo, Stanford Prison Experiment, www.prisonexp.org.

[6]Matt Wells, "BBC halts 'prison experiment'," BBC, January 2002, www.guardian.co.uk/uk/2002/jan/24/bbc.socialsciences.

Spiritual Explanations of Crime and Delinquency

Learning Objective 4.

Explain the source of spiritual explanations of crime.

Spiritual explanations, which are rooted in religion, tend to be favored by many people—"The devil made him do it," "That serial killer is pure evil," or "She was just born bad"—and aspects of the spiritual point of view remain in the formal justice system. One social reason for punishment, especially for heinous offenses, is to satisfy the need of society and the victim (or victims) for revenge by symbolically quelling evil. The custom of and justifications for seeking revenge come from ancient religious texts. For example, in Leviticus 24:17–22 we can observe one of the origins of the Western idea of **lex talionis**, or the law of retribution.[13]

17 And he that killeth any man shall surely be put to death.
18 And he that killeth a beast shall make it good; beast for beast.
19 And if a man cause a blemish in his neighbour; as he hath done, so shall it be done to him;
20 Breach for breach, eye for eye, tooth for tooth: as he hath caused a blemish in a man, so shall it be done to him again.

Religion is a powerful social institution. For much of the recorded history of the Western world, organized religion was vital to political and social control. In western Europe, the Christian Church was linked to royalty in that the royal power was considered a reflection of the will of God, a concept also known as the "divine right of kings."[14] This dual system of Christian church and state survived for centuries because the only people who were educated were royalty, aristocrats, and clergy.

Because of the strong influence of the Christian Church in western Europe and England, the English legal system, on which the US legal system is based, is largely derived from Christian ideas of justice and morality. These ideas explained the nature of humanity and social control as a struggle between good and evil, and crime and deviant behavior were considered to be the works of "the devil" or of human beings who strayed from the will of God.

But just how was "the devil" considered to influence people to break the law and young people to misbehave, and how has society traditionally retaliated? According to Stephen Pfohl, demonic explanations of deviant behavior were of two types.

» **Road of temptation.** According to the theory of demonic influence, each of us is tempted by the devil to engage in deviant acts. Perhaps the most important aspect of the road of temptation, and one which we shall see recur in many other theories of deviance, is the idea that humans have a choice between good and evil. The choices that we make determine our character and are used by the criminal justice system to justify punishment. In other words, those who choose to do the crime also choose to do the time.

» **Road of possession.** In demonic theory, choice is less of a factor when someone is considered to be inhabited by an evil spirit. Here a person's body and mind are believed to be possessed, and this person is no longer deemed to be responsible.[15]

Both of these explanations are especially applicable to young people, who traditionally have been considered to be more subject to both temptation and possession due to youth, inexperience, and vulnerability. Some parents who

Some parents who believe their child to be possessed by an evil spirit might resort to exorcism to evict the entity they believe is troubling their child. In this engraving, the ancient Phoenician god Baal holds a child.

believe their child to be possessed by an evil spirit might resort to supernatural means, commonly known as exorcism, to evict the entity they believe is troubling their child.

These early ideas that people who broke the law were tempted or possessed by an evil spirit are more than historical curiosities. According to Harvard Law School professor Alan Dershowitz, US criminal law can be traced back to the book of Genesis.[16] Religion continues to play a part in the justice system, as well as in the way Americans think about crime and deviance. For example, the Ten Commandments remains an important aspect of the US legal system and, until recently, could be found posted in courthouses around the United States. The existence of the Ten Commandments assumes that people can choose to follow them or not. This idea departs from spiritual theories in which an evil entity is responsible for tempting or possessing people.[17] The offense does not originate with "the devil" but with the offender.

Questions

1. What is evil? Can it be defined? Why or why not?
2. Where do spiritual explanations of crime come from?

The Classical School of Criminology

The spiritual perspective has been largely overtaken in the justice system by other ways of envisioning why people break the law and how society should respond. These alternative perspectives are grounded in the changing economic, political, and social conditions of their times. The first perspective we will study is classical criminology, which grew out of the ideas that fueled the Enlightenment.

Learning Objective 5.

Discuss the effect of the Enlightenment on criminological theory.

Learning Objective 6.

Evaluate the effect of deterrence on juveniles.

History of the Classical School

The Enlightenment, which roughly spanned the 18th century, was a 100-year interlude of energetic thinking and writing based largely on reason, secular ideals, and criticism of all that had gone before. The Enlightenment continues to influence modern science, law, and government. Many of history's great documents were produced during the Enlightenment, including the Declaration of Independence and the US Constitution. Enlightenment philosophy is especially important to the modern US criminal justice system and its treatment of juveniles. The philosophy of Cesare Beccaria and Jeremy Bentham (whom we'll discuss later) emphasized fairness, humaneness, and rationality and was important to the creation of the US juvenile justice system with its laws and legal processes that account for the needs of children and adolescents.

Classical criminology influences the modern criminal and juvenile justice systems with its theories of **deterrence**, emphasis on punishment, and, to a lesser extent, prohibition of torture. Classical criminology is especially present in the continued emphasis on incarceration as a means of deterrence and punishment, as well as the idea that deterrence and punishment are duties of the justice system. Classical criminology uses the idea of **free will** to explain that offenders choose to break the law and that the best way to control lawbreaking is to deter potential offenders.[18] Several Enlightenment-era social shifts fundamentally changed the administration of justice, all of which encouraged the development of classical criminology.

> **Changes in population.** Scholars have learned that the size, density, and **heterogeneity** of a population greatly influence economic and social policies. The population of Europe changed greatly from the 16th to the 18th centuries as people moved from rural areas and cities began to grow. One of the most prominent ways this affected the social control of deviant behavior was through the emergence of anonymity in the cities. In societies where everyone knows each other and where people have strong social bonds, there exist pressure and reward for conforming behavior. As more of the population moved to the cities and the old social networks disintegrated, both juveniles and adults had greater opportunities to break the law without detection. As people of different cultures began to live together, they found that they often viewed behavior differently. Without a shared set of values and history, people were more likely to conflict and less willing to respect one another's privacy, property, and sensibilities.

> **Political and economic changes.** Major political and economic changes happened during the move toward a more rational way of dealing with crime and deviance. The most significant change was the move from feudalism to **capitalism**. The change in the relationship between owner and worker can't be overstated in terms of its effect on social organization and social control. Under feudalism, the workers, called serfs, were bound to the land under the protection and control of a vassal, who obtained his rank by birth. When a vassal sold land, the serfs went with it. The arrangement was binding across generations, so serfs labored on the same lands as their parents, as would their children. This form of communal control was weakened by the trade economy of capitalism, in which labor wasn't attached to serf-vassal loyalty but rather was based on a fixed, impersonal wage. This resulted in an economic individualism in which people fended for themselves and in which young people had the opportunity to determine their own futures for better or worse.

》 **Religious and intellectual changes.** As the Protestant Reformation challenged the authority of the Roman Catholic Church, several developments drastically altered the ways in which society controlled crime. Most significantly, the changes in religious life meant that individuals didn't have to go to the clergy to determine right and wrong. No longer was there just one standard of judging deviance, and people were free to develop their own explanations and reasons for crime. Scholars who sought to develop a more rational view of crime created a philosophy in which people were free to choose their own actions.[19]

These social changes had profound influences on how people viewed their responsibilities to obey the law and deal with lawbreakers. The classical school of criminology grew out of these changes, but it took scholars and public officials to translate these societal changes into theoretical underpinnings that informed policy. The two figures best associated with the classical school of criminology are Cesare Beccaria and Jeremy Bentham.

CESARE BECCARIA

Cesare Beccaria (1738–1794) was an Italian lawyer who became interested in the prison system, which he viewed as repressive, corrupt, and filled with irrationality and injustice.[20] As a reformer, he was concerned with establishing a rational, humane system of social control. His 1764 treatise *An Essay on Crimes and Punishment* influenced many philosophers and early criminologists.[21] In this essay, he laid out nine principles that he claimed would produce more effective and humane justice. Beccaria took the complaints and frustrations that many of his contemporaries had with the medieval penal practices and created a new philosophy. Sociologist Stephen Pfohl summarized these principles in the following points:

》 Society has an interest in making sure that rational punishment is administered in order to preserve the social contract that individuals make with those in the community. If transgressions aren't punished, then there's little incentive to obey the law and expectations of neighbors. The punishment must make sense to the public and not be arbitrary or tyrannical.

》 The law and punishment are to be determined by the legislature and the guilt by the judge. In earlier times, judges had broad discretion in torturing people as part of the fact-finding mission and as part of the punishment. There was little control of overzealous judges who acted in irrational and abusive ways toward defendants, who had few, if any, rights.

》 People are presumed to use a **hedonistic calculus** to maximize pleasure and avoid pain. This simple principle explains a broad range of deviant behavior and serves as a guide to construct punishments designed to prevent crime.

》 Rationally calculated punishment is the best form of social control. If people decide to break the law because they deem the pleasure outweighs the possible punishment, then society needs only to alter the statute to make the punishment more certain, rapid, and severe.

》 Deterrence is the basis for social control. People won't break the law if they think they will get caught and punished.

》 The classical school of criminology is more concerned with controlling the unlawful acts of individuals than with controlling the individual. There's no concern for why someone commits an offense, only with making the punishment severe enough to deter potential offenders. All offenders are thus treated equally according to their infractions, and their social class, gender, age, or personal deficiencies have no part in fashioning the sentence.[22]

It's difficult to overstate Beccaria's contributions to the development of modern legal systems. France was the first country to apply Beccaria's ideas. After the 1789 French Revolution, the new government sought to build a new legal system based on justice and rationality and used Beccaria's ideas to create the French Code of 1791. However, French judges soon found that the classical philosophy was too harsh in some circumstances.[23]

In its zeal for justice, the French Code called for treating all offenders, regardless of age, sex, mental ability, or background, in exactly the same fashion. This meant that a 7-year-old boy who stole a loaf of bread would be treated the same way and given the same sentence as a 37-year-old man who committed the same offense. The French realized that they needed more discretion than classical philosophy allowed and altered the code to accommodate the young, as well as other special offenders. Legislators revised the French Code in 1819 to recognize "age, mental condition and extenuating circumstances."[24]

JEREMY BENTHAM

Another social thinker and reformer who greatly influenced the development of classical criminology was Jeremy Bentham (1748–1832). Bentham developed an approach that, like Beccaria's, was concerned with the way individuals weighed pleasure and pain when deciding whether to commit deviant acts. Bentham reasoned that deterrence theory is a major part of the way that society should respond to crime.[25]

Jeremy Bentham argued that the proper objective of all conduct and legislation is "the greatest happiness of the greatest number."

Deterrence Theory

Deterrence theory is especially important to the classical school of criminology because it's directly connected to the concept of free will. As you'll recall from our earlier discussions, the classical school holds that adult offenders and delinquents freely choose whether to break the law. It follows, then, that those who choose to break the law can also be deterred from doing so. It's just a matter of making the consequences swift, sure, and severe.

Students sometimes make the mistake of thinking that deterrence theory involves only the imposition of more severe sanctions.[26] Bentham and Beccaria both remind us, however, that the certainty of punishment is more influential in controlling crime and delinquency than the severity of punishment. In the modern United States, the certainty of getting caught for many offenses, such as dealing drugs, is relatively low and is offset by the prospect of immense profits. Sometimes the value of the return is subjective. Some youths might consider a $20 return on an offense to be worth the chance they will get caught. In fact, many youths don't even consider the chance that they will get caught.

WHAT IS DETERRENCE?

Does deterrence theory as promoted by classical criminology work? At one level, the answer is yes. Most of us most of the time don't break the law partially because we fear being caught and punished. Certainly, we obey the law for a number of other reasons, such as being bonded to our community and respecting the rights of others, but we're all aware that bad things might happen to us should we seek illegal pleasure at someone else's expense.

We can also contend that, given the crime rate and institutional overcrowding, deterrence theory isn't working well enough. Even with the prospect of the death penalty—or life imprisonment in the case of juveniles—some offenders still commit heinous offenses.[27] In doing this hedonistic calculus, why do so many people make the wrong decision?

For instance, armed robbery is a first-degree felony punishable by a long prison sentence. In some states, an offense as serious as armed robbery will get a juvenile sent straight to criminal court. This brings up an important issue: How do children and adolescents perceive deterrence? Much of deterrence depends on mental maturity and future-time orientation. An adult can consider an offense, then imagine getting caught and punished for that offense, and then imagine how unpleasant a long prison term would be. Research has shown that youths don't imagine the distant future in the same way that an adult does. A 15-year-old obsessing about the homecoming dance isn't thinking about what he will be doing when he's 60. Nor do youths truly comprehend the permanence of some legal consequences, such as a life sentence.

Deterrence is problematic for those who, because of age, are focused on the short term rather than the long term.[28] There is a good chance that someone might get killed in an armed robbery, which can mean a life sentence for a juvenile. One would think then that anyone contemplating armed robbery would pick a target that would yield a great deal of money to offset the possibility of severe punishment. Yet offenders often pick a target, such as a convenience store that keeps only a hundred dollars or so in the cash drawer, for their risk.

Criminologists have spent decades attempting to determine whether deterrence theory works. This is a difficult task because, in effect, they're trying to measure crime that doesn't occur. Some offending varies by season and weather, and some offending varies by **demographic** variables such as the age ratios, neighborhood conditions, and the presence of illegal drugs.[29] It can be extremely difficult to decide which offenses occurred because of a lack of deterrence and which offenses occurred because of a big shipment of cocaine hitting the streets.

So how do researchers attempt to measure the deterrent effects of laws? One method has been to examine the effect of capital punishment on murder rates.[30] Deterrence theory contends that the murder rate would fall after citizens heard about an execution. Because murder rates might rise or fall anyway, researchers compare a state that executes offenders with a neighboring state that doesn't. If the state with capital punishment showed a significant drop in its murder rate while the neighboring state without capital punishment showed no change in its murder rate, researchers could conclude that executing murderers might act as a deterrent.[31]

Another basic concern of deterrence research concerns the accuracy of knowledge of the severity of various sanctions. If we assume that more severe sanctions will deter individuals from breaking the law, we must ensure that we can determine that potential offenders are aware of what the sanctions actually entail. But even this level of understanding can be misleading, because potential offenders don't need an accurate understanding of the sanctions in order to be deterred. All they need is a belief that they will get caught (certainty), get caught swiftly (celerity), and be punished drastically (severity) for deterrence theory to work. Therefore, the perceptions of potential offenders can be as important as their objective knowledge of their situation.[32] In summarizing the deterrent effect of criminal sanctions, Akers and Sellers conclude that certainty of punishment is the most powerful aspect of deterrence theory. Neither the severity nor the swiftness of punishment is as robust as the certainty of getting caught. Imagine a teenager who's planning to shoplift several video games. According to Akers and Sellers, the teenager is more likely to be deterred by the guarantee that she will get caught, than by the threat of a year-long sentence to a detention center or the expectation that she won't have to wait long for that sentence.

DETERRENCE AND JUVENILES

Prior to 1900, juvenile lawbreakers were treated much as adult lawbreakers and subjected to the same punishments. However, youths, according to modern juvenile theory, aren't rational like adults are, and youths' physically immature brains operate differently (see Prevention and Intervention for more on this).[33]

Deterrence theory's hedonistic calculus requires a mature, rational mind to perform it successfully.

3.2 PREVENTION AND INTERVENTION

Deterrence and the Young Brain

The philosophy of deterrence depends on the individual's ability to make a rational choice. Ideally, a person who breaks the law and who is judged to be irrational, usually because of mental illness or intellectual disability, isn't given a typical criminal sentence. Such people are often sent to mental hospitals for medical treatment, and although their freedom is restricted, they aren't punished. But what about a class of people unable to make rational choices? How would deterrence work, then?

Many medical experts and criminological scholars are now questioning the assumption that juveniles are able to make rational decisions. Before the early 20s, the brain not only isn't developed enough to consider long-term consequences, it's also more subject to **impulsivity** and peer pressure and less able to accurately assess risk (a neurological and hormonal condition that continues into young adulthood).[1]

For example, in a driving simulation, young adolescents (ages 13–16), older adolescents (ages 18–22), and adults (ages 24 and older) played the game by driving alone and then with two friends. When driving alone, all of the participants drove in a similar fashion, engaging in similar levels of risk. However, when driving in the presence of two friends, the young adolescents showed a 100 percent increase in risky driving, and the older adolescents showed a 50 percent increase in risky driving, but the presence of friends didn't affect the adults' driving at all.[2]

So if juveniles aren't able to make decisions that are as sound and rational as those of adults, can deterrence efforts prevent delinquent behavior? According to some scholars, juvenile antisocial behavior is actually experimentation with risk and searching for a place in the social hierarchy, a normal part of growing up. In the vast majority of adolescents, this behavior disappears upon adulthood once the brain matures.[3] This means that the deterrence-based consequences of crime that keep most adults within the law—long periods of incarceration, social embarrassment, broken family ties, lost employment, permanent social stigma—don't work as well for youths.

The justice system seems to be catching on to the concept that because of juveniles' reduced ability to resist peer influence, control impulses, and engage in long-term reasoning, they aren't as responsible for their deviant behavior as adults are. In May 2010, the US Supreme Court decided in in *Graham v. Florida* that juveniles couldn't be sentenced to life without parole in cases that didn't involve a homicide.[4] The idea of deterrence is that the threat of a sentence such as life without parole should discourage most people, including juveniles, from committing serious offenses. However, it's questionable as to whether juveniles really understand what "life without parole" really means.

Such developments cast doubt on the role of deterrence-based treatment of juvenile delinquents. More successful efforts at the prevention of delinquency and intervention into delinquent behavior may come from more attentive parenting and increased mentoring from teachers and other authority figures. Some states have also passed legislation aimed at prevention. For example, Connecticut passed driving laws restricting young drivers from having friends in the car.[5] Other states and jurisdictions are experimenting with teen curfew laws that restrict young people from being out after certain hours. As understanding of the juvenile brain increases, it's possible the control of delinquency will involve less deterrence-style, punitive measures and more mentoring and rehabilitative programs.

THINK ABOUT IT

1. Should juveniles be considered less responsible for their actions because of their neurological condition?

2. Create a juvenile delinquency program based on deterrence that takes into account the limitations of the juvenile brain. Why would it work? Why not?

[1] Praveen Kambam and Christopher Thompson, "The Development of Decision-Making Capacities in Children and Adolescents: Psychological and Neurological Perspectives and Their Implications for Juvenile Defendants," *Behavioral Sciences and the Law* 27: 173–190 (2009).

[2] Ibid., 178.

[3] Ibid., 185.

[4] Mark Hansen, "What's the Matter with Kids Today," *ABA Journal* 96, no. 7 (July 2010): 31.

[5] State of Connecticut, Teen Driving Laws for 16- and 17-Year-Olds, www.ct.gov/teendriving/cwp/view.asp?q=413528&a=3369. 7Online.com, "New Teen Driver Laws in Connecticut," July 23, 2008, abclocal.go.com/wabc/story?section=news/local&id=6282909.

This poses a problem for deterrence theory's hedonistic calculus, which requires a mature, rational mind to perform it successfully. There's evidence to suggest that because of these differences between juveniles and adults, deterrence doesn't have much of a deterrent effect on youths. It's possible that they're simply incapable of forming the train of rational thought required for deterrence to work.

At the time much of the basic classical school theory was being formulated, little was known about the neurological differences between children and adults, and even less was known about the brain itself. Early classical theorists expected youths to perform the hedonistic calculus as efficiently as adults. The expectations of the effect of deterrence on juveniles and the way in which juveniles perceive deterrence must be considered differently by criminal justice practitioners.

For example, a small self-report study in Georgia by Richard E. Redding and Elizabeth J. Fuller explored the deterrent effect of juvenile waiver (or transfer) laws, which are laws that allow juveniles to be tried and sentenced as adults (see Chapter 13 for a complete discussion). Several key points emerged from the juveniles who participated in the study.[34]

» The youths were largely unaware of waiver laws.

» The youths believed that knowing about the law might have deterred them from committing their offenses. They also suggested ways that more youths could be made aware of the laws.

» The youths believed that being tried as adults was unfair. About half in the study didn't know why they were being tried as adults. (Many, apparently, were charged with armed robbery, an offense they didn't consider to be serious. When asked to list what they believed were the truly serious offenses, the responses were split between rape and murder.)

» The youths believed that the actual consequences of their offenses were worse than they had imagined. Most of these juveniles had already been through the juvenile system and thought that the sanctions they received there were little more than "a slap on the wrist."

» Other research quoted in the study found that juvenile waiver laws actually weakened **specific deterrence**; that is, **recidivism** among juveniles tried and sentenced as adults increased. The effect on **general deterrence**, however, remained in question.

» Many of the youths who knew about the law didn't think it would apply to them. Redding and Fuller give two possible reasons for this. The first is the general immaturity of juveniles, which includes impulsivity, limited perspective of time, and willingness to take risks.[35] The other is that the youths' prior experience with the juvenile justice system was too gentle and gave the youths the message that there was little consequence to breaking the law.

In an interesting counterpoint to the last item (this will be covered in more detail in Chapter 14), serving "hard time" in an adult facility appears to have a brutalizing effect on juveniles, possibly making them more likely to offend again. So, although the youths quoted in the study said that knowing about the waiver laws might have deterred them, research has found that trying and sentencing them as adults might worsen their rate of recidivism.

Another issue that the study emphasized concerns the fact that deterrence, either specific or general, doesn't work if the target population is unaware of the laws that are supposed to achieve that deterrence. The State of Georgia had produced a video about the waiver laws that was shown intermittently in state schools, in prevention programs, and on television. However, most of the juveniles in the study didn't have a chance to see the video, as they rarely or never attended school. They were truant, or they had been expelled, or they had dropped out. The law's deterrent effect was lost on youths who had no idea that it existed or why it was being applied to them.[36]

In contrast, most adults are generally aware of the consequences of entering the criminal justice system. For the most serious offenses, there are expectations of long prison terms, life sentences, or even execution. Even civil lawsuits worry many adults because of their expense. The juvenile system's focus on rehabilitation means that juvenile penalties can be relatively light and geared toward saving the youth (whether the youth is aware of this or not), so the youth might not perceive them as "serious." However, youths transferred to the criminal justice system can receive decades-long sentences in adult facilities depending on the gravity of the offense.

The Classical School of Criminology Today

The failure of researchers to demonstrate the utility of deterrence theory doesn't mean the classical school of criminology isn't important to the study of contemporary crime and delinquency. Besides setting the framework for many of the rules and procedures used by law enforcement and the courts, the classical school informs new theories of crime and justice system practices. Two of these modern initiatives are **rational choice theory** and **shock deterrence**. Each of these theories is worth examining to see how the present remains firmly entrenched in past ideas and practices.

RATIONAL CHOICE THEORY

Do people choose to break the law or choose to desist from a criminal lifestyle in the same manner that they decide to buy an automobile or join a fraternal organization? In other words, is whether to break the law simply another decision that we make in the context of hundreds of decisions we make every day? Rational choice theory states that the individual decision to offend is susceptible to examination in much the same way as the decision to buy a home. People weigh the costs and benefits of all their decisions and act in their own best interests.

According to Frank P. Williams and Marilyn D. McShane, offenders make two different types of decisions when contemplating an offense.[37] First, they make involvement decisions in which they determine whether they will engage in a particular offense, continue the offense, or desist. For instance, in a study of persistent property offenders, Kenneth D. Tunnell found that money was the primary and almost exclusive motivation for the decision to commit the offense.[38]

Second, offenders make event decisions about what tactics to use. If the tactics to successfully commit the offense appear easy, the offender will decide to become involved, whereas if the tactics appear difficult, the offender will desist. At a certain level, this appears to be simple common sense. For example, banks put money in safes to make the tactics of bank robbery more difficult so that potential bank robbers will pass them by.

The difference between rational choice theory and classical criminology is that rational choice theory is rooted in economics. Economists envision the choice to commit an offense as they would any other choice and try to establish mathematical models to explain the behavior.[39] This can be problematic for several reasons.

》 The researcher has to assume that the variables the offender considers in choosing to offend can be captured in the model. The expected reward isn't really known before the offender commits an offense. Unlike a decision to buy a car in which the value is well established, a mugger who decides to assault someone is uncertain what the payoff will be.[40]

)) Not all individuals bring the same resources to the decision to break the law. Some individuals have money, credit, insurance, and a support network that can affect the decision, while others have few resources and are desperate. These factors seldom enter the decision-making process as envisioned by rational choice models.[41]

)) Many offenders don't adequately weigh the risks of getting caught. They believe they're good at crime and engage in repetitive and reckless behavior that is sure to draw the attention of police. Their irrational patterns almost guarantee they'll eventually be apprehended.[42]

)) It's extremely difficult to factor in variables such as anger, intoxication, boredom, and impulsivity. These variables aren't always available in existing data sets based on official crime reports.[43]

)) Even given the difficulty in obtaining information on the variables that offenders use when deciding to break the law, there's another conceptual flaw in rational choice theory concerning the assumption that the offender does, in fact, make rational choices. Some criminologists believe many offenders act irrationally and do things contrary to their well-being.[44]

It should be noted that these criticisms of rational choice theory don't mean that pursuing this line of research is futile. For certain offenses, such as burglary, in which offenders have the time to plan the event and take precautions against detection, it's useful to attempt to understand what factors they consider. Additionally, when sufficiently large data sets are used, it's possible to observe broad patterns of choice.

Rational choice theory is a relatively new approach, and as more criminologists become familiar with it, we can expect its methodology to become more sophisticated and its applicability more vigorous. Another important question for the study of juvenile delinquency concerns the rationality of the choices that delinquents make. We might find that juvenile delinquents understand their own best interests less than adults understand theirs.

SHOCK DETERRENCE

If offenders are unable to make good choices when considering whether to commit an offense, perhaps they simply lack information on the consequences of getting caught. How much do any of us actually know about the skill of the police in catching offenders, the prosecutors in constructing solid cases that prove guilt, or what life in prison is really like? For the most part, many people get their impressions of the justice system from Hollywood. We watch movies and television and believe they accurately reflect society. How is a 16-year-old youth contemplating robbing a convenience store supposed to have a realistic idea of the costs and consequences of his actions?

The criminal justice system has employed a number of strategies to address this very problem. By giving pre-delinquents or first-offenders a sobering and realistic look at the consequences of breaking the law, some criminal justice administrators reason that potential delinquents will make better choices. The idea behind this technique is to shock youths with a draconian look at what might happen if they continue to break the law. Basically, three types of shock deterrence programs attempt to address delinquency and change behavior in this way.

SHOCK INCARCERATION

Shock incarceration is intended to alter how offenders consider the benefits and costs of breaking the law. Here, offenders are sentenced to long periods behind bars but are released on probation after a few weeks. This experience is intended to demonstrate to the offender how restrictive incarcerated life can be. Presumably, juvenile delinquents will be deterred from further lawbreaking and will cooperate with the probation officer, rather than risk losing their freedom again. One can only imagine the relief a youth must feel after spending two weeks behind bars and suddenly being placed on probation and going home. The shock of short-term incarceration is presumed to give the youngster enough information about incarceration to convince him or her that the risks-and-rewards equation doesn't favor breaking the law.

The major, untested assumption here is that the short-term incarceration does indeed shock the youth. Although many people would find incarceration uncomfortable, some juveniles might benefit from the predictable routine and consistent discipline. We aren't suggesting here that youths enjoy incarceration but rather that the short period of loss of freedom might not be that much of a shock and therefore might not have the intended consequence of deterrence.[45]

SCARED STRAIGHT–STYLE PROGRAMS

In 1975, several inmates serving sentences of 25 years or more in New Jersey's Rahway prison formed the Lifers' Group to give inmates a more sympathetic image. With the help of prison officials, they created the Juvenile Awareness Project to educate youths on the consequences of incarceration. Youths under the age of 18 toured the prison and listened to inmates talk frankly about prison life: "prison violence, including assault and murder, homosexual rape, suicide as a fact of prison life, inedible food, the impersonal atmosphere in which there was no unity between inmates, and the need to live by the bells."[46]

At first, the inmates acted more as counselors, using reasoning and persuasion. Gradually, however, the inmates began to feel they weren't getting through to the youths, and the program escalated to the point that the goal was to "shock" the youths with threats and intimidation and to "scare them straight." The inmates would yell and tell the youths all the terrible things they would do if the young people ever entered the prison as inmates. Threats of rape and brutal beatings were intended to terrorize the youths so much that they wouldn't break the law anymore.

The Juvenile Awareness Project probably would have been eventually discarded if not for a documentary film that made the program famous and spawned dozens of copycat programs across the country. The documentary *Scared Straight!* became an instant hit. The program, based on the classical criminology principle of deterrence, was promoted as a way to deliver real information about incarceration that would alter juveniles' calculations about the feasibility and advisability of breaking the law.

However, besides not deterring youths to the degree claimed by its adherents, the Scared Straight–type program ignored the various reasons that youths break the law. The youths who participated in the program didn't always come from groups who were likely to be serious delinquents but instead tended to be typical middle-class boys. Further, those who were exposed to Scared Straight were arrested five times more than a matched sample of those who didn't participate.[47] James O. Finckenauer of Rutgers University conducted a study that compared two groups of youths with similar histories of delinquency. One group of

46 youths had attended Scared Straight, while the other group of 35 youths had not. Finckenauer reported that 41 percent of the Scared Straight graduates had gotten into trouble again, in contrast with only 11 percent of the control group.[48]

In early 2011, prison officials in California and Maryland suspended their Scared Straight–style programs after the Department of Justice warned that it might halt funding for the programs.[49] Both programs had been featured on the television show *Beyond Scared Straight*, which was based on the original 1978 documentary (see Programs for Children for more on this).

According to two Justice Department officials in a *Baltimore Sun* editorial, a 2002 Campbell Collaboration study reported findings similar to the earlier Finckenauer study: Scared Straight participants were up to 28 percent more likely to break the law than youths who didn't participate. Also, several participants reported that the inmates who were supposed to be "scaring them straight" sexually propositioned them and tried to steal from them.[50] A 2006 review of studies of Scared Straight–style programs by the Florida Department of Juvenile Justice found them to be not only ineffective but actually "criminogenic," that is, likely to cause youths to go out and break the law.[51] In the *Baltimore Sun* editorial, the Justice Department officials wrote that despite the popularity of Scared Straight–style programs, what actually did work was mentoring programs that used positive, teaching-style relationships to reduce delinquency, substance use, and academic failure.[52]

JUVENILE BOOT CAMPS

The most popular of the shock-incarceration techniques is the **juvenile boot camp** strategy, in which offenders are subjected to military-style discipline and routine. Hundreds of these programs have been set up at both the juvenile and young adult levels. We'll discuss juvenile boot camps in greater detail in Chapter 14, but they are worth discussing here to appreciate how they are related to the principles of the classical school of criminology.

Basic training in the military is designed to put enormous physical and psychological stress on recruits to break down their old ways of thinking and to instill the military way of deferring to authority and executing orders. This is necessary to get essentially good teenagers to do something they would not normally consider: kill another human being. Once the recruits are broken down, the training is designed to instill a sense of accomplishment, belonging, and pride in being part of a military organization. Additionally, the shock of basic training is followed by years of military service in which any effects of psychological brutalization are negated, controlled, or ameliorated.[53] Military basic training replaces one attitude and way of life with another.

By contrast, the juvenile boot camp concept fails to provide the redeeming features of military service. Youths are subjected to 90 days of abuse and humiliation as if there's something restorative in the technique itself. Certainly, the youths can be dominated to the point where they obey the commands of the "drill sergeants," but this experience does little to prepare them for life in civil society. National Institute of Justice evaluation studies have shown that neither juvenile nor adult boot camps reduce recidivism, whether they are programs with a heavy military emphasis or treatment-oriented programs. An Office of Juvenile Justice and Delinquency Prevention study found no significant differences in recidivism rates between boot camp participants and juveniles who had participated in other programs. In some cases, boot camp graduates actually had higher rates of recidivism.[54] Criminologists Malcolm Feely and Jonathan Simon have suggested that the one thing juvenile boot camp might be good for is developing drug dealers and gang members.[55]

3.3 PROGRAMS FOR CHILDREN

Scared Straight! Scaring Kids for Over 30 Years

In 1978, 16-year-old Angelo Speziale made it onto national television with a group of other juvenile delinquents and almost-delinquents in the documentary *Scared Straight!* The documentary debuted on television, broadcast uncensored in an era when three networks controlled what the nation watched. Popular and controversial, *Scared Straight!* spawned heated public discussion on the subject of delinquency and what to do about it. In 1979, the film won two Emmys and an Oscar for Best Documentary.[1]

The Scared Straight program received overwhelming public support, and many people wrote to their state legislators demanding similar programs in their own states. The spotlight also brought criticism. Although Scared Straight initially claimed a success rate of 90 percent, this figure didn't withstand subsequent evaluations. By 1980, with program attendance falling, the prison modified the program, dropping confrontational tactics in favor of counseling.[2]

Two sequels to *Scared Straight!* followed up on some of the youths from the original documentary. In *Scared Straight: 20 Years Later* (1999), Angelo Speziale said the experience of being yelled at by hard-core inmates had changed him into a law-abiding person. Some Scared Straight–style programs continued to operate in prisons around the nation even as critics protested that, not only did the program appear to do little good, it might actually be harmful.

In 2005, Angelo Speziale was arrested for shoplifting and subjected to mandatory DNA testing. Because of a large backlog at the lab, it wasn't until 2007 that Bergen County, New Jersey, police were notified that Speziale's DNA matched a semen sample taken from the body of 19-year-old Michele Mika, who was raped and murdered at her home in 1982, just four years after the original *Scared Straight!* documentary. Although Mika and Speziale had been neighbors, the investigation had focused on Mika's boyfriends. In 2010, Speziale was sentenced to 25 years in prison.[3]

Meanwhile, the show goes on. In 2011, Arnold Shapiro, producer of the original documentary, launched the *Beyond Scared Straight* reality-show series on the Arts & Entertainment Network. According to the show's website: "Each one-hour episode focuses on a different inmate-run program in the U.S., and follows four or five at-risk teens before they attend the program, throughout their day inside the prison, immediately afterwards, and then follows up with them one-month later to see the lasting impact of the experience on their lives."[4]

THINK ABOUT IT

1. In your opinion, is Angelo Speziale a good example of whether the Scared Straight program works?
2. Discuss why such a program would be so popular with the public despite evidence to the contrary.

[1] Eileen Keerdoja et al., "Prison Program Gets a New Boost," *Newsweek* 96 (November 3, 1980): 16.

[2] Aric Press and Donna Foote, "Does Scaring Work?," *Newsweek* 93 (May 14, 1979): 131.

[3] Ryan Schill, "Scared Straight! Graduate Plays Starring Role in Cold Case Crime," Juvenile Justice Information Exchange, February 1, 2011, jjie.org/scared-straight-graduate-plays-starring-role/9285. John Holl and Nate Schweber, "DNA Match Leads to Arrest in 25-Year-Old Murder Case," *New York Times*, March 23, 2007, www.nytimes.com/2007/03/23/nyregion/23solve.html. Kibret Markos, "Neighbor Sentenced in Decades-old Ridgefield Park Murder," NorthJersey.com, April 2010, www.northjersey.com/news/040110_Neighbor_sentenced_in_decades-old_Ridgefield_Park_murder.html.

[4] A&E TV, Beyond Scared Straight: About the Show, www.aetv.com/beyond-scared-straight/about/.

CAN MODERN DETERRENCE WORK?

Although deterrence is certainly one of the cornerstones of the criminal justice system, programs designed to alter the way offenders measure the risks and rewards of breaking the law haven't been very successful and in some cases have been counterproductive.[56] The reasons for this lack of accomplishment have to do with the complex nature of deterrence.

Although we might think that all that is necessary to alter one's calculation of risk versus rewards is to make the punishment more severe, deterrence theory is more complicated than that. In addition to the severity of punishment should one get caught, deterrence theory postulates that offenders also calculate the chances of getting caught (certainty) and the swiftness of punishment once caught (celerity). These last two facets of deterrence theory are more difficult to

Even as police agencies add officers and increase security procedures, clever and opportunistic delinquents will adjust their strategies to avoid getting caught in such activities as spray-painting graffiti in public spaces.

produce than severity of punishment. Although police agencies might add more officers and increase security procedures, clever and opportunistic offenders, including juveniles, will adjust their strategies to avoid getting caught.[57] Short of becoming a police state, where everyone's freedoms are curtailed, there are only a limited number of ways we can increase the perception of offenders that they are likely to get caught. In fact, virtually all offenders believe they have taken the necessary precautions to avoid detection when they commit their offenses.

The swiftness of the punishment following arrest and conviction is also difficult for criminal justice administrators to achieve. Because of a combination of procedural laws and the overcrowding of jails, courts, and prisons, it's almost impossible to punish any offender, either juvenile or adult, in a period of time that could affect the likelihood of deterrence. The most extreme example of the lack of swift punishment is the decades it generally takes for an offender on death row to be executed. Certainly this works against deterrence theory and the idea that potential murderers will think twice about taking a life.

Questions

1. How does classical criminology use the idea of free will?
2. How are the ideas of Cesare Beccaria and Jeremy Bentham important to criminology?
3. How did the Enlightenment affect criminological theory?
4. What is deterrence?
5. According to classical criminology, why do offenders break the law?

The Positivist School of Criminology

Learning Objective 7.

Contrast how the positivist and classical schools of criminology approach juvenile delinquency.

Learning Objective 8.

Define determinism.

The classical school of criminology focuses on the offense and treats all offenders as if they have the same motivations. That is, offenders are assumed to possess free will and to break the law for the same reasons. The rate of crime is affected by altering the severity, swiftness, and certainty of punishment, because all offenders react to these changes in the same way. If the consequences are unattractive enough, then potential offenders choose not to break the law.

The positivist school, however, is concerned with the offender's motivations and characteristics. The tracks of positivism can be observed in the statistical study of crime, efforts to rehabilitate offenders, and the initiation of social programs to prevent crime. The positivist school focuses on the offender, rather than the offense or the law, and posits that humans don't necessarily have free will and that human behavior is determined by various external factors.[58] The positivist school considers offenders' motivations and examines their physical characteristics, social background, and moral development to determine why they break the law and what can be done to rehabilitate their behavior.

Positivist criminology considers the circumstances of individuals and states that, as opposed to acting out of free will, some people are influenced to offend because of **determinism**. By this, we mean that someone who is impoverished; suffers from racial, gender, or class discrimination; is undereducated; and is mentally challenged is more likely to break the law than someone without these social disadvantages. A combination of internal factors and external environmental conditions can work to limit opportunities for individual success in the conventional way and compel individuals to meet their needs, desires, and fantasies through illegitimate means.[59]

The other major difference between the classical school and the positivist school is the methodologies they use to explain crime and delinquency. The classical school utilizes philosophy to try to understand why people break the law, while the positivist school uses science as a model on which to base its theories of human behavior. By considering the biological, psychological, and social traits of individuals, as well as the conditions of society, positivist theorists believe it's possible to determine the underlying causes of crime and to prescribe complex treatments that go far beyond altering the severity of punishments.

According to positivist theory, the way to eliminate crime is to eliminate what appears to be causing it. This involves adjusting such external factors as biology (diet, exercise, environment, medication), psychology (therapy, medication), and/or environment (attending to poverty, education, security, sanitation, and cultural ills). In short, the positivist school considers crime to be the product of external factors, and to the extent that these factors can be ameliorated or eliminated, so can crime. As such, the positivist school focuses on rehabilitation, rather than deterrence or punishment.

History of the Positivist School

The positivist school of criminology didn't develop all at once. It was a product of an exciting time in science and the arts when a multitude of accomplishments were amassed in Europe and the United States. In 1859, Charles Darwin published *On*

Positivist criminology states that some people are influenced to break the law because of outside forces rather than free will. According to one theory we'll study later on, children are influenced by their friends. Here, a gang of children smoke and loiter on a Springfield, Massachusetts, street corner in 1916.

the Origin of Species, in which he argued that human beings were basically highly developed animals who were affected by biology and environment. It isn't a coincidence that the positivist school with its scientific perspective on crime and deviant behavior came about during this period. In terms of crime and the criminal justice system, science advanced from several different fronts, and there was considerable error as criminologists developed theories and methods.

ADOLPHE QUETELET

Quetelet, a French mathematician and astronomer who also studied crime statistics, was fascinated by the regularity in property and violent offenses. In what has been called the first true scientific study of crime, Quetelet's *Research on the Propensity for Crime at Different Ages* (1831) argued that poverty wasn't the main cause of crime and demonstrated that wealthy neighborhoods showed more crime than impoverished neighborhoods.[60] He decided that opportunity explained crime rates better than poverty and stated that the government couldn't do much to alter crime rates because criminal behavior was a result of moral defectiveness that was revealed in offenders' biological characteristics.

To deal with the causes of crime, Quetelet recommended that the government institute social reforms that would improve the physical conditions in which people lived and that allowed citizens' moral and intellectual qualities to be fully developed. Quetelet used statistics on offenders' educational levels, gender, and age, as well as the effects of climate and the seasons. According to Quetelet, the primary factor in determining the tendency for criminal offending was age:

> Age is without contradiction the cause which acts with the most energy to develop or moderate the propensity for crime. This fatal propensity seems to develop in proportion to the intensity of physical strength and passions in man. It attains its maximum around 25 years, a period where physical development is pretty nearly ended. Intellectual and moral development, which takes place with more slowness, then moderates the propensity for crime which diminishes still more slowly by the weakening of man's physical strength and passions.[61]

ANDRE-MICHEL GUERRY

Part of the Enlightenment's contribution to science was the development of detailed records that could be studied to find patterns. Guerry, a French lawyer, was appointed as director of criminal statistics for the French Ministry of Justice, where he developed maps of crime rates as they related to other social factors, including poverty and education. Guerry, credited with being the first to use scientific criminology, pioneered the use of crime statistics to graphically represent how social factors contribute to crime rates across jurisdictions.[62]

Both Guerry and Quetelet applied mathematical analysis to explaining and mapping crime rates in relation to other social factors. Although Guerry's and Quetelet's studies aren't sophisticated by today's standards, they're an important part of the development of the scientific method in the study of crime. Modern studies using geographic positioning systems emerged from the work of these two early criminologists.[63]

AUGUSTE COMTE

Comte is credited with being the founder of positivist sociology. A French philosopher and social scientist, he championed several important steps in how social scientists should go about their work so that it could be verified and replicated. These steps included developing testable hypotheses, the use of comparative methods, the classification of societies, a systematic approach to the study of social history, and the study of abnormality as a means of understanding normal behavior.[64]

CESARE LOMBROSO

Lombroso is credited with being the founder of positivist criminology based on his work in trying to find the causes of crime from a multifactor approach. Lombroso is also important because he was one of the first to employ the scientific method in the study of crime.[65]

An Italian physician, Lombroso developed a theory of deviant behavior based on offenders' physical characteristics. Although his later work included a range of variables he claimed were related to crime, such as climate, rainfall, the price of grain, sex and marriage customs, criminal laws, banking practices, national tariff policies, the structure of government, church organization, and religious belief, he will always be remembered for his initial physiological theory of crime.

Lombroso, like many late 19th-century theorists, was influenced by Darwin's theory of evolution. Lombroso postulated that criminals weren't as highly evolved as normal people and that they were predisposed to break the law. Lombroso identified over a hundred supposed physical abnormalities that he called **atavisms**, which he claimed represented the subhuman or primitive features of a biological throwback. The atavisms included a range of measurable physical features such as low cranial capacity and a retreating forehead, as well

Research on the neurological differences between adults and children, as well as other physical differences that may affect behavior, originate from positivist theory.

as features such as tattoos or using excessive gestures. Lombroso's ideas of physical atavisms were based on thousands of precise measurements that he made of Italian offenders. His speculations that individuals who deviated physically from the average Italian were throwbacks to an earlier developed human now seem ludicrous.

Positivism and Juveniles

Positivism considers the external factors that affect juveniles, with the factors affecting juveniles and adults being much the same: employment, poverty, family life, culture, health, and so on. Positivism, however, does focus more on the specific ages of youths than it does the ages of adults. The developmental differences between a 16-year-old and a 14-year-old are vast compared with the differences between a 32-year-old and a 30-year-old.

Family life is also a major issue. Positivist studies consider in detail the effects that divorce rates, mixed families (families with stepparents and stepchildren), single-parent homes, and parents' educational levels and religion have on youths. In fact, studies of youths consider the parents almost as much as the children. Research on the neurological differences between adults and children, as well as other physical differences that might affect behavior, originate from positivist theory. Because positivism considers factors external to offenders, positivist theorists depend on research to develop their ideas. However, research on humans, especially on juveniles, is difficult to do.

Chapters 4 through 6 will deal with positivist ideas in greater detail, fleshing out the many theories of juvenile delinquency that are rooted in positivism. These theories will include biological explanations that were initiated by the early positivists and that continue today as modern science gives researchers increasingly sophisticated tools to examine the reasons for criminal behavior.

Questions

1. What does the positivist school of criminology focus on rather than the offense?
2. What is determinism?
3. What are atavisms?
4. How does positivism treat delinquency?

>> FOCUS ON ETHICS _____

The Devil's Advocate

As a juvenile court judge, you have always been concerned with treating the whole child. You're renowned for your creative sentences that strike to the heart of the problems affecting children and their families. You've received honors from fellow judges, the press, and the community. Proud of your reputation as a cutting-edge jurist, you aren't afraid to impose innovative dispositions that you believe will benefit children and the community.

Now you're sitting in judgment on one of the most fascinating cases of your career. A teenage boy has been accused of a series of despicable offenses spanning five years. These offenses range from small matters, such as four-letter-word graffiti, to serious matters, such as stalking his girlfriend and killing her pets when she rebuffed him. There's no doubt this boy is headed for serious trouble and is becoming a real threat to the community. You're prepared to hold him in a detention center until you read the evaluation from your court caseworker. She provides a complete social history of the boy and his family that reveals that they come from a conservative fundamentalist religion. The parents are adamant that their son is possessed by a demon and that the only hope for him is exorcism.

WHAT DO YOU DO?

1. Let the boy see the exorcist because you think this might be the best chance to keep him out of trouble. It's possible that because exorcism fits within the religious and psychological framework of the youth and his parents, it may help.

2. Remember that you're an officer of the court and that the Constitution has a definitive prohibition against mixing the concerns of church and state. You sentence the youth to detention.

3. Order the youth into temporary foster care. A proceeding such as an exorcism could physically harm the boy and make matters worse, and you fear the parents might try it anyway.

Summary

Summary

Learning Objective 1. List three ways of explaining crime and delinquency.	The classical and positivist schools were developed by scholars looking for rational explanations for crime and delinquency. Spiritual explanations are a third way of thinking about crime and delinquency.
Learning Objective 2. Compare and contrast theories and hypotheses.	A hypothesis is a tentative explanation for an observation or phenomenon. A theory is a way to organize facts and explain data. Theories are based on observations and data and are important tools for understanding the world.
Learning Objective 3. Recall the criteria that must be addressed when evaluating theories.	The criteria that must be addressed when evaluating theories include logical consistency (does the theory make sense?); scope (the amount of deviant behavior that a theory can explain depends on its scope); parsimony (this refers to the economy of an explanation); testability (a good theory should be stated in such a way that the propositions and their relationships can be scientifically tested); empirical validity (evidence that an instrument is measuring what it has been designed to measure); usefulness and policy implications (the thing that keeps criminological theory from being an academic exercise is the degree to which it can guide policy); and ideology (a theory must be considered based on its ideological underpinnings).
Learning Objective 4. Explain the source of spiritual explanations of crime.	Spiritual explanations are rooted in religion. One reason for punishment is to satisfy the need for revenge by symbolically quelling evil.
Learning Objective 5. Discuss the effect of the Enlightenment on criminological theory.	Enlightenment-era social shifts that fundamentally altered the administration of justice included changes in population, politics, economics, religion, and intellectual thought. These changes influenced how people viewed their responsibilities to obey the law and deal with lawbreakers.
Learning Objective 6. Evaluate the effect of deterrence on juveniles.	Research suggests that youths' physically immature brains operate differently than those of adults. Deterrence theory's hedonistic calculus requires a mature, rational mind to perform it successfully. There's evidence to suggest that because of these differences between juveniles and adults, deterrence doesn't have much of a deterrent effect on youths.

Summary

Learning Objective 7. Contrast how the positivist and classical schools of criminology approach juvenile delinquency.	The classical school of criminology focuses on the offense and treats all offenders, including juveniles, as if they have the same motivations. The positivist school is concerned with the offender's motivations and characteristics, which means that adults and juveniles are treated differently, as their motivations and characteristics are different. The classical school utilizes philosophy to try to understand why people break the law, whereas the positivist school uses science.
Learning Objective 8. Define determinism.	Determinism is the philosophical doctrine that human action is determined by external forces and not by free will. Internal factors and external environmental conditions can limit people's opportunities for conventional success and compel them to meet their needs, desires, and fantasies through illegitimate means.

Chapter Review Questions

1. What are the two major schools of criminology?
2. What criteria are used to evaluate theories of juvenile delinquency?
3. What are the steps of the scientific method?
4. What are the major types of spiritual theories of crime?
5. Why is rational choice theory considered a part of the classical school of criminology?
6. Why is deterrence theory considered a major component of the classical school of criminology?
7. What are the policy implications of the classical school of criminology?
8. Who were the major criminological theorists who developed the positivist school of criminology?
9. Why is rehabilitation associated with the positivist school of criminology?
10. In your opinion, which school of criminology is more practical to use for the types of delinquency that today's youth are involved in?

Key Terms

atavism—The appearance in a person of features thought to be from earlier stages of human evolution.

capitalism—An economic system characterized by the private or corporate ownership of production and distribution; the prices and production of goods are determined by competition in a market.

classical school of criminology—A school of thought that uses the idea of free will to explain deviant behavior.

demographics—The study of the characteristics of human populations.

determinism—The philosophical doctrine that human action is determined by external forces and is not a result of free will.

deterrence—The control of behavior through the fear of consequences.

free will—The ability or discretion to make choices that are unaffected by agencies such as fate or divine will.

general deterrence—A method of control in which the punishment of a single offender sets an example for the rest of society.

hedonistic calculus—The idea that potential offenders plan their actions in order to maximize pleasure and minimize pain.

heterogeneity—The quality of consisting of dissimilar elements or parts.

hypothesis—An untested idea set forth to explain a fact or phenomenon. An educated guess.

impulsivity—Acting quickly without considering the consequences.

juvenile boot camp—A short-term prison for juvenile delinquents and young offenders that uses military boot camp techniques for rehabilitation.

lex talionis—A law of retribution and/or retaliation in which an item is taken to make up for an item that has been wrongfully taken or destroyed.

positivist school of criminology—A school of thought that uses scientific techniques to study crime and delinquency and that considers the causes to be external to the offender.

rational choice theory—A perspective that states that people consciously choose deviant or antisocial behavior.

recidivism—Continuing to commit delinquent or criminal offenses after being convicted and sentenced for prior offenses.

scientific method—The rules for the systematic pursuit of knowledge: typically, the recognition and formulation of a problem, the collection of data through observation and experimentation,

the formulation and testing of hypotheses, and the formulation of a conclusion.

shock deterrence—The practice of subjecting minor offenders, often juveniles, to an alarming experience with the justice system in order to convince them to obey the law.

shock incarceration—The practice of sentencing offenders to a long period of incarceration and then granting them probation after a short time without their prior knowledge.

specific deterrence—A method of control in which an offender is prevented from breaking the law further by either incarceration or death.

spiritual explanations—Explanations for crime and deviance that stem from religious belief.

theory—A set of interconnected statements or propositions that explain how two or more events or factors are related to one another. From Daniel J. Curran and Claire M. Renzetti, *Theories of Crime*, 2nd ed. (Boston: Allyn and Bacon, 2001), 2.

Endnotes

1 Peter L. Berger, *The Sacred Canopy: Elements of a Sociological Theory of Religion* (Garden City, NY: Doubleday, 1969).

2 Leslie Stevenson, *Seven Theories of Human Nature* (New York: Oxford University Press, 1994). See also George C. Homans, *The Nature of Social Science* (New York: Wiley, 1967).

3 Thomas J. Barnard, "Twenty Years of Testing Theories: What Have We Learned and Why," *Journal of Research in Crime and Delinquency* 27, no. 4 (1990): 325–347.

4 Daniel J. Curran and Claire M. Renzetti, *Theories of Crime*, 2nd ed. (Boston: Allyn and Bacon, 2001), 2.

5 Ronald L. Akers and Christine S. Sellers, *Criminological Theories: Introduction, Evaluation, and Application*, 4th ed. (Los Angeles: Roxbury, 2004), 5–7.

6 Ibid., 6.

7 Ibid., 7.

8 Ibid., 8.

9 C. Garrett, "Effects of Residential Treatment on Adjudicated Delinquents: A Meta-Analysis," *Journal of Research in Crime and Delinquency* 22 (1985): 287–308.

10 David Lester, "Group and Milieu Therapy," in Patricia Van Voorhis, Michael Braswell, and David Lester, *Correctional Counseling and Rehabilitation*, 3rd ed. (Cincinnati, OH: Anderson, 1997), 189–217.

11 Akers and Sellers, *Criminological Theories*, 12–14.

12 Alvin Gouldner, *The Coming Crisis of Western Sociology* (New York: Basic Books, 1970).

13 King James Version.

14 French bishop Jacques-Benigne Bossuet (1627–1704) originated the theory of the divine right of kings, which claimed that some kings were chosen by God to rule and were accountable only to God.

15 Stephen Pfohl, *Images of Deviance and Social Control: A Sociological History*, 2nd ed. (New York: McGraw-Hill, 1994), 22–23.

16 Alan M. Dershowitz, *The Genesis of Justice: Ten Stories of Biblical Injustice That Led to the Ten Commandments and Modern Law* (New York: Warner Books, 2000).

17 This philosophy provides an interesting addition to Pfohl's statement that, theologically, humans are bad because Adam and Eve succumbed to temptation to eat the fruit of the tree of knowledge. However, it was God who placed the apparently luscious tree in the middle of the Garden of Eden with the command not to touch it (Genesis 1–3, KJV).

18 Donald J. Shoemaker, *Theories of Delinquency: An Examination of Explanations of Delinquent Behavior* (New York: Oxford University Press, 2005), 13.

19 Pfohl (see note 15), 64–67.

Summary

20 Marcello T. Maestro, *Cesare Beccaria and the Origins of Penal Reform* (Philadelphia: Temple University Press, 1973).

21 Cesare Beccaria, *On Crimes and Punishments* (1764), trans. Henry Paolucci (Indianapolis, IN: Bobbs-Merrill, 1963).

22 Pfohl, *Images of Deviance and Social Control*, 71–73.

23 Mark M. Lanier and Stuart Henry, *Essential Criminology* (Boulder, CO: Westview Press, 2004), 78.

24 George B. Vold, Thomas J. Bernard, and Jeffrey B. Snipes, *Theoretical Criminology*, 5th ed. (New York: Oxford University Press, 2002), 20.

25 Jeremy Bentham, *An Introduction to the Principles of Morals and Legislations* (1789) (New York: Kegan Paul, 1948).

26 Daniel S. Nagin and Raymond Paternoster, "The Preventive Effects of the Perceived Risk of Arrest: Testing on Expanded Conception of Deterrence," *Criminology* 28 (1991): 325–346.

27 Scott H. Decker and Carol W. Kohlfeld, "Capital Punishment and Executions in the Lone Star State: A Deterrence Study," *Criminal Justice Research Bulletin* 3, no. 12 (1988): 1–6.

28 Lisa J. Berlin, Jenni Owen, and Geelea Seaford, eds., *Adolescent Offenders and the Line Between the Juvenile and Criminal Justice Systems* (Durham, NC: Center for Child and Family Policy, 2007). Online at www.pubpol.duke.edu/centers/child/familyimpact/07BriefingReport.pdf.

29 Helen Taucher, Ann D. Witte, and Harriet Griesinger, "Criminal Deterrence: Revisiting the Issue of Birth Cohort," *Review of Economics and Statistics* 76 (1994): 399–412.

30 Sam G. McFarland, "Is Capital Punishment a Short-Term Deterrent to Homicide? A Study of the Effects of Four Recent American Executions," *Journal of Criminal Law and Criminology* 74 (1983): 1014–1030.

31 Keith Harries and Derral Cheatwood, *The Geography of Execution: The Capital Punishment Quagmire in America* (Lanham, MD: Rowman and Littlefield, 1997).

32 Gordon Waldo and Theodore Chiricos, "Perceived Penal Sanction and Self-Reported Criminality: A Neglected Approach to Deterrence Research," *Social Problems* 19 (1972): 522–540.

33 Adam Ortiz, "Adolescence, Brain Development and Legal Culpability," American Bar Association Juvenile Justice Center, January 2004, www.abanet.org/crimjust/juvjus/Adolescence.pdf. Bruce Bower, "Teen Brains on Trial," *Science News* 165, no. 19 (May 8, 2004), 299. Online at www.sciencenews.org/articles/20040508/bob9.asp. Carolyn Y. Johnson, "Brain Science v. Death Penalty," *Boston Globe*, October 12, 2004, www.boston.com/news/globe/health_science/articles/2004/10/12/brain_science_v_death_penalty.

34 Richard E. Redding and Elizabeth J. Fuller, "What Do Juvenile Offenders Know About Being Tried as Adults? Implications for Deterrence," *Juvenile and Family Court Journal* 55, no. 3 (Summer 2004):35–44. Online at law.bepress.com/villanovalwps/papers/art29/. Elizabeth J. Fuller isn't related to the author.

35 E. S. Scott, N. D. Reppucci, and J. L. Woolard, "Evaluating Adolescent Decision Making in Legal Contexts," *Law & Human Behavior* 19 (1995): 221–244; L. Steinberg and E. Cauffman, "Maturity of Judgment in Adolescence: Psychosocial Factors in Adolescent Decision Making," *Law & Human Behavior* 20 (1996): 249–272; paraphrased in Redding and Fuller.

36 Redding and Fuller, "What Do Juvenile Offenders Know About Being Tried as Adults?," 35–44.

37 Frank P. Williams III and Marilyn D. McShane, *Criminological Theory*, 4th ed. (Upper Saddle River, NJ: Prentice Hall, 2004), 240.

38 Kenneth D. Tunnell, *Choosing Crime: The Criminal Calculus of Property Offenders* (Chicago: Nelson-Hall, 1992).

39 Erling Eide, *Economics of Crime: Deterrence and the Rational Offender* (Amsterdam: Elsevier/North Holland, 1994).

40 Eric Johnson and John Payne, "The Decision to Commit a Crime: An Information-Processing Analysis," in Derek B. Cornish and Ronald V. Clarke, eds., *The Reasoning Criminal: Rational Choice Perspectives on Offending* (New York: Springer-Verlag, 1986), 170–185.

41 Daniel S. Nagin and Raymond Paternoster, "Personal Capital and Social Control: The Deterrence Implications of a Theory of Individual Differences in Criminal Offending," *Criminology* 32 (1994): 581–606.

42 Julie Horney and Ineke Haen Marshall, "Risk Perceptions Among Serious Offenders: The Role of Crime and Punishment," *Criminology* 23 (1992): 575–592.

43 Paul F. Cromwell et al., "How Drugs Affect Decisions by Burglars," *International Journal of Offender Therapy and Comparative Criminology* 35 (1991): 310–321.

44 Leslie Kennedy and David Forde, "Risky Lifestyles and Dangerous Results: Routine Activities and Exposure to Crime," *Sociology and Social Research* 74 (1990): 208–211.

45 Doris Layton MacKenzie and Alex Piquero, "The Impact of Shock Incarceration Programs on Prison Crowding," *Crime and Delinquency* 40 (1994): 222–249.

46 James O. Finckenauer, *Scared Straight and the Panacea Phenomenon* (Upper Saddle River, NJ: Prentice Hall, 1982), 69.

47 Ibid., 136.

48 James O. Finckenauer, "Scared Crooked," *Psychology Today* 13 (November 1979): 6.

49 David Dishneau, "Md., Calif. Suspend 'Scared Straight' Programs," Associated Press/*Seattle Times*, February 4, 2011, seattletimes.nwsource.com/html/entertainment/2014135003_apusbeyondscared-straight.htm.l. Dan Dearth, "Md. Suspends Programs That Send Young People Into Prisons," Herald-Mail.com (Hagerstown, MD), February 3, 2011, articles.herald-mail.com/2011-02-03/news/27100557_1_mci-h-maryland-correctional-institution-prisons.

50 Laurie O. Robinson and Jeff Slowikowski, "Scary—and Ineffective," *Baltimore Sun*, January 31, 2011, articles.baltimoresun.com/2011-01-31/news/bs-ed-scared-straight-20110131_1_straight-type-programs-straight-program-youths. Anthony Petrosino, Carolyn Turpin-Petrosino, and John Buehler, *"Scared Straight" and Other Juvenile Awareness Programs for Preventing Juvenile Delinquency*, Campbell Systematic Reviews 2004.2. Online at www.campbellcollaboration.org/lib/download/13/.

51 Anthony J. Schembri, *Scared Straight Programs: Jail and Detention Tours*, Florida Department of Juvenile Justice, p. 8, www.djj.state.fl.us/Research/Scared_Straight_Booklet_Version.pdf.

52 Laurie O. Robinson and Jeff Slowikowski, "Scary—and Ineffective," *Baltimore Sun*, January 31, 2011, articles.baltimoresun.com/2011-01-31/news/bs-ed-scared-straight-20110131_1_straight-type-programs-straight-program-youths. Anthony Petrosino, Carolyn Turpin-Petrosino, and John Buehler, *"Scared Straight" and Other Juvenile Awareness Programs for Preventing Juvenile Delinquency*, Campbell Systematic Reviews 2004.2. Online at www.campbellcollaboration.org/lib/download/13/.

53 Gwynne Dyer, *War* (Crown, 1985).

54 Dale G. Parent, *Correctional Boot Camps: Lessons from a Decade of Research* (Washington, DC: US Department of Justice, Office of Justice Programs, National Institute of Justice, 2003), 4, 7. Online at www.ncjrs.gov/pdf-files1/nij/197018.pdf.

55 Malcom Feeley and Jonathon Simon, "The New Penology: Notes on the Emerging Strategy of Corrections and Its Implications," *Criminology* 30(4):449-474.

56 Williams and McShane, *Criminological Theory*, 23.

57 Ernie Thomson, "Deterrence Versus Brutalization: The Case of Arizona," *Homicide Studies* 1 (1997): 110–128.

58 Derek B. Cornish and Ronald V. G. Clarke, "Understanding Crime Displacement: Application of Rational Choice Theory," *Criminology* 25 (1987): 933–947.

59 Ysabel Rennie, "The Positivist Revolution," in *The Search for Criminal Man* (Lexington, MA: Lexington Books, 1978).

60 Sawyer F. Sylvester, Introduction to *Research on the Propensity for Crime at Different Ages*, by Adolphe Quetelet, trans. Sawyer F. Sylvester (Cincinnati, OH: Anderson, 1984), v, xviii.

61 Adolphe Quetelet, *Research on the Propensity for Crime at Different Ages*, trans. Sawyer F. Sylvester (Cincinnati, OH: Anderson, 1984), 64–65.

62 Gillis J. Harp, *Positivist Republic: Auguste Comte and the Reconstruction of American Liberalism, 1865–1920* (University Park, PA: Pennsylvania State University Press, 1995).

63 George B. Wold, Thomas J. Barnard, and Jeffrey B. Snipes, *Theoretical Criminology*, 5th ed. (New York: Oxford University Press, 2002), 21–23.

64 C. Ray Jeffery, "An Interdisciplinary Theory of Criminal Behavior," in William S. Laufer and Freda Adler, *Advances in Criminological Theory 1* (New Brunswick, NJ: Transaction, 1989), 69–87.

65 Marvin E. Wolfgang, "Cesare Lombroso (1835–1909)," in Hermann Manneheim, ed., *Pioneers in Criminology*, 2nd ed. (Montclair, NJ: Patterson Smith, 1972), 232–291.

CHAPTER 4

Biological and Psychological Theories of Delinquency

Why do people break the law? What drives them to break the law and, in some cases, harm others, including their loved ones? The classical school of criminology explanation, that offenders choose to break the law after weighing the risks and rewards of such behavior, can be unsatisfying. The philosophy that those who break the law, including juvenile delinquents and status offenders, are exercising their free will is useful for constructing penalties and designing programs based on deterrence, but there are too many cases in which this explanation appears simplistic and devoid of the policy implications that could effectively address the problems of crime and juvenile delinquency.[1]

Biological Theories

The positivist school of criminology shifts the focus from the offense to the offender and is much more interested in the reasons people violate the law. The positivist school has a long and rich theoretical development, which we will cover in the next three chapters. In this chapter, we will consider biological and psychological theories of crime and human behavior. These theories address the early history of explanations for antisocial behavior, as well as some recent scientific developments in the study of crime and juvenile delinquency. Chapters 5 and 6 will cover established and contemporary sociological explanations of antisocial behavior. In these three chapters, students will find theories that seek to describe and explain human behavior in light of juvenile delinquency.

Learning Objective 1.

Evaluate the assertion that students shouldn't subscribe exclusively to one theory.

Learning Objective 2.

Briefly summarize the first biological theories of crime.

Learning Objective 3.

Explain Fishbein's concerns about the interaction of genes and environment and their relationship to antisocial behavior.

Learning Objective 4.

Discuss the roles researchers believe neurotransmitters and hormones play in antisocial behavior.

Learning Objective 5.

List the criticisms of biosocial theories of crime.

The idea that children are exercising free will when they break the law is useful for constructing deterrence-based penalties and programs, but too often this explanation is devoid of the policy implications that could effectively address the problems of crime and delinquency.

Students are cautioned, however, against subscribing exclusively to one theory. Crime and delinquency are multifaceted phenomena, and no single theory explains all the various behaviors of those who break the law. However, after completing these chapters on criminological theory, the student should have a good idea of the broad range of explanations that criminologists have developed. Although we'll pay particular attention to theories that explain juvenile delinquency, it's important to remember that many of the theories don't distinguish between delinquency and adult crime.

Biological theories of crime seek to provide a physical explanation for the actions of lawbreakers. These theories range from the outdated—atavisms, body types, and phrenology—to today's more advanced theories, which are based on the highly technical study of **neurotransmitters**, hormones, and genetics. (See Table 4.1 for a table of these theories and areas of research.) However, they all seek to answer the same question: Can the desire or urge to violate social laws, customs, and mores lie in the body itself? And if it does, what can be done about it? In this section, we will discuss the history of biological theories of crime, as well as the relationship between juvenile delinquency and theories of heredity, neurotransmitters, hormones, and biosocial theory.

The First Biological Theories of Crime

The first real biological theories of crime were developed in the years after the development of modern methods of scientific research and Charles Darwin's publication of *On the Origin of Species* (1859). The idea that the natural world and all that lived in it could be classified, catalogued, quantified, and predicted became attractive to a number of early social scientists. Ironically, human existence, as well as the societies in which it takes place, seems chaotic to us even as we create it and live it. The need to understand and predict these chaotic behaviors and social processes has always been especially earnest in relation to the study of crime and, more recently, how some children become juvenile delinquents.

CESARE LOMBROSO AND ATAVISMS

Cesare Lombroso's theory of **atavisms** qualifies as a biological theory, although in his later work he also considered sociological factors.[2] Lombroso, an Italian physician who lived from 1836 to 1909, argued that those who broke the law were likely to have certain physical features that could be observed by careful examination and would indicate that offenders weren't as fully evolved as law-abiding people. Lombroso's evidence was based on comparing offenders to other individuals. He performed autopsies on 66 male offenders and concluded that they shared features with primitive humans. He also examined 832 living male and female offenders, as well as 390 law-abiding Italian soldiers.[3]

Lombroso's theory that offenders are physically different from the rest of us hasn't held up to scrutiny. He is remembered as the founder of positivist criminology because he made a concerted effort to ground his research in the **scientific method**. The fact that he was wrong about offenders being throwbacks to an earlier form of human causes many criminologists to devalue his contribution to the field.[4] However, because he continually refined his work over a number of years and stressed a scientific approach, his place as a serious criminologist is assured.

WILLIAM SHELDON AND BODY TYPES

Although Lombroso's theory of atavisms failed to gain acceptance, other theories based on physical differences have been created and discarded over the years.

INSTANT RECALL
FROM CHAPTER 3

atavism

The appearance in a person of features thought to be from earlier stages of human evolution.

INSTANT RECALL
FROM CHAPTER 3

scientific method

The rules for the systematic pursuit of knowledge, typically the recognition and formulation of a problem; the collection of data through observation and experimentation; the formulation and testing of hypotheses; and the formulation of a conclusion.

TABLE 4.1 ⟩ Biological Theories of Delinquency

CATEGORY	AREAS OF RESEARCH	EXAMPLES
genetics/heredity	heritability	impulsivity, hyperactivity, aggression, genes that provide for the regulation of behavior, alcoholism
	evolution	aggression
chemical	pollution	exposure to lead, toxic metals, dioxins, manganese, mercury, pesticides
	hormones and neurotransmitters	low monoamine oxidase (MAO), high testosterone, androgen/estrogen imbalance,[1] dopamine and serotonin disorders
neurological	personality disorders	attention deficit disorder (ADD), antisocial personality disorder, attention deficit hyperactivity disorder (ADHD), conduct disorder, prefrontal cortical dysfunction, bipolar disorder, oppositional defiant disorder
	learning disabilities	low IQ, dyslexia, depression, mental disability
illness & trauma	illness	brain tumor, schizophrenia
	physical injury	premature birth, low birth weight, perinatal trauma, severe head injury; maternal smoking, alcohol, and drug abuse
	structural brain abnormality	abnormalities of the frontal and temporal lobes, hypothalamus, and amygdala
diet	vitamin deficiency	junk food, malnutrition; deficiencies of niacin, pantothenic acid, thiamin, vitamin B6, vitamin C, iron, magnesium, and tryptophan[2]
	food additives	artificial colors[3]
	naturally occurring substances	alcohol, sugar, caffeine, some legal and illegal drugs

Think About It
1. Study these theories' proposed origins of delinquency. In your opinion, which origins are the most easily treated by social intervention?[1]

[1]C. J. Peter Eriksson, Bettina von der Pahlen, Taisto Sarkola, and Kaija Seppa, "Oestradiol and Human Male Alcohol-Related Aggression," *Alcohol and Addiction* 38, no. 6 (2003): 589–596.
[2]Melvyn R. Werbach, "Nutritional Influences on Aggressive Behavior," *Journal of Orthomolecular Medicine* 7, no. 1 (1995): 45–51.
[3]Katherine S. Rowe and Kenneth J. Rowe, "Synthetic Food Coloring And Behavior: A Dose Response Effect in a Double-Blind, Placebo-Controlled, Repeated-Measures Study," *Journal of Pediatrics* (November 1994): 691–698.

Body-type theories postulated a relationship between the physical appearance of the body and the temperament of the mind. These theories of body type were especially popular with criminologists such as William Sheldon (1898–1977), who constructed a physical and mental typology based on the physiology of development.[5] Sheldon's body-type theory had three components (see Figure 4.1):

)) **Endomorphism.** Endomorphic body types are soft, round, and fat. They have tapering limbs, small bones, and smooth skin. Endomorphs tend to be extroverts and seek comfort.

>> **Mesomorphism.** Mesomorphic body types have large muscles, heavy chests, and a hard, lean look. They are active, dynamic individuals who act aggressively and walk, talk, and gesture assertively.

>> **Ectomorphism.** Ectomorphs are skinny individuals who appear fragile and have little body mass. They have small features, delicate bones, and fine hair. Behaviorally, they are introverts who shrink from crowds, are sensitive to noise and distractions, suffer from chronic fatigue and insomnia, and have skin problems and allergies.

According to Sheldon, everyone possesses the characteristics of each of these body types to some degree. Sheldon developed a measure using a scale from 1 to 7 for a person's possession of each type. Therefore, someone with a 1–4–7 somatotype would have few endomorphic characteristics, a healthy dose of mesomorphic characteristics, and many ectomorphic characteristics. This theory tried to explain what offenses each type of offender was most likely to commit. For instance, those individuals with primarily mesomorph characteristics can be expected to engage in street crimes that require aggressiveness and muscle, while an endomorphic offender could be expected to be an embezzler or a forger.[6]

When we consider Sheldon's body-type theory of crime today, it appears simplistic and unworkable. To suggest that body type is destiny ignores our experiences with the vast range of offenders of every size and shape who commit a wide range of offenses. The many psychological and sociological variables that require consideration in determining why individuals violate the law can't be reduced to the body type of offenders.

FRANZ JOSEPH GALL AND PHRENOLOGY

Another way the physical body was thought to indicate a criminal personality was related to the size, shape, and topography of the skull. The pseudoscience of **phrenology** was popular at the beginning of the 19th century and promoted primarily by Franz Joseph Gall. Physicians have long realized that certain parts of the brain are responsible for certain functions, and phrenologists attempted to create a scientific discipline around these observations. Postulating that the outside of the skull could reveal brain structure, the phrenologist would feel for bumps and suggest what type of personality and behavior could be expected. For instance, phrenologists speculated that their science could uncover a penchant for destructiveness, secretiveness, and philoprogenitiveness (love of offspring).[7] Although we seldom hear about phrenology anymore, some still advocate it as a viable scientific approach.[8]

Phrenology fell into disrepute for several reasons. Not only was there limited evidence of effectiveness, phrenology's adherents fought bitter political battles

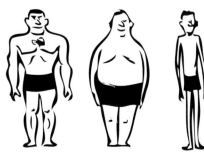

Mesomorph   Endomorph   Ectomorph

Figure 4.1

Think About It
1. What do you think of this theory of personality and body type? Do you agree or disagree with Sheldon's analysis?

THE BOY—WHAT WILL HE BECOME?
FROM A DRAWING BY F. DADD.

The pseudoscience of phrenology was popular at the beginning of the 19th century. Here, a phrenology practitioner tries to determine how a boy's predisposition will affect his adult life.

in the press as they attempted to discredit each other. Additionally, phrenology was co-opted by outright quacks and reduced to a parlor game. The development and popularization of phrenology occurred before modern biological research and scientific practices really took hold. However, phrenology is still discussed because it's probably the earliest cohesive attempt to predict human behavior by considering the body.

Heredity

Early attempts to find a physical reason to explain why someone would violate the law are crude, unscientific, and easy for us to ridicule today because they appear so elementary and superficial. Although a number of other early efforts that attempted to find reasons for crime weren't entirely successful, we don't dismiss them lightly because we are still attempting to make these connections with new and improved scientific tools.

One idea that continues to have appeal is that a tendency to break the law can be inherited by children from parents through their **genes**. This isn't a new idea; in fact, it's over a century old. From about 1900 to World War II, the pseudoscience of **eugenics** was vigorously promoted in the United States as the cure to all social and behavioral human ills. For more about eugenics, see the Crosscurrents feature.

With the decoding of **DNA**, we are continually finding new genetic reasons for how our bodies are structured and how they function, as well as evidence of what traits are inherited. Early attempts to link **heredity** and genetics to crime relied on the use of family trees. Researchers noticed that in certain families crime seemed to be a consistent feature and speculated that it might be inherited. For instance, in independent studies of the Jukes family, two researchers found 7

4.1 crosscurrents

Eugenics

The word "eugenics" was coined in the early 1880s by Francis Galton, who based it on a Greek root word meaning "good in birth."[1] The American eugenics movement, which loosely based its ideas on the work of Galton, became popular in the early 20th century.[2] By 1924, eugenics courses were common in universities, colleges, and high schools.[3] In the early 1930s, American eugenics leaders began receiving mail from a young German politician named Adolf Hitler.[4]

Criminality was a major target for eugenicists. Sterilization of offenders, or those merely deemed offenders, had begun as early as 1899 in Indiana with crude vasectomies performed on the inmates at the Indiana Reformatory at Jeffersonville.[5] In New York, in 1914, a prisons committee began documenting "hereditary criminality," and the New York City Police Department established a eugenic investigations laboratory. Inmates at Sing Sing were examined in a search for criminality in family trees.[6] Eugenics finally lost popularity in the United States after World War II, with the discovery of Hitler's massive eugenics efforts.[7]

THINK ABOUT IT

1. Give one reason that eugenics became so popular in the United States during the early 20th century.

[1] Steven Selden, *Inheriting Shame* (New York: Teachers College Press, 1999), xiv.

[2] Ibid., 2

[3] *Autobiography of Leon. F. Whitney*, unpublished manuscript circa 1973, APS Manuscript Collection, pp. 204–205, as quoted in Black, 75.

[4] Edwin Black, *War Against the Weak* (New York: Four Walls Eight Windows, 2008), 259.

[5] Harry C. Sharp, "The Severing of the Vasa Deferentia and Its Relation to the Neuropsychopathic Constitution," *New York Medical Journal* 8 March 1902: (413–414), as quoted in Black, 64.

[6] Ibid., 96.

[7] Black, *War Against the Weak*, 400.

murderers, 60 thieves, 50 prostitutes, and many other social deviants and offenders.[9] In comparing the Jukes to another family, the Edwards, the researchers found that, in addition to there being no offenders (actually they were mistaken in this observation), the Edwards had governors, preachers, writers, and judges.[10] See Case in Point for *Buck v. Bell*, a 1927 case in which the State of Virginia succeeded in sterilizing a young woman whose family had been deemed feebleminded.

This type of research has two key problems. First, comparing two families doesn't provide a sufficient sample to conclude that genetics produces the observed differences in criminal behavior. Hundreds of randomly chosen families would have to be studied to arrive at such conclusions. The Jukes family was included precisely because of the number of offenses of its members. The second issue has to do with the old problem of separating the influence of genetics (nature) from environment (nurture). If a child is surrounded by family members who break the law, wouldn't it be as likely that they learned to break the law as it would be that they shared criminogenic genes?[11]

So how can we distinguish between inherited behaviors and learned behaviors? To do so, we would have to study individuals with the same genetic makeup but different life experiences. Identical twins provide ideal subjects for such research.

STUDIES OF TWINS AND ADOPTED CHILDREN

Certain traits appear to be transmitted from parents to children through genes rather than learning. A series of studies suggests that traits related to repetitive aggressive behavior, such as impulsivity, drug abuse, alcoholism, and cognitive defects, are heritable. Other studies have found that personality factors such as extroversion, introversion, cognitive deficits, conduct disorder, and anxiety are both heritable and predictive of substance abuse and aggression.

4.2 CASE IN POINT

THE CASE

Buck v. Bell (1927)

THE POINT

This infamous case upheld the right of states to sterilize those determined to be mentally incompetent.

Carrie Buck was a 17-year-old woman in the state of Virginia whose adoptive family committed her to a state mental institution after learning she was pregnant. It was concluded that Carrie, although she had been a good student in school and claimed that the pregnancy was the result of rape, was "feebleminded."

After she gave birth to a daughter, Carrie was sent to the Colony for Epileptics and Feebleminded. Carrie's mother had previously been committed to the same institution under the same diagnosis of feeblemindedness. Carrie's infant was soon declared to be "mentally defective," and doctors concluded that the three females represented three generations of feeblemindedness.

Shortly before Carrie Buck was committed, Virginia passed a law allowing the inmates of mental institutions to be sterilized. Shortly thereafter, an institutional hearing determined that Buck should be sterilized. Buck's counsel claimed that she had been denied due process and equal protection under the Fourteenth Amendment, and the case wound its way through the courts, all of which upheld the new law.

The Supreme Court found that the law did not violate the Constitution and that all legal safeguards had been properly followed. In his opinion, Justice Oliver Wendell Holmes wrote that the issue was not the propriety of the sterilization procedure but the substantive law, which had been followed.

In stating the decision of the court to allow Carrie Buck to be sterilized, Holmes wrote, "It is better for all the world, if instead of waiting to execute degenerate offspring for crime ... society can prevent those who are manifestly unfit from continuing their kind. Three generations of imbeciles are enough."

Source: Edwin Black, *War Against the Weak* (New York: Four Walls Eight Windows, 2003), 108–121.

When considering the differences between fraternal and identical twins, the concept of inherited behavior becomes even clearer. **Fraternal twins** occur when two eggs are fertilized by two sperm. These twins are the same as other siblings, except that they are gestated at the same time and are born within minutes of each other. Identical twins are from the same egg and fertilized by a single sperm and have exactly the same genetic makeup. The presumption is that **identical twins** share more behavioral similarities than fraternal twins.[12]

George Vold and colleagues discussed one significant study that looked at 6,000 pairs of twins to see if antisocial behavior in one twin was indicative of antisocial behavior in the other. The study reported that this happened 35.8 percent of the time in male identical twins, whereas in male fraternal twins it occurred 12.3 percent of the time. In female identical twins, when one was identified as engaging in antisocial behavior, the other also did 21.4 percent of the time. This rate dropped to 4.3 percent in female fraternal twins. In a further look at the data, this relationship was shown to be even more robust for serious antisocial behavior.[13]

We should be careful, however, before we attribute destiny to heredity. This study didn't separate the effects of heredity and socialization. Although the identical twins showed more similarities in breaking the law, we don't know if their

One significant study found that in male identical twins, antisocial behavior in one twin was indicative of antisocial behavior in the other nearly 36 percent of the time.

environments differed greatly from those of the fraternal twins. One way to study this is to look at twins who grew up in different environments. By studying identical twins raised in separate families, it's possible to examine their differences in behavior and then attribute these differences or similarities to genetics or environment.

The largest obstacle to this type of research is finding twins who were separated at birth. Because this is a relatively uncommon occurrence, these studies suffer from having extremely small sample sizes. Vold and colleagues reported on three studies that used this technique. One study reported on 32 sets of identical twins, and another study reported on 8 sets of identical twins.[14] Finally, a study done by Walters used meta-analysis (meaning that a large number of these comparisons were examined), and factors such as sample size, quality of research design, and sex of the twins were controlled for.[15] Vold and colleagues concluded that all three of these studies found some evidence that criminal behavior can be inherited.

A final method for determining the relationship between genetics and environment is to consider the antisocial behavior of adopted children and compare their legal records to those of both the biological parents and the adoptive parents. One would expect to find a similarity to the adoptive parents if environment were the main cause of antisocial behavior, and a stronger relationship to the biological parents if heredity were more important. The studies analyzed by Vold and colleagues reported a consistent relationship between biological parents and their children in terms of antisocial behavior. This held true more often for property crime than it did for violent crime, but this finding might be deceptive. Property offenders typically commit many more offenses than do violent offenders, so they can be expected to show up in official statistics at a much greater rate. Violent behavior might be as easily transmitted as criminal behavior toward property, but this is less likely to be discovered using crime data.[16] What can we conclude from these studies?

》 Separating the influences of genetics and environment on criminal behavior is difficult.

》 The studies that have succeeded in finding research techniques to separate the influences of genetics and environment are limited to small samples.

» There appears to be a consistent relationship between the antisocial behavior of biological parents and their children.

» This relationship holds true even when adoptive parents, fraternal twins, and separate environments are considered.

HEREDITY AND BEHAVIOR

Are genes indeed responsible for antisocial behavior? It's possible to inherit certain diseases from one's parents or even more distant ancestors. Do parents also pass to their children genes that cause them to violate the law?

We can't answer these questions based on the evidence that we have reviewed thus far. Although there might be some association between the antisocial behavior of parents and children, no firm causal link has been identified. What genes or traits could antisocial parents pass to their children? Is it too much testosterone? Not enough of some brain chemical that allows for the child to experience empathy? Are a violent temper, disregard for others' feelings, aggression, and extreme competitiveness inherited? These questions are difficult to answer because something always intervenes between genetics and antisocial behavior. The influence of heredity is always indirect and controlled by a host of factors that might include environmental factors.

Because genetic factors don't exist in a vacuum, it's necessary to consider how these factors interact with the many social and environmental factors that also might play a role in the development of antisocial behavior. Diana Fishbein, one of the foremost criminologists studying biobehavioral perspectives, summarizes these issues in the following points:

1. All human behavior has a genetic component.
2. There are no genes for or biological causes of specific human behaviors. Instead, genes help design our temperament and personality and provide a predisposition to behave according to certain patterns.
3. The environment can modify the expression of genetic and biological traits. No one is predestined to behave in a certain way or to break the law.
4. On a global level, social and economic deprivation, deleterious environmental conditions, psychological trauma, and abuse can lead to antisocial behavior. The deterioration of cities and dissolution of social resources are substantially contributory.
5. Vulnerabilities to antisocial behavior cross all boundaries but will be most abundant where social risks are the highest.[17]

It's important to note that even those who are convinced of the importance of the connection between biology and crime don't contend that the relationship is determinative. Although biology plays a significant part in how our behavior is shaped, it's wise to remember that crime is socially defined. For example, killing another person might mean one is considered a murderer or a war hero depending on the context of the behavior. Although certain individuals might have a biological predisposition to be more violent than others, the circumstances of the behavior will often determine whether it is appropriate or deviant.

Before we conclude our discussion of the relationship between biology and deviant behavior, another crucial concern requires examination. Although there is significant evidence of a relationship between biology and deviant behavior, so far little or no solid theoretical connection has been established. What physical differences exist in the brains of those who engage in criminal or violent behavior

Biology plays a significant part in how our behavior is shaped, but it's wise to remember that crime is socially defined. So far, little or no solid theoretical connection has been established between biology and deviant behavior.

as opposed to the brains of those who don't? What parts of the brain should be examined to determine if these differences exist? To answer these questions, researchers are looking at biochemistry, specifically neurotransmitters and hormones.

Neurotransmitters

Neurotransmitters are chemicals that transmit information between neurons. This function is at least partially determined by genetics. Therefore, we can safely assume that some human behaviors have a biological basis. Some researchers believe that too little or too much of these neurotransmitters might be responsible for neurological and mood disorders, many of which are related to abnormal aggression, crime, and juvenile development. The two neurotransmitters that have received the most attention in the criminological literature are dopamine and serotonin.

» **Dopamine.** We aren't sure exactly how dopamine works in the human body to control behavior. It has been associated with aggressive and violent behavior in animals as well as humans, and some studies have linked increases in dopamine to psychotic behavior. Although we don't know for sure how much dopamine is necessary or desirable, researchers are confident that once its interaction with other neurotransmitters is better understood, it will be possible to predict with more confidence how this important brain chemical relates to behavior.

» **Serotonin.** Low levels of serotonin have been linked to poor impulse control and ultimately to aggressive or violent behavior. This is a complicated issue, because the link between serotonin levels and aggressive behavior is affected by a person's ability to control his or her behavior, and this ability is related to other factors. For instance, underlying hostility or negative moods might be more important than serotonin levels, but they might also interact with serotonin to produce aggression. Complicating this relationship even further is the influence of alcohol. Individuals react differently to the effects of alcohol, and some studies have shown that alcohol can lower serotonin levels. Therefore, there is some confusion as to whether serotonin causes the lack of impulse control that contributes to aggressive behavior or whether alcohol first lowers the serotonin level.[18]

Three additional chemicals in the brain have been found to be related to antisocial behaviors.

» **Norepinephrine and epinephrine.** Norepinephrine and epinephrine are important to the regulation of our reaction to stress. Although not predictive of particular behavioral outcomes, norepinephrine particularly interacts with factors such as individual predisposition, setting, and circumstances to produce such tendencies as impulsivity, sensation seeking, and high activity levels. Although some studies have found an association between norepinephrine and aggression or violence, the direction of this relationship hasn't been established.[19] This means that aggression and violence are as likely to produce norepinephrine as norepinephine is to cause aggression and violence.

» **Monoamine oxidase.** The final brain chemical that might affect antisocial behavior is monoamine oxidase (MAO), an enzyme that metabolizes serotonin, dopamine, epinephrine, and norepinephrine. Low levels of MAO have been associated with psychopathy, aggression, violent behavior, alcoholism, sensation-seeking behavior, and impulsivity.[20]

We can see an example of how researchers analyze the relationship between brain chemistry and behavior in a 2002 study that looked at males from birth to adulthood to determine why some abused boys develop behavior problems while other abused boys don't. The researchers found that a variation in the gene for monoamine oxidase A (MAO-A) ameliorated the psychological effects of abuse. Abused children whose genes expressed high levels of MAO-A were less likely to become antisocial in adulthood. The study concluded that there is evidence that genes can moderate the effects of an abusive childhood environment.[21]

Hormones

Another area in which researchers have found a relationship between the human body and aggression or violence is in the study of sex and stress hormones. In males, the hormone testosterone has been linked to increases in aggression and sex drive.[22] Although testosterone naturally occurs in females, the levels are much lower and the effects substantially different. As with other relationships between the body and behavior, there is a chicken-and-egg dilemma. Do testosterone levels rise when a person engages in aggressive behavior, or does testosterone cause people to become aggressive?

Before puberty, boys and girls have about the same amount of sex hormones. As children grow into adolescents, however, both sexes experience a surge in the production of hormones such as testosterone, which brings on the rapid mood swings that are typically associated with adolescence. Both boys and girls might be more angry, while boys might feel more annoyance and girls more depression.[23] Both boys and girls grow bigger and stronger and typically desire to experiment with new behaviors and seek novel or risky situations. This behavior is affected by neurotransmitters which, in turn, are regulated by sex hormones.[24]

The hormone-modulated behaviors of boys and girls part ways here. After puberty, male testosterone levels are roughly 10 times greater than those of

Do testosterone levels rise when a person engages in aggressive behavior, or does testosterone cause people to become aggressive?

females, so adolescent males end up with far more active testosterone than adolescent females.[25] Researchers believe this high amount of testosterone in young men might be at least partly responsible for the differences in antisocial behavior and the different rate of criminal offenses between adolescent males and females, as well as adult men and women.[26]

Although evidence points to a relationship between sex hormones and antisocial behavior and aggression, especially in adolescent males, researchers still have much to learn. A study that examined the relationship between **androgens** and aggression in prepubescent boys who had been diagnosed with severely aggressive and antisocial behavior concluded that adrenal androgen is important to aggression in boys.[27] Another study found similar links in young males who were at risk for antisocial behavior. Significantly higher androgen levels were found in boys but not in girls, with the boys showing the most antisocial behavior having the highest androgen levels.[28]

Those who advocate the inclusion of biological variables in the study of criminal behavior have a difficult task in unraveling the relationship between hormones and antisocial behavior.[29] Although there is tempting anecdotal evidence, it remains incomplete, and conclusions can be only provisionally drawn.[30]

Biosocial Theory

Another way to consider the influence of biological conditions on crime is **biosocial theory**, which seeks to explain how environmental conditions interact with the body to produce behavior. Biosocial theory is a relatively new field of study that utilizes a Darwinian theoretical framework to explain why behavior is established and why it continues. For the main theories that reside within biosocial theories, see Table 4.2.

The study of biosocial theory considers the effects of **evolution**, including heredity, on the brain and human behavior. A relationship between delinquency and biosocial theory can be derived from the observation that males, especially adolescent and young adult males, are especially risk-prone, competitive, and violent. Researchers have noted that this male behavior peaks during youth, when

TABLE 4.2 ⟩ Three Main Evolutionary Theories of Crime

These biosocial theories of crime are examples of how evolutionary theory is applied to theories that seek to explain crime.

Cheater theory	The theory relies on the different reproductive strategies of men and women. Men can potentially produce more offspring than women. Women seek to maintain a mate to help raise children. A man can help a sole woman raise his children, and have a limited number of children, or he can trick or force a woman into having his children and then move to the next woman. This alternative strategy is the likelier path of criminal offenders and psychopaths even after adolescence. Cheater theory states that antisocial activity is stimulated by the same traits that stimulate a cheater's sexual strategy.
Control adaptation theory	People pursue various reproductive strategies for environmental reasons. A person will be sexually promiscuous if he or she learned during childhood that interpersonal relationships are ephemeral and unreliable. A person will be more sexually restrictive if he or she has matured with the idea that relationships are permanent. Strategies are not chosen consciously, but subconsciously.
Alternative adaptation theory	Human reproductive effort is represented by a continuum. At one end is promiscuity, or "mating effort," and at the other is parenting effort, or effort devoted to raising children. Demographically, the best predictors of both reproductive effort and crime/delinquency are sex and age. Males and young people focus on mating; females and older adults focus on parenting. Deceit, impulsivity, and hedonism are useful for focusing on both mating effort and criminal activity. Empathy and altruism are useful for both parenting effort and noncriminal activities.

Think About It
1. Which theory emphasizes empathy and altruism in parenting effort and law-abiding activities?

there's not only a deluge of testosterone but also male competition for females (and therefore reproductive success) is at its most intense.[31] Researchers have also observed that male violent behavior decreases as testosterone levels and the drive to reproduce decrease with advancement into adulthood and old age.[32]

Some researchers have even argued that rape is a way for a male to spread his genes and, at some level, might be biologically encoded.[33] This isn't to say that biosocial theory asserts the existence of "crime genes." From the biosocial standpoint, almost all the effects of genes on behavior are indirect because their messages are processed through the brain. Antisocial behavior is too complex for there to be one gene, or even a group of genes, to act as a direct cause.[34]

There is a great deal of resistance to biosocial theories from criminologists with backgrounds in legal and sociological traditions. Walsh lists five objections to biosocial theories:

1. Biosocial theories are deterministic and socially dangerous.
2. There can't be any genes for crime because crime is socially constructed.
3. If a problem is considered biological, therapeutic nihilism will ensue. That is, society might give up on trying to rehabilitate delinquents and adult offenders.
4. Crime can't have a biological basis because crime rates change rapidly, and changes in genes require many generations.
5. Biological theories tend to be insensitive to people's feelings.[35]

The second criticism of biosocial theory, that crime, especially delinquency, is socially defined, is especially interesting. The social definitions can be narrow: An action that is considered an offense in one state isn't considered an offense just a few miles away across the state line. So how can genes govern a social phenomenon? Biosocial theorists assert that almost every society with a written criminal code criminalizes a basic set of behaviors. These are behaviors that harm other members of society physically (murder, rape) or harm their property (theft, destruction) and that are basically the same from one society to the next.[36] Biosocial theorists also point out that crime itself might be an adaptation that, while harming society, allows the individual to survive and reproduce.[37]

This discussion of the theories that offer physical reasons for antisocial behavior has only touched on the debate. Although some of the explanations, such as Lombroso's atavisms and phrenology, are no longer applicable, other explanations based on studies of the brain and DNA appear to be more promising.

Questions

1. What does the terminology "biological theories of crime" refer to?
2. How do Lombroso's atavisms and Sheldon's body-type theories qualify as biological theories?
3. What are genes? What is DNA?
4. What are neurotransmitters? Why are they important? What is the role of monoamine oxidase?
5. What is the role of hormones in adolescence?
6. Explain how evolutionary psychology seeks to explain why behavior is established and why it continues.
7. From a biosocial standpoint, how do genes affect behavior?

Psychological Theories

Psychological theories of delinquency and crime are particularly crucial to the study of delinquency. When dealing with adult offenders, a number of assumptions can be made about their level of emotional, cognitive, and moral development. Adults are expected to be able to tell the difference between right and wrong and to curb their temptations and urges to break the law. The principles of deterrence are supposed to work better on adults, who should be able to adequately weigh the rewards of lawbreaking against the likelihood of getting caught.

These assumptions can't be safely made about youths. The ability to recognize right and wrong is the result of a long process of socialization that varies with each individual. Further, the bodies and brains of young people are in constant development until they reach early adulthood.[38] Youths are different when it comes to psychological maturity, and the criminal justice system has spun off a separate juvenile justice system to deal with clients who are deemed to require treatment rather than punishment. The remainder of this chapter considers the following concerns of psychological theories of delinquency:

>> How do the inner and subconscious experiences of childhood affect behavior?

>> At what age do children develop the cognitive ability to comprehend how their behaviors affect others?

>> At what age do children develop their moral foundation to determine what is right and wrong?

>> Do males and females develop cognitive and moral abilities differently?

Learning Objective 6.

Understand how psychological theories of antisocial behavior are particularly crucial to the study of delinquency.

Learning Objective 7.

Briefly describe the psychological theories of Sigmund Freud, Jean Piaget, Lawrence Kohlberg, and Carol Gilligan.

Learning Objective 8.

Summarize the history of research on intelligence and delinquency.

Learning Objective 9.

Explain how the contributions of Sheldon and Eleanor Glueck contribute to the study of personality and crime.

Learning Objective 10.

Discuss the controversy surrounding the use of the psychopathy diagnosis for juvenile delinquents.

》 Does intelligence play a part in how children learn and resist delinquency?

》 What part does the child's personality play in her or his ability to resist delinquency?

Each of these questions is important and is the focus of significant research. Here, only a cursory answer to each question is possible, but we don't mean to minimize the contribution of psychological factors to delinquency. In many respects, these psychological factors are more important to the study of delinquency than they are to the study of adult crime. In this section, we will look at psychodynamic perspective, cognitive development and delinquency, and moral development, as well as the effects of intelligence, intellectual disability, and personality on antisocial behavior.

Psychodynamic Perspective

Have you ever witnessed someone do something really silly and wondered, "Why did they do that?" Or, even more perplexing, have you done something silly and been at a loss to explain your behavior? The first psychological theory to address these questions was Sigmund Freud's psychoanalytic theory, which contends that our behavior is motivated by inner forces, memories, and conflicts of which we have little awareness or control.[39]

Freud suggested that humans go through a process of psychosexual development as they progress from birth to adulthood (see Table 4.3). Children must successfully pass through a number of stages, or they may develop problems later in life with psychological phobias, relating to others, or severe personality disorders. Freud suggested that everyone passes through these stages—oral, anal, phallic (or genital), latency, and genital—and that if an individual has difficulty in any particular stage, behavior problems will manifest themselves either then or at a later stage of life when they can be corrected only by therapy. Although Freud's psychoanalytic theory has its critics, it was the first theory to employ a

TABLE 4.3 〉 Freud's Stages of Psychosexual Development

STAGE	APPROXIMATE AGE	FOCUS	EXPERIENCE
oral	birth to 12–18 months	mouth	The infant needs to be gratified through sucking, eating, mouthing, or biting.
anal	12–18 months to 3 years	anus	Children passing through this stage are concerned with expelling or holding feces and with the process of toilet training.
phallic	3 to 6 years	genitals	At this stage, children are interested in their genitals and come to identify with the same-sex parent. Those who do not successfully negotiate this stage may experience such issues as Oedipal conflicts, in which the son is jealous of his father's sexual access to the mother.
latency	6–12 years	none	At this stage, sexual concerns are largely unimportant.
genital	adolescence to adulthood	genital	Sexual interests reemerge and mature sexual relationships are established.

Think About It
1. At which stage are Oedipal conflicts most likely to occur?

Source: Robert S. Feldman, *Child Development (Upper Saddle River, NJ: Prentice Hall), 23–25.*

purely psychological focus. More recent psychological theories have been developed as extensions to psychoanalytic theory or in reaction to it.

For the purposes of the study of delinquency, psychoanalytic theory is no longer a major focus. However, its contributions to the importance of the psychological perspective, as well as much of its vocabulary, have remained consistent features of how human behavior is considered. Further, to understand why various practices in the juvenile justice system have been developed, it's necessary to understand the history of psychology in which Freud is such a dominant figure. We'll return to Freud a little later when we discuss personality and delinquent behavior.

Piaget's Cognitive Development

Have you ever watched an infant play with food? For most of us, food has a specific purpose, and our contact with it is limited to preparing it and getting it from the plate to our mouths. For infants, food is more multipurpose. It can be a source of amusement as they see how far it can be flung, what happens when it's applied to the head of the cat, or whether it can stick to the wall. For infants, food is another thing to be explored and to learn from.

Swiss psychologist Jean Piaget pioneered the idea that children learn cognitive skills throughout their childhood and that we must appreciate the stages of development when we consider delinquency (see Programs for Children). Children, especially young children, who have delinquency issues might be having trouble with normal cognitive development, even as they cause problems for their parents, teachers, siblings, peers, and themselves.

Piaget pioneered the idea that children learn cognitive skills throughout their childhood. For infants, food is a thing to be explored and to learn from. Here, a baby learns not to eat sand.

According to Piaget, children learn through two primary processes: assimilation and accommodation. Assimilation is a process by which infants learn according to how they already comprehend the world. When presented with new stimuli, they manipulate it by touching it, chewing it, or banging it to determine its properties and fit it into their patterns of thought. Accommodation, on the other hand, occurs when infants encounter new stimuli that don't easily fit into their patterns of thinking, understanding, or behaving. Piaget theorized that infants are limited by their reflexes and that they begin to learn more and more as their motor skills develop and allow them to experiment with stimuli in more sophisticated ways.[40]

Piaget suggested that infants go through six stages of sensorimotor development between birth and age 2. Although there is considerable overlap in the transition from one stage to the next, Piaget argued that each child follows this process at basically the same rate, and the timing of the development is consistent, especially early in their lives. Although later psychological theorists took issue with this tidy timetable of cognitive development, they do credit Piaget with providing a broad outline of sensorimotor development.[41]

Although Piaget was influential in mapping the processes and stages of cognitive development, his scheme has limitations that become more problematic as children age. Most importantly, subsequent psychologists contend that Piaget greatly underestimated the ages at which children are capable of acquiring cognitive abilities.[42] What is important to remember is that cognitive development

4.3 PROGRAMS FOR CHILDREN

Head Start

The Head Start program helps children ages 3 to 5 from low-income families prepare for school through various educational, nutritional, health, and social services. The program is especially focused on helping children develop reading and math skills, and emphasizes parental participation. The related Early Head Start program was launched in 1995 to support infants, toddlers, pregnant women, and their families. Early Head Start promotes children's physical, social, emotional, and intellectual development; helps pregnant women with health care before and after pregnancy; and helps parents become self-sufficient.[1]

Head Start was launched in 1965 as part of President Lyndon B. Johnson's War on Poverty.[2] Today, Head Start, which is the largest publicly financed early childhood education and care program in the United States, serves just over 900,000 low-income children a year at a cost of about $7 billion annually.[3]

Studies have found that Head Start helps children in both their short- and long-term development. One in particular reported "significant" improvements in cognitive development, social competence, and attention problems at age 5.[4] In 2010, the program was criticized when a Department of Health and Human

Services study of first-graders found few differences between Head Start children and children who were eligible for the program but didn't attend.[5] However, the study also reported that children who attended Head Start had more positive experiences in their lives and educational programs than those in the group who didn't attend.[6]

THINK ABOUT IT

1. What is the purpose of Head Start?

[1]Office of Head Start, www.acf.hhs.gov/programs/ohs/index.html.

[2]Jens Ludwig and Deborah A. Phillips, "Long-Term Effects of Head Start on Low-Income Children," *Annals of the New York Academy of Sciences*, Vol. 1136, June 2008, 257–268.

[3]Office of Head Start, Head Start Program Fact Sheet, www.acf.hhs.gov/programs/ohs/about/fy2010.html.

[4]Fuhua Zhai, Jeanne Brooks-Gunn, and Jane Waldfogel, "Head Start and Urban Children's School Readiness:

A Birth Cohort Study in 18 Cities," *Developmental Psychology* 47, no. 1 (2011): 134–152.

[5]*USA Today*, "Fix Head Start Before Throwing More Money At It," July 13, 2010, 10A.

[6]Department of Health and Human Services, "Head Start Impact Study," January 2010, www.acf.hhs.gov/programs/opre/hs/impact_study/reports/impact_study/executive_summary_final.pdf.

follows the child's ability to learn by manipulating his or her surroundings with increasing skill. Table 4.4 depicts Piaget's conception of how infants acquire these abilities. Following sensorimotor development are three further stages through which Piaget believed individuals must progress along the route to adulthood.

Moral Development

When we consider the difference between right and wrong, we assume there's a standard. Right and wrong don't exist in a vacuum but are products of particular cultures that pass values and attitudes from one generation to another. Therefore,

TABLE 4.4 ⟩ Piaget's Stages of Cognitive Development

Sensorimotor stage (birth–2 years)
Intelligence is demonstrated through motor activity without the use of symbols. Knowledge of the world is based on physical interactions and experiences.

SUBSTAGE	AGE	DESCRIPTION
1. Simple reflexes	0–1 month	The infant's reflexes are its focus. For example, the infant sucks at anything placed in its lips.
2. Primary circular reactions	1–4 months	Coordination of separate actions. An infant grasps an object while sucking on it.
3. Secondary circular reactions	4–8 months	Infants begin to act on the outside world. A child may repeatedly pick up a rattle and shake it in different ways to hear how the sound changes.
4. Coordination of secondary circular reactions	8–12 months	Coordinates several schemes to solve a problem. An infant will push away one toy to reach another toy that is lying partially exposed under it.
5. Tertiary circular reactions	12–18 months	Conducting experiments to observe the consequences. A child will drop a toy repeatedly, varying the position from which it falls, observing each time to see where it falls.
6. Beginnings of symbolic thought	18–24 months	Develops symbolic thought. Infants can imagine where hidden objects might be. If a ball rolls under an object, the child can figure out where it may emerge.

Preoperational stage (ages 2–7)
Symbols are used; language use matures, and memory and imagination develop, but thinking is nonlogical and egocentric. From 2 to 4 years, the child can imagine objects that are not present. From 4 to 7 years, the child starts to use reason and ask a variety of questions.

Concrete operational stage (7–11 years)
The child engages in the logical and systematic manipulation of symbols related to concrete objects. Operational thinking develops, and egocentric thought fades. However, the child's ability to apply logic is effective only with concrete objects, not to verbal statements or abstract situations.

Formal operational stage (11 years–adulthood)
The adolescent engages in logical, abstract thinking and can imagine and analyze the possibilities of a situation to determine the best approach. Young adolescents return to egocentric thought early in this stage. Many adults never enter this stage. Even adults capable of higher levels of cognitive thought don't do it all the time. Preoperational thought is present in adult behavior.

Think About It
1. Which stage do some people never enter?

Source: Robert S. Feldman, Child Development, 4th ed., 2007.

when we talk about a "moral compass," we are suggesting that each individual has a culturally learned system of ethics, values, and principles that act as a guide in evaluating behavior. [43]

Where do young people learn these moral values, and, more importantly, how are they developed? In dealing with adult crime it's expected that the offender either did know or should have known what types of behavior are socially approved. In dealing with children, this assumption can't be safely made. Children can be ignorant of the correct behavior for a specific situation, confused by competing demands for their loyalty, or even not understand that their actions are their own choices.

KOHLBERG'S THEORY OF MORAL DEVELOPMENT

Much like cognitive ability, the capacity to make moral judgments and engage in moral behavior is something that is gradually acquired. Human beings don't develop ethical behavior all at once but gain it gradually through experience by engaging in different types of behavior, some of it right, some wrong. Children slowly develop the ability to make the correct decisions, and, until a certain age, they aren't capable of evaluating situations requiring complex moral reasoning.

Developmental psychologist Lawrence Kohlberg, whose work was based on Piaget's, argued that as humans grow and change, they progress through stages of moral development in which they learn to apply ethical behavior and develop a sense of justice and fairness (see Table 4.5). At certain ages, human beings are simply incapable of evaluating moral dilemmas because our moral development hasn't caught up with our cognitive development.

Kohlberg contended that until age 13, children aren't cognitively equipped to move beyond conventional morality and thus may have difficulty in making many of the complex decisions that are required to deal with the problems of crime and delinquency. Stage 4 is where most of our law-abiding behavior is resolved, because, according to Kohlberg, only about 25 percent of adults are capable of moving on to postconventional morality. An important caveat to Kohlberg's theory of moral development is that just because someone can make moral judgments doesn't mean that he or she will automatically engage in moral behavior.[44] Researchers have found that knowing what is morally correct doesn't always mean that moral actions follow.

Another assertion of Piaget and Kohlberg is that children's peer relationships, that is, their relationships with children their own age, are key to developing prosocial attitudes and relating to others. If children are treated well and treat others well, they learn to see other people as caring and themselves as worth caring for.[45]

DOES SEX AFFECT MORALITY?

Like much research on crime and delinquency, research concerning moral development has been done primarily on males. As more research designs have come to include more females, the conventional wisdom has been modified to explain differing outcomes when the ideas, feelings, beliefs, and behaviors of women and girls are fully considered.

Psychologist Carol Gilligan has studied the moral development of girls and found some additional concerns that Kohlberg failed to consider. Specifically, whereas boys consider morality primarily in broad principles, such as justice or fairness, girls consider it in terms of compassion and are willing to sacrifice themselves to help specific individuals within the context of particular

TABLE 4.5 ⟩ Kohlberg's Stages of Moral Development

Level 1	Preconventional	"Reward and punishment"
The individual judges the morality of an action by its direct consequences and doesn't internalize moral values. The preconventional level of moral reasoning is usually observed in children up to age 9. Adults may also engage in this level of reasoning.		
Stage 1	Obey rules to avoid punishment	
	The physical consequences of action determine its goodness or badness. Avoidance of punishment and deference to power are valued in their own right.	
Stage 2	Conform to obtain rewards and have favors returned	
	Correct behavior is defined as what is in one's own best interests. Moral rightness involves an equal exchange. Reciprocity.	

Level 2	Conventional	"Someone else's rules"
The conventional level is typical of children from age 9 (adolescents) and some adults. The individual judges morality by comparing it to social rules and expectations. The individual internalizes and abides by the standards of others, such as parents' rules or societal laws.		
Stage 3	Conform to avoid disapproval and dislike by others	
	The individual tries to be a "good boy" or "good girl" and looks for the approval or disapproval of others. The individual bases moral judgments on trust, caring, and loyalty to others.	
Stage 4	Conform to avoid censure by legitimate authorities and resultant guilt	
	Social systems morality. The individual believes it important to obey laws and social conventions. Moral judgments are based on understanding the social order, law, showing respect for authority, justice, and duty.	

Level 3	Postconventional or Principled	"For the common good"
At the highest level is an effort to define moral values and principles that are valid apart from authority and apart from the individual's own identification with that authority.		
Stage 5	Conform to maintain the respect of the impartial spectator judging in terms of community welfare	
	Free agreement and contract are the binding elements of obligation. That which violates ethical principles is wrong, and laws are considered to be social contracts and must be changed when necessary and if society agrees. This is the morality of the US Constitution.	
Stage 6	Conform to avoid self-condemnation	
	The Golden Rule: "Do unto others as you would have others do unto you." Empathy. The individual develops a moral standard based on universal ethical principles. Kohlberg apparently had difficulty finding anyone who had reached this stage.	

Think About It
1. Which is the lowest level of reasoning at which Kohlberg found some adults to operate?

Source: Lawrence Kohlberg, The Philosophy of Moral Development: Moral Stages and the Idea of Justice (Essays on Moral Development, Vol. 1) (San Francisco: Harper & Row, 1981), 17–19.

relationships. According to Gilligan, girls progress through three stages of moral development:

1. **Orientation through individual survival.** The concern is what is best for oneself.
2. **Goodness as self-sacrifice.** This stage takes into account the needs of others, and the girl may sacrifice her own self-interests to make others happy.

3. **Morality of nonviolence.** The most sophisticated form of reasoning according to Gilligan, this establishes a moral equivalence between self and others. Here, hurting anyone, including oneself, is considered immoral.[46]

Some researchers contend that the differences between the moral reasoning of boys and girls suggested by Gilligan are too sweeping and that both males and females consider justice and compassion in making ethical judgments.[47] Although this question must be addressed by future research, it's important to credit Gilligan for expanding the range of issues that children consider in their moral reasoning. Further, it's crucial to the study of delinquency to keep an open mind, not only about possible differences between the sexes, but also about the fundamental questions concerning the age at which children can make these important decisions. When psychological theories of delinquency are compared to theories of adult crime, age of accountability is a primary concern.

Intelligence and Delinquency

Are delinquents and criminal offenders less intelligent than law-abiding people? Are detention facilities, jails, and penitentiaries filled with the stupid and unlucky? At one time, psychologists argued as such. In the early 1900s, American psychologist H. H. Goddard, a proponent of eugenics who is credited with coining the word "moron," evaluated studies and reported the range of those prison inmates who were "feebleminded" to be from 28 to 89 percent. The median finding was 70 percent, which led Goddard to conclude that most inmates were feebleminded.[48] The following evidence was suggested to support the idea that delinquents and adult offenders were less intelligent than law-abiding people:

» Individuals who lack intelligence can't evaluate or control their behavior. They don't have the mental skills to tell right from wrong and can't rein in their impulses.

» Those with limited intelligence can't compete in the workplace to satisfy their needs through legitimate means. They are compelled to break the law to achieve financial survival and establish their sense of self-worth. Legitimate opportunities are beyond their abilities, so they turn to crime to compete in a capitalist society that requires individuals to provide for themselves.

» Those with low intelligence aren't able to negotiate the rules and procedures of the justice system as well as those with normal abilities and so are likely to end up incarcerated at a greater rate.

But are these assumptions about the intelligence of offenders correct? To answer this question, it's necessary to consider several issues that make judging the mental abilities of offenders problematic. The history of intelligence testing shows that researchers have had to develop inventive ways to get at the difficult target of objectively comparing the innate intelligence of one person to another.

The intelligence test and the concept of mental age were originated by French psychologist and educator Alfred Binet. He was attempting to identify early in their educational careers those students who weren't succeeding in school and therefore required alternative educational methods. He started with students whom teachers had already identified as "bright" or "dull," and through trial and error devised test items that sorted the students into these categories. The strengths and weaknesses of Binet's efforts are still found in today's intelligence tests.[49]

Binet had no theory as to the nature of intelligence. His approach defined intelligence to be whatever the tests measured. This approach allowed researchers to focus on the differences among individuals. The measure of success on Binet's test was success in school. The tests didn't measure alternative attributes that could be a measure of intelligence but were unrelated to academic proficiency. Finally, Binet linked each test to the child's mental age. Therefore, if a 5-year-old child scored at the average of those who were two years older, the child was assigned a mental age of 7.

Binet's test and formula for determining intelligence were later revised by psychologists William Stern and Lewis Terman, who developed a single score called the **intelligence quotient**. Today, intelligence scores are calculated with more sophisticated techniques, but they are still based on a 100-point average at the center of a bell-shaped curve. Figure 4.2 illustrates this principle. Since Binet's time, intelligence testing has improved considerably.

Intelligence researchers are now relatively good predictors of school performance. However, it's important to note that school performance is but one way to assess innate intelligence and that intelligence and school performance aren't the sole indicators of the likelihood of juvenile delinquency or adult criminality. Criminological research has discovered a relationship between low IQ and delinquency.[50] However, although the two factors are related, some researchers say that low IQ doesn't directly cause delinquent behavior but is a risk factor that affects school performance, increases the susceptibility to pressure from antisocial friends, and affects self-control.[51] Perhaps the most perplexing concern when considering relationships between intelligence and crime is the claim that IQ is influenced by race. See Focus on Diversity for more on this controversy.

INTELLECTUAL DISABILITY

Another dimension of intelligence and crime requires consideration. Some individuals who don't have the intellectual ability to engage in normal societal activities often become clients of the justice system. One of these conditions is intellectual disability. The American Association on Intellectual and Developmental Disabilities defines the condition of intellectual disability as "significant limitations both in intellectual functioning and in adaptive behavior, which covers many everyday social and practical skills. This disability originates before the age of 18."[52]

Experts vary widely on whom to label "intellectually disabled." Consequently, the characteristics of people considered to be intellectually disabled range from individuals who can be taught to function and work with

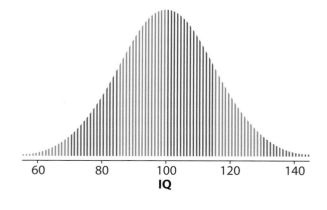

Figure 4.2 Intelligence tests are designed to give normally distributed scores that, when graphed, produce a bell-shaped curve. The intelligence of most people falls within the greater portion of the curve.

Think About It

1. Discuss how the bell curve may be useful when discussing intelligence in a population.

Intelligence testing has improved considerably over the past several decades. Here, two-year-old Joseph Attia, who has an IQ of 140, works on a puzzle at his home in Sydney, Australia.

little attention to individuals who are untrainable. Again, the issue of racial and cultural bias is present when we talk about intellectual disability, and minority children are much more likely to be placed in special education classes than are white children.[53]

A related and persistent issue is that of mentally ill, intellectually disabled, and learning disabled individuals being funneled into the juvenile justice and criminal justice systems instead of into treatment or education. Between 28 and 43 percent of incarcerated juveniles are estimated to need special education, and researchers have found links between learning disabilities and encounters with the juvenile justice system.[54] The population of students in the criminal justice system who have learning disabilities is estimated to be as high as 50 percent.[55]

In the United States, mental health care, which was a fairly centralized institution in the early to mid-20th century, has become a decentralized system of social agencies that comprise mental health, social services, medical, housing, and law enforcement agencies. This means that one or more agencies might end up with a client who needs the services of another set of agencies. This trend, according to Nancy Wolff, not only makes all agencies appear ineffective and inefficient, but sometimes also deepens the client's problems, including the incidence of disorderly or violent behavior.[56]

Freud, Personality, and Delinquent Behavior

Individuals have different personalities. A personality is "a set of relatively enduring behavioral characteristics (including thoughts) and internal predispositions that describes how a person reacts to the environment."[57] Personality is one of the major features by which people judge each other. However, the concept of personality is slippery because it's difficult to quantify. Psychologists and criminologists have sought to use personality to explain why people break the law and as an insight into how to treat or rehabilitate offenders.

As with so many issues that pertain to psychology, the study of personality begins with Freud. Freud didn't directly write about delinquency or criminal

Racial Differences in Intelligence Testing: Why?

One fairly consistent finding of intelligence tests is that the mean score for blacks is about 15 points lower than the mean score for whites.[1] In their controversial book *The Bell Curve*, authors Richard Herrnstein and Charles Murray argued that blacks' lower IQ scores are due primarily to heredity.[2] Critics were unconvinced. In 2009, in *Intelligence and How to Get It*, Richard E. Nisbett asserted that the IQ differences between blacks and whites weren't accounted for by genes at all, but almost totally by environmental and cultural factors.

Nisbett points out that as more blacks enter the middle class, IQ and grades continue to improve.[3] Those who argue for a purely environmental impact on IQ point to the Flynn effect, which is the finding of IQ researcher James Flynn that IQ scores throughout the developed world have been rising with each successive generation.[4] Nisbett states that black IQs today are higher than those of whites in the 1950s, a leap that would be unlikely if IQ were determined by race.[5] In just 60 years, the IQs of children in the United States and several European nations have exceeded those of their grandparents by more than 15 points.[6]

The key to understanding differences in IQ amongst groups around the world (for example, East Asians and Ashkenazi Jews are groups noted to have the highest IQs) may be the idea that "race is not a valid scientific concept."[7] That is, to discuss groups of people in terms of what we call "race" simply isn't useful or even accurate. However, Williams goes on to explain: "For most competent social scientists, race, although not a valid scientific concept, is real—in other words, real in its consequences."[8] This means that if a society believes race is real, that if people with dark skin and people with light skin constitute different races and those groups treat each other accordingly, then the concept of race is real because everyone agrees that it is, not because there's any significant biological basis for it.

So if race exists only socially, but not biologically, where does that leave the debate about race and IQ? There's still a gap between black scores and white scores. If race isn't real, why the gap? When taken into consideration with the Flynn effect and the harmful effects of racism on health, wealth, and social and family stability, the answer likely has more to do with social class than with skin color. Recall that black IQ scores are rising as more black families enter the middle class. Higher social classes not only have more wealth and better health, they also have more social stability, are more invested in the social system, and therefore have more expectation of succeeding. In the future, the questions may shift from asking why there are racial differences in IQ to why the differences seem to be based on class.

THINK ABOUT IT

1. Discuss the relationships between culture, class, and intelligence.
2. Why is intelligence testing such a sensitive subject?
3. Do you agree with the assessment that there's really no such thing as race? Why or why not?

---

[1]Stephen Ceci and Wendy M. Williams, "Should Scientists Study Race and IQ? Yes: The Scientific Truth Must Be Pursued," *Nature* 457, no. 12 (February 2009: 789).
[2]Richard J. Herrnstein and Charles Murray, *The Bell Curve: Intelligence and Class Structure in American Life* (New York: Free Press, 1994).
[3]Richard E. Nisbett, *Intelligence and How to Get It* (New York: WW Norton and Company, 2009), 118.
[4]Stephen Ceci and Wendy M. Williams, "YES: The Scientific Truth Must Be Pursued," *Nature* 457, no. 12 (February 2009: 789).
[5]Nisbett, *Intelligence and How to Get It*, 99.
[6]Ceci and Wendy M. Williams, "YES: The Scientific Truth Must Be Pursued," 789.
[7]Nisbett, *Intelligence and How to Get It*, 3. Vernon J. Williams Jr., "Fatalism: Anthropology, Psychology, Sociology and the IQ Controversy," *Journal of African American Studies* 13 (2009): 90–96.
[8]Williams, "Fatalism," 90–96.

behavior, but he did lay the foundation for conceptualizing the components of personality. According to Freud, the personality comprises three interrelated parts.

» **Id.** The **id** is an unconscious aspect of the personality that is responsible for controlling our two primary instincts: sex and destruction or aggression. The id is present at birth and seeks to maximize pleasure and minimize pain. The id can be thought of as one's natural inclinations that drive behavior prior to socialization. Gradually, as the individual learns the etiquette, norms, rules, and laws of the social group, the id is brought under control, and concern for others is developed. The degree to which the id is controlled varies by individual, and some offenders who are impulsive can be considered as having an underregulated id.

» **Ego.** The **ego** represents the rational part of the personality and responds to the id's drives and instincts in socially acceptable ways. It develops in the first year of life as the individual begins to understand that the needs of others must also be considered. A well-developed ego allows the individual to delay gratification and participate in civil society without always putting his or her immediate concerns ahead of others' concerns. The ego operates on the reality principle.

» **Superego.** The **superego** represents the conscience and operates on the morality principle. It can be thought of as that little voice inside your head that helps you decide what is right and what is wrong. The superego is actually an internalization of society's norms and values that must be considered and balanced when preparing to take action. The superego produces feelings of guilt when an individual behaves in a way that he or she knows contradicts the values of society and his or her own internalized values.[58]

Freud believed that these three components of the personality work in harmony in a psychologically healthy person. The ego keeps the id in check and also makes sure the superego doesn't make one too rigid or too much of a

According to Freud, the id controls aggression and can be imagined as the natural inclinations that drive behavior prior to socialization. Gradually, as the individual is socialized, the id is brought under control and concern for others is developed.

perfectionist. It's easy to see how Freud's components of the personality can be used to explain a variety of delinquency and crime. For instance, those who have an underdeveloped superego have never internalized the rules of society, so their ids run amok. Those who have an overdeveloped superego might break the law because they have a deep desire to be caught and punished. They might actually leave clues at the scene of the crime as a way to be detected and to have their feelings of guilt alleviated.

Freud's ideas concerning the personality have become so popularized that it's difficult to distinguish the musings of armchair psychologists from the findings of learned and serious psychoanalysts. Psychoanalytic theory is complicated and takes years to fully appreciate, and it has suffered from the temptation of many to simplify it to the point where it's commonly considered as pop psychology. However, many experts have serious reservations about Freud's perspective. There are three issues that those concerned with delinquency ought to keep in mind:

1. Freud's components of the personality are difficult to measure. To evaluate the perspective, we must consider therapists' recordings of treatment sessions and rely on their interpretations of what patients say. This becomes especially difficult when dealing with the subconscious. In addition to whatever bias the therapist might introduce, therapists often disagree on interpretations. For these and other reasons, psychoanalytic theory might be considered as much an art as a science.

2. A second concern that is problematic for the study of delinquency is Freud's contention that personality is fixed in early childhood and never really changes. He considered various attributes of the personality to be products of heredity, which ignores the processes of social learning that can drastically alter how people respond to opportunities and temptations throughout life.

3. Freud's understanding of women is a product of the social environment of 19th-century Europe. Given the rigid gender-role expectations of that time, it's understandable that Freud viewed females as passive, inherently jealous, and inferior to men. Today, these views aren't only outdated and misogynist, but are politically untenable for any application to public policy in a time when sex equality is legally required. Although Freud might be forgiven for being a product of his culture, his ideas about women don't translate to the modern era and have been supplanted by more accurate insight into how personalities are formed.[59]

The intent here has been to place Freud's ideas in a historical context and to emphasize that, despite the major limitations of his perspective, his specific contention that personality is formed in childhood is a major feature of the study of juvenile delinquency. It's useful to compare Freud's ideas to an old song: although the lyrics are dated and no longer sung, we still hum the melody.

Is There an Antisocial Personality?

It seems like common sense to assume that personality is related to the propensity to break the law. People, either through the decisions they make or the situations they put themselves in, direct much of their own destiny. Consequently, the aspects of personality that are related to how one interacts with others, handles frustrations, or delays gratification are likely to determine, in large part, the degree to which one may (or may not) break the law. Although there might be agreement that personality should be a clue to an individual's likelihood of engaging in crime, measuring this phenomenon is difficult.

One of the first criminological studies that attempted to understand the link between personality and delinquency was published in 1950 by Sheldon and Eleanor Glueck. The Gluecks compared 500 delinquent boys against a sample of 500 nondelinquent boys and found that although each set had the same personality characteristics, the delinquent boys shared interesting features that not only contributed to their delinquency but also helped them to survive in more conventional ways. These six features were:[60]

1. **Extroversion.** The delinquent boys were found to be more extroverted than those in the control group. This should not be surprising, because the types of delinquency boys typically engage in require social interaction. Those who are shy and withdrawn are less likely to engage in fighting, theft, and robbery than those who can confidently interact with others.

2. **Impulsivity.** Delinquency, especially for juveniles, is often a spur-of-the-moment decision. Young boys also tend to be impatient when wanting something. Although everyone can be impatient to some extent, the Gluecks found that delinquent boys were less able to defer gratification and wait for rewards than were the nondelinquent boys. One by-product of impulsivity is that there's less time to plan the offense, so those delinquents who give in to their whims are more likely to be caught by the police and have their offenses recorded.

3. **Hostility.** Those who have had contact with the juvenile justice system are bound to be resentful of authority and demonstrate negative attitudes toward society.

4. **Fearlessness.** The delinquent boys tended to be less afraid of failure or defeat. Engaging in delinquency takes a bit of nerve. Those who lack confidence and self-reliance are likely to abstain from engaging in risky actions.

5. **Suspicion.** Delinquents are suspicious of the juvenile justice system and often of society. Delinquency is viewed as a way to overcome the inherent inequalities of society.

6. **Low self-esteem.** Some youths who engage in delinquency may consider offending as a way of getting attention or establishing identity. It's understandable that the Gluecks would find that delinquents exhibit feelings of not being recognized or appreciated at a greater rate than nondelinquents.

The size and scope of the Gluecks' study are impressive. The Gluecks found support for differences in the personality of delinquents and nondelinquents by using three types of prediction tables: one based on social background, one based on character traits as measured by the Rorschach test, and a third based on personality traits as determined in psychiatric interviews. Of particular interest, however, is the Gluecks' observation that not all the differences between the two groups were negative.[61] In many ways, the delinquents were found to be as socially likeable as the nondelinquents and not in some way defective, as was consistently assumed by some biological and intelligence theories.

MINNESOTA MULTIPHASIC PERSONALITY INVENTORY

More recently, psychologists and criminologists have attempted to examine the differences between the personalities of offenders and nonoffenders by studying how they answer questions on personality inventories. The most well known of these instruments is the Minnesota Multiphasic Personality Inventory (MMPI-2), which also has a version for adolescents, the MMPI-A.

The MMPI provides an interesting way of assessing an individual's personality and has been found to be accurate in distinguishing offenders from non-offenders.[62] The determination rests in large part on participants' responses to statements such as "I have never been in trouble with the law." However, these types of statements don't measure personality characteristics but rather the respondents' social circumstances. Therefore, it's unclear whether we can conclude from the MMPI-A that there are real personality differences between delinquents and nondelinquents.

A study of adolescent male delinquents did find, however, that the MMPI-A could predict some violent delinquency. Although neither IQ nor MMPI-A scores could predict whether the youths would commit further serious, nonviolent offenses, the MMPI-A did predict whether they would go on to commit any violent offenses. The delinquents who later committed more nonviolent serious offenses had records filled with nonviolent offenses. According to these results, then, personality is a predictor of violent juvenile delinquency, whereas past offending is better at predicting whether a delinquent will continue to commit nonviolent offenses.[63]

PSYCHOPATHY

Some offenses are so heinous they seem to have no explanation. Gruesome rapes or murders in which the offender humiliates or tortures the victim and afterward shows no remorse appear to be so outside the bounds of understandable behavior that we might label these offenders "crazy" or "monster." A common label for extreme offenders is **psychopath**.[64] Because the study of psychopathy is a field of its own, we'll just give a brief description of it and its relation to juveniles.

What is psychopathy? Good question. The definition of psychopathy is much debated in the field of psychology. The study, measure, and definition of psychopathy has typically been drawn from the study of white adult males; however, researchers are focusing increasingly on what has become known as "juvenile psychopathy." The idea is that psychopathy is stable across the lifetime; that is, young psychopaths grow up to become adult psychopaths. The controversial concept that this disorder can be measured in youths is relatively new, and researchers are only beginning to attempt to do so.[65] There are several measures of juvenile psychopathy, each with its own set of defining characteristics. One of the best known is *Psychopathy Checklist: Youth Version* (PCL:YV). This is a version of Robert Hare's psychopathy measure for adults, the *Psychopathy Checklist—Revised*. According to the PCL:YV, the symptoms of juvenile psychopathy include the following:[66]

>> Grandiose sense of self-worth

>> Stimulation seeking

>> Pathological lying

>> Manipulation for personal gain

>> Lack of remorse and empathy

>> Poor anger control

>> Impersonal sexual behavior

>> Early behavior problems

>> Lack of goals

>> Impulsivity

>> Irresponsibility

>> Serious criminal behavior

Most of us probably observe some of these features in our own personality. In fact, most of these characteristics describe typical teenagers during the normal process of rebellion against parents and authority, and the formation of their own identities. Defining these features as psychopathic means we must consider not just the term but the level of involvement in the behavior and the duration of the behavior. Perhaps more important, we must recognize that it's a combination of these features, rather than any single one, that constitutes a viable definition of psychopathy.

Another view of psychopathy in general is offered by the American Psychiatric Association (APA) in its current *Diagnostic and Statistical Manual of Mental Disorders*, also known as the DSM-IV-TR.[67] According to the APA, psychopathy is an aspect of antisocial personality disorder (APD). Diagnostic criteria for APD include:

1. A pervasive pattern of disregard for and violation of the rights of others since age 15, including failure to conform to social norms; deceitfulness; impulsivity; irritability and aggressiveness; consistent irresponsibility; lack of remorse.
2. The individual is at least 18 years old.
3. There is evidence of conduct disorder before age 15.
4. The behavior doesn't occur only during episodes of schizophrenia or manic behavior.[68]

The definitions and lists of psychopathic symptoms are similar, yet professionals still disagree on how they are to be used, especially in the case of juveniles. Note that the APA specifies that only individuals 18 and older can be diagnosed with antisocial personality disorder. Juveniles exhibiting similar symptoms are diagnosed with conduct disorder and presumably treated differently.

Many professionals disagree with the juvenile psychopathy approach, asserting that a juvenile so labeled can expect a tougher time in the justice system.[69] They also point out that youths are unlikely to give honest answers to questions about their thoughts, feelings, and behavior, possibly even wanting to appear psychopathic because they want to look tough or, in the case of a delinquent in custody, to try to avoid incarceration. In *The Psychopath Test*, author Jon Ronson interviewed a 28-year-old man in England named Tony who, at age 17, had badly beaten a man. Fearing he would go to prison for five to seven years, Tony said, he asked other inmates what to do. They advised him to pretend he was "crazy" so he would receive treatment in a hospital rather than a prison sentence. Tony did such a good job of acting crazy that he was labeled a psychopath and committed to a psychiatric hospital for 12 years. When Ronson questioned Tony's doctors about this, saying that Tony didn't seem like a psychopath, they explained that only a psychopath would pretend to be mentally ill to escape a prison sentence. (Tony was eventually released.)[70]

Some researchers advocate for a juvenile psychopathy label because, they say, youths who are found to be psychopathic are much more likely to offend as adults and can receive appropriate medical treatment while they are still young.[71] Although psychopathy measures may identify some youths with psychopathic characteristics who carry these traits into adulthood and even continue to break the law, can they be used to pick out the extreme adult offenders? For example, can a class of sixth-graders be tested and those with psychopathic qualities picked out and treated before they become delinquent or turn into serious adult offenders?

Right now, this is an unlikely scenario. The PCL:YV has been successful in finding psychopathic characteristics in boys, but far less so at finding psychopathy in girls.[72] Also, most, if not all, the research is being done on juveniles who are already delinquent and adult offenders who are already convicted. The problem with these measures is that they're not useful in identifying psychopathic personalities before they offend. It would help if researchers could find a way to identify those who are likely to commit future offenses. It's easy to use hindsight to label a psychopath who is already in custody or at least has a long, serious criminal or delinquent record. To have any public policy implications, we must be able to identify psychopaths before they break the law.

Questions

1. What are Freud's contributions to psychodynamic perspective and the concept of personality?
2. Why did Binet create the intelligence test? What are some concerns when considering the relationship between intelligence and delinquency?
3. What is psychopathy? Why is the terminology controversial?

>> FOCUS ON ETHICS

Why Wait Until It's Too Late?

There has always been something wrong with your 17-year-old son Paul. He failed the 4th, 7th, and 9th grades. He has been arrested for larceny, burglary, robbery, curfew violation, drug possession, drug sales, and now for aggravated assault. You're perplexed about what to do, and when the prosecutor offers you a special program for violent offenders, you convince Paul he needs help and should seize this opportunity.

The violent-offender program finds Paul physically fit and in complete control of his emotions. It rules out any type of chemical imbalance, brain disorder, or dietary deficiency. It concludes that his parents are supportive and the expensive private schools he attended were excellent. The program can't find anything to explain Paul's antisocial behavior and concludes that things are getting worse. It finds that Paul is extremely bright but seriously limited in his ability to relate to others.

After extensive psychological tests, the counselors advise you that Paul has a psychopathic personality. Furthermore, the program director has decided that Paul isn't a good candidate for the violent-offender program, probation, or a halfway house. Because the woman he assaulted dropped the charges and moved out of state, Paul is due to be released and plans to live with you because he has nowhere else to go.

You don't want Paul released. He shows no remorse, and he obeys neither you nor the authorities. Paul has made vague threats against other people. You're afraid if Paul is released, his behavior will accelerate to the point that he does something really terrible.

The prosecutor comes to you with a possible solution. Under a new law, you may be able to place Paul in preventive detention for up to three years although he isn't charged with an offense. It would require you to sign a statement declaring that you fear Paul would do grievous harm if he were released. Paul would spend his time in a prison psychiatric center far from your home and wouldn't be allowed visitors. Paul doesn't like this option and has vowed revenge on you and the rest of the family.

WHAT DO YOU DO?

1. Should you allow Paul to live with you and hope that your love and support will turn him around?
2. Should you tell Paul he's now on his own and not to return until he has learned to obey the law?
3. Should you sign the papers to have your son detained against his will in order to protect yourself, him, and other innocent people?
4. Should you try to get the law changed so that the responsibility doesn't fall on a family member to sign papers allowing preventive detention? Shouldn't the prosecutor or the judge make this decision?

Summary

Summary

Summary

Learning Objective 1. Evaluate the assertion that students shouldn't subscribe exclusively to one theory.	No single theory explains all the various behaviors of those who break the law, so criminologists have developed a broad range of explanations.
Learning Objective 2. Briefly summarize the first biological theories of crime.	Lombroso argued that those who broke the law were likely to have certain physical features that would indicate that offenders weren't as fully evolved as law-abiding people. Sheldon constructed a physical and mental typology based on the physiology of development. Sheldon's body-type theory had three components: endomorphism, mesomorphism, and exomorphism. In the 19th century, Gall and others who promoted the pseudoscience of phrenology postulated that bumps on the outside of the skull could reveal brain structure and personality.
Learning Objective 3. Explain Fishbein's concerns about the interaction of genes and environment and their relationship to antisocial behavior.	All human behavior has a genetic component. There are no genes for or biological causes of specific human behaviors. The environment can modify the expression of genetic and biological traits. On a global level, social and economic deprivation, deleterious environmental conditions, psychological trauma, and abuse can lead to antisocial behavior. Vulnerabilities to antisocial behavior cross all boundaries but will be most abundant where social risks are the highest.
Learning Objective 4. Discuss the roles researchers believe neurotransmitters and hormones play in antisocial behavior.	Some researchers believe that too little or too much of some neurotransmitters may be responsible for neurological and mood disorders. These neurotransmitters include dopamine, serotonin, norepinephrine, epinephrine, and monoamine oxidase.
Learning Objective 5. List the criticisms of biosocial theories of crime.	Walsh lists five objections to biosocial theories: biosocial theories are deterministic and socially dangerous; there can't be any genes for crime because crime is socially constructed; if a problem is considered biological, society might give up on trying to rehabilitate delinquents and adult offenders; crime can't have a biological basis because crime rates change rapidly, and changes in genes require many generations; and biological theories tend to be insensitive to people's feelings.
Learning Objective 6. Understand how psychological theories of antisocial behavior are particularly crucial to the study of delinquency.	Adults are expected to be able to tell the difference between right and wrong and to curb their antisocial temptations and urges. The principles of deterrence are expected to work better on adults. These assumptions can't be safely made about youths. The bodies and brains of young people are in constant development until they reach early adulthood, and the ability to recognize right and wrong is the result of a socialization process that varies with each individual.
Learning Objective 7. Briefly describe the psychological theories of Freud, Piaget, Kohlberg, and Gilligan.	Freud's psychoanalytic theory contends that our behavior is motivated by inner forces, memories, and conflicts of which we have little awareness or control.

Learning Objective 7. (continued)	Piaget pioneered the idea that children learn cognitive skills throughout their childhood and that we must appreciate the stages of development when we consider delinquency. Kohlberg argued that as humans grow and change, they progress through stages of moral development in which they learn to apply ethical behavior and develop a sense of justice and fairness. Gilligan states that whereas boys consider morality in broad principles, girls consider it in terms of compassion and are willing to sacrifice themselves to help specific individuals within the context of particular relationships.
Learning Objective 8. Summarize the history of research on intelligence and delinquency.	In the early 1900s, Goddard concluded that most delinquents and adult offenders were less intelligent than law-abiding people. Binet originated the intelligence test and the concept of mental age; his test and formula were revised by Stern and Terman, who developed a single score called the intelligence quotient. Research has discovered a relationship between low IQ and delinquency. Some researchers say that low IQ doesn't directly cause delinquent behavior but is a risk factor that affects school performance, increases susceptibility to pressure from antisocial friends, and affects self-control.
Learning Objective 9. Explain how the contributions of Sheldon and Eleanor Glueck contribute to the study of personality and delinquency.	The Gluecks compared 500 delinquent boys against a sample of 500 nondelinquent boys and found that the delinquent boys shared some features that contributed to their delinquency and helped them to survive in more conventional ways: extroversion, impulsivity, hostility, fearlessness, suspicion, and low self-esteem.
Learning Objective 10. Discuss the controversy surrounding the use of the psychopathy diagnosis for juvenile delinquents.	Many researchers assert that the psychopathy diagnosis unfairly labels delinquents, who may receive tougher treatment from the justice system because of it. Youths are unlikely to honestly answer questions about their thoughts, feelings, and behavior. Finally, psychopathy measures aren't useful in identifying psychopathic personalities before they break the law, only afterwards.

Chapter Review Questions

1. What is the main concern of the positivist school of criminology?
2. What are atavisms?
3. What was phrenology?
4. What is heredity?
5. How do we study individuals with the same genetic makeup but different life experiences?
6. What is biosocial theory?
7. What idea did Piaget pioneer?
8. What are the three stages of moral development that girls pass through?
9. Explain Freud's concept of id, ego, and superego.
10. According to the Gluecks, what six features do delinquent boys share?

Key Terms

androgen—A general term for male hormones.

biosocial theory—The study of the effects of Darwinian evolution on brain structure and human behavior.

DNA—Deoxyribonucleic acid. The substance inside a cell nucleus that carries the instructions for making living organisms.

ego—In Sigmund Freud's theory of the human psyche, the ego is the conscious part of the personality that one typically identifies as "self," and that mediates between the pleasurable drives of the id and the moral demands of the superego.

eugenics—The idea that human beings can be improved by controlled breeding.

evolution—A gradual process in which the genetic composition of a population changes over many generations as natural selection acts on the genes of individuals.

fraternal twins—Siblings produced by the simultaneous fertilization of two egg cells and who are only as genetically similar as regular siblings.

genes—Short lengths of DNA that determine the inherited characteristics that distinguish individuals.

heredity—The handing down of traits from parents to their offspring.

id—In Sigmund Freud's theory of the human psyche, the id represents the most primitive, irrational instincts and is controlled by the pleasure principle.

identical twins—Siblings produced by the division of a single fertilized egg cell and who are genetically identical.

intelligence quotient (IQ)— A measure of intelligence as indicated by an intelligence test, usually the ratio of mental age to chronological age.

neurotransmitter—A chemical that transmits information between neurons.

phrenology—The outdated study of the skull as an indicator of personality.

psychopath—A person with a personality disorder who behaves without remorse or caring for others.

superego—In Sigmund Freud's theory of the human psyche, the superego internalizes the values and standards of society and represents morality.

Endnotes

1 Daniel J. Curran and Claire M. Renzetti, *Theories of Crime*, 2nd ed. (Boston: Allyn and Bacon, 2001), 9–11. See especially their discussion on neoclassical criminology for an excellent explanation of the need to expand the view of criminology so that the criminal justice system can develop policies to address crime.

2 Gina Lombroso-Ferres, "Criminal Men," in Joseph E. Jacoby, ed., *Classics in Criminology*, 2nd ed. (Prospect Heights, IL: Waveland Press, 1994), 116–131.

3 George B. Vold, Thomas J. Bernard, and Jeffrey B. Snipes, *Theoretical Criminology*, 5th ed. (New York: Oxford University Press), 32–35.

4 Stephen Jay Gould, *The Mismeasure of Man* (New York: Norton, 1981), 121–143.

5 William H. Sheldon, *Varieties of Delinquent Youth* (New York: Harper, 1949), 14–30.

6 Sheldon Glueck and Eleanor Glueck, *Physique and Delinquency* (New York: Harper, 1956).

7 John van Wyhe, *The History of Phrenology on the Web*, pages.britishlibrary.net/phrenology/.

8 *The Phrenology Page*, 134.184.33.110/phreno/.

9 Richard L. Dugdale, *The Jukes: A Study in Crime and Pauperism, Disease, and Heredity* (New York: Putnam, 1877).

10 Arthur H. Estabrook, *The Jukes in 1915* (Washington, DC: Carnegie Institute of Washington, 1916).

11 David C. Rowe and David P. Farrington, "The Familial Transmission of Criminal Convictions," *Criminology* 35, no. 1 (1997): 177–201.

12 Diana Fishbein, *Biobehavioral Perspectives in Criminology* (Belmont, CA: Wadsworth, 2001), 27.

13 Vold et al., *Theoretical Criminology*, 40.

14 Ibid., 41–42.

15 Glen D. Walters, "A Meta-Analysis of the Gene-Crime Relationship," *Criminology* 30, no. 4 (1992): 595–613.

16 Vold et al., *Theoretical Criminology*, 42.

17 Fishbein, *Biobehavioral Perspectives in Criminology*, p. 33.

18 Ibid. Fishbein provides an excellent discussion of how biological factors might be related to crime. This chapter draws heavily on her writings. See Chapter 4.

19 Fishbein, *Biobehavioral Perspectives in Criminology*, p. 40.

20 Lee Ellis, "Monoamine Oxidase and Criminality: Identifying an Apparent Biological Marker for Antisocial Behavior," *Journal of Research in Crime and Delinquency* 28 (1992): 227–251.

21 Avshalom Caspi et al., "Role of Genotype in the Cycle of Violence in Maltreated Children," *Science* 297 (August 2, 2002): 851–854.

22 J. Martin Ramirez, "Hormones and Aggression in Childhood and Adolescence," *Aggression & Violent Behavior* 8, no. 6 (November 2003): 621–645; Alexander McKay, "Testosterone, Sexual Offense Recidivism and Treatment Effect among Adult Male Sexual Offenders," *Canadian Journal of Human Sexuality* 14, no. 1–2 (2005): 43–44; Jean King, Washington De Oliveira, and Nihal Patel, "Deficits in Testosterone Facilitate Enhanced Fear Response," *Psychoneuroendocrinology* 30, no. 4 (May 2005): 333–340; L. H. Studer, A. S. Aylwin, and J. R. Reddon, "Testosterone, Sexual Offense Recidivism, and Treatment Effect among Adult Male Sexual Offenders," *Sexual Abuse: A Journal of Research and Treatment* 17, no. 2 (2005): 171–181.

23 C. M. Buchanan, J. S. Eccles, and J. B. Becker, "Are Adolescents the Victims of Raging Hormones: Evidence for Activational Effects of Hormones on Moods and Behavior at Adolescence," *Psychological Bulletin* 111, no. 1 (January 1992): 62–107; Benjamin L. Hankin and Lyn Y. Abramson, "Development of Gender Differences in Depression: An Elaborated Cognitive Vulnerability–Transactional Stress Theory," *Psychological Bulletin* 127, no. 6 (November 2001): 773–796; Eric Stice, Katherine Presnell, and Sarah Kate Bearman, "Relation of Early Menarche to Depression, Eating Disorders, Substance Abuse, and Comorbid Psychopathology among Adolescent Girls," *Developmental Psychology* 37, no. 5 (September 2001): 608–619.

24 J. R. Udry, "Biosocial Models of Adolescent Problem Behaviors," *Social Biology* 37, no. 1–2 (1990): 1–10; Marvin Zuckerman, "The Psychophysiology of Sensation-Seeking," *Journal of Personality* 58, no. 1 (March 1990): 314–345.

25 Buchanan, Eccles, and Becker, "Are Adolescents the Victims of Raging Hormones"; Udry, "Biosocial Models of Adolescent Problem Behaviors."

26 Anthony Walsh, *Biosocial Criminology* (Cincinnati, OH: Anderson, 2002), 140.

27 Stephanie VanGoozen et al., "Adrenal Androgens and Aggression in Conduct Disorder Prepubertal Boys and Normal Controls," *Biological Psychiatry* 43, no. 2 (January 15, 1998): 156–158.

28 Athanasios Maras et al. "Association of Testosterone and Dihydrotestosterone with Externalizing Behavior in Adolescent Boys and Girls," *Psychoneuroendocrinology* 28, no. 7 (October 2003): 932–940.

29 Alan Booth and D. Wayne Osgood, "The Influence of Testosterone on Deviance in Adulthood: Assessing and Explaining the Relationship," *Criminology* 31, no. 1 (1993): 93–117.

30 Fishbein, *Biobehavioral Perspectives in Criminology*, p. 44.

31 Vernon L. Quinsey, "Evolutionary Theory and Criminal Behaviour," *Legal & Criminological Psychology* 7, no. 1 (February 2002): 3.

32 Ibid.; Margo Wilson and Martin Daly, "Competitiveness, Risk Taking, and Violence: The Young Male Syndrome," *Ethology and Sociobiology* 6 (1985): 59–73; Martin Daly and Margo Wilson, *Homicide* (New York: Aldine, 1988).

33 Lee Ellis, *Theories of Rape: Inquiries into the Cause of Sexual Aggression* (New York: Hemisphere, 1989).

34 Lee Ellis and Anthony Walsh, "Gene-Based Evolutionary Theories in Criminology," *Criminology* 35, no. 2 (May 1997): 229; Lee Ellis, "The Nature of the Biosocial Perspective," in Lee Ellis and Harry Hoffman, eds., *Crime in Biological, Social, and Moral Contexts* (New York: Praeger, 1990).

35 Walsh, *Biosocial Criminology*, 16–22.

36 Ellis and Walsh, "Gene-Based Evolutionary Theories in Criminology," p. 230; Lee Ellis, "Conceptualizing Criminal and Related Behavior from a Biosocial Perspective," in Lee Ellis and Harry Hoffman, eds., *Crime in Biological, Social, and Moral Contexts* (New York: Praeger, 1990), 19; Hans J. Eysenck and Gisli H. Gudjonsson, *The Causes and Cures of Criminality* (New York: Plenum, 1989), 1.

37 Ellis and Walsh, "Gene-Based Evolutionary Theories in Criminology," p. 255.

38 Robert S. Feldman, *Child Development* (Upper Saddle River, NJ: Prentice Hall, 2004).

39 Sigmund Freud, *A General Introduction to Psychoanalysis* (New York: Boni and Liveright, 1920).

40 Jean Piaget, *The Origins of Intelligence in Children* (New York: International Universities Press, 1952).

41 Robert S. Siegler, "How Does Change Occur? A Microgenetic Study of Number Conversion," *Cognitive Psychology* 28 (1995): 225–273.

Summary

42 R. Baillargeon, "Object Permanence in 3 1/2- and 4 1/2-Month-Old Infants," *Developmental Psychology* 23 (1987): 655–670.

43 William Damon, *The Moral Child: Nurturing Children's Natural Moral Growth* (New York: Free Press, 1988).

44 Lawrence Kohlberg, *The Philosophy of Moral Development: Moral Stages and the Idea of Justice* (San Francisco: Harper and Row, 1981).

45 Ervin Staub, "The Roots of Goodness: The Fulfillment of Basic Human Needs and the Development of Caring, Helping and Nonaggression, Inclusive Caring, Moral Courage, Active Bystandership, and Altruism Born of Suffering," Nebraska Symposium on Motivation 51 (2005): 33–72; Emma J. Palmer, "The Relationship Between Moral Reasoning and Aggression, and the Implications for Practice," *Psychology, Crime & Law* 11, no. 4 (December 2005): 356.

46 Carol Gilligan, *In a Different Voice: Psychological Theory and Women's Development* (Cambridge, MA: Harvard University Press, 1982).

47 C. Perry and W. G. McIntire, "Modes of Moral Judgment among Early Adolescents," *Adolescence* 30 (1995): 707–715.

48 H. H. Goddard, *Feeblemindedness: Its Causes and Consequences* (New York: Macmillan, 1914).

49 Feldman, *Child Development*, 365–367.

50 Donald Lynam, Terrie Moffitt, and Magda Stouthamer-Loeber, "Explaining the Relation Between IQ and Delinquency: Class, Race, Test Motivation, School Failure, or Self-Control?" *Journal of Abnormal Psychology* 102, no. 2 (May 1993): 187; Paul D. Lipsitt, Stephen L. Buka, and Lewis P. Lipsitt, "Early Intelligence Scores and Subsequent Delinquency: A Prospective Study," *American Journal of Family Therapy* 18, no. 2 (Summer 1990): 197.

51 Jean Marie McGloin, Travis C. Pratt, and Jeff Maahs, "Rethinking the IQ-Delinquency Relationship: A Longitudinal Analysis of Multiple Theoretical Models," *Justice Quarterly* 21, no. 3 (September 2004): 624; Lisa M. McCartan and Elaine Gunnison, "The IQ/Crime Relationship: An Extension and Replication of Previous Research," *Journal of Crime & Justice* 27, no. 1 (2004): 61.

52 American Association on Intellectual and Developmental Disabilities, Definition of Intellectual Disability, www.aaidd.org/content_100.cfm.

53 D. J. Reschly, "Identification and Assessment of Students with Disabilities," *Future of Children* 6 (1996): 40–53.

54 C. M. Fink, "Special Education in Service for Correctional Education," *Journal of Correctional Education* 41, no. 4 (1991): 186–190; D. I. Morgan, "Prevalence and Types of Handicapping Conditions Found in Juvenile Correctional Institutions: A National Survey," *Journal of Special Education* 13 (1979): 293–295; R. B. Rutherford Jr. et al., "Special Education in the Most Restrictive Environment: Correctional/Special Education," *Journal of Special Education* 19 (1985): 59–71; B. F. Perlmutter, "Delinquency and Learning Disabilities: Evidence for Compensatory Behavior and Adaptation," *Journal of Youth and Adolescence* 16, no. 2 (1987): 89–95.

55 R. Bell, "Tried-and-True Educational Methods Aren't True to the Special Needs of Prison Inmates," *Chicago Tribune*, November 28, 1990, p. 23; Clyde A. Winters, "Learning Disabilities, Crime, Delinquency, and Special Education Placement," *Adolescence* 32, no. 126 (1997): 451–463.

56 Nancy Wolff, "Interactions Between Mental Health and Law Enforcement Systems, Problems and Prospects for Cooperation," *Journal of Health Politics, Policy & Law* 23, no. 1 (February 1998): 133.

57 Vold et al., *Theoretical Criminology*.

58 Feldman, *Child Development*, 23–24.

59 Curran and Renzetti, *Theories of Crime*, 78–79.

60 Sheldon Glueck and Eleanor Glueck, *Unraveling Juvenile Delinquency* (New York: Commonwealth Fund, 1950).

61 Ibid.

62 Gordon P. Waldo and Simon Dinitz, "Personality Attributes of the Criminal: An Analysis of Research Studies," *Journal of Research in Crime and Delinquency* 4, no. 2 (1967): 185–202.

63 Jennifer S. Parker et al., "Predictors of Serious and Violent Offending by Adjudicated Male Adolescents," *North American Journal of Psychology* 7, no. 3 (2005): 407–418.

64 Steven H. Egger, *The Killers among Us: An Examination of Serial Murder and Its Investigation* (Upper Saddle River, NJ: Prentice Hall, 1998), 25–29.

65 Curt R. Bartol and Anne M. Bartol, *Criminal Behavior: A Psychological Approach*, 9th ed. (Upper Saddle River, New Jersey: Pearson Education, 2011), 187–188.

66 A. E. Forth, D. Kosson, and R. Hare, *The Hare Psychopathy Checklist: Youth Version* (New York: Multi-Health Systems, 2003).

67 The full title of the text is *Diagnostic and Statistical Manual of Mental Disorders, 4th ed., Text Revision*, thus the acronym DSM-IV-TR.

68 American Psychiatric Association: *Diagnostic and Statistical Manual of Mental Disorders*, 4th ed., Text Revision (Washington, DC: American Psychiatric Association, 2000), 706.

69 Marcus T. Boccaccini et al., "Describing, Diagnosing, and Naming Psychopathy: How Do Youth Psychopathy Labels Influence Jurors?" *Behavioral Sciences and the Law* 26 (2008): 487–510. Jodi L. Viljoen, Kaitlyn McLachlan, and Gina M. Vincent, "Assessing Violence Risk and Psychopathy in Juvenile and Adult Offenders: A Survey of Clinical Practices," *Assessment* 17, no. 3 (2010): 377–395.

70 Jon Ronson, "How to Spot a Psychopath," *The Guardian*, May 21, 2011, www.guardian.co.uk/books/2011/may/21/jon-ronson-how-to-spot-a-psychopath.

71 Donald R. Lynam et al., "Psychopathy in Adolescence Predicts Official Reports of Offending in Adulthood," *Youth Violence and Juvenile Justice* 7, no. 3 (July 2009): 189–207.

72 Bartol and Bartol, *Criminal Behavior*, 188. Maya K. Krischer et al., "Factor Structure of the Hare Psychopathy Checklist: Youth Version in German Female and Male Detainees and Community Adolescents," *Psychological Assessment* 21, no. 1 (March 2009): 45–56.

Sociological Theories of Delinquency

n the previous two chapters, we examined how theorists looked to the individual to explain deliquency and crime. By considering spiritual, biological, psychological, and other individual explanations, we have seen how people may be compelled or may choose to break the law. These have been some of the most popular theories of crime, and contemporary theorists continue to explore them. Now, we will turn to a different level of explanation for crime and delinquency. Instead of considering the individual as the genesis of deviant behavior, we will study factors outside the offender. Sociological theories contend that the interaction of the individual with the social environment can yield powerful explanations of delinquency and crime.

This chapter covers four types of sociological theories: social structure, social process, subcultural, and social reaction. These theories encompass numerous, more detailed descriptions of crime and delinquency that guide the development of social policies designed to prevent deviant behavior.

Social Structure Theories

Learning Objective 1.

Describe why the early 20th-century Chicago sociologists sought to understand crime and deviant behavior.

Learning Objective 2.

Explain collective efficacy.

At the turn of the 20th century, North America was undergoing a tremendous social change as a result of the Industrial Revolution. The agrarian population was transforming into a more urban population, and the social norms, values, and laws that served a rural setting didn't translate well into guiding a diverse and crowded urban one.[1]

Sociologists at the University of Chicago were the first to recognize this change in the United States. Building on Ferdinand Tönnies's comparisons in Germany of the close-knit rural communities (*Gemeinschaft*) to the impersonal mass society of urban communities (*Gesellschaft*) (see Table 5.1), the Chicago sociologists sought to understand the human condition, especially crime and deviant behavior, in light of the social disorganization they saw in the city.[2]

Social Disorganization

At the heart of the Chicago sociologists' analysis is Ernest Burgess's theory of how cities grow (see Figure 5.1). Burgess theorized that cities develop in

Sociological theories contend that the interaction of the individual youth with the social environment can yield powerful explanations of delinquency and crime.

TABLE 5.1 〉 Gesellschaft and Gemeinschaft Compared

GESELLSCHAFT	GEMEINSCHAFT
Urban	Rural
Social differences are more striking than similarities.	Similar backgrounds and experiences foster a feeling of community.
Social interactions tend to be impersonal and task specific.	Social interactions tend to be familiar and friendly.
Self-interest	Cooperation
Tasks are more important than relationships.	Tasks and personal relationships are mingled and inseparable.
Emphasis on privacy	Little emphasis on privacy
Formal social control	Informal social control
Tolerance of deviance	Intolerance of deviance
Emphasis on achieved statuses	Emphasis on ascribed statuses
Social change is evident.	Social change is limited.

Think About It
1. In which environment is delinquency more likely? Explain your answer.

concentric circles, growing toward outer areas. Each concentric circle represents a zone of development that shares certain features and are in constant transition as the city grows. As the urban area expands toward rural areas, each zone develops certain characteristics, such as an area of working-class homes, affluent homes, commuter neighborhoods, and industrial zones.[3]

Clifford Shaw and Henry McKay theorized that if Burgess was right in his explanation of the fluid and changing nature of the growing city, they could use this model to address juvenile delinquency.[4] Shaw and McKay believed that the core values of society would be sorely tested and strained by persistent poverty,

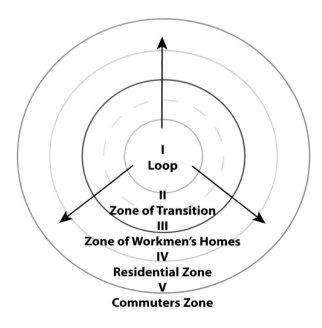

I
Loop

II
Zone of Transition
III
Zone of Workmen's Homes
IV
Residential Zone
V
Commuters Zone

Figure 5.1 Ernest Burgess's Theory of Urban Growth

Think About It
1. According to Shaw and McKay, how could this model be used to explain delinquency?

Burgess theorized that cities grow toward outer areas. As the urban area expands toward rural areas, each zone develops certain characteristics. It's typical for working-class and middle-class suburbs to develop on the outer edges of cities, as seen in this orderly Las Vegas suburb.

rapid population growth, population heterogeneity, and population movement. They hypothesized that delinquency rates would be higher in unstable zones and lower in stable zones. Specifically, Shaw and McKay suggested the following:

)) Weak or nonexistent traditional social controls allow different systems of values to develop.

)) The traditional social controls that worked in primitive societies and isolated, rural communities have been weakened, especially in large cities, by urban growth and the increase in transportation and communication, both of which have accelerated the rate of social change.

)) The city's freedom and tolerance, as well as its emphasis on anonymity and economic values, makes it easier for people to use unconventional methods to improve their status.[5]

URBAN INEQUALITY

Shaw and McKay's social disorganization argument has led others to consider how urban social structural issues may contribute to crime and delinquency. For instance, Robert Sampson and William Julius Wilson introduced race into Shaw and McKay's thesis. Sampson and Wilson rejected the claim that urban culture is an easy way to explain crime and that there is little society can do about it. Rather, they contended that social disorganization creates different ways of considering social dynamics, as well as different norms based on social position that alter how people view their communities. For instance, in areas where drug use, poverty, and substandard housing are part of everyday life, there is greater tolerance for crime and delinquency as a mechanism for individuals to survive, gain status, and pursue the American dream.[6]

By considering the world this way, residents of these areas separate themselves from the greater community. This leads to a social isolation that further impedes these residents' ability to resist crime and delinquency. From a policy perspective, Sampson and Wilson argue for reintegrating the residents or troubled neighborhoods into greater society. This would first mean addressing the

5.1 PREVENTION AND INTERVENTION

Operation Weed and Seed: 1991–2011

Operation Weed and Seed was a federal program initiated in 1991 to provide funding to local agencies to "weed out" violent crime, gang activity, and drug use and trafficking in target areas, then "seed" the area with social and economic revitalization programs. The program reflected sociological theories of crime in acting on the idea that a community's cohesiveness and informal social control largely determined the amount and nature of its crime.[1] The program continued over 20 years, with local groups, agencies, and jurisdictions applying for funding, then applying the program's principles to the crime problems in their communities.

One of the program's ideas was that fear of victimization is a barrier to the safety and renewal of communities: residents may be concerned about their community's safety and be willing to do something about it, but afraid of reprisals from gangs, delinquents, and other antisocial individuals. Although at least two studies, one in 2005 and another in 2010, expressed doubt about the program's effectiveness, some communities reported that it seemed to be working.[2]

» A program in Asheville, North Carolina, reported that "the program's successes include a 34 percent drop in reports of violent crime, a 60 percent drop in calls to police about drug deals, and a revamped community center."[3]

» A Shelby, North Carolina, program reported that calls for service from police had dropped 38 percent since 2006.[4]

» The program in East Chattanooga, Tennessee, was credited with rejuvenating the community, but officials said the area deteriorated when the grant money ran out in 2006.[5]

As of June 2011, Weed and Seed funding was cut, and the program's sponsoring agency, the Community Capacity Development Office, was closed.[6] Although grants extended before 2011 were to be continued, funding after that date was discontinued. It has been stressed that Weed and Seed is more of a strategy than a federal program: that is, any community can implement Weed and Seed tactics. Whether they will continue to do so without federal funding remains to be seen.

THINK ABOUT IT

1. Which sociological theories best describe Weed and Seed's underlying philosophy?
2. Do you think outside funding is critical to the success of such community projects? Why or why not?

[1]Blaine Bridenball and Paul Jesilow, "Weeding Criminals or Planting Fear: An Evaluation of a Weed and Seed Project," *Criminal Justice Review* 30 (May 2005): 64–89.

[2]Ibid. John E. Harmon et al., "Boom to Bust or Bust to Boom? Following the Effects of Weed and Seed Zoning in New Britain, Connecticut, from 1995 to 2000," *Police Quarterly* 13, no. 1 (March 2010): 49–72.

[3]Joel Burgess, "Asheville 'Weed and Seed' program to end," *Asheville Citizen-Times* (North Carolina), May 3, 2011, www.citizen-times.com/article/20110531/NEWS/305310038/Public-safety-project-ending.

[4]Corey Friedman, "Crime Down in Northeast Shelby, Police Credit Weed and Seed Cash," *The Star* (North Carolina), August 23, 2010.

[5]Yolanda Putman, "Wind-down of Weed and Seed Funds Worries Residents," *Chattanooga Times/Free Press* (Tennessee), October 2, 2010.

[6]Community Capacity Development Office, www.ojp.usdoj.gov/ccdo/welcome.html.

structural problem of poverty by developing community, governmental, and corporate programs aimed at providing adequate jobs, housing, and schools.[7] A good real-world example of this idea was Operation Weed and Seed (see Prevention and Intervention), a federal program that operated until 2011.

What is it about a community that encourages or discourages its citizens to break the law? It can't simply be poverty, because many impoverished areas don't have high crime rates. Robert Sampson, Stephen Raudenbush, and Felton Earls studied urban social dynamics and envisioned a concept called **collective efficacy**, which they think is related to crime in a community.[8]

Collective efficacy is a group's shared belief of the extent to which it can successfully complete a task. Collective efficacy occurs at the intersection of two features of a neighborhood. The first of these features is informal social control.

Neighborhoods are more than a collection of buildings with people living in them. Here, a burned-out house is demolished in Detroit. After decades of decline, Detroit is preparing to return much of the city to fields or farmland, like it was in the 19th century.

This refers to citizens who intervene by stopping others' antisocial behaviors and maintaining public order.[9] For instance, keeping a group of youths on a street corner from harassing others requires only the intervention of a shopkeeper or one of the youths' parents. When others in the community speak up or act, potential delinquency can be averted.

This informal social control varies across communities and is related to the other feature of collective efficacy, **social cohesion**, or trust. People are more likely to intervene in situations and attempt to maintain informal social control when they trust their neighbors and can expect support and cooperation. Neighborhoods are more than a collection of buildings with people living in them. The relationships among people are an intangible factor in each neighborhood, and neighborhoods with good relationships are better able to maintain social control. Collective efficacy occurs where individuals are willing to speak up and act when laws are being broken or the community threatened. This informal social control is highly correlated with social cohesion, and the resulting collective efficacy is what makes meaningful communities possible.[10] Social organization of this kind is difficult to measure, but for those who live in a location where the *Gemeinschaft* is high, the connectedness between citizens is evident.

Questions

1. What is the difference between *Gemeinschaft* and *Gesellschaft*?
2. What is Ernest Burgess's theory of how cities grow?
3. How is social cohesion related to collective efficacy?
4. How did Sampson and Wilson extend Shaw and McKay's thesis?

Social Process Theories

Social process theories are concerned not with how society is put together but rather with how it works. Social processes are the ways individuals and groups develop rules of behavior and social norms. Additionally, these social processes enable individuals to comprehend the types of behavior that are expected of them.

Social organization is difficult to measure, but for those who live in a location where the *Gemeinschaft* is high, the connectedness between citizens is evident.

Learning Theories

Several theories assert that antisocial behavior is learned. This learning has many sources, which can be quite different depending on an individual's circumstances and environment. It's common to talk about penitentiaries as "universities of crime," because inmates often learn from other inmates how to be better criminals. For similar reasons, parents will often tell their children not to hang around certain other children because the parents fear a negative influence will be conveyed.[11] Television and the media have also been faulted as providing negative examples for young people, and this tension has resulted in a classification system for movies, television programs, video games, and music.[12]

DIFFERENTIAL ASSOCIATION

The best known of the learning theories of delinquency, and one of the theories that has had a great deal of influence on crime research, is Edwin Sutherland's **differential association theory**.[13] Sutherland's theory is stated in the form of nine propositions in which he argues that crime is learned from others, especially close family members and delinquent peers. These are the nine propositions:[14]

1. Criminal behavior is learned.
2. Criminal behavior is learned in interaction with other persons in a process of communication.

3. The principal part of the learning of criminal behavior occurs within intimate personal groups.

4. When criminal behavior is learned, the learning includes (a) techniques of committing the crime, which are sometimes complicated, sometimes simple; and (b) the specific direction of motives, drives, rationalizations, and attitudes.

5. The specific direction of motives and drives is learned from definitions of the legal codes as favorable or unfavorable.

6. A person becomes delinquent because of an excess of definitions favorable to violation of law over definitions unfavorable to violation of law.

7. Differential associations may vary in frequency, duration, priority, and intensity.

8. The process of learning criminal behavior by association with criminal and anticriminal patterns involves all of the mechanisms that are involved in any other learning.

9. While criminal behavior is an expression of general needs and values, it's not explained by those general needs and values, since noncriminal behavior is an expression of the same needs and values.

Sutherland contended that young people learn two things from their associations with deviant others. First, they learn the attitude that breaking the law is desirable, or what Sutherland called "definitions favorable to the violation of the law." Second, Sutherland contended that youths learn techniques of breaking the law from their interaction with others.

Not all youths turn to delinquency because they have delinquent friends. Clearly, most youths are also influenced to obey the law by law-abiding friends and family members. Sutherland argues that the balance is tipped toward lawbreaking or law-abiding behavior by four factors in youths' exposure to messages about whether crime is good or bad. These factors—priority, frequency, duration, and intensity—are related to what is learned in interaction with significant friends and family members. For example, if a young person spends all his or her time with a juvenile gang that engages in violence, drug use, and vandalism, this youth will be more likely to learn definitions favorable to the violation of the law than if he or she spent the majority of the time engaged in church activities. The gang experience can be intense, allowing little freedom for the youth to form other loyalties. If the youth joins a gang early in life (priority) and stays in the gang for many years (duration), the chances of becoming a delinquent increase drastically.

One main concept of Sutherland's differential association theory that is important to remember is that antisocial behavior is learned in the same way that law-abiding behavior is learned. One point that Sutherland failed to clarify concerns the exact meaning of "definitions favorable to the violation of the law." [15] Did he mean that young people actually have values that say crime is permissible, or did he mean that they hold values that are conducive to crime, such as fighting, thrill seeking, and toughness? It might be that values favoring crime are applicable only to certain situations. These situations might require young people to find excuses to justify their behavior. One theory that looks at these excuses or justifications is called **techniques of neutralization**, which we will discuss later in this chapter.

SOCIAL LEARNING THEORY

Social learning theory is an extension, refinement, and improvement on Sutherland's differential association. According to social learning theory, people learn behaviors by watching other people and mimicking interactions that are rewarded and avoiding those that are punished. Sutherland's eighth proposition states that antisocial behavior is learned like any other attitude or skill, but it doesn't specify exactly how crime is learned.[16] Rather, it's social learning theory that goes on to explain how crime is learned.

Criminologist Ron Akers has spent the better part of his career developing social learning theory well beyond the ideas of differential association. Akers first worked with Burgess to construct a theory that blended the ideas of differential association with the psychological principles underlying **operant conditioning** and **behaviorism**.[17] They were able to combine many aspects of differential association with psychological concepts, such as schedules of reinforcement and behaviors that are voluntary on the part of the respondent, as well as those that are conditioned by involuntary reflex behavior and the principle of rewards and punishment. This advancement on differential association enabled Akers and Burgess to specify how behavior is learned and to develop their theory so it could be put in the form of testable propositions.

Although Akers and Burgess began with differential association, by the time they applied several aspects of psychological theories to social learning, they ended up with a theory that was "closer to cognitive learning . . . than to the radical or orthodox operant behaviorism of B. F. Skinner." As Akers has moved beyond his earlier work with Burgess, he has developed his social learning theory of crime across four dimensions (see Figure 5.2).

» **Imitation.** Akers's social learning theory of crime also includes the idea that individuals learn through imitation. When a person sees someone break a law and escape the negative consequences of punishment, he or she might choose to participate in unlawful behavior as well. Imitation explains how people first decide to engage in crime but has less to do with why they persist or decide to quit.[18]

» **Differential association.** Like Sutherland, Akers contends that individuals learn techniques and attitudes toward breaking the law from others. It's important, however, to specify who these others might be. Clearly, family members, especially parents, are an early influence (priority) on the values

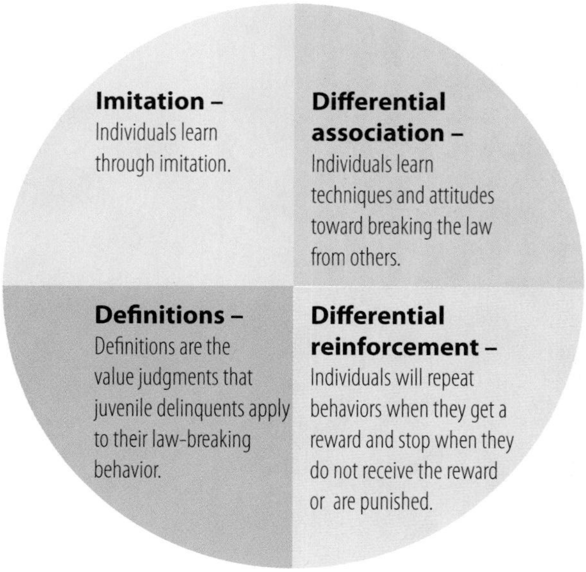

Imitation –
Individuals learn through imitation.

Differential association –
Individuals learn techniques and attitudes toward breaking the law from others.

Definitions –
Definitions are the value judgments that juvenile delinquents apply to their law-breaking behavior.

Differential reinforcement –
Individuals will repeat behaviors when they get a reward and stop when they do not receive the reward or are punished.

Figure 5.2 The Four Dimensions of Ron Akers' Social Learning Theory

Think About It
1. Under which dimension will individuals repeat their activities when they're rewarded?

the youth develops, and peers can exert tremendous pressure (intensity) to conform or not conform to the law. Additionally, numerous other individuals influence young people, including neighbors, members of a church, teachers, or people in the community, as well as figures in the media. Because of the range of media available today, young people might pick up values and attitudes from the Internet, movies, television, and video games, as well as from people on the Internet whom they have never personally met. According to Akers, there is now a greatly expanded range of peer groups from which young people can derive attitudes about the law.

)) **Differential reinforcement.** Individuals will repeat behaviors when they receive a reward and cease the behavior when they don't receive the reward or are punished. This statement is a simplistic synthesis of operant conditioning, but it captures the commonsense logic that underlies the theory. Akers includes this idea in his concept of **differential reinforcement**. Rewards come in many forms, and it's important to understand what individuals consider to be rewarding. The reward might be money, approval, food, or simply a pleasant feeling. These are all considered positive reinforcement and are likely to increase the behavior. The behavior is also likely to occur if it allows the individual to escape unpleasant consequences. This avoidance of disagreeable events is called **negative reinforcement**. Additionally, the likelihood of the behavior continuing is influenced by punishment, which can be either direct or indirect. Direct punishment occurs when something unpleasant is done to the subject, such as incarceration or corporal punishment. Indirect punishment occurs when a planned reward or pleasant consequence is removed.

)) **Definitions.** Definitions are the value judgments that delinquents apply to their antisocial behavior. By excusing such behavior through these accounts, disclaimers, rationalizations, and moral disengagement, young people can maintain positive feelings about their behavior and character. In fact, the youth may be able to completely reframe extremely harmful and

Because of the range of media available today, young people might pick up values and attitudes from movies, television, and video games, as well as from people on the Internet whom they have never personally met.

disreputable behavior. Much like the heroic outlaw of the Old West, Robin Hood, or contemporary international terrorists, delinquents can cleanse their consciences by defining their harmful behavior as harmless, righteous, deserved, or not their fault.

Social learning theory has remained a popular explanation for crime, delinquency, and deviant behavior for two primary reasons:

» Social learning theory has withstood the rigors of empirical testing. It has consistently been shown to explain delinquency at least as well as other theories, and some studies have shown it to be better than most other theories.[19]

» Social learning theory offers obvious policy implications. For instance, many programs use behavior modification techniques that reward the good behavior of inmates or delinquents. Frank Williams and Marilyn McShane point out that these programs are often referred to as "M&M economies" because they use the popular candy as a reward to promote desired behaviors. By rigidly structuring the rewards and punishments of a behavior modification program, administrators can entice participants to exhibit the types of behaviors that are conducive to successfully completing the program.

Despite the popularity of behavior modification programs, there have been several incidents of abusive programs that have impeded rehabilitation efforts. Also, the learned behaviors of delinquents and inmates are often merely adaptations to the artificial environments of the treatment programs and are quickly discarded when the delinquent or inmate returns to the real world.[20] Although behavior modification programs have earned some negative publicity, the underlying utility of social learning theory is still considered useful. The trick is to teach delinquents that their behaviors have long-term consequences and that the short-term reward isn't always the most desirable choice.

TECHNIQUES OF NEUTRALIZATION

Why do people break laws they think are good for society? For some adult offenders and delinquents, it's simply a matter of choosing to participate in behaviors that are contrary to their personal value system. An individual might agree that selling illegal drugs is wrong, but because of the potential to make a great deal of money, she or he might be willing to live with the disjunction of values versus behavior. However, many youths break the law without such a cavalier attitude and are forced to reconcile their values with their offenses. Gresham Sykes and David Matza developed the theory of techniques of neutralization to explain how youths who generally don't approve of delinquency can rationalize or justify their conduct.[21] Youths may construct these defense mechanisms prior to breaking the law as ways of deflecting moral blame.

» **Denial of responsibility.** According to Sykes and Matza, individuals employ denial of responsibility to mitigate their unlawful behaviors in two ways. The first, and least common, is to claim the offense was an accident. By using this rationalization, the offender can avoid responsibility by denying motivation. The second way the offender can claim denial of responsibility is to assert that his or her actions were caused by some outside force. For example, indifferent parents, bad companions, or a socially disorganized neighborhood can be used as reasons why the offender had little choice but to act in the way he or she did.

» **Denial of injury.** Often, delinquents will excuse their actions by claiming that no one was injured. Offenses such as vandalism, even though there is property damage, might be rationalized by asserting that it was done as a prank and that the insurance company will pay for the damages. Additionally, when a youth gets into a fight and doesn't brutally beat the opponent, the rationalization is that no real injury was done and that the fight was simply roughhousing. Although the youth might in fact cause substantial injury to property or other people, the behavior is minimized and blame is deflected by denying that real harm was done.

» **Denial of victim.** Some juvenile delinquents attempt to excuse their actions by claiming that the injured party doesn't deserve true victim status. According to the youth, it's permissible to attack some individuals, such as homosexuals or members of minority groups. The youths see themselves as avengers or retaliators for real or imagined slights. Their logic doesn't have to be consistent provided that they are able to put themselves into the role of a modern Robin Hood who preserves street justice. The injured victim is transformed into someone who deserves contempt, and there is no dishonor in dishing out violence to such a person. The denial-of-victim neutralization technique is also applied to a victim who is physically absent or unknown. The victim is an abstraction, and the youth is able to commit delinquent acts without feeling the blame or dealing with someone's tangible loss or pain.

» **Condemnation of condemners.** Young people are quick to spot hypocrisy. When criticized for smoking marijuana, they point to adults who smoke tobacco and abuse alcohol. They believe those who are guilty of deviance themselves unjustly condemn the deviance of young people. The police who arrest them are viewed as corrupt, stupid, and brutal. Teachers are ineffective and give bad grades to students they don't like while showing favoritism to those who "play the game" and become teachers' pets. Parents are

Some delinquents attempt to excuse their actions by claiming that the injured party doesn't deserve true victim status. Their logic doesn't have to be consistent provided that they are able to put themselves into the role of a modern Robin Hood who preserves street justice.

faulted for condemning in their children the same behaviors they engaged in when they were young. This technique of neutralization works well when youths are encouraged to think critically and find fault with the status quo. It's always much easier for parents and teachers to prescribe the types of behaviors they wish to see, rather than model them.

» **Appeal to higher loyalties.** Sometimes young people understand the logic behind what society holds up as correct behavior, but they are conflicted because another group is competing for their loyalty. The gang, friendship clique, football team, or cheerleading squad may hold a great deal of influence over the youth who wants to do good but who is bonded to a smaller group by identity or a need to belong. Perhaps one of the best contemporary examples of appeal to higher loyalty is the deeply religious individuals who commit violence against abortion clinics or kill doctors who provide abortion services. These individuals conform in other ways but see their duty to their religion and moral code as overwhelming the nation's laws; thus they are able to commit offenses they would reject under any other context. However, society doesn't share this distinction and prosecutes them to the full extent of the law. Although their motivation might be pure in their own eyes, society considers it as terrorism and deals with in the harshest manner. Nevertheless, understanding the appeal to higher loyalties helps us account for the antisocial behaviors of people who otherwise obey the law. Often, members of youth gangs will cite their loyalty to the gang as a reason why they break the law.

Sykes and Matza's techniques of neutralization help answer one of the most interesting questions in criminology. Why do people break laws they believe in? The answer that Sykes and Matza provide is simple, appealing, and understandable. When people break the law, they are able to provide themselves with excuses that minimize their blame. In this way, they are able to escape the full ramifications of their wrongdoing and provide themselves with at least some degree of justification for their antisocial behavior.[22]

The techniques of neutralization aren't always fully effective. Some delinquents who employ them still feel guilty or remorseful even as they continue to break the law, and some delinquents are so isolated from society, they feel no remorse at all. Yet, according to Sykes and Matza, the techniques of neutralization help lessen the constraints of social control to such a great extent that delinquents can justify committing a broad range of unlawful behavior, even while they find fault in others for engaging in similar behavior.

The usefulness of this theory has broad appeal for criminologists. It has been employed to explain the actions of child molesters, bad-check writers, and steroid-using athletes.[23] Anytime there is a disjunction between the ideals taught to young people and the way society actually works, it can be expected that youths will seize on this discrepancy and use it to justify breaking the law.

Anomie and Strain Theory

Anomie is personal anxiety or isolation, also called *normlessness*, which is produced by rapidly shifting moral values. Although anomie and **strain theory** aren't interchangeable, they do refer to the same social processes. Strain theory refers to the personal strain and anger caused by being excluded from economic rewards, which may inspire youths to commit delinquent acts. It's useful to think of strain theory as an extension of anomie. Anomie and strain theory are associated with two important sociologists, Emile Durkheim and Robert

Merton, along with the contemporary work being done on general strain theory by Robert Agnew.

DURKHEIM AND ANOMIE

Durkheim used the term *anomie* to refer to the sense of normlessness that people feel during times of rapid social change, when the usual ways of relating to each other are confused by impersonalization, detailed divisions of labor, and the breakdown of moral order. Deviant behavior occurs when people feel that the traditional ways of relating to others no longer work. People need clear rules to live by, and when these rules are absent or no longer apply, people may feel dissatisfied and frustrated. Durkheim used the term *anomie* to refer to social conditions and not necessarily to individuals. Perhaps his most famous work in which he discussed *anomie* is *Suicide: A Study in Sociology* (1897), in which he looked at the suicide rates of several nations and concluded that the breakdown in social norms as a result of social change was responsible for higher suicide rates.[24]

MERTON AND STRAIN

Merton's strain theory is similar to anomie, but he considers deviance in a slightly different and expanded way. Merton divided social norms into two types of concerns.[25] The first, *social goals*, argued that society teaches individuals to pursue desirable ends. In the United States, the overriding social goal is economic success and accumulating as much wealth as possible. Typically, Americans are socialized from an early age to strive for financial independence. Other societies, however, have different cultural goals. For example, in some traditional Asian societies, getting rich isn't as important as maintaining family obligations and showing the required deference to those in positions of authority.

Merton's second cultural norm deals with the means that one uses to pursue cultural goals. Typically, accumulating wealth isn't considered to be legitimate if it's done through force, coercion, violence, fraud, or duplicity. The culturally approved means for acquiring wealth in American society is study, hard work, and creativity. Although we all may agree with the culturally approved goal of getting wealthy through the culturally approved means of working hard, not everyone has equal access to these means. Because of issues such as racism, sexism, or social-class bias, some young people find their means to the socially approved goals of acquiring wealth to be blocked. This doesn't mean that these young people give up on their goals, however. Rather, they find other, often illegitimate, means for attempting to get what society tells them they need to have. Merton calls these other means *modes of adaptation*. Merton's five modes of adaptation, explained next, are illustrated in Table 5.2.

» **Conformity.** Most of us, including most young people, fall into Merton's category of *conformist*. We have been so heavily socialized into law-abiding behavior that we still strive for our goals by working hard, even if we think the process isn't fair and that we might spend a long time trying to achieve our goals. Because of family upbringing, religious values, or just common decency, most people choose to obey the law and maintain self-respect and a good name. Therefore, according to Merton, we accept both the goals of society and the culturally approved means to obtain these goals.

» **Innovation.** Those who accept the socially approved goals but employ alternative means for achieving these goals are called *innovators*. There are many ways of innovating, the most relevant here being resorting to crime to

TABLE 5.2 〉 Merton's Five Modes of Adaptation

TYPE	ACCEPT GOALS	ACCEPT MEANS
CONFORMITY	YES	YES
INNOVATION	YES	NO
RITUAL	NO	YES
RETREAT	NO	NO
REBELLION	CREATES & SUBSTITUTES NEW GOALS AND MEANS	

Think About It
1. Which types best describe juvenile delinquents?

obtain financial security. Sometimes there's a fine line between legitimate and illegitimate innovation. Aggressive business practices and consumer fraud are difficult to discern and are often decided after the fact by a court of law. Sometimes illegitimate innovations through robbery, theft, and/or lying are more efficient than culturally approved means, and the temptation is high to take such shortcuts to the goal. Some delinquency is actually innovation, such as selling drugs or stealing items to sell for a profit to allow youths to buy things they couldn't otherwise afford.

》 **Ritual.** Some people reject the culturally approved goals but cling tenaciously to the means. These *ritualists* are simply going through the motions of chasing the dream. They long ago gave up on becoming financially successful, but they get a certain satisfaction out of maintaining their positions by doing their jobs in a credible if unimaginative way. These individuals include the professor who never updates classes, the clerk who makes sure every form is filled out completely, and the chef who, while preparing good-tasting food, is unconcerned with how the dish is presented. Because young people haven't had much life experience, few could be called true ritualists.

》 **Retreat.** The American dream is so elusive for some people that they have given up the idea of being successful and no longer pursue the means that would allow them to succeed. Vagrants, drug addicts, and alcoholics are good examples of *retreatists*. They retreat to the bottle or needle and have little hope or care of achieving a respectable job or social position. Historically, this doesn't represent a large social segment, but because of severe dislocations in the economy, it appears to be more prevalent with the increases of the homeless, unemployed, and incarcerated. As with ritualism, retreatism requires a certain amount of life experience. A young person who is this disillusioned might be a victim of mental illness or clinical depression.

》 **Rebellion.** Finally, some people reject society's accepted goals and means and substitute new ones. These people, *rebellionists*, are exemplified by the hippies of the 1960s. The counterculture of that period saw wealth as undesirable or even immoral and attempted to address social inequities through protests and flouting of the dominant society's values. Other rebels might include revolutionaries who advocate the overthrow of governments and the substitution of new leaders who espouse a different set of values. Young people, including juvenile delinquents, are prime candidates to become rebellionists. A majority of the aforementioned hippies, who were members of

Those who accept the socially approved goals but employ alternative means for achieving these goals are called innovators. Some delinquency, such as theft, is actually innovation.

the baby boom generation, adopted their attitudes during late adolescence and young adulthood.

Merton's theory can explain the offenses of the lower class better than the offenses of those who have been economically successful. Those who can successfully compete in the job market don't need to resort to Merton's adaptations because socially approved means to their desired goals aren't systematically blocked. However, just because the middle and upper classes don't experience the strain or anomie of the lower classes doesn't mean they don't break the law. Their strain may be of a different variety—not so much about financial issues as about other concerns, such as reputation among elites, perceived respect, or simple greed.[26]

AGNEW AND STRAIN

Before we leave anomie and strain theory, it's important to consider the theoretical contributions of another criminologist. Robert Agnew considers crime and delinquency as adaptations to stress, and his major contribution to strain theory is the expansion of the types of stress considered to be sources of strain. Specifically, Agnew identifies three major sources of stress.[27]

» **Strain caused by the disjunction between just or fair outcomes and actual outcomes.** This is an interesting point that allows us to consider how people view the type of justice that is allocated to their acts. People have expectations of outcomes based on how hard they have worked and how hard they have seen others work. When it appears that outcomes are allocated not on equity, but rather as a result of inside information such as favoritism, family connections, or class bias, many people may feel strain and disillusionment about the fairness of society.

» **Strain caused by the removal of positively valued stimuli from the individual.** Stress is produced by events other than failure to achieve goals. According to Agnew, a great deal of literature about aggression suggests that strain is caused by the removal of something that is valued. Examples of events that could cause this type of strain include the loss of a loved one, the divorce of parents, the loss of a job, breaking up with a significant other, or suspension from school. When something valuable is removed from one's life, the individual attempts to fill the void through adaptations that can often include crime and delinquency.

》 **Strain caused by the presentation of negative stimuli.** Certain noxious stimuli introduced into an individual's environment can cause strain that results in delinquency. On one level, these noxious stimuli can take a physical form, such as extremely unpleasant odors, disgusting scenes, air pollution, high population density, noise, and heat. At another level, these stimuli can be found in the form of personal interaction in which the individual is subjected to physical or sexual abuse, criminal victimization, physical punishment, negative associations with parents or peers, physical pain, or verbal threats and insults.

Agnew's general strain theory has greatly expanded what is considered stressful. Moreover, Agnew and others have subjected this new way of considering strain to a great deal of empirical investigation.[28] Like Akers's social learning theory, general strain theory provides important insights into why delinquents break the law. It's important to remember that strain theory is concerned primarily with the stresses and concerns of young people.

Social Control Theory

Thus far, the focus of criminological and delinquency theories has been to explain why people break the law. This seems like a straightforward approach that has led to the examination of biological, psychological, and sociological factors that demonstrate differences between delinquents and law-abiding youths. Social control theory, however, approaches the issue from a different perspective. Instead of asking why people break the law, it asks, why don't we all break the law?

In many ways, social control theories are theories of socialization. They consider the extent to which youths have learned the habits, attitudes, and perspectives of society and try to identify deficiencies in this socialization. All groups socialize their members to conform to the group norms, and the health of each group is monitored by the adherence to these norms. Sociologist Emile Durkheim provided the example of a "society of saints," where although each saint was law-abiding, there would still be group norms that would separate the better saints from the less devoted.[29] Inadequate time spent at prayer, being improperly pious, or violating dietary restrictions are all infractions of acceptable behavior in Durkheim's society of saints.

Here, we will briefly review three types of social control theories: personality-oriented control theories, containment theories, and social bonding theories. These theory types demonstrate how social control perspective has gained in sophistication and testability.

PERSONALITY AND SOCIAL CONTROL

Yale sociologist Albert Reiss was one of the first scholars to consider the intersection of personality and social control. Writing in the 1950s, he used the then-fashionable perspective of psychoanalysis to examine the effect of personality on delinquency. More importantly, he identified three aspects of social control that, in interaction with personality, could result in delinquency:

1. **A lack of proper internal controls developed during childhood.** Children who aren't taught to control their temper, defer gratification, or respect the rights of others are likely to engage in delinquent behavior.

2. **A breakdown in internal controls.** A properly socialized youth may become delinquent because he or she follows deviant peers, is tempted by rewards for delinquency, or is influenced by drugs or alcohol.

3. **An absence of, or conflicts in, the social rules provided by important groups such as parents or schools.** Alterations in lifestyle, such as an absent parent or a change in schools, may weaken a youth's social control.[30]

Other theorists have refined Reiss's ideas to explain how individuals are socialized to engage in appropriate and law-abiding behavior.

CONTAINMENT THEORY

Walter Reckless envisioned individuals as being influenced by both inner controls (or inner containment), based on their self-concept and personality, and outer controls (or outer containment), based on the adequacy of their social support systems, such as family, schools, and peers. Reckless suggested that inner containment was bound up in the self-concept of individuals. He thought that those who possess tolerance for frustration, healthy self-esteem, a sense of responsibility, and self-control were psychologically well-armed to resist delinquency. Similarly, outer containment involves family and community advantages, such as proper discipline and effective parental supervision, opportunities for positive social activities, conventional chances for acceptance, and developing a positive identity.[31]

Reckless saw individuals as being pushed because of inadequate inner containment and pulled because of pressures from outer containment, which induced them to commit antisocial acts. According to Reckless, the more important of these two influences to a youth's self-concept was inner containment.[32] Containment theory has appeal because it considers both the individual's personality and the social pressures that can tempt him or her into delinquency. But the crucial question that remained unanswered pertains to what makes a youth believe in society's rules. The theorist who is credited with answering this question is Travis Hirschi, who developed the idea of the social bond.

Hirschi's Social Control Theory

Hirschi's social control theory states that individuals are bonded to conventional society and institutions to varying degrees. Youths who have strong and flexible bonds to society won't engage in delinquent behavior, whereas those who have weak bonds will. The signature factor in Hirschi's theory is the manner in which he identifies the characteristics of the social bond. Hirschi envisioned the social bond as having four dimensions:

» **Attachment.** Delinquent behavior can be inhibited by the extent to which a youth is attached to conventional society. These attachments can take the form of an emotional bond with parents, concern for the opinions of teachers, or respect for peers.

» **Involvement.** Youths who are involved in positive activities have little time and emotional energy to engage in delinquency. Based on the old axiom "Idle hands are the devil's playground," Hirschi saw that keeping youths involved in wholesome activities could prevent bad behavior.

» **Commitment.** Commitment deals with the extent to which an individual is already involved in conventional behavior. People who are invested in conventional society have more at stake than those who don't. Basically, those who have nothing invested in conventional behavior have nothing to lose. Those who succeed at school and have a bright future are less likely to take the chance of committing delinquent acts.

>> **Belief.** People who respect society's rules are more likely to obey them. If rules and social conditions are perceived as fair, people will work within the system to advance themselves. Youths who see society's rules stacked against them due to race, class, or gender inequities are more prone to delinquency.[33]

One reason social control theory became so popular among criminologists is because it could be examined by self-report studies.[34] By asking youths what acts they have committed and recording how bonded they are to conventional society, social control theorists were able to measure the relative influence of each of Hirschi's elements of the social bond. Other measures of delinquency, such as official crime statistics or victimization studies, aren't particularly useful for revealing social control theory.

Questions

1. What two things did Sutherland contend that young people learn from their associations with deviant others?
2. What are the four dimensions of Akers's social learning theory of crime?
3. What defense mechanisms are commonly used in techniques of neutralization?

Subcultural Theories

Let's now turn to another set of theories that explain crime in general but especially seek to explain juvenile delinquency. These theories have a good deal of utility because they explain why youths engage in delinquency as members of gangs. We will examine gangs, especially contemporary gangs, in greater detail in Chapter 10, but it's worthwhile here to observe how criminologists link gang activity to the theoretical development of crime and delinquency.

Subcultural theories of crime and delinquency were among the first explanations of juvenile delinquency offered by American criminologists. Starting in the 1950s and continuing until today, criminologists have observed the nature of group deviance and done considerable research linking gangs to the communities in which they thrived. Here, we will look at five subcultural theories that represent a long tradition of attempting to explain a consistent feature of delinquency: that youths often break the law in the company of friends.

Learning Objective 8.

Understand subcultural theories and their explanations of why youths often break the law with their friends.

Delinquent Boys

Albert Cohen was primarily concerned with lower-class males in gangs. He was particularly interested in the reasons boys break the law in ways that seem to have so little purpose. He contended that much of their behavior was nonutilitarian, malicious, and negativistic. In other words, the offenses did little to gain the boys any advantage, such as money, and seemed to have little payoff. The boys hurt others and took pleasure in their suffering, and their behavior was often a statement that rejected dominant social values. Further, the boys lived for the moment and had little regard for the future. This short-term hedonism meant that most of their actions produced little in the way of useful results. The boys had their own criteria for keeping score and allocating status that were completely at odds with mainstream society.[35]

According to Cohen, children of all social classes compete with each other in school, but children aren't equally prepared for this competition because some have more socially, economically, and educationally advantaged backgrounds than others.[36] Consequently, youths are judged according to a "middle-class measuring rod" that is difficult for disadvantaged youths to attain.

So, when talking about the middle-class measuring rod, what do we mean by "middle class?" Traditionally, the United States is a "classless" society in that social and economic class isn't a barrier to wealth or social status. Americans believe that a person can be born into poverty and become a billionaire CEO or president of the United States or anything that he or she wants to be, with enough hard work. Class does exist in the United States, however informally, and it's loosely defined by economic status. In fact, Americans consider a broad, strong middle class to be the bedrock of a healthy democratic society. According to sociologist Albert K. Cohen, the following nine "norms" are essential to being middle class.

» **Ambition.** A person who isn't ambitious is maladjusted. Ambition also means an orientation to long-term goals and the determination to "get ahead." A parent's first duty is to make his or her children want to "be somebody."

» **Individual responsibility.** The key words here are resourcefulness, independence, and self-reliance. The obligation to assist or share with friends and family is minimal.

» **Achievement.** Outstanding performance of almost any kind is applauded, including athletic achievement and academic achievement.

» **Temperance.** This is the willingness to forgo immediate satisfactions and self-indulgence in the interest of long-term goals.

» **Rationality.** This refers to forethought, planning, scheduling, and the efficient allocation of resources.

» **Courtesy and likeability.** In the middle class, mastery of certain conventions of speech and gesture are important to success. It's interesting that in the early 21st century, as the world of work has become more oriented toward the office rather than the shop or factory floor, classes for adults on etiquette and table manners are becoming common.

» **Less physical aggression.** It's important to have good relations with as many people as possible while remaining competitive in an impersonal, nonphysical way.

» **Educational recreation.** Leisure time should be spent constructively, developing a skill, pursing a worthwhile hobby, or maintaining physical fitness.

» **Respect for property.** This is recognition of the property rights of others, as well as carefully maintaining one's own property so that it's not destroyed or wasted.

When lower-class boys fail to measure up to middle-class standards, they experience status frustration and react in ways that cause delinquent behavior.[37] According to Cohen, this reaction is a defense mechanism that insulates them from feelings of low self-worth. By rejecting middle-class values, the boys are free to excuse themselves from caring about playing the rigged game of middle-class values.

Differential Opportunity Theory

Richard Cloward and Lloyd Ohlin use their theory of differential opportunity to extend the ideas of strain put forth by Merton and Cohen. When lower-class boys experience problems competing in society, they turn to the delinquent subculture to help them adapt to their circumstances. Cloward and Ohlin specify three types of delinquent subcultures (see Table 5.3) in which boys immerse themselves to combat the strain of their class status.[38]

The first delinquent subculture offered by Cloward and Ohlin is called the *criminal pattern*. Here, boys meet their material needs by engaging in activities such as theft. Status is earned by being a good thief and making the "big score." The criminal pattern is closely associated with adult crime and can be a stepping-stone for the youth to becoming a career offender.

The second delinquent subculture is called the conflict pattern. The youth who engages in this pattern is the "warrior" who gains status by fighting at the slightest provocation. He's the gang member who will fight to maintain his reputation and defend the gang's honor. Displays of physical strength, masculinity, fearlessness, and courage are used to frighten others and enhance the prestige of the individual and the gang.

The third type of delinquent subculture is the retreatist pattern in which the drug addict and the alcoholic are the norm. These individuals are after the "kick," which is described as the high that is experienced from drug use or as the rush of adrenalin from lawbreaking. Cloward and Ohlin, writing in the parlance of the 1950s, call this type of delinquent a "cat" and describe another facet of the retreatist subculture that goes beyond simple drug use:

> The successful cat has a lucrative "hustle" which contrasts sharply with the routine and discipline required in the ordinary occupational tasks of conventional society. The many varieties of the hustle are characterized by a rejection of violence or force and a preference for manipulating, persuading, outwitting, or "conning" others to obtain resources for experiencing the kick. The cat begs, borrows, steals, or engages in some petty con-game. He caters to the illegitimate cravings of others by peddling drugs or working as a pimp. A highly exploitative attitude towards women permits the cat to view pimping as a prestigious source of income. Through the labor of "chicks" engaged in prostitution or shoplifting, he can live in idleness and concentrate his entire attention to organizing, scheduling, and experiencing the esthetic pleasure of the kick. The hustle of the cat is

TABLE 5.3 ⟩ Cloward and Ohlin's Three Delinquent Subcultures

The criminal pattern	Boys meet their material needs by stealing. Status is earned by being a good thief.
The conflict pattern	The youth who engages in this pattern is typically the gang member who fights to maintain his reputation and defend the honor of the gang.
The retreatist pattern	The drug addict and the alcoholic are the norm in this pattern.

Think About It
1. In which subculture are drug addicts and alcoholics the norm? Why?

secondary to his interests in the kick. In this respect the cat differs from his fellow delinquents in the criminal subculture, for whom income-producing activity is a primary concern.[39]

The main contribution of Cloward and Ohlin's theory is their contention that youths aren't only pushed toward crime because of lack of legitimate opportunities, but also pulled toward crime by illegitimate opportunities.[40] Just as each youth might have differential access to jobs, mentoring, stable family life, and good schools, so each of them has different exposure to opportunities to know drug dealers and gang members.

Focal Concerns of the Lower Class

Walter Miller is another scholar who locates the source of crime and delinquency in the subculture in which some young people are socialized. According to Miller, the lower-class subculture emphasizes many middle-class values but also has a different set of focal concerns that often puts it in conflict with traditional society. These focal concerns are rooted in the lifestyle in which low-skill labor is common, and the traits and characteristics that enable one to succeed in such an environment are rewarded.[41]

Although Cohen saw deviant lower-class youth as flouting the values of the middle class with negativistic behavior, Miller sees their deviance as simply responding to lower-class subcultural standards. These focal concerns of the lower class shape youth behavior with the following six concepts:

» **Trouble.** Lower-class youths are used to being "in trouble" with the dominant society. Either by being problem students at school, hassled on the street corner by the police, or constantly yelled at by their parents, many of these youths live with a dark cloud of trouble hanging over their heads all the time.

» **Toughness.** Boys' status in lower-class neighborhoods is measured by toughness. Boys must be willing to fight to protect their self-esteem and status on the street. Boys must be brave and fearless and not afraid to fight, even when destined through inferior size and strength to lose.

» **Smartness.** The smartness of the lower class isn't the academic intelligence that is rewarded by middle-class values. Rather, it's the ability to be cunning and to live by one's wits. A youth who displays smartness is the one who isn't taken advantage of by others.

» **Excitement.** Like any youth, lower-class youths crave excitement. Seeking thrills by taking risks and engaging in dangerous activities is a way of generating excitement and a sense of living on the edge.

» **Fate.** To justify their relative lack of success in the dominant society, lower-class youths attribute many of the outcomes of their activities to luck or chance, rather than to skill and knowledge.

» **Autonomy.** Autonomy refers to the independence that the youth values. By not having to rely on others and rejecting the values and rewards of the dominant society, these youths are able to isolate themselves from the expectations and demands of middle-class authority figures.

This discussion of focal concerns of the lower class shouldn't be considered as an indictment of the quality of ethical behavior of this subculture. Rather, Miller intended it simply as an explanation of how lower-class youths might find themselves involved with crime and delinquency as a result of the frustration of living up to middle-class standards and the enhanced opportunities they have in lower-class neighborhoods to break the law. This is especially true for gang activities, in which the peer group often performs functions of belonging and stability that the youth lacks at home.[42] When a male role model is absent in the household, the gang can provide a learning environment that emphasizes the focal concerns of toughness, street smarts, fighting ability, risk taking, and excitement. Although these activities may not be illegal, they do place the youth in positions in which lawbreaking is likely. However, the youth's intent is simply to engage in the adult behaviors of his class, and the law violations are but an indirect result.[43]

Subculture of Violence

Crime and delinquency aren't evenly distributed across the population. Antisocial behavior is more common in some neighborhoods, communities, schools, and subcultures than in others. This phenomenon is particularly easy to see when violence is examined. Marvin Wolfgang and Franco Ferracuti developed their subculture of violence thesis to explain why certain groups consistently produce violent behavior.[44]

Wolfgang and Ferracuti contend that subcultures in which violence is prevalent don't necessarily reject all of the dominant culture's values. In fact, the violence attributed to the subculture is often just a reflection of violence in the larger culture. The differences are that in the greater society the violence is often deemed legitimate, whereas in the subculture it's considered deviant behavior. Also, the subculture's violence is often more intense, widespread, and frequent. According to the subculture of violence thesis, a violent response is

The violence attributed to a subculture is often just a reflection of violence in the larger culture. According to the subculture of violence thesis, a violent response is required in more situations and under a greater range of circumstances in a subculture than in the larger culture.

required in more situations and under a greater range of circumstances than in the larger culture. These circumstances include parent-child relationships, domestic quarrels, street fights, gang conflicts, and other types of assaults. Violence is a learned response that allows the individual to survive in a subculture where the conventional ways of resolving conflicts aren't always effective. According to Wolfgang and Ferracuti, the violent response is concentrated in males who are in late adolescence and who retain the violent response until middle age.

One of the more interesting aspects of the subculture of violence thesis is that it doesn't apply to all young men in the same way. A number of personality characteristics that are shaped by the environment mediate how involved in violence the youth becomes. Some of these young men develop an integrated social-psychological approach that habitually requires violence to resolve conflicts, including those in marriage, child rearing, and relations with neighbors.

The violence that this perspective can best explain is the violence that exists within a subculture or that results from interaction with another violent subculture. Violence, then, isn't considered as something to be avoided but, rather, as a legitimate way of resolving conflict.[45] Status is accorded to those who are willing to use violence for the smallest real or imagined slight, and once one has the reputation as someone who will fight with little provocation, the threat of violence can be sufficient to avoid actual fighting.

It's important to remember that, even in a community that supports the subculture of violence, deadly violence is still rare. Although even law-abiding citizens consider violence to be semilegitimate, there are rules and expectations as to when a violent response is required. People understand what constitutes the need to use legitimate and illegitimate violence. To say that "he had it coming" or "she was asking for it" demonstrates that violence is an expected and, in some ways, functional part of the social order.[46]

We must note that, like many of the sociological theories of crime and delinquency we have studied, the subculture of violence thesis explains only a limited amount of deviance. This perspective is confined only to groups that are either mired in lower-class values or concerned with masculinity rituals. For instance, the environment of the football team or the martial arts club celebrates the use of violence as an expression of one's masculinity. Likewise, in some single-sex subcultures, such as the youth detention facility or the adult prison, the readiness to use violence is a personality feature that protects one from becoming a victim of the informal hierarchy of status roles.[47]

The Code of the Street

The subculture of violence thesis has been given new currency by the groundbreaking work of sociologist Elijah Anderson in his book *The Code of the Street: Decency, Violence, and the Moral Life of the Inner City*. In this book, Anderson claims that disadvantaged black neighborhoods promote a violent code of conduct that young men (and to a great degree young women) must obey. Anderson points out that there are both "decent" families and "street" families who vie for respect in the street. The code requires that individuals feel they are treated "right" by others, which entails being given proper respect. The quickest way to challenge someone is to maintain eye contact for too long as a means of disrespect. The code requires that person to stand up for him- or herself and insist that the one staring announce his or her intentions or motivation. Anderson contends that because inner-city residents lack faith that the police will respond effectively and protect them from danger, they have to do it themselves and be ready to employ violence to ward off street predators.[48]

The origins of this code come from the street parents who are unable to cope effectively themselves and instill in their children the willingness to use violence as a way of displaying power. Anderson explains it this way:

> In these circumstances a woman—or a man, although men are less consistently present in children's lives—can be quite aggressive with children, yelling and striking them for the least little infraction of the rules she has laid down. Often little if any serious explanation follows the verbal and physical punishment. This response teaches children a particular lesson. They learn that to solve any kind of interpersonal problem one must quickly resort to hitting or other violent behavior. Actual peace and quiet, and also the appearance of calm, respectful children conveyed to her neighbors and friends, are often what the young mother most desires, but at times she will be very aggressive in trying to get them. Thus she might be quick to beat her children, especially if they defy her law, not because she hates them but because this is the way she knows how to control them.[49]

Anderson argues that many of these street mothers are sporadic in the care and discipline of their children. Many of them have problems of their own revolving around money, relationships with husbands or boyfriends, and dependence on alcohol or drugs. The children are left to fend for themselves in a violent world with short-tempered adult role models. The children grow up in the streets where their primary socialization comes from other, older children. What they learn is "might makes right" and that verbal and physical aggression is the coin of the realm. Anderson says that when these children learn that the social meaning of fighting entails rewards and the esteem of peers, it's likely that they will internalize this way of adaptation and conflict resolution if it's left unchallenged.

The law-abiding families of the neighborhood provide their children with counteracting role models and messages. The law-abiding families must teach their children the code of the street, lest they fail to pick up on what is happening around them or make a social gaffe that could get them hurt or killed. However, they must also teach their children the values of the dominant society and ingrain in them a sense of ethics and morals that are derived from the church, the extended family, and the middle-class life that they are striving to achieve.

One orienting tenet of the code of the street is manhood. With the idea that someone might attempt to "mess with you" or challenge a youth's manhood, the youth must always be ready to display a willingness to protect himself. The clothes he wears, the way he carries himself, and the way he talks are all indicators of the façade of manhood he is attempting to convey to others. Even when one's self-esteem is low due to an inadequate education, unemployment, and the inability to take care of one's family, one's manhood can be buttressed by displays of temper, violence, or nerve.

Anderson provides an interesting analysis of nerve. Central to the issue of manhood is the widespread belief that one of the most effective ways of gaining respect is to show "nerve." Nerve is shown when one takes another person's possessions (the more valuable the better), "messes with" someone's "woman," throws the first punch, "gets in someone's face," or pulls the trigger. Its proper display helps prevent attacks and also helps build a reputation that prevents future challenges.[50] But since such a show of nerve is a forceful expression of disrespect

5.2 crosscurrents

The Evolution of Delinquency

Most criminological theories envision delinquency as a deviant behavior. It's viewed as an adaptation to circumstances by youths who don't have an adequate education, a suitable upbringing in a stable home, or prosocial friends. These theories are focused on "fixing" the delinquent's personal deficiencies, with the idea that if these can be successfully addressed, the youth will be put on the "right track."

However, there is another way of looking at why some youths, particularly those raised in poverty, are disproportionately involved in delinquency. Evolutionary biologists suggest that delinquency and deviance may be unconscious choices made by youths who feel they can't succeed in conventional society. Arguments for this perspective focus on short life expectancy:

》 **More street crime.** Delinquents don't believe they have a viable and positive future in conventional society, so they're willing to risk crime and violence rather than delaying gratification. If these youths don't try to live fully in the present, they may never get the opportunity to attain their wants and needs given their short life expectancy.[1]

》 **Earlier babies.** For a variety of reasons, impoverished people don't live as long as affluent people. Therefore, poor women are more likely to have babies at a young age and in quick succession. Studies have shown that impoverished women who have children early are actually more successful than impoverished women who wait. This is because motherhood gives these young women a reason to engage in positive behaviors and often motivates them to leave the street life of drugs and violence.[2]

So how does evolutionary theory fit into the argument that poverty results in delinquency? Evolutionary theory argues that organisms adapt to their environments. People who live in economically distressed circumstances have more health problems, are victims of violence, and die sooner than those who live in more affluent circumstances.

Therefore, impoverished people must maximize their reproductive opportunities by having sex earlier and more often to ensure their genes are passed along to future generations. Similarly, there is little incentive to play by conventional society's rules, as the rewards for doing so are limited. Therefore, "living free and dying hard" is actually a rational way of life for those who are marginalized from the conventional society.

However, sociological theorists think this perspective might not be the best way to explain delinquency amongst impoverished and disadvantaged youths. Evolutionary theory argues that organisms adapt to environments over very long periods of time. In the case of delinquency, individuals can change within their own lifetime. This would suggest that evolution is not what is causing youths to adapt to impoverished environments, but something else. For instance, classical strain theory would argue that delinquency is simply a personal choice. Learning theories of crime would state that attitudes toward breaking the law are taught by one generation of disadvantaged persons to the next. Social theory would suggest that impoverished youths are never adequately socialized into conventional behavior.

However, it would be a mistake to think these different perspectives are an either/or proposition. There may be several contributing factors that range across biological, evolutionary, psychological, and sociological explanations. The challenge for criminologists is to assess the contributions of a variety of perspectives.

THINK ABOUT IT

1. What other sociological explanations can you provide for why delinquency is so prevalent amongst impoverished youths?
2. Is "living fast and dying young" an understandable option to a conventional, prosocial life?

[1] T. Brezina, E. Tekin, and V. Topalli, "'Might Not Be a Tomorrow': A Multimethods Approach to Anticipated Early Death and Youth Crime," *Criminology* 47 (2009): 1091–1129.

[2] Mairi Macleod, "Die Young, Live Fast," *New Scientist* 207, no. 2769 (July 17, 2010): 2.

toward the person on the receiving end, the victim might be greatly offended and seek to retaliate with equal or greater force. A display of nerve, therefore, can easily provoke a life-threatening response, and the background knowledge of this possibility has often been incorporated into the concept of nerve.

On a practical level, this code of the street has important implications for life outside the disadvantaged neighborhood and for the juvenile justice system. According to Anderson, the code gives youths a limited view of life that makes them ready to die rather than be disrespected. In interactions with middle-class individuals, youths reared on the code of the street may resort to what is considered unacceptable violence at school, sporting events, concerts, or parks. What is meant to be good-natured teasing by some youths can be considered threats to another's manhood that require instant physical retaliation, often with deadly consequences. When the police deal with these youths, they are often surprised that the youths feel more threatened by their peers' opinions of their toughness than they are by a confrontation with police or even incarceration.[51]

The subculture of violence thesis put forth by Wolfgang and Ferracuti, especially as articulated by Anderson, presents another type of sociological theory that attempts to explain some of the more chronic types of delinquency. Most important is the realization that reforming the youth might require reforming the entire disadvantaged community. To do this would require massive resources aimed at reducing poverty, improving schools, and addressing the issues of dysfunctional families.[52] All these concerns will be discussed in greater detail in Part Three. (For a look at an alternative, conflicting theory on why disadvantaged youths are disproportionately involved in delinquency, see Crosscurrents.)

Questions

1. What is normlessness?
2. What are the six issues pertaining to the focal concerns of the lower class?
3. What does the code of the street require?

Social Reaction Theories

Social reaction theories consider not only the behavior of people but also how that behavior is influenced by others' reactions. The way parents, schools, and the juvenile justice system react to delinquency affects whether this behavior is repeated by the youth. Here, we look at two types of social reaction theories, labeling theory and the more recent shaming theory.

Labeling Theory

A number of theorists have contributed to the development of **labeling theory**, but the first to use this perspective was Frank Tannenbaum in *Crime and the Community* (1938), in which he discussed how juveniles are "tagged" as deviants and how this tag can follow them through the juvenile justice system, as well as life, and influence how others see them.[53] People react to the tag, and this, in turn, influences the youth's self-concept. Robert Merton called this a self-fulfilling prophecy, in which the individual internalizes the label and subsequently acts the part. Because conventional society determines what behavior is appropriate, those who engage in other types of behavior have their actions termed *deviant* and are subject to what Tannenbaum calls the "dramatization of evil."

An important idea of labeling theory is that no behavior is intrinsically deviant, but it is subject to the label placed on it by those who have the power to have their values adopted by the larger culture.[54] For instance, killing another person is a relative act. In some circumstances, such as war, self-defense, or capital punishment, the killing of another person is permissible, valued, or rewarded. In other circumstances, such as in the commission of a crime, the killing of another

Learning Objective 9.

Tell why labeling theory is important.

Learning Objective 10.

Define shaming and give an example.

person is punished, often extremely. The difference lies in the context and the values that are attached to the context by those who have power.

Another important idea behind labeling theory is that the actual behavior isn't as important as the perception of the behavior. For instance, a person doesn't have to break the law to be considered a criminal or a delinquent. Many of us have suffered the consequences, at some time in our lives, when we were accused of something we didn't do and were punished unjustly. Even though we were innocent of the infraction, the label of deviant might have stuck; and perhaps our parents, a school principal, or a juvenile court judge applied a punishment that hurt us just as much as if we had been actually guilty of the offense.[55]

Edwin Lemert added another dimension to labeling theory by distinguishing between primary and secondary deviance.[56] **Primary deviance** is the label that is placed on the delinquent or offender once he or she is caught breaking the law. Primary deviance is useful because it identifies offenders, delinquents, or those who are prone to crime. For instance, prison inmates often must wear distinctive clothing so they can be distinguished from prison staff. Likewise, we keep track of offenders with databases that police officers can consult when they make contact with citizens. Those with prior records or outstanding warrants can be identified and treated appropriately.

Sometimes the effect of primary deviance can appear to be extreme. Adults with sex-offense records are subject to having their neighbors and co-workers know about their past. And even though they may have been to prison and "done their time" or "paid their dues," the label of sex offender sticks to them and prevents them from fully reintegrating into society. Howard Becker referred to this process as a "master status" that overwhelms all other statuses of the individual.[57] Regardless of the fact that the individual is a productive worker, good spouse, reliable taxpayer, church official, or PTA president, the label of sex offender means that society will treat him or her as a dangerous criminal.

The sex-offender label is especially problematic when applied to juveniles. Sex-offender registries were meant to protect youths from predatory adults; however, sometimes juveniles who break sex-offender laws risk not only arrest but ending up on the registries themselves.[58] Sometimes the case involves two teenagers having sex—the ages may be borderline; for example, an 18-year-old boy having sex with his 16-year-old girlfriend—or teenagers sending sexually explicit photographs and messages to each other via cell phones and the Internet (often referred to as "sexting"). For example, 18-year-old Jorge Canal ended up on the Iowa sex-offenders registry because he sent a picture of his penis by cell phone to a 14-year-old girlfriend who had requested it. In another case, a 14-year-old New Jersey girl was charged with possession and distribution of child pornography after posting sexually explicit photographs of herself on the Internet.[59] Many legislators are struggling with the definitions of sex-offender laws and how to enforce them without permanently affecting the lives of children who are likely going through a normal phase of sexual exploration.

Even violent juvenile sex offenders aren't exempt from this concern. Many states have been reluctant to adopt the 2006 Adam Walsh Act, a federal mandate to create a national sex-offender registry. One of the act's requirements is that juveniles age 14 and older who are adjudicated of sex offenses must be placed on the registry for 15 years, 25 years, or even life, depending on the severity of the offense.[60] Some critics worry that the long-term labels will discourage the reporting of such offenses, especially those that occur in families, because parents would be reluctant to have a child—even one who harmed a sibling—marked as a sex offender for so long.[61]

In many ways, the concept of **secondary deviance** is more problematic than primary deviance because it has a long-lasting effect on an individual's psychology. For instance, children who are told they are stupid, lazy, or ugly may internalize these labels, come to believe them, and begin to act them out. Consequently, the youth who is told he is lazy may quit trying to study, and the one who is told she is stupid may drop out of school. These labels can have enduring effects on how young people see themselves, and inaccurate or careless labeling on the part of parents and school officials can be deleterious.

Labeling theory has implications for juvenile justice system policy. By limiting the degree to which young people are inserted into the system and the degree to which labels are applied to them, the degree to which they come to view themselves as deviant can also be limited. Edwin Schur, in his book *Radical Nonintervention*, contends that the best thing that can be done for many minor offenders is to ignore their deviant acts.[62] By not having their behavior treated as serious, the offending youths don't attach their self-concepts to their actions and will often simply outgrow their misbehavior. Just about every person has committed acts for which he or she could have been brought into the juvenile or criminal justice systems. By not getting arrested, processed, and punished, many law-abiding adults escaped the primary and secondary deviance processes and have gone on to be respectable citizens.

Labeling theory also recognizes that there are positive labels. The child who is encouraged to excel will sometimes perform to a degree well past previous expectations. The self-fulfilling-prophecy concept is subject to such positives that it's unwise to underestimate the potential of those who truly believe in their ability to succeed.

Shaming Theory

Labeling theory forms the foundation for the more recent emphasis on **shaming**. Shaming is an old concept that is concerned with applying a mark or stigma on disgraced individuals. One of the most recognized fictional examples of shaming is from Nathaniel Hawthorne's novel *The Scarlet Letter*, in which Hester Prynne is forced to wear a red letter *A* on her clothing to mark her as an adulteress. The shame is expected not to deter the offender, who has already committed the offense, but others. However, this isn't always the case. According to John Braithwaite, an important distinction must be made about shaming. First, there is stigmatizing shaming, which has a negative effect on the offender's behavior. Those who suffer from stigmatizing shaming might join deviant subculture groups, such as street gangs.[63]

Stigmatizing shaming has made something of a comeback in recent years, with judges engaging in what they think is creative sentencing by requiring offenders to march in front of the courthouse or in front of an establishment from which they have stolen wearing a sign that proclaims their offenses. The idea behind stigmatizing shaming is to embarrass and humiliate the offenders so that they don't repeat their behavior.[64] The return of some jurisdictions to making prison inmates wear black-and-white striped outfits is another example of efforts to employ stigmatizing shaming techniques. Stigmatizing shaming is what Harold Garfinkel terms "status degradation ceremonies," which, although designed to deter individuals from committing future offenses, actually so alienate them from conventional society that they end up pursuing crime as a career.[65]

Braithwaite, who is critical of stigmatizing shaming, suggests a more positive way to employ labeling theory to devise policies to reduce crime. According to Braithwaite, shaming can have a reintegrative function. If done right, shaming can help the offender become a productive member of the community again and can help the community accept and forgive the offender. **Reintegrative shaming** is particularly appropriate for youths because it's done in an informal setting. Rather than stigmatizing the youth in an open courtroom with the media recording the event, reintegrative shaming occurs within the youth's own social network. Parents, family members, school officials, community representatives, police officers, and anyone else connected with the youth's problems might be included in the hearing, where all are involved in crafting a solution. When the youth's input is included in the decision, it's presumed the youth will have a greater commitment to seeing that solution succeed.

Through reintegrative shaming, the offender can truly examine his or her culpability in the unlawful behavior and make restitution, apology, and amends to victims and society. This principle is the basis for the restorative justice programs that attempt to repair the harm that crime does to the relationships between offenders and victims. How effective reintegrative shaming can be in preventing future antisocial behavior depends a great deal on other processes, such as the quality of follow-up services. A status degradation ceremony is unlikely to be effective on its own. However, reintegrative shaming applied at a turning point in a youth's life may be useful and effective.

Questions

1. How do social reaction theories consider behavior?
2. What is labeling theory?
3. What is shaming? How does it compare to reintegrative shaming?

>> FOCUS ON ETHICS

Bad Boys

You have always been proud of your 16-year-old son. He has excelled at school and in sports, and you've always liked his friends. Now, however, you are experiencing some concern. He has recently gotten his driver's license and has been using the family car to escape your supervision. He is gone every afternoon after school and doesn't come home until late at night. On the weekends, it's even worse. Although you can't be sure of what he's doing, you've noticed that his choice of friends has changed. Instead of hanging out with his old friends and teammates, he now seems to be running with an older crowd whom you don't know and who are rather tough looking and lack basic social etiquette. These boys exhibit several signs that seem like red flags to you, including numerous tattoos, baggy pants, and multicolored hair. One of the boys has so many body piercings, he looks like he fell face-first into a tackle box.

You consider yourself a person who doesn't judge people by the way they look, but your son's behavior is changing, and you think it's because of the influence of these boys. On the negative side, he hardly talks to you anymore. When he's home, he stays in his room and listens to painful-sounding music. He plays online poker and video games rather than spending time with you and your spouse and his siblings. He seems not to care how he dresses, and his room has become so messy, you don't even go there anymore. His sense of humor has become cynical, and he no longer attends religious services with the family. On the positive side, his grades haven't slipped; he hasn't been arrested; you've detected no sign of smoking, drinking, or drug use; and he says he wants to get a job at a mall store that sells funky clothes.

You aren't sure if you should do anything about this situation. On one hand, you realize that children go through phases and that this might simply be part of growing up. On the other hand, you wonder if you're witnessing the early warning signs of a boy going bad.

WHAT DO YOU DO?

1. Leave him alone. He isn't hurting anyone, and he needs room to find his identity and place in the world. He has to grow up sometime, and you should give him the space he needs.

2. Set a curfew for the car. He can do as he pleases, but the car is yours, and you can demand it be home at a reasonable hour.

3. Insist that he change his set of friends. You don't like the way they look, and you're afraid they will lead him down the path of delinquency.

4. Search his room for drugs or stolen property. Just because he's always been a good kid doesn't mean that he isn't experimenting with bad behaviors. You don't want to be the last one to know that he's making a mess of his life.

Summary

Summary

Learning Objective 1. Describe why the early 20th-century Chicago sociologists sought to understand crime and deviant behavior.	Early 20th-century North America was undergoing social change as a result of the Industrial Revolution. As the agrarian population became urban, the old social norms, values, and laws became outmoded. The Chicago sociologists sought to understand this condition, especially crime and deviant behavior, in light of this urban social disorganization.
Learning Objective 2. Explain collective efficacy.	Collective efficacy, a group's shared belief of the extent to which it can successfully complete a task, occurs at the intersection of two contextual features of a neighborhood: social control and social cohesion.
Learning Objective 3. List the nine propositions of Sutherland's differential association theory.	Criminal behavior is learned; criminal behavior is learned in interaction with other persons in a process of communication; the principal part of the learning of criminal behavior occurs within intimate personal groups; when criminal behavior is learned, the learning includes (a) techniques of committing the crime, which are sometimes complicated, sometimes simple, and (b) the specific direction of motives, drives, rationalizations, and attitudes; the specific direction of motives and drives is learned from definitions of the legal codes as favorable or unfavorable; a person becomes delinquent because of an excess of definitions favorable to violation of law over definitions unfavorable to violation of law; differential associations may vary in frequency, duration, priority, and intensity; the process of learning criminal behavior by association with criminal and anticriminal patterns involves all of the mechanisms that are involved in any other learning; and while criminal behavior is an expression of general needs and values, it isn't explained by those general needs and values, since noncriminal behavior is an expression of the same needs and values.
Learning Objective 4. Explain social learning theory and its relationship to Sutherland's differential association.	Social learning theory is an extension, refinement, and improvement on differential association. According to social learning theory, people learn behaviors by watching other people and mimicking interactions that are rewarded and avoiding those that are punished. Sutherland's eighth proposition states that antisocial behavior is learned like any other attitude or skill, but it doesn't specify exactly how crime is learned.
Learning Objective 5. List the techniques of neutralization.	Denial of responsibility; denial of injury; denial of victim; condemnation of condemners; and appeal to higher loyalties.

Learning Objective 6. Compare and contrast anomie and strain theory.	Anomie and strain theory aren't interchangeable but refer to the same social processes. Anomie is personal anxiety or isolation produced by rapidly shifting moral values. Strain theory refers to the personal strain and anger caused by being excluded from economic rewards.
Learning Objective 7. Discuss Merton's five modes of adaptation to strain.	*Conformity* accepts both the goals of society and the culturally approved means to obtain these goals; *innovation* accepts the socially approved goals but employs alternative means for achieving these goals; *ritual* rejects the culturally approved goals but accepts the means; *retreat* rejects both the goals and the means; and *rebellion* rejects society's accepted goals and means and substitutes new ones.
Learning Objective 8. Understand subcultural theories and their explanations of why youths often break the law with their friends.	Youths often break the law in the company of friends. The five theories are (1) Cohen's delinquent boys, which is concerned with lower-class males in gangs; (2) Cloward and Ohlin's differential opportunity theory, which extends Merton and Cohen's ideas of strain; (3) Miller's focal concerns of the lower class, concerned with the subculture in which some youths are socialized; (4) Wolfgang and Ferracuti's subculture of violence, which seeks to explain why certain groups consistently produce violent behavior; and (5) Anderson's code of the street, which asserts that there are both "decent" families and "street" families who vie for respect.
Learning Objective 9. Tell why labeling theory is important.	Tannenbaum stated that the "delinquent" tag can follow juveniles through the justice system, as well as life, and influence how others see them. People react to the tag, and this, in turn, influences the youth's self-concept. According to Merton, the individual internalizes the label and acts the part.
Learning Objective 10. Define shaming and give an example.	Shaming is concerned with applying a mark or stigma on disgraced individuals. Braithwaite distinguishes between stigmatizing shaming and reintegrating shaming.

Chapter Review Questions

1. What did Sampson and Wilson introduced into Shaw and McKay's thesis?
2. What is collective efficacy?
3. According to learning theories, what is learned?
4. What is social learning theory?
5. What is negative reinforcement?
6. Why has social learning theory remained a popular explanation for crime, delinquency, and deviant behavior?
7. What is containment theory?
8. What is the "middle-class measuring rod?"
9. What are the six major concepts of the focal concerns of the lower class?
10. Define primary and secondary deviance.

Key Terms

anomie—A condition in which people or society undergoes a breakdown of social norms and values. Also, personal anxiety and isolation produced by rapidly shifting moral and cultural values.

behaviorism—A field of psychology that focuses on the study of behavior that is observed.

collective efficacy—A group's shared belief of the extent to which the group can successfully complete a task.

differential association theory—A theory by Edwin Sutherland that states that crime is learned.

differential reinforcement—The rewarding of one behavior and not another, or the rewarding of one behavior and punishment of another.

labeling theory—A theory that describes how a label applied by society can affect an individual's self-perception and behavior.

negative reinforcement—Avoidance of painful or stressful conditions or events.

operant conditioning—A form of learning based on learning from the positive or negative consequences of an action.

primary deviance—A term from labeling theory that describes the label that society places on the offender.

reintegrative shaming—A form of justice in which an offender is confronted and dealt with by those in his or her social network.

secondary deviance—A term from labeling theory that describes the labels that individuals internalize and come to believe as accurate.

shaming—The act of applying a mark or stigma on disgraced individuals.

social cohesion—A condition in which the majority of a given society's citizens respect the law and are committed to social order.

social learning theory—The idea that people learn behaviors by watching other people and mimicking interactions that are rewarded and avoiding those that are punished.

strain theory—The idea that juvenile delinquency is at least partially a result of being excluded from economic rewards.

techniques of neutralization—A theory that describes how some youths who break the law use rationalizations to explain away their deviant behavior.

Endnotes

1 Lincoln Steffens, *The Autobiography of Lincoln Steffens* (New York: Harcourt, Brace, Jovanovich, 1931). Steffens was a muckraking journalist who has colorfully described the social and political upheavals at the dawning of the 20th century. This book can be read profitably on a number of levels. In addition to being entertaining, it provides a detailed picture of the problems and possibilities for youth at the time.

2 Ferdinand Tönnies, *Community and Society* (1887; reprint, Rutgers, NJ: Transaction, 1988).

3 Ernest W. Burgess, "The Growth of the City," in Robert E. Park, Ernest W. Burgess, and Roderick D. McKenzie, eds., *The City* (Chicago: University of Chicago Press, 1925), 47–62.

4 Clifford R. Shaw and Henry D. McKay, "Juvenile Delinquency and Urban Areas," in Francis T. Cullen and Robert Agnew, eds., *Criminological Theory: Past to Present*, 3rd ed. (Los Angeles: Roxbury, 2006), 109.

5 Ibid.

6 Robert J. Sampson and William Julius Wilson, "A Theory of Race, Crime and Urban Inequality," in Francis T. Cullen and Robert Agnew, eds., *Criminological Theory: Past to Present* (Los Angeles: Roxbury, 2006), 111–117. Also see note 4.

7 Ibid., 114–115.

8 Robert J. Sampson, Stephen W. Raudenbush, and Felton Earls, "Collective Efficacy and Crime," in Francis T. Cullen and Robert Agnew, eds., *Criminological Theory: Past to Present,* 3rd ed. (Los Angeles: Roxbury, 2003), 119–123.

9 Robert J. Sampson, Jeffrey D. Morenoff, and Felton Earls, "Beyond Social Capital: Spatial Dynamics of Collective Efficacy for Children," *American Sociological Review* 64 (1999): 633–660.

10 Sampson, Raudenbush, and Earls, "Collective Efficacy and Crime," 122.

11 Delbert S. Elliott and Scott Menard, "Delinquent Friends and Delinquent Behavior: Temporal and Developmental Patterns," in *Delinquency and Crime: Current Theories* (New York: Cambridge University Press, 1996), 28–67.

12 L. Rowell Huesmann et al., "Longitudinal Relations Between Children's Exposure to TV Violence and Their Aggressive and Violent Behavior in Young Adulthood," *Developmental Psychology* 39 (2003): 201–221.

13 Edwin H. Sutherland, Donald R. Cressey, and David F. Luckenbill, *Principle of Criminology,* 11th ed. (Dix Hill, NY: General Hall, 1992).

14 Edwin Sutherland, Principles of Criminology, 4th ed. (Chicago: J. B. Lippincott, 1947), 6–7.

15 Cullen and Agnew, *Criminological Theory: Past to Present*, 125–126.

16 Edwin H. Sutherland and Donald R. Cressey, "A Theory of Differential Association," in Francis T. Cullen and Robert Agnew, eds., *Criminological Theory: Past to Present* (Los Angeles: Roxbury, 2003), 132.

17 Robert L. Burgess and Ronald L. Akers, "A Differential Association-Reinforcement Theory of Criminal Behavior," *Social Problems* 14 (1966): 128–147.

18 Ronald L. Akers, "A Social Learning Theory of Crime," in Francis T. Cullen and Robert Agnew, eds., *Criminological Theory: Past to Present* (Los Angeles: Roxbury, 2003), 142–153.

19 Ronald L. Akers and Gary Jensen, "Social Learning Theory and the Explanation of Crime: A Guide for the New Century," *Advances in Criminological Theory* 11 (Somerset, NJ: Transaction, 2002).

20 Frank P. Williams III and Marilyn D. McShane, *Criminological Theory*, 4th ed. (Upper Saddle River, NJ: Prentice Hall, 2004), 227.

21 Gresham M. Sykes and David Matza, "Techniques of Neutralization: A Theory of Delinquency," *American Sociological Review* 22 (1957): 664–670.

22 Robert Agnew, "The Techniques of Neutralization and Violence," *Criminology* 32 (1994): 555–580.

23 John R. Fuller and Marc L. LaFountain, "Performance-Enhancing Drugs in Sport: A Different Form of Drug Abuse," *Adolescence* 22 (1987).

24 Emile Durkheim, *Suicide: A Study in Sociology* (1897; reprint, New York: Free Press, 1951).

25 Robert K. Merton, "Social Structure and Anomie," *American Sociological Review* 3 (1938): 672–682.

26 Dorothy Meier and Wendell Bell, "Anomie and Differential Access to the Achievement of Life Goals," *American Sociological Review* 26 (1959): 753–758.

27 Robert Agnew, "Foundation for a General Strain Theory of Crime and Delinquency," *Criminology* 30 (1992): 47–87.

28 Robert Agnew, "Building on the Foundation of General Strain Theory: Specifying the Types of Strain Most Likely to Lead to Crime and Delinquency," *Journal of Research in Crime and Delinquency* 38 (2001): 319–361; see also

Velmer S. Burton and Francis T. Cullen, "The Empirical Status of Strain Theory," *Journal of Crime and Justice* 15 (1992): 1–30.

29 Emile Durkheim, *The Rules of the Sociological Method*, trans. Sarah A. Solovay and John Mueller (New York: Free Press, 1885), reprinted 1965.

30 Albert Reiss Jr., "Delinquency and the Failure of Personal and Social Controls," *American Sociological Review* 16 (1951): 196–207.

31 Walter C. Reckless, *The Crime Problem* (New York: Appleton-Century-Crofts, 1955).

32 Walter C. Reckless, Simon Dinitz, and Ellen Murray, "Self-Concept as an Insulator Against Delinquency," *American Sociological Review* 21 (1956): 744–756.

33 Travis Hirschi, *Causes of Delinquency* (Berkeley: University of California Press, 1969).

34 Frank P. Williams III, *Imagining Criminology: An Alternative Paradigm* (New York: Garland, 1999).

35 Albert K. Cohen, *Delinquent Boys: The Culture of the Gang* (New York: Free Press, 1955).

36 Ibid., 86.

37 Albert L. Rhodes and Albert J. Reiss, "Apathy, Truancy, and Delinquency as an Adaptation to School Failure," *Social Forces* 48 (1969): 12–22.

38 Richard A. Cloward and Lloyd E. Ohlin, *Delinquency and Opportunity: A Theory of Delinquent Gangs* (New York: Free Press, 1960).

39 Ibid., 26–27.

40 Roy Fisher, "Borstal Recall Delinquency and the Cloward-Ohlin Theory of Criminal Subcultures," *British Journal of Criminology* 10 (1970): 52–63.

41 Walter B. Miller, "Lower-Class Culture as a Generating Milieu of Gang Delinquency," *Journal of Social Issues* 14 (1958): 5–19.

42 Wilson R. Palacios, "Side by Side: An Ethnographic Study of a Miami Gang," *Journal of Gang Research* 4 (1996): 27–38.

43 Gerald D. Robin, "Gang Member Delinquency: Its Extent, Sequence and Typology," *Journal of Criminal Law, Criminology and Police Science* 55 (1964): 59–69.

44 Marvin E. Wolfgang and Franco Ferracuti, *The Subculture of Violence: Towards an Integrated Theory in Criminology* (London: Tavistock, 1967).

45 Michael Smith, "Hockey Violence: A Test of the Violent Subculture Hypothesis," *Social Problems* 27 (1979): 235–247.

46 Tom W. Rice and Carolyn R. Goldman, "Another Look at the Subculture of Violence Thesis: Who Murders Whom and Under What Circumstances," *Sociological Spectrum* 14 (1994): 371–384.

47 James Gilligan, *Violence: Reflections on a National Epidemic* (New York: Random House, 1996). See especially Chapter 3, "Violent Action as Symbolic Language: Myth, Ritual, and Tragedy," pp. 57–88.

48 Elijah Anderson, *Code of the Street: Decency, Violence, and the Moral Life of the Inner City* (New York: Norton, 1999).

49 Elijah Anderson, "The Code of the Streets," in Francis T. Cullen and Robert Agnew, eds., *Criminological Theory: Past to Present* (Los Angeles: Roxbury, 2003), 162.

50 Ibid., 91–93.

51 Robert J. Sampson and Dawn Jeglum Bartusch, *Attitudes Toward Crime: Police, and the Law: Individual and Neighborhood Differences* (Washington, DC: US Department of Justice, National Institute of Justice, 1999).

52 Charles Murray, *Losing Ground: American Social Policy, 1950–1980* (New York: Basic Books, 1984).

53 Frank Tannenbaum, *Crime and the Community* (Boston: Ginn, 1938).

54 Howard S. Becker, *Outsiders: Studies in the Sociology of Deviance* (New York: Free Press, 1963).

55 Williams and McShane, *Criminological Theory*, 145.

56 Edwin M. Lemert, *Social Pathology: A Systematic Approach to the Theory of Sociopathic Behavior* (New York: McGraw-Hill, 1951).

57 Becker, *Outsiders*, 9.

58 Diane Jennings, "Some Say List Ruins a Juvenile's 2nd Chance," *Dallas Morning News*, July 11, 2009, 11A.

59 Tamar Lewin, "Rethinking Sex Offender Laws for Youths Showing Off Online," *New York Times*, March 21, 2010, late edition, A1.

60 Lori McPherson, *Practitioner's Guide to the Adam Walsh Act* 20, no. 9–10 (2007): 1–7. Online at www.ojp.usdoj.gov/smart/pdfs/practitioner_guide_awa.pdf.

61 Freeman Klopott, "Region Resists Fed Sex Offender Rules," *Washington Examiner*, June 12, 2011, washingtonexaminer.com/local/dc/2011/06/region-resists-fed-sex-offender-rules.

62 Edwin M. Schur, *Radical Non-Intervention: Rethinking the Delinquency Problem* (Upper Saddle River, NJ: Prentice Hall, 1973).

63 John Braithwaite, *Crime, Shame, and Reintegration* (Cambridge, UK: University of Cambridge Press, 1989).

64 David P. Farrington, "The Effects of Public Labeling," *British Journal of Criminology* 17 (1977): 112–125.

65 Harold Garfinkel, "Conditions of Successful Degradation Ceremonies," *American Journal of Sociology* 61 (1956): 420–424.

Critical, Life-Course, and Integrated Theories

n Chapter 5, we studied the foundational sociological theories that have been used to explain crime and delinquency. Now let's turn to other, more recent sociological theories that extend the sociological perspective to explain why individuals and groups violate the law. This chapter covers three types of theories: the first are critical theories. We use the term *critical* to include explanations that are sometimes called conflict, Marxist, or radical.[1] Although the significant distinctions among these theories would become apparent with further study, they are presented here as critical theories.

The second type we will examine are life-course theories. These important theories not only explain delinquency, they also link early crime to the patterns of offending that occur as offenders move through adulthood and into old age. These changing patterns of crime are linked in interesting ways.

Finally, we will study attempts to integrate theories of crime and delinquency. Because most theories explain only a limited amount or type of crime or delinquency, theorists have sought to combine several theories under an organizing perspective to account for a wider variation of deviant behavior and to give a more holistic view.

Critical Theories

Many students are uncomfortable with critical theories because the theories have an unfavorable view of economic systems, gender relations, and the way that some groups use their power to control other groups. Critical theories challenge students to examine their lifestyles, values, and histories to understand how crime happens and is dealt with. Critical theories of crime and delinquency do not distinguish between "bad people" (offenders) and "good people" (citizens). Often, when studying critical theories, students must face the prospect that their behavior and economic and social interests are part of the crime problem. On reflection, some students might remember the axiom "We have met the enemy and he is us." Cullen and Agnew identify five central themes of critical theories that help to differentiate them from other types of sociological theories of crime and delinquency.[2]

1. The concepts of inequality and power are integral to any understanding of crime and its control. The criminal justice system is part of the mechanism of the state, which is controlled by powerful interests and used to enhance the benefits of those who control social institutions.

2. Crime is not a value-free concept, but a political concept. Those who control the political system define what is and is not considered a criminal or delinquent offense. The behaviors of the impoverished are more often considered offenses and are dealt with more severely by the criminal justice system than are the actions of the wealthy and powerful.

3. The criminal justice system ultimately serves the interests of the capitalist class by enforcing laws in a discriminatory manner that favors the wealthy and hurts the impoverished. Further, those working in the system will frequently break the law themselves, often with impunity, to protect the interests of the powerful. The corruption of public officials, wiretapping of protestors, and covert actions to undermine other governments are examples of this official misconduct.

4. Capitalism is a system of economics that causes a large degree of crime. The needs of the poor are ignored under capitalism, and the lax government

Learning Objective 1.

Brief Cullen and Agnew's five central themes of critical theories.

Learning Objective 2.

Describe the relationship between Marx's writings and Marxist criminological theory.

Learning Objective 3.

State the focus of left realism.

Learning Objective 4.

Discuss critical race theory and its narrative approach to the discussion of crime.

Learning Objective 5.

Examine the application of postmodern thought to criminological theory.

Learning Objective 6.

Evaluate how peacemaking criminology affixes responsibility not only to the individuals involved in crime and delinquency, but also to the social structure that accepts, enables, or encourages harm.

Learning Objective 7.

Discuss cultural criminology's emphasis on culture and media.

regulation of businesses results in crimes against those without power, as well as the deterioration of the public environment.

5. The solution to crime, according to critical theories, is the creation of a more equitable society. Many critical criminologists believe that they should take an activist role in exposing the contradictions of capitalism and not simply be armchair theorists.

These five themes, although central to the critical study of crime and delinquency, don't encompass all the critiques modern theorists have developed. This chapter will also include some critical theories that are based not so much in economics as they are in culture, race, age, gender, and lifestyle. Here, we will concentrate on a few of the better-known perspectives. Of particular interest is how these critiques explain delinquency. Sometimes it's difficult to link the broader concerns of the political, economic, and social structure and the reasons individual youths end up in the juvenile justice system.[3] Critical theories can help explain why it always seems that the same sort of youngster ends up in trouble.

Marxist Theory

The political philosophy of Karl Marx has had a great deal of influence on economics and politics for the past century. Although we won't deal with the global dislocations caused by communism, such as the rise and fall of the Soviet Union and the changing economic nature of China, these are important aspects of the universal influence that Marxist thought has had on the world. Here the discussion is limited to the implications of Marx's thinking for the problems of crime and delinquency. Although Marx himself wrote little about crime, other scholars have extended his ideas, and it's fair to say this line of thinking has made important contributions to our understanding of why people break the law and, more significantly, how society responds.[4]

At one level, Marx's explanation of crime is simple. He divides society into two parts, the **bourgeoisie**, who control and own the means of production, and the **proletariat**, the workers who are exploited by this economic system. A key idea of Marxism is that the working class labors under a **false consciousness**, meaning that they believe that such an unequal economic arrangement is legitimate. According to Marx, only when the workers seize the means of production and establish a socialist state where people "work to their ability and get paid according to their needs" will a fair system of government be established.[5]

Willem Bonger was one of the first scholars to link Marxism and crime. Bonger saw egoism as the reason people broke the law in capitalist societies. Because individuals must look out for their own interests and their family's interests, a certain amount of selfish competition is inherent in the system, and concern for others' welfare is secondary. According to Bonger, impoverished people living in a capitalist state are stimulated to break the law for two reasons. First, they break the law to survive. Because wealth and resources are unevenly distributed, the impoverished will break the law, particularly committing property offenses, to secure enough resources to meet their immediate needs and provide for their families.[6]

The second reason Bonger believed that impoverished people are more likely to break the law in a capitalist society is because wealth is the measuring rod by which people are judged. In a society such as the United States, individuals' contributions aren't valued so much as what they have acquired. People are thus encouraged to be manipulative and deceptive to accumulate wealth. The drug dealer or stock market inside trader might live in the same neighborhoods and

The Occupy Wall Street protests of 2011 represented, in essence, a protest on the behalf of impoverished and middle-class citizens who were in debt and unable to find employment, in part because of exploitive capitalist practices.

drive the same model of automobile as those who are successful in legitimate ways. In a capitalist society that judges people on their possessions, the poker player might be more highly regarded than the nurse, and the pimp might be more financially secure than the teacher.

According to William Chambliss, crime serves to divert our attention from the exploitive nature of capitalism and focus it on the offenses of impoverished people. Because the wealthy and powerful can ensure that their interests are encoded in the criminal law, it's the street crime of impoverished offenders that gets most of the legal system's attention. Chambliss contends that the inherent inequalities of the capitalist system and the privileged position of the ruling class go unnoticed, and that the powerful escape the severe sanctions imposed on the lower classes for less harmful behaviors.[7]

Although poverty is linked to crime in capitalist societies, poverty itself isn't viewed as the cause of crime. Raymond Michalowski points out that many impoverished societies have low crime rates. Crime becomes common when there is a vast difference between the impoverished and the wealthy. The relative deprivation felt by those without means and resources is more important than the actual deprivation.[8] In nations where there is not only a wide gap between the wealthy and the impoverished, but where that gap is visible and celebrated, crime is to be expected. When young people see ostentatious displays of wealth on television and the Internet, it makes their own meager living standard seem not only insufficient, but embarrassing.

Marxist criminology has its critics. The perspective has been faulted on many points by both traditional criminologists and critical criminologists. Traditional criminologists contend that Marxism makes some fundamental assumptions about human nature that don't stand up to scrutiny.[9] People don't always act in their economic interests, and to assume that they do reduces the argument to pure economics.

Another criticism of Marxism is that it suggests a utopian, moralistic society. Could the United States jettison capitalism and adopt the ideal socialist state that Marxism suggests? Would this reduce the amount and severity of crime? Critics of Marxism aren't confident that the devil you don't know is better than the devil you do. Critical criminologists worry that Marxist criminologists romanticize criminals and the idea of a revolutionary class. Additionally, the idea that we all live under a false consciousness and can't recognize the boot of oppression on our neck is problematic, according to many critical criminologists.

Our discussion of Marxism and its relationship to crime has been necessarily brief and inadequate. There is a long and rich development of literature in sociological and political science circles that extends the ideas presented here. The primary concern with this discussion has been to point out the contextual nature of crime and delinquency. It isn't enough to consider why a young person has broken the law when the reasons might be mediated by broad social forces beyond the youth's recognition. Like a fish that doesn't realize it's in water, a youth might not comprehend that the reasons he or she breaks the law are because of the pressures of living in a capitalist society.

Left Realism

Many critics of Marxist criminology believe that it romanticizes both offenders and the revolutionary nature of the perspective. In many ways, the idea that the powerful control society and use its laws and institutions to benefit themselves is an attractive perspective that tends to portray impoverished people as noble, and offenders as Robin Hood–type figures who steal only from the wealthy. Left realism theory, however, argues that this perspective is not only fundamentally flawed but also harmful to the people it seeks to benefit.

Left realism contends that the idealism of Marxist criminology sacrifices the interests of impoverished people for the interests of lower-class offenders.[11] Offenders most often victimize those who are in the same social class. When a lower-class youth burglarizes a home, it's usually a neighbor who is equally impoverished. The major issue according to left realist criminologists is that other liberal and critical criminologists are reluctant to blame the offender and instead blame the victim and the system.[12]

The focus of left realists is to ensure that the impoverished aren't further victimized by the criminal justice system and the way that criminologists explain crime. Left realists favor developing social policy over criminal policy. Alleviating the problems of poverty might give impoverished youths fewer reasons to break the law and give impoverished people the means to protect themselves against predators. Left realists believe that empowering impoverished communities helps develop meaningful relationships that can prevent crime and change the outlook of potential delinquents.

Left realist criminologists argue for short-term but immediate reforms that will reduce class inequality and the problems of those without power. According to Walter DeKeseredy, several activities could help lower poverty and unemployment rates, which, in turn, would curb crime and build stronger communities.[13]

》 Job creation and training programs, including publicly supported community-oriented programs

》 A higher minimum wage and universal health care

》 Government-sponsored day care so that impoverished single parents can work without the bulk of their paychecks going to pay for child care

》 Housing assistance, which enables abused women and children to escape their environments without ending up destitute

》 Introducing entrepreneurial skills into high school curriculums

During the Great Depression in the 1930s, several criminal offenders attained outlaw or "Robin Hood" status because their activities were considered a strike at the wealthy on the behalf of the impoverished. Here, bank robber John Dillinger poses with his guns.

A major left realist concern is that government agencies and the justice system, in their efforts to control crime, further victimize the impoverished people who are most affected by crime. Although impoverished people commit many street offenses, most are law-abiding and are overwhelmingly the victims of crime. By instigating "tough on crime" measures, the government often makes the situation worse for the victims, rather than better. The money spent fighting crime and locking up impoverished children could be better spent on alleviating the poverty that contributes to crime.[14]

Finally, it should be noted that left realism criminology argues for the support of impoverished women and children. The patriarchal nature of family relations, in which the father and husband has financial, emotional, and physical control over women and children, is deemed problematic, especially when this control is supported by government policies.[15] Left realism deromanticizes the idea of the "revolutionary bandit," primarily because the victims of crime are usually family members or neighbors.

Critical Race Theory

Critical criminologists look at the problems of crime and justice through a number of lenses. For example, feminist theorists see **gender** as problematic (the ideas and theories of feminists will be dealt with in substantial detail in Chapter 7). Those concerned with social class have used left realism and Marxist critiques to examine the issues of crime and delinquency. As we will see, **critical race theory** focuses on how racial issues determine the quality of justice available to people of color.

Critical race theory is an extension of the field of critical legal studies. Critical legal studies consider how the law has allowed those with power to make and enforce statutes that favor themselves and work against the impoverished.[16] The two perspectives share many characteristics, but critical race theorists contend that race is a dominant factor in the way many legal systems dispense justice.[17] For example, not only have scholarly studies found repeatedly that members of racial minorities are more likely to be arrested than whites (see Focus on Diversity), it's what the American public perceives to be true, which is an interesting, and probably rare, intersection of popular belief and science.[18]

The treatment of people of color has moved through several phases, from ownership of human beings to Jim Crow laws to overt and covert forms of discrimination. Race is at the heart of how the legal system treats citizens, according to critical race theorists. One need only look at issues such as racial profiling, negative attitudes toward interracial dating and marriage, and racial hoaxes such as the Susan Smith case to comprehend how race is a primary determinant of how the legal system treats individuals.[19] One distinguishing feature of critical race theory, and something that has subjected this perspective to a great deal of criticism, is the methodology that supports its arguments. Critical race theory makes no claims to be value free. Race, according to critical race theorists, helps decide how individuals view the justice system. Critical race theory has also been faulted for the type of data used as evidence—including first-person narratives to enhance its arguments. This runs counter to the way many criminologists employ science and statistics to seek the truth. Additionally, critical race theorists use allegories, storytelling, and imagined dialogues to illustrate important concepts. Critics of critical race theory claim that these methods make the perspective more art than science. Critical race theorists would contend that criticism of this sort is simply another example of how those with power define what gets counted as evidence and how truth can be revealed.[20]

For our purposes, we won't take a position on the veracity of the claims of critical race studies or on the objections of its critics. Here, we only aim to alert the reader to this interesting way to consider crime and delinquency.

Postmodern Criminology

Postmodern criminology provides a new and different way of considering crime and justice, because it's concerned primarily with change and how that change is perceived. Specifically, Bruce Arrigo invokes Einstein's theory of relativity to illustrate how postmodern thought can be used to explore delinquency and justice.[21] Here we will present a limited analysis of postmodernism in order to understand its relevance to criminological theory. The reader should be aware that in academic circles, postmodernism is a powerful perspective in many disciplines, particularly in literary criticism and legal and social theory. To some, postmodernism represents the worst case of academic mumbo-jumbo with its precise

FOCUS ON DIVERSITY 〉 *Race and Arrests*

It's a tough statistic to ignore, and even tougher to explain: blacks are arrested disproportionately to whites. This means blacks, both juveniles and adults, are arrested more than their proportion of the general population predicts. Why? No one really knows.

Let's look at the statistics. In 2010, blacks represented 12.6 percent of the US population and whites 72.4 percent.[1] Of the youth population (under 18 years of age) in 2010, blacks represented 15 percent and whites 55 percent. (The remaining 30 percent comprised other racial and ethnic groups.)[2] In 2010, white youths accounted for 66 percent of all arrests under age 18, whereas black youths accounted for about 31 percent.[3] Statistically, the arrest rate of black youths should be about half of what it is.

There are two broad schools of thought on the reasons for the disproportionate arrest rate. One is that the police selectively enforce the law; basically, they arrest more blacks because of racism. The other idea is that blacks simply break the law more often than whites. In searching for answers, researchers have discovered that whatever the answer may be, it isn't an easy one. Here are some examples of the current thinking:

》 *Black youths may be at increased risk of arrest because of their behavior.* One study found that black boys were more likely to exhibit conduct problems and low academic achievement early in their lives, as well as experience poor parent-child communication, their friends' delinquency, and bad neighborhoods, all of which increase the risk of arrest.[4] This finding appears to dovetail with an early study on police that found that disrespectful or hostile people are more likely to be arrested; as blacks were found to be more likely to show less respect to police, they were arrested more than whites.[5]

》 *Black neighborhoods tolerate more deviant behavior from youths.* Black youths tend to live in neighborhoods with more poverty and less **collective efficacy**. It's possible that this social disorganization may lead to more tolerance of deviance, more crime and delinquency, and therefore more arrests.[6]

》 *Black police officers arrest more black suspects than white officers.* When all other factors are equal, a white officer will arrest a white suspect 88 percent of the time, and a black officer will arrest a white suspect 36 percent of the time. When the suspect is black, a white officer will arrest 93 percent of the time, and a black officer will arrest 98 percent of the time.[7]

The disproportionate arrest rate is a difficult subject, and it's quite possible the numbers aren't telling the whole tale. Explaining the phenomenon will require the work of researchers for years to come.

THINK ABOUT IT

1. Why are more black youths arrested than white youths?
2. Explain why collective efficacy may lead to higher arrest rates for black youths.

INSTANT RECALL
FROM CHAPTER 5

collective efficacy

A group's shared belief of the extent to which the group can successfully complete a task.

---

[1] US Census Bureau, State & County QuickFacts, 2010, quickfacts.census.gov/qfd/states/00000.html.

[2] US Census Bureau, The Black Alone Population in the United States: 2010, Table 1: Population by Sex and Age, for Black Alone and White Alone, Not Hispanic: 2010, www.census.gov/population/race/data/ppl-ba10.html.

[3] Federal Bureau of Investigation, *Crime in the United States*, Table 43: Arrests by Race, 2010, www.fbi.gov/about-us/cjis/ucr/crime-in-the-u.s/2010/crime-in-the-u.s.-2010/tables/table-43. These data only categorized youths as white, black, American Indian or Alaskan Native, Asian, and Pacific Islander.

[4] Paula J. Fite, Porche' Wynn, and Dustin A. Pardini, "Explaining Discrepancies in Arrest Rates Between Black and White Male Juveniles," *Journal of Consulting and Clinical Psychology* 77, no. 5 (October 2009): 916–927.

[5] Donald Black, "The Social Organization of Arrest," in *The Manners and Customs of the Police* (New York: Academic Press, 1980).

[6] David S. Kirk, "The Neighborhood Context of Racial and Ethnic Disparities in Arrest," *Demography* 45, no. 1 (February 2008): 55–77.

[7] Robert A. Brown and James Frank, "Race and Officer Decision Making: Examining Differences in Arrest Outcomes between Black and White Officers," *Justice Quarterly* 23, no. 1 (March 2006): 96–126.

meanings and specialized language.[22] For others, postmodernism has opened up new ways of comprehending social life in a complex world. Postmodern criminology is worth reviewing for the insights it can provide for a more informed study of crime.[23]

Postmodern thought would have us believe that there is no objective truth. What we think and why we think it depend on the social, political, religious, and economic context in which we live. We order the world according to models or paradigms into which we have sorted the knowledge that we believe to be true. For instance, one well-known ancient paradigm asserted Earth as the center of the universe; astronomers worked for centuries to prove that the sun is at the center of our solar system and the Earth is the center of little more than the human imagination.[24]

Our social and political life can also be informed by postmodern thought. According to postmodernism, our concepts of justice, law, fairness, responsibility, and authority are all affected by the context in which we live and therefore aren't absolute. To understand how our criminal and juvenile justice systems operate, it's useful to consider some of the ways in which postmodern thought can provide a different angle from which to observe how justice is determined in our era. According to Arrigo, there are three key issues.

» **The centrality of language.** Our language shapes our reality. That is, without language, we have little appreciation for the world around us. An offender entering prison must learn a new system of language to survive, and knowledge of prison argot (or lingo) is required to protect oneself. The ability to use and comprehend language puts some participants in the criminal justice system at a great advantage over others. In the courtroom, the legal-speak can become unintelligible to those without a law degree or experience watching criminal trials. Defendants are at the mercy of the court or their attorney when it comes to deciphering the legal procedures. The specialized system of discourse can have disastrous effects on those who fail to grasp the fine intricacies of language. Words such as *plea*, *continuance*, *objection*, and *stipulate* have meanings in the courtroom that are unknown to anyone who is unfamiliar with modern legal proceedings. According to Arrigo, the issues of language in criminology don't end at the courthouse.

» **Partial knowledge and provisional truth.** Often, in criminal justice system interactions, the participants must act without the benefit of knowing the whole truth. For instance, when the police stop a girl at a bus station and question her about where she came from and whom she is planning to meet in the city, the police are concerned for the girl's safety and welfare. Because pimps and gangsters pick up many runaways at bus stations, it's reasonable for the police to question the girl, detain her, and ensure her safety. This might mean contacting the girl's parents and sending her home. However, the police do this based on incomplete knowledge of the situation. One reason young girls run away from home is because a relative or close friend is sexually abusing them. Running away is a reasonable response to a dangerous and volatile situation. The interaction with the police at the bus station, therefore, is likely to be perceived differently by the girl than by the police. The resulting lies, deception, and miscommunication are tragic, because the police and the girl are working toward the same goal (her safety) without one understanding the other's perspective. Postmodern criminology would have us appreciate this dilemma and construct policies that would help train police officers to understand the contextual nature of their interactions with citizens.

>> **Deconstruction, difference, and possibility.** Because language can be so problematic, postmodern criminologists argue that it's necessary to deconstruct the meanings and implications of any text (written or spoken) to decode the hidden implications. Deconstruction involves a close reading of situations to uncover what biases, hidden values, or contradictory beliefs lie under the surface of the appearance of fact and knowledge. Postmodern thought requires us to appreciate these differences and negotiate reasonable solutions that work for most citizens. How laws are crafted, why offenders break the law, and how law enforcement and courts respond to crime are all subject to different possibilities. The idea that there is one absolute truth and that everyone embraces it or should embrace it is challenged by postmodern thought. Once we are made aware of the variable nature of our understandings of crime, the better we can seek the multiple justices that might be available.

Postmodern criminology, which has only recently gained a foothold in traditional criminological discourse, is fighting an uphill battle for acceptance, because one must invest a good deal of study before understanding its benefits. Postmodern criminology suffers from the same sort of linguistic inaccuracy for which it faults traditional criminology. According to Arrigo, postmodern criminology has been faulted as nihilistic, pessimistic, and fatalistic.[25] As incomplete and fragmentary as our knowledge might be, the criminal and juvenile justice systems still must process cases and decide what to do with offenders. Justice officials don't have the luxury of teasing out everyone's multiple motivations. From a practical standpoint, postmodern criminology is akin to the old philosopher who muddied the water and then complained he couldn't see.

Cultural Criminology

What we know about crime and what we think we know about crime are the result of either our direct experience or what we gather from our culture and the media. However, a new perspective for considering theoretical criminology considers how the media and popular culture intersect with the lives of offenders and the criminal justice system. This perspective, called **cultural criminology**, has been led by criminologist Jeff Ferrell, who has used tools from media analysis and popular culture studies to give new insight into how crime and delinquency affect everyday life.[26]

In many ways, cultural criminology is an outgrowth of postmodern criminology in that it enables us to deconstruct the images and symbols created by offenders, victims, and criminal justice professionals in order to determine the underlying meanings and values associated with offending. Ferrell contends that the media filter the images they present to fit their version of reality and, perhaps more importantly, to fit their need to be entertaining as well as informative. According to Ferrell, this results in a view more like a funhouse of mirrors than a straightforward, objective presentation of the news.[27]

The range of subject matter available to the cultural criminologist is unlimited, ranging from traditional news outlets to technologically based social networking to the cultural artifacts left by powerless youths who spray graffiti on walls, trains, and subway cars. Cultural criminology can expose the assumptions behind the lyrics of music from different genres or uncover the intentions and feelings of individuals who construct informal roadside memorials to mark the location of a loved one's death.

Important to understanding cultural criminology is the appreciation that there is more to these activities than meets the eye. Cultural criminologists help us understand what lies beneath the surface of some of the most taken-for-granted artifacts in society, and, just as important, they help us uncover the textured layers of meaning involved in the media's coverage of crime and delinquency. A few examples can illustrate the range and complexity of this emerging theoretical perspective.

» **Distortion of crime and justice.** Criminologist Gregg Barak has looked at "news-making criminology" to uncover how the media present the picture of crime and justice in such a way that it boosts ratings.[28] He is particularly critical of television programs that focus on the most sensational types of violent crime, stating that they have caused a disconnection in the minds of many people about the nature and extent of serious and violent crime in their communities. Of particular concern is the way these programs indirectly romanticize and glorify violent crime while supposedly reporting and condemning it.

» **Gang fashions.** Clothes are important because they help people present themselves so that others will get a sense of their identity and values. For the most part, this presentation of self is an individualistic concern intended to demonstrate contemporary styles and flattering portrayals of physique. According to criminologist Jody Miller, however, what a gang member in Los Angeles wears can mean a great deal more. Miller interviewed probation officers and was able to construct an idea of how they viewed, or "read," the attire of youths immersed in the gang lifestyle.[29] According to the probation officers, gang members wear clothing styles, often oversized, that emphasize team logos and prison symbolism. The large clothes have two functions: to conceal weapons and to make the gang member appear larger and more intimidating. Sport team logos also have specific meanings. Oakland Raiders attire signals "outlaw," while Georgetown University means "gangster." The dress has consequences for the youth and those around him or her. A young man who adopts the clothing associated with gang involvement alerts everyone who can read his attire that he is ready to defend his gang. This makes him and anyone around him targets for the violence of rival gang members. According to the probation officers, gangs aren't intimately acquainted with members of rival gangs and will consider clothing as a valid reason to shoot another youth.[30] In Los Angeles, it's not a good idea to wear or imitate gang styles because of the potentially deadly consequences.

» **Music and crime.** Cultural criminologists might also look at music as a window into the values and attitudes that individuals hold about the reasons people break the law and society's response. Although it's common today to claim that no one listens to music lyrics, that it's all about the beat, cultural criminologists would dispute this point. Two studies of the effect of music on crime are particularly noteworthy. First, Mark Hamm, an expert on domestic terrorism, examined the American skinhead subculture and drew inferences between the white-power heavy metal music of the 1980s and the racist, anti-Semitic, and homophobic attitudes of this subculture.[31] Hamm makes the important point that skinhead music links skinheads to each other in ways that help them communicate values and attitudes, transcend everyday life, and imbue life with a sense of higher purpose that has far-reaching consequences. Hamm says that the shared values, popular music, and subcultural style of skinheads must be organized to be understood. Further, it must be understood to be controlled. Ken Tunnell did a second form of cultural analysis on music. Looking at what he termed the "murder ballads" of bluegrass music, Tunnell addressed the patriarchal nature of the American Southeast and Appalachian regions. The central theme of these murder ballads served to justify violence in a fatalistic way that often ended up with consequences that involved the criminal justice system. In short, murder was morally, if not legally, permissible under certain circumstances. One interesting feature Tunnell found in the changing nature of bluegrass music was the emphasis on incarceration. Tunnell speculated that this might reflect a change in attitudes about capital punishment and a growing preference for lengthy prison sentences.[32]

As a new and emerging theoretical perspective, cultural criminology shows substantial promise for helping to understand why young people violate the law. It considers both the influence of a wide range of media on the behavior of young people and how youngsters assign meaning to their behavior by using the media to portray symbols and signs significant to them. Cultural criminologists show us how graffiti is not simply vandalism and an eyesore but rather a roadmap to explain a range of political and symbolic messages designed to enable youths to communicate with each other.[33]

Peacemaking Criminology

Another relatively new perspective emerging in theoretical criminology is peacemaking. Although some might argue that **peacemaking criminology** contains little that is actually new, and that its ideas have been around forever in the teaching of major religions, it's worth considering the recent formulation and organization of these ideas as applied specifically to the questions of crime and delinquency. In the book *Criminology as Peacemaking* (1991), scholars Harold Pepinsky and Richard Quinney sought to provide a new way of looking at crime and delinquency that would help relieve the pain and suffering caused to both victims and offenders.[34]

Peacemaking criminology presents a holistic view of the social and personal effect of crime and affixes responsibility not only to the individuals involved but also to the social structure that accepts, enables, or encourages the harm that individuals do to others. As such, peacemaking criminology critiques not just antisocial individuals but also the institutions and cultures that produce the pain and suffering associated with crime.

The peacemaking perspective can be used to examine problems ranging from international conflict and human rights abuses to the interactions of delinquents involved in violence. The idea behind peacemaking is that the same principles apply to conflicts at many levels and thus the solutions to these conflicts are grounded in the same philosophical concerns and practical strategies. The peacemaking pyramid (see Figure 6.1) organizes the tenets of the perspective and presents solutions to crime and conflict. The higher the level reached, the more the process is considered to be peacemaking.[35]

➤➤ **Nonviolence.** The first underlying premise of peacemaking criminology is nonviolence. This means nonviolence not only on the part of the offender but also on the part of law enforcement and the state. When the government uses violence in the form of police brutality or capital punishment, it models the very behavior it's trying to eliminate. Peacemaking criminology

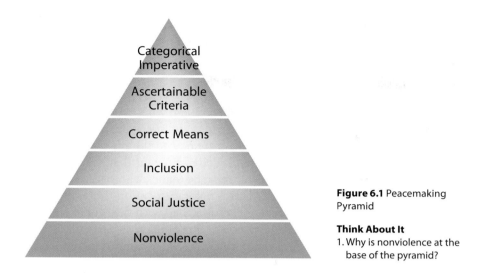

Figure 6.1 Peacemaking Pyramid

Think About It
1. Why is nonviolence at the base of the pyramid?

advocates policies such as increased gun control, rehabilitation, and limits on the state's use of force. The state must use a certain level of violence depending on the circumstances, but violence should be used as a last resort, and the state should help resolve conflicts before employing violence. For instance, although a SWAT team might sometimes be necessary, a law enforcement agency should have trained negotiators to address situations before they escalate.

» **Social justice.** The next premise of peacemaking criminology is social justice. As critical criminology, peacemaking criminology is concerned with the overall sense of fairness and equity in society. The criminal justice system shouldn't simply maintain the privilege of those in power but should increase the rights and welfare of everyone, including those without power. Domestic violence is a good example of an issue in which the criminal justice system has the potential to rectify injustice. Instead of only arresting the one who is violent, the system must protect victims, who are often children, and educate all involved about how to have positive and supporting relationships. The key is to solve the underlying issue, rather than just punish the batterer.

» **Inclusion.** In many ways, justice is in the eye of the beholder. Although the criminal justice system might arrest, try, sentence, and punish an offender, both offenders and victims sometimes feel that the solution isn't really just. The defense attorney, prosecutor, and judge are the experts in dispensing justice, and their decisions about process and results are what usually determine how cases are decided. Peacemaking criminology includes other interested parties in the crafting of a just decision. The victim(s) and the offender, as well as representatives from the school, community, religious organizations, and law enforcement, might also be included in arriving at solutions. By bringing the victim and offender together in an environment that is not so adversarial, it's often possible to solicit both input into the decision and the commitment to abide by it from all interested parties. An offender who agrees to a sentence and has had an opportunity to participate in crafting it might be more likely to keep a promise to stay out of trouble.

» **Correct means.** According to peacemaking criminology, the ends don't justify the means. The criminal justice system is limited in terms of procedural law, which requires that the offender be provided with certain rights, as well as an initial presumption of innocence. Even if the offender is guilty of committing horrendous acts, peacemaking criminology argues that he or she should be accorded the legal safeguards guaranteed by the Constitution. **Correct means** stipulates that the process of arriving at justice must be done in accordance with the model of justice. This premise is illustrated by a quote from Gandhi: "There is no path to peace, peace is the path."

» **Ascertainable criteria.** One intractable problem with the criminal justice system is the vast network of confusing rules and specialized language that make it almost impossible for those who are new to the system to comprehend how decisions are made. **Ascertainable criteria** means that the language and procedures used to pursue justice must be made clear to all. Similar to the prior discussion of postmodern criminology's focus on the centrality of language, peacemaking criminology is concerned with the problem of participants understanding the legal process. This problem is particularly acute in the juvenile justice system, where young people not only don't understand the specialized language, they aren't yet sophisticated enough to appreciate the nature of the proceeding or the consequences. Those appearing before the juvenile court judge often are terrified of a number of things, including their parents, the judge, the possibility of not returning home, and the likelihood of going to a detention center. Given these immediate concerns, coupled with the legal-speak used in the court, youths are often clueless about the decisions that are made concerning their lives.

» **Categorical imperative.** For a system of justice to be perceived as fair and impartial, it must treat similar cases consistently. Although a certain amount of discretion is necessary to fashion effective dispositions for individual cases, the system can't be arbitrary and capricious if it's to maintain the public's trust. The premise of **categorical imperative** is derived from philosopher Immanuel Kant, who wrote that decisions should be made as if the outcome would act as a model for future decisions.[36]

These principles of peacemaking criminology show how this perspective is concerned with reducing the suffering of everyone who is caught up in the criminal and juvenile justice systems. In many ways, the peacemaking perspective requires that the system act as a wise parent and not react to antisocial behavior with violence and revenge, but rather with care and compassion designed to enable victims and offenders to repair the harm done by the criminal or delinquent incident.

All critical theories are concerned with broad sociological issues that consider the relationship between the individual and the political, social, or economic conditions that define how society operates. These theories are important because they extend the inquiry of criminological examination beyond the deficiencies of the individual or the shortcomings of interpersonal relationships to the way the government and the culture affect the creation and violation of laws. The study of these critical theories forces us to evaluate fundamental assumptions about capitalism, race relations, gender issues, and how power is used to maintain social control. The one critical theory that has not been covered in this chapter is feminist criminology, which will be covered extensively in Chapter 7. In the meantime, see Programs for Children for a program that seeks to attain some feminist goals.

Questions
1. How does Marxist theory relate to juvenile delinquency and crime?
2. How does left realism critique Marxist criminological theories?

6.1 PROGRAMS FOR CHILDREN

It's Not Your Mother's Girl Scouts Anymore

Old stereotypes die hard. The Girl Scout program, which originated in the United States and now serves over 3.2 million girls in 90 nations, has traditionally been thought of as a program to teach girls how to exist in a patriarchal society. Not anymore. Today, Girl Scout programs have many initiatives aimed at enhancing the self-esteem of girls and young women and providing them with the tools necessary to compete in a high-tech global society. Girl Scouts seeks to break down the barriers of gender discrimination and prepare girls to become leaders in society.

The Girl Scouts organization seeks to prepare girls to become leaders in society.

》 The Girl Scouts have conducted research on the relationship between gender and technology. In their publication *The Girl Difference: Short-Circuiting the Myth of the Technophobic Girl*, they point out how girls perceive themselves in relation to technology and suggest ways to encourage girls to become more interested in technology and careers.

》 The Girl Scouts are concerned how girls use the Internet. The Girl Scouts provide advice to parents and other adults on how to empower girls to have a safe, positive online experience.

》 The body images portrayed in the media provide unrealistic expectations for girls. The Girl Scouts have conducted research showing that the fashion industry and the media pressure them to be thin. These findings are summarized in the Girl Scout publication *Beauty Redefined*.

》 Promoting leadership has long been a goal of the Girl Scouts. Today the program emphasizes not only skills and qualities but also how those skills make a difference in the world. The Girl Scouts are concerned with girls discovering themselves, connecting with others, and taking action to make the world a better place.

》 The incarceration of mothers affects their daughters. The goals of the Girl Scouts' *Beyond Bars* program are to strengthen the mother-daughter relationship; reduce the stress of separation; foster self-esteem, personal growth, and leadership among girls; and reduce the likelihood of reunification problems following the release.

These initiatives are evidence of the transformation of the Girl Scouts from a program designed to help young women adjust to a historically sexist society to a program geared toward providing positive images of women. Many Girl Scout initiatives are those that have long been articulated by feminists.

THINK ABOUT IT

1. How have the Girl Scouts changed since the time of your mother and your grandmother?
2. What new initiatives should the Girl Scouts consider in order to prepare young girls for the future?
3. In your opinion, are the Boy Scouts as concerned with the limitations of gender roles as are the Girl Scouts?

Source: Girl Scouts of the USA, www.girlscouts.org. Accessed September 16, 2011.

3. What is the focus of critical race theory?

4. In postmodern theory, are our concepts of justice, law, fairness, responsibility, and authority absolute? Why or why not?

5. How does cultural criminology use the media?

6. What are the levels of the peacemaking pyramid?

Life-Course Theories

Learning Objective 8.

Compare and contrast life-course-persistent offenders and adolescence-limited offenders.

Learning Objective 9.

Describe Sampson and Laub's "pathways and turning points" contribution to life-course theory.

Sociologists and criminologists have long used the life-course approach to explain many issues.[37] The life-course perspective represents one of the most robust and potentially important ways to explain delinquency.

The main issue that life-course theories examine in relationship to delinquency and crime is age. Age is a central concern for several reasons. It's an accessible variable for research purposes because it's a core piece of data that is used to keep track of individuals in schools, hospitals, social service agencies, prisons, and funeral homes.[38] Age is a wonderful variable with which to conduct research because it's so stable and well collected. Unlike attitudes toward crime, level of education, chemicals in the body, or relationship with parents, age is an easy variable to track. Age is a reliable marker of physical development and a somewhat reliable marker of social development. Rights and responsibilities have always been allocated on the basis of age.[39] Grade level in school, and the eligibility to drive an automobile, vote, drink alcohol, and collect social security are all age determined, or at least age related.

How is age related to crime and delinquency? We have long known that young children and elderly adults commit few criminal offenses. Between these two ages is a rising curve that peaks from the late teens to the mid-20s (see Figure 6.2). This pattern is consistent in societies across time and cultures. It has to do with several factors, including the increase of testosterone in young males, the transition of adolescents to adult responsibilities and opportunities, and the changing cultural pressures and expectations that go along with one's expected social and emotional development. But what are the important differences in those social conditions that lead to delinquency and crime? Why do most offenders eventually stop breaking the law?[40] Are there interventions that can be aimed at people of a certain age that can affect their proclivities to break the law? All of these questions are important in life-course research.

Before we begin exploring life-course research in delinquency, let's look at an example of a study that has become a hallmark in the analysis of the effects of simple willpower on people's lives. What has become known as the Stanford

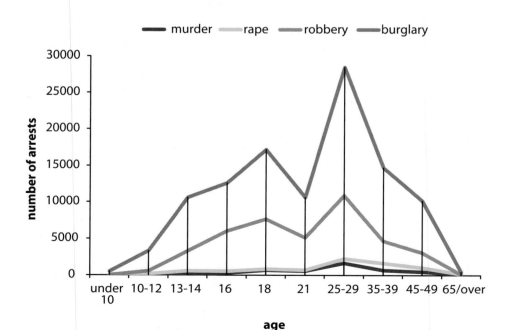

Figure 6.2 Number of Arrests by Age and Offense, 2010

Think About It

1. During what range of ages does criminal activity peak?

Source: Federal Bureau of Investigation, *Crime in the United States, 2010*, Table 38: Arrests by Age, www.fbi.gov/about-us/cjis/ucr/crime-in-the-u.s/2010/crime-in-the-u.s.-2010/tables/10tbl38.xls.

Marshmallow Experiment wasn't conceived as a longitudinal study—that is, a study that follows subjects throughout their lives—or even as a delinquency study. All the researchers did was offer children a tasty treat, then see who could resist it the longest. The ability to resist temptation, it turned out, became a remarkable predictor of who negotiated their adolescent and adult lives the best.

In the late 1960s and early 1970s, researchers at Stanford University's Bing Nursery School enlisted over 500 four-year-olds into a clever experiment. The children were taken into a room and offered a treat, including marshmallows, pretzel sticks, and cookies (many children chose the marshmallow). The researcher then left the child alone in the room with the treat with the promise that if the child resisted eating it while the researcher was gone, then the child would receive a second treat when the researcher returned. The child was allowed to eat the first treat immediately, but would forfeit the second. If the child tired of waiting for the researcher's return, he or she could ring a bell so the researcher could return and allow the child to eat the treat. Many of these tests were videotaped, and the results were interesting. Researchers say most of the children resisted for less than three minutes; some ate the treat immediately, whereas others rang the bell quickly. However, about 30 percent of the children resisted eating the treat the entire 15 minutes the researcher was gone and received the second treat upon his return.

Later, the study's originator, Walter Mischel, noticed from conversations with his own children (who had attended the nursery school) that the "high delayers"— the children who resisted the treat—were more successful in school and in life. The "low delayers" had more behavioral and social problems and often had trouble paying attention in school. The high delayers, on the other hand, had SAT scores about 200 points higher than the low delayers. Over the years, Mischel and other researchers followed up on their data and found that learning to delay gratification to focus on long-term goals is essential not only to social and cognitive development but also to social and economic gain. In other words, the longer people can delay gratification, the more successful their lives are.[41]

So, what does this have to do with delinquency? Although it's difficult to tell if any of the children in the study became delinquents or adult offenders (information about individual subjects has been kept private, and the researchers were unable to find every child who participated), the adolescent lives and achievements of the high delayers versus the low delayers is telling. Could an early ability to resist temptation help predict delinquent behavior? It certainly seemed to predict difficult behavior. Perhaps more important, the study itself points to the value of longitudinal studies and the value of early childhood research. Life-course theorists use these tools to try to understand what creates a delinquent.

In this part of the chapter, we will examine the two most promising life-course theories. First, we look at the work of Terrie Moffitt, who differentiates between those whose offenses are limited to adolescence and those who break the law throughout their lives. Next, we look at the work of Robert Sampson and John Laub, whose work focuses on the transitions and pathways that characterize patterns of delinquency and crime.

Life-Course-Persistent and Adolescence-Limited Crime

Terrie Moffitt developed her life-course perspective of crime by specifying two types of offenders who engage in antisocial behavior in distinctly different patterns: **life-course-persistent offenders** and **adolescence-limited offenders**.[42] Moffitt drew on many other theories, including biological and psychological, to develop a sociological explanation of the patterns of offending that appear to be persistent features of the problems of crime and delinquency.

First, let's examine Moffitt's definition of a life-course-persistent offender. This is the most serious of the two groups, and the theory she uses to explain these offenders' behavior attempts to integrate biological, psychological, and sociological variables.

LIFE-COURSE-PERSISTENT OFFENDERS

Life-course-persistent offenders begin to engage in antisocial behavior at an early age and continue to commit acts that harm others throughout their lives. The context and situations that elicit this negative behavior change over the life course, as does the type of disapproved behavior. A child who bites other children at age 4, hits others at age 10, rapes at age 17, robs liquor stores at 23, and commits child abuse at age 45 is an example of a life-course-persistent offender.[43]

According to Moffitt, such offenders are relatively rare but are capable of harming others a great deal. The life-course-persistent offender may have experienced deficits in neuropsychological abilities at an early age that make him or her more susceptible to weak cognitive abilities, as well as more susceptible to detection by authorities, such as parents, teachers, and police officers. Moffitt has found that these neuropsychological deficiencies are manifested in poor scores on tests of language and self-control, inattention, hyperactivity, and impulsivity. These features are consistent with the emergence of antisocial behavior.

Moffitt goes on to discuss the inadequate environment that many of these life-course-persistent offenders come from. She contends that children with neuropsychological issues tend to be born into environments, such as impoverishment, that aren't equipped to address their problems. When the parents are prone to antisocial behavior, the children will be more likely to exhibit the same attitudes and values. Consequently, Moffitt found a cumulative effect in children who are born with cognitive disabilities, poor parenting, impoverished social and

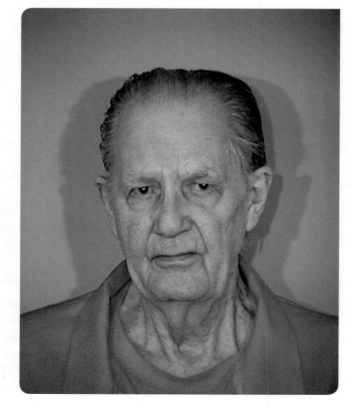

Life-course-persistent offenders begin breaking the law at an early age. Leroy Nash, who was first arrested at age 16 for car theft, spent most of the 20th century breaking the law: writing bad checks, shooting and wounding a police officer, fatally shooting a postman and a store clerk, and repeatedly escaping from prison. Nash, who became the nation's oldest death row inmate, died of natural causes at age 94 in February 2010.

economic neighborhoods, and limited opportunities. The interaction of these factors produces the life-course-persistent offender.

This happens because these youths have developed a limited behavioral repertoire; they both respond inappropriately in many situations and are unable to capitalize on opportunities in which they might acquire and practice prosocial alternatives. Consequently, these children learn to accept rejection and become defensive and embittered. Moffitt claims that if social and academic skills aren't mastered in childhood, it's difficult to make up for it later.

ADOLESCENCE-LIMITED OFFENDERS

Moffitt's second theory of life-course criminology involves the adolescence-limited offender. This group is much larger than the life-course-persistent group and may, in fact, include nearly every juvenile. Because most of us, at one time or another, committed acts for which we could have been brought into the juvenile justice system, we could all be called adolescence-limited offenders. The key idea here is that most youths engage in antisocial behavior for only a short period of time and only in certain situations. They can distinguish when antisocial behavior may benefit them and when it will cost them dearly if they get caught. They can also turn their prosocial behavior on and off as they learn the situations in which it's important to be considered "good." For example, a child may shoplift, smoke marijuana, and fight with or bully other youths, but still earn good grades at school, sing in the church choir, and interact in a positive way with parents. The deviant behavior isn't heavily ingrained in their personality, and after they become young adults, they desist from it altogether.[44]

Moffitt's theory of adolescence-limited offenders suggests answers to different questions than does the life-course-persistent theory. Neuropsychological disabilities aren't the concern when dealing with adolescence-limited offenders. The reasons this group engages in antisocial behavior have to do with mimicry and reinforcement. An interesting thing happens in high school that draws many teenagers into deviant behavior. The life-course-persistent offenders who were previously marginalized by teachers and parents now become more

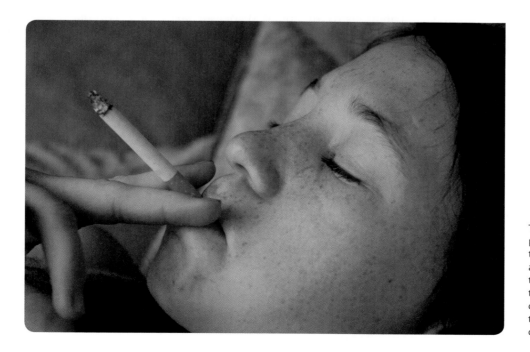

There are no longer any formal puberty rites to mark the transition to adulthood, so adolescents have invented their own ways of marking their change in status. Smoking cigarettes is a common way for teens to try to prove that they can make adult decisions.

interesting to other teenagers because their deviant ways look fun. Drug use, sexual activity, vandalism, car racing, and fighting now become the path to higher visibility and status. The life-course-persistent offenders replace parents, sports heroes, and celebrities as the new role models for many youths who never before broke the law.

Moffitt also claims that many youths are drawn to delinquent activities as a way of proclaiming their independence by flouting conventional social etiquette. Moffitt claims that there is a social and psychological reinforcement in cutting the apron strings and engaging in new challenges and adventures. In fact, Moffitt argues that "every curfew violated, car stolen, drug taken, and baby conceived is a statement of personal independence and thus a reinforcement for delinquent involvement."

In a time when there are no longer any formal puberty rites to mark the transition to adulthood, adolescents have invented their own ways of marking their change in status. These include visible signs such as tattoos, body piercings, and cigarette smoking. They also include delinquent risk-taking activities such as shoplifting, unprotected sex, drug use, intoxication, and driving fast. Moffitt claims that, although these activities may not look appealing to the middle-aged academic, they are precious resources to the teenager who is attempting to establish independence, acquire status, enhance self-esteem, and have fun.[45]

Finally, Moffitt answers the question "Why do adolescence-limited offenders stop breaking the law and adopt a conventional lifestyle?" As the young person ages, he or she finds more legitimate opportunities to acquire the resources that formerly were available only through delinquent behavior. Moffitt contends that adolescents have a maturity gap during which they aspire to the goods and privileges of adults but are prevented because of their age. As they get older, the maturity gap narrows, and youths are more likely to try to meet their needs through conventional behavior because the range of conventional behavior is now much wider. For instance, drinking alcohol is no longer a social taboo but has now become the accepted option of an adult. Drinking alcohol is no longer an act of defiance, so the binge drinking and all-night partying are no longer considered radical behavior that should be mimicked but rather poor choices for the person who has to get up in the morning and go to work.[46]

Moffitt's contributions to life-course theory are significant. Although some might argue that her taxonomy is simplistic, it's useful because it creates a clear demarcation of different types of offending patterns.

Pathways and Turning Points

Robert Sampson and John Laub's pathways and turning points theory of crime combines the current sociological literature on life-course theory with Travis Hirschi's control theory of delinquency and examines these concepts in light of powerful data developed by Harvard researchers Sheldon Glueck and Eleanor Glueck. In the 1940s, the Gluecks studied 1,000 males, ages 10–17, who had been born in Boston. Five hundred of the subjects had entered a correctional facility as youths. The other five hundred, who served as a control group, were law-abiding youths who attended public schools. The Gluecks observed the two groups at the ages of 14, 25, and 32, and published the results of their longitudinal study in their influential book *Unraveling Juvenile Delinquency* (1950).[47]

In the 1980s, Sampson and Laub—who found the Gluecks' original computer cards in the basement of the Harvard library—interviewed 53 of the men and discovered they broke the law less as they aged.[48] Between the ages of 17 and 24, 84 percent of the men had committed violent offenses. The number of violent offenders dropped to 14 percent as the men entered their 40s and to 3 percent when they were in their 60s. On average, a subject committed his first offense at age 12 and stopped breaking the law in his late 30s.

This data helped Sampson and Laub examine how one's connection to conventional society changes over the life course and how these changes influence a person's chances of breaking the law. Life, according to Sampson and Laub, is a progression of age-related responsibilities and opportunities that are available as one moves from infancy to old age. The pathways (career, parenthood, and criminal activity) differ for each individual, as do the turning points (high school graduation, first job, first marriage) that mark changes in status and opportunities. Sampson and Laub use these pathways, turning points, and social controls to examine how a person's commitment to delinquency and crime or a prosocial lifestyle changes over the life span.[49]

» For children, the social controls and turning points focus on parenting styles: supervision, warmth, consistent discipline, and emotional attachment to parents.

» For adolescents, the social controls and turning points are more related to school attachment and peers. Some studies have found motherhood to be a

As children grow, social controls and turning points are related to school attachment and peers. Here, children pledge allegiance on the first day of kindergarten.

significant turning point in that it reduces delinquency and the use of marijuana and alcohol.[50]

》 In adulthood, the social controls and turning points are age, steady employment, marriage, and military service.[51]

In considering how individuals bond to conventional society, Sampson and Laub use Hirschi's social control theory of delinquency and observe how his concepts of attachment, involvement, commitment, and belief determine the strength of a youth's bonds to peers, family, and school.[52] According to Sampson and Laub, the pathways to crime may be interrupted as a youth grows by significant turning points, the most important of which are age, marriage, steady employment, and military service.[53] These turning points are so crucial, they can redirect the trajectory of a life headed down the road of crime. However, most turning points act over time as a process, rather than as a single, dramatic event. Also, turning points can negatively affect one's life course and result in an early trajectory toward delinquency and crime. For example, one study found that juvenile gang membership acted as a negative turning point that could affect the four later turning points. In other words, the longer a youth is involved in a gang, the less likely he or she is to experience the four major adult turning points. Gang involvement could affect the likelihood of marriage, military service (a gang member convicted of a felony couldn't serve in the military), and steady employment. It could even affect age, if the gang member is murdered before reaching adulthood.[54]

Another important feature of Sampson and Laub's theory is the idea of cumulative disadvantage. Problems with the law or authorities early in life may contribute to difficulties later. Youths who are labeled delinquent are cut off from some of the chances or events that might help them make the leap into respectable behavior. For instance, the military doesn't allow felons to enlist. The military has often been a means of cleansing the record of troubled youths. The philosophy of **juvenile boot camps** is based on the expected positive transitions that accompany military discipline. (Unfortunately, juvenile boot camps don't clear the arrest record the way that actual military service does.) Sampson and Laub detail how early issues in the family, school, and juvenile justice system can accumulate and send the youth in a negative direction.[55]

For example, in their reconsideration of the Gluecks' data, Sampson and Laub found the length of incarceration significantly affected the likelihood of finding stable employment later in life. Even when prior crime and excessive juvenile alcohol consumption were considered, those who spent more time behind bars had a tougher time entering and remaining in the labor force than those who were incarcerated for shorter periods of time.

A primary strength of Sampson and Laub's theory is that, because of the longitudinal nature of their research (they were able to follow the same set of males for over 60 years), they were able to link juvenile delinquency with adult crime. This provides a better understanding of the effect of life-course events and allows scholars to speculate on how early interventions might profitably alter the propensity of young people growing up to be what Moffitt calls life-course-persistent offenders. (See Crosscurrents for more about early interventions.)

The Prediction Problem

One perplexing problem for life-course theories is that they are better at looking backward than looking forward. When the data are analyzed at the end of a criminal career, it's easy to pick out the trajectory that resulted in a life

INSTANT RECALL
FROM CHAPTER 3

juvenile boot camp

A short-term prison for juvenile delinquents and young offenders that uses military boot camp techniques for rehabilitation.

6.2 crosscurrents

It Takes a Village

Preventing juvenile delinquency is the business of more than the juvenile justice system. The African proverb "It takes a village to raise a child" has become significant in the United States. Given the complexity of modern urban living, the analogy of a close-knit African village is a poor fit for the institutions and agencies that must deal with the problems of delinquency. Yet it would be a mistake to totally disregard this analogy, because it holds an essential truth that the economic, social, religious, and educational networks of society must work together to accomplish the goal of raising productive and well-adjusted citizens.

Many of the activities of social institutions aren't directly related to delinquency prevention but affect whether children receive the guidance and develop the social skills that will allow them to stay out of trouble with the law. Here, we briefly review the essential activities of social institutions that are aimed at goals other than delinquency prevention, but which still affect the ability of children to accomplish their desires without getting in trouble.

» **Education.** The primary function of schools is to equip children with the tools necessary to become productive citizens. This means teaching them skills such as communicating well orally and in writing. Second, schools help socialize children into society and help them learn to work with others to accomplish group goals. To the extent that schools are successful in these first two goals, they're also advancing the cause of preventing delinquency. Children who don't have the skills to pursue rewarding careers are more likely to engage in delinquency and crime. Furthermore, those who have trouble working with others in school will have trouble working with others as adults.

» **The economy.** When parents lose their jobs, it affects children's ability to stay out of trouble.

For some families, delinquency may be essential to economic survival. When conventional jobs are absent in a community, an underground economy develops in which illegal activities such as drug dealing can become a lifeline. Such activities as shoplifting and stealing food, while illegal, may be deemed by some children as necessary to support their struggling families.

» **The family.** Delinquency is often blamed on the inadequate socialization of children by their parents. However, in a nation where 50 percent of marriages end in divorce, the ideal of a two-parent family is not always realistic. In order to prevent delinquency, other social institutions must compensate for inadequate parental supervision. Ideally, the community would have a network of social agencies that augment families in providing emotional, educational, and social support to children. Programs such as Big Brothers/Big Sisters, recreational programs such as Little League baseball, and religious or community activities such as summer camp or Bible school help prevent delinquency.

The entire community must work to ensure that children don't fall through the social safety net. Although social conditions in a modern society are a far cry from those in a village, the principle is the same. The welfare of children is everyone's responsibility.

THINK ABOUT IT

1. In what ways did the community support your socialization?
2. What are the most important ways in which agencies not directly responsible for juvenile delinquency can have a positive effect on helping children to stay out of trouble?

of crime. What is more difficult, however, is identifying those who are early in their antisocial behavior and projecting who will desist from a life of crime and who will continue. The sophisticated nature of life-course theory promises to rectify this problem. Life-course criminology is a relatively new enterprise, and its potential to yield evidence that can produce effective crime-reduction policies is enormous.

Questions

1. What is the primary issue that life-course theories examine in relationship to crime?
2. According to Moffitt, what is the difference between life-course-persistent offenders and adolescence-limited offenders?

Integrated Theories

Two issues often frustrate students of criminological theory. First, they want to know which theory is the "right" one. With all the competing perspectives, it's only reasonable to look for the one that really explains why people break the law. This is, of course, an ultimately frustrating search, because these criminological theories deal with different aspects of crime. Crime and delinquency are tremendously complicated and involve social behaviors that people engage in for a multitude of reasons. No single theory can encompass such a range of behavior. Once this is understood, students then ask the question, "Can we tie these theories together to come up with a more comprehensive viewpoint?" The answer to this question is a qualified yes.

Although we can't get a complete picture of crime, leading criminologists have tried to integrate theories to expand the scope of explanation. For example, life-course theories draw from other established theories to explain crime and delinquency patterns over the lifetime of individuals. Now we will look at three of the more promising attempts to integrate criminological theory.

Elliott's Integrated Theory of Delinquent Behavior

Criminologist Delbert Elliott has worked with a number of colleagues over the years to formulate his integrated theory. Elliott draws on three leading theories of delinquency: strain, social control, and social learning. The key to appreciating Elliott's theory is that he doesn't accept these theories in the exact manner in which their creators fashioned them. He borrows important aspects from the theories but changes other aspects to fit them into his concept of integration.[56]

For example, when dealing with **strain theory**, he actually expands it to include more than lower-class delinquents. Elliott, therefore, argues that middle-class delinquents suffer from a similar type of strain. Whereas the lower-class youth are chasing the American dream of being financially secure and resort to delinquency when they find their means to success blocked, Elliot argues that middle-class youth are pursuing slightly different goals, such as athletic ability or physical attractiveness. These middle-class youths experience strain when they fail to achieve such goals, which aren't always obtainable by simple hard work. Middle-class boys who have high aspirations are just as susceptible to strain as are lower-class youth, but for different reasons.

Elliott therefore argues that strain theory is not enough to explain delinquency and must be combined with social control and **social learning theories**. In looking at social control theory, Elliott reduces it to two measures, integration and commitment, and argues that those who experience strain will have their bonds to conventional society tested and will turn to delinquent peers from whom they learn antisocial behavior. The three theories, strain, social control, and social learning, are interrelated and act on individuals in different ways depending on factors such as social class, which can strengthen or weaken a person's sense of strain and commitment to conventional society.

Thornberry's Interactional Theory of Delinquency

Terence Thornberry draws on two types of delinquency theories to construct the interactional perspective: social control theory and social learning theory. Thornberry emphasizes the reciprocal relationship between the main ideas in the theories. In terms of interaction, Thornberry contends that the attachment a child has to parents changes as parent and child deal with problems. Attachment is variable: it can't be measured once and treated as if it doesn't change. Thornberry's model accommodates the interaction of youths with attachment to parent, commitment to school, belief in conventional values, and association with delinquent peers.[57] As the youth develops delinquent values because of these interactions, he or she is more likely to break the law.

Of equal importance to Thornberry is the reciprocal nature of these interactions. Although an association with delinquent peers might make a youth more likely to commit delinquent behavior, Thornberry argues that this is not a one-way street. Youths who commit delinquent acts are more likely to find other delinquent peers to associate with. This may be a function of meeting other delinquents in the juvenile justice system, or it may simply be that those who get in trouble often associate at the same locations. Whether it's the street corner, the shopping mall, or the school, those who are likely to break the law will find each other. They may share the same circumstances (broken home, failure at school, or unemployment), but as sources of strain, these conditions aren't as important to Thornberry as are weak bonds of social control and social learning in peer groups.

An additional function of Thornberry's interactional theory that makes it an attractive integrated theory is his attempt to specify how an individual's attachment to society's conventional bonds might change over the life course. This developmental approach allows Thornberry to consider how changes in the expected path of one's life might radically alter the direction in which one is headed. Therefore, the middle-class youth who gets arrested for selling large quantities of marijuana may begin a life of trouble with law enforcement agencies, and the lower-class youth who gets an academic scholarship may escape the negative effects of growing up in an underprivileged neighborhood.

According to Thornberry, changes in the expected path of one's life might radically alter the direction in which one is headed. A middle-class youth who gets arrested for selling large quantities of marijuana may begin a life of trouble with law enforcement agencies.

Tittle's Control Balance Theory

Although Charles Tittle's control balance theory uses a number of other theories to present an integrated explanation of crime, it's important to note that this theory is not a combination of other perspectives but is, rather, a new way of conceptualizing the central reasons for why people break the law. Tittle contends that we control our lives to a certain extent. The control we have is mitigated by the control others have over us. In turn, we feel more in control when we have control of others. The optimum condition is when there is a healthy balance between the control we have over others and the control others (not necessarily the same others) have over us. When there is an imbalance of this control, deviant behavior is one way we attempt to put the condition back into balance.[58]

If we have a deficit in the balance of control, we are likely to take actions that give us a sense of greater control. When we have a surplus of control, we commit deviant acts to extend that control or to take immediate advantage of our current situation. This is an ambitious theory that seeks to explain a broad range of antisocial behavior by explicating the many ways in which individuals seek to redress their perceived imbalance of control. In language reminiscent of Merton's strain theory, Tittle lists a number of ways a person may respond to being humiliated. First, a person might act in a conforming manner, simply endure the humiliation for the present, and over the long term seek to address the alleged personal shortcoming and show the attacker, as well as everyone else, that he or she is a worthy individual and that the insult was inappropriate.

Second, the victim might respond immediately by attacking the attacker. This reaction is called predation, and although it has the advantage of immediate redress and satisfaction, it can cause more trouble than it's worth and make the imbalance of control even greater. When we deal with people who have a great deal more power than we do, it's often necessary to defer our urge to strike back verbally or physically because they control the very resources we strive to accumulate. For instance, if you hit your boss, you could lose your job and the money that you're trying to earn.

A third way to respond, according to Tittle's theory, is to engage in an act of defiance, such as talking behind the attacker's back, giving him or her a bad job-performance evaluation, or showing contempt. Defiance can also have costs associated with it, so it isn't always the optimum option for attempting to restore the balance of control.

A person who feels especially helpless might engage in submission and not even attempt to redress the feelings of being in a control deficit. The victim accepts the attacker's view of the problem and doesn't challenge for control of power. With a bit of luck and some groveling, the attacker might spare the victim further humiliation.

If a victim's social location includes friends, family, or a position of power, he or she might engage in exploitation. The victim might get the attacker fired by arranging for others to boycott the business, hiring a private detective to uncover drug use or marital indiscretions, or hiring others to physically assault the attacker. If the victim is subtle, these activities won't be traced back to him or her, and the victim will get the inner satisfaction of correcting the imbalance of power.

Tittle's control balance theory is complicated because it attempts to do two useful things. First, it tries to explain a range of antisocial behavior. Second, as an integrated theory, control balance accomplishes more than adding the sum of the parts of other theories. It adds an orientation that extends the range of the theory to become one of the most comprehensive explanations available.

These three integrated theories represent different concepts of how criminological theories can be combined to form a more holistic picture of crime and delinquency. Although the authors of these theories are to be commended, they aren't without their critics. One perplexing problem in attempting to integrate theories is that sometimes it's necessary to alter the original theory to make it compatible with other ideas. For instance, Elliott and Thornberry both employ Hirschi's social control theory, but they change key aspects of it to suit their purposes. Can it really be considered social control theory when it has been altered in such a way? Finally, the future of theory integration will almost certainly expand the range of types of theories considered. Like Terrie Moffitt, future criminologists will include biological, psychological, and sociological theories and connect the dots between them to provide new and expanded explanations of antisocial behavior.

Questions

1. Why is it so difficult to integrate theories?
2. Which three theories does Delbert Elliott draw on to formulate his integrated theory?
3. What two delinquency theories does Terence P. Thornberry use to construct the interactional perspective?

>> FOCUS ON ETHICS

Knowing When to Give Children Control

Your two children are both in trouble with the law, and you don't know why. They're different in so many ways, yet here you are in the juvenile court building having to deal with two youngsters who should be model citizens. The judge is a veteran at turning troubled kids around, and she's called you and your spouse into her chambers to discuss your children's cases. You know you'll have to make some tough decisions, but you're surprised at how she considers the issues underlying your children's behavior. The judge explains the cases by applying Tittle's control balance theory and asks you to think about how to address the problems by restoring the balance of control in your children's lives.

Your daughter, a high school junior, is a remarkable student who has suddenly strayed from the straight and narrow. She has been a straight-A student and a leader at her high school. She's captain of the cheerleading squad, on the math team, and has had leading roles in school plays. Everything comes easily for her, and she's used to getting what she wants. The judge believes she hasn't been challenged enough at school or at home and is bored. She's running with a dodgy crowd from the local community college who are influencing her to neglect her old friends and her studies. Now she wants to get body piercings and tattoos and talks not of going to college but of opening a tattoo parlor. She's before the juvenile court for marijuana possession.

Your son is at the opposite end of the spectrum. As a 9th-grader he thinks of nothing but sports although he isn't very athletic. He is a C student and says the only reason he wants to go to school is to practice basketball so he can get a college scholarship and turn pro. When you point out that he barely made the junior varsity squad, he says he is expecting a growth spurt. He's been arrested for shoplifting a Kobe Bryant jersey.

At home, your daughter has always ruled the roost, and your son has been the butt of her sarcastic wit and her friends' jokes. The judge explains that your children suffer from an imbalance of power and control. Your son has too little, and your daughter too much. Your task is to work with the judge to restore some balance into the family dynamics and get your children headed in the right direction.

WHAT DO YOU DO?

1. Send your son to a military school where he will learn discipline and self-esteem. When he returns, he'll be able to compete more equally with your daughter.

Summary

2. Send your daughter to live with her aunt in another state. The aunt is a psychology professor and can match wits with your daughter. With your daughter gone, there will be room in the family dynamics for your son to grow.

3. Have the judge put them on probation. Tolerate no trouble from them and insist they behave appropriately or you will have the judge place them somewhere where they'll have little choice but to obey.

4. Get more involved in their lives and goals. Help your daughter set challenging goals, and send your son to a summer basketball camp where the coaches emphasize the importance of good grades.

5. Lighten up. Your kids are going through a phase. If left alone they'll outgrow their bad behavior.

Summary

Summary

Learning Objective 1. Brief Cullen and Agnew's five central themes of critical theories.	1) The concepts of inequality and power are integral to any understanding of crime and its control. 2) Crime is not a value-free concept, but a political concept. 3) The criminal justice system ultimately serves the interests of the capitalist class by enforcing laws in a discriminatory manner that favors the wealthy and hurts the impoverished. 4) Capitalism is a system of economics that causes a large degree of crime. 5) The solution to crime, according to critical theories, is the creation of a more equitable society.
Learning Objective 2. Describe the relationship between Marx's writings and Marxist criminological theory.	Marx wrote little about crime, but other scholars have extended his ideas to our understanding of why people break the law and how society responds. According to Bonger, impoverished people living in a capitalist state are stimulated to break the law to survive and because wealth is the measuring rod by which people are judged. According to Chambliss, because the wealthy and powerful can ensure that their interests are encoded in the criminal law, it's the street crime of impoverished offenders that gets most of the legal system's attention. Michalowski states that crime becomes common when there is a vast difference between the impoverished and the wealthy.
Learning Objective 3. State the focus of left realism.	The focus of left realists is to ensure that the impoverished aren't further victimized by the criminal justice system and the way that criminologists explain crime.
Learning Objective 4. Discuss critical race theory and its narrative approach to the discussion of crime.	Critical race theory focuses on how racial issues determine the quality of justice available to people of color. It employs first-person narratives to enhance its arguments, which runs counter to the way many criminologists employ science and statistics. Critical race theorists use allegories, storytelling, and imagined dialogues to illustrate important concepts.

Learning Objective 5. Examine the application of postmodern thought to criminological theory.	According to Arrigo, three issues inform postmodernism and critical criminological theory: The ability to use and comprehend language gives some participants in the criminal justice system advantages over others. Often, in criminal justice system interactions, the participants must act on incomplete knowledge. It's necessary to deconstruct the meanings and implications of texts to decode the hidden implications: the making of law, why offenders break the law, and how law enforcement and courts respond to crime are subject to different possibilities.
Learning Objective 6. Evaluate how peacemaking criminology affixes responsibility not only to the individuals involved in crime and delinquency but also to the social structure that accepts, enables, or encourages harm.	Peacemaking criminology critiques antisocial individuals and the institutions and cultures that produce the pain and suffering associated with crime. Peacemaking can be used to examine problems ranging from international conflict and human rights abuses to the interactions of delinquents involved in violence. All peacemaking principles apply to conflicts at many levels, and the solutions to these conflicts are grounded in the same philosophical concerns and practical strategies.
Learning Objective 7. Discuss cultural criminology's emphasis on culture and media.	The critique of cultural criminology ranges from traditional media, to technologically based social networking, to cultural artifacts such as graffiti and gang fashions. Cultural criminologists help reveal the layers of meaning in the media's coverage of crime and delinquency.
Learning Objective 8. Compare and contrast life-course-persistent offenders and adolescence-limited offenders.	Life-course-persistent offenders begin antisocial behavior at an early age and continue throughout their lives. The context and situations involving this behavior change over the life course, as does the behavior itself. Moffitt states that such offenders are rare but may harm others a great deal. Adolescence-limited offenders engage in antisocial behavior for only a short time and in certain situations. This group is much larger than the life-course-persistent group and may include nearly every juvenile.
Learning Objective 9. Describe Sampson and Laub's "pathways and turning points" contribution to life-course theory.	Sampson and Laub's pathways and turning points theory examines how life pathways (career, parenthood, and criminal activity) differ for individuals, as do the turning points (high school graduation, first job, first marriage) that mark changes in status and opportunities. These pathways and turning points examine how a person's commitment to delinquency and crime or a prosocial lifestyle changes over the life span.
Learning Objective 10. Explain the reasons for integrating criminological theories.	Crime and delinquency are complicated and involve social behaviors that people engage in for reasons that no single theory explains. Criminologists have tried to integrate some theories to expand the scope of the explanations for crime and delinquency.

Chapter Review Questions

1. What is false consciousness?

2. What are three key issues of postmodern criminology, according to Arrigo?

3. What does cultural criminology use as its subject matter?

4. What or whom does peacemaking criminology hold responsible for the harm that individuals do to others?

5. How is age related to crime and delinquency?

Summary

6. What happened in the Stanford Marshmallow Experiment?

7. Give an example of a life-course-persistent offender.

8. How did the Gluecks' study contribute to Sampson and Laub's pathways and turning points theory?

9. Which theory is the correct theory?

10. According to Tittle, what do we do if we experience a deficit in the balance of control?

Key Terms

adolescence-limited offender—In life-course criminological theory, youths who engage in antisocial and deviant behavior for only a short period of time and only in certain situations.

ascertainable criteria—In peacemaking criminology, the concept that the language and procedures used to pursue justice must be made clear to all.

bourgeoisie—In Marxist theory, those who own property and the means of production.

categorical imperative—In peacemaking criminology, the concept that a system of justice must treat cases with similar characteristics consistently if the system is to be perceived as fair and impartial.

correct means—In peacemaking criminology, the concept that the process of arriving at justice must be done in a just manner.

critical race theory—A theory that asserts that race is central to law and social justice issues.

cultural criminology—A theory that explores the relationships between culture, media institutions, crime, and social control.

false consciousness—In Marxist theory, the belief that the arrangement of the bourgeoisie owning the means of production and the proletariat working for the interests of the bourgeoisie is legitimate.

gender—The characteristics attributed and accorded to males and females by society and/or culture on the basis of sex.

left realism—A theory suggesting that mainstream criminology underestimates the victimization of the poor and women; it is concerned with why the poor commit offenses mainly against one another.

life-course-persistent offender—In life-course criminological theory, an offender who begins inappropriate behavior at an early age and continues to commit antisocial and deviant acts.

peacemaking criminology—An idea that considers the social and personal effect of crime as a whole; it considers not only the offender and victim but also the social structure that accepts, enables, or encourages the offense.

postmodern criminology—In criminology, a theory that considers justice, law, fairness, responsibility, and authority not to be absolute, but to be mediated by personal contexts.

proletariat—In Marxist theory, the working class.

Endnotes

1   Francis T. Cullen and Robert Agnew, *Criminological Theory: Past to Present* (Los Angeles: Roxbury, 2003), 333–336. Cullen and Agnew present a good description of what makes a theory a critical theory.

2   Ibid., 334–335.

3   David M. Gordon, "Capitalism, Class and Crime in America," *Crime and Delinquency* 19 (1973): 163–186.

4   David F. Greenberg, ed., *Crime and Capitalism: Readings in Marxist Criminology* (Philadelphia: Temple University Press, 1993).

5   Karl Marx, *Selected Writings in Sociology and Social Philosophy*, trans. P. B. Bottomore (New York: McGraw-Hill, 1956).

6   Willem Bonger, *Crime and Economic Conditions*, abridged ed. (Bloomington: Indiana University Press, 1969). [originally published 1916]

7   William B. Chambliss, "Policing the Ghetto Underclass: The Politics of Law and Law

Enforcement," *Social Problems* 41 (1994): 177–194.

8   Raymond J. Michalowski, *Order, Law and Crime: An Introduction to Criminology* (New York: Random House, 1985).

9   Ronald L. Akers and Christine S. Sellers, *Criminological Theories: Introduction, Evaluations, and Application*, 4th ed. (Los Angeles: Roxbury, 2003), 210–213.

10   Jock Young and Roger Matthews, eds., *Rethinking Criminology: The Realist Debate* (New Park, CA: Sage, 1992).

11   Walter DeKeseredy, "Left Realism on Inner-City Violence," in Martin D. Schwartz and Suzanne E. Hatty, eds., *Controversies in Critical Criminology* (Cincinnati, OH: Anderson, 2003), 29–41.

12   Jock Young, "The Tasks of a Realist Criminology," *Contemporary Crisis* 12 (1987): 337–356.

13   DeKeseredy, "Left Realism on Inner-City Violence," 37.

14   Shahid S. Alvi, Walter DeKeseredy, and Desmond Ellis, *Contemporary Social Problems in North America* (Toronto: Addison Wesley Longman, 2000).

15   Martin D. Schwartz and Walter DeKeseredy, "Left Realist Criminology: Strengths, Weaknesses, and the Feminist Critique," *Crime Law and Social Change* 15 (1991): 51–72.

16   Katheryn K. Russell, "Critical Race Theory and Social Justice," in Bruce Arrigo, ed., *Social Justice/Criminal Justice: The Maturation of Critical Theory in Law, Crime, and Deviance* (Belmont, CA: Wadsworth, 1999), 178–187.

17   Katheryn K. Russell, "A Critical View from the Inside: An Application of Critical Legal Studies to Criminal Law," *Journal of Criminal Law and Criminology* 85 (1994): 222–240.

18   Amy Rinehart Kochel, David B. Wilson, and Stephen D. Mastrofski, "Effect of Suspect Race on Officers' Arrest Decisions," *Criminology* 49, no. 2 (May 2011): 473–512. Online at onlinelibrary.wiley.com/doi/10.1111/j.1745-9125.2011.00230.x/full.

19   In October 1994, Susan Smith strapped her 14-month-old and 3-year-old sons into their car seats and rolled the vehicle into a lake. She had originally told police that her car was stolen by a black male who drove off with the boys.

20   bell hooks, "Misogyny, Gangsta Rap, and the Piano," *Race and Ethnicity*, March 1994. Online at race.eserver.org/misogyny.html.

21   Bruce A. Arrigo, "Postmodern Justice and Critical Criminology: Positional, Relational, and Provisional Science," in Martin O. Schwartz and Suzanne E. Hatty, eds., *Controversies in Critical Criminology* (Cincinnati, OH: Anderson, 2003), 43–55.

22   Akers and Sellers, "Criminological Theories," 237.

23   Martin D. Schwartz and David O. Friedrichs, "Postmodern Thought and Criminological Discontent: New Metaphors for Understanding Violence," *Criminology* 32 (1994): 221–246.

24   See *The Galileo Project: Copernican System* at galileo.rice.edu/sci/theories/copernican_system.html for a review.

25   Arrigo, "Postmodern Justice and Critical Criminology," 50–51.

26   Jeff Ferrell, "Cultural Criminology," in Martin O. Schwartz and Suzanne E. Hatty, eds., *Controversies in Critical Criminology* (Cincinnati, OH: Anderson, 2003), 71–84.

27   Ibid., 72.

28   Gregg Barak, *Media, Process, and the Social Construction of Crime: Studies in Newsmaking Criminology* (New York: Garland, 1994).

29   Jody A. Miller, "Struggles Over the Symbolic: Gang Style and the Meanings of Social Control," in Jeff Ferrell and Clinton R. Sanders, eds., *Cultural Criminology* (Boston: Northeastern Press, 1995), 213–234.

30   Ibid., 228.

31   Mark S. Hamm, "Hammer of the Gods Revisited: Neo-Nazi Skinheads, Domestic Terrorism, and the Rise of the New Protest Music," in Jeff Ferrell and Clinton R. Sanders, eds., *Cultural Criminology* (Boston: Northeastern Press, 1995), 190–212.

32   Kenneth D. Tunnell, "A Cultural Approach to Crime and Punishment, Bluegrass Style," in Jeff Ferrell and Clinton R. Sanders, eds., *Cultural Criminology* (Boston: Northeastern Press, 1995), 80–105.

33   Jeff Ferrell, *Crimes of Style: Urban Graffiti and the Politics of Criminality* (New York: Garland, 1993).

34   Harold E. Pepinsky and Richard Quinney, eds., *Criminology as Peacemaking* (Bloomington: Indiana University Press, 1991).

35   John R. Fuller, *Criminal Justice: A Peacemaking Perspective* (Boston: Allyn and Bacon, 1998).

36   Immanuel Kant, "The Categorical Imperative," in Daryl Close and Nicholas

Meier, eds., *Morality in Criminal Justice: An Introduction to Ethics* (Belmont, CA: Wadsworth), 45–50.

37 Glen H. Elder Jr., John Modell, and Ross Parke, eds., *Children in Time and Place: Developmental and Historical Insights* (New York: Cambridge University Press, 1993).

38 David I. Kertzer and Jennie Keith, *Age and Anthropologist Theory* (Ithaca, NY: Cornell University Press, 1984).

39 John Modell, *Into One's Own: From Youth to Adulthood in The United States, 1920–1975* (Berkeley: University of California Press, 1989).

40 Mark Warr, "Life-Course Transitions and Desistance from Crime," *Criminology* 36 (1998): 369–388.

41 Jonah Lehrer, "Don't!: The Secret of Self-Control," *New Yorker*, May 18, 2009, www.newyorker.com/reporting/2009/05/18/090518fa_fact_lehrer. Walter Mischel et al., "'Willpower' Over the Life Span: Decomposing Self-Regulation," *Social Cognitive & Affective Neuroscience* 6 no. 2, (April 2011): 252–256.

42 Terrie Moffitt, "Adolescence-Limited and Life-Course-Persistent Antisocial Behavior: A Developmental Taxonomy," *Psychological Review* 100 (1993): 674–701.

43 Terrie E. Moffitt, "Pathways in the Life Course to Crime," in Francis T. Cullen and Robert Agnew, eds., *Criminological Theory: Past to Present* (Los Angeles: Roxbury, 2003), 452–457.

44 Ibid., 458–459.

45 Ibid., 460–465.

46 Ibid., 466–468.

47 Charles Coe, "Twigs Bent, Trees Go Straight," *Harvard Magazine*, www.harvard-magazine.com/on-line/030491.html.

48 Cullen and Agnew, "Criminological Theory," 470.

49 Robert J. Sampson and John H. Laub, *Crime in the Making: Pathways and Turning Points Through Life* (Cambridge, MA: Harvard University Press, 1993).

50 Derek A. Kreager, Ross L. Matsueda, and Elena A. Erosheva, "Motherhood and Criminal Desistance in Disadvantaged Neighborhoods," *Criminology* 48, no. 1 (February 2010): 221–258.

51 Robert J. Sampson and John H. Laub, "A Life-Course View of the Development of Crime," *The Annals of the American Academy of Political and Social Science* 602, (2005): 12–45.

52 John H. Laub and Robert J. Sampson, *Shared Beginnings, Divergent Lives: Delinquent Boys to Age 70* (Cambridge, MA: Harvard University Press, 2003).

53 John H. Laub and Robert J. Sampson, *Shared Beginnings, Divergent Lives: Delinquent Boys to Age 70* (Cambridge, Massachusetts: Harvard University Press, 2003).

54 Chris Melde and Finn-Aage Esbensen, "Gang Membership as a Turning Point," *Criminology* 49, no. 2 (2011): 513–541.

55 Robert J. Sampson and John H. Laub, "Crime and the Life Course," in Francis T. Cullen and Robert Agnew, eds., *Criminological Theory: Past to Present* (Los Angeles: Roxbury, 2003), 470–482.

56 Delbert S. Elliott, Suzanne Ageton, and Rachelle J. Canter, "An Integrated Theoretical Perspective on Delinquent Behavior," *Journal of Research in Crime and Delinquency*, 16 (1979): 3–27.

57 Terence P. Thornberry, "Toward an Interactional Theory of Delinquency," *Criminology* 25 (1987): 863–891.

58 Charles R. Tittle, *Control Balance: Toward a General Theory of Deviance* (Boulder, CO: Westview, 1995).

Delinquency in Society

Female Delinquency

Women are quickly gaining ground in politics, professions, and the home. For the first half of the 20th century, it was rare to find a woman in law school or medical school. Now, women make up a sizeable proportion of the classes. Women are found in increasing numbers in Congress and in state legislatures. The adage that "a man's home is his castle" is no longer accurate for many households, because there is a sharing of power in marriage that is supported by the economic demands of family life as women work in professions. However, as females have gained ground in prosocial activities, they've also posted higher statistics in antisocial activities such as crime and delinquency.

Girls to Women: A Developmental View

Until recently, the popular view of juvenile delinquency was formed by looking at the antisocial behavior of males. As in other areas of social science and medicine, males were considered the norm, and research in these areas was done almost exclusively on males.[1] This neglect of females has distorted the level and breadth of what we know about half of the human population. The implicit assumption was that males were the standard by which issues were evaluated, and females were an extension of that. Men were legally empowered and physically stronger, so it seemed only reasonable (to men, that is) that they should be considered the standard by which all things are measured.[2] This neglect of females has changed over the past generation, and researchers are now recognizing there is a gender dimension to nearly every social issue.[3]

Generally, females break the law less often than males (see Figure 7.1), but it's still important to study female delinquency for three reasons. First, there is more female delinquency than there used to be: in 1986, girls were involved in about 22 percent of all delinquency arrests, versus about 30 percent in 2009.[4] Second, females are often the victims of crime and delinquency, and it's necessary to understand how and why. Finally, much of male offending is a result of gender issues. As the social roles of men and women continue to evolve, it's interesting to observe how some men have a difficult time with the changing conceptions

Figure 7.1 Inmates Under the Jurisdiction of State or Federal Correctional Authorities by Sex, 2009

Most of the people convicted of criminal offenses and serving time in prison are male.

Think About It

1. This figure uses the number of prison inmates to show which sex is most often convicted of breaking the law. Why is this a better measure than the number of arrests?

Heather C. West, William J. Sabol, and Sarah J. Greenman, *Prisoners in 2009*, (Washington, DC: US Department of Justice Bureau of Justice Statistics, 2010), 16–18. Online at bjs.ojp.usdoj.gov/content/pub/pdf/p09.pdf.

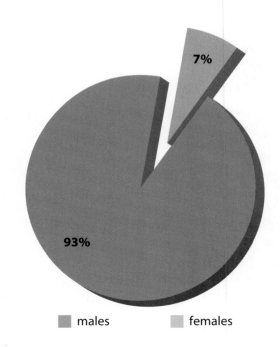

■ males   ■ females

of manhood and with adjusting to the new power that women are demanding in relationships and in the workplace.[5]

It's fair to say that we are in the midst of a gender revolution, and the proper roles for men and women and boys and girls are negotiated on a daily basis. In Durkheim's terminology, it could be said that sex roles in the 21st century are experiencing a state of **anomie**, in which the norms are in flux. It's in this context of sex-role anomie that this chapter examines female delinquency. Although it's also necessary to talk about male delinquency, especially the issue of masculinity, this is done primarily in contrast to female issues to tease out how gender influences delinquency.[6] The chapter is divided into four parts:

1. Girls to Women: A Developmental View
2. The Extent and Nature of Female Delinquency
3. Theories of Female Delinquency
4. Gender and the Juvenile Justice System

When the student is finished with the chapter, it will be apparent that there is such a thing as gender roles and that they are changing rapidly. Additionally, it could be argued that the increase in women's power hasn't necessarily been at the expense of men. Historically, both females and males have been constrained by gender roles. Therefore, this chapter can also shed light on numerous issues that also can be applied to males.[7]

Studying female development is risky because so many of what we thought were biologically and psychologically determined traits actually aren't. Here, we must understand the difference between sex and gender. **Sex** is the biological designation of male or female. **Gender** refers to the characteristics attributed and accorded to males and females by their societies and cultures on the basis of sex. Biology determines sex. Society determines gender. As we learn more about the effects of socialization and the potentials for development if given the right

INSTANT RECALL
FROM CHAPTER 5

anomie

A condition in which people or society undergoes a breakdown of social norms and values. Also, personal anxiety and isolation produced by rapidly shifting moral and cultural values.

INSTANT RECALL
FROM CHAPTER 6

gender

The characteristics attributed to and accorded to males and females by society and/or culture on the basis of sex.

Females are proving to be adept at many sports skills thought to be specific to males. Here, players for women's national soccer teams from Japan and Mexico fight for the ball at a play-off match for the Women's World Cup.

opportunities, we are finding that much of what was thought to be factual about females is actually false.

Take for example the old insult "You throw like a girl." This phrase was used to put girls down and to insult boys who weren't proficient in throwing a ball. One need only look at high school and college softball games to see women who throw a ball perfectly well. What was once thought to be a female limitation has, in fact, turned out to be a limitation placed on females. Given the right coaching, females are proving to be adept at many skills thought to be specific to males. For example, women weren't allowed to run the Olympic marathon until 1976. It was thought that women's bodies couldn't withstand the pounding of running for such a long period of time. In 2000, however, the winner of the women's Olympic marathon posted a time that would have won the men's Olympic marathon in 1956.[8]

Physical Development

Those who study child development look at the physical, cognitive, psychological, and sociological aspects of how children become adults.[9] Here, we will detail how children make this journey, paying particular attention to females. Unraveling the influence of physical and social development of females is difficult because of the rigid gender roles that societies enforce. The greatest differences in the maturation of girls and boys don't appear until adolescence. Our bodies change rapidly during puberty, which influences our psychological self-esteem and sociological interaction with others. One of the first differences between boys and girls is that girls experience a growth spurt in height at about 14 years, whereas boys don't have theirs until about age 16.[10] Additionally, girls develop pubic hair, breasts, and begin menstruation before the age of 14, whereas boys may lag until 16 before realizing any major physical changes. These changes affect the body image of both sexes as they react with horror and/or joy. Few adolescents are neutral about physical changes.

According to Robert S. Feldman, girls in Western society used to react to the onset of menstruation with anxiety because of the negative aspects such as cramps. Now, however, because menstruation is openly discussed, girls often welcome it as a rise in status and react with increased self-esteem and self-awareness.[11] The key to how one reacts to physical development is in the timing. An early- or late-developing body can cause anxiety. For boys, an

Because of their postpuberty physical development, girls were once considered unable to play contact sports. Today, however, more girls are signing up for football and rugby. In 2005, 15-year-old Miranda McOsker threw three touchdown passes as quarterback for her high school team.

early-developing body may mean they excel at sports sooner than their peers. They may also engage in delinquent acts sooner because they associate with older boys who are their size. For girls, early development may mean that older boys seek them out for dates. However, these girls often aren't socially mature and find these situations challenging.

Late-maturing bodies hold different problems for boys and girls. For boys, it means they aren't as tall as their peers and therefore aren't considered to be as physically attractive. For girls, it means they may be overlooked in the dating scene and thus feel themselves to be undesirable. However, when they do finally mature, they are better prepared to deal with dating and may experience fewer emotional problems.[12] Late-maturing girls are also more likely to fit the cultural ideal of being slender and to feel less pressure to diet.[13]

Cognitive Development

During adolescence, young people learn to think in more abstract ways and to understand both the physical and social world around them. More important, however, is that they learn more about their own psychology and begin to see themselves as they believe others see them. Young people develop their **metacognition**, or their own thinking processes, which allows them to have a better idea about how perceptive they are. One downfall of this increase in metacognition is that the adolescent might become particularly introspective and self-conscious.[14]

One observation that applies to many adolescents is that they are quick to find fault with authority figures, such as parents and teachers, and are unwilling to accept criticism. This age-related (but not age-exclusive) fault is a function of **adolescent egocentrism**. Adolescent egocentrism occurs when youths become so absorbed in their own lives, they are unable to view the world from other perspectives. They believe that everybody is scrutinizing them and finding all their real or imaginary faults. A barely noticeable new pimple is a big problem. Likewise, an offhand teasing remark by a popular boy can be the source of extreme embarrassment to the girl who isn't confident of her standing in her school's social order. Adolescents tend to think in terms of an imaginary audience of real and fictitious others who pay attention to every detail of their lives. In reality, nobody is watching, or at least not to the detail and not with the mean-spirited intentions the adolescent imagines.[15]

Another cognitive concern of egocentrism is that many youths believe their problems are unique to themselves. As they endure the predictable crises of growing up, they personalize each event and respond as if no one else could understand their trials and tribulations. This is especially true of their first broken heart or embarrassing *faux pas* in front of their peers. They also tend to see their problems as separate from those of their peers. They don't believe they can get a sexually transmitted disease or a DUI because those things happen to other people, not to them. Their cognitive isolation allows them to become absorbed in their problems as if they were personal fables, and not the growing pains suffered by most adolescents.[16]

Psychological and Social Development

The healthy psychological and social development of young women has several aspects. Like young men, young women are concerned with establishing personal identity, fitting into their peer group, negotiating the pitfalls of dating and sexual activity, cutting the apron strings to parents, and establishing their independence. As young women negotiate these psychological and sociological passages, they're susceptible to feelings of inadequacy and inferiority. These feelings can result in depression and even the contemplation of suicide if they can't be resolved in a positive way.[17] It's worth considering each of these concerns in more detail to appreciate the issues inherent in the change of status from girl to woman.

IDENTITY

It's common for youngsters to ask questions of themselves such as "Who am I?" and "Where do I belong in this world?" As they mature physically and cognitively, they see the world as a more complex place and their role in it as more complicated than it was when they were children. They understand they will be pressured to perform adult activities, and they struggle to acquire a set of values, skills, and abilities in order to interact with others. Girls notice the dramatic changes in their bodies brought on by puberty and the fact that other people are reacting to them differently. These changes challenge their ability to have an accurate self-concept and, even more so, a healthy self-esteem.[18] As their lives become more intertwined with new activities and other people, they may find they have a good idea of where they fit into society but be unhappy with how they see themselves.

According to Feldman, girls have a more difficult time with self-esteem than boys. This is primarily because girls are judged by their physical appearance much more so than boys. This becomes particularly problematic when one discovers that the cultural ideal for the appearance of young women isn't the physical norm.[19] In fact, for most girls, obtaining the "perfect" female body that appears on the covers of magazines would require surgery in the form of breast implants, collagen injections, and liposuction. The social pressures to look a certain way are tremendous and can result in young women engaging in unhealthy and dangerous lifestyles or rejecting the ideal model and adopting a deviant identity.

FITTING IN AND BEING POPULAR

Another aspect of one's social development during adolescence is the forming of reference groups, which enable youths to gather information about the expectations of the adolescent role and compare themselves with other young people. In high school, young people hang out with crowds or smaller cliques to establish their place in the social order. They label each other as a "jock" or "nerd" or "goth," and their position in the informal social order of the school is contingent on how they are perceived to fit into a variety of groups. Their social identity can be fluid as they move from one context (the classroom) to another (the dating scene or the athletic field). Some individuals have limited, rigid identities; others float from one group to another with little effort.[20] Youths can be overly concerned with their reputation and might allow peer pressure to get them into trouble. They also have finely tuned perceptions of who is popular and who isn't. Popularity becomes a goal for some teenagers, and it often proves to be a difficult one as events, styles, and friends change and those who were first become last in the struggle for acceptance.[21]

DATING AND SEX

The ideal function of dating is a practice of courtship that eventually leads to marriage. It gives adolescents an opportunity to get to know each other on a fairly risk-free basis in which the date is limited to a movie, dinner, or party. Parents monitor the selection of a dating partner and set limits on the time, place, and activity of the date. In some cultures, all dating is done under the close watch of a chaperone. However, the reality of dating in the United States

Youths can be overly concerned with their reputation and might allow peer pressure to get them into trouble.

is different from the ideal. Dating for adolescents has little to do with finding a marriage partner. Instead, dating provides the functions of entertainment, establishing intimacy, and often prestige.[22] Being asked out by the football team captain or dating the prettiest cheerleader can consign a degree of status that is coveted by others.

Whether dating encourages intimacy is still an open question for those who are first starting out. Young people are so concerned with guarding their feelings that dating can take on a superficial atmosphere in which little actual communication occurs. As adolescents get older, they are better able to handle their feelings, sometimes long after they have become physically intimate with a partner. As a source of entertainment, dating provides a major departure from family activities. Being outside the scope of adult supervision gives young people the opportunity to establish their identity in new ways, such as engaging in risk-taking behavior by driving fast or consuming alcohol or drugs.

In the 21st century, dating for teenagers has changed. Instead of a boy-girl date with an agreed-on activity, such as seeing a movie, young people now might engage in what amounts to group dating or "hanging out." Here several teens will meet at a friend's house or local mall to talk, shop, flirt, and engage in activities that traditional dating used to encompass. It provides for risk-free emotional interaction during which teens can have fun, get to know each other, and establish their social hierarchy. Two teens might "hook up" and become emotionally or physically intimate, but this doesn't necessarily mean they are a couple. The intimacy is treated as entertainment and is attractive, because there is little in the way of a binding commitment, even for that evening, between them. The dating interaction gets more intense as the teenagers get older, especially when boys start driving and can escape the observation of others. Girls often begin dating older boys who have cars and money, which brings higher social status. Because boys physically and emotionally develop at a slower rate, girls often find themselves attracted to older boys who seem to be more worldly and sophisticated.[23]

Teenagers' first encounter with sex is most often by masturbation. About half of boys and a quarter of girls report sexual self-stimulation. Boys engage in masturbation early and then decrease its occurrence, whereas girls begin slowly in their early teens and reach a maximum later.[24] Sexual intercourse is a major milestone in the lives of most adolescents. It's usually preceded by other sexual activities, such as petting, deep kissing, or oral sex. The age at which adolescents have their first sexual intercourse has been declining for the past 50 years. At least half of adolescents have had sex before age 18, and 80 percent by age 20. One important reason for the earlier onset of sexual activity is the changing nature of the double standard that says sex is permissible for boys but not for girls. Today the double standard has been relaxed, and the new norm is called "permissiveness with affection." Here sexual activity is allowed to girls if it occurs in the context of a long-term, committed, or loving relationship.[25] This new standard isn't rigid, like abstinence, so the definition of what is long-term or loving can vary greatly, giving girls greater autonomy to engage in sex without loss of social status.

To deal with the issues of teenagers having sex, some groups have developed abstinence campaigns to encourage young teens to forgo sexual activity until marriage.

CUTTING THE STRINGS OF PARENTAL CONTROL

The final aspect of girls' healthy psychological and sociological development is the gradual disengagement of parental control that occurs during adolescence and young adulthood. This disengagement is more difficult for girls than it is for boys, because parents generally consider girls to be more fragile and vulnerable than boys, so they tend to try to exert control longer. Traditionally, boys are allowed more flexibility and autonomy at an earlier age than girls.[26] Boys are given later curfews, more access to cars, and less supervision than girls.

The struggle, for girls, typically begins at home with the mother. Predictably, the mother demands that the girl's room be clean and that she help with the domestic duties as preparation for the time when she has a family of her own. The girl might consider her room as the one location where she can establish her own domain and often keeps it messy as a way of proclaiming her independence from parental control. This conflict spreads to skipping religious services, choosing clothing styles, testing curfews, selecting friends, acquiring tattoos and body piercings, and selecting a college or career. Ideally, as the girl gets older, her parents give her graduated responsibilities and autonomy, but from the girl's point of view, this newfound freedom never comes fast enough.[27]

This overview of the development of young females has been brief. Each of the topics could have, and has had, books written about it. Our purpose here has been

Traditionally, boys are allowed more flexibility and autonomy at an earlier age than girls. Girls may respond by engaging in such status offenses as binging on alcohol and smoking.

to alert the student to the major issues and concerns of development. For many of these issues, boys have the same concerns, and many boys find different ways of resolving the tasks of growing up. It's in light of these issues of differential female development that we now turn to the issue of female delinquency. The involvement of young females with crime, delinquency, and the juvenile justice system is different from that of males. Females commit less delinquency and fewer serious delinquent acts, are treated differently by justice officials, and, for the most part, are easier to put back on the right path. However, for a small number of females, delinquency is a serious issue because, whether perpetrators or victims, females have a vastly different experience with the criminal and juvenile justice systems than do males.

Questions

1. What is the difference between sex and gender?
2. What is adolescent egocentrism?

The Extent and Nature of Female Delinquency

Women and girls break the law far less than men and boys. This is one of two reasons they don't show up in the crime statistics at the same rate as males. The other reason is that the justice system treats them differently. Although these statements seem simple, they actually raise a lot of questions. Why do females break the law less than males when they comprise roughly half the population? What offenses and delinquency are females involved in and why? Before moving on to theories of female delinquency, we'll shed some light on these questions, in this brief section.

Although adolescent females break the law less than adolescent males, female delinquency is still a problem; however, the pattern is different across age, type, and seriousness.[28] As one study put it, antisocial behavior in females is "less common, less serious, and less persistent."[29] Of specific interest are the circumstances

Learning Objective 3.

Illustrate how female delinquency is different from that of males.

Women and girls break the law far less than men and boys. According to one study, antisocial behavior in females is "less common, less serious, and less persistent."

that lead young females into trouble. Therefore, we will concentrate on a few types of offenses for which young females are subjected to the most attention from the juvenile justice system. (Also, see Prevention and Intervention for a program that seeks to address female delinquency.)

» **Running away.** One of the two forms of delinquency for which females are arrested more often than males is running away from home (see Figure 7.2; we'll get to the other one, prostitution, next). Running away is considered a **status offense** in that it's a violation of the law only because of age. Once a girl reaches the age of 18, the justice system, as with boys, is no longer concerned about her as a status offender. Girls run away from home more often than boys for two reasons. First, a girl may be running toward something. She may have a romantic partner the parents disapprove of, and she may have to make a choice between the two. This is a classic dilemma, in which the girl is caught up in the romantic passion of first love and in a battle with her parents. The second reason girls run away from home is because they're running away from some sort of physical or psychological abuse. An abuser can make home life so unbearable that a girl feels forced to leave. Sometimes, the romantic partner is used as a way to escape the abuser.[30]

» **Prostitution.** More females, including juveniles, are arrested for prostitution than males (see Figure 7.3). No one knows how many adolescent women and girls are working as prostitutes—the UCR arrest statistics are almost certainly low, and research estimates aren't reliable.[31] The average age at which children are lured into juvenile prostitution is between 11 and 14, although some victims have been reported to be as young as age 5.[32] One study found that risk factors for juvenile prostitution include bad family situations, low IQ, poor school achievement, inadequate social skills, and

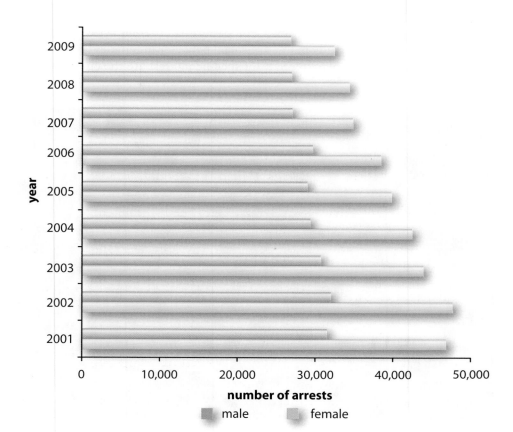

Figure 7.2 Number of Runaway Girls and Boys Arrested, by Year

Think About It
1. Why are more females arrested for running away than males? Discuss your reasoning.

Source: Federal Bureau of Investigation, *Crime in the United States, 2001–2009*, Table 33: Ten-Year Arrest Trends by Sex. Online at www.fbi.gov/about-us/cjis/ucr/ucr#cius.

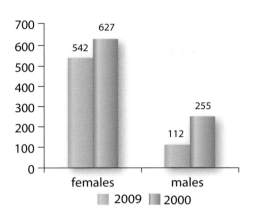

Figure 7.3 Prostitution Arrests, Females and Males Under 18, 2009 and 2000

Note that arrests for both sexes fell.

Think About It

1. Speculate why there are fewer male arrests than female arrests.

Source: Federal Bureau of Investigation, *Crime in the United States, 2010*, Table 33: Ten-Year Arrest Trends by Sex, 2000-2009, www2. fbi.gov/ucr/cius2009/data/table_33. html.

general abuse and neglect.[33] Perhaps the primary source of knowledge about the incidence and circumstances of juvenile prostitution is law enforcement, which apparently is inconsistent in its treatment of juvenile prostitutes. One study reports that law enforcement considers juvenile prostitution not only a delinquency problem but also a problem that isn't worth much attention.[34] Yet another study found that the police treated 60 percent of arrested juvenile prostitutes as victims and 40 percent as offenders. Factors affecting an arrestee's treatment as a victim included her level of cooperation, the presence of identified exploiters (pimps or clients), the existence of an arrest record, and whether she was local. Presumably, youths who were uncooperative, had a record, weren't from the area, and didn't have a readily identifiable exploiter were considered offenders.[35] Currently, many criminal justice practitioners, including legislators, social workers, and researchers, are trying to get the problem recast as an issue of child welfare and victimization rather than delinquency, but attitudes have been slow to change.[36] Part of the movement to change the treatment of juveniles arrested for prostitution is the reclassification of the activity as "domestic minor sex trafficking," with the idea that arrested juveniles will be treated as victims of sex traffickers rather than as delinquents who choose to work as prostitutes.[37]

》 **Shoplifting.** Another form of delinquency that girls engage in at a high rate is shoplifting.[38] The social pressure on young women to wear fashionable clothing and to buy expensive cosmetics is great, and for many young women the only way to acquire these items is to steal them. For some young women, shoplifting is a group activity. They enter shops in pairs or in groups and plan their actions, with some of the girls distracting the clerks, others serving as lookouts, and others committing the theft. Some young women are so proficient at shoplifting, they treat it as a form of job and steal to order. Clients will tell the shoplifter the exact item they desire, including size, color, and accessories, and the shoplifter will steal it for them for a fee. It isn't unusual for young women working in stores to allow their friends to shoplift. This type of delinquency is accessible to young women and has little risk of physical injury.[39]

》 **Fighting.** In her book *Odd Girl Out: The Hidden Culture of Aggression in Girls*, Rachel Simmons details the problems of young women dealing with each other in covertly aggressive ways.[40] Simmons explains the behavior in terms of relational aggression and contends that it starts as soon as girls form meaningful relationships. The aggression can take many forms. In its mildest form, relational aggression can be the silent treatment or the spreading of rumors.

In its more extreme form, it leads to bullying and fighting. Girls, according to Simmons, aren't emotionally prepared to use physical violence in the same way that boys are, so fighting affects them more severely. Fighting is also an important feature of female gang activity. Jody Miller, in her book *One of the Guys: Girls, Gangs, and Gender*, describes how fighting is a form of resolving conflicts with rival gangs.[41] One interesting observation Miller makes is that females limit their violence to fighting, whereas male gang members will engage in deadly violence. Additionally, when there is a conflict with a female from a rival gang, the male gang members will tell the females to do the fighting. Miller points to this gendered nature of gang involvement and links it to the ways the society uses gender to assign status. Beating up a rival female gang member is beneath the male gang members. When they do engage in the rare event of violence against a female gang member, it includes rape, gang rape, or other sexualized violence.

This list is by no means exhaustive. In fact, girls will commit just about every antisocial act that boys will, but at a much reduced level and with different particulars. Take, for example, homicide. In 2009, there were just 69 juvenile female homicide arrests versus 873 male juvenile homicide arrests.[42] The differences don't stop there. The victims of girls tended to be children below age 5, other females, and family members; boys tended to kill other males, strangers, and victims aged 14 to 34. Girls were more likely to use knives, personal weapons (fists, hands, or feet), and asphyxiation, and their homicides were more likely than boys' to be conflict related. Boys tended to kill during the commission of another offense and to use guns.[43]

The examples provided here illustrate the range of female misbehavior and suggest that female delinquency can have a variety of causes, consequences, and

7.1 PREVENTION AND INTERVENTION

Movimiento Ascendencia

Movimiento Ascendencia (Upward Movement), based in Pueblo, Colorado, serves at-risk, delinquent, and gang-involved girls ages 8 to 19 by providing positive alternatives to substance use and gang involvement. The program is headed by the Pueblo Youth Services Bureau.[1] When compared with control groups, girls participating in Movimiento Ascendencia showed improved academic achievement and a marked decline in delinquency, although researchers noted no difference in self-esteem.[2]

When a girl first joins Movimiento Ascendencia, an initial home visit and needs assessment are conducted. Girls are matched with a female mentor with whom they spend at least two hours a week for nine months. The program focuses on teaching conflict resolution skills, recognizing symptoms of drug and alcohol abuse, and providing information on sexuality, pregnancy, and sexually transmitted diseases. Activities are designed around cultural awareness, conflict resolution, and enhancing self-esteem and social support. The tutoring and homework-support program includes training in pregnancy prevention, personal grooming, personal safety and self-defense, dealing with loss and grief, and setting career goals.[3]

THINK ABOUT IT

1. Discuss the reasons a program like Movimiento Ascendencia focuses on raising self-esteem in girls.

[1]Movimiento Ascendencia, Office of Juvenile Justice and Delinquency Prevention, www.ojjdp.gov/mpg/mpgProgramDetails.aspx.

[2]Brendan Groves, "No Panacea, Some Promises, Much Potential: A Review of Effective Antigang Strategies," *United States Attorneys' Bulletin: Gang Issues* 56, no. 4 (July 2008): 38–52. Online at www.justice.gov/usao/eousa/foia_reading_room/usab5604.pdf.

[3]Ibid.

challenges. What is important to remember is that when compared to boys' delinquency, the range, intensity, destructiveness, and frequency of girls' delinquency are much less. This isn't to discount female antisocial behavior but simply to place it in context.

Question

1. What four offenses get females the most attention from the juvenile justice system?

Theories of Female Delinquency

Scholars haven't devoted the time and energy to explaining female antisocial behavior that they have to explaining male antisocial behavior. Because girls and women don't break the law or commit status offenses as often as males, female delinquency and crime haven't traditionally been considered a serious social problem. Further, there was an assumption that females broke the law for the same reasons as males, so all that had to be done was extend the research findings to females. As we will see, this assumption was wrong. There are important distinctions between males and females that account for differences in motivation, technique, and social response. In considering these important differences, scholars have developed a number of biological, psychological, and sociological theories. Here, we will briefly highlight the development of female theories before turning to recent scholarship on feminism.

Biological Theories

Cesare Lombroso set the foundation for much of the study of crime because of his attempts to use the scientific method. Although he made major errors in his science, his contribution to the study of criminology is fundamental, and many of his ideas still resonate today. His major concern was the physical differences between offenders and nonoffenders. Lombroso believed that criminal offenders weren't as highly evolved as other citizens. In adapting Charles Darwin's ideas about evolution, he suggested that offenders were a throwback to a less-developed human. The number of **atavisms** could evidence this lack of development.

In his book *The Female Offender*, written with William Ferrero, Lombroso explored reasons that women break the law.[44] Lombroso found fewer atavisms in females than in males and essentially concluded that female offenders were much like female nonoffenders. This isn't much of a compliment, because Lombroso believed women in general were less intelligent than men and were weak, childlike, jealous, and vengeful. However, some females who committed serious offenses were deemed to be cunning, spiteful, deceitful, and capable of extreme cruelty. Females who committed serious offenses were believed to possess extreme masculine traits, as well as the worst qualities of women. Lombroso believed female offending to be a result of the biological nature of women and, like many later theorists, linked it to sexual issues. A woman's sexuality and anatomy were believed to dictate her actions, and although this view is no longer prevalent today, Lombroso set the stage for its importance for a long time.[45] We'll return to this theme after we examine some of the more recent biological explanations of female deviance.

Criminologist Anthony Walsh contends that males and females engage in antisocial behavior in distinctly different patterns that sociological theories don't fully account for. Walsh claims that fundamental physiological differences between men and women that primarily have to do with the production of testosterone dictate, to some extent, their participation in antisocial behavior.[46]

Learning Objective 4.

Explain the relationship between early puberty and female delinquency.

Learning Objective 5.

Describe the contribution of labeling theory to explaining female delinquency.

Learning Objective 6.

Describe the contribution of life-course theory to explaining female delinquency.

Learning Objective 7.

List the five features of Daly and Chesney-Lind's work in feminist criminology.

Learning Objective 8.

Discuss Curran and Renzetti's explanation of the three feminist perspectives by which female crime and delinquency can be understood.

INSTANT RECALL FROM CHAPTER 3

atavism

The appearance in a person of features thought to be from earlier stages of human evolution.

Both girls and boys have similar stresses related to family life, school, peers, and puberty. However, some of the differences between how boys and girls react to these stresses appears to be biologically based, and sometimes these reactions can lead to delinquency. One fact that may explain why girls break the law less often than boys (and this can probably be generalized to females and males of all ages) is that girls tend to internalize their adverse reactions to stress, whereas boys externalize them. Girls tend to become anxious, depressed, and moody. Boys, on the other hand, will act out and exhibit aggressive behavior. For example, attention deficit hyperactivity disorder (ADHD) is more prevalent in boys than in girls and is strongly associated with delinquency in both sexes. The nature of ADHD in boys tends to be different than in girls: boys with ADHD exhibit hyperactivity and aggression; girls with ADHD tend to be inattentive. Because ADHD girls aren't acting out as boys do, it's possible that the disorder goes largely undiagnosed in girls.[47]

Although girls' and boys' reactions to ADHD are different, as is the likelihood of diagnosis, both can lead to delinquency. So far, the only vulnerability to delinquency that applies solely to girls is early puberty. Although boys may also experience early puberty, it's apparently not the gateway to delinquency—and later criminal offending—that it is for girls.[48]

EARLY PUBERTY AND DELINQUENCY IN GIRLS

Early puberty in girls means an earlier-than-average onset of menstruation, which typically occurs between the ages of 9 and 13. Six factors affect this: heredity, weight and weight-to-height ratio, stressful events, family relations, presence of an adult male in the home, and psychological adjustment. Stress is a particularly important factor in early menstruation. Several things can cause stress for girls, including maternal psychopathology (a mentally ill mother), an absent father, parental rejection, presence of a stepfather, unstable parental bonds, insecurity and mistrust within the family, malnourishment, and poverty. Perhaps not coincidentally, all of these stresses are themselves directly related to delinquency in both sexes. However, some researchers say the way these stresses relate to early puberty is of evolutionary significance. Earlier menstruation means earlier sexual activity and the possibility of more and earlier pregnancies.[49] If you'll recall from Crosscurrents: The Evolution of Delinquency in Chapter 5, more and earlier pregnancies in disadvantaged young women may actually be an adaptation to a lifestyle in which an early death is not unlikely. Another study states a definite genetic component is involved in early puberty, having found that "a common set of genes predisposed girls toward early pubertal maturation and resulted in elevated involvement in both nonviolent and violent forms of delinquency."[50]

Unfortunately, the lifestyle changes that may be brought on by early puberty are also those that tend to lead to delinquency. (Some research has also shown that girls who experienced early puberty were also more likely to become adult criminal offenders.)[51] In what is called the "maturation disparity hypothesis," early-maturing girls are more eager to slip parental bonds and seek out adult status, independence, and possibly an escape from a negative family situation.[52] This is also likely to lead to associations with older males who may already be well into delinquency (and criminal offending if they're young adults). School bonding and academic performance is likely to suffer, and peer relationships are likely to change as the girl drifts away from friends who haven't already "gotten their periods" to friends who have and are more likely to be in the independent, adult-oriented, delinquent-associated peer group that the girl feels she should be a part of.[53]

Some researchers have noted that although early menstruation is a delinquency risk factor for girls who attend mixed-sex schools, it isn't for girls who attend all-girl schools. Several factors may mediate this relationship, including the most obvious one: exposure to males. Other social factors may also be involved. Most same-sex schools are private, and most require families to have significant financial resources to pay the tuition and, often, room and board. Wealthy families are less likely to be exposed to some of the delinquency-risk stresses of impoverished families, such as bad neighborhoods and malnourishment. Also, girls who are living away from home at school may be free from the daily stresses of a troubled family environment. It's possible the risk factors associated with early puberty may be as social as they are biological.

Psychological Theories

In addition to being biologically different from males, females are also subjected to a range of pressures and stimulations that may make them respond in ways that males wouldn't. This is a tricky subject, because it's difficult to untangle the effects of biology and culture from the psychological makeup of individuals. Past efforts to do this can be faulted with the notion that men were considered the norm and that the behavior of females was considered deviant to the extent that it differed from that of males. Given the conventional wisdom at the time and the rigid sex roles that were in place, it isn't surprising to witness this assumed superiority of males. Today, however, it seems to many to be prejudicial.[54]

In his book *The Unadjusted Girl*, W. I. Thomas argued that girls had desires that weren't fulfilled by society. He said they had four categories of wishes: new experiences, security, response, and recognition. In a society that limited their ability to realize these wishes, girls would use their sexuality as a sort of "capital" to accomplish their goals. In this way, they were propelled toward delinquent behavior unless they were successful at selling themselves only once through marriage, as upper-class women were able to do. Thomas claimed that girls considered this arrangement as a way to get the things they wanted in life: attention, pretty clothes, and entertainment. In many ways, it was a deal with the devil because, by using her sexuality to fulfill immediate needs, a girl sacrificed her reputation and self-esteem and was punished later in the marriage market, where her value was considerably diminished by her sexual history. Thomas's solution to this problem was the juvenile court, where he believed the girls could be counseled to engage in more positive behaviors. As one of the **child savers**, Thomas believed the court could compensate for the influence of a bad family and the psychological effects of demoralization that disadvantaged and unsuccessful girls struggled with.[55]

Another study that linked female crime to biological and psychological factors is Otto Pollak's *The Criminality of Women*. In this book, Pollak claimed that women have a precocious biological maturity that leads them to engage in sexual delinquency. He had a negative view of the overall character of women and contended that they are deceitful and manipulating because of their reduced opportunities in society. In addition to concealing sexual arousal, women hide their menstruation. This deceit is learned when girls are young and is a result of not having legitimate outlets for their natural aggression. Pollak's was a patriarchal view of female delinquency. He asserted that women break the law much more than is reported and that men excuse or overlook women's antisocial behavior to protect them. Pollak supported the view that marriage should be a more one-sided affair in which men are allowed the dominant role and women should remain girls in their relationship with their husband, thus allowing a balance in the family power structure. In short,

INSTANT RECALL
FROM CHAPTER 2

child savers

People at the end of the 19th century who were instrumental in creating special justice institutions to deal with juvenile delinquents and troubled youths.

according to Pollak, the dominant culture's gender roles should be maintained to keep girls from going down the path of delinquency and crime.[56]

It's fair to say the history of research on the psychological nature of female delinquency has been flawed. For the most part, studies have viewed females in the traditional gender stereotype of weak, dependent, fragile beings. When strong females were encountered, it was suggested that they had a masculine characteristic that could explain their delinquency.[57]

We turn now to the traditional sociological theories of delinquency, most of which don't denigrate the character and motivation of females as much as simply neglect them. Most of these theories have been focused on lower-class males and have had little to say about females. Yet some would simply apply the theories to females with a caveat that only minor adjustments should be made to account for female delinquency.

Sociological Theories

The **social ecology** school of delinquency characterized by Clifford Shaw, Henry McKay, and Frederick Thrasher was concerned with explaining the geographic distribution of crime. They focused exclusively on male delinquents and illustrated crime patterns by making maps of the city and looking for patterns of offending. This work assumed that females were either prevented from offending because of custom and tradition or because they were more closely supervised by parents and teachers.

Strain theorists considered female delinquency differently. Although Merton and Cloward and Ohlin (see Chapter 5) concentrated exclusively on male delinquents, they also applied the concept of strain to females, although in an offhand way. The central focus of **strain theory** was on men adapting to the culture by adopting roles in which they could achieve their success in a masculine manner. Antisocial women were assumed to want the same things as antisocial men. For the strain theorist, masculinity was at the core of delinquency, and the idea that females might experience other types of strain that propel them toward delinquent behavior wasn't considered.[58]

According to Meda Chesney-Lind and Randall Shelden, many early theorists were themselves locked into the gender roles of the time, and explained any female delinquency as the inability of girls to adopt their natural role. For instance, Albert Cohen is quoted as saying that women want not only to excel, but to excel as women. The dominant gender roles of the 1950s are taken by Cohen as a given, and his sexism is therefore encoded in his view of delinquency.[59]

Other popular sociological theories, such as differential association and control theory, were also constructed and tested without females in mind. Although it's possible to retrofit these theories to include female delinquents, they simply assume that the premises behind the theories are applicable to females as well as males, and all that is required is to find a data set of female delinquency and apply the theory. (For a look at efforts in sociological theory to account for the differences of females, see Crosscurrents.)

Still, other sociological theories have more to say about female delinquency. For instance, **labeling theory** has been used to explain a variety of concerns of female delinquency. **Primary deviance**, the label put on a youth by parents, teachers, peers, or the courts, tags a girl with the label of "tramp," "slut," or "thief," and, consequently, others treat her that way. When the girl internalizes the label, which is **secondary deviance**, she believes it's an accurate description of her moral character and thus acts in the way she believes others see her.[60] Labeling theory, unlike many of the other sociological theories, can be used to explain a

7.2 **crosscurrents**

Why *Don't* Girls Become Delinquent?

In Chapter 5, we discussed Hirschi's social control theory. In that theory, Hirschi doesn't ask why youths break the law, he asks instead, why don't they? According to Hirschi, levels of attachment, involvement, commitment, and belief keep youths bonded to society. Although these factors are generally the same for both boys and girls, the specific factors that bond youths to society are slightly different for girls than they are for boys.

The Girls Study Group, which is part of the Department of Justice, looked at girls' "resiliency," which, in the context of delinquency, is the ability to adapt to, or succeed in spite of, negative situations such as abuse, neglect, or poverty. In other words, resiliency is what keeps girls from falling into delinquency.

Research has found that the most effective protection against violent delinquency for both boys and girls is academic success, which is best measured by grade point average. After that, the picture of resiliency diverges. After school success, girls—but not boys—are most protected by family connectedness, school connectedness, and religiosity. Let's look at these factors more closely.

》 **Family connectedness.** The presence of a caring adult, especially one who's aware of a youth's daily activities and associations, provides an important support system for girls. The adult doesn't even have to be a parent; in fact, a caring adult outside the family can provide support against a negative family situation.

》 **School connectedness.** This is closely related to academic success, but goes further to include a positive perception of school and interactions with the people there, including teachers and peers. In this case, social success is as important as academic success. This is especially important for girls with negative home situations, as school may be one of the few places where their achievements are recognized.

The presence of a caring adult, especially one who's aware of a youth's daily activities and associations, provides an important support system for girls.

》 **Religiosity.** Although some studies found that religious faith only protected youths against minor offenses, it's an important factor in the lives of many youths and helps to increase girls' resilience against delinquency.

Although these factors help increase girls' resilience, they aren't perfect and don't affect all girls at all ages, or even in all situations. For example, these factors may work during early adolescence but not be strong enough to protect a girl against severe adversity, such as gang involvement or prostitution, in later adolescence. Researchers are still trying to understand these protective factors and the points during girls' lives at which they are most effective.

THINK ABOUT IT

1. Which factor most affects girls' resilience against delinquency?

Source: Stephanie R. Hawkins et al., "Resilient Girls—Factors That Protect Against Delinquency," *Girls Study Group: Understanding and Responding to Girls' Delinquency* (Washington, DC: US Department of Justice, 2009). Online at www.ncjrs.gov/pdffiles1/ojjdp/220124 .pdf.

variety of delinquency offenses and is able to account for the reaction of society to the girl's antisocial behavior.

Life-course theory may also be applied to explanations for female delinquency. Although many of the "turning points" into delinquency may be the same as they are for boys (bad family situations and neighborhoods, academic failure, impoverishment), we've discussed at least one (early puberty) that is specific to girls. Some turning-point research, however, has focused on what brings young delinquent women out of delinquent trajectories, and one turning point that shows particular promise is motherhood. Even marriage hasn't shown the ability that motherhood has to change the lives of impoverished, delinquent young women headed for lives of crime. Researchers speculate that motherhood is an effective turning point for three possible reasons: (1) the identity of being a mother and caring for a child become more important than anything else; (2) the risk of arrest is too great, and the effect it would have on the child too serious; and (3) the young women stay at home more often and refrain from partying, because to do so is to be a good mother.[61] Although motherhood doesn't absolutely protect all young women from further delinquency and crime—some women do continue deviant lives—children seem to motivate them to continue trying to change their lives and set a positive example.[62]

Critical theories have also been applied to the explanation of female delinquency. When looking at social class as a reason for the disparity in opportunities afforded individuals in society, gender can be considered as one of the indicators of class. Men have always held a privileged position in society, and it's axiomatic that lower-class women and children are the most affected by the inequitable distribution of wealth, power, and status. For instance, Chesney-Lind and Shelden state:

> Much of the "delinquent" behavior that girls engage in can be understood as an attempt by oppressed people to accommodate and resist the problems created by capitalist institutions, especially the family (since so many girls begin their "careers" in delinquency by running away from an oppressive family situation). Many of these girls adapt to their disadvantaged positions by their involvement in "accommodative" and "predatory" criminal behavior (e.g., shoplifting, prostitution, drug use).[63]

This accommodation to capitalist structures can be further exacerbated by the social conditions in which many females find themselves as a result of their overall social location. According to Chesney-Lind and Shelden, many females are at a fourfold disadvantage by being a person of color (race), young (age), a girl (sex), and impoverished (class). In this way, the critical theories speak to the issues of female delinquency but only as part of an overall pattern of discrimination by the powerful. Although sympathetic to the economic plight of women, most critical theories concern themselves with overall social justice and neglect explanations that cast females in a unique light. There are, however, theories that do focus on women and girls. Feminist theories of crime and delinquency are emerging to plug the gender gap in what we think we know about antisocial behavior.

Feminist Theories

To appreciate the contributions made by feminist criminologists to the understanding of crime and delinquency, it's necessary to back up a bit and make sure we're all considering the same concerns. Feminist scholarship refers to a specific way of looking at problems and doesn't indicate the physical sex of the scholar. Also, it would be a mistake to think of feminist criminology as solely the study of females and crime. Feminist criminology is more about approaching the serious study of how gender influences the reasons people break the law and how the criminal and juvenile justice systems respond. Therefore, we find that criminologists who study masculinity are also considered to be feminist scholars. Feminist criminologists study how sex and gender shape the social world, and, according to Kathleen Daly and Meda Chesney-Lind, their work can be differentiated from traditional criminology because it focuses on five features:

-)) Gender isn't a natural fact but is a complex social, historical, and cultural product; it's related to, but not simply derived from, biological and sex differences and reproductive capabilities.

-)) Gender and gender relations order social life and social institutions in fundamental ways.

-)) Gender relations and constructs of masculinity and femininity aren't symmetrical but are based on an organizing principle of men's superiority and social and political-economic dominance over women.

-)) Systems of knowledge reflect men's views of the natural and social world. The production of knowledge is gendered.

-)) Women should be at the center of intellectual inquiry, not peripheral, invisible, or appendages to men.[64]

Feminist scholars also recognize that the inequalities women face are only part of their problems. Women who are members of racial minorities and are impoverished face additional and interlocking disadvantages. Therefore, let us proceed with the recognition that feminist criminology is more inclusive than we might first suspect. It's a complicated line of inquiry that sheds light on the criminal and juvenile justice systems in ways that traditional theories don't.[65]

Because knowledge is gendered, it's important to understand some of the obstacles faced by feminist criminology. By saying "knowledge is gendered," we mean that much of what we know about the world is a result of research that has focused on males and been generalized to females. This is a problem because of the marked differences in the experiences and makeup of males and females. Also, it's interesting that the research done on females isn't automatically applied to males. Recall that, in research, males have been considered the norm, and females, when they are considered, are treated as a subcategory of males. In criminology, because male offenders so outnumber female offenders, the study of female offending hasn't been in the mainstream.

In traditional criminology, according to Jody Miller and Christopher Mullins, women are considered as either an identical subcategory (the old "add women and stir" adage) of the crime problem, or they are seen as different only because of assumptions about how women differ from men.[66] These assumptions about the emotional character and physical makeup of women historically have been used to relegate them to second-class citizenship.

Not all feminist criminologists consider the problems of crime and justice in the same way. There are distinct differences in why feminist criminologists believe women commit the offenses they do and in how they see the justice system dealing with female offenders. Further, feminists might disagree on what needs to be done to make the criminal and juvenile justice systems more equitable and effective. Daniel Curran and Claire Renzetti highlight three ways in which criminal offending can be understood from feminist perspectives.

1. **Liberal feminism.** Liberal feminists make two critiques about how gender influences crime and delinquency. The first argues that men control power and privilege in society. Men use that power to act in sexist ways to keep women "in their place" and to preserve the power and benefits of power for themselves. Liberal feminists have made strides toward breaking down the male-dominated and entrenched power structure but argue that much more needs to be accomplished before there is gender equity in society and in the juvenile justice system. The second critique concerns the way that boys and girls are socialized into adult roles. Given the highly gendered institutions in society where sex-role differences are systematically reinforced, it isn't

surprising that more progress hasn't been made. The women's movement has broken down many barriers and has educated parents, teachers, and decision makers on the dysfunctional ways that boys and girls get socialized, but much remains to be done. It's important to add here that not everyone shares the goals of the liberal feminists, and there's considerable backlash in the form of maintaining distinct feminine and masculine sex roles.

2. **Radical feminism.** Radical feminists call for a major overhaul in the systems of gender relations in society. They would wipe out many of the patriarchal structures that put women at such a disadvantage in obtaining positions of power and in controlling their own destinies. For instance, in the military, the radical feminist would eliminate all job discrimination based on gender and allow women to engage in combat alongside men. This would give women the opportunity to gain the experiences that are used to decide promotion to a higher rank. In the criminal justice system, the radical feminist would argue that the traditional system hasn't been responsive to women's needs. Crimes such as rape and domestic violence have historically been decided in ways that advantage male perpetrators. In recent decades, the feminist movement has corrected some of these injustices, but the radical feminist argues that justice is still gendered.

3. **Socialist feminism.** The combination of social class and gender is used as a "double whammy" to deny women access to positions of power in society. Being both female and impoverished has meant that women are perpetually kept from getting a decent education and job promotions, are saddled

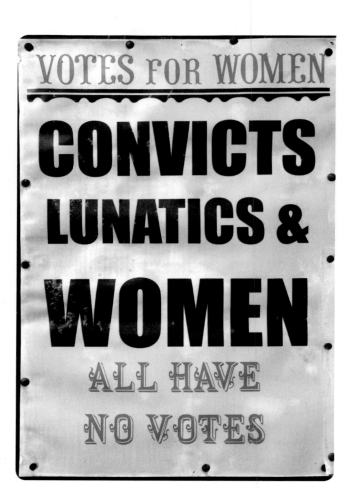

Liberal feminists have criticized men for controlling power and privilege in society. For instance, women weren't allowed to vote in the United States until ratification of the Nineteenth Amendment in 1920.

with the burdens of child care, and are denied control of important decisions affecting their lives by parents, boyfriends, husbands, and government authorities. Because impoverished women don't have access to power, their concerns are overlooked and neglected. Impoverished women who are also members of racial minorities experience an extra dimension of discrimination.[67]

In considering the problems of juvenile delinquency, the feminist perspective is poised to make major contributions to our understanding of how the juvenile justice system operates and how it affects girls even more negatively than it does boys. The juvenile justice system is similar to the family and the school in making assumptions about the basic nature of males and females and how society should treat them differently. In 1975, criminologist Freda Adler advanced an idea called the liberation hypothesis, which stated that as females gained more power in society, they would break the law more often and commit the types of offenses once believed to be the province of males.

Historically, women and girls have committed fewer offenses and different types of offenses than males. As such, they're not represented in the criminal and juvenile justice systems to the extent that males are. But why? Could the rigid gender roles that women traditionally have been forced to occupy have something to do with it? Do females commit fewer and less serious offenses simply because they've had no opportunity to do so?

In the liberation hypothesis, Adler speculated that as rights and opportunities for females increased, they would begin to commit more offenses that had been thought to be solely the domain of males, including violent offenses such as assault, murder, and robbery. According to Adler, the delinquency gap between males and females would shrink, and the statistics would merge as females not only committed "male" offenses but committed them more often. At first glance, the statistics seem to support this. According to FBI data, the percentage of under-18 females who were arrested rose about 4 percent from 2000 to 2009, from 26 percent of all juvenile arrests to 30 percent. However, such an increase isn't really that startling, given the overall decrease in juvenile arrests over the same period, with boys' arrests dropping nearly 23 percent and girls' arrests dropping 13 percent.[68]

Meda Chesney-Lind disagrees with the liberation hypothesis. She believes girls aren't becoming more delinquent, it's just that now society is more willing to deal with their offenses formally. The factors at work in the appearance of increased girls' delinquency are relabeling, rediscovery, and upcriming.

>> **Relabeling.** Some status offenses are now being considered as criminal offenses. Also, the mandatory arrest policies that some jurisdictions have for domestic violence have resulted in more female arrests. Research supports this idea, pointing to evidence that, since 1980, the year girls' arrests began to rise, behaviors that the juvenile court formerly handled as status offenses began to be considered as criminal offenses.[69] At least one study stated that the increase of judicial control over girls was a move by the juvenile court to make up for the drop in boys' offenses and "maintain operational stability."[70]

>> **Rediscovery.** Girls have always been violent, but neither the public, obsessed with boys' violence, nor the juvenile justice system, geared toward boys, have noticed. Girls are now being arrested for behaviors they wouldn't have been arrested for 10 or 20 years ago.

>> **Upcriming.** Schools are now sending cases to the police instead of dealing with them informally. More juveniles, and more juvenile girls, are

being arrested and facing more severe dispositions. For example, in 1986, a small pocketknife on a girl's key chain would have gone unnoticed in most schools. Now it can be grounds for arrest and expulsion from school.[71]

There is general agreement, however, that girls' motivation is markedly different than that of boys, with experts reporting that girls' violence is more controlled by their relationships with family, friends, and intimate partners. Drawing on the work of Daly and Chesney-Lind, Miller and Mullins laid out three ways in which feminist scholarship can inform how we consider the relationship between gender and offending.[72]

» **Gendered pathways to lawbreaking.** Drawing on insights from the life-course theories of crime, feminist scholars have examined the individual histories of female offenders and found that their pathways to crime and delinquency are often different than for males.[73] The remarkable thing is that many females become involved with the juvenile or criminal justice system for the first time as victims. There are "blurred boundaries" between offending and victimization. For instance, when a girl runs away from an abusive family situation, she commits a status offense, which could leave her fate in the hands of a justice system that might punish her for running away from home when that might be her best or only realistic choice. Mary Gilfus argues that many women start out as victims, then become survivors, and finally become perpetrators of street crime. Some young women must engage in prostitution or drug sales as a means to survive, and they are drawn into the justice system as offenders, although their behavior could be considered as something that victims or survivors have no choice but to engage in.[74] Victimization is but one pathway to crime for women. Drug and alcohol use, economic marginality, and experiences at school can also put girls in contact with the juvenile justice system. One other important pathway to delinquency for girls is association with a gang. This could be in the form of belonging to an all-girl gang or being involved with male gang members.

» **Gendered crime.** Feminist scholars are interested in how offending is often organized by gender. When males and females offend together, are some aspects of the offense reserved for males and some for females? For instance, in cases in which the male customers of female prostitutes are robbed, the prostitutes tend to steal the money while their customers are asleep, while male pimps are more likely to use physical force. In a support role, such as lookout or getaway-car driver, females are likely to remain in that task while males are allowed to move on to more instrumental tasks. Like the rest of society, the world of crime has some deeply entrenched ideas about which roles are appropriate for females. Even when girls rebel against the social order by breaking the law, they're still constrained by the social expectations of their male partners in the offense and often by the social expectations they learned as young girls.[75]

» **Gendered lives.** Finally, feminist scholars consider how gender is a factor in how men and women experience their lives. Because of the opportunities and limitations of gender roles, males and females are pressured in different ways that shape how they see themselves, their place in the world, and their relationship to the opposite sex. Girls and young women are more likely to be sheltered from many of the ways in which youngsters are recruited into delinquency. They are also initially more likely to be the victim of a street crime, rather than the perpetrator. This isn't to say that females don't choose to break the law. Although their victimization is real and harmful, there are also reasons to credit females with being active and creative in choosing delinquency. It's often a limited, poor, or contradictory choice based on circumstance, but it's a choice nevertheless.[76] Feminism isn't so narrowly focused on gender relations that it overlooks accountability for one's decisions. It does, however, explain how gender is a factor in many decisions and that a theoretical overview of crime and delinquency wouldn't be complete without considering how feminist criminology addresses the issues in ways that challenge the traditional and the customary.

Questions

1. According to labeling theory, what are primary and secondary deviance? How can these labels affect girls?

2. What is meant by the phrase "knowledge is gendered"?

3. By what pathway do females often first become involved with the criminal or juvenile justice system? What are some other ways?

4. What is your opinion of Adler's liberation hypothesis? How about Chesney-Lind's hypothesis that society is treating female delinquency more seriously?

Gender and the Juvenile Justice System

Does the juvenile justice system treat females differently than males? The answer isn't only yes, but also yes with a number of qualifications, explanations, and amplifications. Every institution of society treats females differently, so we shouldn't be surprised that the legal system reflects many of the same sex-role demands that are found throughout the culture.

Girls are treated differently for a structural reason. Because the juvenile justice system handles so many fewer girls than boys, the system has fewer alternatives for processing and sentencing girls. Municipalities have built intake and detention centers to accommodate all the male delinquents, and the facilities that deal with females are usually of a much lower quality. Policy makers might try to excuse the inferior facilities for girls by claiming that the delinquency problem is primarily male and that there aren't enough females to justify the construction of separate facilities, but this tells only part of the story. The additional argument is that the lack of female facilities reflects the aversion society has to locking up girls and the willingness of officials to find alternative ways of handling girls' cases.[77]

One explanation for the differential treatment of girls in the juvenile justice system is the "chivalry hypothesis." This argument states that girls are treated more leniently than boys because officials consider girls to be weaker, helpless, and less threatening. Girls, when they are caught and processed in the system, don't appear to be physically dangerous.[78] Officials tend to consider them more as accessories or indirect victims of the offense, rather than as full-fledged perpetrators, and consequently give them lighter sentences. By treating them more like ladies, juvenile justice officials intend to diminish the effect of case processing on girls. Based in part on labeling theory and in part on lack of resources, the chivalry option looks beneficial for females but might not always be so. There is a fine distinction between chivalry and paternalism.

Chivalry is associated with placing an individual on a pedestal and behaving gallantly toward that person, whereas paternalism involves taking care of

Learning Objective 9.

Explain what may happen to female delinquents at critical points in the justice system.

Learning Objective 10.

State some reasons the juvenile justice system treats girls differently.

The "chivalry hypothesis" states that girls are treated more leniently than boys because officials consider girls to be weaker, helpless, and less threatening.

the powerless and dependent. Both chivalry and paternalism, however, imply weakness and a need to protect another person or group, which can have dangerous repercussions when "protect" becomes "control." It's often difficult to tell whether preferential treatment of female defendants, when it occurs, is due to chivalry or paternalism, some combination of the two, or other factors.[79]

One interesting aspect of the chivalry hypothesis is that it isn't available to all females. It's mostly accorded to females who conform to traditional gender stereotypes. In a sense, then, a male authority extends chivalrous behavior to women who are deemed helpless, attractive, and harmless. Females who challenge established gender roles are more likely to be treated harshly and not have the benefits of chivalry offered to them.

The corollary to the chivalry hypothesis, the "evil-woman hypothesis," is reserved for females who commit serious offenses. Because chivalrous treatment of murderers and child abusers would be deemed inappropriate for serious offenders and because females who commit these types of offenses quickly fall out of the traditional gender stereotype, the justice system treats them more harshly.[80]

The point in the juvenile justice system at which sex discrimination occurs is an important concern for those who want to unravel how bias is subtly introduced into the process. Criminal and juvenile justice officials use discretion at many points in the system, and it's necessary to look at each point at which females are processed to see if there is differential handling of offenders based on gender. Here we will take a look at areas in which discretion is exercised.

» **Decisions made by law enforcement officers.** The police are the first contact a girl has with the juvenile justice system. She is likely to be treated differently than a boy in two ways. First, she is likely to be questioned about her sexual activities. Running away from home, incorrigibility, curfew violation, and such are considered status offenses, and girls who violate them are likely to be held to a different standard than boys.[81] Because a girl is more likely to be a victim of sexual offenses, she's dealt with more severely when she commits a status offense, such as running away, that could expose her to victimization. Although the police officer might mean well in the desire to protect the girl, the result is actually blaming and punishment. The second way in which a girl might be treated differently is the sexual exploitation and sexual abuse sometimes committed by police officers. According to Kraska and Kappeler, some police officers will exploit females when they follow them from a party or bar and offer to exchange overlooking a DUI or other offense for sexual favors.[82] The females most often confronted with such dilemmas are young and impoverished.[83]

» **Predisposition court decisions.** A number of decisions are made before a case goes before the judge. Many of these decisions can determine the outcome of the case. Other decisions, such as granting conditional release, reflect the attitudes and opinions of court workers toward the dangerousness and vulnerability of the juvenile. Although in past decades girls were more likely to be released to their parents than boys, this has changed since 1985.[84] One study found that girls were increasingly referred to juvenile courts from 1985 to 1997, and more of their cases were formally processed and adjudicated.[85]

» **Disposition.** At one time, girls were more likely to get probation and boys were more likely to be sentenced to detention. This was considered a sign of paternalism and chivalrousness by the courts. In recent decades, however, research has found that girls receive more punitive treatment than boys. Compared to boys, girls adjudicated delinquent were far more likely to be committed to a residential correctional facility. They were also more likely to be committed for status offenses and technical violations of probation, and were committed to facilities at much younger ages than boys.[86] Paradoxically, this might be a sign of the same sort of old-style court paternalism, just applied in a different way. That is, the court no longer entrusts the parents with the girls' rehabilitation and, in an effort to protect the girl, moves in earlier and with harsher dispositions than it does for boys.

This disparity of treatment, it may be argued, is simply a reflection of society's values and the perception that girls are more vulnerable than boys and need greater protection. However, in a system in which the ideal is to be free of bias based on gender, race, and social class, this differential treatment is considered a serious problem. What is most remarkable here, however, is the idea that there are good reasons to treat delinquents differently according to gender. There are far fewer female delinquents than male; girls commit less serious delinquency than boys, and privacy concerns dictate that they have separate facilities. Feminist scholars strive to ensure that the differential treatment doesn't remain invisible and that the juvenile justice system operates in ways that don't simply reflect traditional gender roles but instead promote justice for females, the poor, and people of color.[87]

Questions

1. What is the chivalry hypothesis?
2. Should female delinquency be treated as seriously as that of males?
3. What issues do girls face at the different discretion points in the juvenile justice system?

>> FOCUS ON ETHICS

Sex Talk

You are a single parent with 15-year-old twins. They're approaching the age and emotional maturity of youngsters who begin to think about the opposite sex, dating, and all the other issues you have neglected to consider because you really don't want to talk to them about adult topics. However, because you found a condom in your daughter's sock drawer, you know the time has come to have that "sex talk" with them.

As twins, your son and daughter are much alike in some ways and different in others. They're wonderful kids who do well in school, stay out of trouble, and provide you with emotional support since your spouse died four years ago. Until recently, they have been best friends and have always done things with the same group of peers.

Now, however, your daughter has started to attract the interest of older boys. She's streaking ahead of your son in her social and physical development, and this has started to concern you.

Her 18-year-old boyfriend isn't someone you would have picked for her. Although he seems like a nice and respectful young man, his life's ambition is to be a drummer in a rock band. He already has all the tattoos, body piercings, and raggedy clothes that make him look the part, but he has a problem in not being able to keep a beat. His band kicked him out because of his poor playing, and now he sulks around your house all day. Your daughter has fallen for his "woe is me" attitude and fancies herself as the only one who sees his hidden genius.

Your son has come to you and complained about how this "loser" has brainwashed your daughter and how he wants him out of the house because he's eating everything in sight. Your son further informs you that the young man and your daughter spend a lot of time in her bedroom behind a locked door. Although you have known this day was going to come, you are uncertain about how to proceed.

WHAT DO YOU DO?

1. Sit your daughter down and have that difficult talk about sex; you provide her with the scientific facts and make her aware of your expectations. Give your son the same talk about sex even though he seems to be a year or two from developing his own interest in girls.

2. Tell her to dump the boyfriend. Lay down the law of the house, and inform her she isn't to entertain males in her bedroom when you aren't home.

3. Do nothing and let her find her own way in the world. She is a good child, and you want to show her that you have confidence in her decisions.

4. Tell your son to stay out of your daughter's business.

Summary

Learning Objective 1. Explain how research typically focuses on males and is then applied to females.	Males have long been considered the norm, and, until recently, research has been done almost exclusively on males. The assumption was that males, being legally empowered and physically stronger, were the standard by which issues were evaluated, and females were an extension of males.
Learning Objective 2. Compare and contrast the basic differences between the female and male maturation processes.	he greatest differences in the maturation of girls and boys don't appear until adolescence. Girls typically experience growth, develop pubic hair and breasts, and begin menstruation before or at the age of 14, whereas boys lag until 16 before realizing any major physical changes. For boys, an early-developing body may mean they excel at sports sooner than their peers. They might also engage in delinquency Tsooner because they associate with older boys who are their size. For girls, early

Learning Objective 2. (continued)	development may mean that older boys seek them out for dates. Late-maturing boys aren't as tall as their contemporaries and therefore aren't considered to be as physically attractive. For girls, late maturity means they may be overlooked in the dating scene and thus feel undesirable. However, when they do finally mature, later, they may experience fewer emotional problems.
Learning Objective 3. Illustrate how female delinquency is different from that of males.	Females don't show up in the crime statistics at the same rate as males for two reasons: (1) females break the law far less than males, and (2) the justice system treats them differently. Female delinquency patterns are different across age, type, and seriousness, and tend to be less common and less persistent.
Learning Objective 4. Explain the relationship between early puberty and female delinquency.	Six factors affect early puberty: heredity, weight and weight-to-height ratio, stressful events, family relations, presence of an adult male in the home, and psychological adjustment. Several things can cause stress for girls, including maternal psychopathology, an absent father, parental rejection, presence of a stepfather, unstable parental bonds, insecurity and mistrust within the family, malnourishment, and poverty. Lifestyle changes related to early puberty may also lead to delinquency. As described by the "maturation disparity hypothesis," early-maturing girls are more eager to seek out adult status, independence, and possibly an escape from a difficult home life. Early-maturing girls may associate with older males who are already well into delinquency or criminal offending. School bonding and academic performance are likely to suffer, and peer relationships are likely to change as the girl drifts toward friends who may be in independent, adult-oriented, delinquent-associated peer groups.
Learning Objective 5. Describe the contribution of labeling theory to explaining female delinquency.	Primary deviance, the label put on a youth by parents, teachers, peers, or the courts, tags a girl with the label of "tramp," "slut," or "thief," and, consequently, others treat her that way. When the girl internalizes the label (secondary deviance), she believes it accurately describes her, and she acts in the way she believes others see her.
Learning Objective 6. Describe the contribution of life-course theory to explaining female delinquency.	According to some life-course research, motherhood can bring some young women out of delinquent trajectories. Researchers speculate that motherhood is an effective turning point for three reasons: (1) the identity of being a mother and caring for a child become more important than anything else; (2) the risk of arrest is too great, and the effect it would have on the child too serious; and (3) the young women stay at home more often and refrain from partying, because to do so is to be a good mother. Although motherhood doesn't protect all young women from further delinquency and crime—some women do continue deviant lives—children seem to motivate them to continue trying to change their lives.
Learning Objective 7. List the five features of Daly and Chesney-Lind's work in feminist criminology.	(1) Gender isn't a natural fact but a complex social, historical, and cultural product; it's related to, but not simply derived from, biological and sex differences and reproductive capabilities. (2) Gender and gender relations order social life and social institutions in fundamental ways. (3) Gender relations and constructs of masculinity and femininity aren't symmetrical but are based on an organizing principle of men's superiority and social and political-economic dominance over women. (4) Systems of knowledge reflect men's views of the natural and social world. The production of knowledge is gendered. (5) Women should be at the center of intellectual inquiry, not peripheral, invisible, or appendages to men.

Summary

Learning Objective 8. Discuss Curran and Renzetti's explanation of the three feminist perspectives by which female crime and delinquency can be understood.	(1) Liberal feminism. Liberal feminists make two critiques about how gender influences crime and delinquency. The first argues that men control power and privilege in society. The second critique concerns how boys and girls are socialized into adult roles. (2) Radical feminism. Radical feminists would wipe out many of the patriarchal structures that put women at such a disadvantage in obtaining positions of power and in controlling their own destinies. (3) Socialist feminism. Because impoverished women don't have access to power, their concerns are overlooked and neglected.
Learning Objective 9. Explain what may happen to female delinquents at critical points in the justice system.	(1) Decisions made by law enforcement officers. A female is likely to be treated differently than a male in two ways. First, she is likely to be questioned about her sexual activities. Second, she may be sexually exploited or abused by the officers themselves. (2) Predisposition court decisions. One study found that girls were increasingly referred to juvenile courts from 1985 to 1997, and more of their cases were formally processed and adjudicated. (3) Disposition. Compared to boys, girls adjudicated delinquent were more likely to be committed to a residential correctional facility. They were also more likely to be committed for status offenses and technical violations of probation, and were committed to facilities at much younger ages than boys.
Learning Objective 10. State some reasons the juvenile justice system treats girls differently.	There are far fewer female delinquents than male; females commit less serious delinquency than males, and females must have separate facilities from males. This means the justice system has fewer alternatives for processing and sentencing girls.

Chapter Review Questions

1. In what ways has the study of female delinquency been historically neglected?
2. How do males and females develop differently both biologically and cognitively?
3. Why do girls have more problems with self-esteem than boys?
4. What is the delinquency rate of females as opposed to males?
5. How did Lombroso consider female offending?
6. In what ways is early puberty for females related to delinquency?
7. How can labeling theory be applied to female delinquency?
8. According to life-course theories, how do females have different turning points in their lives that may be related to delinquency?
9. According to Curran and Renzetti, how can criminal offending be understood from feminist perspectives?
10. What is relabeling? What is upcriming?

Key Terms

adolescent egocentrism—The belief common to many adolescents that they are the focus of attention in social situations.

metacognition—The act of thinking about one's processes and means of thinking.

sex—The biological designation of male or female.

social ecology—The study of the relationships between people, their behavior, their social groups, and their environment.

Endnotes

1 Claire M. Renzetti, "On the Margins of the Mainstream (or, They Still Don't Get It, Do They?): Feminist Analysis in Criminal Justice Education," *Journal of Criminal Justice Education* 4 (1993): 219–249.

2 Carol Travis, *The Mismeasure of Woman* (New York: Touchstone Books, 1992).

3 Roslyn Muraskin, "Ain't I a Woman?," in Roslyn Muraskin, ed., *It's a Crime: Women and Justice*, 3rd ed. (Upper Saddle River, NJ: Prentice Hall, 2003), 3–11.

4 Federal Bureau of Investigation, *Crime in the United States, 1995*, Table 33: Total Arrest Trends, Sex, 1986–1995, www.fbi.gov/about-us/cjis/ucr/crime-in-the-u.s/1995/95sec4.pdf. Federal Bureau of Investigation, *Crime in the United States, 2009*, Table 33: Ten-Year Arrest Trends by Sex, 2000–2009, www2.fbi.gov/ucr/cius2009/data/table_33.html.

5 Tony Jefferson and Pat Carden, eds., "Masculinities, Social Relations and Crime," *British Journal of Criminology* 36 (1996): 337–444.

6 James W. Messerschmidt, *Masculinities and Crime: Critique and Reconceptualization of Theory* (Lanham, MD: Rouman and Littlefield, 1993).

7 Judith Lorber, *Paradoxes of Gender* (New Haven, CT: Yale University Press, 1994).

8 On December 1, 1956, Alain Mimoun O'Kacha of France won the men's Olympic marathon in Melbourne, Australia, with a time of 2:25:00. On September 24, 2000, Naoko Takahashi of Japan won the women's Olympic marathon in Sydney, Australia, with a time of 2:23:14. See MarathonGuide.com at www.marathonguide.com/history/records/index.cfm.

9 Robert S. Feldman, *Child Development*, 3rd ed. (Upper Saddle River, NJ: Prentice Hall, 2004).

10 Ibid., 413.

11 Jodee McCaw and Charlene Y. Senn, "Perception of Cues in Conflictual Dating Situations," *Violence Against Women* 4 (1998): 609–624.

12 A. C. Petersen, "Those Gangly Years," *Psychology Today* (September 1998): 28–34.

13 H. M. Wellman and S. A. Gelman, "Cognitive Development: Foundational Theories of Core Domains," Annual Review of Psychology 43 (1992): 337–375.

14 C. Lightfoot, The Culture of Adolescent Risk-Taking (New York: Guilford Press, 1997).

15 J. J. Arnett, "Adolescent Storm and Stress, Reconsidered," American Psychologist 54 (1999): 314–326.

16 R. H. Aseltine, Jr., S. Gore, and M. E. Colten, "Depression and the Social Developmental Con-text of Adolescence," Journal of Personality and Social Psychology 67 (1994): 252–263.

17 B. Byrne, "Relationships between Anxiety, Fear, Self-Esteem, and Coping Strategies in Ado-lescence," Adolescence 35 (2000): 201–215.

18 Feldman, Child Development, 416–418.

19 Naomi Wolff, *The Beauty Myth: How Images of Beauty Are Used against Women* (New York: Random House, 1991).

20 Wayne Wooden and Randy Blazch, *Renegade Kids, Suburban Outlaws: From Youth Culture to Delinquency*, 2nd ed. (Belmont, CA: Wadsworth, 2000).

21 Thomas P. George and Donald P. Hartmann, "Friendship Networks of Unpopular, Average, and Popular Children," *Child Development* 67 (1996): 2301–2316.

22 J. K. Skipper and G. Nass, "Dating Behavior: A Framework of Analysis and an Illustration," *Journal of Marriage and Family* 28 (1966): 412–420.

23 Grace Palladino, *Teenagers: An American History* (New York: Basic Books, 1996).

24 I. M. Schwartz, "Sexual Activity Prior to Coital Interaction: A Comparison between Males and Females," *Archives of Sexual Behavior* 28 (1999): 63–69.

25 J. S. Hyde, *Understanding Human Sexuality*, 5th ed. (New York: McGraw-Hill, 1994).

26 William Strauss and Neil Howe, *Generations: The History of America's Future, 1584–2069* (New York: Morrow, 1991).

27 J. G. Smetana, "Adolescents' and Parents' Reasoning about Actual Family Conflict," *Child Development* 60 (1989): 1052–1067.

28 Kimberly Kempf-Leonard and Paul E. Tracy, "Gender Differences in Delinquency Career Types and the Transition to Adult Crime," in Roslyn Muraskin, ed., *It's a Crime: Women and Justice*, 3rd ed. (Upper Saddle River, NJ: Prentice Hall, 2003), 544–569.

29 N. Fontaine et al., "Research Review: A Critical Review of Studies on the

Summary

Developmental Trajectories of Antisocial Behavior in Females," *Journal of Child Psychology and Psychiatry* 50 (2009): 363–385.

30 Meda Chesney-Lind and Randall G. Shelden, *Girls, Delinquency and Juvenile Justice*, 3rd ed. (Belmont, CA: Wadsworth, 2004), 40–43.

31 Kimberly J. Mitchell, David Finkelhor, and Janis Wolak, "Conceptualizing Juvenile Prostitution as Child Maltreatment: Findings from the National Juvenile Prostitution Study," *Child Maltreatment* 15, no. 1 (February 2010): 18–36.

32 Kimberly Kotrla, "Domestic Minor Sex Trafficking in the United States," *Social Work* 55, no. 2 (April 2010): 181–187.

33 Sarah E. Twill, Denise M. Green, and Amy Traylor, "A Descriptive Study on Sexually Exploited Children in Residential Treatment," *Child Youth Care Forum* 39 (2010): 187–199.

34 Mitchell, Finkelhor, and Wolak, "Conceptualizing Juvenile Prostitution as Child Maltreatment."

35 Stephanie Halter, "Factors That Influence Police Conceptualizations of Girls Involved in Prostitution in Six U.S. Cities: Child Sexual Exploitation Victims or Delinquents?" *Child Maltreatment* 15, no. 2 (May 2010): 152–160.

36 Mitchell, Finkelhor, and Wolak, "Conceptualizing Juvenile Prostitution as Child Maltreatment."

37 Kotrla, "Domestic Minor Sex Trafficking in the United States."

38 Ronald Chilton and Susan K. Datesman, "Gender, Race, and Crime: An Analysis of Urban Trends," *Gender and Society* 1 (1987): 152–171.

39 However, it's important to note that the research shows that males shoplift more than females. See Chesney-Lind and Shelden (see note 30), p. 101.

40 Rachel Simmons, *Odd Girl Out: The Hidden Culture of Aggression in Girls* (New York: Harcourt, 2002).

41 Jody Miller, *One of the Guys: Girls, Gangs, and Gender* (New York: Oxford University Press, 2001).

42 Federal Bureau of Investigation, *Crime in the United States, 2009*, Table 39: Arrests Males, by Age, 2009, and Table 40: Arrests Females, by Age, 2009, www2.fbi.gov/ucr/cius2009/arrests/index.html.

43 Kathleen M. Heide et al., "Male and Female Juvenile Homicide Offenders: An Empirical Analysis of U.S. Arrests by Offender Age," *Feminist Criminology* 6 (2011): 3–31.

44 Cesare Lombroso and William Ferrero, *The Female Offender* (London: Fisher Unwin, 1895).

45 Carol Smart, *Women, Crime and Criminology: A Feminist Critique* (London: Routledge and Kegan Paul, 1976).

46 Anthony Walsh, *Biosocial Criminology: Introduction and Integration* (Cincinnati, OH: Anderson, 2002), 210–212.

47 Diana Fishbein et al., "Biopsychological Factors, Gender, and Delinquency," in Margaret A. Zahn, ed., *The Delinquent Girl* (Philadelphia: Temple University Press, 2009), 84–106.

48 Ibid.

49 Ibid.

50 K. Paige Harden and Jane Mendle, "Gene-Environment Interplay in the Association Between Pubertal Timing and Delinquency in Adolescent Girls," *Journal of Abnormal Psychology* (June 2011). Advance online publication.

51 Ibid.

52 Avshalom Caspi et al., "Unraveling Girls' Delinquency: Biological, Dispositional, and Contextual Contributions to Adolescent Misbehavior," *Developmental Psychology* 32 (1993): 631–635.

53 Fishbein et al., "Biopsychological Factors, Gender, and Delinquency."

54 Christine Rasche, "The Female Offender as an Object of Criminological Research," in A. M. Brodsky, ed., *The Female Offender* (Beverly Hills, CA: Sage), 9–28.

55 W. I. Thomas, *The Unadjusted Girl* (New York: Harper and Row, 1967).

56 Otto Pollak, *The Criminality of Women* (Philadelphia: University of Pennsylvania Press, 1950).

57 Dorie Klein, "The Etiology of Female Crime: A Review of the Literature," in S. K. Datesman and F. R. Scarpitti, eds., *Women, Crime, and Justice* (New York: Oxford University Press, 1980), 70–105.

58 Joanne Belknap, *The Invisible Woman: Gender, Crime, and Justice* (Belmont, CA: Wadsworth, 2001), 4.

59 Chesney-Lind and Shelden, *Girls, Delinquency and Juvenile Justice*, 107–118.

60 Edwin Schur, *Labeling Women Deviant* (New York: Random House, 1984).

61 Derek A. Kreager, Ross L. Matsueda, and Elena A. Erosheva, "Motherhood and Criminal Desistance in Disadvantaged Neighborhoods," *Criminology* 48, no. 1 (February 2010): 221–258.

62 Charlotte Lyn Bright, Sara K. Ward, and Nalini Junko Negi, "'The Chain Has to Be Broken': A Qualitative Investigation of the Experiences of Young Women Following Juvenile Court Involvement," *Feminist Criminology* 6, no. 1 (2011): 32–53.

63 Chesney-Lind and Shelden, *Girls, Delinquency and Juvenile Justice*, 119.

64 Kathleen Daly and Meda Chesney-Lind, "Feminism and Criminology," *Justice Quarterly* 5 (1984): 497–538.

65 Martin D. Schwartz and Dragan Milovanovic, *Race, Gender, and Class in Criminology: The Intersection* (New York: Garland, 1996).

66 Jody Miller and Christopher W. Mullins, "The States of Feminist Theories in Criminology," in Francis T. Cullen, John Paul Wright, and Kristie R. Blevins, eds., *Taking Stock: The Status of Criminological Theory* (New Brunswick, NJ: Transaction, 2006), 217–249.

67 Daniel J. Curran and Claire M. Renzetti, *Theories of Crime*, 2nd ed. (Boston: Allyn and Bacon, 2001), 209–228.

68 Federal Bureau of Investigation, *Crime in the United States, 2009*, Table 33: Ten-Year Arrest Trends by Sex, 2000–2009, www2.fbi.gov/ucr/cius2009/data/table_33.html. Federal Bureau of Investigation, *Crime in the United States, 2000*, Table 38: Arrests by Age, 2000, www.fbi.gov/about-us/cjis/ucr/crime-in-the--u.s/2000/00sec4.pdf.

69 Barry C. Feld, "Violent Girls or Relabeled Status Offenders? An Alternative Interpretation of the Data," *Crime and Delinquency* 55 (2009): 241–265.

70 K. H. Federle, "The Institutionalization of Female Delinquency," *Buffalo Law Review* 48 (2000): 881–908.

71 Meda Chesney-Lind and Katherine Irwin, *Beyond Bad Girls: Gender, Violence and Hype* (New York: Routledge, 2008), 28–29.

72 Miller and Mullins, "The States of Feminist Theories in Criminology," 228–242.[73]

73 Peggy Giordano, Stephen A. Cherkovich, and Jennifer Rudolf, "Gender, Crime, and Desistance: Toward a Theory of Cognitive Transformations," *American Journal of Sociology* 107 (2002): 990–1064.

74 Mary E. Gilfus, "From Victims to Survivors to Offenders: Women's Routes of Entry into Street Crime," *Women and Criminal Justice* 4 (1992): 63–89.

75 Sally Simpson and Lori Ellis, "Doing Gender: Sorting Out the Caste and Crime Conundrum," *Criminology* 33 (1995): 47–81.

76 Lisa Maher, *Sexed Work: Gender, Race, and Resistance in a Brooklyn Drug Market* (Oxford, UK: Clarendon Press, 1997).

77 Nguine Naffine, "Towards Justice for Girls: Rhetoric and Practice in the Treatment of Status Offenders," *Women and Criminal Justice* 1 (1989): 3–20.

78 Deborah Curran, "Judicial Discretion and Defendant's Sex," *Criminology* 21 (1983): 41–58.

79 Belknap, *The Invisible Woman*, 133.

80 Christy A. Visher, "Gender, Police Arrest Decisions, and Notions of Chivalry," *Criminology* 21 (1983): 5–28.

81 Ibid.

82 Peter Kraska and Victor Kappeler, "To Serve and Pursue: Exploring Police Sexual Violence Against Women," *Justice Quarterly* 12 (March 1995): 85–111.

83 Marvin Krohn, James P. Curry, and Shirley Nelson-Kilger, "Is Chivalry Dead? An Analysis of Changes in Police Dispositions of Males and Females," *Criminology* 21 (1983): 417–437.

84 Katherine S. Teilmann and Pierre H. Landry, "Gender Bias in Juvenile Justice," *Journal of Research in Crime and Delinquency* 18 (1981): 47–80.

85 Paul E. Tracy, Kimberly Kempf-Leonard, and Stephanie Abramoske-James, "Gender Differences in Delinquency and Juvenile Justice Processing: Evidence from National Data," *Crime & Delinquency* 55 (2009): 171–215.

86 Ibid.

87 K. H. Federle and Meda Chesney-Lind, "Special Issues in Juvenile Justice; Gender, Race, and Ethnicity," in I. M. Schwartz, ed., *Juvenile Justice and Public Policy: Toward a National Agenda* (New York: Macmillan, 1992), 165–195.

The Family and Delinquency

The family is the most basic institution. Although the economic system, religion, and government have varied greatly over the centuries, the family has remained the most stable institution. All societies and cultures have families, but the institution of the family has undergone some changes of its own. Today, we tend to idealize the family as a unit consisting of the biological parents and their immediate offspring. However, this isn't the dominant type of family in either the United States or the world.[1]

The type of family we consider to be traditional is really a modern adaptation to the industrial age.[2] It requires that a married couple exclude extended family members and concentrate on themselves and their children. This structure is supported by the lifestyle of an era in which houses are built without extra rooms to accommodate the couple's parents, their siblings, the "spinster" aunt, or the "confirmed-bachelor" uncle. The three-bedroom home ensures that the family lives without all the supporting members of the extended family. However, it's interesting to note that the postmodern family, which includes a number of variations on the traditional theme, is replacing the traditional American family and differs significantly from it. There is a proliferation of family types that include two-earner, single-parent, blended, gay, and cohabiting couples and couples without children.

With all these variations, it's a wonder that the term "family" has any objective meaning. It may mean a wide variety of living arrangements with a range of individuals who may or may not be related by blood or legal contract. Other institutions have been forced to adjust to the family's changing nature. Schools must include after-school programs for children who don't have a caregiver at home in the afternoon, many corporations provide health insurance for people who are only tangentially related, and the government must decide who can be legally married and enjoy the benefits of this legal status.

The family is significant to our study of delinquency because it's both a buffer against the influences that propel young people toward antisocial behavior and a source of antisocial behavior in its own right. The family is a place where young

We tend to idealize the family as a unit consisting of the biological parents and their immediate offspring. The Huxtable family from *The Cosby Show* in the 1980s and 1990s is an example of such an idealized family on television.

The postmodern family, which includes a number of variations on the traditional theme, is replacing the traditional American family and differs significantly from it.

people can be both protected and victimized. Although we often talk in a romantic way about family values and the long-lasting positive influences of coming from a good home, the family can also be a place where young people are neglected, exploited, or abused.[3] Even for children who aren't victims of family violence, the context in which they grow up might contribute to their being antisocial and dysfunctional individuals. For example, racism, social inequality, poverty, and language barriers can all negatively affect children. To fully understand delinquency, we must look at the history, structure, and function of the family and its relationship to delinquency.

Functions of the Family

Society invests important functions in the family. In fact, we may expect too much from families. In an age when there is a tension between our freedoms and government intervention, a decided bias exists toward keeping government out of our lives and allowing individuals the chance to direct their own destinies. Historically, society has believed that "a man's home is his castle." This has meant that the husband and father has been the lord of the household with complete discretion in how he treats his family. Over time, this complete authority has been challenged, and the government has stepped in to correct abuses and ensure that women and children have rights and opportunities.

This government intervention isn't complete, and dominant males still have a great deal of latitude to rule the household, but we have come to realize there is more to being a family than simply allowing the husband and father to dictate the terms of family life.[4] Because the family is such a primary institution, it's expected to fulfill certain obligations in meeting its members' needs. Strong

Learning Objective 1.

Tell why the traditional, Western nuclear family isn't the most common type of family.

Learning Objective 2.

Discuss the effects of poverty on parenting.

Learning Objective 3.

Go over Wallace's differences between parents who neglect their children and parents who don't.

Learning Objective 4.

List the four types of injuries common to physical child abuse.

Learning Objective 5.

Explain the connection between child sexual abuse and the power relationship between adults and children.

families help protect children from delinquency.[5] When the family fails to do this, other institutions, including the juvenile justice system, must step in to ensure these functions are accomplished. The important functions of the family can be summarized by the following:

» **To raise children responsibly.** Human beings have a long period in their life cycle in which they're dependent on their parents and during which parents must pass on necessary skills and values. Unlike many species in the animal kingdom, for whom parenthood ends at birth or shortly thereafter, human beings invest many years and considerable physical and emotional energy into preparing their young to survive on their own. The first task is to socialize the children into the culture's prescribed ways of doing the work of society and finding their role and identity in the world. During this socialization process, children must learn the values and skills that enable them to fit into their social context. For instance, a child must learn to share with others, pull his or her own weight in economic and social endeavors, and fulfill a variety of demands from family, peers, and society. Another function the family must perform is to provide children with a set of moral values consistent with social norms and laws.[6] Ideally, children learn the values of honesty, hard work, respect for others, and responsibility. Although it's true that the church, school, and other institutions contribute to children's acquisition of moral values, these values are first modeled and taught in families. Included in these moral values is the appropriate way of expressing sexual desires and engaging in the reproduction of the species. By the age of 18, the youth should be ready to engage in responsible sexual activity that will result in her or his own family.

» **To provide economic support.** At one time, this was the family's primary function. Long ago, in fact, the family was the sole unit of economic production in society and was essentially self-sufficient. It provided food, clothing, and shelter for its members and protected them from other groups. Today, family members support each other and pool their resources into shared household finances to provide for the necessities of life and to save for the future when they won't be so economically productive. Additionally, family members provide for each other when one gets sick and needs to be cared for or transported to the doctor. Therefore, it's the family one generally first turns to for economic and material support. This support is shared, and it isn't a commodity as it might be with friends and acquaintances. An individual supports family members because they need it, not because he or she expects to be paid back.[7]

» **To provide emotional support.** As children struggle to find their place in the world, they turn to their families for the unconditional positive regard that enables them to weather life's inevitable storms. Throughout childhood and adolescence, young people require the emotional support of family members when stiff competition, high obstacles, or disappointments challenge them. Ideally, family members can be counted on to stick by one another whether one is right or wrong, and although there might be severe disagreements between family members, the family puts on a united face to the rest of the world. This is true to varying extents for most families. Certainly, family members can tire of the ne'er-do-well who continually takes advantage of the family's trust and resources. At times, stress within the family can sap more emotional energy than the family can support; but, for the most part, the family is a reliable provider of emotional support and love.

Can the family perform all these functions? The answer is yes, to some extent. Although there are wide variations in how well families live up to these expectations, it's assumed that all families attempt to fulfill these important roles. However, many families are prevented from being successful. For instance, some families have fewer economic and social resources than others to do this work. Also, there is an issue of changing gender roles in which husbands and wives, or parents and children, may not agree on the proper roles for males and females. Finally, there is the concern of family violence.[8] Instead of being the solution to that problem, the family might be the source.

It's important to realize that variations in social class, race, and ethnic identity can make families perform differently in attempting to accomplish these functions.[9] Again, we're faced with the illusion of the idealized family, and it's difficult but necessary to consider the vast differences in how families function. This leads to the issue of how families are structured. The number of individuals in the family and the roles they carve out for themselves can greatly influence the family's dynamics.

Challenges in Families Today

Many challenges that families face today differ from the problems that influenced family life in the past. Perhaps the most basic concern that confronts families today is that of structure and stability. In the past, there were limits on what families could do when faced with a crisis. Marriage was considered a permanent union, and those who sought to dissolve the arrangement were met with negative sanctions by society. Divorce could mean the end of a promising career for men, social devaluation for women, and abject poverty for children. Couples stayed together because they believed it was in their children's best interests. Today, couples are much quicker to end an unsuccessful marriage and seek their happiness elsewhere. There is no longer a severe social cost to divorce, and society is generally more tolerant of alternative family structures. In lieu of the traditional intact nuclear family, today's families come in an assortment of structures.[10]

》 **Single-parent families.** Single-parent families can be either male headed or female headed. In terms of children (recall that not all households have

Today, couples are much quicker to end an unsuccessful marriage. There is no longer a severe social cost to divorce, and society is generally more tolerant of alternative family structures.

children), 23 percent live with their mother only and 3 percent live with their father only (see Figure 8.1). These figures can be misleading, however, because they don't reflect the situation in which other adults may live in the home, such as grandparents or other relatives, or the common arrangement in which mothers or fathers live in another household. The reasons for a single-parent family are many, and we must be cautious about lumping such families together. Some single-parent families are the result of a divorce. The divorce may have been traumatic and may have deeply scarred the parents and children, or it may have been amicable, with everyone adjusted to the new living arrangement.[11] Divorce doesn't necessarily mean that the family suffered debilitating trauma. The single-parent family might be the result of a sexual union in which the father is unknown or has abandoned his responsibilities. The single-parent family may also be the result of the death of a parent, leaving the other to raise the children. Although a single-parent family departs from the nuclear-family ideal, it can't be automatically assumed that it's dysfunctional or an inferior type of family. Many single-parent families succeed in accomplishing the functions of family life. Although single-parent families are found at all levels of economic class, those with sufficient wealth and income have a better time of overcoming the problems of having only one parent.[12] From a delinquency point of view, it's assumed that having both parents at home helps keep children out of trouble if both parents present positive role models and each spends time with the children.

» **Cohabitating parents.** Some families include two adults who live together without being formally married.[13] These unions might contain the children of one or both of the partners from a previous relationship that might or might not have been a marriage. Often, this cohabitation is a prelude to a formal marriage, but the couple also might continue in the relationship for

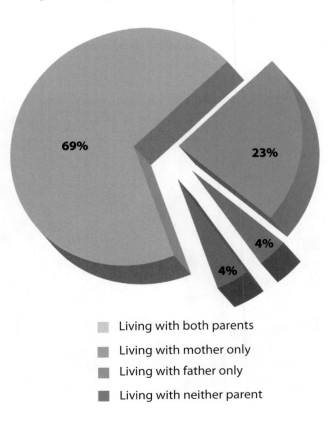

Figure 8.1 Household Relationship and Living Arrangements of Children, Under 18 Years, 2010

These figures don't include other types of households, such as nonchild households or post-child-rearing married couples or people living alone. It also doesn't distinguish between married and unmarried partners.

Think About It

1. Which living arrangement has the lowest percentage? Discuss reasons for this.

Source: US Census Bureau, America's Families and Living Arrangements: 2010, Table C2, www.census.gov/population/www/socdemo/hh-fam/cps2010.html.

69%

23%

4%

4%

☐ Living with both parents

☐ Living with mother only

■ Living with father only

■ Living with neither parent

many years without being formally married.[14] Many issues confront those who cohabitate, including health insurance, tax issues, and legal matters. Some agencies and businesses have policies prohibiting cohabitation, but, for the most part, these policies are difficult to enforce.

» **Blended families.** Blended families are typically composed of adults who bring their children from a former marriage to a new marriage. Blended families face a number of adjustment issues because the children must deal not only with a new adult in the home but also with other children whom they haven't grown up with. There is nothing intrinsically negative about blended families, but there is always a period in which the new family dynamics must be worked out, something that children can find particularly stressful. Adjusting to a stepparent is one challenge, but accommodating the needs and desires of other children who are also under the stress of change is often difficult. One way in which children manifest this stress is through rebellion and delinquency.[15]

» **Gay and lesbian families.** Gay and lesbian couples are families also. They might have children from previous heterosexual relationships, or they might adopt children or bear children by a surrogate parent. There is considerable debate about whether these families are suitable for raising children, but the reality is that they do raise children and that thousands of these families must confront the daily trials and tribulations of family life burdened with the negative attitudes of others.[16] Gay and lesbian families aren't immune from concerns such as family violence, and they may have the additional problem of dealing with many in society who are unsympathetic or even hostile to their situations. Children in these families might experience problems at school that range from embarrassment to harassment. It should also be noted that many of these children experience few or no problems as a result of their family structure.

These alternative family structures make it difficult to discuss the typical family because, counted together, the alternative structures outnumber traditional families. This makes for an interesting and difficult public policy debate. Should the school, church, and government devise policies based on the assumption that the family has a traditional structure? Does supporting families with these alternative structures encourage people to engage in relationships that deviate from the idealized family? Does society have an interest in shaping policies that benefit the traditional family structure and disadvantage alternative structures in an attempt to reduce divorce, make parents more responsible for the well-being of their children, and promote the idealized lifestyle? Regardless of how we answer these questions, the nature of the American family will continue to change, and the effect of family concerns on the delinquency of children will continue to be a challenge for those involved in schools, recreational programs, and the juvenile justice system.

Another major challenge to the family, in addition to the range of family structures, is concerned with parenting (see Prevention and Intervention for a look at a program designed to help young mothers raise healthy babies). A number of issues are of concern when discussing parents. The most fundamental issue is the entry barrier to becoming a parent. There is none. Anyone can become a parent regardless of his or her parenting skills, responsibility, maturity, sanity, motivation, criminal record, or economic resources. The right to reproduce is absolute, and society hasn't established a required educational program, fitness test, or maturity level that prospective parents must meet. The result is that there is great variation in the adequacy of parents.[17] Most are good, but some are so incompetent, clueless, and dangerous that society has to take away their children to prevent injury or death.

Society establishes a threshold for driving a car, flying a plane, trading on the stock market, and becoming a teacher. Yet adolescents who are barely out of childhood themselves are free to produce children they can't nurture, support, or guide. This is the major challenge faced by the juvenile justice system. The family isn't always a decent and safe place for children to grow up in, and it can set the child off on a trajectory toward delinquency.[18]

What does it take to be a good parent? This is a complex question, because families have multiple goals for their children. For our purposes here, we will concentrate on how parents might keep their children from delinquency. Sometimes, parents might go overboard in controlling their children. At least, good parenting requires the following tasks:

>> **Providing a positive role model.** The parent's influence on the child's behavior is crucial. Although many parents lecture their children on being truthful, dependable, and law-abiding, the parents' behavior often paints a different picture. Children are quick to see the contradictions between what parents say and what they do, and it's difficult for anyone to engage in entirely consistent behavior. Children get mixed messages when parents cheat, lie, or steal in some situations and not in others. In their efforts to teach their children how to survive in a competitive capitalist society, parents often inoculate their children with skills, values, and attitudes that test the boundaries of ethical and legal behavior.[19] There is no easy answer to dealing with matters of economic survival, and each parent struggles with striking a balance between making his or her children effective citizens and making them potential law violators.

>> **Encouraging productive behavior.** One role of parents is to ensure their children grow into responsible adults who will one day be self-sufficient and help to support other family members. During the productive working years, between the ages of 21 and 65, society expects adults to support themselves, pay taxes, and provide leadership in civic activities. Parents gradually socialize their children to take on these adult roles by encouraging productive behavior starting at an early age. Requiring a three-year-old to pick up her toys can take more work to enforce than it would for the parent to do it herself. However, keeping the child's room clean isn't as important as it is to instill in the child a sense of responsibility. This message is continued throughout childhood and can be a source of conflict between parents and children. During the adolescent years, young people must learn several crucial lessons before they're ready to engage in the full range of adult behavior. Adolescents must learn to make decisions on their own concerning activities such as driving a car, engaging in intimate relations, handling money, and solving problems and negotiating conflicts in ways that preserve and strengthen important relationships with family members, peers, and co-workers. Learning productive behavior as opposed to selfish, wasteful, or destructive behavior is a lifelong process that is shaped in early childhood by parents and adults who understand the value of teaching children responsibility, accountability, and the idea of serving others.[20]

>> **Engaging in adequate supervision.** Encouraging responsible and productive behavior is pointless unless the parent is prepared to supervise and make corrections when the child falls short of the goal. Providing adequate

8.1 PREVENTION AND INTERVENTION

Nurse-Family Partnership

Nurse-Family Partnership provides free registered nurses and training to low-income, first-time mothers. The average age of the mothers is 19. Only about half of them have a high school degree, and 88 percent are unmarried.[1] The program's developer, David Olds, designed the program to begin during pregnancy so babies could receive good prenatal care, and he asked nurses to make home visits so mothers wouldn't have to travel. Specifically, the program seeks to do the following:

» Improve pregnancies by teaching mothers how to get prenatal care, improve their diet, and reduce their use of cigarettes, alcohol, and drugs.

» Improve families' economic self-sufficiency by helping parents develop an economic vision, plan future pregnancies, continue their education, and find work.

The nurses may also provide other help as needed. In one case, a nurse helped a client with an abusive boyfriend find a new apartment and enroll in college.[2] Typically, the nurse begins visiting the mother twice a month during the first trimester and continues until the child is two years old. This is one of the most critical stages during a child's life, as basic brain functions related to vision, hearing, and language are developing.

The program, which costs about $4,500 per family per year, receives state and federal funding. It currently serves over 23,000 families and employs over 1,200 registered nurses. As of 2011, Nurse-Family Partnership operated in 32 states, including Alabama, Arizona, California, Colorado, Delaware, Florida, Illinois,

Nurse-Family Partnership provides free registered nurses and training to low-income, first-time mothers. In this photo, a nurse from Nurse-Family Partnership (left) meets with a baby girl's mother and grandmother.

Iowa, Kentucky, Louisiana, Maryland, Michigan, Minnesota, Missouri, Nevada, New Jersey, New York, North Carolina, North Dakota, Ohio, Oklahoma, Oregon, Pennsylvania, Rhode Island, South Carolina, South Dakota, Tennessee, Texas, Utah, Washington, Wisconsin, and Wyoming.[3]

THINK ABOUT IT

1. In your opinion, can good prenatal care and parent training help prevent delinquency? Why or why not?

[1] Fiona J. Kirk, "Return of the House Call," *The Daily*, www.thedaily.com/page/2011/07/19/071911-arts-health-nurse-family-partnership-1-2/.

[2] Ibid.

[3] Nurse-Family Partnership, www.nursefamilypartnership.org/.

supervision is tricky, because although heavy-handed oversight can make children follow directions, it fails to get them to think for themselves and to internalize the desired values of hard work, sacrifice, deferred gratification, and service. A child or employee who does good work only when there is a parent or boss standing around isn't effective. Although extensive supervision might be necessary early in a child's life when being responsible is a novel idea or when there is potential for harm, such as playing near a busy street, good supervision structures the situation so that the child is given the opportunity to apply the lessons learned.[21] Michel Foucault refers to the internalized grids of discipline that we unconsciously employ when we perform what we believe is the correct and appropriate behavior. According to Foucault, these grids of discipline can cause an oversocialization that can rob us of our creativity and humanity. For instance, when we criticize children for coloring outside the lines in an effort to teach them art skills, we also might be squeezing the artistic genius out of them and depriving society of the next Georgia O'Keeffe or Pablo Picasso.[22]

» **Instituting effective discipline.** Another task of parenting is discipline (see Focus on Diversity for a look at how cultures discipline children). The problem with discipline is that if it's done poorly, it can actually do more harm than good.[23] Ineffective discipline can be counterproductive because it sends the wrong message to children, which can be manifested in later years in a variety of ways, including delinquency, crime, and other deviant behaviors. Many individuals equate discipline with spanking. This seems like a reasonable and responsible way to address misbehavior, and it's administered by most parents with a sense of obligation and love. However, according to noted child authority Alice Miller, children don't experience spanking in the way adults mean for them to; hitting children begins a cycle by which they learn that violence is the way powerful people deal with the powerless.[24] Although we won't go into all the negative effects of spanking, it's worth noting here that some groups have advocated against the corporal punishment of children. If spanking isn't a good way to discipline children, then what should a parent do? A number of strategies are more effective than corporal punishment in both the short and long term in shaping children's behavior. At the core of these alternative methods of discipline is the establishment of a safe, supportive, and loving home in which children are nourished and nurtured.[25]

Parenting is a complex task and everyone does it differently. Even within families, parents can treat one child differently than another depending on age, sex, level of maturity, or birth order. Sometimes parents supervise their first children to a much greater degree than those who follow because the parents have become more confident in their own abilities, less afraid of the natural ups and downs of childhood, and better able to predict how younger children will respond.

Parents also have different resources available to them for their parenting tasks. Poverty greatly restrains the ability of parents to meet all the physical, psychological, and social needs of their children. Families living in poverty are more likely to have only one parent, lack health insurance, and have their children drop out of school. Problems caused by poverty have a cumulative effect on the family when the parents are required to work longer hours to support the children and thus deprive them of support and supervision.[26]

Impoverished families can be contrasted with those who are wealthy. Wealthy parents can purchase help in raising their children in the form of nannies, coaches, tutors, and babysitters. Instead of coming home to an empty apartment in a dangerous neighborhood, the children of wealthy parents might go to soccer practice one afternoon, violin lessons on another afternoon, a French tutor on a third afternoon, and yet other activities for the remaining days of the week. Although all this activity might be more beneficial than the circumstances of the impoverished child, it may still be problematic. Overscheduled children can lack the time to simply play with their friends. Additionally, children can be placed in positions in which they must constantly perform, whether it's on the piano or the soccer field or in school.[27]

Although both impoverished and wealthy parents love their children, they aren't always available to love them. Work obligations or social duties may require the parents to leave the children alone or place them in day care, an afternoon recreational program, or with a babysitter. Unfortunately, some children's

Parents Who Use the Rod in Cultures That Don't

It's fair to say that every culture considers how it controls and socializes children to be the "right way" to do so. Parents socialize and control their children much the way their parents socialized and controlled them. However, many child-rearing traditions have been put to the test in multicultural, multireligious American society.

Parents not only may be challenged about how they socialize and control their children, they may sometimes be punished themselves. This scenario has been repeated throughout US history with the settlement of various waves of immigrants. Immigrant parents have variously been considered too harsh in their discipline, and sanctioned for child abuse, and not harsh enough, and criticized for not controlling their children.

The development of the US juvenile justice system has created an interesting dynamic between the government, parents, and children. After the mid-20th century, the right of parents to treat their children as they saw fit was increasingly questioned. Some forms of physical punishment once tolerated by society became considered abuse. The government began to step into family situations in which violence was being used by one family member against another. Today, it's not unusual to hear of a child being removed from a home and placed in foster care because authorities deemed the physical punishment the child was receiving to have been too harsh.

Although spanking and other forms of striking children seems to be falling out of style in the United States, this attitude rankles not only many Americans from traditional cultures—including some religious and regional cultures—but also immigrants from traditional cultures around the world.[1] Here are some examples of how parents from some other cultures physically discipline children. Many of these parents consider some forms of American child rearing—such as yelling at children, not feeding children between meals, or letting infants cry themselves to sleep at night alone in their own rooms—as abusive.

》 In the Pacific Island nation of Palau, parents commonly tie a toddler's leg to a post or door when they can't supervise the child. Palau parents also use a broom to spank children, breaking the skin and leaving bruises.

Although many parents in the United States do not use spanking, some believe forms of discipline other than spanking are too permissive.

》 Some African women eschew anger, cursing, or screaming at a child—which they consider a form of child abuse—for a tap with a hand or a switch.

》 Korean immigrants to the United States have reported slapping the child's face or pulling the child's hair. Chinese immigrant parents may pinch their children, whereas Puerto Rican parents may place a toddler having a tantrum into a cold bath.[2]

In 2011, the publication of *Battle Hymn of the Tiger Mother* raised controversy as author Amy Chua described how she tried to get her seven-year-old daughter to perfect a piano piece by making her practice through dinner. Chua criticizes American-style parenting as too "soft" and focusing too much on the child's self-esteem.[3]

Observers point out it's true that American child raising focuses on individualism, whereas other cultures consider children as a more integral part of the family, their purpose being to carry on the family name, carry on cultural and religious traditions, and provide for parents in their old age. Family and community are so important in other cultures, parents worry they will "lose" their children to American culture, which values peers and individualism at least as much as the family.

THINK ABOUT IT

1. American parents have been criticized as not disciplining their children harshly enough. Do you agree or disagree?
2. Must children be spanked to learn how to act in society? Why or why not?

[1]Lisa Aronson Fontes, *Child Abuse and Culture: Working with Diverse Families* (New York: The Guilford Press, 2005), 113.
[2]Ibid., 116–117.
[3]Amy Chua, "Why Chinese Mothers Are Superior," *Wall Street Journal*, January 8, 2011, C1.

parents would rather be at the bar, country club, or racetrack having their own fun, rather than spending time with their children.

Challenges outside the family can also affect the likelihood of youths engaging in delinquency. Communities and neighborhoods can inadvertently pressure children into delinquency, or they can provide support and programs that shield children from the temptations of the street. In communities where drug sales flourish, youths are commonly employed as couriers because the juvenile justice system will penalize them less—or not at all, if they're young—if they're caught.[28]

Finally, challenges to the family have been increased over recent years by the reduction, or even removal, of the social safety net the government provides for those who experience temporary difficulty. For instance, in 1997 the federal aid available under the Aid to Families with Dependent Children (AFDC) ended and was replaced by the Temporary Assistance for Needy Families (TANF) program. The new legislation limited assistance to five years and required adults to begin working within two years. The intention was to get "welfare mothers" off public assistance and to decrease the number of female-headed households by removing the perceived incentive of receiving welfare for having children. However, research indicates that because of these women's lack of job skills and the lack of jobs in the community, the desired reform of welfare has yet to take place.[29]

Child Victimization in the Family

Because the family is such an important institution, we shouldn't be surprised that it's also a place where bad things happen along with the good. As Tolstoy reminds us, a family can be dysfunctional in many ways, with devastating effects on children.[30] All families are affected by outside forces, such as the quality of the neighborhood, the availability of jobs, and the availability of good schools. There are also sources of conflict within families that include its structure, problems of drug or alcohol abuse, and family violence. Understanding the functioning of families is important because among the most prominent risk factors for delinquency are poor parental supervision, punitive or erratic parental discipline, cold parental attitude, physical abuse, parental conflict, family disruption, antisocial parents, large family size, and low family income.[31] We'll start with three concerns that deeply influence children's quality of life.

First, we consider the issue of neglect. Some parents lack the skills to meet their children's needs, and some parents simply don't place a priority on their children's welfare because of problems of their own. Second, we look at the issue of physical child abuse, one of the greatest threats to a child's welfare and safety. Finally, we'll look at the issue of sexual child abuse. It seems almost ironic that the family, the presumed source of love and nurturing for children, can also be one of the most dangerous places for them.

CHILD NEGLECT

Child neglect is less visible than child abuse, so it's difficult to determine its exact prevalence in society. Although more child fatalities are caused by neglect only (see Figure 8.2), the common definition of child neglect isn't as well established as that of child abuse. One person might consider leaving a child alone at home after school to be neglect; another person might consider it a case of demonstrating to the child that he or she is trusted with personal responsibility. For our purposes here, we will adopt the definition used by criminologist Harvey Wallace, who states, "Child neglect is the negligent treatment or maltreatment of a child by a parent or caretaker under circumstances indicating

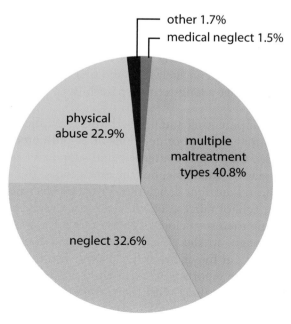

Figure 8.2 Child Abuse and Neglect Fatalities by Maltreatment Type, 2010

Fatal child abuse may involve repeated abuse over a period of time, or it may involve a single, impulsive incident. In cases of fatal neglect, the child's death results from a caregiver's failure to act. Like abuse, the neglect may be long-term, or it may be the result of a single incident.

Think About It

1. Discuss why neglect is such a pervasive form of child abuse.

Source: U.S. Department of Health and Human Services, Administration for Children and Families, Administration on Children, Youth and Families, Children's Bureau, *Child Maltreatment, 2010* (Washington, D.C.: U.S. Department of Health and Human Services, 2010), 71. Online at www.acf.hhs.gov/programs/cb/pubs/cm10/cm10.pdf.

harm or threatened harm to the child's health or welfare." This neglect, according to Wallace, runs a continuum from momentary inattention to gross action or inaction.[32]

Although we typically think of poverty as the best indicator of neglect, economic resources are a misleading measure. Children from extremely impoverished families can be well cared for emotionally and supported in all their endeavors, whereas children of wealthy parents can be made to feel that, despite their material opulence, they're unloved and ignored by their busy parents. How do parents who neglect their children differ from those who take good care of their children? Wallace suggests the following factors:

» **Inability to plan.** Some parents can't adequately plan for either the near- or long-term future. They don't establish goals, provide direction, or defer gratification. They lack a future orientation and live for the moment, which results in not having groceries for the week, clean clothes for school, or money for emergencies.

» **Lack of knowledge.** Many people have children when they're young and have little knowledge of how to run a household and meet the family's needs. Their skills at cooking, nurturing, and housekeeping can be limited. Having grown up eating fast food, they don't know how to cook a variety of nutritious foods and don't understand their children's emotional and psychological needs.

» **Lack of judgment.** Parents who neglect their children sometimes lack the judgment to decide at what age the children should be given responsibilities to look after themselves. By not setting curfews for young children, giving fast cars to young adolescents, or overlooking and condoning drug or alcohol use, some parents allow their children to enter dangerous situations in which they may injure themselves or others. These parents might reason that children need to be entrusted with the responsibility of learning to take care of themselves, and although they might be partially right, they thrust this burden on children too early and without adequate supervision.

» **Lack of motivation.** Some parents have given up on life themselves and have little interest in helping their children succeed. These parents might be more interested in their own drug or alcohol consumption, their favorite football team, or their own love life than they are in their children. At best, they might simply be clueless about their children's needs; at worst, they might consider their children to be a drain on their time and finances and resent the fact that, as parents, they have a long-term responsibility.[33]

What is the difference between poor parenting and neglect? This is a difficult question to answer. Although parents may make poor decisions or be indifferent to their children's needs in some areas, they may be attentive and supportive in others. The intentions of the parents may be honorable, but the execution of their plans might be haphazard, ineffective, and outright dangerous. Professionals who deal with children, such as teachers, school nurses, and recreational directors, constantly face judgment calls regarding their suspicions of child neglect.

Sometimes they notice subtle changes in the child's behavior, and sometimes it's clear the child isn't functioning at his or her full capacity. These professionals look for a number of clues before reporting cases of child neglect. For instance, children who don't physically grow along with their peers might lack proper nutrition. Of course, this single indicator is problematic because children go through growth spurts at different stages in their lives, so it's necessary to check for other indicators of neglect. Is the child constantly hungry, or are there indications of malnutrition? Does the child have lice, body odor, or old and torn clothing? Other indicators of physical child neglect include listlessness or falling asleep in class, and unattended medical needs, such as poor vision, dental problems, or lack of proper immunizations. If the child is left unattended for long periods of time or in situations of imminent danger, it may signal that the parents aren't adequately supervising the child.[34]

There are also a number of behavioral indicators of child neglect. The child may steal or beg for food because there aren't adequate meals at home. The child may be destructive to self or others and show extremes in behavior ranging from inactivity to aggressiveness. If the child assumes adult responsibilities for self or siblings, it may indicate a lack of responsible adult supervision at home. The child might exhibit hypochondria as a way of getting attention.[35] And, of course, delinquent behavior can be an indicator of child neglect. The Study of National Incidence and Prevalence of Child Abuse and Neglect has sought to standardize the definitions of the various forms of neglect (see Table 8.1). The following are some of the more common forms of child neglect:

Failure-to-Thrive Syndrome. Failure-to-thrive is a controversial issue. The symptoms might indicate a real medical problem rather than ineffective parenting. It's an identifiable medical diagnosis that classifies the child's physical development as deficient in relation to the established norms for children of that age. It might indicate a malfunction of one of the child's organs or a disease, or it might be the result of a nonorganic problem such as poor parenting. **Nonorganic failure-to-thrive** (NFTT) is indicated when the child is below the 20th percentile in both height and weight provided that the child was within the established norm at some point in her or his life. Children suffering from NFTT are physically emaciated, pale, and have little subcutaneous fat. Behaviorally, they appear listless and apathetic.

Still, a number of physical ailments might cause the same symptoms. Kidney disease, allergies, and congenital heart problems must be ruled out before NFTT can be diagnosed. The primary problem causing NFTT is lack of caloric intake, which can be reversed by adequate meals. School meal programs and policies such as replacing junk food with fruit in school vending machines are aimed at this problem. The problems originating from NFTT can be long-term even if the condition is eventually addressed and the symptoms disappear.[36]

Emotional Neglect. **Emotional neglect** in children is extremely hard to detect and even harder to prove. It's defined as "acts or omissions of acts that are judged by community standards and professional expertise to be psychologically damaging to the child."[37] Because emotional neglect leaves no marks, scars, bruises, or broken bones, the problems can go unrecognized by authorities, the parents, and the child. The parents might believe they're simply arming their children with emotional toughness when they overly criticize or demean their children's character and behavior, but in reality, the parents may be doing severe emotional damage that prevents their children from establishing a positive and healthy sense of self-esteem.

Emotional neglect can take several forms. One form is spurning or rejecting the child. Here the parent tells the child that he or she is stupid, worthless, and otherwise inadequate. Being compared unfavorably to siblings and having one's emotional needs ignored by parents can be extremely harmful to the child's sense of worth. A second type of emotional neglect consists of terrorizing the

TABLE 8.1 〉 Forms of Neglect

PHYSICAL NEGLECT

Refusal of Health Care	Failure to provide or allow needed care in accord with recommendations of a competent health care professional for a physical injury, illness, medical condition, or impairment.
Delay in Health Care	Failure to seek timely and appropriate medical care for a serious health problem which any reasonable layman would have recognized as needing professional medical attention.
Abandonment	Desertion of a child without arranging for reasonable care and supervision. This category included cases in which children were not claimed within 2 days, and when children were left by parents/substitutes who gave no (or false) information about their whereabouts.
Expulsion	Other blatant refusals of custody, such as permanent or indefinite expulsion of a child from the home without adequate arrangement for care by others, or refusal to accept custody of a returned runaway.
Other Custody Issues	Custody-related forms of inattention to the child's needs other than those covered by abandonment or expulsion. For example, repeated shuttling of a child from one household to another due to apparent unwillingness to maintain custody, or chronically and repeatedly leaving a child with others for days/weeks at a time.
Other Physical Neglect	Conspicuous inattention to avoidable hazards in the home; inadequate nutrition, clothing, or hygiene; and other forms of reckless disregard of the child's safety and welfare, such as driving with the child while intoxicated, leaving a young child unattended in a motor vehicle, and so forth.

SUPERVISION

Inadequate Supervision	Child left unsupervised or inadequately supervised for extended periods of time or allowed to remain away from home overnight without the parent/substitute knowing (or attempting to determine) the child's whereabouts.

EMOTIONAL NEGLECT

Inadequate Nurturance/Affection	Marked inattention to the child's needs for affection, emotional support, attention, or competence.
Chronic/Extreme Abuse Or Domestic Violence	Chronic or extreme spouse abuse or other domestic violence in the child's presence.
Permitted Drug/Alcohol Abuse	Encouraging or permitting drug or alcohol use by the child; cases of the child's drug/alcohol use were included here if it appeared that the parent/guardian had been informed of the problem and had not attempted to intervene.
Permitted Other Maladaptive Behavior	Encouragement or permitting of other maladaptive behavior (e.g., severe assaultiveness, chronic delinquency) in circumstances in which the parent/guardian had reason to be aware of the existence and seriousness of the problem but did not attempt to intervene.
Refusal Of Psychological Care	Refusal to allow needed and available treatment for a child's emotional or behavioral impairment or problem in accord with competent professional recommendation.
Delay In Psychological Care	Failure to seek or provide needed treatment for a child's emotional or behavioral impairment or problem which any reasonable layman would have recognized as needing professional psychological attention (e.g., severe depression, suicide attempt).
Other Emotional Neglect	Other inattention to the child's developmental/emotional needs not classifiable under any of the above forms of emotional neglect (e.g., markedly overprotective restrictions which foster immaturity or emotional overdependence, chronically applying expectations clearly inappropriate in relation to the child's age or level of development, etc.).

EDUCATIONAL NEGLECT

Permitted Chronic Truancy	Habitual truancy averaging at least 5 days a month was classifiable under this form of maltreatment if the parent/guardian had been informed of the problem and had not attempted to intervene.
Failure To Enroll/Other Truancy	Failure to register or enroll a child of mandatory school age, causing the school-aged child to remain at home for nonlegitimate reasons (e.g., to work, to care for siblings, etc.), an average of at least 3 days a month.
Inattention To Special Education Need	Refusal to allow or failure to obtain recommended remedial educational services, or neglect in obtaining or following through with treatment for a child's diagnosed learning disorder or other special education need without reasonable cause.

Think About It
1. What form of neglect is abandonment? Inadequate nurturance?

Sources: US Department of Health and Human Services, Study of National Incidence and Prevalence of Child Abuse and Neglect, www.childwelfare.gov/pubs/usermanuals/neglect/neglectb.cfm. US Department of Health and Human Services, Child Neglect: A Guide for Intervention, 1993.

child with threats of violence, abandonment, or humiliation. Some children live in fear that their parents will expose their secrets or physically harm them. A third type of emotional abuse is isolating the child. Sometimes done as an alternative to physical punishment, isolating the child by placing him or her in a closet, bedroom, or tool shed for long periods of time can be harmful. A fourth type of emotional neglect involves corrupting children by exploiting them. Some parents abuse their children sexually or allow others to touch, fondle, or film their children in sexual acts. This type of exploitation can have harmful and long-lasting effects on the children's emotional condition. Finally, emotional neglect can consist of denying the child's emotional responses. Parents who fail to talk to, touch, look at, or otherwise interact with their children can greatly harm their emotional development. Some parents believe their children should be "seen but not heard" and set up stringent rules concerning behavior in the home that prevent the children from playing, experimenting, or otherwise exploring their emotional boundaries.[38]

Unsafe Home Environment. Some children suffer from neglect by being raised in a home that is unfit because of filthy conditions, unsafe wiring, broken plumbing, or lice and rodents. Some homes are physically deteriorated and a real threat to the children's health and welfare. Parents who don't clean up animal feces, broken glass, or dirty dishes expose their children to injury and disease. Police officers, welfare workers, and teachers who make home visits are authorized to remove children from homes that are an immediate danger to them. The reasons homes can be inadequate living quarters can range from the effects of poverty to neglectful landlords to parents who simply don't know how to keep a home clean and safe or understand how an unsafe home harms their children.

Drug and Alcohol Use. Parents and caretakers who use drugs and alcohol put their children at risk. The first serious problem of abuse and neglect related to drug and alcohol use is the transference of the substances from the parent to the fetus or newborn child. Although this problem has been overstated by some war-on-drugs publicity, no one seriously suggests that drug use by pregnant mothers is risk-free. The drugs pass through the placenta and affect the fragile fetus, and it's difficult, if not impossible, to gauge the actual effect on the child.

Most states now have legislation that mandates the reporting of newborns who have been exposed to drugs by the mothers, and have established punishments that include removing the baby and placing it with family members or a foster home. The effect of alcohol on fetuses is better established than that of other drugs. **Fetal alcohol syndrome** (FAS) is suspected of being one of the primary causes of mental retardation. There is considerable debate about what to do with families in which the mother has used drugs or alcohol during pregnancy. Some would take the child away to be raised by others because of the likelihood of relapse by the mother. Others contend that treatment for new mothers can be effective because they're motivated to clean up their bodies in order to be allowed to keep the child.[39]

Medical Neglect. Sometimes parents fail to seek medical care for their children even when they're extremely ill. This should not be particularly surprising when we consider the inadequate system of medical insurance in this country. Medical care is expensive, and many can't utilize preventive services. Many parents take their child to a doctor only when the problem gets acute, and this is usually to a hospital emergency room. Children make up the majority of those

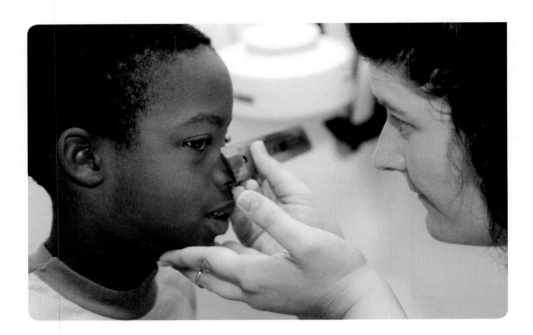

Fetal alcohol syndrome is suspected of being one of the primary causes of mental retardation.

without insurance and suffer from a variety of ills that regular medical treatment and checkups could prevent.

Often, parents don't choose to neglect their children's medical needs but simply can't afford proper medical care. Other cases are more problematic. Some parents, for religious reasons, choose to forgo the advantages of advanced medicine in favor of letting their belief in supernatural forces decide the child's fate. A number of religions are suspicious of modern medicine or believe illness and death are the will of God. Often these cases escape attention, and the children simply suffer and even die because no one recognized or reported their plight to authorities. Other times, relatives, schools, or hospitals will become aware of the situation and implore the courts to intervene. The state will invoke its *parens patriae* authority and order medical treatment. The reasoning is that the child's well-being supersedes the parent's right to practice a religious doctrine that might result in grave illness or death.

Abandonment. A final form of child neglect is abandonment. Periodically, the media report a case in which a newborn is found in a restroom or a trash bin. This is a clear case of abandonment, and the parent or parents, if they are found, usually lose parental rights. Sometimes, the case isn't so straightforward. A parent may leave the child in the care of a relative or a friend for an extended period of time, have no contact, and provide no material support, then show up years later wanting the child back. In such cases, the court must decide on several important issues. The primary concern of what is best for the child must be balanced with the biological parents' legal rights.

Another common form of abandonment results in what has been termed "throwaway youth." For some reason, a child, usually an adolescent, is told to leave the home. It may be because the child is incorrigible, and the parent(s) find him or her uncontrollable. The child may be alcoholic or drug-dependent. Or a parent may have married a new spouse who dislikes the child, and the parent must send the child away to save the relationship. Often, there are no alternative living arrangements for these children, so they must find their own way in the world. To say that children in such situations are vulnerable is an understatement. Often, they're rendered homeless and must stay with friends' families and

INSTANT RECALL
FROM CHAPTER 1

parens patriae

Latin for "father of his country." Refers to the philosophy that the government is the ultimate guardian of all children or disabled adults.

work low-paying, part-time jobs to survive. In this condition, many are unable to continue to attend school. It's not surprising that throwaway youths often resort to delinquency and have higher levels of delinquency than the general youth population.[40]

Child neglect is a substantial social problem in the United States. It's more prevalent than the actual physical abuse of children, although it's much less visible. The juvenile court, which we discuss in greater detail in Chapter 13, is vested with deciding how to deal with cases of neglect.

PHYSICAL CHILD ABUSE

The family is ideally a place of safety and comfort. Increasingly, however, we are becoming aware that the family can also be a place where physical violence is perpetrated by one member of the family on another. Family violence takes several forms, but for our study of juvenile delinquency, we won't deal with family violence that doesn't directly affect children.[41] In this section, we cover the family abuse that might contribute to delinquency.[42] These forms of family violence include physical child abuse and sexual child abuse. Each form of family violence has its own causes, solutions, and ramifications.

Our definition of **physical child abuse** is taken from Harvey Wallace's *Family Violence: Legal, Medical, and Social Perspectives.* Wallace defines physical child abuse as "any act that results in a non-accidental physical injury by a person who has care, custody, or control of a child."[43] The distinguishing features of this definition are the aspects of physical injury and intent. A child slipping in the tub during a bath wouldn't qualify as physical child abuse. Although the child might be hurt in the accident, the parent didn't intend to hurt the child, so the act might qualify as simply an accident instead of abuse.

The physical abuse of children has long been an established practice in human societies and, until recently, was institutionalized in some cultures. By that, we mean it was part of accepted social policy to kill or injure children. Many

The family can be a place where physical violence is perpetrated by one member of the family on another. Here, Julie Schenecker, accused in 2011 of shooting to death her 16-year-old daughter and 13-year-old son, is escorted into court.

ancient societies, including those of Greece and Rome, accepted infanticide, most infamously by exposure, as a parental right. Infanticide might have served as a form of birth control, especially in times of scarcity.[44] In other societies, especially those that valued boys over girls, the killing of girls might have been officially frowned on but was practiced anyway by parents who wished to have a boy instead.

The history of physical abuse of children must be put in context, however. It was once considered appropriate for parents to beat or even kill their children, but when we measure the behavior of older civilizations by our modern standards, we are guilty of what historians call **presentism**. Social conditions, value systems and ethics, and the economic feasibility of having large families have changed over time, and what was considered necessary or appropriate in one era can be considered a crime in another.[45] Physical abuse of children can be likened to slavery or armies pillaging the lands they conquered. As despicable as these actions seem to us today, they were sanctioned and rewarded by the authorities of the time.

Parents are the most frequent physical abusers of children (Figure 8.3), far more than other relatives or caregivers, with mothers perpetrating the most fatalities (Figure 8.4). Physical child abuse is more obvious than neglect because the injury is visible. The problem becomes one of determining how the injury occurred. Because children injure themselves all the time, there is always the question whether the adult inflicted the injury or it happened by accident. There are a number of warning signs that abuse has occurred based on how the injury is explained.

>> **Unexplained injury.** If the caretaker can't explain how the injury happened, there is a good chance that he or she inflicted it on the child. Especially if the child is too young to give his or her own account, the caregiver who abused the child may claim to have no knowledge. Certainly, there are times when a child is injured out of the adult's sight, and the caregiver's claim of having no knowledge is legitimate, but most caregivers are eager to tell medical personnel all they can about the circumstances of the injury.

>> **Impossible explanations.** If the caretaker's story is inconsistent with the type and extent of the child's injury, it might be a sign that the caregiver is lying. For example, a minor accident shouldn't cause a life-threatening

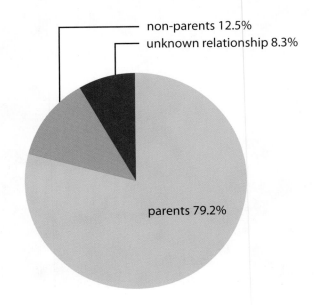

Figure 8.3 Parents Are the Most Frequent Child Abusers

Think About It

1. Discuss reasons that parents are the most frequent abusers of children.

Source: U.S. Department of Health and Human Services, Administration for Children and Families, Administration on Children, Youth and Families, Children's Bureau, *Child Maltreatment 2010* (Washington, DC: U.S. Department of Health and Human Services, 2011), 69. Online at www.acf.hhs.gov/programs/cb/pubs/cm10/cm10.pdf

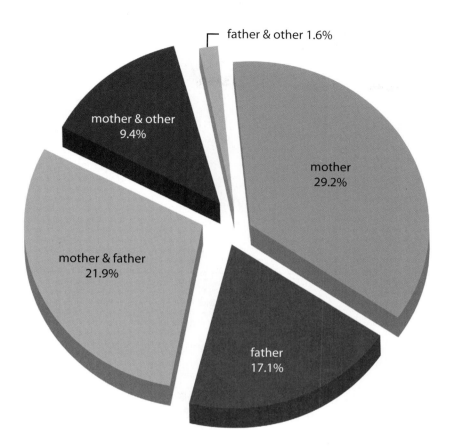

father & other 1.6%

mother & other 9.4%

mother 29.2%

mother & father 21.9%

father 17.1%

Figure 8.4 Child Fatalities by Perpetrator Relationship

Most child abuse fatalities result from abuse by the mother, followed by abuse by both parents.

Think About It

1. Discuss why fathers perpetrate child fatalities less often than either mothers or mother/father pairs.

Source: U.S. Department of Health and Human Services, Administration for Children and Families, Administration on Children, Youth and Families, Children's Bureau (Washington, DC: U.S. Department of Health and Human Services, 2011), 69. Online at www.acf.hhs .gov/programs/cb/pubs/cm10/ cm10.pdf.

injury. Common sense and good medical judgment can often alert professionals to the possibility of child abuse.

» **Different versions of the incident.** One tactic that police officers use to determine if child abuse has occurred is to talk to the parents separately and compare their versions of how the accident happened. Minor inconsistencies in which the parents didn't get the details of their stories straight can lead to an unraveling of the explanation upon further investigation.

» **Different explanations.** When the caregiver must repeat the story of the incident to several people at different times, the story might change. The circumstances of the truth never change, but when one must remember what lies were told, keeping the cover story consistent becomes difficult. As police officers talk with emergency room technicians and child protective service workers, they might find that on repeated explanations the story gets embellished and the facts become inconsistent or contradictory.

» **Delay in seeking medical attention.** Officials consider it a red flag when someone who has a child with life-threatening injuries does not seek immediate medical attention. The person might hope the bump on the head or the sore ribs will heal with time, but this only puts the child in more pain and more danger. Concerned parents are more likely to err on the side of caution and overreaction than to delay getting the child to a doctor.[46]

Unfortunately, the youngest children, infants, bear the most physical abuse, with the numbers tapering off sharply once the youth advances into adolescence (see Figure 8.5). The types of physical child abuse are limited only by the imaginations of the abusers. Typically, however, the physical abuse fits into well-known categories because the abuse is spontaneous most of the time. According

Figure 8.5 Victims by Age, 2010

Victimization was split between the sexes. Boys accounted for 48.5 percent of victimizations and girls for 51.2 percent.

Think About It

1. Why are children less than a year old at such risk for maltreatment? Discuss your reasoning.

Source: U.S. Department of Health and Human Services, Administration for Children and Families, Administration on Children, Youth and Families, Children's Bureau, *Child Maltreatment, 2010* (Washington, DC: U.S. Department of Health and Human Services, 2011), 23. Online at www.acf.hhs.gov/programs/cb/pubs/cm10/cm10.pdf.

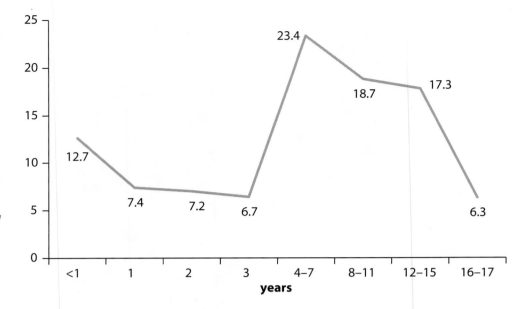

to Harvey Wallace, physical child abuse is normally associated with one or more of four types of injuries.

》 Bruises are the first common type of physical child abuse and the one that is hardest to distinguish from the normal bruises of an active child. The first thing that professionals look for on a bruised child is the injury's location. A child who falls off a swing, trips on the rug, or fights with his or her sibling will acquire bruises where there is little flesh. The shins, forehead, elbows, and knees are where normal bruising occurs. Bruises on the abdomen or buttocks, on the back of the arms or legs, or on the genitals might indicate injuries sustained when a child is being physically abused. Experts also look at the pattern of the bruising. Certain weapons such as belts, paddles, or cords leave distinctive marks, and a handprint on a child's face or bottom is a clue the injury wasn't self-inflicted. Finally, bruises heal at a predictable rate and change color as they do so. This leaves a history of the trauma suffered by the child and shows the professional the recent history of the abuse.[47]

》 Another injury common to physical child abuse is burns. Some parents, as a way of punishing a child, place the child in hot water or, in some cases, use a lighted cigarette. The seriousness of the burn is measured according to a scale that runs from first degree (looks like mild sunburn) to fourth degree (penetrates to the muscle or bone). Like bruises, burns leave a history of trauma on the child's skin that can alert professionals to the abuse.[48]

》 Bone fractures are another common result of physical abuse. The most common type of fracture indicating abuse is the spiral fracture, in which the child's arm has been grabbed and twisted. In young children whose bones haven't fully developed, a fracture is relatively rare. It takes a good deal of force to twist an arm to the extent that it breaks. Most likely, the adult didn't intend to break the child's bone but nevertheless exerted enough power to do this level of damage.

》 Finally, physical abuse can injure the head and internal organs, ranging from black eyes and skull fractures to kidney and liver damage. These injuries can occur when children are hit with a fist or weapon or when they're thrown into a wall or to the floor. These types of injuries can be the most life threatening but the hardest to prove were a result of child abuse.[49]

SEXUAL CHILD ABUSE

The sexual abuse of children generates a lot of media attention these days. Whether it's a case in which a child is abducted, abused, and killed, a case in which members of the clergy or a scouting organization take advantage of those under their care, or a case of incest, the media give a great deal of coverage to the sensational and lurid nature of these offenses. Part of the reason for this interest is the power relationship between children and adults. Children aren't legally or emotionally capable of giving informed consent for the sexual encounter.[50] Although some abusers will claim the sex was loving in nature and agreed on by both parties, it's viewed by the courts, parents, and the public as one of the most despicable criminal offenses.[51] Child sexual abuse is also an offense seized on by politicians to show they're tough on crime.

We tend to think of the perpetrator as male and the victim as female. However, recent studies show that the incidence of male victims and female abusers is higher than originally thought.[52] There have been a few high-profile cases of female teachers having sexual affairs with male high school students, which has led people to question whether this type of behavior is as serious and detrimental as when the teacher is male and the victim female. Boys might not report sexual abuse as often as girls for a number of reasons. First, they aren't questioned as closely as girls. They're given greater freedom to travel and stay out late, and parents don't automatically worry that they may be taken advantage of sexually. The second reason boys might not report sexual abuse is that they're afraid of looking weak. Boys are taught to take care of themselves, and if they're seduced or forced into sex, they may endure more embarrassment than girls who realize immediately that they've been victimized.[53]

Younger children are more likely to be sexually victimized than older children. By age 4, children are sexually curious and can be manipulated by an adult, and by age 9 they have a desire to please and are willing to trust adults. Sexual abuse of children tapers off sharply at age 14, because the child is likely to either run away or threaten disclosure.[54] Although sexual child abuse takes several forms, we're most concerned here with incest because of its connection to families and delinquency. Actually, statistics show that parents are less likely to commit sexual abuse than other adults the child knows. Nonparental relatives show the highest rate of sexual abuse, with 30 percent of perpetrators, followed by day care staff, with 23 percent of perpetrators. Parents represented only 3 percent of sexual-abuse perpetrators.[55]

The juvenile court is concerned with all types of juvenile victimization, but the crucial issue here is how family relations encourage or protect against delinquency. Incest involves sexual relations between blood relatives. Incest has an uneven history, because it was encouraged in some societies and outlawed in others. It's generally thought that incest is prohibited for biological reasons because of the strong possibility of passing along recessive genes that result in physical or mental disabilities. Most states have laws prohibiting marriage between relatives closer than first cousins.[56]

Incest is also prohibited for psychological reasons. When fathers dominate the family dynamics, daughters have little power to resist sexual advances either physically or emotionally. Therefore, a social proscription against incest allows fathers to internalize a supportive and protective role and prevents them from viewing their daughters as potential sex partners. This incest taboo creates order and cooperation within the family unit and allows children to grow up trusting their parents and to later enter into intimate relationships with a member of a different family.[57] Because the incest taboo is so firmly entrenched in modern Western society, it's difficult for us to imagine incest without being revolted. However, what we must realize is that the norms of society are socially constructed and that what is appropriate in one time and place may be inappropriate in another culture or century. In modern Western society, sexual relations with children are considered abuse and are likely a causative factor in delinquency. According to Andrea Sedlak and Diane Broadhurst, girls are sexually abused almost three times more often than boys.[58] The median age at which girls report first becoming victims of sexual assault is 13.[59] Another study found that 92 percent of juvenile female offenders interviewed had experienced emotional, physical, and/or sexual abuse.[60]

Questions

1. What does the term "family" mean?
2. What are the important functions of the family?
3. What are the barriers of entry to becoming a parent?
4. What is the difference between child neglect and child abuse?
5. What are some of the more common forms of child neglect?
6. What are the warning signs of physical child abuse?

Families and Delinquency

Learning Objective 6.

Describe the effects of divorce on delinquency, as well as the effects of social support, family conflict, and parents and siblings.

Learning Objective 7.

Understand how a child might not necessarily be the recipient of family violence or conflict, but the cause.

What is the link between the type and quality of the family and the likelihood the children will engage in some kind of delinquency? The quality of family life is clearly related to the victimization of children. This leads to the question of whether such victimization can propel the child toward victimizing others. So far, research points to a number of possible causes of delinquency within the family besides victimization. Ideas about other sources include Michael R. Gottfredson and Travis Hirschi's theory of low self-control—a product of weak parent-child bonds and ineffective parenting—and Ron Akers's modeling theory, in which children mimic their antisocial parents' behavior.[61] It seems obvious that coming from a bad family where one is the victim of abuse or neglect would eventually result in further deviance, but the nexus is complicated and deserves close examination.[62] To examine the dynamics of the relationship between the family and delinquency, we consider four historically associated areas. First, we look at the effects of divorce on children. Second, we examine how well the family provides emotional and economic support to children. Third, we look at conflict within the family, and finally, we consider the influence of parental and sibling deviance on the delinquent behavior of children.

Divorce

More than half of marriages don't last "until death do us part." Divorce is such a prevalent feature of American family life today that it no longer carries the social stigma that it once did. Still, dissolving a marriage is no easy task. It has social, economic, and emotional costs that make adults endure infidelity, emotional estrangement, public embarrassment, and feelings of betrayal and worthlessness, rather than seek divorce. Although some may contend getting divorced is too easy, almost everyone who has endured one will attest that it's an unpleasant and heart-wrenching task.

Difficult as a divorce may be on the parents, it's the children who have the most difficulty adjusting to this monumental change in their family structure and living conditions. Many children react to divorce with the feeling that it's somehow their fault, and they may experience a sense of misplaced guilt. Other children blame one of the parents and develop a sense of loyalty and protectiveness toward the other. Still other children see divorce as abandonment and feel as if the bonds of social control have slackened and that they're free to engage in delinquent behavior.[63]

Not all children are affected in the same manner by divorce. The age and sex of children play an important role in how they adjust, and some studies suggest that boys are affected more than girls. With the male role model leaving the home, boys are more likely to test the mother's authority and to feel that they're now the "man of the house" and not subject to rules as they were when the father was at home.[64] With only one parent around to enforce discipline, discover deviance, and solve problems, it's not surprising that there is a clear relationship between divorce and delinquency. Research has shown that when the number of single-parent households goes up dramatically, so too does the incidence of status offenders and delinquents.[65] For example, one study found that 2 percent of female respondents who lived with both biological parents had been arrested in the last year, as opposed to 5 percent of female respondents who lived in families with alternative structures. For males, the number was 4 percent (who lived with both biological parents) versus 10 percent (who lived in families with alternative structures).[66] See Figure 8.6 for further comparisons.

Still, it's not wise to paint all divorces with the same brush. There is the concept of a "successful" divorce in which the partners and the children adjust and grow emotionally in their new living situations. The components of a successful divorce include both parents playing a positive role in their children's lives.[67]

Social Support

Each family environment is unique, and it can change over time depending on its structure, size, and economic conditions. When new children are added to the family, the dynamics are altered and the future changed as parents and siblings learn to accommodate the new members. Each family provides a range of support to every member, and this support greatly influences the chances that the child won't engage in delinquency.

Figure 8.6 The Relationship Between Family Structure and Problem Behavior

Think About It

1. For which sex and behavior exists the greatest difference between behavior in families with both biological parents and other types of families?

Source: Adapted from C. McCurley and H. Snyder, *Risk, Protection, and Family Structure* (Washington, DC: US Department of Justice, Office of Justice Programs, Office of Juvenile Justice and Delinquency Prevention, forthcoming) by Howard N. Snyder and Melissa Sickmund, *Juvenile Offenders and Victims: 2006 National Report* (Washington, DC: US Department of Justice, Office of Justice Programs, Office of Juvenile Justice and Delinquency Prevention, 2006), 72. Online at www.ojjdp.ncjrs.org/ojstatbb/nr2006/downloads/NR2006.pdf.

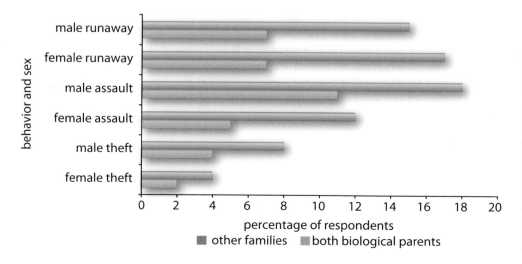

The primary issue of social support revolves around the setting of rules and the enforcement of discipline. People tend to behave better when they understand the boundaries of what is considered appropriate behavior for each social context. Many parents teach their children that there is one volume of voice for recreation outside (the outside voice) and another for home, school, and church (the inside voice). We expect parents to correct children who use the outside voice while inside. It's the manner and nature of this correction that determines how the child will react in the future. If a child starts screaming in a restaurant, the parent may quietly tell the child to use the "inside voice," yell at the child to be quiet, strike the child, or remove the child by taking him or her outside. This circumstance, in which the parent shapes the behavior of the child, is repeated endlessly each day and forms a pattern of correction and discipline that both creates the self-esteem of the child and forms his or her future reactions to rules and rule violation.

Previously, we covered the concerns of using physical punishment on children, and although that discussion is pertinent, we are concerned with the broader scope of support and discipline. Physical punishment can be a sign that the important lessons to be learned have already been lost. Children whose behavior can be corrected only with the infliction of pain can grow up to be problematic. One key to keeping children out of trouble is teaching them to evaluate and modify their own behavior. We all learn this at some point and to varying degrees, but those who break the law are either unable to control their impulses or don't care if their behavior is inappropriate or harmful.

Another issue related to family discipline is parents' availability to nurture and supervise children. Some parents work incredibly long hours to succeed in their careers. Their jobs require them to travel, bring work home at night and on the weekends, stay connected to the office through e-mail or cell phones, and to be on call and ready to drop family obligations to rush back to the office for an emergency. Although jobs like this may provide plenty of economic support for children and model hardworking behavior, they aren't without their own cost. The parents' indulgence in their own careers comes at the expense of their children's needs. These parents miss school plays, soccer games, reading to their children, and countless other opportunities to form crucial relationships and provide positive supervision. Much of the work of being a parent is outsourced to teachers, coaches, nannies, and the computer.[68]

Other parents face the same issues of poor supervision but for different reasons. Some parents work more than one job to simply pay the bills. It isn't a matter of making a choice between careers and family; it's a matter of economic survival. Their children spend long periods of time without adult supervision and might be influenced by older children to engage in antisocial or delinquent behavior.[69] Even in two-parent families, the economic demands can be so acute, both parents must work instead of one staying home with the children. It's difficult to blame families for delinquency when the economic effects of globalization have disrupted patterns of work and family stability. In many ways, the ideals of American family values are at odds with the economic realities of the 21st century.[70]

Family Conflict

Previously, we discussed child neglect and abuse in the context of children as victims of faulty parenting. Another dimension to this problem that bears further discussion is the effect of neglect and abuse on future delinquency. When there is a high degree of family conflict, it shouldn't surprise us that the children end up having problems with school officials, community leaders, and the police. In environments where aggression and violence are rewarded, children learn that power and abusive behavior allow one to achieve goals. These are hard lessons for children to learn because they're often the recipients of the violent behavior. Such lessons are also difficult to correct later because, to the children, they have become common sense.[71]

Children don't necessarily have to be physically abused themselves to learn that violence is a way to get what one wants. Witnessing the victimization of one parent at the hands of another demonstrates to a child that it's permissible to control and dominate by physical force. Family conflict can also teach a child impulsivity. When a parent "flies off the handle" for no apparent reason or resorts to violence with little provocation, children learn to be constantly on their guard and to be quick to react to real or imagined insults with violence. Additionally, these children have a difficult time learning to solve problems without turning to anger. Skills such as humor, physical and verbal support, and active listening aren't part of the repertoire of children from families that suffer from a high level of conflict.

Children aren't always the recipient of family violence; sometimes they're the cause. Conflict might be a symptom of an underlying issue for children who are constantly creating problems and calling the family to the attention of authorities. For instance, if a daughter is sexually promiscuous and defying her parents, the family conflict might help to address these concerns. Parents who are so disengaged that the daughter can do anything she wants are simply a different type of faulty parents. Many good parents struggle with adolescent children, and family conflict is necessary as children test their parents' will to enforce rules.

Families are dynamic institutions, and the many factors that influence family conflict are subject to change. For instance, younger siblings might find that their parents are tired of enforcing bedtimes, curfews, and chores. Older siblings can become resentful of how the younger children are given more flexibility and latitude. The reasons for this increased freedom are many. Sometimes, the economic status of the family has improved, and they live in a better, safer neighborhood where extremely close supervision is no longer required. Other times, the parents feel they can depend on the older siblings to assume some of the supervision, and don't monitor the younger children as strictly as they did

Families are dynamic institutions, and the quality of family life is related to the victimization of children. Less family conflict helps children be happier.

the older ones. Also, parents can become more confident in their judgment of when to intervene in their children's lives. Although they might have felt that they had to know about every friend and activity of their older children, the parents now feel they can assess their younger children's lives with much less information and intrusion into their affairs. This results in less family conflict and presumably happier children who don't manifest their anger and frustration in committing delinquent acts.

Parents and Siblings

Antisocial parents are poor role models. The children see the advantages of a quick gain with little work and are unlikely to see police officers as trustworthy individuals. Exploring the link between lawbreaking parents and delinquent youths raises a number of interesting issues. First, is the link between the antisocial behavior of the parent and the children genetic or sociological in nature? Are aggressive tendencies inherited or learned? Should delinquent children be returned to a home with a parent who has a criminal record?

These questions are difficult to answer, but some factors can shed light on intergenerational crime. Professionals who work with delinquent children consider the quality of parenting as a means to decipher the atmosphere in the home. In fact, parents have long been considered a source of delinquency, and various approaches over the 20th century have sought to address this (see Crosscurrents). Today, all 50 states have civil and/or delinquency statutes that penalize parents who "cause," "aid," "encourage," or "contribute" to their child's delinquency.[72] Even if the child isn't delinquent, the home can be considered a negative influence, such as the homes of parents who are addicted to drugs or who sell drugs. Drug-using and drug-selling parents put their children at risk of falling into the same habits and attitudes, as well as exposing them to the dangers of the drug trade. Criminal justice authorities, including judges and law enforcement, are viewed as the enemy, and respect for any authority but the parent is discouraged.

The children of antisocial parents, even when they are good kids, are subjected to more scrutiny and surveillance from teachers, school administrators, and police. The old adage that "an acorn doesn't fall far from the tree" can become a self-fulfilling prophecy when youths whose parents have been identified as antisocial are subjected to greater supervision and given fewer breaks than children whose parents aren't known to authorities.

A youth's siblings might also exert a negative influence. Older children can stay out later, range in a wider geographic circle, and engage in more risky behavior than younger children. When a boy runs around with his older brother, he may be exposed to deviant behavior at an early age, before he has the emotional maturity and judgment to evaluate the effect it might have on his life. Younger siblings are eager to gain the approval of older siblings and might break the law in order to be allowed to associate with the older crowd.[73] Because most youths eventually give up delinquency as they become more involved in society, the age at which they began delinquent behavior is important. Youths who start their delinquent career early have more time to progress into serious crime and are likely to miss some of the positive aspects of childhood as they engage in antisocial behavior with their older siblings. In effect, they grow up fast and lose their innocence early, making it more likely that by the time they are ready to get married, start work, and enter into a respectable lifestyle, they already have the emotional and legal baggage of someone who has spent too much time in an antisocial lifestyle. It's not as easy for them to transition into respectable adulthood as it was for their older siblings who had a shorter delinquent period.[74]

8.2 **crosscurrents**

Sending Parents to School

Parents are often blamed for the delinquency of their children, and the juvenile justice system has long focused on the home as a source of delinquency. Although there tends to be some social resistance at punishing parents for every act of delinquency (unless the parent actively encourages it), the justice system has taken some stabs at reforming parents of delinquent children.[1]

American society endured deep social upheaval during World War II. Fathers were sent overseas and were largely absent from their children's lives from 1941 to 1944. Many mothers, now single parents, worked full-time to help support their families and assist the war effort. In this atmosphere of weakened parental supervision, the authorities worried about a surge in juvenile delinquency. Casting about for solutions—to a delinquency problem that never actually came about—some cities tried to institute parenting classes to help show parents of delinquent children the error of their ways.[2]

> "How can a child be delinquent? The answer is that he isn't. But his father and mother are. Let's go after them." (George Jarrett, founder, San Francisco Parental School)[3]

The model San Francisco Parental School opened its doors in 1943 with the aim of helping youths by addressing family deficiencies. Parents were referred to the school by the juvenile court, police and social agencies, the district attorney's office, and schools. The school operated on the principles that the parents had failed their children and didn't know how to use community resources for themselves and their children. At least one other city, Minneapolis, seriously tried the San Francisco model, which apparently didn't run as smoothly as the California program. After two years, what had been envisioned as a multisite, compulsory school for parents of delinquents ended as voluntary classes offered at two sites.[4]

Sending parents of delinquents to parenting school seems to be an on-again, off-again idea in juvenile justice. For example, a 1997 study describes a series of classes held at a juvenile probation facility in Northern California. At the time, the program had operated for more than six years. Typically, the court ordered parents to attend the 10-session series within three months of the juvenile's sentencing. The study noted that parents resisted many of the program's strategies—such as trying to convince them to testify in court against their children—and that the program's unintended side-effect of providing a support group was its most productive result.[5]

THINK ABOUT IT

1. Are parenting schools a good idea? Do some parents need to be taught how to parent?
2. What did you think of George Jarrett's quotation? Are parents completely to blame for a child's delinquency?

[1] Sarah K. S. Shannon, "Dereliction of Duty: Training Schools for Delinquent Parents in the 1940s," *Journal of Sociology & Social Welfare* 37, no. 3 (September 2010): 11–27.

[2] Ibid.

[3] Ibid.

[4] Ibid.

[5] Laurie Schaffner, "Families on Probation: Court-Ordered Parenting Skills Classes for Parents of Juvenile Offenders," *Crime and Delinquency* 43 (1997): 412–437.

Questions

1. What four issues are related to the quality of family life and delinquency?
2. What effect do age and sex have on children whose parents divorce?
3. How might poor supervision be considered neglect?
4. How may family conflict affect a child's impulsivity?

>> FOCUS ON ETHICS

Pierced

As you are walking through a large store, you pass the jewelry counter and hear a commotion. A man and woman who appear to be in their early 20s have their three-year-old child propped up on a stool while the clerk attempts to use an instrument to pierce the child's earlobe.

"No, no, I don't want to," screams the child.

"It will only hurt for a little while," says the man.

"Sit still and make mommy proud. You will look so pretty in your new earrings."

"I don't want earrings, they will hurt. Please don't do this to me mommy."

The father puts the little girl in a bear hug while the mother holds the girl's head. The clerk slips the girl's earlobe into a device that pierces her ear with a popping sound. The girl lets loose a bloodcurdling scream that can be heard throughout the store. She wiggles free of her father's embrace and runs down the aisle with a tiny trickle of blood flowing from her earlobe. The father runs after her, scoops her up, and brings her kicking and screaming back to the stool. By this time, it's clear the child wants no part of having her other ear pierced.

You're in a quandary as to what to do. On one hand, you understand this is a family matter and the parents have the authority to have the child's ears pierced. On the other hand, you have sympathy for the little girl, and your heart breaks for the terror she's experiencing. In the back of your mind is the question whether this activity for the sake of appearance constitutes child abuse. The child clearly doesn't want her ear pierced, and the parents are using physical force in a public place. You're tempted to intervene.

WHAT DO YOU DO?

1. Do you decide the situation is none of your business and walk away?

2. Do you confront the parents and tell them their child isn't old enough to consent to mutilation and that they should wait until she's old enough to decide if she wants her ears pierced?

3. Do you confront the jewelry clerk and tell her what she's doing to this little girl is wrong?

4. Do you call the police and report that a child is being abused?

Summary

Summary

Learning Objective 1. Tell why the traditional, Western nuclear family is no longer the most common type of family.	In the past, marriage was considered a permanent union, and those who sought divorce were met with negative sanctions by society. Couples stayed together because they believed it was in their children's best interests. There is no longer a severe social cost to divorce, and society is generally more tolerant of alternative family structures.
Learning Objective 2. Discuss the effects of poverty on parenting.	Poverty hinders parents in meeting their children's physical, psychological, and social needs. Impoverished families are more likely to have one parent, lack health insurance, and have their children drop out of school. Impoverishment has a cumulative effect on the family when the parents must work longer hours to support the children and thus deprive them of support and supervision.
Learning Objective 3. Go over Wallace's differences between parents who neglect their children and parents who don't.	Inability to plan: Some parents can't adequately plan for the future. Lack of knowledge: Many don't know how to run a household. Lack of judgment: Parents are sometimes unable to decide when children should be given responsibilities to look after themselves. Lack of motivation: Some parents have little interest in helping their children succeed.

Learning Objective 4. List the four types of injuries common to physical child abuse.	Bruises on the abdomen or buttocks, on the back of the arms or legs, or on the genitals may appear when a child is being physically abused. Some parents use burns for punishment by placing the child in a bowl of hot water or in some cases using a lighted cigarette. The most common type of bone fracture indicating abuse is the spiral fracture, in which the child's arm has been grabbed and twisted. Physical abuse can also hurt the head and internal organs, with injuries that include black eyes, skull fractures, and kidney and liver damage.
Learning Objective 5. Explain the connection between child sexual abuse and the power relationship between adults and children.	Children aren't legally or emotionally capable of giving informed consent for sexual encounters. Younger children are more likely to be sexually victimized than older children. Child sexual abuse tapers off sharply at age 14, because the child is likely to run away or threaten disclosure.
Learning Objective 6. Describe the effects of divorce on delinquency, as well as the effects of social support, family conflict, and parents and siblings.	Some children see divorce as abandonment and feel free to engage in delinquent behavior, which may be easier with only one parent around to enforce discipline, discover deviance, and solve problems. Each family provides a range of social support to every member, which includes the setting of rules and the enforcement of discipline, as well as the parents' availability to nurture and supervise children. A high degree of family conflict may lead to children having problems with school officials, community leaders, and the police. In aggressive, violent environments, children learn to try to achieve their goals through power and abusive behavior. Finally, parents and siblings who feel free to break the law may influence other children in the family to become delinquent.
Learning Objective 7. Understand how a child might not necessarily be the recipient of family violence or conflict, but the cause.	Conflict might be a symptom of an underlying issue for children who are constantly creating problems and calling the family to the attention of authorities. Many good parents struggle with adolescent children, and family conflict is necessary as children test their parents' will to enforce rules.

Chapter Review Questions

1. Do fathers have complete discretion in the affairs of their families?
2. What are the alternative ways in which families are structured?
3. What roles does a parent need to assume in order to be a good parent?
4. What challenges from outside the family may influence delinquency?
5. What challenges inside the family may influence delinquency?
6. How do parents who neglect their children differ from those who take good care of their children?
7. Do states have the authority to provide medical attention to children against parents' wishes?
8. What do we mean by "throwaway youth"?
9. Are older children more likely to be victims of sexual abuse than younger children?
10. How does the behavior of parents and siblings influence the way children are treated by schools and the juvenile justice system?

Key Terms

child neglect—According to criminologist Harvey Wallace, "the negligent treatment or maltreatment of a child by a parent or caretaker under circumstances indicating harm or threatened harm to the child's health or welfare."

emotional neglect—From Harvey Wallace: "Acts or omissions of acts that are judged by community standards and professional expertise to be psychologically damaging to the child."

fetal alcohol syndrome (FAS)—The National Institutes of Health defines this condition as a pattern of mental and physical birth abnormalities found in some children of mothers who drank excessively during pregnancy.

nonorganic failure-to-thrive (NFTT)—This medical term describes an infant or child who has a measurable lag in height, head size, and/or development due to environmental factors and not an illness or disorder.

physical child abuse—According to criminologist Harvey Wallace, "any act that results in a nonaccidental physical injury by a person who has care, custody, or control of a child."

presentism—Believing that people of an earlier time should be accountable to the standards of present time.

Endnotes

1 Judith Stacey, *Brave New Families: Stories of Domestic Upheaval in Late Twentieth Century America* (New York: Basic Books, 1990).

2 Philip S. Gutis, "What Is a Family? Traditional Limits Are Being Redrawn," *New York Times*, August 31, 1989, C1.

3 James Garbarino, Cynthia J. Schellenbach, and Janet M. Sebes, *Troubled Youth, Troubled Families: Understanding Families At-Risk for Adolescent Maltreatment* (New York: Aldine, 1986).

4 L. Gorden, *Heroes of Their Own Lives: The Politics and History of Family Violence: Boston 1880–1960* (New York: Viking, 1988).

5 Stavros P. Kiriakidis, "Child-Rearing Practices and Delinquency in Children and Adolescents," *International Journal of Special Education* 25, no. 1 (January 1, 2010): 94–105.

6 Robert Coles, *The Moral Intelligence of Children* (New York: Random House, 1997).

7 Suzanne Bartholomae and Jonathan Fox, "Economic Stress and Families," in Patrick C. McKenry and Sharon J. Price, eds., *Families and Change: Coping with Stressful Events and Transitions*, 3rd ed. (Thousand Oaks, CA: Sage, 2005), 205–225.

8 Denise Kindschi Gosselin, *Heavy Hands: An Introduction to the Crimes of Family Violence* (Upper Saddle River, NJ: Prentice Hall, 2005).

9 Terri L. Orbuch and Sandra L. Eyster, "Division of Household Labor among Black Couples and White Couples," *Social Forces* 75 (1997): 301–332.

10 Barbara Dafoe Whitehead, *The Divorce Culture* (New York: Knopf, 1997).

11 Constance R. Ahrons and Richard B. Miller, "The Effect of the Post-Divorce Relationship on Paternal Involvement: A Longitudinal Analysis," *American Journal of Orthopsychiatry* 63 (1993): 462–479.

12 Joyce A. Arditti, "Women, Divorce and Economic Risk," *Family and Conciliation Courts Review* 35 (1997): 79–92.

13 Jennifer Steinhauer, "No Marriage, No Apologies," *New York Times*, July 6, 1995, C1.

14 Judith Seltzer, "Families Formed Outside of Marriage," *Journal of Marriage and Family* 62 (2000): 1247–1268.

15 Howard Wineberg and James McCarthy, "Living Arrangements after Divorce: Cohabitation Versus Remarriage," *Journal of Divorce and Remarriage* 29 (1998): 131–146.

16 James Q. Wilson, "Against Homosexual Marriage," in Henry L. Tischler, ed., *Debating Points: Marriage and Family Issues* (Upper Saddle River, NJ: Prentice Hall, 2001), 123–127.

17 Lori Kowaleski-Jones and Frank L. Mott, "Sex, Contraception and Childbearing among High Risk Youth: Do Different Factors Influence Males and Females?" *Family Planning Perspectives* 30 (1998): 163–169.

18 Marshall Jones and Donald Jones, "The Contagious Nature of Antisocial Behavior," *Criminology* 38 (2000): 25–46.

19 Donald West and David Farrington, *Who Becomes Delinquent?* (London: Heinemann, 1973).

20 John Wright and Francis Cullen, "Parental Efficacy and Delinquent Behavior: Do Control and Support Matter?" *Criminology* 39 (2001): 601–629.

21 Sung Jang and Carolyn Smith, "A Test of Reciprocal Causal Relationships among Parental Supervision, Affective Ties, and Delinquency," *Journal of Research in Crime and Delinquency* 34 (1997): 307–336.

22 Michel Foucault, *Discipline and Punish: The Birth of the Prison* (New York: Pantheon, 1977).

23 Robert Brooks and Sam Goldstein, *Raising Resilient Children: Fostering Strength, Hope, and Optimism in Your Child* (New York: Contemporary, 2001).

24 Alice Miller, *For Your Own Good: Hidden Cruelty in Child-Rearing and the Roots of Violence* (New York: Farrar, Straus, and Giroux, 1983).

25 Murray A. Straus, *Beating the Devil Out of Them: Corporal Punishment in American Families and Its Effects on Children* (New Brunswick, NJ: Transaction, 2001).

26 William Julius Wilson, *The Truly Disadvantaged: The Inner City, the Underclass and Public Policy* (Chicago: University of Chicago Press, 1987).

27 Thomas J. Stanley and William D. Danko, *The Millionaire Next Door: The Surprising Secrets of America's Wealthy* (Atlanta, GA: Longstreet, 1996).

28 Elijah Anderson, *Code of the Street: Decency, Violence, and the Moral Life of the Inner City* (New York: Norton, 1999).

29 Janet M. Currie, *The Invisible Safety Net: Protecting the Nation's Poor Children and Families* (Princeton, NJ: Princeton University Press, 2006).

30 "All happy families resemble one another, each unhappy family is unhappy in its own way." Leo Tolstoy, *Anna Karenina* (Mineola, New York: Dover Publications, 2004), 1.

31 Joseph Murray and David P. Farrington, "Risk Factors for Conduct Disorder and Delinquency: Key Findings from Longitudinal Studies," *Canadian Journal of Psychiatry* 55, no. 10 (October 2010): 633–642.

32 Harvey Wallace, *Family Violence: Legal, Medical, and Social Perspectives*, 4th ed. (Boston: Allyn and Bacon, 2005), 90–110.

33 Ibid., 94.

34 J. Myres, *Evidence in Child Abuse and Neglect*, 2nd ed. (New York: Wiley, 1992).

35 D. J. Hansen and V. M. MacMillan, "Behavioral Assessment of Child Abuse and Neglectful Families: Recent Developments and Current Issues," *Behavior Modification* 14 (1990): 225–278.

36 I. W. Hutton and R. K. Oates, "Nonorganic Failure to Thrive: A Long Term Follow-up," *Pediatrics* 8 (1977): 73–77.

37 Wallace, *Family Violence*, 98.

38 S. N. Hart and M. Brassard, "Developing and Validating Operationally Defined Measures of Emotional Maltreatment: A Multimodal Study of the Relationships between Caretaker Behavior and Child Characteristics across Those Developmental Levels" (Washington, DC: Department of Health and Human Services, 1986).

39 D. Wiese and D. Daro, *Current Trends in Child Abuse Reporting and Fatalities: The Results of the 1994 Annual Fifty State Survey* (Chicago: National Committee to Prevent Child Abuse, 1995).

40 Katherine L. Montgomery, Sanna J. Thompson, and Amanda N. Barczyk, "Individual and Relationship Factors Associated with Delinquency among Throwaway Adolescents," *Children & Youth Services Review* 33, no. 7 (July 2011): 1127–1133.

41 Although understanding forms of family violence such as spouse abuse, elder abuse, and abuse by gay and lesbian partners is important, they're only indirectly pertinent here. Students are advised to look elsewhere for a full discussion.

42 Timothy Ireland, Carolyn Smith, and Terence Thornberry, "Developmental Issues in the Impact of Child Abuse on Later Delinquency and Drug Use," *Criminology* 40 (2002): 359–396.

43 Wallace, *Family Violence*, p. 33.

44 W. V. Harris, "Child-Exposure in the Roman Empire," *Journal of Roman Studies* 84 (1994): 1–22.

45 S. Radbill, "A History of Child Abuse and Infanticide," in R. Helfer and C. H. Kempe,

eds., *The Battered Child*, 2nd ed. (Chicago: University of Chicago Press, 1974).

46 Wallace, *Family Violence*, 43–44.

47 H. Schmitt, "The Child with Nonaccidental Trauma," in R. Kempe and R. Helfer, eds., *The Battered Child*, 4th ed. (Chicago: University of Chicago Press, 1987).

48 J. Showers and K. M. Garrison, "Burn Abuse: A Four Year Study," *Journal of Trauma* 28 (1988): 1581–1583.

49 John Longstaff and Tish Sleeper, *The National Center on Child Fatality Review* (Washington, DC: Office of Juvenile Justice and Delinquency Prevention, 2001), FS-200112.

50 David Finkelhor, *Sexually Victimized Children* (New York: Free Press, 1984).

51 B. Dermott, "The Pro-Incest Lobby," *Psychology Today* (March 1980): 12.

52 Mic Hunter, *Abused Boys: The Neglected Victims of Sexual Abuse* (Lexington, MA: Lexington Books, 1990).

53 E. Porter, *Treating the Young Male Victims of Sexual Assault* (Syracuse, NY: Safer Society Press, 1986).

54 C. A. Courtios, "Studying and Counseling Women with Past Incest Experience," *Victimology: An International Journal* 5 (1980): 322–324.

55 Adapted from Walter R. McDonald and Associates, *Child Maltreatment 2003: Reports from the States to the National Child Abuse and Neglect Data System* (Washington, DC: US Department of Health and Human Services, Children's Bureau, 2004) by Howard N. Snyder and Melissa Sickmund, *Juvenile Offenders and Victims: 2006 National Report* (Washington, DC: US Department of Justice, Office of Justice Programs, Office of Juvenile Justice and Delinquency Prevention, 2006), 55. Online at /www.ojjdp.ncjrs.org/ojstatbb/nr2006/downloads/NR2006.pdf.

56 B. Justice and R. Justice, *The Broken Taboo: Sex in the Family* (New York: Human Services Press, 1979).

57 G. Lindsey, "Some Remarks Concerning Incest, the Incest Taboo, and Psychoanalytic Theory," *American Psychologist* 22 (1967): 1051–1059.

58 A. J. Sedlak and D. D. Broadhurst, *Executive Summary of the Third National Incidence Study of Child Abuse and Neglect* (Washington, DC: US Department of Health and Human Services, Administration for Children and Families, 1996), 2.

59 Leslie Acoca, "Investing in Girls: A 21st Century Strategy," *Juvenile Justice* 6, no. 1 (October 1999): 8.

60 L. Acoca and K. Dedel, *No Place to Hide: Understanding and Meeting the Needs of Girls in the California Juvenile Justice System* (San Francisco: National Council on Crime and Delinquency, 1998).

61 James D. Unnever, Francis T. Cullen, and Robert Agnew, "Why Is 'Bad' Parenting Criminogenic? Implications from Rival Theories," *Youth Violence and Juvenile Justice* 4, no. 1 (January 2006): 3–33.

62 Ronald Simons, Leslie Simons, and Lora Wallace, *Families, Delinquency and Crime: Linking Society's Most Basic Institution to Antisocial Behavior* (Los Angeles: Roxbury, 2004).

63 Jackson Toby, "The Differential Impact of Family Disorganization," *American Sociological Review* 22 (1957): 505–512.

64 Lawrence Rosen, "The Broken Home and Male Delinquency," in M. Wolfgang, L. Savitz, and N. Johnston, eds., *Sociology of Crime and Delinquency* (New York: Wiley, 1970), 489–795.

65 Edward Wells and Joseph Rankin, "Families and Delinquency: A Meta-Analysis of the Impact of Broken Homes," *Social Problems* 38 (1991): 71–93.

66 Howard N. Snyder and Melissa Sickmund, *Juvenile Offenders and Victims: 2006 National Report* (Washington, DC: US Department of Justice, Office of Justice Programs, Office of Juvenile Justice and Delinquency Prevention, 2006), 72. Online at www.ojjdp.ncjrs.org/ojstatbb/nr2006/downloads/NR2006.pdf.

67 Constance Ahrons, *The Good Divorce* (New York: Harper, 1995).

68 Susan Byrne, "Nobody Home," *Psychology Today* 10 (1977): 40–47.

69 Lawrence Steinberg, "Latchkey Children and Susceptibility to Peer Pressure," *Developmental Psychology* 22 (1986): 433–439.

70 Jody Miller, "Global Prostitution, Sex Tourism, and Trafficking," in Claire M. Renzetti, Lynne Goodstein, and Susan L. Miller, eds., *Rethinking Gender, Crime, and Justice, Feminist Readings* (Los Angeles: Roxbury, 2006), 139–154.

71 Carolyn Smith and David Farrington, "Continuities in Antisocial Behavior and Parenting across Three Generations," *Journal of Child Psychology and Psychiatry* 45 (2004): 230–247.

72 Eve M. Brank, Stephanie Carsten Kucera, and Stephanie A. Hays, "Parental Responsibility Statutes: An Organization and Policy Implications," *Journal of Law & Family Studies* 7, no. 1, (2005): 1–55.

73 David Rowe, Joseph Rogers, and Sylvia Meseck-Bushey, "Sibling Delinquency and the Family Environment: Shared and Unshared Influences," *Child Development* 63 (1992): 59–67.

74 Marshall Jones and Donald Jones, "The Contagious Nature of Antisocial Behavior," *Criminology* 38 (2000): 25–46.

Schools and Delinquency

School is a primary institution of **socialization**, and the one that formally educates children. Besides the family, the school is where children spend the greatest amount of time and where they learn values and ideas that can protect them from delinquency. This also means that the school is where children can fall victim to other children, teachers, and outsiders. Parents are concerned with both the quality of education their children receive and with their children's safety.[1]

Society has set an ambitious role for schools, one that states and jurisdictions don't fulfill to the same degree. In fact, school quality is one of the most pressing social concerns facing the United States because it influences the extent and seriousness of delinquency.[2] Ineffective or inadequate schools don't serve students well, especially students who are marginal in terms of economic status, intellectual ability, maturity, or physical or mental health. These are the teenagers who are most likely to drop out of school or turn to delinquency. Young high school dropouts are nearly 10 times as likely as high school graduates and nearly 63 times as likely four-year college graduates to be incarcerated.[3] Let's begin by discussing how school affects the victimization of children and antisocial behavior.

The Purpose of School

Learning Objective 1.

List and explain the goals
of school that affect
delinquency.

Learning Objective 2.

Tell why a school might
be unable to meet the
needs of all its students.

Schools have a number of goals that affect delinquency. When schools accomplish these goals—that is, to educate and socialize children—we expect delinquency to decrease, and when schools fail to accomplish these goals, we shouldn't be surprised to see delinquency and victimization increase. The goals of schools can be roughly divided into the following categories:

» **Academic goals.** Schools strive to help students reach two academic goals. First is the attainment of basic skills such as reading, writing, and math, along with the skills to communicate ideas. The second set of goals concerns the abilities to think rationally, independently, and critically. Schools encourage students to be curious, to accumulate knowledge, and to solve problems. Students who attain these goals are better equipped to make good decisions as adults and compete in society for good jobs.

» **Vocational goals.** Students acquire many vocational skills in school (see Programs for Children for a look at an antidelinquency, national vocational program). In addition to learning the academic skills necessary for almost all jobs, students are expected to learn appropriate work attitudes and habits and to select a career in which they can utilize their particular skills. It's generally accepted that adults who enter satisfying and meaningful careers are less tempted to engage in crime and antisocial behavior.

» **Social, civic, and cultural goals.** Schools also attempt to instill in students the ability to develop meaningful relationships, appreciate and contribute to the culture, and acquire important social values. Schools encourage participation in citizenship activities, such as making informed choices in elections and voting, learning about representational government, contributing to the welfare of fellow citizens, and acting responsibly to preserve the environment. Ideally, schools also teach moral and ethical behavior. Schools encourage students to develop integrity and to evaluate their conduct in light of how it affects others.

» **Personal goals.** These goals include the development of physical and emotional well-being, including self-awareness, physical fitness, self-esteem, and coping skills. Additionally, schools teach students to explore their creativity and to appreciate it in others, as well as to tolerate new ideas. Finally, schools ask students to be responsible for their decisions, set reasonable personal goals, and continually evaluate their abilities and limitations.[4]

Clearly, not all students accomplish these goals to the same degree, and it's unrealistic to expect all students to benefit from their educational experiences in the same way. Several factors affect a student's level of academic and social accomplishment, including differences in mental abilities, economic opportunities, and simple desire and motivation. However, differences in attaining these goals become a major social issue when recurring problems based on race, social class, and gender appear generation after generation.[5] The reasons for such disparities in school quality are largely based on how schools are funded.

9.1 PROGRAMS FOR CHILDREN

Career Academies

Career academies have been used in high schools for about 40 years to help students better prepare for college and work. Although intended to provide vocational training to truant students and students at risk of dropping out of school, career academies are now in operation in schools throughout the nation, serving students from all income levels. Funding for career academies is usually acquired through the state, although some federal funding is available. For example, in 2011, the State of Georgia provided $9 million in grants for career academies.[1]

Designed as "schools within schools," career academies offer small, tight-knit learning environments with academic and technical curricula organized around careers, job training, and work-based learning. About 2,500 career academies are estimated to be in operation around the nation.[2]

Many career academies target youths who have trouble in large, impersonal school environments. Students remain in "small learning communities" with a core group of teachers throughout high school while also attending some regular high school classes. Career academies also partner with local employers to provide career development and work opportunities for students.[3] Research has shown that career academy programs reduce dropout rates, improve attendance, and increase students' likelihood of graduating on time.[4]

THINK ABOUT IT

1. Did you attend a career academy in high school? If so, discuss your experience. If not, do you think a career academy would have increased your interest in school?

At the King Career Center in Anchorage, Alaska, a student grinds a piece of metal in a construction class.

[1]GeorgiaCAN, Career Academies Continue to Grow–$9 Million in Funding Approved in 2011 State Budget, June 2010, www .georgiacareeracademies.org/documents/GeorgiaCAN_June_2010 .pdf.

[2]James J. Kemple and Cynthia J. Willner, "Career Academies Long-Term Impacts on Labor Market Outcomes, Educational Attainment, and Transitions to Adulthood," MDRC, June 2008, www.mdrc.org/ publications/482/overview.html.

[3]Office of Juvenile Justice and Delinquency Prevention, Model Programs Guide, www.ojjdp.gov/mpg/mpgProgramDetails.aspx.

[4]Virginia Child Protection Newsletter, *Truancy and Dropout Prevention* 84, (Fall 2008): 4. Online at psychweb.cisat.jmu.edu/ graysojh/volume%2084.pdf.

School money comes from several sources and levels of government, but schools are mainly under local control. Local property taxes provide most school funding, and local school boards decide many school issues. One main idea behind local control is that the people closest to the schools get to have the most authority. Although local control is a deeply held value, it sometimes results in disparities in school quality.[6] For instance, prosperous communities have more money to spend on schools than impoverished communities, and schools in low-crime areas are likely to have fewer delinquency issues than schools in high-crime areas. These disparities directly affect the quality of education, which can be seen in standardized test scores and other indicators like school safety and rates of dropout and delinquency.[7]

As the United States becomes more racially and ethnically diverse, schools struggle to maintain a level of quality and discipline that meets the needs of all students and keeps them in school and away from serious delinquency. A school or a school district might be unable to do this for many reasons, however.[8]

» **Inappropriate curricula and instruction.** Particularly diverse schools have students who don't speak English or don't speak it well. There is a debate between those who advocate English-only classes as a means of rapid assimilation and those who believe foreign students should be taught at least partly in their native languages. It's much easier for youths who don't speak English to give up on school and instead confine themselves to cultural and linguistic enclaves and possibly the youth gangs that inhabit them.

» **Differences between parental and school norms.** Children from ethnically diverse groups might not have absorbed American middle-class norms. This can cause problems ranging from children who study all the time and do little else, to children who don't value education at all. Additionally, some parents have fixed ideas about the values they want schools to teach their children, and they resist efforts to teach subjects such as evolution and sexual health. Much like the language issues, this difference in norms can alienate students from their schools, separating them from a major socializing institution. Youths with little or no investment in society are more likely to rebel against it and its norms.

» **Lack of previous success in school.** Some students have trouble with difficult subjects because they missed important steps in earlier grades or failed those grades completely. Although rapid progress is possible, some students are discouraged and pessimistic about their chances of succeeding in school because they have failed in the past. Many of these youngsters drop out as soon as possible. Although a school dropout isn't automatically a delinquent, a young adult who doesn't have the diploma to pursue the many good jobs that require one is more likely to be attracted to crime.

» **Teaching difficulties.** Lack of student preparation and effort frustrates teachers. This can be particularly acute if there is a language and/or cultural gap between teachers and students. Student behavioral problems often reflect these concerns.

» **Teacher perceptions and standards.** Teachers assigned to ethnically or economically diverse groups might not expect these students to do well. These expectations might be based on the teacher's own experiences or on data that measure student success. The key is that a teacher's perception is important to how children learn. Teachers with low expectations might find that their students work only to that level, regardless of their economic or ethnic status. A teacher who isn't prepared for the diverse backgrounds of his or her students may have trouble keeping classroom order or keeping students in class at all.

)) **Segregation.** Children from ethnically diverse backgrounds are likely to go to the same school if they live in the same jurisdiction. This means that patterns of learning and attitudes toward authority from the culture at home are likely to be altered as students attempt to fit into the school environment. Youngsters who do well in school may be ostracized by family and friends because they adopt new perspectives. This is especially true when gangs are prominent in the school.

These issues are important to understanding how delinquency happens in schools and how schools encourage social environments that produce delinquency. As a pivotal social institution, the school is both the victim and creator of the atmosphere that allows or encourages young people to engage in antisocial behavior and delinquency. However, blaming schools for delinquency is much like blaming the victim of a crime. When schools are overcrowded, underfunded, and burdened with multiple and conflicting mandates, they shouldn't all be expected to function at the same high level.[9]

Questions

1. What are the goals of schools?
2. How does local control of schools affect school quality and juvenile delinquency?

Keeping Control

The first and most obvious concern about schools is how they control students. During the 2008–2009 school year, about 55.6 million students were enrolled in pre-kindergarten through 12th grade.[10] Without some type of social order, maintaining any learning environment would be impossible, and delinquency would be rampant. Schools have different ways of establishing and maintaining social order, which helps them keep their students safe. Children learn early that they must rein in their immature tendencies and start acting in a more adult manner when they enter school.

In his influential essay "Kindergarten as Academic Boot Camp," sociologist Harry Gracey said the purpose of kindergarten isn't to teach children how to write numbers and letters, but rather to establish the patterns of behavior that make learning possible. They learn to take turns, share materials, be quiet while the teacher is talking, and many other behaviors that convert them from narcissistic five-year-olds to well-behaved students. This is because social order in school is impossible without the cooperation of students.[11] Some experts now believe that attending preschool before kindergarten improves a child's chances of not only doing well in public school but also avoiding delinquency and becoming a successful and productive adult.

A long-term University of Wisconsin study compared urban children who didn't attend preschool with those who did. The children who completed preschool had 41 percent fewer arrests for violent offenses and were 29 percent more likely to graduate from high school.[12] A landmark study, the 1962 Perry Preschool Study, looked at 123 Michigan children, ages 3 and 4, who were at high risk of failing school. Fifty-eight of the children went to preschool for two years, while the rest of the children didn't. Researchers met with the children

Learning Objective 3.

Explain what is meant by "The purpose of kindergarten is to establish the patterns of behavior that make learning possible."

Learning Objective 4.

Describe the pressures that affect teachers.

annually until they were 11, then again at ages 14, 15, 19, 27, and 40. Of the preschoolers, 65 percent graduated from a regular high school, compared with 45 percent of the nonpreschoolers. In the late 1990s, researchers returned to the group, now age 40, to find that over 76 percent of the preschooled men had jobs, compared with 62 percent of the men from the control group. Those who hadn't attended preschool were more likely to be arrested for drug offenses, to be repeat offenders, and to have committed more than one violent felony.[13]

Preschool appears to affect delinquency and crime, but why? Some researchers say teaching children as early as possible about things as simple as holding a book and how to wait turns encourages good behavior and gets children emotionally ready for school. As they mature, youngsters with this increased confidence in school may be less likely to use drugs and alcohol, and get involved with gangs or become delinquent, even if they're from places where crime and delinquency are common.

Although schools need a certain degree of structure, some people believe it comes with a social cost. Two important American values are individualism and creativity, and too much structure can snuff out these qualities, especially in impressionable young children. Schools encourage appropriate behavior by using some tools and techniques that are criticized for sacrificing student welfare for the sake of social control. So how do schools balance the need for control with the desire to foster students' creativity? Here are a few of the more controversial measures.

» **School uniforms.** One problem that school districts face is the disparity in the income of students' families. In what sociologist Thorstein Veblen calls "conspicuous consumption," some students wear expensive clothes that other students' parents can't afford.[14] Some experts believe this visible disparity in social class disrupts learning by creating an obvious caste system within the school. With required uniforms, the economic advantages of some families aren't broadcast by their children. An additional presumed benefit of uniforms in schools where gang activity is a problem is to prevent some youths from displaying gang affiliations. However, not everyone agrees. Research has shown that uniforms can have the opposite effect.[15]

» **Corporal punishment.** Spanking isn't confined to the family. Some schools have policies specifying that disruptive students may be struck with an object as a form of discipline. The object is usually a paddle, and the student is usually struck on the buttocks. The youth's pain and embarrassment are believed to deter future misbehavior. Many states and school districts have set up stringent guidelines on **corporal punishment**, whereas others have dispensed with the practice altogether. School paddling is less related to delinquency—serious delinquency is typically handled by the juvenile justice system, not by schools—than it is to what some experts criticize as the formalized victimization of children.[16] The concern is that victimization of this sort in a major socializing institution sends the message that "might makes right" and that it's acceptable to assault people to make them do what you want. This has interesting implications in an institution whose major problems include bullying, fighting, and sometimes gang violence.

» **Zero-tolerance policies.** An extreme reaction to delinquency is **zero-tolerance policies**. For example, students who bring things to school that can be considered weapons or drugs face severe penalties. The penalties, which can include suspension and expulsion, don't give administrators a lot of discretion. For instance, some jurisdictions treat toy guns as they would firearms, and aspirin as they would cocaine. The severe penalties for minor

INSTANT RECALL
FROM CHAPTER 2

*zero-tolerance
policies*

School regulations that give teachers and administrators little to no discretion in dealing with rule infractions.

Whippings and paddlings have long been used in schools as a form of discipline. In this 19th-century illustration of ancient Rome, a teacher whips a student. Today, more schools are eschewing corporal punishment for more creative disciplinary measures.

or technical rule infractions often make school districts and administrators look foolish. Whether zero-tolerance policies have actually stopped any extreme violence is questionable, but they do send the message that school administrators and teachers are concerned about student safety and that they are doing the best they can to ensure it.[17]

These policies are a response to what many consider to be deterioration in the social climate of the school. Many parents believe that schools were safer and more effective in their day than they are now. But adults might forget, or not realize, that their schools "back in the old days" might have been better funded or had fewer students in the classes. Each year, schools must deal with issues that past generations didn't have to contend with or even be aware of. The next two sections look at the internal constraints and external pressures that limit school effectiveness and contribute to behaviors associated with delinquency.

Preventing Delinquency in School

Children and teenagers spend a lot of time in school, which increases their chances of committing some types of delinquency on school property. For example, middle and high school students are more likely to be victims of crime at school. Although they are more likely to suffer serious violence or homicide away from school, there were 1,135,500 thefts and violent offenses among students ages 12–18 in 2008 at school versus 804,300 offenses away from school (see Figure 9.1).[18] However, serious violent crime still occurs at school. From July 2008 through June 2009, there were 38 school-associated violent deaths among youths ages 5–18. ("School-associated violent death" is a homicide, suicide, or police intervention in which a fatal injury occurs on an elementary or secondary school campus. Victims include students, staff members, and other nonstudents.) In 2008, there were 113,300 serious violent offenses among students ages 12–18. In 2009, nearly 8 percent of students reported being threatened or injured with a weapon on school property.[19]

Schools are also often the target of vandals, who strike on weekends or after school. They pick schools because of bad experiences in the classroom, rebellion against authority, or because they wish to damage a rival's property. A great

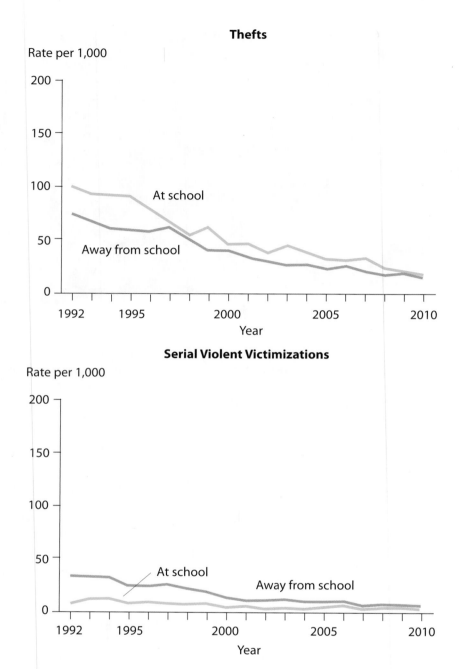

Figure 9.1 Rate of Nonfatal Victimizations Against Students Ages 12–18 per 1,000 Students, by Type of Victimization and Location: 1992–2010.

Think About It

1. Were more or fewer serious violent offenses committed against students in 1992 than in 2010?

Source: Simone Robers, Jijun Zhang, and Jennifer Truman, *Indicators of School Crime and Safety: 2011* (Washington, DC: National Center for Education Statistics, US Department of Education, and Bureau of Justice Statistics, Office of Justice Programs, US Department of Justice, 2012), 11. Online at nces. ed.gov/pubs2012/2012002.pdf.

deal of resources have been devoted to making school a safe learning environment while addressing the needs of students who have the potential to commit a variety of delinquent acts. However, delinquency often consists of spontaneous acts committed against vulnerable targets. Teenagers are especially tempted to have some fun by breaking a window, spray painting a wall, or destroying classroom furniture. Recall from Chapter 5 that criminologist Albert Cohen referred to much of this activity as negativistic, malicious, and of no use, meaning that the reasons and motivations behind school vandalism are often unclear and inconsequential.[20]

Much of this kind of delinquency can be prevented by **target-hardening**, that is, making it more difficult for students to access the school after hours and better monitoring the property. Additionally, it's important during school hours to keep track of where children are and how they're being supervised. As of

2008, 90 percent of schools controlled access to buildings during school hours by locking or monitoring doors, and 43 percent controlled access to the grounds. Also, 55 percent of schools used security cameras for monitoring.[21] Statistics suggest that at least some of these measures, plus increased attention to the prevention of bullying, have decreased the number of children who experience violence at school. The rate of violent-crime victimizations against students ages 12 to 18 at school dropped from 48 per 1,000 students in 1992 to 26 in 2008.[22]

Several commonsense steps can be taken to make vandalism and other forms of delinquency more difficult. School safety goes beyond target-hardening, however. Well-trained staff and teachers who understand the need for safety and are willing to implement a security plan can significantly increase the students' sense of safety. School safety doesn't just happen. It must be carefully planned and have plenty of resources allocated to it. Teachers and students who aren't afraid of disruptive students or outside troublemakers can focus on teaching and learning. One study suggests that commonsense initiatives such as supportive leadership, dedicated teachers and administrators, behavior management for the entire school, and good academic instruction go a long way toward reducing the chances for delinquency.[23]

Another hypothesis that has shown some promise is that of **school bonding**, which is the connection students have to their schools, their lives there, and their academic work. One study has found that high levels of school bonding might decrease student use of drugs and alcohol. Major aspects of school bonding include the following:

1. Attachment to school (how much the student cares about the school)
2. Attachment to personnel (the quality of the student's connection with the teachers, staff, and administration)
3. School commitment (how much the student participates in school activities and how important these activities are for the student)

The bond students have to their schools can affect drug and alcohol use, delinquency, antisocial behavior, academic performance, and self-esteem. Students who are more attached to their schools, according to research, enjoy better self-esteem and better grades. In turn, schools that successfully bond with their students often see less antisocial behavior, as well as lower levels of drug and alcohol use and delinquency.[24] Research on youth substance abuse found that students who were poorly bonded to school were less likely to believe the use of drugs or alcohol would prevent them from achieving their life goals.[25]

What About the Teachers?

Teaching has long been considered an honorable profession that attracts talented individuals who are intelligent and have a calling to serve others by doing an important job. However, several factors have greatly compromised the ability of teachers to teach according to their standards. These factors include pressure from administrators, parents, and government. Well-meaning programs, such as the federal government's **No Child Left Behind Act** initiative, have had unintended consequences that have made the job of teaching less attractive. Here are some other internal pressures when teaching school:

» **Standardization and regimentation.** Schools are required to account for the money they spend and the learning activities they present to students. Financially, this is a good idea, but unfortunately it limits teachers' discretion to design individualized lessons. In an attempt to standardize the curricula, schools have adopted a one-size-fits-all philosophy that doesn't take advantage of the unique skills of individual teachers. One reason teenagers drop out of school, often to become involved in delinquency, is because they're bored and believe the lessons aren't relevant to their lives.

» **Standardized testing.** School systems, schools, administrators, and teachers are evaluated on how well students perform on nationwide standardized tests. Schools that don't measure up can lose funding or even their accreditation. Critics of standardized testing say it ignores important factors such as the amount of resources and quality of funding that schools get and how well students are prepared when they arrive at school.

» **Tracking.** Given the wide range of student abilities, interests, and motivations, many school districts group students with similar needs and abilities. **Tracking** youths with similar abilities and interests allows teachers to teach at a pace that is appropriate for everyone. Tracking has been criticized, however, for preventing some students from succeeding in school by forcing them into tracks that offer little academic challenge. Here, a bit of labeling theory can be applied. Although these tracks might have value-free titles, everyone in the school knows which tracks are for students who have special needs, have low IQs, are academically slow, or simply wish to prepare for a vocation rather than college. Students in these tracks might meet with derision from their classmates and lower expectations from everyone else. This puts extra pressure on teachers to make sure these students don't lose faith in their schools and decide to drop out at the first opportunity, increasing their risk of delinquency.[26]

» **Limited teacher authority.** Despite being held responsible for what happens inside the classroom, teachers have limited authority to discipline students. Because of past abuses and society's increasingly litigious attitude, teachers must maintain classroom order without a great deal of formal authority. Formal procedures for dealing with problem students involve school administrators who are trained and mandated to dispense discipline. Unfortunately, teachers and administrators have only limited authority to deal with students who are disruptive or who commit minor delinquency, and much of the success of their disciplinary procedures depends on parental support. Severely disruptive or delinquent students might be referred to law enforcement.

These internal pressures make delinquency more likely because school officials often don't have the authority and resources necessary to maintain safe and effective schools. Teacher burnout can make an exemplary school mediocre and a poorly performing school dangerous.[27]

Schools must also respond to outside pressures that affect the way they handle students. These outside pressures have many sources, and it's difficult to tell if the threat is legitimate, significant, or potentially harmful. As an example, let's discuss the relationship between schools and parents. Parental involvement is important to school success. Schools work hard to get parents to reinforce the educational mission and to keep them involved in the encouragement of their children's education. Not all parents, however, are equal to this task. Parents have a range of educational experiences of their own and possess different degrees of ability to appreciate the efforts of schools and teachers. Some parents are school dropouts and are limited in their ability to help their children prepare for and negotiate the challenges of school. Other parents are extremely well educated and have high expectations for their children's school, some of which may be unrealistic.[28]

Teachers sometimes find themselves dealing with parents who are clueless about what the school can and can't deliver in terms of a quality education. Affluent parents often abandon public schools and enroll their children in private schools. Although the property taxes of these parents still support the public school, their involvement is lost. Still other parents become deeply involved in their schools and communities. The intent isn't to blame parents for the failure of the schools to provide a quality education, but rather to point out that schools get a variety of input from parents, not all of it positive. Sometimes, parents might refuse to recognize the limitations they have placed on their children with their own biases and lack of support. Some parents may turn a blind eye to their children's delinquent behavior and refuse to allow the school to correct it. In some instances, parents are confrontational or even violent with teachers or school administrators.[29]

Another external factor that affects the school's ability to educate is gangs. Schools aren't immune from community problems, and because they are where youngsters are legislated to be, a community's gang activity often follows. Chapter 10 deals with gangs in detail, but it's important here to understand that schools aren't always equipped to handle serious gang problems and are often where gang issues are contested. The external stresses of drugs, violence, and rebellion that accompany gang life not only complicate the school's mission, but also might change the environment to the point where the school is more like an armed camp than a place of learning.[30]

Questions

1. What might prevent a school or school district from maintaining high quality and discipline?
2. How do schools control and discipline students? What are some controversial measures?
3. What is school bonding?

School Safety

When parents send their children to school, they have every right to expect that their children will be safe from physical and psychological harm. Most schools meet this expectation. School officials and teachers work hard to provide students with a safe learning environment. There are, of course, exceptions. Some teachers harm students; some students harm teachers; and some students harm each other.

Fortunately, students are rarely seriously harmed at school. So why is the impression that the school is a dangerous place for children so widespread? Part of this impression comes from the way the media sensationalize school crime. Although these events are rare, school crime has been elevated from local news to national news. In many rather routine situations, the media have focused on linking unrelated cases in distant physical locations as if some sort of national trend were afoot. The most visible of these attempts is the coverage of school shootings.

School Shootings

Over the past two decades, there have been several well-publicized cases in which students have murdered several other students and teachers.[31] School shootings in Littleton, Colorado; Red Lake, Minnesota; and Jonesboro, Arkansas, have affected the entire nation. Each case represents different issues in

Learning Objective 5.

Understand why school shootings don't represent typical juvenile delinquency, and outline the more pertinent issues of juvenile delinquency and schools.

Learning Objective 6.

Discuss why bullying hasn't been taken seriously until recently and how it's related to delinquency.

Technological security measures have increased at schools in recent decades. Metal detectors and security cameras are common sights.

terms of the motivation of the shooter(s), number of people killed, and effect on the community, and all are worth exploring in their own right. However, for our purposes, we will take a look at the case that has become the signature case of school shootings: Columbine High School in Littleton, Colorado.

On April 20, 1999, two high school seniors, Dylan Klebold and Eric Harris, walked into Columbine High School carrying two 20-pound propane bombs in duffel bags that they placed in the cafeteria. They set the timers and went outside to wait for the explosions. When the bombs didn't explode, they went back inside with an assortment of weapons and proceeded to shoot people indiscriminately. Over the next hour, they fired 188 rounds of ammunition and threw 76 bombs, 30 of which exploded. Klebold and Harris killed 13 people, then themselves.[32]

Two remarkable aspects of this case inspired school administrators and law enforcement to develop new procedures for ensuring that schools will be better protected from this type of attack. The first aspect is the apparent absence of any compelling motivations on the part of Klebold and Harris. No one saw this attack coming. The boys were well behaved at school, and their parents didn't know they were making bombs in the garage. The second remarkable aspect of the case is the inadequate response of law enforcement. With no coordinated plan, police took a long time to fully comprehend the extent of the threat and to try to remove the attackers. Each of these aspects bears further examination in terms of how it has compelled authorities to plan for the prevention of and response to future incidents of extreme school violence.[33]

Were there warning signs that indicated that Klebold and Harris were capable of committing such a violent act? This question can never be fully answered. Klebold and Harris were unremarkable students who appeared to inhabit the fringes of several marginal groups. Much was made of the trench coats the boys wore to conceal their weapons and bombs. They were believed to be part of a clique called the "trench-coat mafia," and after the incident, others in this clique were questioned. In reality, the boys had given no indications that they were planning the attack. It's tempting to speculate that the boys were predisposed to violence because of their marginality and their preoccupation with video games, and because they were picked on by athletes in the school. But are these really substantial indicators of potential violence? Thousands of youths fit this profile, never harm anyone, and grow up to become normal and productive adults.

Robert Wooden and Randy Blazek deal with youth alienation in their book *Renegade Kids, Suburban Outlaws*. One central idea is that teenagers are alienated from society, especially the school, so they seek meaning in various subcultures that fulfill their need for identity, empowerment, and relationships with others similar to them. Much of youth culture exists in response to the feelings that teenagers have of being unconnected to the dominant culture.[34] For instance, body piercing and tattoos reflect attempts to express alienation with parents, schools, and society.

One problematic feature of this alienation related to delinquency is how the bar of deviance is continually raised. What used to shock people in the 1960s—bell-bottom pants, marijuana, long hair, and loud rock music—is now so common that it goes unnoticed. To attract attention and express the right amount of alienation, some music has become more socially offensive, fashions and hairstyles have fragmented to the point where anything may be considered okay, and today's degree of scarring, branding, tattooing, and piercing was unimaginable in the 1960s.[35] So how does a youth filled with rage get attention in a society where nothing is shocking? Shooting one's schoolmates certainly fits the bill. More common, however, is membership in a particularly dangerous gang, petty theft, promiscuous sex, binge drinking, and dropping out of school altogether, all of which are hallmarks of delinquency.

This observation brings us back to Harris and Klebold. Writings of theirs that were released in 2006 reveal not a pair of psychotic adolescents, but young men who were normal teenagers in many ways. Both were deeply depressed: Harris because he felt no one liked him and that everyone made fun of him, and Klebold because of an unrequited crush on a girl and the fact that one of his friends now preferred spending time with a new girlfriend. These adolescent concerns are typical, and usually evaporate with adulthood. Why Klebold and Harris chose the path that they did, spectacular violence rather than typical rebellion or delinquency, and why millions of teenagers with the same problems go on to successful adulthoods will probably remain a mystery.[36]

High school students line up before school for a security check. The week before, the school had failed to use a metal detector to check students' property, and a gun went off in a student's backpack, wounding two classmates.

Perhaps the most important thing to realize about school shootings is that they don't represent any typical aspect of delinquency. Like serial killers, young people angry enough to commit mass murder at school do exist, and school shootings have happened. However, they represent extreme exceptions within delinquency, just as serial killers represent the extreme exception among felons and even among convicted murderers. This is one reason the police response to Columbine was so inadequate. The officers had never faced anything like it before, and the incident was outside their training. Most police officers, most parents, and most children will never have to deal with a school shooting. Most of us will experience school shootings, if there ever are any more, only from our television sets and computer screens in the form of media coverage.[37]

The real issues of delinquency and schools are those that we hear about every day: gangs, status offenses, bullying, drug and alcohol use, and relatively minor delinquent behaviors such as theft and fighting. Behavior that leads to school violence, such as bringing a weapon to school, has actually declined in the past several years (see Figure 9.2), as has the number of youngsters who kill their acquaintances (although youngsters still murder their acquaintances more than they do strangers or family members).[38] And, as we learned in Chapter 8, most children who are murdered die at the hands of adults, not other children and not at school.

Bullying

Although school shootings are rare, they have gotten a great deal of publicity, altered school safety policies, and generated fear. An issue related to school safety that hasn't received the coverage of school shootings but is more prevalent and worthy of increased attention is **bullying**. Bullying is the victimization of youths by their peers. It can range from verbal taunts, threats, and put-downs to deadly physical assaults. For some children, the experience of being bullied can result in severe trauma that affects them for many years. Some youths even commit suicide because they can't see their lives as ever improving. See Focus on Diversity for a look at the work of the It Gets Better Project in helping teens look ahead to adulthood.[39]

Bullying is nothing new. It has been part of the experience of school children for as long as there have been schools. Unfortunately, until recently, bullying was considered a normal part of growing up and the way youngsters establish social hierarchy. However, bullying is a serious problem among children and in schools

Figure 9.2 Percentage of Youths Who Have Carried a Weapon onto School Property, 1993–2009

Think About It

1. Discuss reasons why the number of youths who have carried weapons onto school property has been dropping.

Source: National Center for Chronic Disease Prevention and Health Promotion, Youth Risk Behavior Surveillance System, Unintentional Injuries and Violence: Carried A Weapon On School Property On At Least 1 Day, apps.nccd.cdc.gov/youthonline/App/Default.aspx. Accessed April 2012.

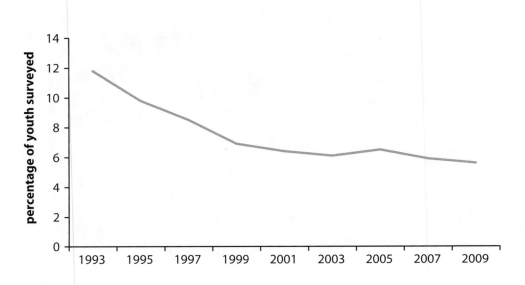

around the world. Although bullying itself might not constitute delinquency, the US Department of Health and Human Services reports that delinquency and early criminal offending seems to be rooted in childhood aggression, of which bullying is one aspect.

Although bullying can take physical and psychological forms, experts say physical bullying isn't as common as psychological forms, such as exclusion, name-calling, and gossip. International experts say bullying happens the same way in every school, everywhere. Norway began its antibullying campaign in 1982 after three adolescents committed suicide as a result of bullying. The nation instituted what became known as the Olweus Bullying Prevention Program, which established classroom rules governing acceptable behavior, teacher-development groups, and counseling for bullies, victims, and parents. In three years, school bullying was reported to have fallen by 50 percent.[40] The program calls on elementary and middle school teachers and staff to create a caring and involved environment and to act as both authority figures and role models. It also sets firm limits on disruptive behavior and handles violations of the rules in a nonviolent manner.[41]

Several other nations have developed antibullying programs that use a variety of methods. Israel has had success merely by increasing adult supervision. Studies there found bullying occurs most often when adults aren't around to stop it: in hallways, restrooms, on the playground, after school, and when the teacher has left the room. In some cases, bullying can be controlled merely by giving a problematic situation some specific attention. In one study, carried out in a very small rural school that consisted of one teacher and 28 students, acquaintances of the bully were asked to keep an eye on the bully and physically restrain the youth from further harassing the victim. The bully ceased the harassment thanks to the immediacy and intentionality of the response by the bully's peers.[42]

We will deal with bullying in detail for two reasons. First, bullying, although not restricted to schools, is most common there and has the greatest effect there. The second reason is that bullying can deeply affect both the victim and the school's social environment. Bullying is related to delinquency because it often includes actual criminal offenses and can influence victims or bullies to become delinquent themselves.

Young people have a desperate need to belong. In school, especially, they establish cliques that share their viewpoints, social status, and biases. Youngsters work hard to establish identity by rigidly enforcing the in-group exclusiveness of their **clique**.[43] After all, how cool are you and your friends when anyone is allowed to join? A clique's initiation is usually informal and can range from mild to severe. Initiations usually entail mild forms of physical or psychological assault and can be recognized by anyone who has endured grade school. Here are a few ways youngsters bully others and try to establish social dominance.

» **Name-calling.** Young people establish social hierarchy in a number of ways. One is to exclude others by designating them as undesirable based on some characteristic they might or might not control. For instance, race is an obvious way that youths divide themselves. Despite the efforts of administrators and teachers, race continues to be a major sorting mechanism. Racial epithets are used to remind victims they are outside a particular clique and that they are considered inferior regardless of their accomplishments. Name-calling also singles out those with physical abnormalities or alternative lifestyles, or who participate in specific activities. For instance, playing tuba in the band might be socially rewarded by some peers but derided by others. Name-calling can be a cruel and debilitating experience and is used to terrorize those without much social capital.[44]

FOCUS ON DIVERSITY 〉 *It Gets Better*

In July 2010, 15-year-old Justin Aaberg, a gay student who had frequently been bullied at school for his sexual orientation, hanged himself in his room at home.[1] Then, in September, another 15-year-old, Billy Lucas, hanged himself in his parents' barn when other students picked on him for being gay.[2] Then, three more youths—Tyler Clementi, 18; Asher Brown, 13; and Seth Walsh, 13—committed suicide.[3] These incidents were the last straw for gay and antibullying activists across the nation.

Just weeks later, columnist and author Dan Savage and his partner Terry Miller began the It Gets Better Project with an Internet video describing their experiences as gay teenagers in high school, how their lives improved once high school ended, and how an adult can live a positive life free of bullying.[4] What followed was a series of Internet videos recorded by entertainers, actors, athletes, politicians, and even President Obama urging young people to endure high school and wait for their adult lives to begin.

Lesbian, gay, bisexual, and transgender (LGBT) students have particularly difficult issues with bullying. Over 85 percent report being harassed because of their orientation, and over 20 percent report assault and battery. Unfortunately, teachers and school administrators have a reputation for doing little or nothing to protect these students, even if parents get involved. Facing daily verbal and physical attacks, LGBT students commit suicide at rates three to four times higher than straight students.[5]

Today, the It Gets Better Project continues to produce videos, raise funds for LGBT charities, and provide hope to bullied youths. With all the attention, schools are beginning to pay more attention to the problems of bullying and the struggles of LGBT youths, as well as other youths who just "don't fit in."

In this photo, Tammy Aaberg holds a photo of her son Justin. Aaberg has set up a support group called Justin's Gift for young people who are bullied for their sexuality.

THINK ABOUT IT

1. Go to the It Gets Better Project (http://www.itgetsbetter.org) and watch some of the videos. Do you think this project will help decrease bullying? If not, what would?

---

[1] David Crary, "Suicide Surge: Schools Confront Anti-gay Bullying," AP/MSNBC, 2010, www.msnbc.msn.com/id/39593311/ns/us_news-life/t/suicide-surge-schools-confront-anti-gay-bullying/.
[2] Kara Brooks, "Bullied Greensburg Student Takes His Own Life," Fox59, September 13, 2010, www.fox59.com/news/wxin-greensburg-student-suicide-091310,0,1101685.story.
[3] John Cloud, "Bullied To Death?" *Time* 176, no. 16 (October 18, 2010): 60–63.
[4] It Gets Better Project, www.itgetsbetter.org.
[5] Stuart Biegel, Sheila James Kuehl, and the National Education Policy Center, University of Colorado at Boulder, "Safe at School: Addressing the School Environment and LGBT Safety through Policy and Legislation," National Education Policy Center (October 1, 2010).

》 **Practical jokes, shoving, and other forms of physical dominance.** Some youths bully others by making them the object of jokes or mild physical aggression. A boy who knocks the books out of another boy's hands when passing him in the hallway sends the message that the aggressor is dominant and that the victim dare not challenge the affront. Although it's tempting to dismiss this as typical "kids will be kids" behavior, it can have real consequences for the victim. Humiliation in front of your peers can be devastating. Being a victim of such attacks can cause a child to lose focus on his or her schoolwork and avoid going to school. This type of bullying may even be learned by the victim and used on younger and weaker children. It's important to break the consistent cycle of bully–victim–bully.[45]

》 **Assault.** This type of bullying worries adults the most. Some children are severely injured by beatings from older or bigger students. As with all types of bullying, this isn't confined to boys but is also common among some groups of girls. The beating usually isn't the first time the victim has been attacked. These incidences are often the result of a pattern of ever-increasing aggressive behavior against the victim. It's difficult to satisfy the committed bully because each day the victim reappears, and a new and more aggressive act is expected by the bully's friends. After a time, the bully has to physically harm the victim or risk losing his or her tough reputation. In the most extreme cases, this violent escalation can result in the victim's death.

A final consequence of bullying is, perhaps, suffered by the bully. Bullies who are allowed to continue their behavior and profit from it socially risk taking it with them into adulthood.[46] Bullying worked for them when they were young, so why wouldn't it work as an adult? The bully might become accustomed to gaining social capital from the behavior and continue it in some form into adult life. Although some adult bullies stop physically tormenting others, they may continue to psychologically intimidate their spouses, co-workers, employees, and children. Depending on the personalities around them, these bullies can go on to lead successful and law-abiding adult lives, even while causing those who live and work with them a lot of stress. Adult bullies who never graduate from physical bullying invariably find themselves in trouble with the law. Or the bully may finally stumble on a more powerful person, perhaps another bully, who won't be pushed around. If the adult bully is particularly violent and has enough run-ins with the law, this meeting might happen in prison.[47]

Questions

1. How do school shootings relate to general school safety?
2. How do youngsters try to establish social dominance?

School Failure and Juvenile Delinquency

Students who fail in school are more likely to have a difficult time for the rest of their lives, even if they never break the law. Academic failure, disciplinary practices such as suspension and expulsion, and dropping out are the important factors in the **school-to-prison pipeline**.[48] (See Crosscurrents for more about the school-to-prison pipeline.) A high school diploma or **GED** (general education diploma) is a vital requirement for a number of occupations, and people who don't have a diploma, degree, or certificate can be automatically excluded from many jobs. Professions like medicine, law, architecture, and education cooperate

Learning Objective 7.
Tell what the "school-to-prison" pipeline is.

Learning Objective 8.
Outline the reasons youths have for dropping out of school.

with legislators to ensure that those who want to work in those professions meet certain standards.

Many tasks that require little in terms of advanced skill or education still require a high school diploma or GED. This requirement is assumed to ensure that the applicant can read instructions and has enough problem-solving skills to work independently. Although a diploma is not always a reliable indicator that someone will be a good employee or will find a good job—many people who haven't finished high school find well-paid, satisfying work—most employers require a high school diploma, which can be a barrier for many young people who drop out of school.

School failure can have severe consequences. A youngster who is identified as an academic failure can suffer troubling psychological and sociological problems. For instance, when a student doesn't meet the minimal standards to finish a grade and is made to repeat classes, go to summer school, or drop back a grade level, the student might be labeled by teachers and peers as "dumb." It's true that some students may not be smart, but it's more likely that students who fall behind just aren't able to flourish under their school's conditions.[49] The psychological damage done to these youths, the not-very-smart and the smart-but-not-responding, can be devastating. In Chapter 5, we learned in the discussion of **labeling theory** that people treat deviants differently because of the label (primary deviance) and that the deviant will internalize the label and act as if it were true (secondary deviance).[50]

INSTANT RECALL
FROM CHAPTER 5

labeling theory

A theory that describes how a label applied by society can affect an individual's self-perception and behavior.

Students who have trouble in school experience primary deviance in several ways. First, the student might be placed in a classroom with other students who aren't expected to succeed. This means that expectations for everyone are lowered, and when one of the students does learn something, he or she may be ignored or even picked on for exceeding the class norms or teacher expectations. It doesn't take too many times of being right but getting ignored or punished before the student will learn to not stick out, and become withdrawn or rebellious. This type of student is further labeled as problematic, and his or her every action is under supervision and review.

Secondary deviance is even more of an issue in delinquency. Youths who are labeled as failures often give up on their educations because they come to believe they aren't cut out for school. They might express this belief through delinquent acts aimed at the school or classmates, or they might simply withdraw from all school activities. Negative early school experiences can convince children who have learning disabilities or who are late bloomers that they will never be able to compete with those who do well in school early on. Whether these youths drop out of school or not, the ramifications of early failure can continually plague their self-esteem and prevent them from even trying to do well in school.[51]

Suspension and Expulsion

There is a special relationship between delinquency and the traditional school punishments of suspension and expulsion. A common outcome for misbehaving students is a series of suspensions that culminate in expulsion. Students who are suspended from school are often the least likely to have an adult at home to supervise them. According to 2009 census data, children from impoverished homes were more likely to have been suspended than children from homes at or above poverty level (see Figure 9.3).[52] Perhaps not coincidentally, youngsters who do the sort of things to get suspended or expelled—use drugs, commit delinquent acts, threaten or commit violence—aren't only poor but have been abused, are depressed, or are mentally ill. Between 45 and 60 percent of incarcerated juveniles

9.2 **crosscurrents**

Shutting Off the School-to-Prison Pipeline

Many kids don't like school. In fact, children often go through a phase in which they don't make the best grades and hate being in a classroom. However, most of them don't end up in front of a judge. For some children, bad grades, a dislike of school, and classroom disciplinary problems aren't a phase, but a regular occurrence. Unfortunately, many of these children cross over into delinquency.

A common term to describe the cycle of academic failure and poor school bonding that ends in delinquency is the "school-to-prison pipeline." The frequency of school discipline is one good indicator of who ends up in the pipeline: the more disciplinary action a child receives, the less likely he or she is to make good grades and feel like he or she belongs in the school environment.

Unfortunately, research has shown that black youths—who are already arrested at rates disproportionate to whites (see Chapter 6, Focus on Diversity: Race and Arrests)— are more likely than children of other races to be disciplined at school.[1] One study, which found that the behavior of black students was no worse than the behavior of students of other races, noted that research had shown that black students' behavior was often *perceived* as being more hostile and thus attracted more disciplinary action.[2] This differential perception and treatment may begin as early as elementary school and build until the students, who eventually realize they're being punished more than white students, disengage from school entirely.

In many cases, black students (as well as Hispanic and special-needs students) are simply expelled from school. According to a Texas school report, during the 2008–2009 school year, more than 8,000 students were expelled from the state's schools. Of these expulsions, black students weren't only overrepresented, they tended to be expelled for vague, subjective reasons.[3] A Georgia Appleseed report found that black students were more than three times as likely as students of other races to receive an out-of-school suspension.[4] Nationally, black students are nearly three times as likely to be suspended and three and a half times as likely to be expelled as white students.[5]

These statistics and reports raise more questions than they answer. Why is disciplinary treatment disproportionate? Could such treatment be directly responsible for feeding the school-to-prison pipeline?

Research has shown that black youths are more likely than children of other races to be disciplined at school, often because their behavior was perceived as being hostile.

In an attempt to address these concerns, the US government announced the Supportive School Discipline Initiative, a national effort at improving school discipline procedures. According to US Secretary of Education Arne Duncan, kids "don't need to be pushed out the door or to start a criminal record."[6]

THINK ABOUT IT

1. Have you heard of the "school-to-prison" pipeline? Has it affected anyone you know? If so, discuss your answer.

[1] Black youths comprise about 15 percent of the under-18 population (according to the 2010 Census, The Black Alone Population in the United States: 2010, http://www.census.gov/population/www/socdemo/race/ppl-ba10.html, Table 1), but 31 percent of under-18 arrests in 2009 (Crime in the United States, 2009, Table 43, http://www2.fbi.gov/ucr/cius2009/data/table_43.html). Michael Rocque and Raymond Paternoster, "Understanding the Antecedents of the 'School-to-Jail' Link: The Relationship between Race and School Discipline," *Journal of Criminal Law and Criminology* 101, no. 2 (August 2011): 633–665.

[2] Rocque and Paternoster, "Understanding the Antecedents of the 'School-to-Jail' Link."

[3] Texas Appleseed, *Texas' School-to-Prison Pipeline: School Expulsion: The Path from Lockout to Dropout*, April 2010, 3–4, http://www.texasappleseed.net. Forrest Wilder, "Too Black for School? How Race Skews School Discipline in Texas," *Texas Observer*, May 5, 2010, http://www.texasobserver.org/cover-story/too-black-for-school.

[4] Georgia Appleseed Center for Law & Justice, *Effective Student Discipline: Keeping Kids In Class*, June 2011, 7, /www.gaappleseed.org/keepingkidsinclass/executive-summary.pdf.

[5] American Civil Liberties Union, "ACLU Hails Obama Administration's Supportive School Discipline Initiative," July 21, 2011, /www.aclu.org/racial-justice/aclu-hails-obama-administrations-supportive-school-discipline-initiative.

[6] Ben Firke, "Ending the School-to-Prison Pipeline," July 22, 2011, ED.gov Blog, www.ed.gov/blog/2011/07/ending-the-school-to-prison-pipeline.

Figure 9.3 Percentage of Children Aged 12 To 17 Years Who Have Ever Been Suspended From School, By Level Of Poverty

Children who live below poverty are suspended from school more often.

Think About It

1. Why would impoverished children be suspended from school more often than other children? Discuss your reasoning.

Source: US Census Bureau, A Child's Day: 2009, Table D18: Academic Performance and Experience of School Age Children— Characteristics of Families and Households with Children Age 6 to 17: 2009. Online at www.census.gov/hhes/socdemo/children/ data/sipp/well2009/tables.html.

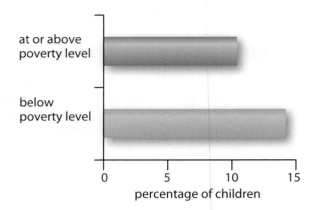

have learning disabilities or brain-based disorder.[53] These are the children who need an adult the most, or even professional help. Isolating them from peers, friends, concerned adults, the culture of the school, and possibly any mental health professionals on staff who might be able to help is unlikely to correct the youth's behavior and might even make it worse.

This is especially important to the issue of delinquency because suspensions and expulsions separate the youngster with problems from the society he or she ultimately has to live in. The boy or girl who is increasingly estranged from socializing institutions, such as the school, may eventually see little point in trying to do what society expects and instead turn to delinquency. At this point, the next social institution the youngster is likely to encounter is law enforcement. Generally, a child or teenager who is home alone all day will find other things to do, and these things may include running with a gang or becoming involved in other kinds of delinquency.[54] According to a Centers for Disease Control and Prevention study, youths who aren't in school are more likely to get into fights, use drugs, smoke cigarettes, and carry weapons.[55]

Still, schools must have a way to deal with disruptive students and to protect and nurture students who aren't disruptive. Removing the problem student is often the easiest and most efficient way to do this. However, several school districts have dispensed with traditional suspension and expulsion. Some transfer problem students to supervised suspension areas or require a student's parents to attend school with him or her for part of the day. Others have the students do community-service work at the school when classes aren't in session.[56]

Dropping Out

The reasons for dropping out of school cover a broad range of motivations, some the fault of the youth and the family and others attributable to the school climate and administrative procedures. Let's review some of the reasons teenagers drop out of school and how these reasons are related to crime and delinquency.

>> **Academic failure.** Many students drop out because they simply can't keep up. They are held back a grade while their friends advance. They find themselves in classrooms with children one or two years younger, and although they can compete on the playground or athletic fields, they're still unable to keep up in the classroom. This repeated and visible failure takes its toll

on the student's self-concept and often results in a teenager dropping out the first chance he or she gets. Table 9.1 provides an interesting look at the earliest age that each state allows a student to quit school. Although some dropouts might eventually return to school and earn a GED, many never return. For all practical purposes, their formal education is over, and their reading, math, and logic abilities are fixed. These limitations can decide what types of work they can get, making delinquency and crime attractive alternatives. Further, dropping out of school can be alienating and cause the youth to distrust authority and to scorn the ethos of working hard, saving money, and planning for the future.[57]

)) **Unmet special needs.** Schools sometimes miss the opportunity to recognize students' special needs. Those with learning disabilities and attention-deficit issues go undiagnosed, and their issues get attributed to low IQ or behavioral problems. For many of these youngsters, school is frustrating. Without successful interventions, dropping out is an escape from a climate where they are the victim of forces beyond their control. It's often a short step to delinquency and crime for those whose special needs went unrecognized and unmet. Sometimes the schools can diagnose the problem but don't have the facilities, staff, or programs to solve it. These youngsters can become bitter when they see resources going to athletes, cheerleaders, the band, and other extracurricular activities while their basic needs appear to be ignored.[58]

)) **Cultural issues.** Often, schools can do little to prevent some students from dropping out. This is especially true when the students come from diverse social and cultural backgrounds. Although a school might try to foster a multicultural climate, sometimes the subculture of the student's family or peers is too strong to overcome. For instance, parents may require their children to quit school and work in the family business, or they may believe that daughters don't need as much education as sons and remove their daughters from school. Some parents just don't care if their children are in school or not. A youngster's involvement in gangs can also be a problem. The gang can be a **greedy institution** that demands time and loyalty. Gangs generally don't value academic success, and the gang might be successful instead in coercing youngsters with a chance to succeed in school into deviant and antisocial behaviors. Dropping out of school and joining the local gang might seem like an obligation.[59]

)) **Boredom and questions of relevance.** Many students find that school isn't exciting enough to keep them interested. The school routine of classes, homework, sitting for an hour being lectured at, and taking tests is boring. Many youngsters feel alive only when outside the classroom, on the ball field, in some student club, or just hanging out with friends. They long for the time when they can have greater control of their daily schedule and don't have to adhere to the demands of teachers, administrators, and parents. The early signs of dropping out of school are truancy, behavioral problems in the classroom, refusing to do homework, not caring about grades, and taking shortcuts such as cheating and plagiarism. These youngsters are in danger of turning to delinquency as a response to the feeling that school can't give them what they want out of life and is, in fact, standing in the way. To them, school is just another opportunity for failure, and the sooner they can get out and on to something important, the better. Unfortunately, many of these youngsters have no realistic plan for something better. They

TABLE 9.1 〉 Ages that School Attendance is Required, by State

STATE	REQUIRED ATTENDANCE AGES	EXEMPTIONS
Alabama	7	legally and regularly employed under child labor laws
Alaska	7	none
Arizona	6	14 with parental consent and gainfully employed
Arkansas	5	17*	*must complete school year; otherwise no exceptions
California	6	18	none
Colorado	7	16	with current age and school certificate or work permit
Connecticut	5	18	16 with parental consent
Delaware	5	16	none
D.C.	5	18	none
Florida	6	16	16 with parental consent
Georgia	6	16	none
Hawaii	6	18	15
Idaho	7	16	none
Illinois	7	17	employed and excused by school official
Indiana	7	18	16 with consent of parent and principal; 14 if parent agrees and state labor bureau issues certificate; must return to school within 5 days of termination of employment
Iowa	6	16	none
Kansas	7	18	17 or 16 with parental consent
Kentucky	6	16	none
Louisiana	7	18	17 with parental consent
Maine	7	17	15
Maryland	5	16	none
Massachusetts	6	16	14
Michigan	6	18	none
Minnesota	7	16	none
Mississippi	6	17	none
Missouri	7	17	14
Montana	7	16*	*or completion of 8th grade, whichever is later; otherwise, no exceptions
Nebraska	7	18	14 and 16 with parental consent; special legislation for home schooling

Schools and Delinquency | **CHAPTER 9** 305

State			
Nevada	7	18	14 and excused by board of trustees; 14 if work is necessary for own or parents' support.
New Hampshire	6	16	none
New Jersey	6	16	none
New Mexico	5, or 8 if parents and school board agree	High school graduation	17 if excused by school board and gainfully employed; or student is in alternative schooling with parental consent; otherwise no exceptions
New York	6	17*	*in cities with population of 4,500 or more and union-free school districts; 16 if approved by local school board; otherwise, no exceptions
North Carolina	7	16	none
North Dakota	7	16	necessary to family support
Ohio	6	18	16 with parental and superintendent permission
Oklahoma	5	18	16 with written joint agreement
Oregon	7	18	or excused by district school board; 16 with school administration and parental consent
Pennsylvania	8	17	16 with certificate and regular employment; 15 in farm work or domestic service in private home with permit; 14, employed as above if completed elementary school with permit recommended by district superintendent or private school principal
Rhode Island	6	18	16 with written parental consent
South Carolina	5	17	16; further attendance is determined by court to be disruptive, unproductive or not in child's best interest
South Dakota	6	16	or completion of 8th grade if member of certain religious organizations; otherwise no exceptions
Tennessee	6	18	none
Texas	6	18	none
Utah	6	18	16 and 8th grade completed; home-schooled minors exempt from attendance
Vermont	6	16	15, completed 6th grade and needed for family support
Virginia	5	18	exempt with parental consent along with that of principal or superintendent or a court ruling that the minor can't benefit from school
Washington	8	18	16 and parent agrees that child should not be required to attend, or child is emancipated, or child has certificate of competence
West Virginia	6	16	none
Wisconsin	6	18	none
Wyoming	7	16	none

Think About It
1. Which is the only state that, with a few allowances, requires high school graduation?

Source: U.S. Department of Labor, Employment Related Provisions in State Compulsory School Attendance Laws - January 1, 2010, www.dol.gov/whd/state/schoolattend2010.htm.

Many students find that school isn't exciting enough to keep them interested.

are ill-equipped financially, emotionally, and intellectually to enter the workforce with the skills and work habits it takes to succeed. Teenagers who drop out of school face two problems connected to delinquency. The first involves getting enough money to buy what they want. The second is what to do with their time. Dropouts can quickly get bored with hanging out with their friends, in much the same way they were bored in school. They crave excitement and fun, as well as the money to buy it, which can lead them into taking lawbreaking risks.[60]

» **Delinquency and crime.** Finally, many teenagers drop out or are thrown out of school because of criminal or delinquent acts. Schools are obligated to provide a safe learning environment, so they can't tolerate students who pose a threat to other students or the school staff. The behaviors that lead to expulsion range from serious acts of delinquency to minor pranks. Depending on the school district, expulsion is the punishment for a wide range of behaviors. Clearly, criminal offenses such as murder, rape, and robbery are grounds for dismissal. Often, the school doesn't have to do anything with these cases because the juvenile court will take the delinquent out of school and place him or her in a secure detention facility. Other criminal offenses, such as drug use and drug sales, carrying a weapon to school, or making threats, are covered by school policies (usually zero-tolerance policies) and leave administrators little choice but to remove the student. Other offenses seem designed to rid schools of students even before they commit serious infractions. Wearing clothes that violate the school dress code can result in suspension. For instance, in school districts with youth gang problems, a student wearing gang colors can be suspended or expelled. Although the necessity of such a punishment might be debated, the school must try to prevent disruptions. Students who are removed from school will find it difficult to return, at least to a regular school. Students are forced either to go to another school district or to attend an alternative school with other youths who had trouble with traditional school. Some alternative schools are excellent educational institutions that provide the specialized educational experiences and behavioral treatment these students required in the first place. Unfortunately, other alternative schools are dumping grounds for youngsters who are **aging out** of the juvenile court system.[61]

Regardless of the specific cause, most dropouts will face challenges in entering the workforce with the skills that will give them a reasonable chance to become self-supporting adults. Most schools employ a number of strategies to keep students in the classroom and provide them with the chance to earn the high school diploma that can mean the difference in getting a good job and a job that won't even pay the bills. Sometimes it can take a young person a year or two away from school to figure out the value of an education and develop the motivation to return to school with a positive attitude.

Questions
1. How does labeling theory relate to failure in school and delinquency?
2. Why do some teenagers drop out of school?

Education and Juvenile Delinquency

Childhood and early adolescence are crucial points in the life course when people are best able to learn. **Longitudinal studies** have shown quality day care and other early childhood intervention programs help prevent delinquency and adult crime.[62] Without early opportunities, youngsters may face a trajectory of delinquency, crime, and even incarceration as adults.

Learning Objective 9.

Discuss how education can protect youths from delinquency or help them out of it.

A prominent 1974 study, the University of North Carolina's Abecedarian Project, showed the long-term positive effects of day care. The project studied a group of 57 children who received high-quality day care and a group of 54 children who received no day care. Children who received day care were enrolled as early as 4 weeks old and remained in the program until kindergarten. At age 21, the adults from the day care program had significantly higher scores on IQ and reading tests compared to the participants who had been in the control group.[63] As we have discussed previously in this text, there is a strong connection between academic failure, poor school bonding, and delinquency. It's fair to say that a child who receives the academic advantage of quality day care early is more likely to be successful in later schooling and, thus, less likely to become delinquent.

Unfortunately, the United States doesn't have a comprehensive day care or early education system, so many youths never receive any quality, early academic intervention. Later, as teenagers, many youths see getting an education as something they must do to get a job. Then there are other youngsters who are so far into a delinquent career, they never have the opportunity to get an education, much less a job. Many of these youths are incarcerated in juvenile detention facilities where they can't get traditional schooling. This is even more of a problem when the youth, who may by this time be a young adult, returns to society still further behind in his or her education. Getting a job at that point does not necessarily help, either. According to David Brown of the National Youth

Employment Coalition, low-skill jobs don't protect youths from delinquency, nor do they reduce **recidivism**.[64]

Recognizing this problem, some states have taken steps to help delinquent youths get some kind of education. Each state has a different way of educating delinquents. Here are some examples:

» **Louisiana.** The state Office of Juvenile Justice, Division of Education educates youth in secure facilities. Youths in nonsecure placement are educated by community providers and in partnership with local school districts.[65]

» **Arizona.** Juvenile detention education is assigned to the county. The county school superintendent and the presiding juvenile court judge agree on how to deliver the education program in juvenile detention facilities.[66]

» **Florida.** Delinquent youths are educated in one of 22 regional juvenile detention centers, all of which have a school funded by the local school district.[67]

Delinquents are more likely to miss getting an education than nondelinquent youngsters. The No Child Left Behind Act, which, as you will recall, mandates a series of reforms for the nation's school systems, includes the requirement that delinquents in juvenile justice schools get the same consideration as students in regular schools. The legislation provides additional money for educational programs that serve students in state institutions or community day programs, and additional funding for school programs that cooperate with local correctional facilities.

However, No Child Left Behind has yet to fulfill its promise in this respect. The act's limitations are, unfortunately, more pronounced for delinquents than for public school students.[68] Delinquent youths tend to have higher rates of learning disabilities and mental health disorders than nondelinquent youths. In one study, researchers found that nearly 40 percent of a group of youths admitted to a long-term, secure-custody facility had learning disabilities.[69]

If delinquents get an inferior education or inadequate attention to special needs, is it surprising that they continue to break the law? A good education program can reduce delinquent recidivism rates. Thomas Blomberg and George Pesta's study of 4,794 juveniles released from 113 Florida residential facilities shows that quality education programs "serve as a turning point in the life course" of many incarcerated juveniles. According to another study by Blomberg and others,

» incarcerated youths with higher levels of education were more likely to return to school after release;

» youths who returned to school and attended regularly were less likely to be rearrested within 24 months; and

» among rearrested youths, those who had attended school regularly following release were arrested for significantly less serious offenses compared to those who didn't attend school or attended less regularly.[70]

The educational services provided to delinquents can be improved in a number of ways. These improvements require a rethinking of the role of education in rehabilitating delinquents, primarily by putting a greater emphasis on quality schooling early on in their difficulties.

» **Early identification and remediation.** It's important to identify students at the beginning of their educational difficulties and try to correct their problems immediately. The longer a student suffers declining grades and a sense of failure, the harder it will be to get him or her back on track. Additionally, the longer a student has this sense of failure, the more he or she is vulnerable to delinquency.

)) **Instructional methods and classroom management.** Individualized instruction plans can quickly bring some delinquent students back into the norm. Teachers should be trained in how to deal with high-risk students by instituting classroom management techniques designed to keep the troublemaker's attention and get him or her involved in group activities.

)) **School discipline.** Traditionally, the easiest way of dealing with a disruptive student has been to remove the student from the classroom. Although there will be incidents in which other students' safety is a primary concern, removal shouldn't be the only recourse. Sometimes removal better serves the teacher, rather than actual school safety. It may take more patience, understanding, and risk, but often the situation can be handled in such a way that the tension is reduced, and the delinquent or disruptive student is allowed to stay in class.[71]

Dealing with the educational problems of delinquents is one of the most difficult issues facing schools and the juvenile justice system. Finding the balance between safety and the needs of disruptive, abusive, or dangerous students is a challenge. Administrators and teachers must think about both what is good for the individual delinquent and what is good for all students. Both parties must be considered, and schools that sacrifice the delinquent youth for school safety may be missing the opportunity to prevent further delinquency and perhaps more serious crime.

Question

1. What effect does good day care have on delinquency?

>> FOCUS ON ETHICS

Punishing a Poet

As a high school English teacher you have taught thousands of students over the past 20 years, but you haven't yet had one like Carlos. Carlos is a wonderful poet who can instantly understand the rhythm and the structure of any poem. When he reads Byron's *Prisoner of Chillon*, it's as if he's experiencing the pain of incarceration himself. Unfortunately, you fear that he may soon be incarcerated himself because of his gang involvement, drug dealing, and attitude toward any type of authority.

Carlos has been your student for several years. He's taken every writing, literature, and poetry class you have taught. Although he's a mediocre student in other classes, he shines in English and literature and is a good candidate to go to college. However, as much as he likes literature, the call of the streets is more powerful. He fancies himself as a romantic warrior struggling to achieve justice for his gang. He's completely wrapped up in local turf wars and is constantly in trouble for fighting, drinking, and being involved in dealing drugs.

You have a plan to save Carlos. You've convinced him that his talent for poetry can be used for many things. He likes rap music, and you've managed to hook him up with a record producer that your sister knows through a friend. This producer thinks Carlos has potential and is willing to help him make a demo.

But there's a problem. Carlos has surrounded himself with an entourage of his gang friends. They think they're all rebel artists and entitled to the adulation that comes after someone is a big star, not before. You've heard they've been selling drugs at school to finance their rap-star lifestyle, but turned a blind eye to this possibility because you were trying to wean Carlos away from the gang with music. Now it seems all your efforts have been in vain because you've heard about Carlos giving drugs to several sophomore girls.

Although you believe Carlos is immensely talented, you realize you've overestimated your influence. You thought that by presenting him with an alternative to gang life, you could divert him from delinquent activities. Now you aren't so sure. The principal vows to expel Carlos and his gang buddies if they get in trouble again. Without school and your small influence to add some structure to Carlos's life, you know that he'll disappear into his gang and probably end up dead or in prison.

WHAT DO YOU DO?

1. Turn Carlos over to the school authorities. Your first obligation is to the school and all students to provide a safe learning environment.

2. Give Carlos another chance and try harder to convince him that he's in danger of losing his future.

3. Recognize you can no longer make good judgments in this case. Carlos has become almost like a wayward son, and you have trouble distancing yourself emotionally. You decide to seek professional help.

Summary

Summary

Learning Objective 1. List and explain the goals of school that affect delinquency.	Academic goals: Schools help youths attain basic skills such as reading, writing, math, communicating ideas, and thinking rationally, independently, and critically. Vocational goals: Students are expected to learn appropriate work attitudes and habits and to select a career in which they can utilize their particular skills. Social, civic, and cultural goals: Schools attempt to instill in students the ability to develop meaningful relationships, appreciate and contribute to the culture, and acquire important social values. Personal goals: These goals include the development of physical and emotional well-being, including self-awareness, physical fitness, self-esteem, and coping skills.
Learning Objective 2. Tell why a school might be unable to meet the needs of all its students	Inappropriate curricula and instruction; differences between parental and school norms; lack of previous success in school; teaching difficulties; teacher perceptions and standards; segregation.
Learning Objective 3. Explain what is meant by "The purpose of kindergarten is to establish the patterns of behavior that make learning possible."	In kindergarten, children learn to take turns, share, be quiet while the teacher is talking, and other forms of behavior that make them well-behaved students. The cooperation of students is necessary for social order in school.
Learning Objective 4. Describe the pressures that affect teachers.	Standardization and regimentation may limit teachers' discretion to design individualized lessons for students' specific needs. Standardized testing may ignore important factors such as the amount of resources and quality of funding schools get and how well students are prepared. Students may be tracked into groups according to their needs and abilities. Teachers may have limited authority to discipline students.

Learning Objective 5. Understand why school shootings don't represent typical juvenile delinquency, and outline the more pertinent issues of delinquency and schools.	School shootings are rare and represent extreme exceptions within delinquency. The more pertinent issues are typical delinquency problems such as gangs, status offenses, bullying, drug and alcohol use, and relatively minor delinquent behaviors such as theft and fighting.
Learning Objective 6. Discuss why bullying hasn't been taken seriously until recently and how it's related to delinquency.	Bullying was once considered a normal part of growing up and how youngsters establish social hierarchy. The US Department of Health and Human Services reports that delinquency and early criminal offending seems to be rooted in childhood aggression, of which bullying is one aspect.
Learning Objective 7. Tell what the "school-to-prison" pipeline is.	The school-to-prison pipeline is a phenomenon in which children leave school or are expelled because of inappropriate behavior and poor academic performance and turn to lawbreaking, which eventually leads to incarceration. Students who fail in school are more likely to have a difficult time for the rest of their lives.
Learning Objective 8. Outline the reasons youths have for dropping out of school.	Academic failure: Many students drop out because they can't keep up with the work. Unmet special needs: Those with learning disabilities and attention-deficit issues go undiagnosed, and their issues get attributed to low IQ or behavioral problems. Cultural issues: Sometimes the subculture of the student's family or peers is too strong to overcome. Boredom: Many students find that school isn't exciting enough to keep them interested. Delinquency and crime: Many youths drop out or are thrown out of school because of criminal or delinquent acts, and schools must provide a safe learning environment.
Learning Objective 9. Discuss how education can protect youths from delinquency or help them out of it.	Research has shown day care and other early childhood intervention programs help prevent delinquency and crime. These early opportunities help prevent delinquency, crime, and further incarceration as adults. Many youths who turn delinquent are incarcerated in juvenile detention facilities where traditional schooling isn't available. The low-skill jobs these youths are eligible for when they leave detention won't keep them from further breaking the law. According to Blomberg and others, incarcerated youths with higher levels of education were more likely to return to school after release; youths who returned to school and attended regularly were less likely to be rearrested within 24 months; and among rearrested youths, those who had attended school regularly following release were arrested for significantly less serious offenses compared to youths who didn't attend school or attended less regularly.

Chapter Review Questions

1. Which school goal do you think is most important?
2. Why are schools primarily under the control of local government? Is this a good idea?
3. What are the advantages of preschool and kindergarten in developing productive future citizens?
4. Would you allow a school to use corporal punishment on your child?
5. What are your ideas for increasing the bond between students and their schools?
6. What procedures did the schools you attended take to ensure school safety?
7. Why do sensational cases of shootings at schools distort our understanding of school safety?
8. To what extent is bullying a problem in contemporary schools?
9. How is failure in school related to future delinquency?
10. How successful has the federal program No Child Left Behind been in increasing the quality of education in American schools?

Key Terms

aging out— In juvenile justice, reaching the age at which the system no longer serves a person, usually age 18.

bullying—The psychological or physical victimization of youths by other youths.

clique—Any small, exclusive group of people that controls how and if others may join.

corporal punishment—The infliction of physical harm on a person who has broken a rule or committed an offense.

GED—General education diploma. A document that certifies that a student has passed a high school equivalency test.

greedy institution—A formal or informal group or organization that demands undivided loyalty from its members.

longitudinal study—A type of study or survey in which the same subjects are observed over a long period of time.

No Child Left Behind Act of 2001—A federal law passed in January 2002 that seeks to improve the performance of K–12 schools.

school bonding—The connection that students have to school and their academic work.

school-to-prison pipeline—A phenomenon in which children leave school or are expelled because of inappropriate behavior and poor academic performance and turn to lawbreaking, which eventually leads to incarceration.

target-hardening—Making a focus of crime or delinquency as difficult as possible for potential offenders to access.

tracking—Educational paths that schools use to group students into classes with other students who have similar needs.

Endnotes

1   Carolyn S. Anderson, "The Search for School Climate: A Review of the Literature," *Review of Educational Research* 52 (1982): 368–420.

2   Adam Gamoran, "American Schooling and Educational Inequality: A Forecast for the 21st Century," in Jeanne H. Ballantine and Joan Z. Spade, eds., *Schools and Society: A Sociological Approach to Education*, 2nd ed. (Belmont, CA: Wadsworth, 2004), 249–264.

3   Andrew Sum, Ishwar Khatiwada, and Joseph McLaughlin, "The Consequences of Dropping Out of High School," Center for Labor Market Studies Publications, 2009. Paper 23. hdl.handle.net/2047/d20000596.

4   Roberta M. Berns, *Child, Family, School, Community: Socialization and Support*, 6th ed. (Belmont, CA: Wadsworth, 2004), 213.

5 Jeanne H. Ballantine, *The Sociology of Education: A Systematic Analysis* (Upper Saddle River, NJ: Prentice Hall, 2001). See especially Chapter 4, "Race, Class, and Gender: Attempts to Achieve Equality of Educational Opportunity."

6 Harold Wenglinsky, "How Money Matters: The Effect of School District Spending on Academic Achievement," in Jeanne H. Ballantine and Joan Z. Spade, eds., *Schools and Society: A Sociological Approach to Education*, 2nd ed. (Belmont, CA: Wadsworth, 2004), 213–219.

7 Martin Carnoy and Henry M. Levin, "Educational Reform and Class Conflict," *Journal of Education* 168 (1986): 35–46.

8 Myra P. Sadker and David M. Sadker, *Teachers, Schools, and Society* (New York: McGraw-Hill, 2003).

9 Denise C. Gottfredson, "An Empirical Test of School-Based Environmental and Individual Interventions to Reduce the Risk of Delinquent Behavior," *Criminology* 24 (1986): 705–731.

10 Simone Robers, Jijun Zhang, and Jennifer Truman, *Indicators of School Crime and Safety: 2010* (Washington, DC: National Center for Education Statistics, US Department of Education, and Bureau of Justice Statistics, Office of Justice Programs, US Department of Justice, 2010), iii. Online at nces.ed.gov/pubs2011/2011002.pdf.

11 Harry L. Gracey, "Learning the Student Role: Kindergarten as Academic Boot Camp," in Jeanne H. Ballantine and Joan Z. Spade, eds., *Schools and Society: A Sociological Approach to Education*, 2nd ed. (Belmont, CA: Wadsworth, 2004), 144–148.

12 Brian Mattmiller, "Study: Early Intervention Cuts Crime, Dropout Rates," *University of Wisconsin-Madison News*, May 8, 2001, www.news.wisc.edu/6148.

13 High/Scope Perry Preschool Study Lifetime Effects, www.highscope.org/Content.asp?ContentId;eq219.

14 Thorstein Veblen, *The Theory of the Leisure Class* (New York: Penguin, 1994).

15 David L. Brunsma and Kelly A. Rockquemore, "The Effects of Student Uniforms on Attendance, Behavior Problems, Substance Abuse, and Academic Achievement," *Journal of Educational Research* 92 (1998): 53–62.

16 Murray A. Straus and Denise A. Donnelly, *Beating the Devil Out of Them* (San Francisco: Lexington Books, 1994).

17 Russell Skiba, *Zero Tolerance, Zero Effectiveness* (Bloomington: Indiana Education Policy Center, 2000).

18 Simone Robers, Jijun Zhang, and Jennifer Truman, *Indicators of School Crime and Safety: 2010* (Washington, DC: National Center for Education Statistics, US Department of Education, and Bureau of Justice Statistics, Office of Justice Programs, US Department of Justice, 2010). Online at nces.ed.gov/pubs2011/2011002.pdf.

19 Ibid.

20 Albert K. Cohen, *Delinquent Boys: The Culture of the Gang* (Glencoe, IL: Free Press, 1955).

21 Robers, Zhang, and Truman, *Indicators of School Crime and Safety: 2010*, 11.

22 Ibid., 10.

23 Christine A. Christle, Kristine Jolivette, and C. Michael Nelson, "Breaking the School to Prison Pipeline: Identifying School Risk and Protective Factors for Youth Delinquency," *Exceptionality* 13, no. 2 (2005): 69–88.

24 Samuel J. Maddox and Ronald J. Prinz, "School Bonding in Children and Adolescents: Conceptualization, Assessment, and Associated Variables," *Clinical Child & Family Psychology Review* 6, no. 1 (March 2003): 31–49.

25 K. L. Henry, R. C. Swaim, and M. D. Slater, "Intraindividual Variability of School Bonding and Adolescents' Beliefs about the Effect of Substance Use on Future Aspirations," *Prevention Science* 6, no. 2, (2005): 101–112.

26 Delos Kelly, *Creating School Failure, Youth Crime, and Deviance* (Los Angeles: Trident Shop, 1982), 11.

27 Berns, *Child, Family, School, Community*, especially Chapter 7, "Ecology of Teaching," 249–288.

28 J. L. Epstein, *School and Family Partnerships* (New York: Basic Books, 1996).

29 Robert J. Rubel and Peter D. Blauvelt, "How Safe Are Your Schools?" *American School Board Journal* 181 (1994): 28–31.

30 Daryl A. Hellman and Susan Beaton, "The Pattern of Violence in Urban Public Schools: The Influence of School and Community," *Journal of Research in Crime and Delinquency* 23 (1986): 102–127.

Summary

31 Katherine S. Newman et al., *Rampage: The Social Roots of School Shootings* (New York: Basic Books, 2004).

32 *New York Times*, "Columbine High School," April 17, 2008, topics.nytimes.com/top/reference/timestopics/organizations/c/columbine_high_school/index.html.

33 Mary W. Green, "The Appropriate and Effective Use of Security Technologies in U.S. Schools: A Guide for Schools and Law Enforcement Agencies," in William L. Turk, ed., *School Crime and Policing* (Upper Saddle River, NJ: Prentice Hall, 2004), 173–201.

34 Wayne Wooden and Randy Blazek, *Renegade Kids, Suburban Outlaws: From Youth Culture to Delinquency* (Belmont, CA: Wadsworth, 2000).

35 Patricia Hersch, *A Tribe Apart: A Journey into the Heart of American Adolescence* (New York: Ballantine, 1999).

36 Susannah Meadows, "Murder on Their Minds: The Columbine Killers Left a Troubling Trail of Clues," *Newsweek* 148, no. 2 (July 17, 2006): 28.

37 Ted Chiricos, Kathy Padgett, and Marc Gerty, "Fear, TV News, and the Reality of Crime," *Criminology* 38 (2000): 755–785.

38 Analysis of FBI Supplementary Homicide Reports, 1980–2002, by Howard N. Snyder and Melissa Sickmund, *Juvenile Offenders and Victims: 2006 National Report* (Washington, DC: US Department of Justice, Office of Justice Programs, Office of Juvenile Justice and Delinquency Prevention, 2006), 68.

39 Cheryl E. Sanders, "What Is Bullying?," in Cheryl E. Sanders and Gary D. Phye, eds., *Bullying: Implications for the Classroom* (Boston: Elsevier), 2–19.

40 Marianne D. Hurst, "When It Comes to Bullying, There Are No Boundaries," *Education Week* 24, no. 22 (February 9, 2005): 8.

41 Paul R. Smokowski and Kelly Holland Kopasz, "Bullying in School: An Overview of Types, Effects, Family Characteristics, and Intervention Strategies," *Children & Schools* 27, no. 2 (April 2005): 101.

42 Peter Edward Gill and Max Allan Stenlund, "Dealing with a Schoolyard Bully: A Case Study," *Journal of School Violence* 4, no. 4 (2005): 47.

43 Maurissa Abecassis, "I Hate You Just the Way You Are: Exploring the Formation,

Maintenance, and Need for Enemies," in Ernest V. E. Hodges and Noel A. Card, eds., *Enemies and the Darker Side of Peer Relations* (San Francisco: Jossey-Bass, 2003).

44 Diana Boxer and Florencia Cortés-Conde, "From Bonding to Biting: Conversational Joking and Identity Display," *Journal of Pragmatics* 27 (1997): 275–294.

45 David S. J. Hawker and Michael J. Boulton, "Subtypes of Peer Harassment and Their Correlates: A Social Dominance Perspective," in Jaana Juvonen and Sandra Graham, eds., *Peer Harassment in School: The Plight of the Vulnerable and Victimized* (New York: Guilford Press, 2001), 378–397.

46 R. Loeber and D. Hay, "Key Issues in the Development of Aggression and Violence for Childhood to Early Adulthood," *Annual Review of Psychology* 48 (1997): 371–410.

47 James Gilligan, *Violence: A Reflection on a National Epidemic* (New York: Viking, 1997).

48 Christle, Jolivette, and Nelson, "Breaking the School to Prison Pipeline," pp. 69–88.

49 Jonathan Kozol, *Savage Inequalities: Children in America's Schools* (New York: Crown, 1991).

50 Ross L. Matsueda, "Reflected Appraisals, Parental Labeling, and Delinquency: Specifying a Symbolic Interactionist Theory," *American Journal of Sociology* 6 (1992): 1577–1611.

51 Delbert S. Elliott, "Delinquency, School Attendance, and School Dropout," *Social Problems* 13 (1966): 307–314.

52 US Census Bureau, A Child's Day: 2009, Table D18: Academic Performance and Experience of School Age Children—Characteristics of Families and Households with Children Age 6 to 17: 2009. Online at www.census.gov/hhes/socdemo/children/data/sipp/well2009/tables.html.

53 National Institute of Child Health and Human Development, Cognition, Brain Function, and Learning in Incarcerated Youth Workshop, July 2010, www.nichd.nih.gov/about/meetings/2010/072310.cfm.

54 Howard L. Taras et al., "Out-of-School Suspension and Expulsion," *Pediatrics* 112, no. 5 (November 2003): 1206–1209.

55 Centers for Disease Control and Prevention, "Health Risk Behaviors among Adolescents Who Do and Do Not Attend School—United States, 1992," *Morbidity and Mortality Weekly Report* 43 (1994): 129–132.

Online at www.cdc.gov/mmwr/preview/mmwrhtml/00025174.htm.

56 Jo Anne Grunbaum et al., "Youth Risk Behavior Surveillance—National Alternative High School Youth Risk Behavior Survey—United States, 1998," *Morbidity and Mortality Weekly Report* 48 (1999): 1–44. Online at www.cdc.gov/mmwr/preview/mmwrhtml/ss4807a1.htm.

57 Alan McEvoy and Robert Welker, "Antisocial Behavior, Academic Failure, and School Climate: A Critical Review," *Journal of Emotional and Behavioral Disorders* 8, no. 3 (Fall 2000): 130–140.

58 Aaron M. Pallas, Gary Natriello, and Edward L. McDill, "The Changing Nature of the Disadvantaged Population: Current Dimensions and Future Trends," *Educational Researcher* 5 (1989): 16–22.

59 Robert A. Peña, "Cultural Differences and the Construction of Meaning: Implications for the Leadership and Organizational Context of Schools," *Educational Policy Analysis Archives* 5, no. 10 (April 8, 1997). Online at epaa.asu.edu/epaa/v5n10.html.

60 James D. Raffini, "Student Apathy: A Motivational Dilemma," *Educational Leadership* 44, no. 1 (September 1986): 53–55.

61 Lawrence M. DeRidder, "How Suspension and Expulsion Contribute to Dropping Out," *Education Digest* 56, no. 6 (1991): 44–47.

62 David R. Katner, "Delinquency and Daycare," *Harvard Law & Policy Review* 4 (2010): 49–72.

63 Ibid.

64 David Brown et al., *Barriers and Promising Approaches to Workforce and Youth Development for Young Offenders* (Baltimore: Annie E. Casey Foundation, 2002), 5. Online at www.aecf.org/upload/publicationfiles/barriers_and_promising.pdf.

65 State of Louisiana Youth Services Office of Juvenile Justice, Overview of Education Services, ojj.la.gov/index.php?page;eqsub&id;eq104.

66 Arizona Judicial Branch, Detention Education, www.azcourts.gov/jjsd/CorrectionalEducation/DetentionEducation.aspx.

67 Florida Department of Juvenile Justice, Frequently Asked Questions: Education Service, www.djj.state.fl.us/AboutDJJ/faq.html#Education.

68 Juvenile Justice Educational Enhancement Program, "No Child Left Behind and Its Implications for Schools Serving Florida's At-Risk and Delinquent Youths," in *2003 Annual Report to the Florida Department of Education: Juvenile Justice Educational Enhancement Program* (Tallahassee, FL: Juvenile Justice Educational Enhancement Program, 2003). Online at www.criminologycenter.fsu.edu/jjeep/research-annual-2003.php.

69 Keith R. Cruise, Lisa J. Evans, and Isaiah B. Pickens, "Integrating Mental Health and Special Education Needs into Comprehensive Service Planning for Juvenile Offenders in Long-Term Custody Settings," *Learning and Individual Differences* 21, no. 1 (February 1, 2011): 30–40.

70 Thomas G. Blomberg et al. "Incarceration, Education and Transition from Delinquency," *Journal of Criminal Justice* 39, no. 4 (July 2011): 355–365.

71 Xia Wang, Thomas G. Blomberg, and Spencer D. Li, "Comparison of the Educational Deficiencies of Delinquent and Nondelinquent Students," *Evaluation Review* 29, no. 4 (2005): 291–312.

Youth Gangs and Delinquency

ny discussion of juvenile delinquency must include the subject of youth gangs. According to US law enforcement, about 28,100 gangs and 731,000 gang members operated throughout 3,500 jurisdictions in the United States in 2009.[1] Although the number of gangs declined from 1996 to 2003, their numbers have been rising steadily since then (see Figure 10.1).

According to the *National Survey of American Attitudes on Substance Abuse XV: Teens and Parents*, 45 percent of high school students and 35 percent of middle school students say there are gangs in their schools or students in their schools who consider themselves to be in a gang.[2]

Gangs present the juvenile justice system and law enforcement agencies with their most difficult challenges in limiting the harm done by youths to each other and to society.[3] Gang members are among the toughest offenders to rehabilitate. Because the gang problem has been around for the past century, we may be tempted to think we know how to deal with gangs. However, we would be mistaken. Despite extensive efforts by scholars, law enforcement, schools, and community groups, gangs are a social problem not only in big cities, but also in smaller communities.[4] Although police reports of gangs have leveled off in recent years, the extent of the gang problem is still significant (see Figure 10.2).

Gang crime poses special challenges for criminal justice agencies for two reasons. The first concerns the motivation of youths to engage in gang activity. It's not enough to contend with the personal issues and shortcomings of the individual gang member; rather, the social context of group dynamics that involve gang membership must be addressed. This means not only must the educational, family, drug and alcohol, and psychological issues of the youth be treated, but also the network of gang peers must be severed and the youth introduced to a more supportive and positive social group. Breaking down the context for gang membership requires resources that are seldom available to criminal justice agencies, so unless or until communities develop comprehensive approaches to the problem of gang activity, the connection between delinquency and gangs will continue.[5]

A second reason that juvenile gang activity concerns criminal justice agencies is because, unless effective steps are taken to address gang crime while the youths are still young, chances are good that they will continue to break the law when they become adults. Some gang members don't outgrow their involvement, develop other interests and leave the gang. Some gangs are lifelong organizations that include family members from several generations.[6]

Figure 10.1 Estimated Number of Gangs, 1996-2009

The 2009 estimate of more than 28,000 gangs is the highest since 1997.

Source: National Gang Center, National Youth Gang Survey Analysis, Measuring the Extent of Gang Problems, www.nationalgangcenter. gov/Survey-Analysis/ Measuring-the-Extent-of-Gang-Problems#estimatednumbergangs.

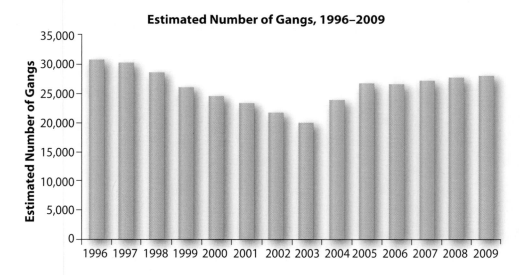

Estimated Number of Gangs, 1996–2009

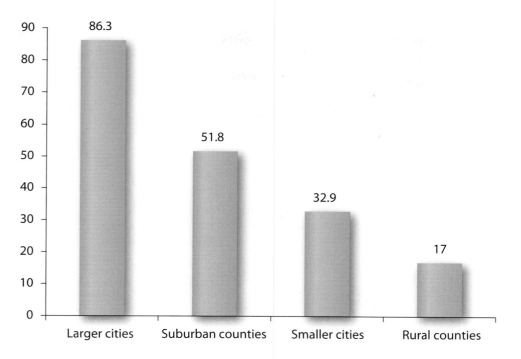

Figure 10.2 Gang Activity Reported in 2009

This figure shows the percentage of types of cities in which gang activity was consistently reported in 2009. For example, gang activity was consistently reported in 86.3 percent of larger U.S. cities.

Think About It

1. Discuss reasons why smaller cities have a lower percentage of gang reports than suburban counties.

Source: Arlen Egley, Jr., and James C. Howell, *Highlights of the 2009 National Youth Gang Survey*, Table 1. Law Enforcement Reports of Gang Activity, 2005–09, June 2011, p.2, www.ncjrs.gov/pdffiles1/ojjdp/233581.pdf.

In this chapter, we'll first present the problem of defining gangs. Although you might think this would be easy, there's considerable debate about just what constitutes a gang. Second, we'll discuss the glue that holds gangs together, **peer relationships**. Gang loyalty depends on several complex factors, and these factors can be different for various gangs. Third, we look at joining the gang. The size and level of commitment for individual gangs vary and have many implications. Fourth, we consider the different types of gangs. Some gangs are based on race or ethnicity, some on the local neighborhood, and some on the type of illegal activity they pursue, if any. Finally, we look at efforts to control gangs, focusing on the work of youth service workers, police, and the juvenile justice system to find strategies for resolving the issues that lead to gang activity.

What Is a Gang?

Criminologists have never agreed on exactly what constitutes a youth gang. Although most people think they know a gang when they see one, the problems of measuring gang behavior require specifying the exact parameters of a number of characteristics. That is, before something can be measured, we must know what it is. Because scholars can't agree on which characteristics to include in a definition and they can't agree on how the characteristics that they do agree on should be measured, a widely accepted definition remains elusive.[7] Therefore, we present one definition that includes many of the characteristics we generally expect of gangs.

Walter Miller asked youth service agency workers, police officers, community outreach workers, judges, criminal justice planners, probation officers, prosecutors, public defenders, city council members, state legislators, ex-convicts, and past and present gang members about their definitions of a gang. The resulting list of characteristics was long, but 85 percent of those surveyed agreed on the following six:

1. **A self-formed association of peers.** This would exclude something like a football team or church group where there is adult supervision, financing,

Learning Objective 1.

Detail Miller's six characteristics of a gang.

Learning Objective 2.

List and explain the two aspects of the definition of a gang member.

Learning Objective 3.

Discuss how gangs vary.

Two gang members, Antonio Hernandez (wearing a hat) and Salvador Agron, ages 17 and 16 respectively, are booked in the fatal stabbing of two teens in New York City in September 1959. Hernandez, called himself the "Umbrella Man" because he used one as a sword, and Agron, called himself "Dracula."

or other support. These peers choose to form gangs because of functions they believe the gang can provide that they can't get in their traditional relationships.

2. **Bound by mutual interests.** These interests can be as simple as living on the same block of a street or being members of the same ethnic or minority group. Gang members see their fellow gang members as having the same kinds of concerns that they do.

3. **Well-developed lines of authority and other organizational features.** All gangs have some level of organization that includes leadership, division of labor, and lines of communication. Depending on the gang's size and complexity, the organization might have such roles as lookouts, drug couriers, drug sellers, money launderers, and street fighters. The leadership might be structured along military or corporate models.

4. **Acting together to achieve a specific purpose or purposes.** For a gang to be successful, its members must work together to achieve their goals. This differs from a loose gathering of people who might, or might not, decide to participate in the group's activities.

5. **Involvement in illegal activity.** This is one of the primary distinguishing features of a gang. Members engage in delinquent or criminal offenses that range from drug sales to murder. The illegal activities are often oriented toward making money but are sometimes simply efforts to establish the gang's identity.

6. **Control over a particular territory, facility, or type of enterprise.** Gangs usually protect some geographical area. It may be a section of their neighborhood, a shopping mall, school grounds, or even the exercise yard at a youth detention facility. Their goal is to preserve the integrity of their turf and to signal to others that they rule their limited domain. When gangs contest the ownership of a particular location, it can be a defining moment in the viability of their leadership and organization.[8]

These gang characteristics have a certain commonsense appeal. They include many of the features that anyone might use to identify a gang. If we asked

Gangs can be defined in many ways, one of which is by the graffiti that many gangs leave on public property.

a random selection of people to give us their definitions of a gang, their answers would vary.[9] However, Miller asked those who are intimately involved with gang behavior, which suggests a certain level of expert opinion. A couple of other elements could be added to the definition of a gang. Today, gangs use symbols to communicate their members' involvement. These symbols might be as simple as wearing certain colors (someone who is in the Bloods gang, for example, would wear red) or wearing the jerseys of a particular professional sports team. The flashing of gang signs also allows members to identify their loyalty to a gang, and graffiti can mark the boundaries of their turf or signify the gang's presence in public areas.[10]

Gangs can be defined in many other ways, but it's beyond the scope of this chapter to explore them all. However, there is concern that the definition of a gang depends on who is doing the defining.[11] The police may have one set of criteria that is useful to their mission of suppressing gang activity, and schools may have a different definition that is useful in targeting youths who are beginning to have academic and behavioral problems. Additionally, a youth detention facility may need to consider different criteria to separate potential gang members from each other or from the institution's general population. So, while recognizing its limitations, we will use Miller's definition because it contains information from across the juvenile justice system.

Studying Gangs

What we know about gangs isn't clear. A number of studies over the past 80 years have informed academics and criminal justice practitioners about the development and seriousness of gang activity. The US government also funds the Regional Information Sharing Systems program (RISS), which links thousands of criminal justice agencies and provides information-sharing resources and investigative support to deal with multijurisdictional offenses, including gang activity. The RISS National Gang Intelligence Database provides police with information about gangs, including suspects, organizations, weapons, locations, and vehicles, as well as visual material of gang members, gang symbols, and gang graffiti.[12]

What has the research on gangs concluded? The definition of a gang member has two aspects. The first aspect is involvement in crime.[13] Young people have a natural propensity to bond in friendship groups and cliques, but gang researchers are interested only in those groups who break the law. This is a crucial distinction that helps to differentiate gangs from other adolescent groups. The second aspect is bonding. Gang members show an affiliation with their gang through some cultural aspects that bond them with a family-like loyalty (see Crosscurrents). This bonding can be exemplified by the wearing of gang apparel, getting gang tattoos, or communicating with gang signs. Additionally, gang bonding includes spending time together in both criminal and noncriminal activities and swearing allegiance and loyalty to the gang. Members see the gang as what sociologists call a **primary group**, whereby the gang comes first in how members identify themselves and is a relationship that supersedes all others except for (in some cases) the family.[14]

It's tempting to typify gangs based on ethnicity. This is because the membership of many gangs is racially or culturally homogeneous. However, researcher Malcolm Klein has developed a gang typology (see Table 10.1) based on gangs' activities and formation, which he asserts are more important and telling than the members' color or culture.

Varying levels of involvement in gang activities can complicate the definition of certain youths as gang members. Some police agencies have claimed that they don't have a real gang problem but simply have some "wannabes" who like

TABLE 10.1〉   Characteristics of Five Street-Gang Types

According to Malcolm W. Klein, typing gangs by their ethnic or racial compositions is misleading, as what the group does and how it does it is far more important than its members' ethnicity.

TYPE	SUBGROUPS	SIZE	AGE RANGE	DURATION	TERRITORIAL	CRIME VERSATILITY
traditional	yes	average 180	wide (20–30 years)	long (>20 years)	yes	yes
neotraditional	yes	average 75	no pattern	short (<10 years)	yes	yes
Traditional and neotraditional gangs aren't the most common type of gang, but they are the largest, longest-enduring, most violent, and commit the most offenses. These are large, inner-city gangs, such as the Crips and Bloods.						
compressed	no	average 35	narrow (<10 years)	short (<10 years)	no pattern	yes
Compressed gangs are mainly adolescent groups of 50 to 100 members. These are the most common and are found in both large and small cities.						
collective	no	average 55	medium-wide (>10 years)	medium (10–15 years)	no pattern	yes
Collective gangs are the least common, are large, but have little internal structure. They're sometimes bonded by loose neighborhood ties and extensive drug dealing.						
specialty	no	average 25	narrow (<10 years)	short (<10 years)	yes	no
Specialty is the smallest type, but the most tightly structured. These gangs perpetrate a narrow pattern of offending and are devoted to certain types of crimes, such as robbery, burglary, car theft, or racial hate.						

Think About It
1. Which type of gang is the most common? The least common?

Source: Malcolm W. Klein, Chasing After Street Gangs: A Forty-Year Journey (Upper Saddle River, New Jersey: Prentice Hall, 2007), 55–56.

10.1 crosscurrents

The Grip of the Gang

The loyalty some youngsters have toward their gang is remarkable because the kids are willing to give up so much to be considered a respectable gang member. One might compare gangs to a football team or a Boy Scout troop, considering the way members display loyalty, connectedness, and a common purpose. Gangs, however, transcend the commitment their members have to legitimate institutions, and can even be compared to religion in how they involve their members. Although this analogy may seem extreme, a look at the sociology of religion shows that it's not far off the mark.

Looking at Emile Durkheim's *The Elementary Forms of Religious Life*, we can see how gangs perform many of the same functions for their members that religions do for their adherents. According to Durkheim, religion meets eight basic human needs. With a bit of imagination we can apply five of these functions of religion to gangs.

» **Questions about ultimate meaning.** What is the purpose of life? Why are we here? Why do we have to suffer? These are the cosmic questions that religions answer for their followers. For gang members' questions such as "Why does society discriminate against me?," "How do I deal with being poor?," and "How do I act like a man?," gangs can supply the answers.

» **Emotional comfort.** Religion comforts people by providing support in times of sickness, trouble, and death. For gang members, the rituals of the organization provide similar comfort. The loss of a gang member in gang warfare might be commemorated with graffiti or a tattoo. For a gang member who loses a loved one, such as a parent or sibling who isn't involved in the gang,

the gang can be an outlet for his or her grief and aggression.

» **Social solidarity.** Religious teachings and practices unite believers into a community that shares values and perspectives. Likewise, a gang's activities bring its members closer together. Fighting with another gang can illustrate to fellow gang members that "I got your back and you got mine."

» **Guidelines for everyday life.** Six of the Ten Commandments are instructions for living everyday life. The gang also has rules on how to interact with others, especially rival gang members. In some cities, a gang member who encounters a rival is almost always required to pick a fight to defend his gang's honor.

» **Social control.** Religion controls the activities of adherents and wider society if a majority of that society adheres to the religion. For example, in many parts of the United States, "blue laws" restrict the sale of alcohol on Sundays. Gangs are able to enforce their own rules by claiming playgrounds or streets as territory. Additionally, gangs can enforce a dress code that prohibits members of other gangs or nonaffiliated youths from wearing gang colors.

THINK ABOUT IT

1. Compare and contrast gangs with religions.
2. Does gang membership have positive aspects?

Source: Emile Durkheim, *The Elementary Forms of Religious Life* (New York: Free Press, 1965, first published in 1912)

---

to dress in gang clothing and hang out looking like a gang. Curry and Decker don't like the wannabe concept and contend this designation obscures the fact that gangs have core members and fringe members. The fringe members may be young, emerging members and quite capable of committing violent offenses. By claiming they have only wannabe gang members, police departments lose valuable time and intelligence in building a response to gang crime and violence.[15]

Once researchers identify gang members, they must gather information. This can be precarious, because those involved in illegal behavior have good reasons for not talking about themselves and their activities. Researching gangs can be dangerous, as well as difficult. In addition to getting limited, inaccurate, and purposely slanted information from gang members, researchers might be exposed to intimidation or violence should the gang members not want to be studied or dislike the researchers' conclusions.[16]

Many research strategies can be employed to study gangs, but the two most common ones are (1) to examine records and talk to criminal justice administrators or schools, and (2) to talk directly to youths and gang members through surveys or interviews. Each strategy is useful for gathering information about gang activity and will yield different types of information. Researchers decide which to use depending on the issues they want to explore. For example, the question "Are there gangs in your city?" might get a vastly different response from the chief of police than it does from a gang member.

When researchers ask law enforcement officials about the prevalence and seriousness of gang activity in their cities, the researchers encounter some difficulties. The police may be reluctant to admit a gang problem. The police are vested with the responsibility to keep the community safe, and admitting a gang problem may be interpreted as admitting that the police department is failing. However, when money is available in the form of grants or other aid to fight gang activity, police agencies may claim to have gangs simply to become eligible for the funding.[17]

A more difficult problem for gang researchers involves determining how much crime is gang related. Law enforcement agencies don't always separate crime incidents according to whether they're gang related. Even more problematic is that it's usually impossible to determine whether an offense involves gang activity if there's no arrest. Drug sales, muggings, and larcenies are committed by gang members and non–gang members alike.[18] Unless a witness is capable of identifying gang monikers or colors, or there is an arrest of a gang member, police can't attribute criminal activity to gangs. This makes police records unreliable for determining the level of gang-related crime. These records capture police activity better than gang activity. Therefore, it's almost certain that police records will underreport the level and intensity of any gang problem.[19]

Field studies that interview or observe gang members offer a different perspective. Field studies aren't particularly well suited to collecting large amounts of data that can compare gangs between cities. Rather, they're useful for scholars concerned with the circumstances in gang members' lives, how the gang members interpret their circumstances, and how their behaviors and activities are shaped.[20] This micro-level research provides the foundation for most of what we know about gangs. The long and informative history of ethnographic research done on American street gangs demonstrates the difficulties and pitfalls of doing research on deviant populations. Starting with Frederic Thrasher's seminal 1927 study of Chicago gangs and continuing through Jody Miller's significant study of female gangs in Columbus, Ohio, and St. Louis, Missouri, researchers have shown amazing ingenuity in discovering how gangs are structured and why they break the law.

Field researchers confront three problems when attempting to study gangs; the first is finding gang members who are willing to talk. Police officers, youth service workers, and teachers may identify gang members and sometimes have relationships with them that can help researchers talk to them. Once the trust of one key informant gang member is secured, this gang member can vouch for the researcher and introduce her or him to other gang members who can in turn provide further introductions. This method of finding research subjects, the **snowball sample**, is useful in getting into the gang subculture and targeting subjects who can provide relevant observations, opinions, and perspectives about gang activity. The crucial step in developing a snowball sample is gaining the trust and support of that first informant who will open doors into the gang and provide not only access but also safety. Without this connection, the researcher would probably meet with suspicion, distrust, and resistance.[21]

A second concern of field research has to do with **generalizability**. When studying one particular gang, it's risky to attribute the findings to other gangs, especially in other places. Although the findings from studying a particular gang may be rich in detail and reveal intimate and fascinating insights, the likelihood that these findings can be transferred to other gangs in other cities is low. This doesn't mean the research is flawed but only that it needs to be carefully considered before generalizations are made.

A third limitation of field studies has to do with the researcher's effect on the setting. Merely by being there and recording observations or interviews, the researcher can subtly influence the responses or behaviors of the subjects.[22] In sociology, this is called the **Hawthorne effect**. For example, the gang members may decide against a drive-by shooting or robbery because they think the researcher will report them to the police or, at least, record their behaviors in less-than-flattering terms.

We should be aware of the issues that are inherent in doing gang research, but we shouldn't be quick to dismiss the value of what has been reported about gangs. As gangs have become a serious problem in many large and medium-sized cities, scholars have invested a great deal of time and attention into learning why gangs form and how they can be controlled.

Delinquency, Peers, and Group Activity

By definition, gang delinquency is group behavior. To fully understand gangs, it's necessary to appreciate how and why juveniles pursue peer friendships and how nongang groups avoid becoming enmeshed in delinquent behavior.

American society is an age-graded society. This means that we mainly interact with others of our own age. This is particularly true during childhood, when schools group students into classes according to age. Occasionally, some students advance a grade level or two because of exceptional ability, and students who don't make satisfactory progress may have to retake a grade. We see the same age-grading among the elderly who move to retirement communities or nursing homes, where others around them share their concerns for medical care and safety.

For young people, this constant exposure to others who share their inexperience, immaturity, and long-term perspective means they may be occasionally tempted into delinquent behavior when adults aren't around to supervise their decisions. As young people get opportunities through school and recreational activities to develop relationships outside the family, these peer bonds become extremely important to their emotional development. Part of growing up involves cutting the strings to our parents and finding new freedom to make decisions, be they good or bad.[23] Significantly, some research has shown that for youths who join gangs, stable membership—meaning that the youth joins the gang regularly and for good—typically occurs at age 13, exactly the time when puberty begins changing the child into an adult, and the child begins to seek separation from his or her parents.[24]

Generally, children and adolescents form cliques that center around activities, geography, or intimate feelings. For example, the eighth-grade basketball team, street-corner hustlers, computer club, or staff at a fast-food restaurant may find they have more in common with each other than with their families or classmates. These friendship groups establish norms that dictate appropriate styles of

Gradually, a child's friends play an increasing role in forming the child's values. As parents lose control, they fear their child will fall in with the wrong crowd, such as a gang. This photo, displayed during a news conference by the Los Angeles Police Department, shows suspected gang members being sought during raids in 2011.

dress, how members should express themselves, and attitudes toward breaking the law. It's little wonder that parents are constantly concerned with their children's friends. Gradually, a child's friends play an increasing role in forming the child's values, and as parents lose control, they fear their son or daughter will fall in with the wrong crowd.[25]

Teenagers in gangs are more likely to break the law than those who are not. Although this statement seems so obviously true that it's redundant to even make it, an important distinction should be considered. This distinction sets up a classic chicken-and-egg dilemma: Does delinquency make youths more likely to join a gang, or does gang membership tempt youths into delinquency?[26] The answers to these questions are yes and yes. Because delinquents often have co-delinquents, they tend to develop close relationships that take on ganglike features. Loyalty to one another, rejection of conventional society, and increasing social isolation from schools and family mean that it's a short step for delinquent youths to become involved with existing gangs or to begin one of their own. Additionally, once in a gang, fighting, drug use, drug sales, motor vehicle theft, and larceny are all activities that youths are encouraged to commit to become respected members.[27]

There is evidence that boys who join gangs are more delinquent before they join than are boys who don't join gangs. Also, teenagers in gangs participate in more delinquency than those who aren't in gangs. But just as delinquent acts increase significantly for boys who join a gang, they also decrease once the boy leaves the gang, dropping to the level prior to when the boy joined the gang.[28]

Basically, delinquent peers commit more delinquency together than apart. This is because young people, especially teenagers, have a desperate need to fit in with their peer groups. Those who participate in deviant behaviors, such as drug use and delinquency, seek out others who do the same to get a sense of belonging. One reason gangs become so highly structured with symbols, signs, and rules is that the gang is replacing other institutions such as the family, school, and community. Belonging to a gang provides the youth with a sense of identity, a supportive network of friends, and a feeling of love and purpose. As some gang members get older and move into more conventional relationships, such as marriages and jobs, these replace the functions the gang plays in their lives, and eventually their involvement declines.[29] For those youths who have trouble finding these more conventional relationships, the possibility of a criminal career looms, especially if they have been periodically incarcerated and exposed to other, perhaps more serious delinquents.

One obvious strategy for helping young people avoid gangs is to ensure they choose their friends wisely. Getting children involved in prosocial activities, such as sports, extracurricular activities, church groups, and employment, can take up their discretionary time and creative energies so they have little opportunity or need to seek out delinquent friends.[30] Additionally, parental supervision can play an important role in helping youngsters make good choices in whom to hang out with. Parents can be instrumental in spotting early gang activity. However, not all youths have equal support from parents and schools, and some are left on their own to occupy their time and choose their friends and activities. Those who live in disadvantaged neighborhoods without legitimate after-school activities or whose parents are both working find more occasions to participate in delinquent behaviors than those youths with more conventionally structured lives.[31]

Some youths fail to find supportive friends in conventional society because their peers reject them. As children form cliques, they might adopt rigid rules about who and what is acceptable and cool, and those who are the slightest bit different may be left out. When a youth's family moves to a new town, a youth might have trouble replacing the old set of friends and the niche he or she had carved out in the school's social structure.[32] New classmates may find the youth's clothing to be old-fashioned or speech to have a funny accent. Youths who experiment with body piercing or tattoos may discover that their new classmates consider such fashion statements to be silly or passé. Finding ways to fit into a new social system can be overwhelming and propel the youth into seeking out others who don't fit in. Those who are socially rejected often use delinquent behaviors as way to establish and reinforce their deviant status in school.[33]

Joining the Gang

Joining a gang has been envisioned as a turning point in the life course that is associated not only with delinquency but with significant changes in emotions, attitudes, and social controls.[34] The reasons young people join gangs can provide insight into how to find more conventional activities to replace the functions that gangs play in young people's lives. Not all gangs fill the same needs, and the range of youths who join gangs spans the continuum of race, social class, sex, and age. Here, we discuss several reasons why a youth may join a gang, with the understanding that no single reason is sufficient to describe all youths. Also, it's probable that some youngsters will have many reasons for joining a gang, which may be categorized as "pushes" and "pulls." Some factors push a youth toward joining a gang, such as protection, friendship, and family tradition, while others pull the youth into the gang, such as status, money, and excitement.[35]

》 **Pull: The gang as a buffer against poverty.** One of the most obvious features of gangs is that many of them comprise youths from disadvantaged neighborhoods. In a society where wealth and privilege are constantly celebrated, these youths find that they can't compete for status because of their families' social and economic situation. Rather than accept their circumstances, these youths join gangs to provide themselves with the things their families can't. Gang activity gives the youths a certain status at school and in the community, because the gangs are seen as exclusive clubs that not everyone can join. In the view of gang members, gangs become elite organizations that only those with the right set of skills are allowed into. These skills may not be the ones that allow them to excel in school or get a job, but they're valued for gang activity. The willingness to fight, break the law, use drugs, and have an attitude that rejects the conventional society's values is useful for gang membership. The gang provides not only a sense of belonging and status but also material items. Gangs that shoplift, commit robberies, or sell drugs can give the members the money, clothes, and other goods that allow them to feel on an economic par with their more conventional peers.[36]

》 **Pull: The gang as a tribe.** The social organization of gangs suggests that they assuage a deep psychological need to belong to an extended group that provides meaning. Anthropologists have noted how groups, clans, and tribes have rituals and ceremonies for young males to mark the passing from adolescent to adult.[37] These ceremonies or rituals may be formal rites of passage or simply a recognition that the youngster has done something significant and can now leave the mother and start hanging out with the tribe's adult males.[38] Although it might be a stretch of theory to contend that gangs are simply modern tribes, it's worth considering the social organization and rituals of gangs as such. One measure of a group is the types of symbols worn by members to denote status. Although there might be a formal system of symbols akin to rank insignias in the military, some group members select their own accoutrements, and the very act of wearing the gang colors or getting a gang-related tattoo becomes a mark of status. Gangs might have elaborate or simple initiation rites that require newcomers to prove they have what it takes to belong. These rites might be as simple as showing how much one is willing to sacrifice for membership by submitting to a "beat down," in which gang members beat up the inductee to gauge how much heart and fight he or she has.[39] Some gangs also have a generational component. In cities that have had gangs for many years, brothers, uncles, fathers, and sons are all members of a gang at one time or another. The gang in these neighborhoods acts like a community club (although somewhat more deviant) and provides its members with a sense of history, commitment, and belonging. Youngsters join gangs in these circumstances because they see it as being loyal to the family and they wish to carry on the protection of the neighborhood, much like a child of a more conventional upbringing might join the military out of a sense of patriotism.

》 **Push: Gangs as a response to social change.** Sociologists use the term **anomie** to refer to the individual and societal feeling of aimlessness, alienation, or normlessness that occurs when there is rapid social change in a society. When change upsets the old rules and the old status systems, people look for new and emerging norms to guide them. Two good examples of this are found in the 19th-century gangs that existed in New York City and the gangs that emerged during the late 1960s. Both periods saw a tremendous amount of social upheaval. In New York City in the late 1800s, European immigrants were entering the United States by the shipload at Ellis Island, bringing with them the languages, habits, and customs of their homelands. In the late 1960s, it seemed the young generation was bent on breaking, then rewriting, all the social rules their parents had carefully constructed and followed. Both of these periods gave birth to gangs or ganglike institutions, some of which are still with us today, such as the Mafia, the Crips, and the Bloods (these last two are discussed later in the chapter). Some youths are attracted to gangs because they seem to provide a way to negotiate life's challenges in times of stress and change. When suspended from school, kicked out of the home by a new stepparent, or moving to a new city, a young person can see gang involvement as an attractive way to find certainty and structure.[40]

INSTANT RECALL
FROM CHAPTER 5

anomie

A condition in which people or society undergoes a breakdown of social norms and values. Also, personal anxiety and isolation produced by rapidly shifting moral and cultural values.

» **Pull: Gangs as deviant "birds of a feather."** Some youngsters join gangs because that's where they can find others who share their deviant worldview. Some research has found that aggressive children make friends with other, similarly aggressive children by the age of 10.[41] For those who are selfish, have few feelings of empathy or guilt, and prefer to manipulate others for their self-gain, the gang provides like-minded others who not only tolerate these behaviors but share them. Many youths feel rejected by conventional society and suffer from limited life skills and low self-esteem. By participating in delinquent and criminal activities with fellow gang members, these youths feel that they're in control of their situation and can define their behaviors as supportive of the subcultural goals of the gang, thus increasing their feelings of self-worth.[42]

» **Pull: Gangs as success.** Failure in school, specifically the middle grades, when children are entering puberty, can be a warning of later gang involvement, especially when paired with peer rejection.[43] Or, more harshly: you're getting bad grades and no one likes you. These devastating things, especially when they're happening at such a vulnerable, malleable time as puberty, can lead to the aforementioned pull, or the grouping of deviant "birds of a feather." Children who are getting failing grades, who have behavior problems, who tend to be aggressive, and who have been rejected by the prosocial in-crowds will probably find each other and reinforce what they consider to be positive and exciting about each other. Not coincidentally, these are the things they consider to be positive and exciting about themselves.

» **Push: Gangs as a rational choice.** Some youths feel at a disadvantage in conventional society because of their race, ethnicity, social class, or other variables beyond their control. They don't see life as a level playing field when they observe middle-class and affluent peers being able to take better advantage of legitimate opportunities. These youths think gang activity is an acceptable compensation for the discrimination they feel. Some gang members break the law with their eyes wide open and with the intention of profiting from it. The gang is simply a mechanism for doing better and more lucrative crime. Gang membership provides the youths with a ready-made set of partners in crime to party with, as well as a way to find sexual liaisons with the gang's network of sisters, relatives, and neighbors. Gang members see this extended social network as something akin to a family, and the choice to join is considered rational. Gang life can be fun and exciting, prompting youths to seek out gang activity as a release from the boredom of living in disadvantaged neighborhoods where there is little to do. Additionally, some might make a choice to join a gang because they're victimized by other gangs in the area. Gang membership can provide physical security. This security can be especially important in female decisions to join a gang. Whether it's an all-girl gang or an ancillary of a male gang, membership can signal to others that messing with this young woman means messing with the gang.[44]

» **Push: Gangs as the only game in town.** Some youths don't have specific reasons for joining a gang. They don't even realize they're choosing delinquent behavior. Like fish in water, they're clueless about alternative lifestyles. In many communities, gangs are such stable features of the institutional landscape that the question is not whether to join a gang, but which one. In communities where the governmental, educational, family, and religious leaders have failed to provide adequate education and recreational facilities, the gang becomes the one organization that speaks to the problems and needs of young, disenfranchised people.[45]

Gangs fill a perceived need in the lives of their members for a period of time. Many gang-involved youths say they join gangs for protection from criminal victimization and from other gangs. However, gang members are actually victimized more often than youths who aren't in gangs.[46] Probably for this reason and others, most gang members eventually leave the gang. In fact, most youths leave the gang after a year or less.[47] For the most part they **age out**, meaning, as they grow older, they find other activities that are more important than being in the gang. They get good jobs, get married and have children, move to a new city, or simply tire of the gang lifestyle. With the exception of some intergenerational gangs, the gang culture is a young person's game.[48] Unfortunately, gang involvement may permanently damage a youth's social networks, which can have long-term consequences.[49] For example, if a youth joins a gang, drops out of school, and gets arrested, the youth's education and ability to get a job are affected even if the whole episode lasts only a year. The youth must straighten out his or her life, return to school having fallen behind in his or her studies and lost nongang friends, then spend a great deal of time trying to rebuild broken family ties and other community relationships. The longer the youth is in the gang, the more difficult this becomes.

Types of Gangs

Gangs vary in several ways. Size, racial and ethnic makeup, criminal activity, organization, and geographic location are all factors that scholars use to differentiate among types of gangs. Although many gangs demonstrate stability across these factors, some gangs change as circumstances change. For instance, a gang might allow females to participate at some level, then change its attitude and exclude them from gang status, allowing them to participate only as girlfriends. Likewise, a gang might gradually move its geographic base as neighborhoods change in racial composition or social class. As gang members get older, they may participate in more serious delinquent activities.[50]

With these dynamic changes in mind, let's now look at developing a typology of gangs based on race. Most gangs are racially homogeneous groups that are

INSTANT RECALL
FROM CHAPTER 9

aging-out

In juvenile justice, to get too old for the system, which is usually the age of 18. This also can refer to growing too old for any organization, such as a gang. Also "age-out."

In this photo, young adult gang members are celebrating a truce. Most gang members eventually leave their gangs.

largely the result of urban geographic segregation. For example, ethnically defined neighborhoods such as San Francisco's Chinatown produce Asian gangs. The ethnic background of gangs has changed over time. Most of the Irish, German, and Italian youth gangs that were prevalent in the first half of the 20th century no longer exist in any quantity. These groups have largely been assimilated into American society and are no longer subject to the economic and racial discrimination they previously experienced. Today, gangs are composed of other groups that are readily identifiable by perceived racial and cultural characteristics.[51]

BLACK AND HISPANIC GANGS

There are black gangs in many cities in the United States. However, Los Angeles is home to the two largest and best known. Bitter rivals, the Crips and the Bloods have franchised their gangs to several other communities in California and beyond. It's difficult to know the exact size of these gangs, but because estimates of their combined membership exceed 30,000, they have been labeled as supergangs. Other gangs in large cities, such as the Folks in Chicago, are also included in the supergang category, but it's worth looking at each of these gangs separately to discern how they vary. It's also important to note that although these gangs aren't necessarily youth gangs, they recruit their members at young ages, thus contributing to delinquency.

Crips. The inspiration for the Crips was the 1960s Black Panther political party, which became famous for its confrontations with authorities over a number of social issues. The Black Panthers transcended traditional street gangs and promoted itself as a prosocial group that defended disadvantaged people in the black community. Additionally, they provided a free breakfast program in some cities and generated a tremendous amount of goodwill from the community and the press, if not from the police. The party's Los Angeles chapter, established in 1968, was the model for several other gangs, such as the Avenues and Baby Avenues, who

A member of the Grape Street Crips in Los Angeles shows off a tattoo reading "Tha Hood Die Young."

eventually became the Crips.[52] The gang's unusual name is said to be shortened from "Cripples," a name that recalls a time during the 1960s when gang members carried walking canes as weapons because guns were more difficult to obtain. The cane was used as a weapon to "cripple" anyone who crossed them.[53]

Currently, the Crips are involved in a number of illegal enterprises, such as murder, armed robbery, and the distribution of illegal drugs, and have been selling crack cocaine ever since it appeared in the 1980s. Stanley "Tookie" Williams sat on California's death row from 1981 to 2005, where he wrote a series of children's books. Williams publicly denounced his gang affiliation and was nominated for a Nobel Peace Prize but was executed in 2005 for the 1979 murders of four people during an armed robbery.[54] According to Delaney, the Crips are the largest street gang in the world and have extended their reach from Los Angeles to every large US city. Their organizational structure has become so unwieldy that the various Crips factions battle each other almost as much as they fight other gangs.[55]

Bloods. The Bloods originated in Compton, California, and have a severe disadvantage in numbers when compared to the Crips. There are three Crips to every Blood, but the Bloods are able to compete because they're so violent.[56] Although primarily black, the Bloods, unlike the Crips, have accepted members from other racial groups, including Hispanic, white, and Asian. Like the Crips, the Bloods have spread nationwide. They're extremely strong in the Northeast, where they're affiliated with a gang based in Riker's Island Prison in New York called the United Blood Nation. In 2000, they had at least 500 members in New York City alone.[57]

The Bloods are known for their violence against other gangs, as well as against innocent civilians. To become a member, the individual must "blood in," which entails spilling someone else's blood. This is typically done by walking up to a stranger and slashing him or her across the face with a box cutter. In 1997 during a three-day sweep, the New York Police Department arrested 167 gang members and attributed 135 slashings to gang initiation rituals.[58]

The Bloods sell a variety of drugs, including heroin, LSD, PCP, and crack cocaine. The Bloods also commit other offenses, including robberies, car thefts, rapes, and murders. In addition to their presence on the streets of major cities, they're one of the most feared prison gangs in the United States. They take over the prison's underground economy and intimidate other inmates into joining the gang. In California, the Bloods and the Crips were routinely sent to different prisons because of the certainty of violence should they find themselves together in the prison yard or the cafeteria.[59] As the Bloods expand their territory into smaller cities, they bring their drug distribution enterprise and a reputation for backing it up with deadly violence. Because the Crips are expanding alongside the Bloods, drug- and gang-related violence will continue to be a problem in smaller cities as well as major ones.

The People, Latin Kings, and Vice Lords. Two large gangs based in the Midwest comprise what is loosely known as the People. The People Nation and the Folk Nation represent a different form of gang structure than found with the Bloods and Crips. First, People-style gangs are more racially heterogeneous than the California gangs. The People includes individuals from a variety of racial and ethnic backgrounds. Additionally, these supergangs comprise smaller gangs that have their own names and can change allegiance from one supergang to another. They're found in Chicago and Milwaukee, primarily, but have expanded to other cities, such as Detroit, Michigan; Cleveland, Ohio; and Columbus, Ohio.

The largest of the People-style subgangs is the Latin Kings. It's mainly composed of Hispanic youths, particularly Mexican and Puerto Rican, and is one of the oldest and most powerful gangs in the country. (See Focus on Diversity for more on the police and their treatment of Latinos and Latino gangs.) Originally based in Chicago, they formed alliances with other gangs such as the Vice Lords and grew to as many as 25,000 members in cities and states across the East and Midwest, including New York, Connecticut, New Jersey, Iowa, Indiana, Ohio, Florida, and Massachusetts. Of particular interest is the Latin Kings' well-formed organizational structure, which is patterned after the military. The hierarchical structures include foot soldiers and officers with titles such as lieutenant and sergeant. The Latin Kings have religious and mystical overtones that they mix with gang symbols and activities and a belief that God looks favorably on them because of their ethnic background. They're the most violent of the Hispanic gangs and participate in many criminal activities, such as drug and weapons sales, assault, robbery, intimidation, and murder.[60]

The Vice Lords also fit under the People umbrella. The Vice Lords is a predominantly black gang that started in the 1960s in Chicago. Somewhat like the Black Panther Party in California, the Vice Lords had overtones of a prosocial gang that attempted to eliminate crime and violence in the community and increase legitimate job opportunities in urban areas for disadvantaged youths. They even secured $1.4 million in federal antipoverty funds, which ultimately was channeled into illegal gang activities. The structure of the Vice Lords differs in some respects from that of other supergangs. Local leaders command the respect of members based on their power to persuade, rather than on violence. Consequently, leadership within the gang is always in flux, and power is based on how many followers a leader can point to at any one time.[61]

Folks. The Folks is a supergang that resulted from a coalition between the Simon City Royals, a white gang well known for burglary in Chicago, and the Black Gangster Disciples. The Folks are aligned with the Crips, while their rivals, the People, are loosely connected to the Bloods. Started in Chicago, the Black Gangster Disciples are estimated to have 30,000 members. Their founder, Larry Hoover, is serving a life sentence but is still considered to be the gang's leader. The Black Gangster Disciples are a sophisticated criminal organization that uses legitimate false-front businesses to conceal their drug distribution network. Stores and businesses such as car washes, music stores, barbershops, and apartment buildings are outlets for the drug enterprise or launder the money from criminal endeavors. In 1997, it was estimated the gang's revenues were close to $100 million a year. When the revenues for all Chicago gangs are considered, federal officials estimate the profits for drug sales exceed $1 billion.[62]

ASIAN GANGS

Traditionally, Asian gangs in the United States were confined to the various Chinatowns of the nation's largest cities. These gangs were derived from secret Chinese societies that formed in the 1600s. The two primary kinds of Chinese gangs, triads and *tongs*, were originally formed as patriotic and nationalistic organizations in China, but they were viewed by US law enforcement as criminal organizations. Over 80,000 members of triad gangs are active in China, Taiwan, and the United States.[63] Because they're extremely secretive organizations, little is known about their actual numbers and activities. The criminal activities of the triads are widespread and include not only traditional gang activities but also more high-tech crimes, such as credit card fraud, counterfeiting, software piracy, human smuggling, prostitution, loan sharking, and home-invasion robbery.[64] The most common offense committed by triads is the extortion of Asian businesses and other wealthy Asians. Triads are a juvenile delinquency problem because

FOCUS ON DIVERSITY 〉 *Gangs, Race, Stereotypes*

Racial stereotypes present a significant concern for the justice system. When police give selective treatment because of how individuals look rather than what they do, there are injustices that have consequences far beyond a single case. Whether it's being stopped by the police for "driving while black," being frisked at an airport for wearing traditional Muslim clothing, or being targeted for wearing baggy pants, oversize shirts, and baseball caps of a certain color, selective treatment causes resentment and a sense of unfairness among minority populations. The feeling that one is being racially profiled results in a lack of trust in the impartiality of the justice system.

According to Eduardo L. Portillos, Latinos experience differential treatment at every stage of the juvenile justice system regardless of their involvement in gang activity or drug use. Although Portillos acknowledges that Latinos are involved in illegal activities in some communities, he also recognizes most are not. The difficulty is that police cannot readily identify those involved in gangs and drug-dealing from their physical appearance. When skin color, mannerisms, styles of dress, and tattoos are used to single out individuals for increased surveillance and detainment, many innocent people are subjected to feeling that they're being hassled by the police. Portillos recommends the following policies to alleviate these feelings of injustice:

》 Officials must realize that being a member of the Latino community doesn't mean one is involved in gangs and drugs even though there may be Latinos who are.

》 Officials must recognize Latino diversity. The Latino population includes people from many regions and countries, including Mexico, Central America, South America, Puerto Rico, and other Caribbean nations. Although they share a common language, there are differences in dialect and culture.

》 There is a need for more Spanish-speaking officers who understand the difficulties of life in the barrio. Also, the courts need translators not only for youths, but also for their parents.

》 There is a need for bilingual attorneys who can not only represent youths but also help their families understand the proceedings.

》 Finally, there is a need to change the "get tough on crime" and "three strikes" policies that have a differential impact on blacks and Latinos in the justice system. More resources spent on education and social services can help prevent crime.

THINK ABOUT IT

1. What other minority populations experience discrimination from the criminal and juvenile justice systems?
2. What additional solutions do you suggest for making the justice system appear to be unbiased and impartial?

Source: Eduardo L. Portillos, "Latinos, Gangs, and Drugs," in *Images of Color, Images of Crime*, Coramae Richey Mann, Marjorie S. Matz, and Nancy Rodriguez (Los Angeles: Roxbury Publishing Company, 2006), 212–220.

they recruit members as young as 13. Unlike many gangs, in which members age out when they reach their 20s and get legitimate jobs and marry, triads retain gang members until they're well into their 30s.

Tongs are Chinese social clubs that law enforcement officials suspect of being associated with illegal gambling, drug trafficking, extortion, and robbery. They started in places like San Francisco's Chinatown in the 1860s, where they ran gambling houses, opium dens, and brothels. They perform many positive functions for the Chinese community in the United States but are so secretive it's difficult to judge the balance between their prosocial activities and their criminal and delinquent interests.[65]

One of the most interesting facets of contemporary Chinese gangs is the competition from the arrival of new immigrants. Those coming to US shores in recent times have little in common with the members of old established gangs who speak English and who have access to legitimate employment opportunities and education. The newer Asian immigrants find much of American society, even Chinese American society, closed to them, so they form gangs that don't honor decades-old agreements, protocols, and territorial claims. These contemporary Chinese gangs, which started to form in the late 1960s, borrowed their patterns of behavior from the traditional triads and from watching movies. This has given them an atmosphere based on clichés and stereotypes rather than on necessity and tradition. Some new arrivals can enter the older gangs because of their willingness to provide the muscle for criminal enterprises that entail a high risk of violence or detection.

Some of the newer gangs have discarded the secrecy of traditional Chinese gangs and have developed styles of dress and tattoos that allow them to be readily identified as gang members. In New York, the American Eagles gang favors tight, straight-legged jeans and satin jackets, and its members bleach the tips of their hair blond. Although they are a relatively small gang, their visibility makes them appear more prevalent, and they're easier for victims to identify and for police officers to track. Chinese gang members have now adopted many of the accoutrements of the hip-hop culture and have their own rappers, who brag about being shot and about their run-ins with the law.[66]

Yakuza is the collective name for 2,500 Japanese gangs. These gangs have an estimated 200,000 members worldwide and are active in the United States, primarily on the West Coast and in Hawaii. The *Yakuza* are an exclusively male organization, preferring that women be wives and mothers rather than gang members. Its roots can be traced to the 14th century, when outcasts banded together for protection from the authorities. *Yakuza* members are heavily involved in prostitution, including the smuggling of underage girls for wealthy businessmen, and are deeply involved in weapons trafficking, particularly to Japan, where gun laws are extremely strict. The *Yakuza* invest their profits in legitimate businesses and have large holdings in several companies that are traded on the New York Stock Exchange. In the United States, they commit offenses generally within the Japanese American community and are extremely secretive and difficult for law enforcement to infiltrate. Delaney relates an interesting way in which the *Yakuza* discipline those who violate the rules. Rather than killing violators, the *Yakuza* perform a ceremony called a *yubizume*, in which the offender cuts off his little finger and presents it to the insulted party as an apology. The offender is then kicked out of the gang forever.[67]

In the past 20 years, the Asian gang problem has shifted from those controlled by traditional Chinese and Japanese semilegitimate organizations to newer gangs composed of youths from Vietnam, Laos, and Cambodia. These youths are feeling the stress common in many recent immigrant groups for which there isn't a large enclave of fellow countrymen with established, stable ethnic subcultures. They experience problems in school and in the community because of language and cultural differences and turn to gangs to find protection, identity, and ways of coping with a new and strange society.

Asian youths are joining gangs in increasing numbers and engage in a variety of offenses but seem to specialize in home invasions. Home invasions entail breaking into the homes of wealthy families and terrorizing them until they produce money, jewelry, and other valuables. The perpetrators will beat the men and rape the female family members in crime sprees that can last for hours. The victims, who are also Asian, are reluctant to call the police, because in the countries they come from, the police are often corrupt and linked to criminal organizations.[68]

Vietnamese gangs are credited with being the most violent of the Asian gangs. Their main base of operation is in Orange County, California, which has a robust Vietnamese population. Vietnam doesn't have a history of organized criminal gangs, but Vietnamese who migrated to the United States after the Vietnam War were mostly linked to the South Vietnamese government, which was riddled with corruption, bribery, and violence. As new immigrants, the parents of gang members worked long hours to obtain an economic toehold in the United States, and the children were subjected to racial discrimination and hostility in the schools. Not surprisingly, these children coalesced into secretive and violent gangs that preyed on legitimate Vietnamese businesses and restaurants. The Vietnamese gangs, which are only loosely organized, sometimes form what is known as a "hasty gang" that is quickly put together for a brief crime spree and then disbands. This makes gathering intelligence on the gangs a difficult task for police gang units.[69]

Finally, there are a number of Filipino gangs on the West Coast and in Las Vegas. Large numbers of Filipinos were admitted to the United States because of their backgrounds in nursing or the military. Many Filipino men served in the US Army during the Vietnam War and were rewarded with permission to move to the United States. Because of a shortage of nurses during the 1970s, immigration laws became more liberal for nurses, and many Filipino women took advantage of the economic and social opportunities available in US hospitals. By 1988, 14 percent of all gang-related incidents in the United States involved Filipino youths, who committed robberies, drug sales, car theft, and drive-by shootings.[70]

As the Asian population in the United States grows, so does the gang problem. Although Asians have long been considered the "model minority" because of their commitment to working hard and achieving success, there is an underside to immigration in which some youths quickly shed the traditions of the old culture and adopt the behaviors of the street as a way to survive and protect themselves in circumstances in which they're continually victimized. As the more recent Asian immigrants are assimilated into American society, it's likely that gang behavior will decrease. However, this doesn't mean that Asians, as well as youths from every other racial group in the country, will not participate in gang activity. At some point, gangs might not be organized according to race as they are now but will depend more on geography or a specific delinquent and criminal behavior.

WHITE GANGS

White youths have traditionally joined gangs as a way to escape poverty or secure protection from other gangs. White youths commonly join mixed-race gangs where they're in the minority. Although whites have an easier time being assimilated into the dominant culture and overcoming the effects of poverty by doing well in school or finding gainful employment, they often reject society and find meaning, satisfaction, and excitement in gang life. Three types of white gangs bear examination: skinheads, stoners, and taggers. Each of these provides white youths with alternative ways of coping in a society where they're unable to find an outlet for their angry and violent behavior.

》 Neo-Nazi skinheads. Skinheads get their name because they shave their heads. They may also wear steel-toed boots and tight, straight-legged jeans. They pattern themselves after similar groups in Europe and commonly adhere to a racist agenda, claiming that minorities get preferential treatment in the United States and that whites should remain "racially pure" and not intermarry with other races. They picture themselves as neo-Nazis and often use the swastika in their literature or as tattoos. Additionally, they look on Adolph Hitler as a visionary whose racism and anti-Semitic teachings are worthy of following. Skinhead music also celebrates the plight of working-class youth and is often racist, misogynistic, and violent. In areas with significant immigration from Hispanic and Asian countries, skinhead gangs often form in an attempt to protect what they see as a threatened white culture. In addition to being racist, most skinhead groups are homophobic and quick to use violence against gays and lesbians.[71]

》 Stoners. Stoners are youths who come from middle-class or upper-middle-class families and are unable to succeed in traditional ways. They're commonly high school dropouts who exist on the fringes of conventional society. Funded by parents and minimum-wage jobs, stoners are loosely organized groups that are heavily into drugs and alcohol. Like other juveniles, they commit burglary, larceny, and sell drugs, and their drugs of choice are speed, LSD, rock cocaine, and PCP. Additionally, they're likely to inhale anything from glue to paint thinner. They might declare their independence and counterculture attitudes by harming animals and committing ritual-style offenses, such as desecrating churches or graveyards. Their music and dress can have overtones of Satanism, and their purpose is to declare their rejection of traditional values. They don't compete with street gangs for territorial dominance and don't engage in high levels of violence. Rather, they congregate in smaller groups and are sometimes indistinguishable from other youths hanging out in the local mall. What makes stoners fall under the rubric of being a gang are the offenses they commit and the reliance on drugs and alcohol to define their worldview.[72]

》 Taggers. Taggers use graffiti to call attention to themselves. They use spray paint to deface road signs, walls, railroad cars, or sidewalks. Their goal is to leave their mark where other people can see it. Although most people are oblivious to the meanings of this graffiti, tagger crews have a highly structured symbolic language that allows them to recognize each other's work and appreciate the skill or risk it took to mark the surfaces. The tagger subculture in Southern California predominantly comprises young, white males. They range in age from 10 years old up to the early 20s, but most teenagers stop tagging at 15 or 16. An estimated 600 tagger crews with upward of about 30,000 youths live in Southern California. With numbers like this, it's impossible for police to keep track of all the taggers or to prevent their actions. The taggers' goal is to mark as many places as possible. Extra status is gained by putting graffiti in hard-to-reach, guarded, or dangerous places. Tagger crews will do battle with each other, not by violence, but by attempting to outdo each other in putting their graffiti in more places. Some taggers carry weapons for protection from other tagger crews, but violence isn't the norm. Taggers are hard to identify because they aspire to a chameleon-like quality so that they can put their tags on surfaces and get away without being noticed. Like the stoners, taggers aren't particularly dangerous. Their delinquency is painting graffiti on public and private property, but they don't engage in gang warfare and drive-by shootings. Next to graffiti, their most common offense is larceny, whereby they steal a lot of spray paint. They have an almost inexhaustible appetite for paint, and many large retail stores have had to take special precautions to prevent taggers from wiping out their inventories.[73]

GANGS AND FEMALES

Historically, gang activity has been considered a young man's game. Females weren't considered full gang members and existed only in ancillary roles that served the male members' interests. This secondary gang status was thought to be primarily as a sex object, with limited participation in delinquent activities.

Little is known about female participation in gangs, but several surveys estimate that around 10 percent of gang activity can be attributed to girls and young women. Other studies put the figure closer to 30 percent. Female gang members participate in delinquent and criminal activities as part of male gangs and also can be found operating all-female gangs. Although we don't know the exact number of female gang members, we do know they participate in a variety of ways and can be just as violent as male gang members.[74] According to researchers, girls who are active in gangs become the most serious, violent, and chronic delinquents of all girls.[75]

Females report a number of reasons for joining a gang. A primary reason is protection. Young women are often the victims of abuse by fathers or other family members, and joining a gang serves as a refuge from unwanted attention.[76] Often, female runaways can choose only between joining a gang and becoming the property of a pimp. The gang gives them higher status and more control over their sexual activities. Rebellious girls join gangs as a way to spite what they perceive to be overprotective parents. Sometimes the reason a young woman joins a gang is because her boyfriend is already a member, and she can either follow him into the gang or lose him to another female gang member. Finally, economic reality provides females with a reason to join a gang. By participating in gang behaviors such as shoplifting, drug sales, and larcenies, the girls can improve their marginal economic status and obtain the stylish clothes, fast food, and other items valued by teenagers. The females most likely to join a gang are those who suffer from low self-esteem, come from dysfunctional families, and have a history of victimization. Unlike males, who are often seeking thrills and action, females typically join gangs for defensive reasons.[77]

Females aren't recruited into gangs in the same way as males. They typically aren't coerced or forced to join but do so because they have family ties in the gang or seek a buffer from poverty. At an age when many teenagers are experiencing major biological and physical changes, joining a gang gives girls a sense of commitment and belonging that is absent in other areas of their lives. There are three types of initiation rites for females who join gangs:

» **Jumped-in.** This involves physical fighting. Sometimes the girl must fight other gang members, and because she is outnumbered, she inevitably gets beaten severely. The idea is to test her willingness and ability to fight. Sometimes being jumped-in means the girl has to commit some offense, such as assault on someone from a rival gang or a law enforcement authority. Drive-by shootings, face slashing, or muggings are ways females can show their willingness and toughness.[78]

» **Born-in.** Because of family ties, a recruit might be admitted to the gang without having to prove her toughness. With the blessing of established gang members, she can simply get some gang tattoos and verbally commit to the gang. Sometimes, these girls are second- or third-generation gang members who have been around the gang all their lives and are allowed to join as a matter of family status.

» **Trained-in or sexed-in.** Young women are required to have sex with several male gang members. The gang leaders have sex with her first, and others follow according to their rank. This is the least desirable way to become a gang member, and it carries a stigma. Girls who are trained-in seldom become fully accepted by other female gang members and might be continually abused by the males. It's certainly cause for a loss of respect, and these girls remain the most marginalized and exploited ones in the gang.[79]

Not every gang uses these methods of initiation, and the methods differ according to whether the individual is male or female. Female gang members fall into three categories: some are regular members of a mixed gang, some are members of independent female gangs, and some are auxiliaries to male gangs. These types of gang affiliation affect the type and seriousness of the female's delinquent or criminal behavior.[80]

With the exception of murder, female gang members break the law at rates similar to that of males. Their offenses differ by type but not so much by frequency. For instance, Miller found that girl gangs in St. Louis, Missouri, and Columbus, Ohio, were as likely as boy gangs to commit larcenies, steal cars for joyriding, intimidate people, and commit vandalism. Although they don't seek out violence in the same manner as boys, violence is part of gang life, and girls will use it to establish themselves within the gang culture and at school. Girls will sometimes be used by male gang members to help in fighting other gangs by seducing rival gang members in secluded areas so that the gang can jump them. Girls are also used to gather gang intelligence by sleeping with rival gang members.[81]

Drug sales and drug use are common features of gang life for many females. Girls sell drugs to get money to party, to buy clothes, and for personal use. When they break away from home and live on their own or with a boyfriend, the drug sales may be the only stable source of income for rent and groceries. Selling drugs is a dangerous enterprise, and girls willing to undertake the risks must be tough and ready to use or respond to violence. They must protect their drugs, money, and lives by being aggressive and capable of convincing others that they will use deadly force. Often, girls assist the drug dealing of boy gang members.[82]

Questions

1. What are the six commonly accepted characteristics of gangs?
2. What are the two aspects of the definition of a gang member?
3. What are the various pushes and pulls that can lead to a child joining a gang?
4. Why do gang members leave their gangs?
5. Why do girls join gangs? What are the three main ways that girls join gangs?

Dealing with Gangs

Although there are some broadly agreed-on strategies, the efforts to stem the growth of gangs and the damage they do to other young people and society have been largely unsuccessful. Gangs continue to plague large cities, and appear to be spreading to smaller communities. For the rest of this chapter, we review some of the prevention, suppression, and treatment methods that have been used to deal

Learning Objective 4.

Describe primary gang prevention.

Learning Objective 5.

Understand how secondary gang prevention works.

Learning Objective 6.

Discuss the focus of tertiary gang prevention.

with gangs. Although the success of these strategies is questionable, they might have a greater effect with the proper funding and support. With this in mind, how might a prosocial gang affect the scene? Recall that the Crips has its roots in the prosocial activities of the 1960s-era Black Panthers.

Prevention, Suppression, and Treatment of Gangs

Community efforts to prevent the formation and sustainability of gangs fall into three categories: primary, secondary, and tertiary (see Figure 10.3). On a broad level, these categories are useful for examining the prevention of a wide variety of social and public health problems. By categorizing these community crime-prevention efforts, we may appreciate how different levels of crime prevention are aimed at distinct target groups. (See Programs for Children for a federal program that practices primary, secondary, and tertiary gang prevention.)

PRIMARY GANG PREVENTION

The idea behind primary gang prevention is to remove factors from the community that are suspected to breed gang involvement. This is a broad strategy that is aimed at more than gang prevention. By improving schools, developing a healthy local economy and employment, and providing recreational opportunities, communities seek to improve the lives of all citizens. When meaningful communities meet the needs of children, gangs aren't necessary to fill the gaps in identity, purpose, and protection. Much of what we call primary prevention of gangs isn't really aimed at gangs at all but rather is designed to help all children in the community.

It can be argued that primary prevention is worthwhile even if these efforts don't prevent gangs, because they provide so many other benefits. For instance, mandatory schooling until the age of 16 helps all children, even those who might join gangs. Later, it will be easier to rehabilitate gang members if they have some skills that will help them get a job.

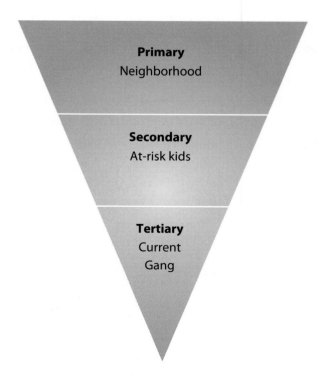

Primary
Neighborhood

Secondary
At-risk kids

Tertiary
Current
Gang

Figure 10.3 Community Gang Prevention

Different levels of crime prevention are aimed at distinct target groups. Here, an instructor leads a session on video production as part of a program designed to offer Los Angeles kids an alternative to gangs.

SECONDARY GANG PREVENTION

Secondary prevention of gangs involves focusing on potential gang members and intervening specifically to improve their attitudes toward conventional society and to alter the behaviors that might get them into trouble. One of the most effective secondary-prevention programs is Head Start, a federally funded program for disadvantaged children. Head Start provides preschool education for children from needy families. It is designed to get these children up to speed in social and academic development so that they can start the first grade with the same capabilities as children from more privileged families.

A number of other school-based programs target at-risk children, including social-skills training, law-related education, classroom-management programs, alternative schools, cooperative learning programs, and antidrug programs. One school-based program that is specifically designed to address the problems of gangs is the Gang Resistance Education and Training (G.R.E.A.T.) program. Patterned after the D.A.R.E. (Drug Abuse Resistance Education) program, G.R.E.A.T. has uniformed police officers interact with children by providing community-based activities and classroom instruction. This program is intended to provide life skills that empower adolescents to resist the pressure to join gangs.[83]

Another school-affiliated program that has demonstrated some success is Broader Urban Involvement and Leadership (BUILD). This program distributes information on gang violence, substance abuse, gang recruitment strategies, and the consequences of gang membership. BUILD recruits youths who may be gang affiliated, delinquent, or encountering risks such as violence, substance abuse, truancy, poor academic performance, or other problematic issues in their schools and communities. The program offers in-school and out-of-school activities, as well as after-school activities and community outreach efforts.[84]

TERTIARY GANG PREVENTION

What can be done with youths who are already in gangs? Here, we briefly review a couple of techniques, but the main material for answering this question is reserved for the following chapters, which deal with the juvenile justice system's response to crime and delinquency. Tertiary prevention involves convincing youths to give up their gang affiliation and become responsible members of the community. This is difficult to do, because a committed gang member considers the gang to be the primary institution in his or her life, replacing even the family. To lure youths away from an organization that has such a strong grip on loyalty is difficult. See Prevention and Intervention about a

The Gang Reduction Program

In 1987, the Office of Juvenile Justice and Delinquency Prevention (OJJDP) launched the Juvenile Gang Suppression and Intervention Research and Development Program, in which researchers developed a model youth gang program based on findings from a national assessment. The resulting Comprehensive Community-Wide Gang Program Model implements progressive practices in gang prevention, intervention, suppression, and reentry. In detail, these are the practices:

» Prevention targets high-risk and high-crime communities, as well as children who are at risk, with school-based activities and community events.

» Intervention targets active gang members and associates with aggressive outreach, recruitment, and support services, such as mentoring, job training, mental health and substance services, and tattoo removal.

» Suppression seeks to remove the most dangerous and influential gang members from the community. An example of suppression technique is the use of crime statistics and data logs to determine high-crime days and times in specific areas. During these times, law enforcement adds foot, bicycle, motorcycle, and walking patrols to the target area, resulting in a significant decrease in crime.

» Reentry provides services to and monitoring of serious offenders who are returning to the community after incarceration. Returning gang members who may attempt to rejoin their gangs are especially targeted. Activities include self-sufficiency skill training, as well as job training and placement.[1]

In 2003, OJJDP implemented the program in four demonstration cities: Los Angeles; Richmond, Virginia; Milwaukee, Wisconsin; and North Miami Beach, Florida. As of 2010, researchers found that although the program's success varied from site to site, they all successfully built local partnerships to raise awareness of gang and crime issues.[2]

THINK ABOUT IT

1. Discuss possibilities for the long-term effectiveness of the prevention, intervention, suppression, and reentry strategy. For example, do you think close monitoring of gang members who are returning to the community after incarceration will help prevent them from rejoining their gangs?

[1]National Gang Center, *Best Practices to Address Community Gang Problems: OJJDP's Comprehensive Gang Model* (Washington, DC: US Department of Justice, Office of Justice Programs, Office of Juvenile Justice and Delinquency Prevention, 2010). Online at www.ncjrs.gov/pdffiles1/ojjdp/222799.pdf.

[2]Meagan Cahill and David Hayeslip, Findings from the Evaluation of OJJDP's Gang Reduction Program (Washington, DC: US Department of Justice Office of Justice Programs Office of Juvenile Justice and Delinquency Prevention, 2010). Online at www.ncjrs.gov/pdffiles1/ojjdp/230106.pdf.

Chicago group, the "violence interrupters" who work with a program known as CeaseFire, entering dangerous neighborhoods and trying to convince gang-involved youths to stop the violence.

Research suggests that merely getting youths to leave gangs isn't enough to restore their place in law-abiding society. Programs must help restore the youths' social bonds with their nongang friends, families, schools, and the rest of conventional society. Because gang membership is such an integral part of gang members' personal identity, reorienting that identity is also important.[85] A good example of reorientation is tattoo-removal programs. Programs that remove tattoos for a reduced cost, in exchange for community service, or even for free now operate in many large cities. The most common stated reason for removing gang tattoos is to get a job or to get a better job.[86] According to a Texas plastic surgeon, "They want to get a job beyond dishwasher and realize no one will hire them with a swastika on their arm."[87]

10.4 PREVENTION AND INTERVENTION

The Violence Interrupters

It's difficult to try to tell a young gang member that he or she doesn't have to fight or kill a kid in another gang. Not just anyone can do it. In Chicago, the violence interrupters are people from the community and former gang members who work with the CeaseFire organization to try to stop youths from killing each other.

The violence interrupters have been doing just that for 11 years. Their mission is a bit different from that of other antigang organizations. They don't try to convince kids to leave gangs. They don't try to get gangs off the streets. They simply enter potentially violent situations and try to talk the combatants down. Their mission is about saving the lives of youths who feel they must avenge any disrespect with escalating violence.

CeaseFire takes a public health approach to preventing violence. The group's website states, "Violence is a learned behavior that can be prevented using disease control methods." Using "proven public health techniques," the group advocates three steps to stop violence:

>> Identification and detection
>> Interruption, intervention, and risk reduction
>> Changing behavior and norms[1]

So far, the approach has worked. In its first year, CeaseFire communities enjoyed a 45 percent decrease in shootings, compared to a 10 percent reduction in all of Chicago.[2]

One of the violence interrupters is Ameena Matthews, a former gang enforcer and daughter of a Chicago gang leader. Matthews says that often the youths don't even want to fight, much less kill. She says that thanks to her fierce reputation, when she steps in as a mediator, it gives the youths a good excuse to back down. Still, gang youths have a warlike mentality when it comes to protecting their honor and their gang's

Two CeaseFire violence interrupters attempt to stop retaliatory gang violence.

honor. Says Matthews, "It's like Afghanistan to them. And if one of their brothers or sisters die[s] out there, it's like a fallen soldier over there across the waters. They feel that this is something that is honorable, and that I served well."[3]

THINK ABOUT IT

1. Discuss why community members and ex–gang members are successful at "violence interruption," in ways that outsiders might not be.
2. Is simply stopping violence a good goal? Shouldn't CeaseFire seek to dismantle the gangs, as well? Why or why not?

[1]CeaseFire, CeaseFire: A Public Health Approach to Public Safety, ceasefirechicago.org/how-it-works. Accessed August 31, 2011.
[2]Sheridan Lardner, "An Examination of Gangs and Urban Violence," *Centennial*, University of Chicago, ssacentennial.uchicago.edu/features/features-crimelab.shtml.
[3]National Public Radio, "Gang 'Interrupters' Fight Chicago's Cycle Of Violence," August 1, 2011, www.npr.org/2011/08/01/138888371/gang-interrupters-fight-chicagos-cycle-of-violence.

The juvenile justice system uses two approaches to stem gang activity: deterrence and treatment. Law enforcement agencies have developed specific gang units that gather intelligence on gang activities and attempt to arrest and convict gang members. The idea is that getting gang members off the street and punishing them for their criminal activities will deter others from joining gangs.

Although law enforcement authorities have been successful in incarcerating thousands of gang members, there is little evidence that this has stemmed the development of gangs. Once a gang member goes to prison, officials provide

A young former gang member with his wife's name tattooed on his neck stands outside Homeboy Industries in Los Angeles. Homeboy Industries employs ex-gang members as a way of keeping them off the street.

opportunities for education, job training, drug and alcohol counseling, and a variety of other rehabilitative efforts. However, there are two problems with this approach. First, effective treatment programs are expensive, and few states have allocated the money to provide comprehensive programs in all youth detention facilities and prisons.[88] These programs can sometimes be effective, but they simply don't have enough resources. The second problem with trying to rehabilitate gang members is that many youth detention facilities and prisons have highly organized gang subcultures that have a great deal of influence on inmates. Rehabilitation, then, takes a back seat to continued gang involvement. Often, young people become further involved in gangs as a result of incarceration, rather than receiving the treatment they need to break away.

To be truly effective, a comprehensive program that involves all three levels of prevention—primary, secondary, and tertiary—must be utilized in a thoughtful, coordinated, and well-funded approach. In cities with racially and ethnically diverse populations, the large disparities in income and wealth, large geographic areas, limited tax bases, and ineffective politicians affect the commitment to seriously address all three levels of crime and gang prevention.

Questions

1. What are the three categories of gang control? Describe each.
2. What is the role of gangs when communities meet the needs of children?
3. Name and describe one of the most effective secondary gang-prevention programs.
4. How can gang loyalty be compared to religious conviction?
5. Why are programs that help restore the youths' bonds with conventional society important?

>> FOCUS ON ETHICS

The Prosocial Gang

As the police chief of a medium-sized city, you're concerned with the gang problem. You have assigned two of your experienced officers to form a gang unit to suppress emerging gang activity. These officers have come to you with an interesting problem, and you're unsure what to do about it. A gang called the Li'l Bad Boys has recently changed its focus of activities, and now instead of selling drugs and committing larcenies, the Li'l Bad Boys have appointed themselves as protectors of their downtrodden neighborhood.

It seems one of the leaders has been recently re-leased from prison, where he had an epiphany: he now believes it's his mission in life to help those in need. He has convinced the Li'l Bad Boys to clean up the neighborhood. The gang now bullies both drug dealers and drug users and has unilaterally declared the neighborhood a drug-free zone.

Although you agree with their goals, you can't condone their tactics. They have beaten some youths severely and invaded several homes they suspected of being crack houses and meth labs. Twice they made mistakes and broke into the houses of law-abiding citizens, doing considerable damage and injuring three people.

Overall, however, this gang has had a positive effect on the community. Crime is down, drug sales have moved to a nearby small town, and citizens are once again enjoying being on the streets and in the parks during the day and early evening hours.

Your two experienced gang officers are divided as to what to do. One claims the Li'l Bad Boys are cleaning up the area and are actually doing the work of the police. She's willing to tolerate a level of crime against drug dealers and says the few mistakes where law-abiding citizens are inconvenienced are just collateral damage. In her view, it's better to have this gang working toward a safe neighborhood instead of against one.

Your other officer has a different opinion. He says vigilante justice shouldn't be condoned. The gang members break the law when they assault drug dealers, and although he has little sympathy for the victims, he says the police must investigate and respond to all crime. Additionally, he's suspicious about the gang's motives: he fears they may be trying to eliminate the competition under the guise of being a prosocial gang but will ultimately revert to traditional gang behavior. He urges you to target this gang for special surveillance.

WHAT DO YOU DO?

1. Let the gang continue to clean up the community by victimizing offenders and drug dealers.
2. Crack down on the gang and require them to obey the law like everyone else.
3. Call the gang leaders into a meeting and see if you can take advantage of their prosocial activities but channel them into appropriate methods. For instance, if the gang members know about drug activity, they are welcome to inform the police and help gather evidence.

Summary

Learning Objective 1. Detail Miller's six characteristics of a gang.	A self-formed association of peers. These peers form gangs because of functions they believe the gang is able to provide that they can't get in traditional relationships.
	Bound by mutual interests. Gang members see their fellow gang members as having the same kinds of concerns that they do.
	Well-developed lines of authority and other organizational features. All gangs have some level of organization that includes leadership, division of labor, and lines of communication.
	Acting together to achieve a specific purpose or purposes. For a gang to be successful, its members must work together.
	Involvement in illegal activity. This is one of the primary distinguishing features of a gang.
	Control over a particular territory, facility, or enterprise. Gangs usually protect some geographical area.

Summary

Learning Objective 2. List and explain the two aspects of the definition of a gang member.	The first aspect is involvement in crime, a crucial distinction that helps to differentiate gangs from other adolescent groups. The second aspect is bonding. Gang members show an affiliation with their gang with a family-like loyalty. This bonding can be exemplified by gang apparel, gang tattoos, or communicating with gang signs. Members see the gang as a primary group, whereby the gang comes first in how members identify themselves.
Learning Objective 3. Discuss how gangs vary.	Scholars differentiate among types of gangs by size, racial and ethnic makeup, criminal activity, organization, and geographic location. Although many gangs remain stable across these factors, gangs may change as circumstances change. A gang may move as its neighborhood changes in terms of racial composition or social class, or as gang members grow older, they may commit more serious delinquency and crime.
Learning Objective 4. Describe primary gang prevention.	The idea behind primary gang prevention is to remove community factors that are suspected to breed gang involvement. By improving schools, developing a healthy local economy and employment, and providing recreational opportunities, communities seek to improve the lives of all citizens.
Learning Objective 5. Understand how secondary gang prevention works.	Secondary gang prevention involves focusing on potential gang members and intervening to improve their attitudes toward conventional society and to alter the behaviors that might get them into trouble. This includes school-based programs that target at-risk children.
Learning Objective 6. Discuss the focus of tertiary gang prevention.	Tertiary gang prevention focuses on youths who are already in gangs by convincing them to give up their gang affiliation and become responsible members of the community. In doing so, it's important to help restore the youths' social bonds with their nongang friends, families, schools, and the rest of conventional society.

Chapter Review Questions

1. What are the two special challenges juvenile gangs pose for criminal justice agencies?
2. What are the two most common research strategies used to study gangs?
3. How do generalizability and the Hawthorne effect interfere with researchers' efforts to study gangs?
4. What factors go into an individual's decision to join a gang?
5. How is race related to an individual's decision to join a gang?
6. Why is it difficult for researchers to determine how much crime is gang related?
7. Why might police officials be reluctant to admit they have a gang problem?
8. What motivations might police agencies have for overstating a gang problem?
9. How do female gangs differ from male gangs?
10. How do primary, secondary, and tertiary gang-prevention strategies differ?

Key Terms

generalizability—The degree to which the results of an individual study or investigation sample can be applied to other studies and samples.

Hawthorne effect— The tendency of research subjects to act differently than they normally would as a result of their awareness of being studied.

peer relationships—The connections between those of equal standing within a group.

primary group—A small social group whose members share personal, enduring relationships.

snowball sample—A method of field research in which information is gathered by asking each person interviewed to suggest additional people for interviewing.

Endnotes

1 Arlen Egley Jr. and James C. Howell, Highlights of the 2009 National Youth Gang Survey, Table 1: Law Enforcement Reports of Gang Activity, 2005–09, June 2011, p. 1, www.ncjrs.gov/pdffiles1/ojjdp/233581.pdf.

2 National Center on Addiction and Substance Abuse at Columbia University, *National Survey of American Attitudes on Substance Abuse XV: Teens and Parents*, August 2010, p. 2, www.casacolumbia.org/templates/publications_reports.aspx.

3 Tom Hayden, *Street Wars: Gangs and the Future of Violence* (New York: New Press, 2004).

4 Ralph A. Weisheit and L. Edward Wells, "Youth Gangs in Rural America," *NIJ Journal* 5 (2004): 2–6.

5 Finn-Aage Esbensen, *Evaluating G.R.E.A.T.: A School-Based Gang Prevention Program* (Washington, DC: National Institute of Justice, 2004).

6 Laura Caldwell and David M. Altschuler, "Adolescents Leaving Gangs: An Analysis of Risk and Protective Factors, Resiliency and Desistance in a Developmental Context," *Journal of Gang Research* 8 (2001): 21–34.

7 Richard A. Ball and G. David Curry, "The Logic of Definition in Criminology: The Purpose and Methods for Defining 'Gangs,'" in G. Larry Mays, ed., *Gangs and Gang Behavior* (Chicago: Nelson-Hall, 1997), 3–21.

8 Walter B. Miller, "Gangs, Groups and Serious Youth Crime," in David Schichor and Delos H. Helley, eds., *Critical Issues in Juvenile Delinquency* (Lexington, MA: D. C. Heath, 1980), 115–138.

9 Malcolm W. Klein and Cheryl L. Maxson, "Street Gang Violence," in Neil A. Weiner and Marvin E. Wolfgang, eds., *Violent Crime, Violent Criminals* (Newbury Park, CA: Sage, 1989), 198–234.

10 Tim Delaney, *American Street Gangs* (Upper Saddle River, NJ: Prentice Hall, 2006). See especially Chapter 6.

11 G. David Curry and Scott H. Decker, *Confronting Gangs: Crime and Community* (Los Angeles: Roxbury, 1998).

12 Regional Information Sharing Systems (RISS) program, www.riss.net/Default/Overview. RISS National Gang Program, www.riss.net/Documents/RISSGang.Brochure.pdf. Accessed August 31, 2011.

13 Curry and Decker, *Confronting Gangs: Crime and Community*, 13.

14 Martin Sanchey-Jankowski, *Islands in the Street: Gangs and American Society* (Berkeley: University of California Press, 1991).

15 C. Ronald Huff, "Youth Gangs and Public Policy," *Crime and Delinquency* 35 (1989): 524–537.

16 Robert J. Bursik Jr. and Harold G. Grasmick, "Defining and Researching Gangs," in Arlen Egley Jr. et al., eds., *The Modern Gang Reader*, 3rd ed. (Los Angeles: Roxbury, 2006), 2–13.

17 Richard C. McCorkle and Terance D. Miethe, "The Political and Organization Response to Gangs: An Examination of a 'Moral Panic' in Nevada," *Justice Quarterly* 15 (1998): 41–64.

18 Jerome H. Skolnick, "The Social Structure of Street Drug Dealing," *American Journal of Police* 9 (1990): 1–41.

19 G. David Curry, Richard A. Ball, and Scott H. Decker, *Estimating the National Scope of Gang Crime from Law Enforcement Data* (Washington, DC: National Institute of Justice, 1996).

20 George J. McCall, *Observing the Law: Field Methods in the Study of Crime and the Criminal Justice System* (New York: Free Press, 1978).

21 Frederic Thrasher, *The Gang: A Study of 1,313 Gangs in Chicago* (Chicago: University of Chicago Press, 1927); Jody Miller, *One of the Guys: Girls, Gangs, and Gender* (New York: Oxford University Press, 2001).

22 William F. Whyte, *Street Corner Society* (Chicago: University of Chicago, 1943). Although somewhat dated now, Whyte's appendix in this book detailing how his field research was done provides an excellent review of how to get access to street youths and win their trust.

23 Malcolm Klein, *Street Gangs and Street Workers* (Upper Saddle River, NJ: Prentice Hall, 1971), 151.

24 Wendy M. Craig et al., "The Road to Gang Membership: Characteristics of Male Gang and Nongang Members from Ages 10 to 14," *Social Development* 11, no. 1 (2002): 53–68.

25 Albert Cohen, *Delinquent Boys: The Culture of the Gang* (Glencoe, IL: Free Press, 1955).

26 Kate Keenan et al., "The Influence of Deviant Peers on the Development of Boys' Disruptive and Delinquent Behavior: A Temporal

Analysis," *Development and Psychopathology* 7 (1995): 715–726.

27 Scott Decker, "Collective and Normative Features of Gang Violence," *Justice Quarterly* 13 (1996): 243–264.

28 Rachel A. Gordon et al., "Antisocial Behavior and Youth Gang Membership: Selection and Socialization," *Criminology* 42, no. 1 (2004): 55–88.

29 Scott H. Decker and Janet L. Lauritzen, "Leaving the Gang," in Arlen Egley et al., eds., *The Modern Gang Reader* (Los Angeles: Roxbury, 2006), 60–70.

30 Peggy Giordano, "The Wider Circle of Friends in Adolescence," *American Journal of Sociology* 101 (1995): 661–697.

31 Thomas Vander Ven et al., "Home Alone: The Impact of Maternal Employment on Delinquency," *Social Problems* 48 (2001): 236–257.

32 Penelope Eckert, *Jocks and Burnouts: Social Categories and Identity in the High School* (New York: Teachers College Press, 1989).

33 Daneen Deptula and Robert Cohen, "Aggressive, Rejected, and Delinquent Children and Adolescents: A Comparison of Their Friendships," *Aggression and Violent Behavior* 9 (2004): 75–104.

34 Chris Melde, Terrance J. Taylor, and Finn-Aage Esbensen, "'I Got Your Back': An Examination of the Protective Function of Gang Membership in Adolescence," Criminology 47, no. 2 (2009): 565–594.

35 Scott H. Decker and Barrick van Winkle, *Life in the Gang: Family, Friends, and Violence* (New York: Cambridge University Press, 1996).

36 Felix M. Padilla, *The Gang as an American Enterprise* (New Brunswick, NJ: Rutgers University Press, 1992).

37 Joseph F. Kett, *Rites of Passage: Adolescence in America 1790 to the Present* (New York: Basic Books, 1978).

38 Lowell Sheppard, *Boys Becoming Men: Creating Rites of Passage for the 21st Century* (New York: Authentic Media, 2003).

39 Curry and Decker, *Confronting Gangs*, 65–67.

40 Tim Delaney, *American Street Gangs*, 145–148.

41 R. B. Cairns and B. D. Cairns, "Social Cognition and Social Networks: A Developmental Perspective," in Debra J. Pepler and Kenneth H. Rubin, eds., *The Development and Treatment of Childhood Aggression* (Hillsdale, NJ: Erlbaum, 1991), 389–410.

42 Stephen W. Baron, "Self-Control, Social Consequences, and Criminal Behavior: Street Youth and the General Theory of Crime," *Journal of Research in Crime and Delinquency* 40 (2003): 403–425.

43 Thomas J. Dishion, Sarah E. Nelson, and Miwa Yasui, "Predicting Early Adolescent Gang Involvement from Middle School Adaptation," *Journal of Clinical Child and Adolescent Psychology* 34, no. 1 (2005): 62–73.

44 Karen Joe Laidler and Geoffrey Hunt, "Violence and Social Organization in Female Gangs," *Social Justice* 24 (1997): 148–187.

45 Lawrence Rosenthal, "Gang Loitering and Race," *Journal of Criminal Law and Criminology* 91 (2000): 99–160.

46 Melde, Taylor, and Esbensen, "'I Got Your Back.'"

47 Chris Melde and Finn-Aage Esbensen, "Gang Membership as a Turning Point in the Life Course," *Criminology* 49, no. 2 (2011): 513–552.

48 Decker and Lauritzen, "Collective and Normative Features of Gang Violence," 60–69.

49 Melde, Taylor, and Esbensen, "'I Got Your Back.'"

50 Pamela Irving Jackson, "Crime, Youth Gangs, and Urban Transition: The Social Dislocations of Postindustrial Economic Development," *Justice Quarterly* 8 (1991): 378–397.

51 Finn-Aage Esbensen and L. Thomas Winfree Jr., "Race and Gender Differences Between Gang and Nongang Youths: Results from a Multi-Site Study," in Arlen Egley Jr. et al., eds., *The Modern Gang Reader*, 3rd ed. (Los Angeles: Roxbury, 2006), 162–175.

52 Madeleine Brand, "Tookie Williams and the History of the Crips," National Public Radio, December 7, 2005, www.npr.org/templates/story/story.php?storyId;eq5042586.

53 Wilson Gray and Gerald Cohen, "Origin of the Gang Name 'Crips,' " *Names* (American Name Society) 55, no. 4 (December 2007): 455–456.

54 Jennifer Warren and Dan Morain, "Crips Target of Prison Lockdown," *Los Angeles Times*, July 1, 2003, B1.

55 Delaney, *American Street Gangs*, 184.

56 Randall G. Shelden, Sharon K. Tracy, and William Brown, *Youth Gangs in American Society* (Belmont, CA: Wadsworth, 2004), 54.

57 Howard Safir, *Security: Policing Your Homeland, Your City* (New York: St. Martin's Press, 2003).

58 Peg Tyre, "New York Turns Up the Heat on Crips, Bloods," *CNN Interactive,* August 27, 1997, www.cnn.com/US/9708/27/crips.bloods/.

59 John Irwin, *Prisons in Turmoil* (Boston: Little Brown, 1980).

60 John H. Richardson, "The Latin Kings Play Songs of Love," *New York* 30, no. 6 (February 17, 1997): 28.

61 Delaney, *American Street Gangs,* 189–191.

62 Frank Main and Carlos Sadovi, "Gangs Channel River of Cash from Streets to Shops, Studios—Even Vegas," *Chicago Sun Times,* April 7, 2002, 6A–9A.

63 Gerald L. Posner, *Warlords of Crime: Chinese Societies—The New Mafia* (New York: McGraw-Hill, 1988).

64 Dennis J. Kenney and James O. Finckenauer, *Organized Crime in America* (Belmont, CA: Wadsworth, 1995).

65 J. Keene, "Asian Organized Crime," *FBI Law Enforcement Bulletin* 58 (1989): 12–17.

66 Ko-Lin Chin, "Chinese Gangs and Extortion," in Arlen Egley Jr. et al., eds., *The Modern Gang Reader* (Los Angeles: Roxbury, 2006).

67 Kenney and Finckenauer, *Organized Crime in America.*

68 Gregory Yee Mark, "Oakland Chinatown's First Youth Gang: The Suey Sing Boys," in Rebecca D. Peterson, ed., *Understanding Contemporary Gangs in America* (Upper Saddle River, NJ: Prentice Hall, 2004).

69 Illinois Police and Sheriff's News, Organized Crime & Political Corruption, "Asian Street Gangs and Organized Crime in Focus: A Rising Threat from the Far East," www.ipsn.org/asg08107.html.

70 Bangele D. Alsaybar, "Deconstructing Deviance: Filipino Youth Gangs, 'Party Culture,' and Ethnic Identity in Los Angeles," *Amerasia Journal* 25 (1999): 116–138.

71 Wendy L. Hicks, "Skinheads: A Three Nation Comparison," *Journal of Gang Research* 11, no. 2 (2004): 51–73.

72 Wayne Wooden and Randy Blazak, *Renegade Kids, Suburban Outlaws: From Youth Culture to Delinquency* (Belmont, CA: Wadsworth, 2000).

73 Wayne S. Wooden, "Tagger Crews and Members of the Posse," in Malcolm W. Klein et al., eds., *The Modern Gang Reader* (Los Angeles: Roxbury, 1995), 65–68.

74 Finn-Aage Esbensen, Elizabeth Piper Deschenes, and L. Thomas Winfree Jr., "Differences Between Gang Girls and Gang Boys," in Rebecca D. Peterson, ed., *Understanding Contemporary Gangs in America* (Upper Saddle River, NJ: Prentice Hall, 2003).

75 Pernilla Johansson and Kimberly Kempf-Leonard, "A Gender-Specific Pathway to Serious, Violent, and Chronic Offending? Exploring Howell's Risk Factors for Serious Delinquency," *Crime & Delinquency* 55, no. 2 (2009): 216–240.

76 Johansson and Kempf-Leonard, "A Gender-Specific Pathway to Serious, Violent, and Chronic Offending?"

77 Mary G. Harris, *Cholas: Latino Girls and Gangs* (New York: AMS Press, 1988).

78 Eduardo Luis Portillos, "Women, Men, and Gangs: The Social Construction of Gender in the Barrio," in Meda Chesney-Lind and John M. Hagedorn, eds., *Female Gangs in America* (Chicago: Lake View Press, 1999).

79 Jody Miller, *One of the Guys: Girls, Gangs, and Gender* (New York: Oxford University Press, 2000).

80 Ibid.

81 Ibid.

82 Mark D. Tatten, *Guys, Gangs, and Girlfriend Abuse* (Orchard Park, NY: Broadview, 2001).

83 Finn-Aage Esbensen et al., "Evaluation and Evolution of the Gang Resistance Education and Training (G.R.E.A.T.) Program," *Journal of School Violence* 10 (2011): 53–70. Online at www.nationalgangcenter.gov/Content/Documents/GREAT-Evaluation-and-Evolution.pdf.

84 BUILD: Broader Urban Involvement and Leadership Development, www.buildchicago.org/. Accessed August 15, 2011.

85 Melde, Taylor, and Esbensen, "'I Got Your Back.'"

86 Nancy Pasternack, "Erasing Ink First Step Toward New Life," *Appeal-Democrat* (Marysville, CA), March 14, 2011. Chris Havens, "New Life Without Ink," *Star Tribune* (Minneapolis, MN), June 16, 2010.

87 Melissa Schorr, "Removing Tattoos from Gang Members," ABC News, October 17, 2009, abcnews.go.com/Health/story?id;eq117891&page;eq1.

88 John R. Fuller, *Criminal Justice: A Peacemaking Perspective* (Boston: Allyn and Bacon, 1998).

Substance Abuse

There is considerable controversy about the most effective approach to dealing with drugs and the harm they do. Some parties claim that drugs are a scourge on society and approaching epidemic proportions. Others argue that drugs are a natural part of life, that societies have used them for centuries, and that it's modern-day drug policy that harms society. They contend that if it weren't for the war on drugs, drugs wouldn't be such a problem. Evaluating the relative merits of each side is beyond the scope of this chapter. Regardless of where one comes down on the question of how drugs affect society and how detrimental they are to human health, it should be remembered that the debate is primarily concerned with the issues of freedom of choice and how adults control their own bodies.

Drugs Youths Use

Learning Objective 1.

Explain why there should be different drug laws for adults and youths.

Learning Objective 2.

Discuss the relative dangers of the drugs youths typically use.

There is almost universal consensus that this good-versus-bad debate about drugs and drug laws doesn't pertain to young people. Youths should be excluded from any debates concerning the reform of drug laws for several reasons. When it comes to young people, the problems of drug use are different than those for adults in the following ways:

> **Age of reason.** Young people don't have the emotional maturity to make rational decisions about drugs. Several factors are at work here. The first is that young people are susceptible to fads and are more likely to use drugs because they don't have the experience and background to comprehend how drug use can affect their future. Young people are susceptible to the influence of older peers who may pressure them into drug use. Young people have limited means of generating discretionary income, and the sale of drugs to their peers is one of the few ways they can meet their personal needs and, in many cases, their family's needs. Consequently, it's viewed that young people haven't developed the discipline or perspective to make informed decisions about using drugs. If drugs were to become **decriminalized** (have the legal penalties removed) or **legalized** (changed from illegal to legal), it's unlikely these reforms would include youths.

> **Physical development.** Substances such as alcohol, tobacco, and most illegal drugs are considered dangerous to physical development. The medical community, as well as the mental health community, has consistently documented the harmful effects of drug use on young bodies.

> **Interaction with parents.** Parents and society expect parents to control the behavior of their children. Allowing youths access to drugs would loosen this control and create tension between the state, parents, and children. In addition, parents would be reluctant to legalize drugs for youths because they may be legally liable for their children's actions. Short of legalizing all drugs for all people, the legalization of certain drugs will be restricted to adults.

Some drugs are more devastating to the body and mind than others and have deleterious effects on behavior. Other drugs have beneficial effects. Taken to extremes, however, just about all drugs are problematic in some way. The key is to differentiate between drugs as medicine, drugs as harmless recreation, and drugs that damage individuals and society. The discussion is complicated because we're talking about a wide range of drugs, as well as a continuum of behavior in terms of dosage, context in which the drugs are used, and the reaction of parents, police, teachers, and peers.

A single chapter can't sufficiently cover all the issues concerning drugs and US drug laws. So, we'll limit our discussion to how drugs affect juvenile delinquency. The rest of this chapter is divided into four sections. The first section deals with the types of drugs juveniles commonly use. Here, we'll discuss the **gateway drug** idea, which suggests that young people who use less-harmful drugs eventually use more more-harmful drugs. The second section discusses the context in which youths use drugs. We'll cover issues such as peer pressure, families, neighborhoods, and problems related to establishing identity and individuality. The third section deals with drugs and their relationship to juvenile delinquency. The final section discusses the efforts of the legal system to deter and punish drug users, the efforts of teachers and parents to prevent drug use, and the availability and effectiveness of drug-treatment programs. Of particular interest here is the relationship between legal drugs, such as alcohol and tobacco, and illegal drugs in terms of how they're encouraged or discouraged by society.

Although few people would encourage children and adolescents to use alcohol or drugs, there is, in general, an ambivalence as to what to do about it. The media are replete with advertisements aimed at developing markets for alcohol and tobacco among the younger population, and some people consider a certain amount of legal and illegal drug use as simply a rite of passage as young people experiment with adult behaviors.

The medical, legal, and social issues surrounding drug use are well documented and debated. We'll focus on the drugs that affect youths the most, as well as the context in which they're used. For example, high school students who don't plan to go to college are far more at risk for using illegal drugs, drinking alcohol, and smoking cigarettes than students who do plan to go to college. As for race, black 8th-, 10th-, and 12th-grade students have substantially lower rates of drug usage, including alcohol and especially tobacco, than white students.[1] (See Figure 11.1 for the percentage of 8th-, 10th-, and 12th-grade students who reported using illicit drugs in the past 30 days.) Still, according to the National Center on Addiction and Substance Abuse at Columbia University, 75 percent of high school students have tried cigarettes, alcohol, or other substances, and nearly half are current substance users.[2]

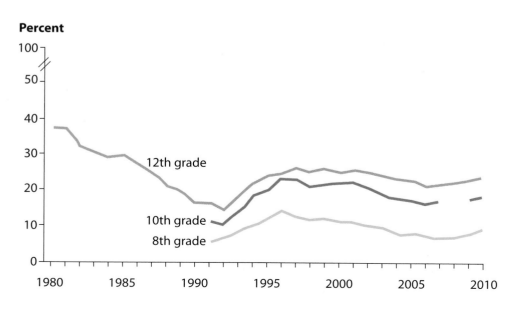

Percent

Figure 11.1 Students Who Use Drugs

Percentage of 8th-, 10th-, and 12th-grade students who reported using illicit drugs in the past 30 days by grade, 1980–2010.

Think About It

1. Reason why more 12th-graders use drugs than younger children.

Source: Federal Interagency Forum on Child and Family Statistics, America's Children: Key National Indicators of Well-Being, 2011 (Washington, DC: US Government Printing Office, 2011), 43. Online at www.childstats.gov/americaschildren/beh3.asp.

We won't distinguish between legal and illegal drugs because youths are prohibited from using any substances (except for medications with a parent's OK or doctor's prescription), even legal drugs such as tobacco and alcohol. Still, the availability of some legal drugs makes their control problematic. Adding to the difficulty is the way corporations market them not only to adults but also to young people.

This section will focus on the drugs youths most commonly use and the efforts to discourage it. We'll also attempt to distinguish why youngsters are singled out for more prevention efforts than adults. Finally, we'll highlight the unintended consequences of focusing antidrug efforts on youths who don't use any substances.

Tobacco

The harmful effect of tobacco on the human body is clear. Lung cancer and heart disease are two of the most well-documented and lethal consequences of smoking.[3] However, tobacco use remains legal for adults. Youths under age 18 (all 50 states have established this age limit) are prohibited from buying and using tobacco products. Merchants who sell cigarettes to minors are subject to fines and imprisonment. Nevertheless, smoking and other forms of tobacco use remain a major health problem for young people despite the fact that the percentage of high school students who have ever smoked a cigarette has decreased by about 34 percent since 1999 (see Figure 11.2 for youths who smoke cigarettes daily).[4] The reasons youths use tobacco are varied but can be summarized as a way for young people to attempt to claim adult status. Basically, tobacco use is a way to "look cool" and independent from adult control. Although both males and females smoke cigarettes at roughly equal rates, males use smokeless tobacco at a much higher rate than females.[5] The use of tobacco among young people is considered more problematic than adult use for several reasons:

>> Smoking dangers are cumulative. The longer a person smokes, the more deleterious the physical effects. Once a smoker stops, the body begins to repair itself. Within 10 years the lung cancer death rate drops to about half that of a continuing smoker.[6]

>> The age a youth begins to smoke is important. Almost 90 percent of smokers start smoking by age 18.[7] The psychology of smoking suggests that

Figure 11.2 Students Who Smoke

Percentage of 8th-, 10th-, and 12th-grade students who reported smoking cigarettes daily in the past 30 days by grade, 1980–2010

(Data for 10th-graders during 2008 are missing because estimates were considered unreliable due to sampling error.)

Think About It

1. During which years did cigarette-smoking among the students peak? Discuss reasons why reports of smoking dropped after those years.

Source: Federal Interagency Forum on Child and Family Statistics, America's Children: Key National Indicators of Well-Being, 2011 (Washington, DC: US Government Printing Office, 2011), 41. Online at www.childstats.gov/americaschildren/beh1.asp.

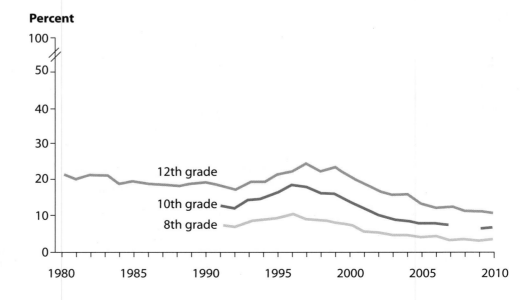

individuals who start smoking in their early teens adopt a self-image of a smoker and continue much longer than those who start smoking later. Of smokers younger than 18, more than 6 million will die prematurely from a smoking-related disease.[8]

» Those who start smoking at a young age find it harder to quit. Almost all smokers begin smoking before age 18. The younger they start, the more likely they are to continue. If a young person can resist smoking until the senior year of high school, it is less likely he or she will ever smoke at all.[9]

Efforts to reduce the onset of smoking in young people are varied. The juvenile justice system can't solve the problem alone. Discouraging smoking and tobacco use by youths requires a comprehensive effort at prevention, education, and control. The Centers for Disease Control and Prevention promotes the following policies:

» Counteradvertising mass media campaigns such as TV and radio commercials, posters, and other media messages targeted toward youth to counter pro-tobacco marketing

» Comprehensive school-based tobacco-use prevention policies and programs such as tobacco-free campuses

» Community interventions that reduce tobacco advertising, promotions, and commercial availability of tobacco products

» Higher costs for tobacco products through increased excise taxes[10]

Almost all smokers begin smoking before age 18. Those who start smoking at a young age find it harder to quit.

Authorities are concerned about underage smoking for reasons other than juvenile health. When youths break smoking laws, it can be an indication that they're likely to break other laws. Underage smoking has been related to alcohol use, high-risk sexual behavior, and other drug use.[11] The idea isn't that smoking is a gateway drug that inevitably leads to these other high-risk behaviors, but rather that smoking leaves little room for strong bonds to conventional society. Smoking at an early age can indicate that something is amiss in a youth's life that may be contributing to other deviant behaviors.

Most of the responsibility for the prevention and treatment of underage smoking lies with institutions such as family, schools, and the media. The glorification of smoking in advertisements helps motivate youths to smoke. When smoking is ubiquitous in adult society, it's only natural that young people smoke too. When the laws against underage smoking are inconsistently enforced and the punishments are relatively mild, the perceived rewards for smoking outweigh its negative consequences.

The effects on human health are so deleterious, there's no longer any debate on whether smoking is bad for you. According to the Centers for Disease Control and Prevention:

» The adverse health effects from cigarette smoking account for nearly one of every five deaths each year in the United States.

» More deaths are caused each year by tobacco use than by human immunodeficiency virus (HIV), illegal drug use, alcohol use, motor vehicle injuries, suicides, and murders combined.

» Smoking causes about 90 percent of all lung cancer deaths in men and 80 percent of all lung cancer deaths in women.[12]

Still, tobacco companies spend millions of dollars attempting to create new smokers in order to increase profits. The political muscle of those who have a vested interest in tobacco use ensures that it will continue to be widely available to young people. Because tobacco has chronic rather than acute effects, it causes death and disease over decades rather than immediately. Unfortunately, tobacco isn't considered the problem that other drugs are. Now we'll move on to another damaging, but legal, drug.

Alcohol

Alcohol is hard to keep away from children and teenagers because it's legal to consume for those over age 21. Despite a drop in the use of alcohol by high school students, alcohol is the most common mind-altering substance used during adolescence.[13] Almost 75 percent of high school students have ever had a drink, and just over 40 percent currently use alcohol.[14] The distribution network for alcohol is so large and sophisticated, it's a pervasive feature of American society. Alcohol advertising is often aimed at audiences likely to contain minors, a problem that has been increasing in recent years.

Youth exposure to alcohol advertising on U.S. television increased 71 percent between 2001 and 2009, more than the exposure of either adults ages 21 and above or young adults ages 21 to 34, according to an analysis from the Center on Alcohol Marketing and Youth (CAMY) at the Johns Hopkins Bloomberg School of Public Health. Driving this increase was the rise of distilled spirits advertising on cable television. Youth exposure to all distilled spirits TV advertising was 30 times larger in 2009 than in

The alcohol industry has been criticized for marketing its product to children and teens. Here, a Michigan store owner holds a can of an alcohol-based drink (left) next to similarly packaged alcohol-free drink. In 2010, Michigan was among the first states to investigate alcohol energy drinks, which are also under federal scrutiny over concerns about whether they are marketed to minors.

2001, with significant growth occurring in distilled spirits ads on cable. By 2009, the majority of youth exposure to advertising for all alcoholic beverages on cable was occurring during programming that youth ages 12 to 20 were more likely to be watching than adults 21 and above.[15]

The alcohol industry, sensitive to criticism that it markets to young people, established a policy to advertise in programs that expect an audience composed of less than 30 percent of viewers under the age of 20. This policy is difficult to measure, and there is skepticism as to its effectiveness.[16]

Patterns of alcohol use vary from one nation to another. These patterns are a result of the type of alcohol preferred, the nation's history and religion, and the prevalence or scarcity of other types of intoxicants. Charles Ksir and his colleagues make the following observation about how culture influences drinking patterns:

A comparison of Irish-Americans with Italian-Americans is of interest: the Irish forbid children and adolescents from learning to drink, but they seem to expect adult men to drink large quantities. They value hard liquor more than beer and promote drinking in pubs, away from family influences. By contrast, Italian families give children wine from an early age in a family setting but disapprove of intoxication at any age.[17]

Educators, parents, and law enforcement are concerned about underage drinking for several reasons, ranging from the effects of alcohol on physical and mental development to concerns about public safety, early sexual activity, and interpersonal violence. These concerns can be categorized as follows:

》 School problems, such as higher absence and poor or failing grades
》 Social problems, such as fighting and lack of participation in youth activities
》 Legal problems, such as arrest for driving or physically hurting someone while drunk
》 Physical problems, such as hangovers or illnesses
》 Unwanted, unplanned, and unprotected sexual activity
》 Disruption of normal growth and sexual development

» Physical and sexual assault

» Higher risk for suicide and homicide

» Alcohol-related car crashes and other unintentional injuries, such as burns, falls, and drowning

» Memory problems

» Abuse of other drugs

» Permanent changes in brain development

» Death[18]

One of the most surprising things about juvenile alcohol use is that girls use it more than boys, at certain ages. In a study that measured whether high school students had used alcohol within the last 30 days, 8th-grade girls have had higher rates than boys since 2002, and equivalent rates at 10th grade since 2005.[19] Those who start drinking before age 15 are more likely to develop problems with alcohol abuse than those who start after age 21.[20] There are also questions as to whether alcohol is a gateway drug. Do youths who use alcohol eventually turn to drugs such as heroin, cocaine, and methamphetamines? This is a difficult question. The concept of gateway drugs may be popular among those engaged in the war on drugs, but its empirical and logical evidence has been questioned. The concept of gateway drugs involves two scenarios:

1. Drug users constantly seek a more powerful high. As the body adjusts to alcohol intoxication, the user seeks something more effective, such as marijuana or cocaine. Studies of drug-using patterns reveal that those who use harder drugs also use less serious drugs such as alcohol and marijuana. The connection here is envisioned to be one of progression from milder drug use to more serious drug use.

2. Deviance causes deviance. Society stigmatizes those who use mild drugs and label them as deviant. Users believe they have reduced opportunities to succeed in conventional society and are motivated to seek out others with the same experiences and engage in other deviant subcultures. They try other drugs because they're involved in social networks that introduce them to other types of drugs.

Although tobacco and alcohol are considered legal for adults and illegal for juveniles, the rest of the drugs we'll consider in this chapter are controlled for both. Perhaps the drug over which there is the most debate is marijuana. Like tobacco and alcohol, it's often considered a gateway drug.

Marijuana

The most commonly used illegal drug in the United States, marijuana ranks second only to alcohol and tobacco as the most commonly used substance by adolescents.[21] Marijuana proponents contend it's less harmful than alcohol and tobacco and should be legalized for adult use. Opponents argue that marijuana has no benefits and should continue to be banned. Somewhere in the middle are those who believe marijuana has legitimate medical uses and should be legalized for that purpose (see Crosscurrents for more about the controversy surrounding the use of medical marijuana for children).

What isn't disputed, however, is that marijuana should remain illegal for young people. The reasons for this are similar to the reasons for prohibiting the juvenile use of alcohol and tobacco. It's a question of physical and emotional maturity. Therefore, marijuana use among young people is a significant issue for the juvenile justice system. Although the percentage of high school students who report ever trying marijuana has declined since 1999, the government reports that youths' perceptions of the harms associated with marijuana has continued to erode.[22] That is, youths now think it's less harmful than youths did a few years ago. It isn't surprising, then, that between 2009 and 2010, daily use of marijuana among 8th- , 10th- , and 12th-graders increased.[23]

One of the problems of prohibiting a substance is that it opens an underground economy. For marijuana, this underground economy includes juveniles. (We'll discuss this later in the chapter when we talk about drug dealing among juveniles.) Marijuana use has been linked to several medical and social problems in adults and young people. First is the problem of mental and physical impairment. In ways similar but not identical to alcohol, marijuana may cloud judgment, slow reaction time, and make users unaware of dangerous situations. For instance, driving under the influence of marijuana can be as problematic as driving under the influence of alcohol.[24] Marijuana impairment is harder to detect in drivers than alcohol impairment. Although Breathalyzers can quickly, easily, and cheaply measure someone's blood alcohol level, there are no similar tests for marijuana. When a police officer suspects a driver has been using marijuana, the officer must resort to a more expensive and time-consuming blood test—one that can't be administered and evaluated in the field.

From an academic perspective, the causal link between poor school performance and marijuana use isn't well established. Some researchers contend that students who do poorly in school are more likely to use marijuana, which is different than saying that students who use marijuana are more likely to do poorly in school. It amounts to the old chicken-and-egg dilemma. Which comes first?

Methamphetamine

Methamphetamine, or meth, often referred to as "crank" or "ice," can have devastating physical effects. A central nervous system stimulant similar in structure to amphetamine, meth is classified as a Schedule II drug—substances with a high potential for abuse—because it's so easily abused. Meth is a white, odorless, bitter, crystalline powder that easily dissolves in water or alcohol and is taken orally, snorted, injected, or smoked. Meth can be purchased legally only through a prescription that can't be refilled.[25] According to the National Institute of Drug Abuse, the effects of meth include the following:

- » Addiction
- » Violent behavior
- » Anxiety
- » Confusion
- » Insomnia
- » Psychotic events (paranoia, hallucinations, delusions)
- » Cardiovascular problems (rapid heart rate, irregular heartbeat, increased blood pressure, stroke)

Meth can be manufactured with a few easily obtained ingredients. Meth laboratories have sprung up in many cities and rural areas to address the high demand. The stovetop labs are particularly dangerous because they exude highly combustible toxic fumes, and cleaning up "meth labs" is expensive and dangerous. Meth may cause a great deal of collateral damage to personal finances,

11.1   crosscurrents

Medical Marijuana for Children

The legalization of marijuana is a controversial topic. Marijuana has been considered as a recreational drug that, although not as problematic as cocaine or heroin, still must be prohibited. A new crosscurrent to the marijuana legalization debate has arisen around the purported medical uses of this drug. Fourteen states now have some type of medical marijuana law that allows doctors to prescribe marijuana to their patients. Although there still is considerable controversy about the efficacy of marijuana as a medicine, public opinion is becoming more tolerant.

However, when it comes to prescribing medical marijuana for children, things are different. Many people are concerned with the potential harmful effects that marijuana could have on children's developing bodies. Critics such as Dr. Steven Sager, a child psychologist, claim that giving marijuana may mask symptoms and cause anxiety and depression.[1] Proponents of medical marijuana for children claim to have found that it has had beneficial effects in addressing specific types of problems where other medicines have seemed ineffective.

As of 2011, 14 states had laws allowing doctors to prescribe marijuana to their patients. Here, volunteers in Oregon trim marijuana grown at a cooperative that serves 70 medical marijuana patients.

» In California, a child diagnosed with one of the rare pediatric autoimmune neuropsychiatric disorders associated with streptococcal infections, or PANDAS, which causes severe obsessive-compulsive disorder (OCD), takes a medical marijuana capsule each day. The mother claims that the marijuana doesn't completely eliminate the OCD but allows the child to cope with it.[2]

» A Montana father whose son was undergoing chemotherapy for cancer became distressed by how his son had lost his appetite and was quickly losing weight. Without the doctors' knowledge, the father began slipping cannabis oil into his son's feeding tube. Nausea drugs had not prevented the boy from vomiting eight to ten times a day, but the cannabis oil helped, and the boy recovered. Marijuana proponents claim the drug reduces the nausea associated with chemotherapy and increases the patient's appetite.[3]

» In Rhode Island, a mother used medical marijuana to treat her child's autism. The marijuana reduced the child's aggressive behavior so that he was no longer hitting, biting, and kicking other children at school. The drug also seemed to eliminate the constant pain the child was in

and helped decrease his tendency to eat objects that weren't food.[4]

Medical marijuana, particularly when used for children, remains a controversial topic. Much of the evidence about the benefits of medical marijuana is anecdotal. Until serious rigorous research is conducted, these controversies will continue.

THINK ABOUT IT

1. What is your opinion on the use of medical marijuana for children? Should more research be conducted?

[1] Jennifer Joseph, Astrid Rodrigues, and Chris Connelly, "Marijuana From Mom: Mother Says Drug Helps Son Cope with Severe OCD," ABC News 20/20, July 23, 2010, abcnews.go.com/2020/MindMoodNews/marijuana-alternative-treatment-children-ocd-autism/story?id;eq11227283.

[2] MSquared, msquaredinc.info/Alternative_Treatment.html.

[3] ABC News, "Montana Dad Gives Cancer-Stricken Boy Marijuana Behind Doctor's Back," May 5, 2011, abcnews.go.com/Health/montana-father-medical-marijuana-cancer-stricken-toddler-son/story?id;eq13529490.

[4] Lisa Belkin, "Medical Marijuana for Children," *New York Times*, October 20, 2009, parenting.blogs.nytimes.com/2009/10/20/medical-marijuana-for-children/.

This pipe, used for smoking methamphetamine, was for sale at a gas station near a Minnesota school. This type of pipe is often called a "bubble."

family relationships, and education. It has been linked to illegal activities necessary to obtain the money for its use, such as prostitution, burglary, and robbery.

Meth can be particularly devastating for children and adolescents, affecting them in terms of being a user and being a victim of adult users. A study that compared meth-using teens with other drug users found that meth users more often had parents who used drugs, and higher rates of attempted suicide.[26] Another study of meth users in grades 6–12 found that the meth users, regardless of shared characteristics such as race, income level, or sex, had far more police contact and legal trouble than drug users who didn't use meth.[27] Those who use methamphetamine often make it a central focus of their life, to the detriment of their roles as mother, father, breadwinner, protector, or positive role model. Additionally, the underground market exposes users and their children to other types of deviant behavior that have social and legal consequences.

Inhalants

Inhalants include a number of products that can be found in ordinary household chemicals. Inhalants are drugs of choice for many young people because they're relatively inexpensive and easy to obtain. Youths often inhale spray paint, glue, gasoline, canned air, and a number of other readily available products. The fumes can be inhaled in a number of ways:

>> "Sniffing" or "snorting" fumes from containers
>> Spraying aerosols directly into the nose or mouth
>> "Bagging" (sniffing or inhaling fumes from substances sprayed or deposited inside a plastic or paper bag)
>> "Huffing" from an inhalant-soaked rag stuffed in the mouth
>> Inhaling from balloons filled with nitrous oxide[28]

One of the major concerns for police, teachers, and parents is that inhalants are readily available and, unlike alcohol or tobacco, aren't often recognized by parents as drugs. Unlike nearly all other drug use, inhalant use is most common among younger adolescents and declines as youths age (see Figure 11.3).[29] A reason for this may be that it's easier for older adolescents than younger children to

Common inhalants include spray-paint, glue, gasoline, or canned air.

purchase alcohol, marijuana, and other drugs, and they no longer depend on a substance being as easily available and cheap as inhalants. Also, girls are likelier than boys to have tried inhalants.[30] The exact level of inhalant use by youths is difficult to measure, but estimates are in the thousands:

> In 2009, there were 813,000 persons aged 12 or older who had used inhalants for the first time within the past 12 months, which is similar to the numbers in prior years since 2002; 67.9 percent were under age 18 when they first used. The average age at first use among recent initiates aged 12 to 49 was also similar in 2008 and 2009 (15.9 and 16.9 years, respectively).[31]

Discouraging the use of inhalants is difficult to do because it's hard to know when common household products are being abused.

Recreational use of inhalants in the United States increased in the 1950s and is now widespread amongst adolescents. More than 3000 abusable products containing volatile chemicals are legal and readily obtained; these include solvents, adhesives, fuels, dry-cleaning agents, cigarette lighters, permanent markers, correction fluid, and aerosols with propellants used in whipped cream, deodorants, paints, electronic cleaning sprays, and cooking sprays. These products are readily available, easy to purchase, not illegal to possess, easy to conceal, and are found in every household or garage. They

Percent

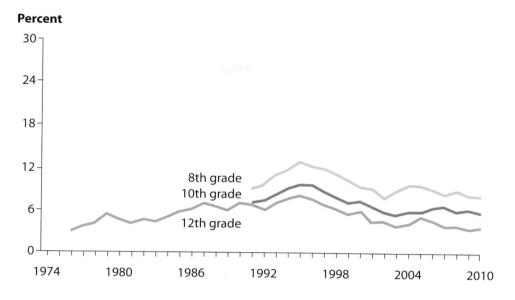

8th grade
10th grade
12th grade

Figure 11.3 Students Who Use Inhalants

Percentage of 8th-, 10th-, and12th-graders who used inhalants in the last 12 months

Think About It
1. Discuss reasons that inhalants are used more often by younger students.

Source: Lloyd D. Johnston et al., *Monitoring the Future National Results on Adolescent Drug Use Overview of Key Findings, 2010*, (Ann Arbor: Institute for Social Research, The University of Michigan, 2011), 15. Online at monitoringthefuture.org/pubs/monographs/mtf-overview2010.pdf

offer a quick-onset high of brief duration, lessening the chances of getting caught. Prosecution of offenders tends to be minimal, and few states have laws prohibiting inhalant abuse.[32]

The problems inhalants cause differ according to type because they produce several acute and chronic effects. At the extreme end of the continuum are death, and brain and lung damage. Because youngsters can obtain inhalants easily and without their parents' knowledge, it's often difficult to link symptoms of their use to physical and behavioral problems. Often, behavioral issues, including delinquency, occur without any indication that specific inhalants are responsible.

Prescription Drugs

The fourth most commonly misused substance among adolescents is prescription drugs.[33] As with inhalants, it's often difficult to tell when youths are abusing prescription drugs. This is because, for the most part, youths don't attempt to purchase these drugs but rather steal them from the medicine cabinets of their parents or their friends' parents. It's even harder to detect because one strategy for stealing these drugs is to steal only a few of them so the owner doesn't realize that the drugs are missing.

Prescription drugs are controlled substances that require a doctor's prescription to obtain. These drugs have many beneficial uses but can also be abused either in quantity or purpose. Commonly abused prescription drugs fall into three main categories:

» Opioid painkillers
» Sedatives and tranquilizers
» Stimulants

Each of these types of drugs will produce different experiences, as well as different evidence of drug abuse. The evidence might be depression, confusion, anxiety, constipation, high blood pressure, poor judgment, insomnia, or a host of other symptoms depending on the type, amount, and combination used. However, most juveniles who take these drugs are just looking for a high. Prevention of prescription drug use among teens is most effective when parents are vigilant.

An additional dimension of the use of prescription drugs by youths should be highlighted here. Often, prescription drugs are used in conjunction with other substances, especially alcohol. The combined effects of alcohol and prescription drugs can be unpredictable and serious, especially when teens are partying, driving, or experiencing problems such as depression. Alcohol lowers inhibition and impairs judgment. Because of teenagers' inexperience, they may drink alcohol in combination with multiple types of prescription drugs to get high or appease their peers. Because it's so difficult to judge dosages and the interaction of these drugs, overdoses are common, and serious impairment, including death, is possible.

Performance-Enhancing Drugs

Not all drug abuse is aimed at getting high. Some drugs are used for other purposes. For instance, **performance-enhancing drugs** are used by some athletic adolescents to increase power, endurance, or strength. Performance-enhancing drugs include anabolic steroids; the hormones androstenedione, human growth hormone, and erythropoietin; diuretics (substances that alter the body's fluid balance); creatine (a nutritional supplement); and stimulants.[34] Once thought to be in the purview of elite professional athletes, the use of performance-enhancing drugs has filtered down to colleges and high schools. Performance-enhancing drugs such as anabolic steroids are used mostly by males.[35]

Although athletes may conform in other aspects of their lives, such as earning good grades, maintaining a healthy diet, and getting regular physical activity, performance-enhancing drugs may jeopardize their bodies and their lives on a number of levels:

» Performance-enhancing drugs are illegal. Young athletes who use performance-enhancing drugs are subject to sanctions by the juvenile justice system. This means they can be arrested and receive remedial interventions by the juvenile court. It may also mean placement in a treatment facility, probation, or other sanction. Furthermore, this interaction with the juvenile court may limit their opportunities for university athletic scholarships.

» Performance-enhancing drugs are cheating. Young athletes who use performance-enhancing drugs are breaking the rules of competition. This may result in their being barred from future athletic competitions. They and their teams may be stripped of whatever accomplishments they have accrued.

» Performance-enhancing drugs are a health risk. The health risks for performance-enhancing drugs are well documented. They include an increased risk of heart problems, issues with the digestive and reproductive systems, and behavioral deviancy. The term "roid rage" is used to describe the uncontrollable anger the increased testosterone associated with performance-enhancing steroids has on the personality of athletes.[36]

Despite the dangers associated with steroid use, many people believe that performance-enhancing drugs are here to stay. They contend that the negative health effects are overstated and that if these drugs are used properly and under a physician's supervision, they can be beneficial in developing superior athletic performance. They further claim that the use of performance-enhancing drugs shouldn't be considered an unfair advantage in athletic performance. Athletes have a variety of resources available to them in terms of coaches and trainers, workout facilities, nutritionists, and parental funding. They view performance-enhancing drugs as simply another tool serious athletes can employ to make themselves more effective. Additionally, because performance-enhancing drugs are so pervasive, their proponents suggest that legalizing them would make competitions more fair, and serious research could be done on the effects of these drugs on athletes' bodies.[37]

Lacking the knowledge necessary to fully evaluate the health effects of performance-enhancing drugs, there is little reason to embrace the philosophies of those who advocate their use. When athletes, especially young ones, self-medicate with performance-enhancing drugs, the potential for serious abuses is obvious.

Other Substances

Youths experiment with a variety of substances. We don't have enough space to deal with each of these drugs in detail, so we're limited to the substances young people most commonly use. This in no way diminishes the danger of the many other drugs that at least some young people use. Foremost among these drugs are the ones more commonly associated with adult drug abuse, such as rock cocaine (crack), powder cocaine, and heroin.

There will always be some youths who use these substances. The reason cocaine and heroin aren't usually associated with youths is because they are extremely expensive. Typically, youths don't have the resources to develop a dependency on these drugs. Later in this chapter, we'll deal with some of the collateral damage youths may suffer from the more adult drugs. Specifically, youths may become engaged in some lower-level positions of the drug trade that deal with cocaine, heroin, and other drugs that comprise the illegal drug market.

Questions

1. Why does society restrict the use of alcohol and tobacco by children but not by adults?
2. Is the argument that children's bodies are still developing a good reason to restrict them from using recreational drugs?
3. What types of drugs do young people use most frequently?
4. What is the most commonly used illegal drug in the United States?
5. Why are inhalants often drugs of choice for many young people?
6. Why do some youths use performance-enhancing drugs?

Why Do Youths Take Drugs?

In order to successfully prevent drug use among young people and to effectively offer treatment for those who do use drugs, it's necessary to fully understand the social pressures and personal motivations that encourage drug use (see Focus on Diversity for more on this). First, we must recognize there is no single source of the juvenile drug problem in the United States. The problem is multifaceted and extremely complicated. Let's look at why.

Peer Pressure

Youth drug use is typically a group activity. Seldom does an individual decide to initiate drug use without some type of pressure, motivation, or encouragement from friends. Often, this is the result of having older siblings who initiate the idea of smoking, marijuana use, or drinking alcohol. Other times, it's picked up

Learning Objective 3.

Discuss why peer pressure is such a powerful influence on why young people use drugs.

Learning Objective 4.

Distinguish individual drug-abuse factors from social drug-abuse factors.

FOCUS ON DIVERSITY 〉 *Who Uses What Drugs*

Kids use drugs in various patterns. Not all youths who use drugs use the same drugs, in the same social settings, and with the same consequences. As with many other aspects of juvenile delinquency, drug use and abuse is related to the participant's **social location** (an individual's class, race, and sex). How is this so?

》 **Social class.** Economic resources greatly determine what drugs a youth can get. For instance, juveniles in rural areas are more likely to use inhalants or methamphetamine because they have more access to these substances than designer drugs such as ecstasy. Also, it is easier for rural delinquents to grow marijuana than it is to get hooked up to the heroin trade, which stems from Central and East Asia.

》 **Race.** America's black population has been affected by the disparity in punishments for crack cocaine and powder cocaine. During the 1980s, the use of crack cocaine became associated with the black population. An offender possessing 5 grams of crack got the same five-year mandatory minimum sentence as an offender possessing 500 grams of powder cocaine. That's a disparity of 100:1. The Fair Sentencing Act of 2010 decreased that ratio to 18:1. (The act also eliminated the five-year mandatory minimum sentence for first-time simple possession of crack.)[1] So, why wouldn't some crack users switch to powder cocaine? It may have to do with the drug's effects. It's reported that a "crack high" is faster and more intense than one induced by powder cocaine. Crack has fallen out of style amongst adolescents in recent years, and being a "crackhead" is no longer desirable. Today, crack users are most likely to be males in their late 20s or early 30s.[2]

》 **Sex.** Young females are more likely to steal prescription drugs from their parents' medicine cabinet and young males are more likely to get drugs from their friends on the streets. Another difference is that girls may smoke cigarettes with the idea that it could help them control their appetites, while boys are more likely to binge drink.

These examples are not mutually exclusive or exhaustive. People from different races, sexes, and social classes participate in a variety of drug-taking patterns. Some drugs are inexpensive compared to others, and the amount of money a juvenile has access to or can steal will influence drug choice. In addition, peer pressure can play a role in deciding what drugs are used.

THINK ABOUT IT

1. If you were to decide to use illegal drugs, which ones would you have the greatest access to?
2. In your opinion, how would your social class, race, and sex influence the decision to use illegal drugs?

---

[1]Danielle Kurtzleben, "Data Show Racial Disparity in Crack Sentencing," *US News and World Report*, August 3, 2010, www.usnews.com/news/articles/2010/08/03/data-show-racial-disparity-in-crack-sentencing.
[2]Howard Abadinsky, *Drug Use and Abuse: A Comprehensive Introduction* (Belmont, CA: Thomson Higher Education, 2008), 135.

from school friends who model drug use on the playground, while waiting for the bus, or during after-school hours in their homes.[38] Why is peer pressure such a powerful contributor to delinquency? Why are young people so influenced by their friends? This robust relationship between peers and delinquency exists for several reasons:

» **Establishing identity.** Juveniles have a desperate need to fit in. Their identity is constructed according to a complex pattern of how they relate to their peers. Juveniles establish many social roles in order to find a place in the hierarchy of their schools and neighborhoods. Some of these roles value deviant behavior and are attractive to youths who might not be star athletes or very popular. These roles can range from goth and punk subcultures to skinhead and street-gang lifestyles. Included in many of these roles is a large component of illegal drug use.[39]

» **Thrill seeking.** One way young people test the boundaries of appropriate behavior is to engage in risky and dangerous activities. Drug use is socially supported by peers and is a way for youngsters to try on the cloak of adulthood. By smoking cigarettes and drinking alcohol, they think they're demonstrating to themselves and others that they're fully capable acting adult at an early age. Unfortunately, as we have already indicated, youths' drinking patterns may include dangerous activities such as driving under the influence or **binge drinking**, a pattern of alcohol consumption that raises the blood alcohol concentration to at least 0.08 gram percent, which typically happens when men consume five or more drinks and when women consume four or more drinks in two hours.[40] (See Figure 11.4 for 8th- , 10th- , and 12th-grade students who reported binge drinking during the past two weeks.) For many teens and young adults, binge drinking is proof that they can meet the challenges of adulthood, even if binge drinking actually prevents or delays the development of adult competencies.[41] In 2009, nearly a quarter of high school students were binge drinkers.[42] The other aspect of thrill seeking is the possibility of getting caught and sanctioned. The mere fact that substance use is illegal for them and not for adults motivates some young people to risk using the substances to prove they're clever enough not to get caught. In some European cultures where children are introduced to

Figure 11.4 Students Who Drink Alcohol

Percentage of 8th-, 10th-, and 12th-grade students who reported having five or more alcoholic beverages in a row during the past two weeks by grade, 1980–2010

Think About It
1. Compare this figure with Figure 11.2 (Students Who Smoke). Which substance, alcohol or drugs, do students use the most?

Source: Federal Interagency Forum on Child and Family Statistics, America's Children: Key National Indicators of Well-Being, 2011 (Washington, DC: US Government Printing Office, 2011), 42. Online at www.childstats.gov/americaschildren/beh2.asp.

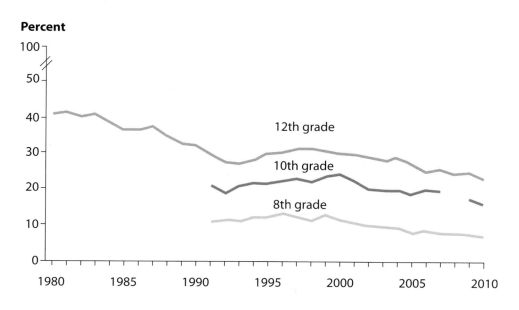

Percent

For many teens and young adults, binge drinking is proof that they can meet the challenges of adulthood, even if binge drinking actually prevents or delays the development of adult competencies.

alcohol at an early age in a family setting, this risk-taking behavior isn't as pronounced as it is in the United States.[43]

》 Shared intimacy. Peers who use drugs together share a bonding experience in which they picture themselves as outsiders and dependent on each other for mutual support. In fact, a whole subculture of drug using arises in which the qualities of trust and honor are emphasized within the group and a level of paranoia about those outside the group is engendered.

Family

In addition to peers, family influences may encourage youths to use alcohol and drugs. Parents may set a poor role model by using cigarettes and becoming dependent on alcohol or prescription drugs. Children learn that these are natural behaviors and that they're positively rewarded as indications of successful adulthood. Children may attempt to jump-start their adulthood by using tobacco and alcohol as signifiers that they have achieved a status beyond their age.

Tobacco, alcohol, and drug use may also indicate that the child is rebelling against family norms. By using these illegal substances, he or she may be crying out for attention, rebelling against family discipline, or simply following the family path of alcoholism or addiction. The family may have other conflicts, such as disruption or violence, and substance use may be a symptom of deeper problems.

Finally, the influence of the family on drug and alcohol use among their children may be unintentional. Parents who lead productive lives but drink socially may be modeling the behaviors of successful people; however, these behaviors may be interpreted by youths as glamorous and socially desirable and the reason for their parents' success rather than as a perk. Sometimes these messages get a bit twisted in the minds of young people, who may think that the more they model these behaviors (the more they drink), the more successful they'll be.

Neighborhoods

In socially disorganized neighborhoods, youngsters are often left to their own devices. Lacking adequate schools, recreational activities, and competent adult supervision, youths are free to engage in a variety of deviant behaviors that may bring them into contact with law enforcement and the juvenile justice system. In neighborhoods with few job opportunities for young people, an underground economy that includes drug selling may emerge. However, we shouldn't be too quick to claim that poverty equals drug abuse. Several intervening factors complicate the relationship.

Drug and alcohol use includes a wide variety of behaviors. People who live in affluent neighborhoods are just as likely to use drugs and alcohol as those in disadvantaged neighborhoods. The exact type and pattern of use may be different according to different residential settings, but a broad range of activities must be discussed. For instance, we think of disadvantaged neighborhoods as experiencing unemployment, poverty, and violent crime and expect juvenile drug use to be high in such places. However, other factors mediate between the type of neighborhood and juvenile drug use. For example, in one study it was found that American Indian youth showed lower levels of drug use than non-Indian youth. It's speculated that the connection to the American Indian culture provided a sense of ethnic pride and close family relationships that protected youths from becoming engaged in drug use.[44]

It's difficult to untangle the effect of neighborhoods from the effects of families and peers. Disadvantaged neighborhoods don't necessarily result in broken homes, delinquent children, and negligent parents. Neighborhoods with a high degree of **collective efficacy** can protect their young people from crime, delinquency, and drug abuse. By taking responsibility not only for one's own children but for the children of others, neighbors can ensure that public places are adequately supervised and safe.

Individual Factors

Peers, family, and neighborhood are all external factors that may contribute to juvenile drug use. However, internal factors may also influence a youth's decision to use drugs. These individual factors are both physical and psychological.

The first type of physical factor is genetic. Some people appear to be "hardwired" to use alcohol or drugs. It has long been noted that alcoholism appears to run in families. This is a difficult relationship to understand because rather than being genetic, alcoholism may also simply be a matter of **social learning** and cultural patterning. Nevertheless, several studies have shown that many individuals have a genetic predisposition to drug and alcohol use.[45]

At the emotional level, some individuals appear to have an addiction-prone personality. This type of personality disorder may be manifested in a variety of ways, including obesity, overdependence on approval from parents, or drug or alcohol abuse. Individuals who suffer from this condition often have a low tolerance for frustration and little confidence in their abilities. Thus, they turn to drugs or alcohol for the psychological support that is missing from their lives.

In the case of adolescent males, substance abuse is considered a way to achieve masculinity. Unfortunately, this can become a problem later in adulthood, when many of these men find themselves addicted to tobacco, drugs, or alcohol. According to one study, males who become addicted as adolescents find that, to recover from addiction, they must change their definitions of manhood and realize that substance abuse isn't part of a successful adult life.[46]

Finally, some individuals choose to use drugs for reasons that aren't entirely attributable to either outside forces or internal motivations. **Rational choice theory** suggests that the decision to use drugs or alcohol is based on the calculated costs and benefits of the activity. The calculation may not be entirely accurate, in that the youngsters don't have the maturity, knowledge, and reasoning power to

INSTANT RECALL FROM CHAPTER 5

collective efficacy

A group's shared belief of the extent to which the group can successfully complete a task.

INSTANT RECALL FROM CHAPTER 5

social learning theory

The idea that people learn behaviors by watching other people and mimicking interactions that are rewarded and avoiding those that are punished.

INSTANT RECALL FROM CHAPTER 3

rational choice theory

A perspective that holds that people consciously choose to break the law.

make a truly rational choice, but to them it seems like the logical decision. For instance, they like the high they get from marijuana and believe it makes them more creative and interesting. Or, drinking gives them a feeling of invincibility and power. The effects of these drugs appear to them to be positive, whereas, for adults, it's easy to see how the drugs cloud the their judgment and often produce negative consequences.

Questions

1. What do we mean when we suggest that some individuals are "hardwired" to use drugs?
2. How does peer pressure influence a young person's decision to use recreational drugs?

Drugs and Delinquency

Learning Objective 5.

Examine the relationship between delinquency and the drug trade.

Learning Objective 6.

Show how having a drug dependency may lead to delinquency.

For those interested in juvenile delinquency, the question as to whether substance abuse is a causal factor in breaking the law is important. At a superficial level this question is easy to answer. Because underage drinking and using prohibited substances constitute delinquency, there is a direct relationship between substance abuse and delinquency. However, the discussion becomes a bit more complicated when the question is whether substance abuse *causes* delinquency.

According to the Pathways to Desistance study, which followed more than 1,300 serious juvenile delinquents for seven years after conviction, serious and chronic delinquents are much more likely than other delinquents to be substance users and to have substance-use disorders. Also, substance use and delinquency at a young age consistently predicted continued serious offending later on. However, substance use and serious delinquency fluctuate in similar patterns, which suggests some kind of relationship, but not necessarily a relationship in which one behavior causes another.[47]

As we have discussed previously, youths who make bad grades and are poorly bonded to their schools are more likely to become delinquent. Again, the **causality**, or relationship between an event and a following event, is uncertain. Do students turn to delinquency because they don't like school, or do they not like school because they're delinquent? The causality question is similar for students who do poorly in school and use alcohol and drugs. That is, students with good grades are less likely to use substances than their less academically successful classmates, and students who don't use substances get better grades than their classmates who do. The question here is, are better students simply too academically successful to be interested in drugs, or is the performance of students who might do well in school affected by drugs and alcohol? It seems that substance abuse, poor grades, and delinquency are somehow connected, but the nature of that connection hasn't yet been determined.[48]

The Drug Trade

Unless you're a licensed pharmacist filling a physician's prescription, selling drugs is illegal. Selling recreational drugs in the underground economy can bring trouble from the law. These activities include selling alcohol to minors, selling large quantities of marijuana, cocaine, or heroin to mid-level dealers, or being a street dealer who sells or barters minor amounts of drugs to users. Curiously enough, the risks and rewards for each of these types of drug transactions vary enough to make it difficult to assess the pattern of punishment the justice system applies.

For instance, US prisons are full of low-level drug dealers serving long mandatory sentences while others who profited from lucrative drug transactions escaped the severe punishment.

Often, selling drugs isn't as risky for young people as it is for adults. This is because the juvenile justice system is geared more toward treatment than punishment. The idea is that youths are more amenable to rehabilitation and that an intervention by the juvenile justice system can turn the wayward youth around and place him or her on a more positive path. Young people are often recruited into the drug trade as low-level dealers because they aren't subject to the severe sanctions adult dealers face.

Another aspect of the drug trade is more problematic than being caught up in the juvenile justice system: the routine violence. This comes in two distinct forms. First, there is the violence related to drug deals that go bad. Users may be addicts who don't have the money to pay the young drug dealers, so they may try to take the drugs by force, sometimes deadly force. Therefore, drug dealing entails a great physical risk. Drug addicts are often irrational and sometimes kill young dealers to get their fix. Consequently, youngsters are motivated to arm themselves to ensure they aren't victimized. This can result in the young dealers hurting or even killing someone. Self-defense isn't a claim that can be made when selling illegal drugs.

The other aspect of the drug trade that can lead to delinquency involves the stabilization of the drug market. For example, in the 1980s and 1990s, a good deal of violence was associated with the drug trade in **crack cocaine** (a highly addictive form of cocaine that is processed into a crystal that can be smoked) as dealers fought over territory and customers. This increased the price of crack cocaine and made drug dealing even more profitable. For some youths, these drug wars provided not only opportunities for financial remuneration but also opportunities to establish one's "street cred." In neighborhoods with few legitimate opportunities, selling drugs looked like an attractive alternative. Although the stereotype of drug dealers may be one of conspicuous displays of jewelry, expensive cars, and designer clothes, often the money was put to more conventional uses such as paying rent and buying food for the family. We expect parents to ensure that their children don't become involved in the drug trade, but in some circumstances, the youth is able to bring in much-needed money for the family.

Supporting a Drug Habit

Another drug-related source of crime and delinquency involves drug users acquiring the money to support their habits. Here, the offenses can range from armed robbery to burglary to stealing money out of Mom's purse. A drug habit can be expensive. Once users go through their discretionary income, they may be motivated by withdrawal symptoms to spend the rent money, steal money from their employers, or otherwise break the law to get the money to buy drugs. Desperate drug users will steal copper piping out of homes under construction, break into automobiles, and mug strangers. Addicts may also forge prescriptions or rob pharmacies.

Alcohol is also strongly linked to aggression. Those under the influence often engage in behavior such as brawls and domestic violence. Drug addicts can be the most unpredictable and violent offenders. They suffer from a diminished capacity to think rationally and do things they would never consider when sober.

Proponents of drug legalization argue there wouldn't be nearly the amount of crime and delinquency if drugs were readily and cheaply available, because users wouldn't need so much money to buy them. If drugs were treated as other commodities there would be a legitimate market for them, and the government could control and tax it. Drug addicts could obtain their fix without resorting to crime and violence.

Opponents of drug legalization or decriminalization contend that crime would increase if drugs were more available. Although drug-trade crime might decrease, it's argued that drug legalization or decriminalization would greatly increase the number of people under the influence and there would be more DUIs, automobile accidents, bar fights, and the community in general would be more dangerous.

Questions

1. What roles do young people play in the drug trade?
2. What is the relationship between participating in the drug trade and delinquency?
3. Are people who use illegal drugs more likely to break the law?

Prevention and Treatment

Learning Objective 7.

Describe the types of drug-use prevention efforts.

Learning Objective 8.

Identify some critical issues that may impede successful drug treatment

Drugs are a significant problem for young people. Of high school students ages 18 and younger who have ever used tobacco, alcohol, or other drugs, nearly 20 percent have a substance-use disorder, meaning they have become dependent on alcohol, drugs, or nicotine. Among 14-year-old high school students, over 5 percent meet the criteria for substance-use disorder.[49] Substances not only affect youths' health and quality of life but also bring them into contact with the law. Therefore, many youth agencies and the juvenile justice system have developed programs to address the issues of drug use and abuse among juveniles early in their lives.

Prevention

Youth drug-prevention programs have been developed across a wide range of public and private agencies. These prevention efforts are also aimed at various points in the drug-use continuum in an effort to prevent early drug use and to deter those who are more advanced and sophisticated in their illegal drug taking behavior. It's useful to think of drug-use prevention programs in accordance with what the Institute Of Medicine calls the "continuum of prevention efforts."

» **Universal-prevention strategies.** These programs are aimed at all youths. Even though most youths have never had experience with illegal drugs, the prevention efforts are designed to fortify them against the temptations they may face in school or in their neighborhoods. This will be the first time many of these youths ever hear the names of specific drugs they may later come in contact with. The idea is that early education about the dangers of drug use will enable youngsters to make wise decisions when confronted with drug-taking opportunities and peer pressure.

» **Selective-prevention strategies.** These drug-prevention strategies are aimed at juveniles who are deemed to be at high risk of using illegal drugs. Typically they are doing poorly in school, live in disadvantaged neighborhoods, or come from families with a history of drug abuse or crime involvement. An intervention may prevent drug use before it even starts.

» **Indicated-prevention strategies.** These drug-prevention strategies are aimed at youths who are clearly on the road to getting in trouble. Young people who are smoking cigarettes at an early age or engaging in underage drinking are the prime targets. Other indications that a young person may be a candidate for this program include a DUI or excessive truancy. These minor status offenses signal that the young person needs some type of intervention to prevent graduation into serious delinquency.

Several program models can be employed to prevent young people from using drugs. One common model found in schools and communities is the **knowledge model of drug-use prevention**, or the idea that educating individuals about the potential harms will stop them from using substances. Some critics contend this model is just propaganda designed to scare youth into avoiding drugs. Inaccurate messages, such as "Using crack cocaine once results in addiction," are common in knowledge models. (Addiction is a medical condition that requires the body to develop a physical dependence and doesn't occur with one use.) However, some believe that the distinction between psychological dependence and physical addiction doesn't need to be made clear to youth and may be confusing. Therefore, it's permissible to prevent youths from using drugs by providing them with stark, if somewhat inaccurate, messages about the dangers.

The knowledge model has three major problems. The first has to do with the assumption that young people don't have prior knowledge about drugs and that introducing them to the desired knowledge early will shield them from developing pro-drug attitudes. For many young people, drugs are ubiquitous in their families, peer groups, and schools. Their attitudes toward drugs are already well established, and such programs are considered as simple propaganda that doesn't consider the realities of their lives.

The second problem with the knowledge models is that they ignore the features of large parts of American society. Poverty, unemployment, blighted cities, and other pressing factors can have a larger influence on the drug problem than the knowledge and attitudes of young people. For instance, drug dealing is crucial for the financial survival of many families, and dealing is so ingrained that more than messages about the dangers of drug use would be required for prevention. Providing good jobs for parents may be much more effective in dealing with drug use than instructing the kids to "just say no."

The third problem has to do with the legitimacy of those giving the message. Young people are bombarded from every quarter with lectures, advice, and demands concerning what others think is appropriate behavior for them. Many young people become jaded or immune from parents, teachers, coaches, and school administrators who don't understand the pressure youths receive from their peers and the media. Three categories of drug-prevention messengers can be problematic:

1. **Former drug users.** Many drug-prevention programs employ former drug users to talk to young people about the dangers and problems of drug use and abuse. The idea is that if young people hear from those who experienced the downside of drug abuse, this knowledge will change their attitudes and behavior. The problem with this approach is twofold. First, the former drug users might not be effective public speakers and their message can get muddled. For many young people, the message is either hypocritical or attractive. For instance, when a former drug dealer says, "I had plenty of money, girls, and nice cars, but drugs took over my life and ruined it," youths sometimes hear the first part of the message and not the second. For those who come from impoverished families, drug dealing and using are interpreted as

being attractive alternatives rather than dire problems. The second concern has to do with employing former drug users as role models. Youths may consider them as interesting but flawed individuals who have led exciting lives. In spite of their problems with drugs, these former users are now in front of the classroom demonstrating that there is a life after drug use and such an adventurous experience is survivable.

2. **Police officers.** Several drug-prevention programs feature police officers. The most well-known of these programs is Drug Abuse Resistance Education (D.A.R.E.). Started in 1983 in Los Angeles, it had uniformed police officers work with teachers to teach students refusal skills, alternatives to drug use, and the building of self-esteem. It was thought that the presence of uniformed officers would impress students as to how serious drug use is. Furthermore, the sight of a friendly uniformed officer dispensing good advice was thought to inspire trust and a positive attitude toward the police. This program has been replicated nationwide and a great deal of hope and resources has been invested in it. Unfortunately, the results haven't been as robust as the hype. Although these programs seem to increase drug knowledge and social skills, the effect on drug use was negligible. In effect, although some positive outcomes were reported, the true mission of the D.A.R.E. program, the prevention of drug use among young people, wasn't accomplished.[50]

3. **Celebrities and athletes.** A Nike advertisement from a few years back featured basketball player Charles Barkley stating, "I am not a role model. Parents should be role models. Just because I dunk a basketball, doesn't mean I should raise your kids." Barkley and Nike were criticized for this ad, but given the many celebrities and athletes who have been in trouble with the law, particularly for substance abuse, there seem to be some good reasons to applaud this approach. Many celebrities and athletes do good work with charities and giving back to the community. However, these celebrities and athletes are human, too, and when their indiscretions happen, they are often the subject for headlines and media exposés. Drug-prevention programs with celebrities and athletes risk sending the wrong message to children when those individuals end up on television for undesirable reasons.

Many scholars and researchers have criticized DARE for failing to prevent drug usage amongst children and teens.

Preventing young people from taking illegal drugs is difficult to accomplish, and it's hard to know what is effective. Most children will grow up without developing alcohol or drug dependencies, but history has shown that many youths will use drugs, and the earlier in life they are exposed to drugs, the more likely they are to develop problems as adults. The real test for drug-prevention programs is to target those who are likely to develop drug problems. The difficulty is in knowing which youths are in danger of future drug problems and which ones aren't. Too much exposure to drug-prevention programs too early may actually be counterproductive in that the children are desensitized to the message and end up thinking that drugs are an exciting and normal part of growing up.

At a broader level, programs that can prevent substance abuse may address issues that aren't concerned with drug use at all but rather with some of the antecedent factors, such as poverty, lack of recreational opportunities, inadequate schools, and blighted neighborhoods. Programs that increase the quality of life for everyone can have a direct and indirect effect on youth drug use. In this context, it's useful to think of youth drug use as a symptom of larger social problems. By providing challenging opportunities in schools, safe, clean neighborhoods, and clear expectations of rewarding jobs in the future, communities can deal with the underlying issues that influence delinquency and youth drug use. Unfortunately, the juvenile justice system has little influence on these broader social initiatives.

Treatment

Drug-treatment programs vary widely depending on the type of drug being addressed. They also vary according to criteria such as age, motivation (voluntary or court-ordered), and financial resources (see Programs for Children to learn about one form of treatment, residential treatment programs).

Additionally, the goals of drug treatment differ according to the methodology applied to drug use. For instance, some drug-treatment programs are aimed at total abstinence whereas others are aimed at controlled usage. In dealing with underage substance abusers, this distinction isn't particularly important. Because social drinking (and drug usage) is illegal for minors, the goal is to get the youth to abstain from any substance use. However, we shouldn't be blind to the benefits of partial success when someone starts drinking less or using less harmful drugs. Several issues concerning drug treatment require elaboration:

1. **Motivation.** Conventional wisdom says people have to want to quit using alcohol and drugs in order to be successful. Still others contend that the user's motivation to quit isn't required. Many, if not most, substance abusers are in denial about their addictions. They deny they have a problem and resent parents, teachers, and police who demand they seek treatment. In fact, many programs spend a considerable amount of time and resources convincing abusers that they have a substance-abuse problem and that this problem is affecting their lives. Many court-ordered programs and other interventions require only that the individual participate, holding that the motivation will come later.

2. **Detoxification (or detox).** The first step in getting some people to engage in successful drug treatment is to place them in a secure facility without access to drugs. Detox is a process in which the body is denied drugs and allowed to recalibrate itself to its normal functions. Often, this involves going through withdrawal, in which the body can be uncomfortable as it craves the drug. Depending on the type of substance, detox can last from days to

11.2 PROGRAMS FOR CHILDREN

Residential Treatment Programs

Even under the best circumstances the transition from child to adolescent can be rocky. Parents often find that their children are uncommunicative, associating with questionable peers, neglecting their work, and experimenting with alcohol, tobacco, or illegal drugs. Much of this behavior is expected as teenagers seek to establish their own identity and break the "apron strings." However, for some families, this rebellious behavior signals something more serious and potentially devastating when the teen become addicted to drugs.

One option for parents is to send their child to a residential treatment program. This is a difficult decision because many parents fear their child will resent them for sending him or her away to what the child considers to be a prison. However, many parents don't have the resources to monitor their children's behavior 24 hours a day. Residential treatment programs, which are typically staffed with treatment experts and educational experts, seek to deliver academic programs in a secure environment where access to illegal drugs is restricted and exposure to the temptations of the school and street are denied.[1]

The services available at residential treatment programs range widely. Some have specialties such as wilderness adventure programs designed to increase the youth's self-esteem, as well as strong academic programs aimed at ensuring that the teen can succeed once back in his or her regular school. Many programs use 12-step methodologies commonly found in Alcoholics Anonymous programs.[2]

But residential treatment programs aren't the whole answer. Often, a teen's problems are vested in the family or school, and even after successful treatment, the child may return to his or her normal environment to find the factors that caused the addiction are still present. Some parents use boarding schools as a way to pass their parental duties on to others, but this is only a short-term fix. Another problem is that some of these schools aren't properly supervised and may abuse their charges.[3]

Between 1990 and 2007, the Government Accountability Office reported on allegations of abuse at residential treatment programs throughout the

Here, teens work in the garden of a Michigan residential treatment program that uses Christianity as part of its treatment plan.

nation. In several case studies, teens attending the programs died of causes such as internal bleeding, dehydration, hyperthermia, and other physical trauma. In a 2008 investigation, federal investigators also found that at least ten private residential programs and four referral services engaged in deceptive marketing that made the cost of the programs appear less expensive. Currently, there are no federal laws or regulations specific to the residential program industry that govern marketing practices.[4]

THINK ABOUT IT

1. Can teen drug abuse be treated successfully without addressing family and neighborhood influences?
2. Will sending a child to a therapeutic boarding school cause resentment toward the parents?

[1]Teen Boarding Schools, www.teenboardingschools.com.

[2]12 Step Treatment, www.12-step-treatment.com.

[3]Ken Dilanian, "GAO Finds Abuses at 'Tough Love' Camps for Troubled Kids," *USA Today*, October 10, 2007, www.usatoday.com/news/nation/2007-10-10-boot-camps_N.htm

[4]Government Accountability Office, *Residential Treatment Programs: Concerns Regarding Abuse and Death in Certain Programs for Troubled Youth*, October 2007, www.gao.gov/new.items/d08146t.pdf.

months. For the severely addicted, detox may involve a gradual withdrawal so that the body doesn't react in such a negative way that the person experiences severe discomfort.

3. **Lifestyle adjustment.** Many people in drug treatment do well in a secure setting or a highly structured environment. When rules are clear, opportunities controlled, and social support forthcoming, these individuals are able to successfully address their drug problems. The time comes, however, when they must leave the support network of the drug-treatment group and return to the home and neighborhood where the drug problems flourished. Part of the treatment protocol is aimed at equipping substance abusers with the skills to deal with the negative environment to which they must return. These skills may include anger management, developing better relationships, or education and job training, to facilitate finding alternative ways of meeting their financial, social, and emotional needs.

4. **Relapse.** Drug treatment often isn't successful the first time. In fact, it might not be successful the second or third time, either. It might never be successful. However, relapse doesn't mean that drug treatment can't be successful with a particular person. For many, ceasing drug or alcohol use is a lifelong struggle and repeated relapses are common. Sometimes, substance abusers are successful after many relapses simply because they get tired of the drug lifestyle and desire a conventional life. Sometimes, substance abusers experience life-changing events, such as arrest, marriage, or childbirth, that make them refocus their determination.

Drug treatment is a promising strategy to deal with adolescent substance abusers. Although substance abuse is a problem for people of all ages, it's of particular concern for youths. Substance-abuse problems become more difficult to address as users age. Furthermore, substance abuse at a young age increases the likelihood of involvement with the juvenile justice system. Programs that successfully treat substance abuse and divert the youth from the normal processing of the juvenile justice system benefit both the individual and society. Treating substance abuse as a medical problem while the individual is young may reduce the likelihood that the abuse will need to be treated as a criminal justice problem later.

Questions

1. Is it possible to prevent youths from using illegal drugs?
2. What types of individuals are best able to provide drug-prevention education to juveniles?
3. Is drug treatment for juveniles a realistic strategy?

>> FOCUS ON ETHICS

The Lesser of Many Evils

As a juvenile probation officer you have had a great deal of success in dealing with young people who have been using drugs. You're especially proud of your record in reforming juveniles who abuse inhalants. You have seen the devastating effect of inhalants on your probationers, and the probation office channels inhalants-users to you because of your successes. You go above and beyond the call of duty by working on weekends to monitor your charges at their homes to ensure they're not using drugs.

Now you have a special case that is causing you great frustration. Eric is a chronic inhalant abuser who's finally showing the motivation to stop using this drug. However, in your last visit to his home, although you didn't find evidence of inhalant use, you did find a bag of marijuana in his sock drawer. When you confronted him, he claimed he could not go "cold turkey" off drugs and that he was using marijuana to gradually wean himself. He claimed he was using less marijuana than he had been for the past few months and that he would be marijuana-free within three more months if given the chance.

What should you do? Marijuana is clearly illegal, and as an officer of the juvenile court you clearly can't condone Eric's use of it. However, your gut feeling tells you this substitution of marijuana for inhalants is better for Eric's health, and you believe he is making a good-faith effort to get off drugs completely.

WHAT DO YOU DO?

1. Violate Eric's probation and send him back to court for his marijuana use.
2. Turn a blind eye to Eric's marijuana activity and hope he's successful in developing a drug-free lifestyle.
3. Turn a blind eye to Eric's illegal activity, monitor his marijuana use to ensure it's decreasing each week, and establish a deadline for him to stop smoking it.
4. Report this activity to your supervisor, request the opportunity to implement your plan to monitor Eric, and establish your deadline for cessation of all drug use.

Summary

Learning Objective 1. Explain why there should be different drug laws for adults and youths.	Age of reason. Young people don't have the emotional maturity to make rational decisions about drugs.
	Physical development. Alcohol, tobacco, and most illegal drugs are considered dangerous to healthy physical development.
	Interaction with parents. Allowing youths access to drugs would create tension between the state, parents, and children.
Learning Objective 2. Discuss the relative dangers of the drugs youths typically use.	Lung cancer and heart disease are two of the most well-documented and lethal consequences of smoking.
	Alcohol may cause school problems; social problems; legal problems; physical problems; unwanted, unplanned, and unprotected sexual activity; disruption of normal growth and sexual development; physical and sexual assault; higher risk for suicide and homicide; alcohol-related car crashes and other unintentional injuries; memory problems; abuse of other drugs; permanent changes in brain development; and death.
	Marijuana may cloud judgment, slow reaction time, and make users unaware of dangerous situations.
	Methamphetamine may cause addiction, violent behavior, anxiety, confusion, insomnia, psychotic events, and cardiovascular problems.
	Inhalants may cause brain and lung damage, and death.
	Prescription drugs may cause depression, confusion, anxiety, constipation, high blood pressure, poor judgment, and insomnia.
	Performance-enhancing drugs may cause increased risk of heart problems, digestive and reproductive issues, and behavioral deviancy.

Learning Objective 3. Discuss why peer pressure is such a powerful influence on youth substance use.	Establishing identity. Juveniles have a desperate need to fit in. Thrill seeking. Youths test the boundaries of appropriate behavior by engaging in risky and dangerous activities. Shared intimacy. Peers who use drugs together share a bonding experience.
Learning Objective 4. Distinguish internal drug-abuse factors from external drug-abuse factors.	Peers, family, and neighborhood are all external factors that may contribute to juvenile drug use. One internal factor is genetic. At the emotional level, another internal factor, some youths appear to have an addiction-prone personality. For adolescent males, substance abuse is a way to achieve masculinity. Finally, rational choice theory suggests that the decision to use drugs or alcohol, an internal factor, is based on the calculated costs and benefits.
Learning Objective 5. Examine the relationship between delinquency and the drug trade.	Selling drugs might not be as risky for youths as it is for adults, because the juvenile justice system is geared more toward treatment than punishment. Youths are considered more amenable to rehabilitation, and juvenile justice intervention may place a wayward youth on a more positive path. Youths are often recruited into the drug trade as low-level dealers because they aren't subject to the severe sanctions that adult dealers face.
Learning Objective 6. Show how having a drug dependency may lead to delinquency.	Young drug users may break the law to acquire the money to support their habits. Those under the influence of alcohol often engage in violent behavior. Drug addicts can be the most unpredictable and violent offenders because they may do things they never would consider when sober.
Learning Objective 7. Describe the types of drug-use prevention efforts.	Universal-prevention programs are aimed at all youths. Selective-prevention strategies are aimed at youths who are deemed to be at high risk of using illegal drugs. Indicated-prevention strategies are aimed at those who are clearly on the road to getting in trouble.
Learning Objective 8. Identify some critical issues that may impede successful drug treatment.	Motivation. Conventional wisdom says people have to want to quit using alcohol and drugs in order to be successful. Detoxification. Some people must be placed in a secure facility where they don't have access to drugs. Lifestyle adjustment. Many people in drug treatment do well in a secure setting or a highly structured environment. Relapse. Drug treatment can still be successful, even if a person relapses.

Chapter Review Questions

1. Is restricting alcohol and tobacco use for young people equivalent to age discrimination?

2. What are the health risks of tobacco use for young people?

3. What are the health risks of alcohol use for young people?

4. Is marijuana use psychologically or physically addicting? Why or why not?

5. What is meant by a "continuum of prevention efforts"?

6. Which is more responsible for delinquency, selling drugs or using drugs? Why?

Summary

7. Why are former drug users sometimes problematic when giving drug-prevention education to young people?

8. Is it realistic to expect drug treatment to work when people must still live in the environment in which their drug use flourished?

9. Does someone have to want to stop using drugs for drug treatment to work?

10. Would drug use increase or decrease if drugs were legalized?

Key Terms

binge drinking—A pattern of consuming alcohol that brings a person's blood alcohol concentration to 0.08 gram percent or above.[51]

causality—The relationship between an event and a following event.

crack cocaine—A highly addictive form of cocaine that is processed into a crystal that can be smoked.

decriminalize—To remove the legal penalties from a prohibited activity.

gateway drug—A term to describe a less-harmful substance that is believed to lead to abuse of more-harmful substances.

knowledge model of drug-use prevention—The idea that educating individuals about the potential harms of substance use will stop them from using substances.

legalize—To make an illegal activity legal.

performance-enhancing drugs—Substances typically taken by athletes to increase power, endurance, or strength.

methamphetamine—A white, odorless, crystalline powder that stimulates the central nervous system.

social location—An individual's class, race, sex, and age.

Endnotes

1   Lloyd D. Johnston et al., *Monitoring the Future: National Results on Adolescent Drug Use, Overview of Key Findings, 2010* (Ann Arbor: Institute for Social Research, University of Michigan, 2011), 44. Online at www.monitoringthefuture.org/pubs/monographs/mtf-overview2010.pdf.

2   National Center on Addiction and Substance Abuse at Columbia University, *Adolescent Substance Use: America's #1 Public Health Problem* (New York: National Center on Addiction and Substance Abuse at Columbia University, 2011), i.

3   Department of Health and Human Services, *The Health Consequences of Smoking: Nicotine Addiction. A Report of the Surgeon General* (US Department of Health and Human Services, Public Health Service, Centers for Disease Control, Center for Health Promotion and Education, Office on Smoking and Health, 1988). Online at profiles.nlm.nih.gov/ps/access/NNBBZD.pdf. Accessed September 1, 2011.

4   National Center on Addiction and Substance Abuse at Columbia University, *Adolescent Substance Use: America's #1 Public Health Problem* (New York: National Center on Addiction and Substance Abuse at Columbia University, 2011), 22.

5   Johnston et al., *Monitoring the Future*, 14.

6   Charles F. Levinthal, *Drugs, Society, and Criminal Justice*, 3rd ed. (Boston: Prentice Hall, 2011), 368.

7   Federal Interagency Forum on Child and Family Statistics, *America's Children: Key National Indicators of Well-Being, 2011* (Washington, DC: US Government Printing Office, 2011), 41.

8   Ibid.

9   Campaign for Tobacco-Free Kids, "The Path to Smoking Addiction Starts at Very Young Ages," December 2009, www.tobaccofreekids.org/research/factsheets/pdf/0127.pdf.

10 Centers for Disease Control and Prevention, "Smoking & Tobacco Use," July 2011, www.

cdc.gov/tobacco/data_statistics/fact_sheets/youth_data/tobacco_use/index.htm.

11 Campaign for Tobacco-Free Kids, "How Parents Can Protect Their Kids from Becoming Addicted Smokers," February 2011, www.tobaccofreekids.org/research/factsheets/pdf/0152.pdf.

12 The 2004 Surgeon General's Report, *The Health Consequences of Smoking*, www.cdc.gov/tobacco/data_statistics/sgr/2004/pdfs/whatitmeanstoyou.pdf. Accessed September 2011.

13 Federal Interagency Forum on Child and Family Statistics, *America's Children*, 42. Office of National Drug Control Policy, *2010 Monitoring the Future Study Highlights*, December 2010, www.whitehouse.gov/sites/default/files/ondcp/Fact_Sheets/monitoring_the_future_2010_fact_sheet_12-16-10.pdf.

14 National Center on Addiction and Substance Abuse at Columbia University, *Adolescent Substance Use*, 24.

15 Johns Hopkins Bloomberg School of Public Health, "Youth Exposure to Alcohol Advertising on Television, 2001–2009," executive summary, December 2010, www.camy.org/research/Youth_Exposure_to_Alcohol_Ads_on_TV_Growing_Faster_Than_Adults/index.html.

16 Ibid.

17 Charles Ksir, Carl L. Hart, and Oakley Ray, *Drugs, Society, and Human Behavior* (Boston: McGraw Hill, 2006), 207.

18 Centers for Disease Control and Prevention, "Alcohol and Public Health," July 2010, www.cdc.gov/alcohol/fact-sheets/underage-drinking.htm.

19 Johnston et al., *Monitoring the Future*, 44.

20 Centers for Disease Control and Prevention, "Alcohol and Public Health."

21 National Center on Addiction and Substance Abuse at Columbia University, *Adolescent Substance Use*, 26.

22 Ibid.

23 Office of National Drug Control Policy, *2010 Monitoring the Future Study Highlights*.

24 J. G. Ramaekers et al., "Dose Related Risk of Motor Vehicle Crashes after Cannabis Use," *Drug and Alcohol Dependence* 73 (2004): 109–119.

25 National Institute of Drug Abuse, NIDA InfoFacts: Methamphetamine, March 2010, www.nida.nih.gov/infofacts/methamphetamine.html.

26 D. J. Yanosky II et al., "Differentiating Characteristics of Juvenile Methamphetamine Users," *Journal of Child & Adolescent Substance Abuse* 18, no. 2 (June 2009): 144–156.

27 Ruth Gassman, Carole E. Nowicke, and Jun Mi Kung, "Individual Characteristics of Adolescent Methamphetamine Users in Relation to Self-Reported Trouble with the Police," *Journal of Alcohol & Drug Education* 54, no. 1 (April 2010): 76–92.

28 National Institute on Drug Abuse, Research Report Series: "Inhalant Abuse: What Are Inhalants?," www.drugabuse.gov/ResearchReports/Inhalants/whatare.html. Accessed September 1, 2011.

29 Johnston et al., *Monitoring the Future*, 14.

30 National Center on Addiction and Substance Abuse at Columbia University, *Adolescent Substance Use*, 30.

31 Substance Abuse and Mental Health Services Administration, *Results from the 2009 National Survey on Drug Use and Health, Volume I: Summary of National Findings* (Rockville, MD: Office of Applied Studies, NSDUH Series H-38A, HHS Publication No. SMA 10-4856 Findings, 2010). Online at oas.samhsa.gov/NSDUH/2k9NSDUH/2k9Results.htm#5.7.

32 Edward C. Jauch, "Inhalants," *Medscape Reference*, September 2, 2010, emedicine.medscape.com/article/1174630-overview.

33 National Center on Addiction and Substance Abuse at Columbia University, *Adolescent Substance Use*, 31.

34 Mayo Clinic, "Performance-enhancing Drugs: Know the Risks," December 2010, www.mayoclinic.com/health/performance-enhancing-drugs/HQ01105.

35 Johnston et al., *Monitoring the Future: National Results on Adolescent Drug Use*, 42.

36 John R. Fuller and Marc J. LaFountain, "Performance-Enhancing Drugs In Sport: A Different Form of Drug Abuse," *Adolescence* 22, no. 88 (1987): 969–976.

37 For a fascinating discussion about the pros and cons of performance-enhancing drugs, see "Legalizing Performance Enhancing Drugs" at sportsanddrugs.procon.org/view.resource.php?resourceID;eq002352#Legalizing.

38 James Jaccard, Hart Blanton, and Toya Dodge, "Peer Influences on Risk Behavior:

An Analysis of the Effects of a Close Friend," *Developmental Psychology* 41 (2005): 135–147.

39 Wayne S. Wooden, *Renegade Kids, Suburban Outlaws: From Use Culture to Delinquency* (Belmont, CA: Wadsworth Publishing, 1995).

40 National Institute on Alcohol Abuse and Alcoholism, "NIAAA Council Approves Definition of Binge Drinking," *NIAAA Newsletter* no. 3 (2004): 3. Online at pubs. niaaa.nih.gov/publications/Newsletter/winter2004/Newsletter_Number3.pdf.

41 Edward P. Mulvey, Carol A. Schubert, and Laurie Chassin, "Substance Use and Delinquent Behavior Among Serious Adolescent Offenders," *Juvenile Justice Bulletin* (US Department of Justice, Office of Justice Programs, Office of Juvenile Justice and Delinquency Prevention, 2010), 7. Online at www.ncjrs.gov/pdffiles1/ojjdp/232790.pdf.

42 National Center on Addiction and Substance Abuse at Columbia University, *Adolescent Substance Use*, 24.

43 G. Vaillant, "Cultural Factors in the Etiology of Alcoholism: A Prospective Study," in T. F. Babor, ed., *Alcohol and Culture: Comparative Perspectives from Europe and America* (New York: New York Academy of Sciences, 1986).

44 S. T. Yabiku et al., "The Effect of Neighborhood Context on the Drug Use of American Indian Youth of the Southwest," *Journal of Ethnic Substance Abuse* 6, no. 2, (2007): 181–204.

45 Kate Kelland, "Scientists Find Gene Link to Alcohol Consumption," Reuters, April 4,

2011, www.reuters.com/article/2011/04/04/us-alcohol-gene-idUSTRE7335CK20110404.

46 Jolene M. Sanders, "Coming of Age: How Adolescent Boys Construct Masculinities Via Substance Use, Juvenile Delinquency, and Recreation," *Journal of Ethnicity in Substance Abuse* 10, no. 1 (2011): 48–70.

47 Mulvey, Schubert, and Chassin, "Substance Use and Delinquent Behavior Among Serious Adolescent Offenders," 1.

48 Centers for Disease Control and Prevention, "Alcohol and Other Drug Use and Academic Achievement," www.cdc.gov/HealthyYouth/health_and_academics/pdf/health_risk_behaviors.pdf. Accessed September 2, 2011.

49 National Center on Addiction and Substance Abuse at Columbia University, *Adolescent Substance Use: America's #1 Public Health Problem* (New York: National Center on Addiction and Substance Abuse at Columbia University, 2011), 33.

50 Steven L. West and Keri K. O'Neal, "Project D.A.R.E. Outcome Effectiveness Revisited," *American Journal of Public Health* 94, no. 6 (2004): 1027–1029.

51 National Institute on Alcohol Abuse and Alcoholism, "NIAAA Council Approves Definition of Binge Drinking," *NIAAA Newsletter* no. 3 (2004): 3. Online at pubs. niaaa.nih.gov/publications/Newsletter/winter2004/Newsletter_Number3.pdf.

Juvenile Justice System and Cultural Comparisons

PART IV

The Police

Police officers have an uneasy relationship with juvenile delinquents. In many ways, the police face contradictory and confusing demands when dealing with children and adolescents who break the law or are victims of abuse and neglect. The job is further complicated by the fact that police often don't know the age of the suspect when they must take action. This can be dangerous for officers, because hesitating in a violent situation may result in injury or death. In this chapter, we'll learn more about the ambiguous nature of the relationship between law enforcement and juveniles, with an eye toward appreciating the fine line police officers walk between protecting society and acting in the best interests of young people.

At this point, we should also discuss the word "juvenile," a legalistic term used throughout the book to refer to a person under the age of 18 (in most states). Parents with children never refer to the "juveniles" in their home, but the law does. So, in keeping with this custom, we will use "juvenile" to refer to young people who are involved in the juvenile justice system.

A Short History of Juvenile Policing

The history of the police handling of juveniles delineates an important overall shift in juvenile justice, from the informal to the formal, from families to the police and the courts. In the early North American colonies, juvenile justice was handled by parents with the support of local authorities, such as the constabulary, if any, or religious leaders. As the nation grew and became more diverse, it became necessary for a single authority to handle wayward and disruptive youths, especially in cities like New York City, Los Angeles, and Chicago. However, juvenile justice was formalized much more slowly than adult (criminal) justice. Recall from Chapter 2 that there was no juvenile court or even separate juvenile **detention** until the 20th century. Thus, in the formalization process, police served as the intermediate step between local institutions and the 20th-century juvenile court.

Learning Objective 1.

Detail how the police dealt with youths in three ways during the late 19th and early 20th centuries.

Learning Objective 2.

Understand the role of "policewomen" in working with juveniles during the early 20th century.

Police officers walk a fine line between protecting society and acting in the best interests of young people.

In the late 19th and early 20th centuries, the police dealt with youths in three general but important ways:

1. The police decided which cases they would handle informally within their own departments and which to push to the (adult) courts. Only a small percentage ever went to the courts.

2. The police used their discretion and power to round up youths for minor offenses and attempt to scare them onto the "straight and narrow," then release them on informal probation or even no probation at all.

3. The police made most detention decisions, using detention as a swift punishment for the youth rather than for the protection of society or any long-term rehabilitative effort.

During the early 20th century, the police resolved a large percentage of juvenile delinquency cases without involving the juvenile court. Many departments even supervised youths directly in a sort of informal probation. Sometimes the cases never hit the station house. The officers, using substantial discretion, would lecture and release the youth on the spot. For example, between 1930 and 1940, the juvenile bureau of the Los Angeles Police Department disposed of well over half its cases within the department. Chicago's revolutionary juvenile court system saw only a small percentage of the city's delinquents, because the police resolved most cases themselves.

During the late 19th and early 20th centuries, juvenile policing was order-maintenance policing, with most arrests being for public-order violations and what we now call **status offenses**, such as running away and truancy. According to David Wolcott, "Arresting juvenile offenders was less a means of introducing them into the criminal justice system for punishment or rehabilitation, than of satisfying aggrieved citizens and of officially reprimanding disorderly youth."[1]

The police could also use their discretion to detain a juvenile for as long as they saw fit, with little court interference. Evidence points to the police using detention as a reprimand or a scare tactic. The detentions, which came prior to disposition or release to a juvenile court, typically lasted only days or weeks. In 1920s Chicago, despite overcrowding, "the police officers who controlled admission to the Juvenile Detention Home still used it as if it were a jail, holding youth there as a swift and secure form of punishment." In 1926, this detention home admitted 7,115 juveniles, but the court heard only 2,265 cases. Nearly half the juveniles admitted were released within two days.[2]

After 1940, the police handling of juveniles shifted from the maintenance of order to ensuring that the law wasn't broken. This change in attitude resulted more from police professionalization than from the rehabilitative goals of the new juvenile courts. As a result, the police began arresting older juveniles and more juveniles suspected of felonies and sending them to the courts, rather than rounding up bands of 12-year-olds for petty thefts and letting them go after a couple days of detention.[3]

A final aspect of the order-maintenance function was social work. Much of police work, even today, involves helping people in difficult circumstances, such as refereeing explosive domestic situations, rescuing **dependent** children from bad homes, protecting the mentally ill from harming themselves and others, and preventing suicides.

A big part of law enforcement's work with juveniles includes protecting dependent and neglected children, not just delinquents. In the early 1900s, this social work with nondelinquent children was provided by "policewomen" trained in

INSTANT RECALL FROM CHAPTER 1

status offense

An act considered to be a legal offense only when committed by a juvenile; it can be adjudicated only in a juvenile court.

INSTANT RECALL FROM CHAPTER 1

dependent

A term describing the status of a child who needs court protection and assistance because his or her health or welfare is endangered due to the parent or guardian's inability, through no fault of their own, to provide proper care and supervision.

social work. According to Albert Roberts, "There is no evidence that policemen were assigned to perform social work functions during the first quarter of the 20th century. At that time social work was predominantly a female profession, and it's understandable that the first police social workers were women." [4] There was a division of labor in which male police officers rounded up delinquents, while female officers had the task of assisting neglected, abused, and dependent juveniles.[5]

Questions

1. How did the police deal with juveniles in the late 19th and early 20th centuries?

2. What was the role of discretion in policing during the early 20th century?

The Police: Dealing with Juvenile Delinquents and Victims

The juvenile court revolutionized the legal processes for youths, but the police had no such revolution. Although many police departments have juvenile officers, there is no specialized juvenile police force, and police departments aren't required to have juvenile officers. Police management of juveniles is most often dictated by the courts, legislation, and the officers' own **discretion**.

The police are typically the first contact that young victims and delinquents have with the juvenile justice system. As with adults, law enforcement serves as the gatekeeper to the justice system. This is especially important, because this gatekeeper function often results in youths being labeled as delinquent, which can have profound consequences. The importance of a police officer's decision to introduce a child into the juvenile justice system can't be overemphasized.

In 2010, police arrested 1,040,453 suspects under 18 years of age, a decrease of nearly 24 percent since 2001. Juvenile arrests comprised about 12 percent of all arrests. Most were arrested for **larceny-theft**, assaults, and drug-abuse violations.[6] Like the rest of the juvenile justice system, police must balance what is best for the youth with what is best for the community. However, unlike juvenile-oriented courts and corrections, the police have to function almost atypically because much of the treatment of delinquents has a social-work aspect. Many police officers (and whole departments) prefer to focus on the justice aspects of police work: getting offenders off the streets, responding to emergencies, scoring big drug busts, and generally "catching the bad guys."[7]

A situation involving a delinquent, however, is often complicated simply because the juvenile is considered to be a child and not completely responsible for his or her actions. The youngster might have an untenable home life involving abuse or maybe a single parent who just can't cope; live in a neighborhood overrun by gangs; attend a poor school; have learning or behavioral issues; or all of the above. Whereas our society accepts that an adult is, in most cases, solely responsible for his or her actions, it also stipulates that a child or adolescent is not. This automatically brings in numerous other social factors. The police must deal with some or all of the major socializing institutions—parents, families, schools, and neighborhoods—with nearly every juvenile arrest, whether the individual officers or departments are equipped to do so or not.

It's also important to keep in mind that much of law enforcement's interaction with young people concerns the maintenance of public order, such as controlling youths in public, rather than criminal law enforcement. This requires

Flash Mobs

A new type of crime is emerging in several large cities that has law enforcement agencies perplexed: flash-mob violence. Flash-mob violence entails large groups of people coordinating their movements on the Internet, then converging on an area to riot, loot, or commit thefts. What is new about flash-mob violence is that social media enable perpetrators to gather together people who may not even know each other.

A flash mob can quickly communicate, organize, then gather in a store, where they overwhelm store managers and workers, and steal merchandise worth hundreds or thousands of dollars. This is similar to the way social media have been used in insurrections in the Middle East. Flash mobs have left law enforcement wondering how to effectively get ahead of the curve and prevent this type of crime.[1] There is a tension between the First Amendment rights to gather and the creation of these flash mobs.

» In August 2011, hundreds of black teenagers not only got into fights amongst themselves but also beat and robbed white patrons of the Wisconsin State Fair as they exited the fairgrounds.[2]

» In Philadelphia, after violent attacks by teenagers, the police started enforcing a 9 PM curfew for teens under 18 and began monitoring social-media pages in an effort to determine if flash-mob violence was brewing.[3]

» In Maryland, a flash mob raided a 7-Eleven store and took drinks, snacks, and candy. Store surveillance cameras provided pictures that allowed police to identify many of the suspects, including 14 teenagers.[4]

Several ideas have been put forth to combat flash-mob violence. One idea is to enforce local curfews to keep juveniles off the streets at night. Another idea is to have law enforcement monitor social media to see when these incidents may occur. This idea is heavily criticized by civil liberties defenders because it treads on issues of privacy and freedom of assembly.

THINK ABOUT IT

1. Should the government monitor social media in order to prevent flash-mob violence?
2. In your opinion, is flash-mob violence just a fad, or can it turn into a more substantial type of crime?

---

[1] Patrik Jonsson, "'Flash Robs': How Twitter Is Being Twisted for Criminal Gain," *Christian Science Monitor*, August 3, 2011, www.csmonitor.com/USA/2011/0803/Flash-robs-How-Twitter-is-being-twisted-for-criminal-gain-VIDEO.
[2] NPR, "Wis. State Fair Latest Target Of Violent Flash Mob," August 13, 2011, www.npr.org/2011/08/13/139600667/wis-state-fair-latest-target-of-violent-flash-mobs.
[3] Rick Jervis, "'Flash Mobs' Pose Challenge to Police Tactics," *USA Today*, August 19, 2011, www.usatoday.com/news/nation/2011-08-18-flash-mobs-police_n.htm.
[4] Dan Morse, "Viral Flash-mob Theft Video Leads to Charges," *Washington Post*, August 26, 2011, www.washingtonpost.com/local/viral-flash-mob-theft-video-leads-to-charges/2011/08/26/gIQAIQt4gJ_story.html.

many low-visibility, discretion-based decisions from the police, which means the police are almost a juvenile court unto themselves.[8] See Focus on Diversity for how police are challenged with incidents involving juveniles who are using social media to break the law.

Dealing with Juveniles

The manner in which police interact with youths presents a number of problematic issues. Perhaps the most pressing is the attitude the police have developed in the wars on crime and drugs, which have put delinquents in the position of being considered as dangerous as adult suspects and offenders. It's understandable that police are concerned for their safety as they confront juvenile delinquents. Youths who carry weapons are just as dangerous as adults, and some boys are so big and strong they pose a physical challenge to the police officers who have to apprehend them. From the officer's viewpoint, age is an artificial criterion for determining danger. A 15-year-old can be as problematic as an adult, and until the encounter can be evaluated, the police must ensure their safety. From time to time, this might lead to a well-publicized case of excessive force, but that is a regrettable and inherent part of the job. Thus, juveniles occupy a difficult and challenging place in police work for three reasons:

1. The police must deal with juveniles often, especially teenagers.
2. Juveniles are more likely than adults to hold negative attitudes toward the police.
3. Juveniles commit a significant percentage of offenses.[9]

A major issue in the relationship between law enforcement and juveniles is "situational ambiguity"; that is, when juveniles encounter the law, the situation and what to do about it are often ill-defined. The opposite of this concept is "situational clarity," when the situation and what to do about it are well-defined.

Sometimes no one, from the parents to the courts, is sure what's best for the child, or, even more complicating, everyone is positive as to what's best for the child. Often, the status of the situation itself is unclear. For instance, a missing youth can be a runaway, abducted by a stranger or an acquaintance, or abducted by a parent. In all three cases, the youth can be a victim, offender, or both. For instance, if a teenager runs away from home to escape an abusive parent and steals a car while doing so, the teenager is both an offender and a victim. In this case, the police must still act in the youth's best interests.

In their interactions with juveniles, the police are guided by the mission of the juvenile justice system to rehabilitate delinquents and divert those on the path to delinquency. This directive is largely unofficial and indirect—after all, it's a philosophy rather than a law or a rule—but it's endorsed by juvenile court judges, many of whom would rather see disputes and complaints settled without referral.[10] The police are indirectly guided by the Juvenile Court Act, which states that juveniles are "taken into custody," not arrested. This is interpreted to mean the police's role is to salvage and rehabilitate youth, a role indirectly sanctioned by many judges.

Another issue when dealing with juveniles is that of determining if the subject is a juvenile. Often, juveniles in trouble claim that they're adults, especially in the case of status offenses. Let's consider, for example, a group of teenagers drinking beer in a parking lot. The teens might claim to the inquiring officers that they are adults, hoping they will only be charged with violation of an open-container ordinance and issued a ticket, instead of being taken to the police station or driven home to their parents. Better yet, in some jurisdictions, there

Police use of force often results in potentially coercive relationships in encounters between the police and lawbreakers. This issue becomes even more difficult when the lawbreakers are juveniles. Sometimes, the police don't even know suspects are juveniles. Here, a firefighter stabilizes the neck of one of three 17-year-old males who stole a car and wrecked it while fleeing state troopers.

might be no charge at all for adults drinking alcohol in public. In either case, identifying themselves as juveniles only means more trouble.[11]

A final issue that requires consideration is the potential use of force by the police. The police are one of the few agencies sanctioned to use force. It can be said that police have a monopoly on the legitimate use of force, and this results in potentially coercive relationships in encounters between the police and lawbreakers.

Specialized Juvenile Policing

Two units within police departments have the most contact with juveniles: patrol and special juvenile units. Patrol officers cruise a regular beat and are the ones who most often deal with status offenders and take juveniles into custody. Larger departments have special juvenile units.[12] The amount of special attention delinquency gets from police departments depends a lot on the department's size. The smaller the department is, the fewer juvenile specialists it has. This is simply a function of the size of the department and jurisdiction and the department's budget. A small department might have only one or two juvenile officers; a large, urban department will have a whole juvenile unit, and perhaps even separate units for juvenile victims and missing children. The larger the department is, the greater the possibility it will have some officers who specialize in certain types of problems. Small police departments are unlikely to have juvenile officers assigned solely to motor vehicle theft, homicide, drugs, gangs, or juveniles. However, very large departments will have these special units and more.

JUVENILE OFFICERS

Typically, juvenile officers are drawn from the ranks of the patrol staff. These officers may have little or no extra training in dealing with delinquency and may only repeat the lessons they learned as patrol officers. However, some of these officers are chosen because they have a special talent for dealing with delinquency. They may have backgrounds in social science, child psychology, adolescence, child-parent conflict, or sex offenses. Such officers can be extremely valuable in detecting, preventing, and treating delinquency and abuse cases.

Often, these officers don't enjoy high status in the department because they "work only juvie crimes." However, experienced juvenile officers are typically more skilled at classifying and dealing with delinquents than are regular police officers. Research has found that juvenile officers prefer prevention and intervention tactics, including more discretion and referrals to external agencies; a more proactive approach with prevention programs; and fewer referrals to juvenile courts. Juvenile officers also use less intrusive measures when handling juvenile incidents and are more offender oriented.[13] Here is a summary of what juvenile officers do:

1. The juvenile officer is skilled at interrogating juveniles. Although a regular officer might have trouble categorizing a juvenile episode, the juvenile officer, because of his or her experience, usually does not.

2. The juvenile officer has many types of juvenile contacts, such as school officials, parents, neighbors, and victims.

3. The juvenile officer is experienced at handling difficult parents and dispositions, as well as a variety of delinquents and their situations.

4. Because of a knowledge of juvenile court procedures and dispositions, a juvenile officer is better able to handle juvenile interrogations. Given the same information from a juvenile about a situation, the juvenile officer might make an entirely different recommendation than a regular officer.[14]

JUVENILE UNITS

Large police departments have specialized units that respond to offenses they suspect are committed by juveniles. Offenses such as bicycle theft, drug sales in schools, and fighting are investigated by juvenile-unit officers. Some officers might be assigned as school resource officers, where they maintain a presence in one or more schools and try to get to know the students in order to develop a positive relationship between youths and the police. The officers are also responsible for handling cases of abuse and neglect, as well as investigating offenses committed against juveniles. Working closely with the juvenile court and youth service workers, members of juvenile units typically attain a working knowledge of the problems of delinquency.[15]

Gang Units. In cities with gang problems, police departments may assign several officers to the gang unit, where they develop strategies to prevent and solve gang crime. By developing intelligence about the structure and behaviors of the gangs in their jurisdictions, gang-unit officers can provide other officers, schools, and the community with information for stemming the tide of gang activities. These officers work gang-related cases and are in a much better position to interpret gang graffiti, understand gang rivalries, and apprehend gang members than are regular police officers.[16]

Neglected and Abused Children

Although not all are juvenile delinquents, neglected and abused children often come into contact with the police. This is because police officers, who are first responders in times of crisis or emergency, are often the first officials to become aware of cases of child abuse or neglect. For example, during the arrest of adults at their home for drug offenses, the police may discover that their children are living in squalid conditions. Or because the parents are going to jail, the police may have to deal with the children because the children have nowhere else to go. The officer's role in these situations is limited and predicated on doing what is best for the child. It may mean arresting a parent or guardian or removing the child from the home. These cases are quickly turned over to a child protective services agency, so police officers have only a tangential role as compared to their involvement with delinquency cases.

Status Offenders

Status offenders may be the easiest type of juvenile case for police because of the wide range of discretion and the situational clarity. A status offense, as you'll recall, applies only to juveniles. Twelve-year-olds are prohibited from drinking beer because we believe they are harmed by inebriation and alcohol more than adults are. A police officer who catches a 12-year-old drinking beer has to do something about it, but has a range of choices:

1. End the status offense (in this case, take the beer away), and release the youth.
2. Take the youth into custody with release to the parents; this may involve simply taking the youth home, with an explanation of what he or she was up to, or having the parents retrieve him or her from the station.
3. Take the youth into custody but with referral to counseling or other social service.
4. Take the youth into custody with formal charges and referral to juvenile court.

Police officers are likely to go easier on juveniles caught committing simple status offenses, because most status offenses aren't serious from a public safety perspective. Recall the prior example of teenagers drinking beer in a parking lot. Let's say the teenagers are out past curfew. The curfew and alcohol-consumption violations are status offenses, but the teenagers, while they may be loud and obnoxious, aren't endangering anyone with these activities alone. However, if one of the teens gets in a car and drives away while drunk, then the teen is a danger to public safety—but the offense has gone beyond being a simple status offense. Driving while drunk is illegal and dangerous for everyone, not just teenagers. At this point, the police have less discretion and must take the matter more seriously, with greater consequences for the drunk teenager.

Other status offenses, besides curfew violations and underage drinking, include underage driving, truancy (not being in school), and running away. Unless some other offense was committed, runaways generally don't incur much police involvement, other than locating the runaway and taking the child home. If abuse at home is obvious, then police are concerned with the abuser(s), not the runaway.

Violent Juveniles

In 2009, the serious violent crime rate among juveniles was 11 offenses per 1,000 youths ages 12–17, a substantially lower rate than the 1993 peak rate of 52 violent offenses (see Figure 12.1). When looking at these statistics, it's important to understand how authorities arrive at these figures. More than one offender was involved in over half of all serious violent juvenile offenses that victims reported in 2009. Therefore, this rate of serious violent offending doesn't represent the number of juvenile offenders, but rather the rate of violent offenses involving a juvenile.[17]

Recall that police officers have a great amount of discretion, especially with status offenders, which generally leads to one of four outcomes. The first is doing nothing and ending the status offense, and the other three involve taking the

Figure 12.1 Rate of Serious Violent Offenses by Juveniles Ages 12–17

The offense rate is the ratio to the number of juveniles in the population of the number of violent offenses (aggravated assault, rape, and robbery) reported to the National Crime Victimization Survey that involved at least one offender perceived by the victim to be 12–17 years of age plus the number of murders reported to the police that involved at least one juvenile.

Think About It

1. About when did the rate of offenses peak?

Source: Federal Interagency Forum on Child and Family Statistics, *America's Children: Key National Indicators of Well-Being, 2011* (Washington, DC: US Government Printing Office), 45. Online at www.childstats.gov/pdf/ac2011/ac_11.pdf.

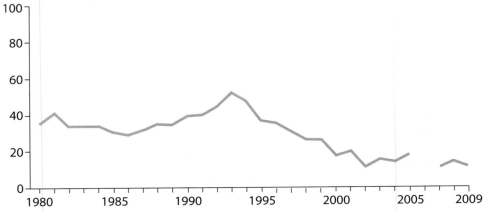

Youth offending per 1,000 youth ages 12-17

juvenile into custody with (1) release to parents, (2) referral to an alternative social program, or (3) referral to juvenile court. A violent juvenile greatly curtails police discretion, however. If the violence is bad enough, the police have only the last option, referral to juvenile or criminal court, although the third option, referral to an alternative social program, may be possible in some circumstances. A violent juvenile will almost certainly be placed in detention.

Gun violence is a troubling aspect of juvenile violence. As part of its guides for police, the Justice Department's Office of Community Oriented Policing Services (COPS) details police strategies for dealing with juvenile gun violence. The two types of strategies are offender-oriented responses and place-oriented responses.

» **Offender-oriented responses.** The "pulling levers" deterrence strategy, which began in Boston as the Boston Gun Project/Operation Ceasefire, targets a small group of serious offenders with a specific message that violence won't be tolerated. The strategy requires, in part, community support, effective communications, providing social services and opportunities, and searching for and seizing juveniles' guns.

» **Place-oriented responses.** Aside from community support, this strategy requires that police focus on "high-risk places at high-risk times." This strategy also involves intensive search and seizure of guns, as well as high contact with potential offenders, gang suppression, and gun buy-back programs.[18]

Learning Objective 5.

List and discuss the two standards juveniles must meet to be introduced into the juvenile justice system.

Learning Objective 6.

Tell why there's no particular age at which a juvenile is considered to be able to consent to a search.

Questions

1. What is usually the first contact young victims and offenders have with the juvenile justice system?
2. Which police units have the most contact with juveniles?
3. How are the police most likely to handle status offenders?
4. What are police likely to do with a violent juvenile?

Procedure: What the Police Do

Juveniles can be referred to the system in other ways, but police referral is the most common. In 2008, law enforcement sent 66 percent of all delinquency cases to juvenile court, with parents, victims, schools, and probation officers

If juvenile violence is bad enough, the police must refer youths to juvenile or criminal court. Here, a teenager and two 10-year-old boys leave their first judicial appearance after being accused of attacking a homeless man and smashing a concrete block into his face. The three boys were charged with aggravated battery.

responsible for the rest of the referrals.[19] This percentage seems high, but remember that police also divert many juveniles from the system through the use of discretion. Sometimes the police department deals with the juvenile's offense and then releases the juvenile, a process called **station adjustment**.

Taking into Custody

Taking a juvenile into custody is an important decision for the police officer because it affects not only the juvenile's freedom but also the justice system itself. Most juveniles taken into custody are referred to juvenile court (see Figure 12.2). About 2 percent are referred to a welfare agency or to another police agency.[20] The police can't take into custody every juvenile who is suspected of

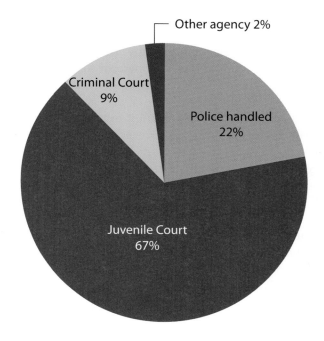

Other agency 2%
Criminal Court 9%
Police handled 22%
Juvenile Court 67%

Figure 12.2 The Disposition of Arrested Juveniles

In 2009, police handled 22 percent of all juvenile arrests and released the youths; in 67 percent of the arrests, the cases were referred to juvenile court. Nine percent of arrests were referred directly to criminal court, and the rest went to a welfare agency or another police agency.

Think About It

1. What percentage of cases went to other agencies?

Source: Charles Puzzanchera and Benjamin Adams, *Juvenile Arrests 2009* (Washington, DC: U.S. Department of Justice Office of Justice Programs Office of Juvenile Justice and Delinquency Prevention, 2011), 5. Online at www.ojjdp.gov/pubs/236477.pdf.

Taking a juvenile into custody involves a decision to either send the matter further into the justice system or divert the case.

an offense because this would swamp the system with too many cases. In deciding to introduce the juvenile to the system, the custody must meet one of two standards:

1. **Probable cause. Probable cause** simply means a reasonable person would conclude that there is a high probability an offense is being or has been committed. One doesn't need absolute proof of guilt here, but only a probability of over 50 percent that the juvenile is responsible.

2. **Reasonable suspicion. Reasonable suspicion** is a lower standard than probable cause. Here, the officer needs at least a 30 percent suspicion that an offense has been committed or that the youth needs supervision.[21]

Although police don't need probable cause or a warrant to take a juvenile into custody, many, if not most, departments notify the juvenile's parents after the fact. Many state laws require police to notify parents.[22] With this exception of notifying the parents, police follow the same procedures when taking a juvenile into custody as they do when arresting an adult. Two general classes of encounters are common in juvenile cases:

1. **Patrol.** Police who are on the street might be called to the scene by dispatchers passing on complaints from citizens, or they might witness infractions themselves that they view as suspicious.

2. **Investigations.** Juvenile officers make telephone or personal inquiries in the field or at the station when they investigate problems that are part of their caseload.[23]

In the case of situational ambiguity, the officer might arrest everyone involved for further interrogation or detention. Depending on the type and size of the department, a juvenile officer or detective might continue the investigation.[24]

Taking a juvenile into custody involves a decision to either send the matter further into the justice system or divert the case, often into an alternative program. The officer generally makes this decision after talking to the victim, the juvenile, and the parents and reviewing the juvenile's prior contacts with the juvenile justice system. Sometimes the police take into custody juveniles who aren't suspected of delinquency, such as in cases of abuse, neglect, or dependency. This area doesn't have an analog in the criminal justice system and illustrates why juveniles have a separate system, with slightly different rules and different terminology.

Booking

Once a juvenile has been taken into custody, the case is evaluated in several stages and processed into the system. These activities differ from those of the criminal justice system in a few significant ways.

FINGERPRINTS AND PHOTOGRAPHS

Officers may fingerprint or photograph youths or collect their DNA under specific conditions. Until recently, juvenile law was particular about how these records were handled, stating basically that they couldn't be kept or, in some states, even collected in a central database. Confidentiality has been considered crucial to juvenile system philosophy, with the idea that a stigmatized youth is more difficult to rehabilitate and that behavior changes significantly with age. Imagine being turned down for a job at age 36 because your potential employer finds out through a record check that you shoplifted a video game at age 13.

However, as juveniles are charged with increasingly serious and violent offenses, this attitude is changing. Several states have opened some juvenile court proceedings to the public, especially for serious offenses. Many states now retain juvenile records, not allowing them to be sealed, expunged, or destroyed, and some states allow sealed records to be opened.[25] These records include evidence

Officers may fingerprint or photograph youths or collect their DNA only under specific conditions.

collected by the police, such as statements, fingerprints, photographs, and DNA samples. States' rules for collecting such information vary widely, with many specifying certain ages under which information such as fingerprints can't be collected at all. Local police must be well aware of their state laws concerning juveniles when collecting this information.

Search and Seizure

An officer may conduct a search without a warrant or probable cause if the subject, either a juvenile or adult, gives **consent**. There is no set age at which a juvenile is considered to be able to consent to a search, and simply being young or immature isn't necessarily enough to excuse juveniles from consent in states that allow juvenile searches. Courts evaluate a juvenile's ability to consent by considering whether the search was voluntary based on the **totality of circumstances**. This means that courts consider the juvenile's consent in light of several factors, including age and maturity level, intelligence, the type of offense, and whether the juvenile has had prior contact with the justice system. A 16-year-old who consents to a search that turns up marijuana and who has been taken into custody for the same offense before will probably be considered by the courts to be able to give consent.

If, for some reason, a court finds a juvenile's consent to be invalid, all evidence turned up in the search will be thrown out. It's important to remember that juvenile searches and consent are yet another gray area in how police deal with juveniles, and that the rules vary from state to state. Some states allow no juvenile searches, regardless of consent, while others allow them only when a parent or attorney is present.[26] Most states allow the consent of parents or guardians who give police permission to search the room and possessions of a juvenile who lives in their home without paying rent. If the child is paying for room and board—for instance, a 17-year-old who has a job—then courts usually require the youth's consent. The difference isn't necessarily age but ownership of the property in question. Parents are considered to be the owners of their child's property, so the consent to search an 8-year-old's room must come through the parents. The 17-year-old, however, is considered to own the room he rents, even if it's from his parents.[27]

It's important to remember that juvenile searches and consent are yet another gray area in how police deal with juveniles.

The other major special consideration of juvenile consent involves school searches. Basically, a juvenile may be searched while at school, including his or her possessions and locker, without a warrant, probable cause, or consent as long as administrators have reasonable grounds. The reason for this is that the safety of everyone else in the school outweighs the juvenile's right to privacy or consent.

Interrogation

Juveniles have the same **Miranda rights** as adults: the right to remain silent, the right to counsel, the right to know the specific charge, and the right to confront witnesses. Some states and the federal government even have "juvenile Miranda" requirements, which we'll cover later. The rules regarding juvenile interrogation are much like those for adults, with a few key differences, such as ensuring that the youth understands the situation, the presence and concern of parents or guardians, and waiver of Miranda rights. This is part of the "totality-of-circumstances" test, in which courts consider all the circumstances of a case, including the juvenile's age, life experience, intelligence, maturity, and juvenile record, if any.

The reality of how police interrogate youths may be much different, however. An American Psychological Association study of 1,828 police officers found that although they acknowledged that youths and adults are developmentally different, and that these differences may affect the reliability of information obtained from interrogated youths, the officers didn't consider this during interrogations. According to the study, it appeared the officers believed that youths can be interrogated in the same way as adults.[28]

The US Supreme Court uses three amendments to regulate police interrogation:

» **Fifth Amendment.** Privilege against self-incrimination.

» Sixth Amendment. Right to counsel.

» **Fourteenth Amendment.** Right to due process. This amendment received the most exercise up until the early 1960s. The Supreme Court's concern was that young age, maturity, and overall competence affected the ability to waive rights and give confessions, thus violating the juvenile's rights of due process and equal protection.[29]

Haley v. Ohio (see Case in Point 12.1), one of the seminal juvenile cases to reach the Supreme Court, set forth an important rule regarding coerced confessions.

MIRANDA AND JUVENILES

Miranda rights, which stem from the 1966 landmark case *Miranda v. Arizona*, apply to "custodial interrogation by law enforcement officers."[30] Everyone who is arrested (or taken into custody) must hear a Miranda warning. The following is the basic text of the warning; however, it may vary slightly by state.

> You have the right to remain silent. Anything you say can and will be used against you in a court of law. You have the right to speak to an attorney, and to have an attorney present during any questioning. If you cannot afford a lawyer, one will be provided for you at government expense.

The police must ensure that arrestees understand the warning. Some states have officers also say something like, "Do you understand these rights?" If the arrestee doesn't understand English, then the warning and the arrestee's response

12.1 CASE IN POINT

THE CASE

Haley v. Ohio (1948)

THE POINT

Coerced confessions violate the due process clause of the Fourteenth Amendment. This case is also the first time the Supreme Court extended to juveniles the constitutional rights of adults, determining that juveniles must also receive due process.

In 1945, William Karam was shot and killed in his store by either Alfred Parks, 16, or Willie Lowder, 17. John Haley, 15, was with both youths before they went into the store and was waiting for them outside when the shooting occurred. Five days later, Haley was arrested at his home just after midnight on Saturday and taken to the police station.

After his arrival at the police station, police questioned Haley, alone, for about five hours in relays of one or two officers at a time. Haley confessed at around 5 AM, Saturday morning, after being shown the alleged confessions of Lowder and Parks. The police never advised Haley of his right to see a lawyer, although the confession the police typed began with a statement informing Haley of his constitutional rights. According to Haley and his mother, the police beat him, and his mother testified that the clean clothes Haley was wearing when he was arrested had become torn and bloodstained. She also testified that he was bruised and skinned when she first saw him after his arrest. The police denied beating Haley.

Haley was jailed early Saturday morning. Over the next few days, a lawyer his mother had retained tried to see Haley twice but was refused by police. The police didn't allow Haley's mother to see him until Thursday. Haley didn't see a judge, nor was he formally charged, until three days after signing the confession.

Haley was convicted of first-degree murder and sentenced to life imprisonment. The Ohio Court of Appeals sustained the conviction over the objection that the admission of the confession at the trial violated the Fourteenth Amendment. The US Supreme Court reversed the decision, holding that "the Fourteenth Amendment prohibits the police from using the private, secret custody of either man or child as a device for wringing confessions from them."

must be translated. Also, an arrestee's silence doesn't constitute waiver of Miranda rights.

These rights generally apply equally to juveniles and adults, with some exceptions (see the discussion of juvenile Miranda rights that follows). The key terminology here is "custodial" and "law enforcement officers." The courts have found that Miranda rights don't apply if the subject isn't in police custody or the interrogator isn't a police officer or acting as an instrument of the police (this would include some personnel who work with juveniles but aren't sworn police officers). Miranda rights don't apply in casual conversations with police officers or when the subject isn't in custody. They don't apply if the interrogator isn't a police officer but is a parent, teacher, or school principal. In short, Miranda rights apply only to a narrow range of circumstances that still, according to some critics, haven't been clearly defined.

For examples of how complex the issue of *Miranda* and the interrogation of minors can be, see Case in Point 12.2, *Yarborough v. Alvarado* (2004) and Case in Point 12.3, *J. D .B. v. North Carolina* (2011). In *Alvarado*, the police interviewed 17-year-old Michael Alvarado, who wasn't officially in custody. Alvarado confessed, and his statements to police were used to convict him. The Supreme Court ruled that the police weren't required to read Alvarado his Miranda rights because he was never in custody and that his age wasn't an issue in the matter.

In *J. D. B.*, police questioned a 13-year-old youth at his school without advising him of his Miranda rights. The youth, who wasn't in custody, confessed and was adjudicated delinquent. In this case, however, the Court held that J. D. B.' s age did make a difference in his understanding of whether he was in custody. The question is, does *J. D. B.* overturn *Alvarado*? According to the Court, not really. Age must be considered, but it doesn't absolutely determine what a child knows or how he or she should be treated in an interrogation. Thus, the 17-year-old Alvarado who was questioned at a police station was treated differently than a 13-year-old in a school. Essentially, the rules of interrogating juveniles must be considered on a case-by-case basis.

WAIVER OF MIRANDA RIGHTS

A juvenile may waive Miranda rights, but this waiver must be intelligent and voluntary. The juvenile must understand what he or she is doing and what is at stake, and must not have been coerced. Here, most courts once again use the totality-of-circumstances test. Some states require courts to consider various other circumstances: whether parents are present, the length of the detention, and the offense for which the juvenile is being questioned.[31]

A court will probably closely examine a juvenile waiver at some point, especially one given by a young child or a juvenile accused of a serious offense.[32] Also, both juveniles and adults must be clear in refusing to waive Miranda rights, especially in states without strict requirements for juvenile waiver, such as per se (discussed in the next section) or lawyer requirements.

12.2 CASE IN POINT

THE CASE

Yarborough v. Alvarado (2004)

THE POINT

Only suspects in police custody require a Miranda warning. Suspects who aren't in police custody don't require Miranda, although their statements to police may be held as evidence. The police aren't required to consider a suspect's age and experience.

In 1995, Michael Alvarado, 17, helped another youth attempt to steal a truck. The owner of the truck was shot and killed, although Alvarado didn't pull the trigger. The Los Angeles police called Alvarado's mother, and took him to the station for questioning. At this time, Alvarado was a high school student with no arrest record.

At the station, Alvarado's parents asked to be with their son during the interview but were denied. They waited in the lobby for two hours while a detective questioned Alvarado. The detective didn't advise Alvarado of his Miranda rights. Alvarado admitted he helped during the robbery and to hide the gun after the murder. Alvarado, who was never arrested, went home with his parents after the interview.

Alvarado was convicted of second-degree murder and attempted robbery in a California state court. Although Alvarado didn't receive a Miranda warning, the court didn't allow Alvarado to suppress the statements he made in the interview. Alvarado stated that he was deprived of his Fifth Amendment rights in violation of Miranda. Ultimately, the Ninth Circuit Court of Appeals held that the state court didn't consider Alvarado's age and inexperience when evaluating whether a reasonable person would have felt free to leave the interview.

The US Supreme Court reversed the Ninth Circuit decision in a 5–4 opinion, finding that Alvarado's interview didn't constitute custody and didn't require a Miranda warning, and that age and experience made no difference in this matter.

12.3 CASE IN POINT

THE CASE

J. D. B. v. North Carolina (2011)

THE POINT

A juvenile's age is relevant in determining whether the youth is "in custody" for Miranda purposes.

J. D. B., a 13-year-old special education student in 7th grade, was suspected of a series of burglaries. He was brought to his school's conference room, where he confessed to two police officers and two school administrators after questioning. Only after J. D. B.'s confession did the police tell him he could refuse to answer questions and was free to leave. Until then, J. D. B wasn't informed of his Miranda rights or his right to leave the room. He wasn't allowed to call his guardian or advised that he could have an attorney present during questioning. During the state trial, his public defender moved to suppress his confession on the grounds that J. D. B. had been interrogated while in police custody without Miranda warnings. The trial judge denied the motion, and J. D. B. was declared delinquent.

At issue is whether J. D. B. understood his Miranda rights and the nature of custody. The Supreme Court held in a 5–4 decision that a youth's age must be considered when determining if he or she understands his or her Miranda rights. Writing for the majority, Justice Sotomayor argued that "Children will often feel bound to submit to police questioning when an adult in the same circumstances would feel free to leave."

Apparently, most youths without representation waive their Miranda rights. Studies have found that most children under age 15 simply don't understand the right to remain silent and to have a lawyer. They may think their counsel is working for the court and not for them, and that their right to silence might be later revoked in court.[33] Another reason could be related to the expectations of children from parents and teachers. They have no "right to remain silent" when being questioned for breaking a vase at home or cheating on a test at school, nor do they have the right to an attorney. So, from the child's viewpoint, why would they have these rights with police?

THE JUVENILE MIRANDA

The federal government and some states have rules that give arrested juveniles a bit more protection than adults. These juvenile Miranda rules, which vary by state, usually allow a juvenile to waive Miranda rights only after being informed of the right to consult with someone, such as a parent or guardian, who is interested in his or her welfare. Some rules allow extra protection only for very young juveniles, such as those under the age of 12. Some states require juveniles to consult with a parent, guardian, or "interested adult" before or during interrogation for a Miranda waiver to be valid. This is called a **per se requirement**, although it can be called an interested adult test, friendly adult test, or concerned adult test.[34] A few states require juveniles to consult with a lawyer before waiving their Miranda rights.[35] The following is a summary of the guidelines for federal law enforcement officers to ensure that juvenile confessions aren't suppressed in court:

Once a juvenile is in custody, the arresting officer must make a good faith effort to notify the juvenile's parents or guardian to tell them that the child has been taken into custody, what offense the child was accused of committing and the juvenile's *Miranda* rights. A juvenile's *Miranda* rights must be given in a language that the juvenile can understand. The confession must also be otherwise voluntary. If the juvenile requests an attorney or invokes his or her right to remain silent, the interrogation must stop immediately. The juvenile must appear before a magistrate "forthwith." If the juvenile is not afforded these due process rights, the confession may be suppressed.[36]

In essence, these are the same rights adults have, with the exception of the requirement of notification of parents or guardians.

Custody

Police must treat juveniles in custody differently than adults in custody. In Chapter 14, we will cover the punishment and treatment functions of juvenile incarceration, but first we must examine police detention. In reference to detention, the 2002 reauthorization of the Juvenile Justice and Delinquency Prevention Act holds that states must comply with four "core protections" to receive grants. These protections are the following:

》 Deinstitutionalization of status offenders
》 Separation of juveniles from adults in institutions (separation)
》 Removal of juveniles from adult jails and lockups (jail removal)
》 Reduction of disproportionate minority contact where it exists[37]

All these protections apply to state juvenile justice systems as a whole, but one, the separation of juveniles from adults in jails and lockups, applies specifically to police and the way they handle juveniles in custody.

> Federal regulations discourage holding juveniles in adult jails and lockups. If law enforcement must detain a juvenile in secure custody for a brief period to contact a parent or guardian or to arrange transportation to a juvenile detention facility, federal regulations require that the juvenile be securely detained for no longer than 6 hours and in an area that is not within sight or sound of adult inmates.[38]

A juvenile who is taken into custody isn't necessarily "arrested." The juvenile might be placed under the state's control for his or her own protection. However, if the juvenile is suspected of unlawful behavior, he or she may be placed in detention.

In 1980, Congress ordered that status offenders and nondelinquents (juveniles who are in custody because they are dependent, neglected, or abused) had to be removed from all secure facilities and that delinquents, status offenders, and nondelinquents couldn't be detained in jails and lockups. The fundamental rule for juveniles in custody is that they must be kept well separated from adult offenders, regardless of the facility.[39] (These requirements don't apply to juveniles who have been transferred from the juvenile justice system to the criminal justice system; we'll discuss this in Chapter 14.) There are two major reasons for keeping juveniles and adults separate (and this is true for prisons and other secure facilities, as well as jails and lockups). The first is to ensure the juveniles' physical and psychological safety, and the second is so the facilities don't become crime schools.

Let's take a closer look at these two reasons. First, mixing delinquents with adults isn't only traumatic, but dangerous. According to the *National Prison Rape Elimination Commission Report*, "More than any other group of incarcerated persons, youth incarcerated with adults are probably at the highest risk for sexual abuse." [40] One study found that youths in adult facilities were sexually assaulted five times more often than those in juvenile facilities, as well as assaulted by staff twice as often and assaulted with a weapon 50 percent more often. [41]

The second reason concerns the simple risk of adult offenders helping youths improve their crime skills, from, say, better ways to break and enter a residence to expanding a market for selling drugs. Housing adults and juveniles together offends the philosophy of juvenile rehabilitation. These two problems are a risk at any confinement area, from a rural lockup, where the police are responsible, to a big state penitentiary at the corrections level. Remember, the juvenile justice system, at all points in the system, including the police, should be devoted to the protection and rehabilitation of juveniles.

Questions

1. What is probable cause? Reasonable suspicion? Why are they important?
2. What special considerations are involved in taking a juvenile's fingerprints, photographs, and DNA?
3. What special conditions apply to juvenile waiver of Miranda rights? What is the "juvenile Miranda"?

Discretion: How the Police Decide What to Do

Learning Objective 7.

Explain juvenile Miranda rights.

Learning Objective 8.

List and describe the three types of police discretion.

The police don't take into custody every juvenile suspected of breaking the law. The police use a certain amount of professional judgment or discretion in deciding whom to arrest. When examining the factors that affect police discretion, it becomes clear there is great variation in how the juvenile justice system processes cases. For the police officer, discretion can be divided into three types, based on demands of the law, demands of the situation, or bias.

Demands of the Law

The three legal factors that most influence taking a juvenile into custody are these:

1. **The seriousness of the offense.** This is the most important factor. Generally, as the seriousness of the offense increases, police discretion decreases, and custody becomes more likely.
2. **Frequency of offense.** If an officer sees a juvenile frequently in suspicious circumstances or if the juvenile is already known to be a frequent offender, the officer is more likely to take the juvenile into custody.
3. **Prior or current involvement with the juvenile justice system.** A juvenile with a history of custody and detentions or one who's under juvenile probation is more likely to be arrested if the officer suspects something. [42]

Demands of the Situation

A number of situational factors involving police discretion can influence whether an officer takes a juvenile into custody.

> The body motion, facial expressions, voice intonation, a known past record by the juveniles involved provide the officer with an initial basis for inferences, judgments, routinized evaluations as revealed in the language categories he employs. [43]

Different officers use this discretion in different ways. Experience teaches them what to look for in the behavior of suspects and how the local juvenile justice system responds to particular issues and concerns. The situational factors the officer considers when dealing with juveniles include these:

1. **Attitude.** A juvenile's attitude can make a big difference in police response, depending on the offense. Serious or frequent offenders are more likely to be taken into custody regardless of their attitude toward the police, simply because the police have less discretion in the matter. But if the offense isn't serious, such as certain status offenses, the amount of deference the youngster shows toward an officer can, in turn, affect the officer's attitude toward the youth and the decision to take him or her into custody.

2. **Family.** We have all seen movies or television shows, especially old ones, in which a police car pulls up to a house and the officer escorts a shamefaced boy or girl to the door and explains to a pair of stern and displeased parents what the child has done. It's usually something minor or silly, like breaking a window or running away after a family spat. This scenario isn't just something that happens on television. This is what officers do when the offense is minor enough and they can be relatively sure that the youth's family will dispense discipline. Such discretion is more likely in small jurisdictions or neighborhoods where the officers know the local residents and vice versa.

3. **Complaint.** If someone, especially a victim, complains about a juvenile's behavior, police are more likely to take the juvenile into custody. Most of the decisions police make are invisible to the public, so the police are free to use more discretion. However, a complaint or an obvious victim can throw a bright light on police discretion. If there is a complaint and no arrest, especially if neighbors are standing around and watching, the officer risks the appearance of not doing his or her job, which can damage the department's relationship with the community.

4. **Style of policing.** In 1968, political scientist James Q. Wilson defined three policing styles: legalistic, watchman, and service. The legalistic style describes officers or departments who work strictly "by the book" and use little discretion. If a situation legally calls for an arrest, the officers arrest and follow the letter of the law. The watchman style is nearly the exact opposite. This style depends on discretion, and watchman-style officers act only on serious or obvious offenses. If a watchman-style officer doesn't see trouble, then trouble is not there as long as public order is not disturbed. The last style, service style, is a combination of the other two. The service-style officer arrests (or takes into custody) offenders when it's called for but is also more likely to use alternative solutions or diversion, rather than sending the offender straight through the system. So, as you can see, a department's style can affect how officers treat juveniles. Consider a young teenager who is sitting outside a house drinking what appears to be a beer and smoking what might or might not be tobacco. A legalistic-style officer will attempt to take the status offender into custody, determine if she's smoking tobacco or marijuana, then proceed as the law specifies. A service-style officer may question the juvenile and determine where her parents are and what her juvenile status is (including her exact age, where she goes to school, where her home is, record of offending if any, etc.). The service-style officer will probably take the juvenile into custody but then may try to find the parents and/or refer her to an alternative program, rather than seek a formal disposition. The watchman-style officer will ensure the neighborhood is calm and keep driving.

5. **Friends.** If a youngster is associating with known troublemakers, delinquents, or gang members, custody is more likely.

6. **Individual traits.** An officer might decide to pursue custody based on the youngster's age, physical appearance, and level of maturity. This also depends on the offense. A shoplifting 10-year-old may only be sent home to his parents with a stern warning, whereas a 16-year-old who commits the same offense may face more serious sanctions because he's closer to adulthood. On the other hand, a bedraggled and frightened-looking 10-year-old at a bus station will most certainly be taken into custody for her own protection, whereas a 16-year-old with enough confidence and physical size may appear to be an adult and not be approached by the police at all.

7. **System characteristics.** These are extremely practical considerations. Custody is less likely, especially for a minor offense, if the police don't have a proper juvenile detention area or if this area is already crowded with more serious delinquents. If the community has few or no community referral programs or is having a problem with delinquency, even gangs, then custody and formal processing are more likely.

Bias

Police officers dealing with delinquency must constantly operate on their best intuition. The law and departmental policy go only so far in guiding the police in doing a difficult job. At some point, officers must rely on their own judgment, background, and feelings. Although most officers do their jobs as objectively as possible, data suggest that a certain level of bias is inherent in the juvenile justice system, including the phase in which police officers interact with juveniles. This bias is both overt and unconscious on the part of the officers, and it can include racial, sex, and social-class dimensions. It's overt in the sense that police officers participate in proactive policing in which they target specific neighborhoods, gangs, and offenses. It's unconscious because many police actions are predicated on issues that are, to a large degree, organized by race; therefore, racial bias is introduced into the activities of the police.

RACIAL DISCRIMINATION BY THE POLICE

Police officers will argue that illegal behavior, not race, is their motivation. However, a disproportionate number of minority youths are arrested. Officers will also argue they're making the community safer when they target juveniles. Citizens demand that law enforcement officials provide adequate coverage to their neighborhoods and not let teenagers take over the streets. However, when police officers engage in racial profiling, their justifications for arresting greater proportions of minorities are suspect. Black youths complain of being stopped by police for "driving while black."[44] In other words, they believe they're specifically targeted because of their race and that white youths don't suffer the same level of suspicion even though they're doing the same things. One study found that black teens encountered police discrimination most frequently in predominantly white neighborhoods, especially those in which the black population was growing.[45]

Similarly, the actions of police officers have an unconscious dimension because of society's bias against minorities. This principle can be demonstrated in two ways:

1. In his classic book *Justice without Trial*, Jerome Skolnick introduces the idea of **symbolic assailant**.[46] This is the mental picture that many people have

of what criminals look like. To a disturbing degree, this symbolic assailant is a young, black male. People are so willing to accept this description of a criminal that when Susan Smith drowned her two children in South Carolina, she was successful for weeks at getting police officials to search for a black male who didn't exist.

2. The unconscious bias against minorities is also demonstrated in a study cited by Everette Penn in his discussion of why race matters in juvenile justice. According to Penn, this study involved sending identical résumés to 1,300 places that advertised job openings. Some résumés had "white-sounding" names such as Brad, Matthew, Sarah, and Emily, while others had "black-sounding" names such as Rasheed, Tyrone, Jamal, and Lakisha. The "white" names had a 50 percent greater callback rate than the "black" names, although the résumés bearing the black names showed superior qualifications, such as better schooling and more awards.[47]

Racial bias will become a constant theme in our discussion of the juvenile justice system throughout the remainder of this book. The effects of discrimination, which begin with law enforcement, compound throughout the system. According to Penn, "being black" becomes a variable that explains the cumulative effect for black youths once they're inside the juvenile justice system. Discriminatory practices by individuals applied at various decision points throughout the system create insurmountable hurdles for black youths to overcome in order to exit it. In the end, these hurdles produce an invisible wall that in its current state cannot be fully seen, avoided, destroyed, or changed.[48]

The bias toward minority youths isn't limited to black people. Youths of other ethnic and racial groups have also been treated differently by police. However, because of the way official records are collected, it's difficult to measure the amount of bias in the juvenile justice system. For instance, Myrna Cintrón lists reasons why Latinos are underreported in the juvenile justice system and why we know so little about how they are treated by criminal and juvenile justice agencies:

1. The criminal justice system lacks a uniform definition for the Latino group. "Latino" and "Hispanic" are used interchangeably, and many jurisdictions use terms of national origin (such as Puerto Rican and Cuban) for identification.

2. The system doesn't separate ethnicity from race. (Persons of Latino origin can be of any race.) As a result, counting Latinos as white inflates the proportion of whites in the criminal justice system while underreporting the proportion of Latinos in the system.

3. There is evidence that Latino youths are disproportionately arrested, detained, and tried in adult criminal courts. Their sentences are harsher, and their commitments are longer than those for white youths who have committed the same offenses. Latinos are significantly overrepresented in federal and state facilities, although arrest data are lacking or inconsistently collected across jurisdictions.

4. The juvenile justice system must recognize and address the challenge the Latino population represents. The growth of the population, coupled with the effects of age, low educational attainment, immigration, acculturation, poverty, language, and discrimination, place Latino youths and their families at a greater risk for juvenile justice intervention.[49]

Cintrón's observations of the difficulties the juvenile justice system has in dealing with Latino or Hispanic youths reveal the problems of official definition and personal identity. The terminology issues are magnified by the lack of attention given to the cultural uniqueness of each group of Latino youths. Youths whose families have been in the United States for generations find themselves stopped and questioned by police and immigration officers who suspect that they aren't legal citizens. Having a Spanish surname might single one out for suspicion and extra surveillance in schools and the juvenile justice system. The cultural lifestyle and dress preferences of Latino youths are sometimes interpreted by the police as signifying gang involvement.

SEX DISCRIMINATION BY THE POLICE

Girls aren't involved in nearly as much delinquency as boys. There are several reasons for this disparity, all of which are related to the biological differences and cultural experiences of growing up female in the United States. Generally, there are two aspects of the police treatment of juvenile girls. The first involves chivalry, and the second involves protection.

From the chivalry aspect, girls get more lenient treatment than boys because they're presumed to be less dangerous, and their delinquent behavior is assumed only to support boys. For instance, a girl who sells drugs is thought to be under the influence of a boyfriend, rather than simply working independently for a dealer. Therefore, the police are less likely to arrest her and to use her as an informant. Police officers act on their stereotypes of females: they don't expect them to be serious delinquents and, therefore, don't proactively target them for arrest.[50]

The other side of sex discrimination concerns protection. This is most apparent with status offenses. Girls who commit status offenses are dealt with more harshly than boys. Running away from home is a status offense in which girls are arrested and referred to the juvenile court at a greater rate than boys. In the view of law enforcement and court officials, this is done for the girls' protection. Girls on the street are considered to be at a greater risk of victimization than boys. Being raped, recruited into prostitution, or otherwise victimized for sexual reasons is thought to be more likely for girls.

Often, police officers act on their stereotypes of females and don't proactively target them for arrest.

Researchers have confirmed that a double standard exists at many levels in the juvenile justice system whereby males are arrested more for delinquency, while girls are more likely to be processed for status offenses.[51] Like racial discrimination, sex discrimination is part of the discretion that police officers and other juvenile justice professionals introduce into the way they do their jobs. Whether overt or unconscious, this discretion results in young people being treated differently by the system based on extralegal factors. This discretion might be limited or controlled in a number of ways.

Controlling Police Discretion

For the juvenile justice system to be applied fairly to the problems of delinquency, juveniles suspected of similar offenses and who have similar delinquent backgrounds should be treated similarly. Although it's true the juvenile justice system is more focused on treating each case on its individual merits, police discretion often results in practices that not only are racially or sexually biased but also spend resources on the wrong juveniles. By arresting, adjudicating, and incarcerating juveniles based on who they are rather than on what they have done, the system risks neglecting those who desperately need intervention and may even be dangerous.

What are the best ways to ensure that the juvenile justice system, especially the police, exercises discretion in the most effective and fair way? The police should have clear guidelines that cover or include the following:

>> **Restricting the law.** One reason the police can use so much discretion in dealing with juvenile suspects is because youths are subjected to so many laws. In addition to the criminal code, juveniles also have the full range of status offenses that apply to them because of their age. These are well-meaning laws designed to protect youths from danger but, when used aggressively by police officers, may result in greater surveillance and arrests. Instead of helping young people and channeling them toward the resources they need, the overreach of criminal and juvenile laws often sucks them into the juvenile justice system. Some scholars have suggested that the best thing we can do for some delinquents is to ignore their behavior, because they will most likely grow out of their deviance as they grow older and become more integrated into society.

>> **Written guidelines.** Ninety percent of police departments have written policies on how to deal with juveniles.[52] Ideally, these guidelines are developed with the collaboration of juvenile court judges and youth service workers. By specifying the conditions under which a juvenile should be stopped, searched, or arrested, the guidelines largely eliminate police discretion that focuses on sex, race, or ethnicity. The result is a fairer pattern of police-juvenile interaction.

>> **Training.** Finally, police discretion could be controlled by properly training officers on the law, departmental procedures, and the youth development process. It's understandable that police officers consider juveniles to be as dangerous and intractable as adult suspects, but the police should be trained to use a certain amount of judgment and discretion in deciding which juveniles actually need intervention. There are behavioral reasons to bring the youth before the court that are independent of race, class, and sex. It's important to admit that discretion is inevitable and to train and educate officers in how it can best be applied to the problems of delinquency and the protection of children.[53]

The interaction between juveniles and police is problematic for several reasons. Although police might stop and question juveniles, their discretion is hard to keep track of until they take specific action and make a referral. The discretion used in deciding whom to stop, question, and refer rests on several factors.

First, youths who act suspiciously are most likely to attract police attention. Additionally, youths loitering in or near high-crime areas will arouse police interest. Once stopped, youths who are polite and well mannered will have an easier time than those who are impolite and challenge the officers' authority. The youth's style of dress, especially if it signifies gang involvement, could be deemed a sufficient reason for questioning, although no offense has been committed. Still, few youths are actually arrested, compared to the vast numbers who have street contact with police. These stops are used as a filtering device, and the exact reasons for the stops and arrests are hard to determine.[54]

Questions

1. What three legal factors most influence taking a juvenile into custody?
2. What are the concerns about racial and sex discrimination by police?

Prevention: What the Police Do to Help

Learning Objective 9.

Detail the best ways to ensure police officers exercise discretion in the most effective and fair way.

Learning Objective 10.

Describe the most widely used police strategies to address juvenile delinquency.

Generally, research shows that police are more successful in keeping the peace when they're closer to and more involved in the communities they're policing. To this end, a number of philosophies, theories, and official programs seek to integrate officers into their communities in several ways.

In traditional modern policing, officers are separate from their communities and react to situations. That is, they respond as offenses occur or are reported. Community-policing-style programs and initiatives seek to make officers more proactive, trying to solve problems before they occur. Law enforcement agencies have long struggled to maintain order on the streets using a number of successful and not-so-successful approaches. Because a suspect's age isn't known until the time of police contact or arrest, these strategies are aimed broadly at both adult crime and juvenile delinquency. Here, we review three police strategies to address delinquency that are widely used, although with mixed results: community policing, problem-oriented policing, and zero-tolerance policing. These strategies involve different patterns of interaction between the police and juveniles.

Community Policing

Law enforcement agencies struggle with the problems of gaining the community's trust and cooperation. This is especially true when dealing with juveniles who see police officers as authority figures with little tolerance for youthful behavior. As populations have grown larger in cities, and technological advances, such as the patrol car, have put more social distance between the police and citizens, the bond between the police and the community has weakened. As the police have become more professionalized and bureaucratic, they have also lost close contact with their neighborhoods.[55]

Community policing is aimed at reestablishing the positive relationship between police and citizens. The idea is to get the police back on the streets, where they can return to the roots of policing: the "neighborhood cop." Community policing covers a wide range of activities in which the police take an active part in the community, and it constitutes a major role change.[56] Community policing represents what we expected of the police in the past, before they became so focused on "fighting crime." The police are servants of the community, rather than an invading army, according to this perspective. Police scholar David Carter contends:

> It must be recognized that community policing is a philosophy, not a tactic. It's a proactive, decentralized approach to policing, designed to reduce crime, disorder, and fear of crime while responding to explicit needs and demands of the community. Community policing views police responsibilities in the aggregate, examining consistent problems, determining underlying causes of the problems, and developing solutions to those problems.[57]

On a daily basis, the work of the community police officer includes a variety of activities in addition to traditional law enforcement and responses to calls for service. These activities are concerned with making the officer a more integral part of the community and are designed to increase the interaction between the police and citizens. Many of the activities are aimed at crime prevention, whereas others are used to ensure that citizens have knowledge, confidence, and trust in the individual officers who are responsible for their community. According to Stephen Mastrofski, a community police officer's day includes the following:

» **Operating neighborhood substations.** One way police departments have decentralized is by putting substations in neighborhoods, housing projects, and shopping malls. The idea is to have officers responsible for a consistent area, rather than having them roam throughout the city. This way the officers can become familiar with the people of the community, and citizens see a visible police presence in their neighborhood. In terms of juvenile justice, substations allow officers to become familiar with school personnel, youth service workers, and neighborhood youths.

» **Meeting with community groups.** A range of community groups can assist the police in maintaining order in the community. Often, parents form groups that are concerned with their children's safety and welfare, and by including community police officers in their meetings, they can understand law enforcement's concerns.

» **Working with citizens on crime-prevention programs.** The most notable of the crime-prevention programs is Neighborhood Watch. Here, officers help citizens "harden the target" by advising them on locking their homes, installing burglar alarms, and making sure they have emergency phone numbers handy. In addition, police officers help neighbors establish procedures for looking after each other's homes when one is away.

» **Talking with students in schools.** There are a number of programs in which police officers enter schools in an attempt to become more effective in preventing and dealing with juvenile delinquency. These programs range from the traditional Officer Friendly school-resource officers to the D.A.R.E. program. When a police presence is maintained in schools, children are able to see at an early age that police officers are part of the social fabric of the school and community and will presumably be people they learn to trust and depend on.

» **Meeting with local merchants.** By maintaining close contact with local merchants, the police can gather a great deal of intelligence about what goes on in the community. Merchants are in their stores on a daily basis and are attuned to the patterns of interaction on the streets. Merchants depend on the police for timely responses to the problems of shoplifting and robbery, and forming a working relationship with the police is in their best interest.

Even merchants who hire their own security guards find that a good relationship with the police is advantageous. At the same time, police officers who have intimate knowledge of those who work in the community are in a good position to see which liquor store owners, tavern keepers, or restaurant servers sell alcohol to underage youths.

» **Dealing with disorderly people.** Community police officers perform a number of order-maintenance functions. Rather than arresting every citizen who's teetering on the line between inappropriate behavior and violation of the law, community police officers attempt to settle disputes on the spot and channel disorderly people to agencies where they can get help.[58]

It's clear that community policing is aimed at more than the problems of juvenile delinquency. However, many of its activities affect juveniles who are delinquents or victims. Community policing is a broad philosophy aimed at building socially and physically healthy neighborhoods that allow citizens to communicate effectively with the police. When specific problems are identified, community policing gives way to another type of police action, problem-oriented policing.

Problem-Oriented Policing

Problem-oriented policing, first developed by Herman Goldstein in 1979, is related to community policing but is different in substantial ways. The major difference lies in the proactive focus of problem-oriented policing. Rather than deal with improving relationships with the entire community to prevent crime, problem-oriented policing deals with specific recurring patterns of criminal or delinquent activity and addresses the underlying causes that promote law violations. For instance, in a downtown area that has a number of fights and muggings in the early-morning hours, the traditional police response would be to set up increased patrols to protect people from predators. However, problem-oriented policing would take another approach. Looking at the patterns of fights and muggings surrounding several downtown bars, police would investigate to see if minors and obviously drunk patrons are being served and if closing times are being strictly observed. By conscientiously enforcing existing liquor laws, the problems of muggings and assaults can be addressed through problem-oriented policing, which operates on the following principles:

» Focusing attention on substantive issues in the community

» A more analytical and empirical approach to the functions of the police

» Focusing on underlying problems instead of only individual incidents

» Employing a wider range of problem solutions instead of relying exclusively on the criminal law and its actual or threatened enforcement[59]

In dealing with juvenile delinquency, problem-oriented policing can be an effective strategy. Police have advised convenience store operators and owners on methods to prevent teenagers from loitering in their parking lots. For example, by playing classical music on the loudspeakers outside the store instead of music generally preferred by teenagers, some store owners have discouraged them from hanging around. The attractive part of this tactic is that it didn't result in interaction between youths and police. By altering the environment, the police and store owners were able to alter the conditions that led youths to engage in delinquent activity. The advantages of problem-oriented policing lie in analyzing a problem and finding ways to resolve it without increased police resources or invoking the criminal law for minor delinquent acts.

Similar successes have been obtained when the police worked with other local and state officials to pressure landlords to bring their apartment buildings up to code and provide a clean, safe place for residents. As the housing improved, so did the overall quality of life in the neighborhood, making the neighborhood more responsive to police efforts to address the problems of crime and drug sales. Problem-oriented policing encourages police departments to work with other government agencies as well as citizen groups to target hot spots where specific offenses occur because of underlying problems. By working on the causes of crime, problem-oriented policing can often prevent or greatly limit it.[60]

Zero-Tolerance Policing

Zero-tolerance policing is a form of community policing, but it's much more aggressive and proactive. The discretion that police use in zero-tolerance policing is aimed at adults and juveniles suspected of minor offenses. Rather than handling these minor offenses informally, zero-tolerance policing uses discretion to invoke the full brunt of the law. It's presumed that delinquents and adult offenders won't be motivated to commit major offenses if they know that the minor ones are being dealt with so harshly.

Zero-tolerance policing is based on the **broken-windows** idea developed by James Wilson and George Kelling.[61] Wilson and Kelling contend that run-down neighborhoods, that is, neighborhoods with broken windows, invite crime and delinquency. When people see that no one repairs the windows, they think no one cares about the property and that further vandalism won't be punished. By contrast, a neighborhood of well-kept homes signifies the area is occupied and cared about.

Wilson and Kelling apply broken-windows to public social interactions. This is where the analogy becomes problematic and of interest in our discussion of the interaction between police officers and young people. Broken-windows suggests that streets populated with homeless people, con artists, and loitering youths are rife with minor crime and are unattractive places for law-abiding people to spend time. Streets and neighborhoods where socially marginal people are absent will be populated with families enjoying a walk outdoors and people window-shopping, and encourage an atmosphere of positive and socially connected exchanges between citizens.[62]

Broken-windows was the perspective behind the police efforts in New York City in the 1990s when Mayor Rudy Giuliani instituted a zero-tolerance policy. The police made misdemeanor arrests for offenses such as panhandling, public drunkenness, prostitution, jumping subway turnstiles, and public urination. By aggressively prosecuting these offenses, it was felt that many offenders would get the message that deviant behavior wouldn't be tolerated. Additionally, this policy left a paper trail so the police could keep track of those who committed minor infractions. The trail of arrest summonses and court hearings was useful for rounding up suspects when serious offenses occurred. This perspective has a certain logic, especially when crime rates decrease and citizens feel safe on the streets again. But there is reason to be cautious in judging its value.

Critics of broken-windows think it's biased against young people, the poor, and the socially marginal. By aggressively protecting the interests of the majority in the community, this perspective adversely affects the least powerful. In communities with few recreational activities for youths, does it make sense for the police to introduce them to the justice system when they commit minor offenses because they are alienated and bored? Constant police harassment can force youths to internalize the label of delinquent and make crime a self-fulfilling prophecy.[63]

A final concern with zero-tolerance policing that requires mention is **net-widening**, which refers to including increasing numbers of individuals under the control of the state. Under zero-tolerance policing, those who before were simply warned and released are now processed into the juvenile justice system and given some sort of minor sanction. A good deal of time, effort, and resources are devoted to dealing with offenses so inconsequential, they're often dismissed by a judge or diverted at the intake phase of the juvenile court.[64] As a police strategy, zero-tolerance policing alienates juveniles and provides them with reasons to distrust and hate the police. This is exactly the opposite of what community policing was envisioned to accomplish. It's interesting, however, that police departments with specialized juvenile units show little or no evidence of net-widening.[65]

These various strategies the police use to interact with juveniles produce different outcomes. With community policing, problem-oriented policing, and zero-tolerance policing, it's possible to see the range of approaches that can be used to attempt to prevent crime. Although these approaches aren't specifically aimed at juveniles, they're important initiatives that greatly affect how police officers handle delinquency.

Questions

1. What three police strategies are most widely used to address juvenile delinquency? Discuss each.
2. What is the broken-windows perspective?

>> FOCUS ON ETHICS

Shoot or Don't Shoot?

As a police officer with over 12 years of experience you've never had to fire your weapon in the line of duty. You qualify on the police pistol range every year, and your abilities have allowed you to win the expert rank for the past four years.

Recently you've been distressed because the family of a young gang member who was shot during an armed robbery has sued a good friend who went through the police academy with you. The shooting review board ruled the killing as justified, but the publicity has made the police force wary. Your friend is taking the incident badly, because he wonders if he might have been able to handle the situation differently. He's depressed, has started drinking heavily, and has regular sessions with a psychologist who is trying to help him with his feelings of guilt.

This is on your mind on the night you're called to a domestic disturbance at the home of an immigrant family who doesn't speak English. As you and your partner forcibly subdue the intoxicated husband, the wife runs into the back bedroom screaming at an unknown number of children. You follow her down the hall, and out of the corner of your eye you see a gun being pointed at you from a side bedroom. As you draw your weapon, several things flash through your mind:

» The figure holding the gun is small and can only be a child.

» The gun could be a plastic toy pistol.

» In the darkened bedroom, you can't be sure of the exact nature of the threat.

» If the gun is real, and if the person pointing it at you is serious about shooting, you have a split second to act without properly evaluating the degree of threat.

» If you shoot and it's a child with a toy gun, your career will be over. Regardless of what the shooting board rules, you won't be able to deal with shooting a child.

» A child with a real gun can still kill you.

WHAT DO YOU DO?

1. Shoot to kill. This is a predictable crisis that all police officers are trained to anticipate and navigate.
2. Shoot to wound. After all, you're an expert shot, and they do this on television all the time.
3. Don't shoot. As a firearms expert, you believe a responsible person shoots only when he or she knows exactly what he or she is shooting at. You are wearing a bulletproof vest, so you are willing to take your chances before pulling the trigger and making a big mistake.

Summary

Summary

Learning Objective 1. Detail how the police dealt with youths in three ways during the late 19th and early 20th centuries.	The police decided which cases they would handle and which to push to criminal court. The police used discretion to round up youths for minor offenses, attempt to scare them into law-abiding behavior, then release them on informal probation or no probation. The police made most detention decisions, using detention as a swift punishment rather than for the protection of society or rehabilitative effort.
Learning Objective 2. Understand the role of "policewomen" in working with juveniles during the early 20th century.	Much of police work with juveniles includes protecting dependent and neglected children. In the early 1900s, "policewomen" trained in social work dealt with nondelinquent children and women. Male police officers rounded up delinquents, and female officers assisted neglected, abused, and dependent juveniles.
Learning Objective 3. Describe how the police are guided by the mission of the juvenile justice system to rehabilitate juvenile delinquents and divert those on the path to delinquency.	This directive is largely unofficial and indirect, a philosophy rather than a law or a rule. The police are indirectly guided by the Juvenile Court Act, which states that juveniles are "taken into custody," not arrested. This is interpreted to mean the police's role is to salvage and rehabilitate youth, a role indirectly sanctioned by many judges.[1]
Learning Objective 4. Discuss how the amount of special attention that delinquency gets from police departments depends on the department's size.	Small police departments have few or no juvenile specialists. This is a function of the size of the department and jurisdiction and the department's budget. A large, urban department will have a whole juvenile unit, often with separate units for juvenile victims and missing children.
Learning Objective 5. List and discuss the two standards juveniles must meet to be introduced into the juvenile justice system.	Probable cause means a reasonable person would conclude that there is a high probability that an offense is being or has been committed. Absolute proof of guilt isn't needed at this point, only a probability of over 50 percent that the juvenile is responsible. Reasonable suspicion is a lower standard than probable cause. The officer needs at least a 30 percent suspicion that an offense has been committed or that the juvenile needs supervision.

Summary

Learning Objective 6. Tell why there's no particular age at which a juvenile is considered to be able to consent to a search.	An officer may conduct a search without a warrant or probable cause if the subject, either a juvenile or adult, gives consent. There is no set age at which a juvenile is considered to be able to consent to a search, and being young or immature isn't enough to excuse juveniles from consent in states that allow juvenile searches. Courts evaluate a juvenile's ability to consent by considering whether the search was voluntary based on the totality of circumstances, or factors including age, maturity level, intelligence, type of offense, and whether the juvenile has had prior justice system contact.
Learning Objective 7. Explain juvenile Miranda rights.	Juvenile Miranda rules, which vary by state, usually allow a juvenile to waive Miranda rights only after being informed of the right to consult with someone, such as a parent or guardian. Some rules allow extra protection only for very young juveniles, such as those under the age of 12. Some states require juveniles to consult with a parent, guardian, or "interested adult" before or during interrogation, for a Miranda waiver to be valid. This is called a per se requirement. A few states require juveniles to consult with a lawyer before waiving their Miranda rights.
Learning Objective 8. List and describe the three types of police discretion.	Demands of the law: The three legal factors that most influence taking a juvenile into custody are (1) seriousness of the offense, (2) frequency of offense, and (3) prior or current involvement with the juvenile justice system. Demands of the situation: The situational factors an officer considers when dealing with juveniles include attitude, family, complaint, style of policing, friends, individual traits, and system characteristics. Bias: Bias is both overt and unconscious on the part of the officers, and it can include racial, sex, and social-class dimensions. It's overt in the sense that police officers participate in proactive policing in which they target specific neighborhoods, gangs, and offenses. It's unconscious because many police actions are predicated on issues that are, to a large degree, organized by race.
Learning Objective 9. Detail the best ways to ensure police officers exercise discretion in the most effective and fair way.	Restricting the law: One reason the police can use so much discretion in dealing with juvenile suspects is because youths are subject to so many laws. Written guidelines: Ninety percent of police departments have written policies on how to deal with juveniles. Training: Police discretion could be controlled by properly training officers on the law, departmental procedures, and the youth development process.
Learning Objective 10. Describe the most widely used police strategies to address juvenile delinquency.	Community policing covers a wide range of activities in which the police take an active part in the community; it constitutes a major change in the role of police. Problem-oriented policing deals with recurring patterns of criminal or delinquent activity and addresses the underlying causes that promote law violations. Zero-tolerance policing uses discretion to invoke the full brunt of the law and aggressively attack minor offenses.

Chapter Review Questions

1. How did order-maintenance policing affect the handling of juveniles prior to the 20th century?

2. How did police use their social-work orientation to deal with juveniles in the 20th century?

3. How is working with juveniles challenging for the police?

4. What are the typical duties of a juvenile officer?

5. What strategies do police use to deal with violent offenders?

6. How is the entry of a juvenile into the juvenile justice system different than the entry of an adult into the criminal justice system?

7. Are juveniles capable of understanding their legal rights, according to the Supreme Court?

8. What three factors do police take into account in using discretion?

9. Is there a double standard used by police in dealing with females versus males?

10. What are some of the common crime-prevention strategies that police use when dealing with juveniles?

Key Terms

broken-windows—This perspective states that aggressively pursuing minor offenses and offenders prevents neighborhoods from deteriorating into major crime.

consent—The voluntary agreement by a person of age or with requisite intelligence who is not under duress or coercion and who understands the proposition to which he or she is agreeing.

detention—The temporary care of a child alleged to be delinquent who requires secure custody in physically restricting facilities pending court disposition or execution of a court order.

discretion—The power of a legal authority to decide what to do at any given point in the justice process.

larceny-theft—The completed or attempted taking of property or cash without the owner's consent.

Miranda rights—The rules concerning arrest and police interrogation that stem from the 1966 criminal case *Miranda v. Arizona.*

net-widening—Describes measures that bring more offenders and individuals into the justice system or cause those already in the system to become more involved.

per se requirement—The legal requirement that an arrested juvenile consult with a parent, guardian, or other "interested adult," before or during interrogation, to waive Miranda rights.

probable cause—Sufficient reason for a police officer to believe an offense has been committed, and which must exist for an officer to arrest (or take into custody) without a warrant, search without a warrant, or seize property.

reasonable suspicion—Doubt that is based on specific facts or circumstances and that justifies stopping and sometimes searching an adult or juvenile thought to be involved in criminal activity or, in the case of a juvenile, a status offense.

station adjustment—When a juvenile delinquent is handled within a police department and released.

symbolic assailant—The mental picture that many people have of criminal offenders.

totality of circumstances—The consideration by the court of all the conditions surrounding an issue, such as police interrogation or juvenile consent to a search or interrogation.

Endnotes

1 David Wolcott, "' The Cop Will Get You': The Police and Discretionary Juvenile Justice, 1890–1940," *Journal of Social History* 35, no. 2 (Winter 2001): 356.

2 Ibid., 359–360.

3 Ibid., 349–371.

4 Albert R. Roberts, "Police Social Workers: A History," *Social Work* 21, no. 4 (July 1976): 294.

5 Ibid., 294–299.

6 Federal Bureau of Investigation, Uniform Crime Reports, *Crime in the United States, 2010*, Table 32: Ten-Year Arrest Trends, www.fbi.gov/about-us/cjis/ucr/crime-in-the-u.s/2010/crime-in-the-u.s.-2010/tables/10tbl32.xls

7 Samuel Walker and Charles M. Katz, *The Police in America: An Introduction*, 7th ed. (New York: McGraw-Hill, 2011), 249.

8 Barry C. Feld, *Juvenile Justice Administration in a Nutshell* (St. Paul, MN: West Group, 2003), 54–55.

9 Walker and Katz, *The Police in America*, 249.

10 Kären M. Hess and Robert W. Drowns, *Juvenile Justice* (Belmont, CA: Wadsworth, 2004), 216.

11 Ibid., 219–220.

12 Walker and Katz, *The Police in America*, 250.

13 Jennifer L. Schulenberg and Deirdre Warren, "Police Discretion with Apprehended Youth: Assessing the Impact of Juvenile Specialization," *Police Practice and Research* 10, no. 1 (February 2009): 3–16.

14 Aaron V. Cicourel, "Process and Structure in Juvenile Justice," in David L. Parry, ed., *Essential Readings in Juvenile Justice* (Upper Saddle River, NJ: Pearson Prentice Hall, 2005), 137. Appeared in *The Social Organization of Juvenile Justice* (New Brunswick, NJ: Transaction, 1968; first published by Heinemann Educational Books Ltd., 1968).

15 Walker and Katz, *The Police in America*, 250.

16 Vincent J. Webb and Charles M. Katz, "Policing Gangs in an Era of Community Policing," in *Policing Gangs and Youth Violence* (Belmont, CA: Wadsworth, 2003).

17 Federal Interagency Forum on Child and Family Statistics, *America's Children: Key National Indicators of Well-Being, 2011* (Washington, DC: US Government Printing Office), 45. Online at www.childstats.gov/pdf/ac2011/ac_11.pdf.

18 Anthony A. Braga, *Problem-Specific Guides Series, No. 23: Gun Violence among Serious Young Offenders* (Washington, DC: US Department of Justice, Office of Community Oriented Policing Services, 2004). Online at www.cops.usdoj.gov/files/RIC/Publications/e0507882-web.pdf.

19 Charles Puzzanchera, *Juvenile Arrests 2008* (Washington, DC: US Department of Justice, Office of Justice Programs, Office of Juvenile Justice and Delinquency Prevention, 2009), 5. Online at https://www.ncjrs.gov/pdffiles1/ojjdp/228479.pdf.

20 Ibid.

21 Rolando V. del Carmen and Chad R. Trulson, *Juvenile Justice: The System, Process, and Law* (Belmont, CA: Thomson Wadsworth, 2006), 75.

22 Ibid., 73, 76.

23 Cicourel, "Process and Structure in Juvenile Justice," 137.

24 Ibid.

25 del Carmen and Trulson, *Juvenile Justice: The System, Process, and Law*, 102.

26 Ibid., 88–89.

27 Ibid., 89.

28 N. Dickon Reppucci, Jessica Meyer, and Jessica Kostelnik, "Custodial Interrogation of Juveniles: Results of a National Survey of Police," in *Police Interrogations and False Confessions: Current Research, Practice, and Policy Recommendations* (Washington, DC: American Psychological Association, 2010), 67–80.

29 Feld, *Juvenile Justice Administration in a Nutshell*, 98.

30 Sarah H. Ramsey and Douglas E. Abrams, *Children and the Law* (St. Paul, MN: Thomson West, 2003), 527.

31 Feld, *Juvenile Justice Administration in a Nutshell*, 54–55.

32 del Carmen and Trulson, *Juvenile Justice: The System, Process, and Law*, 101.

33 Ramsey and Abrams, *Children and the Law*, 531–532.

34 Thomas Von Wald, "No Questions Asked! *State* v. *Horse*: A Proposition for a Per Se Rule When Interrogating Juveniles," *South Dakota Law Review* 48 (2003): 143–171.

35 del Carmen and Trulson, *Juvenile Justice: The System, Process, and Law*, 100.

36 Joey L. Caccarozzo, "Juvenile *Miranda* Rights" (Federal Law Enforcement Training Center, 2006), www.fletc.gov/training/programs/legal-division/the-informer/research-by-subject/5th-amendment/juvenilemirandarights.pdf.

37 Office of Juvenile Justice and Delinquency Prevention, *Guidance Manual for Monitoring Facilities Under the Juvenile Justice and Delinquency Prevention Act of 1974, as amended* (Washington, DC: US Department of Justice, Office of Justice Programs, 2009), 5. Online at www.ojjdp.gov/compliance/guidancemanual2010.pdf.

38 Howard N. Snyder and Melissa Sickmund, Juvenile Offenders and Victims: 2006 National Report (Washington, DC: US Department of Justice, Office of Justice Programs, Office of Juvenile Justice and

Delinquency Prevention, 2006), 104. Online at www.ojjdp.ncjrs.org/ojstatbb/ nr2006/ downloads/NR2006.pdf.

39 Office of Juvenile Justice and Delinquency Prevention, *Guidance Manual for Monitoring Facilities Under the Juvenile Justice and Delinquency Prevention Act of 1974, as amended*, 5.

40 *National Prison Rape Elimination Commission Report*, June 2009, 18, https://www.ncjrs.gov/pdffiles1/226680.pdf.

41 Dale Parent et al., *Conditions of Confinement: Juvenile Detention and Corrections Facilities, Research Summary* (Office of Juvenile Justice and Delinquency Prevention, 1994); Martin Forst, Jeffrey Fagan, and T. Scott Vivona, "Youth in Prisons and Training Schools: Perceptions and Consequences of the Treatment-Custody Dichotomy," *Juvenile & Family Court Journal* 40, no. 1 (1989).

42 del Carmen and Trulson, *Juvenile Justice: The System, Process, and Law*, 77–78.

43 Cicourel, "Process and Structure in Juvenile Justice," 137.

44 Richard L. Lundman and Robert L. Kaufman, "Driving While Black: Effects of Race, Ethnicity, and Gender on Citizen Self-Reports of Traffic Stops and Police Actions," *Criminology* 41 (2003): 195–220.

45 Eric A. Stewart et al., "Neighborhood Racial Context and Perceptions of Police-based Racial Discrimination among Black Youth," *Criminology* 47, no. 3 (2009): 847–887.

46 Jerome Skolnick, *Justice without Trial: Law Enforcement in a Democratic Society*, 3rd ed. (New York: Macmillan, 1994).

47 Everette B. Penn, "Black Youth: Disproportionality and Delinquency," in Everette B. Penn et al., eds., *Race and Juvenile Justice* (Durham, NC: Carolina Academic Press, 2006), 47–64.

48 Ibid., 60.

49 Myrna Cintrón, "Latino Delinquency: Defining and Counting the Problem," in Everette B. Penn et al., eds., *Race and Juvenile Justice* (Durham, NC: Carolina Academic Press, 2006).

50 Christy A. Visher, "Gender, Police Arrest Decisions and Notions of Chivalry," *Criminology* 21 (1983): 5–28.

51 Barry Krisberg, *Juvenile Justice: Redeeming Our Children* (Thousand Oaks, CA: Sage, 2005),

113–114. See especially Chapter 6, "Young Women and the Juvenile Justice System."

52 Brian A. Reaves, *Local Police Departments, 2007* (Washington, DC: US Department of Justice, Office of Justice Programs, Bureau of Justice Statistics, 2010), 16.

53 Samuel Walker, *Taming the System: The Control of Discretion in Criminal Justice 1950–1990* (New York: Oxford University Press, 1993).

54 David A. Klinger, "Demeanor on Crime: Why 'Hostile' Citizens Are More Likely to Be Arrested," *Criminology* 32 (1994): 475–493.

55 Robert C. Trojanowicz and Bonnie Bucqueroux, *Community Policing: A Contemporary Perspective* (Cincinnati, OH: Anderson, 1990).

56 Walker and Katz, *The Police in America: An Introduction*, 301.

57 David L. Carter, *The Police and the Community*, 7th ed. (Upper Saddle River, NJ: Prentice Hall, 2002), 49.

58 Stephen D. Mastrofski, "What Does Community Policing Mean for Daily Police Work?" in Willard M. Oliver, ed., *Community Policing: Classical Readings* (Upper Saddle River, NJ: Prentice Hall, 2000), 318–324.

59 Herman Goldstein, *Problem-Oriented Policing* (New York: McGraw-Hill, 1990).

60 Gordon Bazemore and Allen W. Cole, "Police in the 'Laboratory' of the Neighborhood: Evaluating Problem-Oriented Strategies in a Medium-Sized City," *American Journal of Police* 3 (1994): 119–147.

61 James Q. Wilson and George L. Kelling, "Broken Windows: Police and Neighborhood Safety," *Atlantic Monthly* 249, no. 3 (March 1982): 29–38.

62 Robert Panzarella, "Bratton Reinvents, 'Harassment Model' of Policing," *Law Enforcement News* (June 1998): 13–15.

63 Lorraine Green, "Cleaning Up Drug Hot Spots in Oakland, California: The Displacement and Diffusion Effects," *Justice Quarterly* 12 (1995): 737–754.

64 Thomas Blomberg, "Diversion and Accelerated Social Control," *Journal of Criminal Law and Criminology* 68 (1977): 274–282.

65 Schulenberg and Warren, "Police Discretion with Apprehended Youth," *Police Practice and Research*.

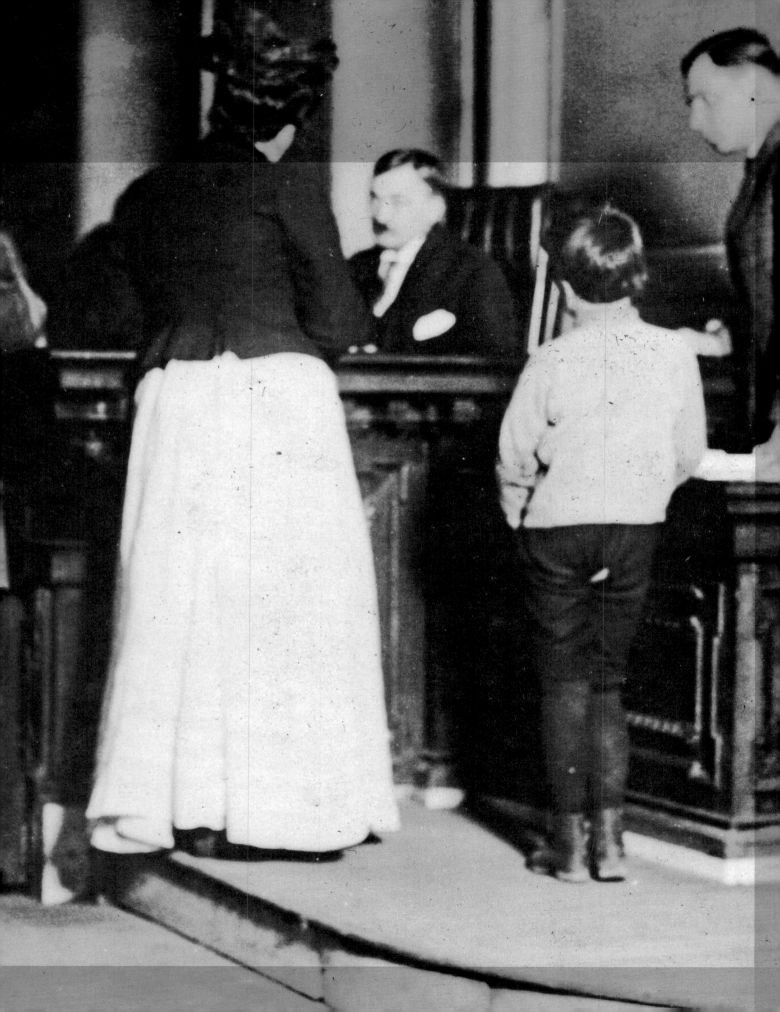

The Juvenile Court

The greatest differences between the criminal justice system and the juvenile justice system are apparent in the juvenile court. Although each system is charged with essentially the same task, dealing with violations of the law, the juvenile justice system has an even broader mandate. It also has a different operating philosophy, more complicated relationships with other institutions, and, perhaps most important, the deep suspicion of many observers that it coddles young criminals and lets them get away with bad behavior.[1] The juvenile court has a complex role, so we will focus not only on how it works, but also on some of its shortcomings and challenges. By gaining an appreciation of the juvenile court's difficult and ambiguous mission, you will better understand why it has always been a source of controversy in society's attempts to curb crime and delinquency.

Organization and Jurisdiction

Learning Objective 1.

Discuss the problem of juvenile court fragmentation.

We covered juvenile court development in Chapter 2, so we won't repeat it here. However, it's important to remember the reasoning behind the invention of the court and its proposed goals. The idea was that a juvenile court would deal with juvenile delinquency more effectively, as well as protect children from the dangers of being handled in parallel with adult offenders.[2] Additionally, it was presumed that having child specialists address juvenile delinquency and dependency would prevent the justice system from victimizing children. These goals still haven't been fully accomplished, despite the well-meaning activities of generations of juvenile court judges, youth service workers, and child advocates. Part of the difficulty of achieving effective and humane juvenile courts can be found in their organization and jurisdictional structure.[3]

Learning Objective 2.

Explain the relationship of the federal government to juvenile courts.

The structure of juvenile courts varies widely. In some populous jurisdictions, they're part of a juvenile justice system that works in conjunction with other youth agencies. In other places, they're a specialized court that operates in a central courthouse along with other courts. Usually, they're called "juvenile courts," but in some places they're referred to as "family courts" or "magistrate courts."

Juvenile courts are almost exclusively a state and county responsibility. The federal government specifies some of the rules and laws that apply to juvenile courts, especially in dealing with status offenders; but, for the most part, the federal government defers to the states on juvenile delinquency. For certain offenses, such as the killing of a federal officer, offenses on a military or American Indian reservation, and violation of a federal law, the federal government may become

The purpose of the juvenile court was to deal with delinquency more effectively and protect children from being handled alongside adult offenders. In this juvenile court scene from 1910, an 8-year-old boy is charged with stealing a bicycle.

involved under the Federal Juvenile Delinquency Act. For a juvenile to be tried in the federal court system, certain conditions must be met to show a "substantial federal interest."

》 The state has no jurisdiction or refuses jurisdiction.

》 The state with jurisdiction doesn't have adequate programs or services for juvenile delinquents.

》 The offense is a violent felony, a drug trafficking or importation offense, or firearm offense.

For the most part, the federal government doesn't prosecute juveniles because it has no juvenile court or juvenile correctional system. If the juvenile has to be incarcerated, the federal government must coordinate with a state-run juvenile correctional facility. The federal government can also certify the juvenile as an adult, in which case the proceedings are held in federal court. In this case, the juvenile is afforded all the rights of an adult in the federal court system, including a jury trial.

Sometimes, however, the federal government is eager to assert its jurisdiction over juveniles who break federal laws. The 2002 "DC Sniper" case involved an adult and a juvenile who shot and killed several people from ambush over a period of several weeks in several states. Also, one of the victims worked for the FBI, and because the case involved firearms, the federal government filed charges along with the states of Virginia and Maryland.

After the arrests of Lee Boyd Malvo, 17, and John Allen Muhammad, 44, US Attorney General John Ashcroft ordered federal agents to transfer Malvo from federal custody to local authorities in Fairfax County, Virginia. Ashcroft said it was "imperative" that the death penalty be an option. Neither federal nor Maryland state law allowed the death penalty for offenders who were juveniles at the time of their offense, but Virginia law did.[4] Although Malvo wasn't sentenced to death, this case still illustrates how the federal and state governments collaborate to handle juveniles who have committed offenses that fall under the jurisdiction of both levels of government.

The federal government is sometimes eager to assert its jurisdiction over juveniles who break federal laws. The 2002 "D.C. Sniper" case involved an adult and a juvenile who shot and killed several people in different states. Lee Boyd Malvo, then 17, pleaded guilty and was sentenced to two life sentences.

It's difficult to discuss typical juvenile court structure because states vary so much in how they organize jurisdictional responsibilities. Some states use the juvenile court for serious delinquency and another court, such as a limited-jurisdiction juvenile court, for minor delinquency. Family matters such as divorce or child-custody disputes will go to domestic-relations court, and cases involving status offenses, dependency, and neglect go to probate court.[5] Some jurisdictions have an interesting alternative to juvenile court called "youth court," in which other youths decided what to do with juveniles who have committed some minor delinquency (see Programs for Children).

This fragmentation of juvenile court structure is a problem with two possible fixes. The first involves some sort of coordinating function in which the various judges dealing with the same family meet and discuss the case. This allows the judges to schedule the case in a way that permits the issues to be decided in a progressive fashion. For instance, it makes little sense for one judge to set up an expensive family counseling program under the assumption that the juvenile will be returned to his or her parents, only to have another judge send the juvenile to a secure detention facility. Coordination would save resources, time, and duplication of services.

A second solution to the fragmented nature of the juvenile court is to institute a unified court system in which one judge handles all the issues and concerns of a case. This one-stop justice would ensure that the case would be dealt with holistically, rather than piecemeal. Theoretically, this single judge would become familiar with the dynamics of the family and craft solutions to its various problems. By knowing the family's history, how the siblings influence each other, and the parents' capabilities, the judge could construct long-term programs for remediation. This one judge, responsible for all the problems faced by a family, would presumably claim ownership for the results of the court's dispositions.[6]

If having a coordination council or a unified court would help solve the problems of fragmentation in the juvenile court, why don't more states institute such solutions? The answer to this question can be summarized by one word: politics. Court structures have evolved with state legislators determining the composition of the court system. Change in court structures is opposed by several groups for various reasons:[7]

» **Jobs.** Streamlining and consolidating courts could take jobs from judges and court workers. Making the courts more efficient would require a prolonged look at how cases are processed and who provides needed and unneeded services.

» **Power.** Having a coordinating counsel means that judges would have to agree on the best way to dispose of cases. Although this might be in the best interests of the juveniles and might save money for the government, not all judges will see things in the same way.

» **Philosophy.** Some juvenile court judges believe the fragmented nature of the court system, while inefficient, is desirable. A single judge or court isn't always equipped to deal with all the problems a youth exhibits. A family court judge might be effective in determining which parent should receive custody in a divorce but know little about how to deal with a child who is addicted to drugs. Although only one family might be the focus, its problems can be the purview of several different courts, each of which believes it has the optimal philosophy, temperament, and skills to deal with individual concerns.

This discussion of the different juvenile court structures and the relative advantages of each highlights some of the complexity of the juvenile court process.

Questions

1. Is the structure of juvenile courts the same in every state?
2. How does the federal government regard juvenile courts?
3. Why is juvenile court fragmentation undesirable? Why is it desirable?

13.1 PROGRAMS FOR CHILDREN

Youth Courts

Youth courts are programs in which young lawbreakers accept sentences from their peers for minor delinquent and status offenses, as well as other problem behaviors. Youth courts may also be called teen, peer, or student courts. As of 2010, more than a thousand youth courts were operating, in every state but Connecticut.[1] Youth courts may be run by private nonprofit organizations, but most are based in juvenile justice system agencies and schools.[2]

In most cases, juvenile lawbreakers are given a choice to enter the regular juvenile justice system or participate in youth court.[3] Most youth courts require juveniles to admit guilt prior to participating in the court. A few programs allow juveniles to plead "not guilty," and the court will conduct a hearing to determine guilt. More than half of youth courts dismiss the charges when juveniles successfully complete the program, and nearly a third expunge the juvenile's record.[4]

The four typical youth-court models are the adult judge, youth judge, peer jury, and youth tribunal. The two most common are the adult judge and the peer jury. The most common offense accepted by youth courts is theft, followed by vandalism, alcohol, disorderly conduct, and assault. Typical dispositions are community service, apologies, essays, educational workshops, youth-court jury duty, and restitution. More than half of youth courts close their hearings to the public, and 70 percent hold hearings all year long, whereas the rest are in session only during the school year.[5]

There hasn't been much rigorous study on the effectiveness of youth courts, but some research questions their effectiveness despite their popularity. One study claimed no significant differences in recidivism between juveniles who completed youth court and those who completed regular diversion programs; an additional finding was that the court seemed to work better for older youths and girls than younger youths and boys.[6] Another study found that youth courts actually increased male delinquency and had no effect on female delinquency.[7]

In this Redmond, Oregon, youth court, a teen bailiff writes down the punishments agreed to by jurors. The court fits into a broad range of juvenile justice programs in the city, including school resource officers and a dedicated juvenile police officer.

THINK ABOUT IT

1. Teen courts are popular, but researchers question their value. Would further study reveal their value, or is it possible that youth courts are simply a "feel-good" program?

2. What is your opinion of most youth courts' requirement that juveniles plead "guilty" as a condition of participation?

[1]Scott Bernard Peterson, "Made in America: The Global Youth Justice Movement," *Reclaiming Children and Youth* 18, no. 2 (2009): 48–52.

[2]National Association of Youth Courts, Facts and Stats, www.youthcourt.net/?page_id=24.

[3]Peterson, "Made in America: The Global Youth Justice Movement," 48–52.

[4]Ibid.

[5]Ibid.

[6]Michael Norris, Sarah Twill, and Chigon Kim, "Smells Like Teen Spirit: Evaluating a Midwestern Teen Court," *Crime & Delinquency* 57, no. 2 (March 1, 2011): 199–221.

[7]Denise M. Wilson, Denise C. Gottfredson, and Wendy Povitsky Stickle, "Gender Differences in Effects of Teen Courts on Delinquency: A Theory-guided Evaluation," *Journal of Criminal Justice* 37, no. 1 (January 2009): 21–27.

Key Players

Learning Objective 3.

Tell why the players in the juvenile court aren't as adversarial as those in the criminal court.

Learning Objective 4.

Describe the typical youth whose case goes to juvenile court.

Learning Objective 5.

Understand why the prosecutor exercised important discretion in the juvenile court after the 1960s.

Learning Objective 6.

Discuss the relationship between the concept of *parens patriae* and the juvenile court judge.

Learning Objective 7.

List and explain the two roles of juvenile probation officers.

The various actors in the juvenile justice system differ across jurisdictions. Let's take a look at the roles of those responsible for representing the interests of the parents, the state, and, most important of all, the juvenile, as well as at the cases that wind through the juvenile court.

The key players in the juvenile court represent varying interests but must work together to achieve the goals of ensuring justice, providing for the best interests of juveniles, and moving a high volume of cases through the system. The players in the juvenile court have a greatly reduced adversarial relationship when compared to their counterparts in the criminal justice system, but because of their elected or appointed positions, they may have vastly different ideas about how to proceed in specific cases.

Juveniles

Who are the youths whose cases go to juvenile court? The juvenile courts handled about 1.7 million cases in 2007, a caseload that climbed steadily from 1962 (about 400,000 cases) to 1997 (over 1.8 million) (see Figure 13.1). From 2000 to 2007, the number of cases handled by juvenile courts remained steady. Although more females are involved in the juvenile court than ever, they still represent a relatively small proportion of the delinquency caseload. White juveniles comprised 64 percent of the cases, and 33 percent involved black juveniles, 1 percent Asian juveniles, and 1 percent American Indian juveniles.[8]

The general offense categories are person offenses, property offenses, drug offenses, and public-order offenses. Most of the drug cases involved white juveniles, at 72 percent. Most black juveniles were involved in person-offense cases (murder, forcible rape, robbery, and assault), at 41 percent.[9]

Juveniles younger than 16 at the time of referral accounted for 54 percent of all cases. This age group accounted for 61 percent of person-offense cases, 56 percent of property-offense cases, 50 percent of public-order cases, and 39 percent of drug cases. The category with the largest proportion of young juveniles (younger than age 14) was person-offense cases.[10]

Figure 13.1 The Rise and Fall in Juvenile Court Caseloads

So far, the juvenile court caseload has peaked at over 1.8 million in 1997.

Think About It

1. Try to give some reasons for the steady rise in juvenile cases since the 1960s. In your opinion, why did the caseload drop in the late 1990s?

Source: Benjamin Adams and Sean Addie, "Delinquency Cases Waived to Criminal Court, 2007," OJJDP Fact Sheet (Washington, DC: U.S. Department of Justice Office of Justice Programs Office of Juvenile Justice and Delinquency Prevention, 2010), 1. Online at www.ncjrs.gov/pdffiles1/ojjdp/230167.pdf.

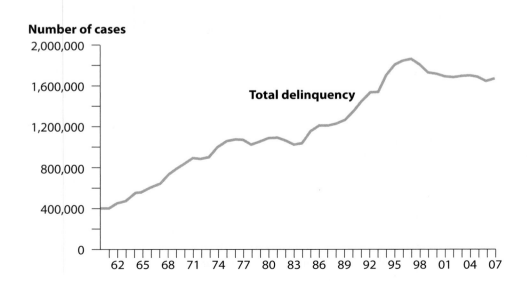

Number of cases

Juvenile Court Judge

The nature of the work of the juvenile court judge varies greatly depending on the state and the court's organization. However, all juvenile court judges have some things in common regardless of jurisdiction. First, the juvenile court judge has discretion in how to conduct the courtroom's business (see Crosscurrents for a story about how two Pennsylvania judges used the juvenile court to conduct their own business). Some judges are extremely formal and legalistic, emulating the criminal court, while other judges are informal and nonadversarial. Because judges are such key actors in the juvenile court, they set the tone of the proceedings. The judge embodies the principle of *parens patriae* in a way no other participant in the court does.[11]

This concept requires the judge to act as a surrogate parent for the juvenile to ensure his or her best interests are addressed. In cases in which a juvenile's parents have failed in their duty to care for, protect, and control their child, the judge assumes the responsibility to take a holistic look at the case and make decisions that provide for the juvenile's welfare, even if it means removal from the home or placement in secure detention.

Like a criminal court judge, the juvenile court judge is responsible for ensuring that juveniles receive due process. To this end, juvenile court judges rule on pretrial motions that challenge the circumstances of the arrest, interrogation, and search-and-seizure. The judge must also decide if the juvenile will be kept in custody while the case is processed or returned to the parents' supervision. Plea-bargain arrangements must be approved by the juvenile court judge, as well as trials or hearings concerning the facts of the case and the juvenile's **culpability**. Finally, the judge must decide on the disposition and be prepared for appeals. Sometimes, the judge has to ensure that the juvenile's best interests are guarded, because the parents are absent or in conflict with their child. Here the judge may appoint a **guardian *ad litem*** who can advocate for the youth's best interests in custody or abuse cases.[12]

Qualifications to be a juvenile court judge vary by state, but most states require the judge to have a law degree. Most juvenile court judges have experience in the court as defense lawyers, although some might be politically appointed with little or no juvenile justice experience or expertise.

Prosecutor

The prosecutor represents the state's interests in juvenile court hearings. Historically, the juvenile court didn't have prosecutors, and cases were presented directly by police officers, school officials, or caseworkers. After the 1960s due process revolution, the prosecutor became a fixture in the juvenile court and has evolved into a key player who exercises important discretion.

As in the criminal court, the prosecutor is the gatekeeper in the juvenile court. As cases are referred to the prosecutor, she or he decides if there is enough evidence to proceed, if that evidence was gathered in a legal manner, and if the case is serious enough to warrant the court's attention. Sometimes the prosecutor will use discretion to divert the case to another agency, where it will be handled in a nonlegal way. Because the prosecutor's power is so great, some states have taken steps to curtail or circumvent the decision-making authority of this key player. Especially in serious cases in which the juvenile could be waived to criminal court, legislators have indicated a lack of trust in the prosecutor's discretion and have passed laws requiring mandatory waiver for certain offenses.

Such legislation is part of the get-tough-on-crime movement of the criminal court that has filtered into the juvenile court. This shift in discretion in the

13.2 crosscurrents

Kids for Cash

For people to have faith in the juvenile justice system, it's necessary that those who work in the system be of good character and high integrity. For the most part, they are. Working in the juvenile justice system doesn't pay particularly well, and those who do it are usually committed to helping children turn their lives around. Occasionally, however, individuals abuse their positions. Such a case was revealed in Pennsylvania, where two juvenile court judges sentenced youths to incarceration in private facilities and received over $2 million worth of kickbacks.[1]

Judges Mark A. Ciavarella Jr. and Michael T. Conahan sent 2,500 juveniles to two private detention centers owned by a friend of theirs. These elected officials incarcerated juveniles at twice the state average. Ciavarella was sentenced to 28 years and ordered to pay $1.7 million in restitution. In September 2011, Conahan was sentenced to 17 1/2-years in federal prison and nearly $900,000 in fines and restitution.

Conahan, who had authority over the courthouse budget, saw to it that the proposed county detention center was never built, thus allowing the judges to rely exclusively on the private facilities. Juveniles, many of whom had committed minor offenses, were sent to the private center over the objections of other court personnel. Lawyers advised parents that they shouldn't hire them because they wouldn't be allowed to speak on behalf of their child in court. Many youths appeared without legal representation because of the judges' reputation for ignoring lawyers' arguments.[2] Between 2003 and 2007, juveniles appeared before the court without lawyers at 10 times the state average. The average proceeding took less than two minutes.

In one case, a 17-year-old was sentenced to five months in juvenile boot camp for serving as a lookout

Judge Mark A. Ciavarella Jr., who sent 2,500 juveniles to private detention centers owned by a friend, was sentenced to 28 years and ordered to pay $1.7 million in restitution.

for a friend who stole DVDs from Wal-Mart.[3] In another case, a 16-year-old girl went to detention for six months for gesturing with her middle finger to a police officer during a custody battle involving her sister and her parents. The State Supreme Court has ordered that the records be cleaned for hundreds of such juveniles that Ciavarella sentenced.

THINK ABOUT IT

1. What should happen to officials who violate the public trust in this way?
2. Are the youths who were sentenced for minor offenses by these judges entitled to compensation?

[1] Ian Urbina, "Despite Red Flags About Judges, a Kickback Scheme Flourished," *New York Times*, March 27, 2009, www.nytimes.com/2009/03/28/us/28judges.html.
[2] Ibid.
[3] Ibid.

judicial and executive branches of the government is a direct result of sensational offenses committed by juveniles who are seen as literally "getting away with murder." Nevertheless, the prosecutor remains a key figure who must represent the state's interests, which are considerable, even though the juvenile court operates under a vastly different philosophy than the criminal court.[13]

Juvenile Defense Counsel

When juvenile courts were first instituted, defense counsel for juveniles wasn't considered necessary. The judge and caseworkers were assumed to be working for the juvenile's best interests. Still, the informality of the proceedings often resulted in due process violations and troubling inconsistencies. In a series of cases decided by the Supreme Court, due process protections concerning standards of proof and the right to confront hostile witnesses required juveniles to be represented by competent counsel. Today, many jurisdictions have juvenile courts that mirror the adversarial proceedings found in the criminal court. Defense lawyers are serious about their mandate to protect juveniles from abuses resulting from well-meaning but punitive decisions by the state. Although many judges wish to maintain the juvenile court's informality, in cases in which serious offenses are at issue, it's almost always necessary for the juvenile to be represented by counsel.[14] The quality of the defense counsel for juveniles varies greatly both within and across juvenile courts. As in the criminal justice system, youths may be represented by either their own lawyer or one appointed by the state.

PUBLIC DEFENDERS

Lawyers appointed by the state may be private lawyers who are appointed as part of a court rotation system, or they may be **public defenders**. Public defenders are full-time state employees who represent the interests of those who can't afford private counsel. Typically, public defenders work under oppressive caseloads and have little support staff. Public defenders often don't have the resources to take very many cases to trial and so often encourage their clients, especially if they're guilty, to **plea bargain**. Private lawyers appointed by the court work under many of the same constraints as public defenders. Their compensation may be set by the court, which discourages private lawyers from spending a great deal of time and resources on cases when the pay is substantially limited. Further, the type of private lawyer who seeks work from the court is often new and inexperienced.

This haphazard system of supplying lawyers for juvenile cases means the lawyer is often unaware of the juvenile court's specialized procedures or the various treatment and dispositional options available to the client. Finally, the public defender or court-appointed lawyer may have little knowledge or appreciation of the problems juveniles have in communicating their concerns, constructing their self-image, or negotiating the challenges of schools, gang activity, or bad parenting. Although many public defenders and private court-appointed lawyers provide excellent representation for juveniles, there is no system to ensure a uniform level of expertise.[15]

Before moving on to the other juvenile court players, we must consider the low level of prestige and status that goes with practicing law in the juvenile court. For many judges and lawyers, the juvenile court is the "low-rent district" of the criminal justice profession. It's where one goes to gain experience and techniques that will be useful later in the practice of criminal law. Because many of the cases are low-stakes propositions, there is a general belief that new and inexperienced judges and lawyers cut their teeth in juvenile court, where mistakes and poor judgment don't have the dire consequences they do in criminal court. We can see evidence of this in the movement to waive serious felony cases to criminal court. This is unfortunate, because decisions made at the juvenile court level can profoundly affect the lives of juveniles, and those who practice law at this level should be committed to the process and the children.[16]

Juvenile Intake Officers

Juvenile intake officers occupy another important gateway in the juvenile justice system. Intake is the stage at which it's decided whether to dismiss the case, handle it informally (without filing a petition), or handle it formally by filing a petition requesting an adjudicatory or waiver hearing. When police officers, schools, nurses, or other individuals who have contact with children send cases to juvenile court, it's the juvenile intake officer who recommends to the judge whether the case should be moved to the juvenile justice system.

Several factors must be weighed in determining if the case should proceed. Issues such as the juvenile's personal safety, the risk of flight, and the risks to the public if the juvenile is released must be considered by the intake officer before deciding to place the juvenile in detention.[17] In 2007, 19 percent of all cases were dismissed at intake, generally because of weak legal standing, and another 26 percent were handled informally, with the juvenile agreeing to a sanction such as restitution. In more than half of the cases, 56 percent, a petition was filed, and the case went to juvenile court.[18]

Juvenile Probation Officers

Juvenile probation officers have two roles. One role is to craft supervised-treatment plans for juveniles placed on probation (this will be discussed in greater detail in Chapter 14). The other role is to act as an officer of the court by investigating juveniles' social backgrounds and making recommendations to the judge on appropriate dispositions. In some jurisdictions, probation officers may act as intake officers, or they may mediate out-of-court settlements between juvenile delinquents and victims of delinquency. In other instances, the probation officer works with parents in cases of abuse or neglect to solve the problem before it gets to the point of official referral to the juvenile court.[19] These key players are the ones who process the cases. The ideal is that each case gets careful attention, and the juvenile's best interests are weighed against the protection of society. Unfortunately, the ideal is elusive, and decisions are often made based on expediency and available resources. These key players don't always agree on the outcome, and the juvenile court often has more adversarial interaction than was envisioned by its creators.

Questions

1. Who are the key players in the juvenile court?
2. What do all juvenile court judges have in common regardless of jurisdiction?
3. When juvenile courts were first instituted, why was defense counsel for juveniles considered unnecessary?
4. What do intake officers do?

Juvenile Court Process

Now let's look at the actual process of the court. We will trace the stages each case goes through and identify some of the issues and concerns that must be overcome. Although this process differs slightly from jurisdiction to jurisdiction, essentially the same functions are accomplished as cases move through the system. The process may seem unwieldy and inefficient, and it is, but these stages are necessary to protect the juvenile's rights and to allow the juvenile justice system time to evaluate the case and options for disposition. The juvenile court process is similar in many respects to that of the criminal court, but there are also stark differences based on the core philosophies of each institution.

Custody and Detention

As we learned in Chapter 12, taking a juvenile into custody is the equivalent of arresting an adult, with some minor qualifications. It's similar in that the juvenile may be taken into custody if the police officer sees a law being broken, if there

Learning Objective 8.

Compare and contrast the taking of a juvenile into custody with the arrest of an adult.

Learning Objective 9.

List and discuss the three types of juvenile court hearings.

Once in custody, the juvenile may be held in detention until the intake officer and the juvenile court judge can evaluate the case. Here, 12-year-old Michael Nichols is escorted out of court. Nichols, who was adjudicated delinquent in the shooting of a police officer while heading toward his school with a shotgun, was sentenced to a youth correctional program.

is a court order, or if a complaint has been filed. Juveniles, but not adults, also may be taken into custody for their own protection in cases of abuse, neglect, or dependency.

Once in custody, the juvenile is subject to being held in detention until the intake officer and the juvenile court judge can evaluate whether the youth should be returned to parents or guardians until the hearing. If the juvenile is held in detention, the parents must be notified of the reasons for custody. Most juveniles are released to their parents, and only in circumstances in which the juvenile is in danger or a threat to others is detention preferred at this stage.[20]

Petitions and Summonses

Petition is the term used to refer to the filing of charges against a juvenile. Remember that there are additional reasons to file a petition besides actual delinquency. A petition may be filed to protect a child from harm if the parents are abusive or absent. A number of people, including police officers, teachers, parents, or nurses and doctors, may bring petitions to the court, but it's the court-appointed intake officer (often in consultation with the juvenile court judge) who decides to file a petition.

Once a petition is filed, a hearing date is set, and summonses are issued for those concerned with the case. Typically, the summons is sent by registered mail, and failure to appear can result in a warrant from the judge.

Juvenile Court Hearings

The three types of juvenile court hearing are the preliminary hearing, the adjudicatory hearing, and the dispositional hearing. Each state has its own rules on how these hearings are conducted, each judge has a different standard of formality, and the lawyers demonstrate varying levels of adversarial behavior. In some cases, the hearings are combined. For instance, a judge who is familiar with the

INSTANT RECALL
FROM CHAPTER 2

petition
In juvenile court, a document that alleges that a juvenile is delinquent and that asks the court to assume jurisdiction over the juvenile, or asks that an alleged delinquent be waived to criminal court to be prosecuted as an adult.

juvenile may combine the adjudicatory and dispositional hearings. The judge doesn't need a new predispositional report if the juvenile has been before the court numerous times and the judge has already exhausted the available remedies short of secure detention.

PRELIMINARY HEARING

The **preliminary hearing** is the initial preadjudicatory hearing in which the judge decides if the case should be further processed. The judge reviews the intake officer's report and consults with the probation officer on the particulars of the case and the juvenile's social history and circumstances. The judge must determine that the parents and juvenile understand their rights and the nature of the charges, and whether the juvenile is likely to show up for further hearings. Additionally, the judge must decide if further detention is in order, and if so, in what type of facility the juvenile should be confined. For instance, juveniles who have committed serious offenses are typically sent to a secure detention facility similar to jail, and juveniles charged with status offenses or who need protection may go to foster homes. In large jurisdictions with heavy caseloads, the judge may be assisted by a court referee who will hear the less serious cases and make recommendations to the judge. At this stage, in some cases where there is conflict with the parents or the parents aren't available, the judge will appoint a guardian *ad litem* to represent the juvenile's interests.

ADJUDICATORY HEARING

The **adjudicatory hearing** is similar to a criminal trial, with one major difference: there is no jury. Only in the rarest cases are juries used in juvenile court, and it's the judge who decides on the issue of culpability. Guilt and innocence aren't as important in juvenile court as they are in criminal court. The juvenile could be factually innocent of the charges, or the state might not present a convincing case, but the juvenile still may be placed in further detention. For example, in a case in which the judge decides the youth's home environment is dangerous or unsuitable, or the youth is in danger of becoming a serious delinquent, the judge might decide not to wait until the youth commits a serious offense before intervening. In 2007, juveniles were adjudicated delinquent in 63 percent of petitioned cases.[21]

The judge has the latitude to craft solutions that are in the best interests of the juvenile and society regardless of what happens in the hearing.[22] However, the judge is concerned that the allegations be based on fact, and will apply one of two standards of proof:

1. For status-offense cases, the judge will look for a **preponderance of evidence**. This is a fairly low standard that allows the judge to weigh the evidence and decide on the case if it's believed the juvenile likely committed the offense or needs supervision.

2. In cases in which the juvenile is accused of a delinquent act that would be considered a criminal offense for an adult, the standard of proof is **beyond a reasonable doubt**. As in the criminal court, this standard ensures that there is convincing evidence that the juvenile committed the offense. The juvenile is given an opportunity to admit or deny the charges, and the juvenile's lawyer may engage in plea bargaining to get a reduced disposition. If the juvenile denies the charges, the judge will consider the facts of the case and render a finding of fact stating that the court believes that the juvenile committed the offense or needs supervision.

Once the judge is convinced that a case is serious enough to warrant further processing, a **predispositional report** is ordered. The probation officer prepares this report to aid the judge in fashioning an appropriate disposition. Depending on the resources and the seriousness of the case, a great deal of information may be gathered and analyzed in the predispositional report, but basically two types of information are used:

1. **Legal.** The probation officer reviews the circumstances of the delinquency, such as what offenses were committed, the presence of co-defendants, victim input, and any aggravating or mitigating circumstances. Also included in the legal section is a review of any past delinquency, including the type and seriousness of the behavior, the disposition of the case, and whether there is a pattern of increasing seriousness of delinquency.

2. **Social history and present circumstances.** Information is collected on the parents, siblings, educational success and failure, use of alcohol or drugs, mental health problems, and housing situation. Depending on the case, the predispositional report will delve into every conceivable factor in order for the judge to get a clear picture of the juvenile so that problems can be corrected and a plan constructed that will allow the juvenile to thrive.[23]

DISPOSITIONAL HEARING

The **dispositional hearing** can take place weeks after the adjudicatory hearing while the probation officer prepares the predispositional report. In the dispositional hearing, the juvenile court specifies what should be done with the juvenile. In 2007, formal probation was the most severe disposition ordered in 56 percent of the cases. Twenty-five percent of youths adjudicated delinquent were ordered to residential placement as the most severe disposition. The rest of the cases received some other disposition.[24]

In criminal court, the sentence details the offender's punishment, but in the juvenile court, the disposition is designed to help the juvenile. Although a delinquent who is sent to a secure detention facility may perceive the disposition as punishment, this isn't the intent. Sometimes it's believed that removing the youth from society and locking him or her up is the best way to correct the delinquency. However, the court's philosophy is to assist the juvenile in developing good behavior, not to punish bad behavior. Sometimes this distinction isn't appreciated by the juvenile who is behind bars.[25]

In the dispositional hearing, the juvenile court specifies what should be done with the juvenile.

One study of juvenile court dispositions found that six factors tend to predict decisions to commit a juvenile to a secure facility:

» the number of prior complaints

» being black

» being young (older juveniles with serious cases are likely to be transferred to criminal court)

» living in foster care

» having a father who was or is incarcerated

» a court assessment of the family as dysfunctional

According to the study, these factors relate to court officials' ideas of what is a "good" family and what is a "bad" family and, ultimately, to their assessments of whether the family can care for, supervise, and control the juvenile. An especially important factor is race: black juveniles were more likely than white juveniles to be removed from the home (see Focus on Diversity). Another particularly important factor is the incarceration of fathers, but not of mothers, possibly because of the greater effect (in the eyes of court officials) on family financial stability.[26]

Jury Trials and Plea Bargaining

Jury trials and **plea bargaining** for juveniles are two procedures that account for how culpability is decided in the juvenile court. Juveniles don't have a constitutional right to a jury trial, but some states allow it under certain conditions. Plea bargaining can be considered a necessary evil because, although it sometimes appears to thwart justice, it helps move a large number of cases through court.

JURY TRIAL

There are good reasons to allow a juvenile a jury trial. The most significant one concerns the juvenile's potential loss of freedom if convicted. The Sixth Amendment specifies that citizens charged with an offense be allowed an impartial jury. Although juveniles don't have all the rights of adults, contested cases may either be waived to criminal court for a jury trial or receive one in the juvenile court. In both cases, the juvenile's due process rights are enhanced by the procedures inherent in a jury trial.[27] Some of the reasoning for a jury trial for juveniles is articulated in the dissenting opinion of Justice William Douglas in *McKeiver v. Pennsylvania* (see Case in Point 13.1).

» **Equal protection.** Equal protection under the law shouldn't exclude juveniles. In cases of serious felonies, in which the juvenile can be deprived of freedom, the court considers a jury trial to be part of equal protection.

» **Traumatic experiences.** One reason juveniles have been denied jury trials is that it was presumed the trial could be a traumatic experience. In a dissenting opinion, Justice Douglas remarked, "The fact is that the problems which are now followed in juvenile cases are far more traumatic than the potential experience of a jury trial. Who can say that a boy who is arrested and handcuffed, placed in a lineup, transported in vehicles designed to convey dangerous criminals, placed in the same kind of cell as an adult, deprived of his freedom by lodging him in an institution where he is subject to be transferred to the state's prison and in the 'hole' has not undergone a traumatic experience?"

Compound Risk

A government study reveals some troubling figures regarding how the court treats black juveniles versus white juveniles.

》 In 2007, black juveniles were referred to juvenile court 140 percent more often, and the rate at which the referred cases were petitioned was 12 percent greater for black youth.

》 The cases of black juveniles were waived to criminal court 9 percent more often.

》 Black youths were ordered into residential placement 27 percent more often, but received probation 14 percent less often.[1]

It appears that black juveniles are treated more harshly in the juvenile court system. What's going on? According to one study, large caseloads and other complicating factors mean that court staff must quickly assess cases using limited information. This forces court staff to use "shortcuts" that may result in intentional or unintentional discrimination. For example, staff will categorize juveniles who share surnames, or ethnic or racial origins. These shortcuts can appear to be racially based. Other shortcuts may be based on the juvenile's attitude, physical appearance, and the quality of family support. Sometimes, what may look like racial discrimination may actually be an effort by court workers to provide minority juveniles with resources.[2]

Although the effect of such shortcuts may be slight, it may contribute to something called "compound risk." This means that although racism may be slight, even unintended, at every stage of the system, these incidences compound. If police take proportionately more black juveniles than white juveniles into custody, then more black juveniles than white juveniles may be petitioned. Ultimately, more black juveniles than white juveniles in the system means proportionately more are at risk of being sent to criminal court or adjudicated delinquent.[3]

THINK ABOUT IT

1. Discuss ways to prevent or lessen racism within the juvenile court system.
2. In your opinion, what can be done about compound risk?

[1]Benjamin Adams and Sean Addie, "Delinquency Cases Waived to Criminal Court, 2007," OJJDP Fact Sheet (Washington, DC: US Department of Justice, Office of Justice Programs, Office of Juvenile Justice and Delinquency Prevention, 2010), 2. Online at www.ncjrs.gov/pdffiles1/ojjdp/230167.pdf.
[2]Stephanie K. Matsumura, "Justice for All? How Race Influences the Intake Process in Juvenile Court," *Dissertation Abstracts International* Section A, 2010.
[3]Samuel Walker, Cassia Spohn, and Miriam DeLone, *The Color of Justice: Race, Ethnicity, and Crime in America* (Belmont, California: Thomson Wadsworth, 2007), 394–395.

》 **Case backlog.** One reason most states don't provide jury trials for juveniles is because it would hold up the flow of cases. Justice Douglas argued that "the very argument of expediency, suggesting 'supermarket' or 'assembly-line' justice is one of the most forceful arguments in favor of granting jury trials. It will provide a safeguard against the judge who may be prejudiced against a minority group or who may be prejudiced against the juvenile

13.1   CASE IN POINT

THE CASE

McKeiver v. Pennsylvania (1971)

THE POINT

Juveniles have no constitutional right to a jury trial during adjudication in a state juvenile court delinquency proceeding.

In May 1968, Joseph McKeiver, 16, was charged with robbery, larceny, and receiving stolen goods as acts of juvenile delinquency. McKeiver was represented by counsel during the adjudication hearing. The court denied his request for a jury trial, and McKeiver was adjudicated delinquent in juvenile court and placed on probation. The state superior court later affirmed the decision.

In January 1969, Edward Terry, 15, was charged with assault and battery on a police officer and conspiracy as acts of juvenile delinquency. As with McKeiver, the court denied Terry's request for a jury trial, and Terry was adjudicated delinquent. Terry was committed to a juvenile institution. The state superior court later affirmed the decision.

The two cases were consolidated for the purposes of appeal and for the consideration of the question of "whether there is a constitutional right to a jury trial in juvenile court." The US Supreme Court held that "trial by jury in the juvenile court's adjudicative stage is not a constitutional requirement."

brought before him because of some past occurrence which was heard by the same judge."

» **Jury of peers.** A fair jury trial means that the jury comprises one's peers. But what, exactly, does a "jury of peers" mean? Should a juvenile have only other juveniles on the jury? Should a teenage female delinquent have only teenage females? Would a youth charged with delinquent behavior get a fair hearing from a 16-year-old who hasn't had a US history class? Should juveniles be subject to jury duty just like adults? These are interesting questions that complicate the task of providing jury trials for juveniles. However, a "jury of peers" simply means that no one is systematically excluded. The local and federal jury pools are selected from the voting rolls, so anyone who votes is eligible to serve on a jury. In some cases, this might mean the gender or racial composition of the jury doesn't reflect the local population, but this is permissible as long as there is no systematic exclusion. In the case of juvenile delinquents, there is the potential for 18-year-old voters to be placed on the jury along with everyone else. For the purposes of jury selection, "peers" is defined simply as citizens, and no one has a right to a jury that looks like them, has had the same life experiences, or has the same political or religious tastes.

» **Public trial.** Juvenile proceedings are generally held in closed-door sessions for the juvenile's protection and privacy. Justice Douglas argued that juvenile proceedings are far from private. In fact, witnesses for both the prosecution and the defense, social workers, court reporters, students, police trainees, probation counselors, and sheriffs are present in the courtroom. Further, the police, armed forces, and FBI have access to the court and police records. Having a public trial, therefore, wouldn't destroy confidentiality any more than the exceptions that already exist, according to Justice Douglas.[28]

The Supreme Court has stopped short of requiring jury trials for all jurisdictions and allows the states to decide the matter. The State of California has set forth two main reasons why the Supreme Court should resist making the juvenile court identical to the criminal court. First, the juvenile already has the right to waive his or her juvenile rights and go to criminal court and enjoy more procedural safeguards. Second, if the Supreme Court wanted to extend all due process rights to juveniles, it would have to consider giving precise definitions to terms such as "neglect," "abuse," "dependent," and "delinquent." The discretion and informality enjoyed by the juvenile court can accommodate the vagueness in these terms, but they would become contentious in the criminal court. The State of California, therefore, has decided that how and when jury trials are used for juveniles should be encoded in state law rather than decided on a case-by-case basis by judges.[29]

PLEA BARGAINING

Although it would be preferable to give each case the time, attention, and resources required to bring it to a satisfying resolution, the sheer number of cases in both the criminal court and the juvenile court makes this goal impossible.[30] Other mechanisms must be found to control the vast number of cases that enter the system. One way might be to limit the scope of the criminal law and make permissible some currently illegal behaviors that don't constitute a threat to public safety. Drug laws are continually being placed under public scrutiny because of all the precious prison space being taken up by those who use or deal drugs but haven't actually hurt anyone. Other offenders in victimless crimes might also be handled by institutions other than the criminal or juvenile justice systems. But this solution to limit the scope of the law is a political one that would require legislative action. The juvenile justice system can't unilaterally make the decision that it isn't going to respond to certain cases. Therefore, plea bargaining occurs at two points in the juvenile court:

» **Intake.** The intake officer has broad discretion in deciding what charges to bring against the juvenile. Because up to half of the cases brought to the court never make it past the intake officer, it's evident that important decisions are being made at this crucial stage of the process. In looking at the circumstances of the case, the intake officer is concerned with making a recommendation that fits the juvenile court's philosophy. The intake officer usually isn't qualified to determine the quality of the legal evidence against the juvenile and is instead focused on deciding what interventions are best, rather than factual guilt or innocence. The intake officer can reduce the charges or divert the case to a community-based agency. This is the stage where drug treatment, restitution, or any of a number of other sanctions can be pressed on the juvenile and parents to avoid filing a petition. Parents who insist on pressing the facts of the case are warned that handling the case in a more formal manner could result in a more severe sanction. However, one study has shown that those who contest the charges actually end up with lighter sanctions than those who acquiesce to the intake officer.[31]

» **Adjudication and disposition.** Once a petition is filed and the case brought before the juvenile court judge, plea bargaining takes on a whole new and different urgency for the juvenile and parents. Defense lawyers are aware of how serious it is to have the juvenile adjudicated delinquent and will attempt to strike a deal with the prosecutor to reduce the charges and avoid the stigma.[32] For example, in cases involving sexual misconduct, the defense lawyer will try to get the prosecutor to agree to a plea bargain to charges that won't expose the youth to sex-offender laws that could affix a label perhaps carried for life. Both the defense lawyer and the prosecutor have an interest in plea bargaining. The defense lawyer wants the most lenient sanction possible, while the prosecutor wants to impose a sanction that doesn't require a great deal of time or effort. The prosecutor must push a big caseload through the system, so as long as the case can be counted as a "win," the prosecutor isn't interested in holding out for the most severe sentence. Both the defense lawyer and the prosecutor are looking for ways to claim that they didn't lose a case, and the compromise inherent in the plea bargain allows each of them to claim this type of victory.[33]

Although the juvenile can benefit from a plea bargain in terms of reduced charges or reduced punishment, there is concern about this type of negotiated justice. What gets lost is the *parens patriae* objective of looking out for the youth's best interests. When juvenile justice is reduced to a zero-sum game between the defense lawyer and the prosecutor, the most basic and underlying idea of the juvenile court is forfeited. As stated by one justice in *In re Gault* (see Case in Point 13.2), the child gets the worst of both the juvenile and the criminal justice systems. To compensate for the juvenile court's informality, reformers have concentrated on introducing more due process into the management of juvenile delinquents.

Due Process

Giving juveniles the constitutional right to due process is a controversial issue. Doing so changes the atmosphere and philosophy of the court from one in which

---

13.2 CASE IN POINT

THE CASE

In re Gault (1967)

THE POINT

The US Supreme Court established juveniles' right to an attorney, right to confront accusors, and protection from self-incrimination.

In 1964, Gerald Gault, 15, and another boy were accused of making an obscene telephone call to a female neighbor. Gault was arrested without the knowledge of his parents, who were both at work, and questioned by police at the jail. He was held in detention for four or five days, then released to his parents. In the court proceedings, Gault was not allowed to cross-examine his accuser, who was never present, or to testify on his own behalf, nor was he advised of his rights. He was sentenced to the Arizona State Industrial School until he was 21. No appeal was permitted in juvenile cases in Arizona at that time. In 1967, the Supreme Court reversed the decision on appeal and established that juveniles have a right to an attorney, a right to confront accusers, and a right to protection from self-incrimination.

In this 1967 photo, Gerald Gault, then age 18, studies automotive and heavy equipment operation.

juvenile justice officials collaborate in deciding how the juvenile might best be rehabilitated to one that is more adversarial. This treatment model is contrasted with the due process model, which results in often contentious adversarial proceedings in which the judge sits as a neutral party while the prosecution and defense lawyers battle to win the case.

Juveniles enjoy due process rights comparable to those of adults only in adjudicatory proceedings. Although many states don't provide for a trial by jury, other rights are expected in the juvenile court. For example, the prosecution must, if requested, share evidence with the defense lawyer that is favorable to the juvenile's case. Exculpatory evidence that shows the juvenile defendant wasn't at the scene of the offense or didn't have knowledge that co-defendants were planning a robbery can't be hidden from the defense. Due process is concerned with fundamental fairness and stems from the Fourteenth Amendment.

The question for the juvenile justice system is, how universal are due process protections when dealing with youths? Juvenile rights are an evolving matter as the courts continually struggle with squaring the philosophies of the juvenile court with those of the Constitution. The court has left it to the states to decide what level of due process is given to juveniles at many points in the proceedings of the juvenile justice system. Although juveniles are allowed many due process rights in the adjudicatory hearing, there are other decision-making points in the system where their rights are unclear and subject to interpretation by judges and state legislatures. For example, in deciding the revocation of probation or a disciplinary action in a secure institution, the juvenile won't enjoy exactly the same due process rights as an adult in a similar situation.

Until 1967, the US Supreme Court maintained a hands-off policy toward the juvenile justice system. It wasn't until the landmark case *In re Gault* that the Supreme Court ruled that juveniles should have four constitutional rights if curtailment of their freedom was possible:

1. Right to a lawyer
2. Protection against self-incrimination
3. Right to notice of charges
4. Right to confront and cross-examine witnesses

In cases involving offenses where incarceration isn't likely, the Supreme Court has allowed the juvenile court to proceed without giving the juvenile the benefit of these four due process rights.

RIGHT TO A LAWYER

There is an old saying in legal circles that anyone who acts as his own lawyer is a fool. When one is a principal party in a case, one loses objectivity and can't make decisions in one's own best interest. It's better to enlist a professional who not only knows the law but can argue the case without seeming to be acting out of self-interest. For example, when lawyers are accused of criminal offenses or sued, they hire other lawyers to represent them. In the juvenile court, self-representation is also a concern. A juvenile doesn't have the legal training, the self-awareness, or the emotional temperament to provide an adequate defense. Additionally, parents lack objectivity and intimate knowledge of juvenile justice system proceedings. To protect the juvenile's liberty, the Supreme Court has ruled in several cases that a lawyer may be retained to present the youth in the best possible light and to challenge the state's case.

However, there are some concerns with how the juvenile's right to a lawyer is applied.[34] The key issue is whether the juvenile could be incarcerated. In the case of serious delinquency, a lawyer for the juvenile is fairly standard. In less serious cases, in which the judge doesn't anticipate placing the youth in a detention facility, the proceedings might be conducted in a less adversarial manner without the juvenile being represented by counsel. However, some critics believe that abused and neglected children, especially in cases involving parental rights, need legal representation to ensure that their best interests are met.

The juvenile may also waive the right to a lawyer. Again, this happens in minor cases in which the intake officer or judge convinces the juvenile and parents that a less serious disposition is imminent and that securing a lawyer will delay the proceedings, cost money, and make the whole thing more adversarial. While stopping short of coercing the juvenile and parents with threats of more severe treatment by the court, the suggestion that a lawyer isn't needed can place subtle pressure on the juvenile and parents to waive this right. One study found that 80 to 90 percent of juveniles waive their right to counsel because they simply don't understand the consequences of waiving this right or even what the term "waive" means.[35]

The Supreme Court specified in *Gault* that juveniles have the right to be represented by a lawyer at the adjudicatory stage of the proceeding when there is a possibility of curtailed freedom. This leaves the juvenile's right to a lawyer greatly limited when compared to the rights of adults to be represented by a lawyer at "every critical stage of the case." For example, we have already discussed the substantial discretion enjoyed by the intake officer in deciding which cases are inserted into the juvenile justice system and which cases are adjusted or dismissed. This is a crucial stage of the proceedings that juveniles seldom benefit from as they are often not made aware of their right to a lawyer. Because so many cases get informally plea bargained at intake, a lawyer can be of tremendous value to the juvenile at this critical point.

Some parents can afford private lawyers, some private lawyers are appointed by the juvenile court judge based on a rotation system, and some larger jurisdictions have public defender offices that represent indigent clients. Juveniles without the financial resources to hire a lawyer are deemed to be indigent (poor) and can have a lawyer appointed by the court. However, all jurisdictions don't evaluate indigence in the same way. Judges consider many factors to determine if a juvenile or his or her family can afford to retain counsel. Are the parents employed? Do they own a house? What are the family's financial obligations? These considerations all go into the judge's decision on declaring a family indigent and thus having the state provide a lawyer.

Once the juvenile has a lawyer, the court proceedings might alter the traditional lawyer-client relationship. Although a lawyer is a zealous advocate for the client in criminal court, the philosophy of the juvenile court alters the lawyer's role. There is a tendency to look out for the juvenile's best interests, even when this might mean subjecting him or her to sanctions. For instance, when a juvenile needs drug rehabilitation, the defense lawyer might be persuaded to go along with this recommendation even though the state's case is weak. The defense lawyer is subtly influenced by the court to shift in occupational role from being a bulldog in defense of the juvenile's rights to being a surrogate family member or social worker involved in getting the youth into a physically and socially healthy environment.[36]

PROTECTION AGAINST SELF-INCRIMINATION

Another constitutional right guaranteed to adults is the right against self-incrimination. This means that a defendant doesn't have to answer questions that could be used as evidence against him or her in a criminal case. The protection against self-incrimination stems from language in the Fifth Amendment that states, "nor shall be compelled in any criminal case to be a witness against himself." The Supreme Court extended this privilege to juveniles because it deems the protection to be unequivocal and without exception. Again, as in other rights granted to juveniles, the Supreme Court ruled that this protection against self-incrimination applies only to the adjudicatory stage of the juvenile court proceedings. The protection against self-incrimination protects both adults and juveniles in two ways:

1. **Privilege of the accused.** A person doesn't have to testify in a criminal case in which he or she is the defendant. Additionally, this choice not to testify can't be used by the prosecution to impugn the defendant's integrity or motives. By this, we mean the prosecutor can't say to the jury (or to the judge in a bench or juvenile trial), "If the defendant is truly innocent, why doesn't he take the stand and proclaim so? His silence betrays his guilt." If the juvenile does take the stand, however, he or she must answer questions truthfully, and the right against self-incrimination is forfeited. Further, the prosecution may then cross-examine the juvenile, who must answer hostile questions even if the answers are incriminating.

2. **Privilege of a witness.** Witnesses can be subpoenaed to appear before the court and required to answer questions from the prosecutor and the defense lawyer. However, if the answer to a question would implicate the witness in a criminal offense, he or she can refuse to testify. This protection against self-incrimination is extended to witnesses because they aren't the ones on trial and don't have the advantage of being prepared for the case and having a lawyer to look out for their rights. However, this protection is limited to criminal liability. The protection from self-incrimination doesn't apply to issues of civil liability or the possibility of shame or disgrace.[37]

For instance, if a teenage boy is testifying as a friendly witness for a friend accused of an offense, the boy would have to admit that he'd snuck out of the house at night, even though he might get in trouble with his parents.

RIGHT TO NOTICE OF CHARGES

To properly defend yourself in a criminal case, you have to know what you are accused of. The right to notice of charges stipulates that the state has to provide you with written notice of the exact offenses or behaviors you are alleged to have committed. Further, this notice has to be provided far enough ahead of time so that you can prepare the case, research your alibi, and identify supporting witnesses.

For example, if the state accused me of stealing diamonds from a large department store in New York City at noon on July 21, 2011, I would need time to check my daily planner so I could show that at that particular time I was actually at home in another state writing these very words. Further, I might be able to produce the credit card statements showing I bought gasoline for my car, food for my cat, and a dozen new golf balls for the water hazards on my local golf course. Without the advance written notice of the particular charges against me, I might not remember the events of this day or my whereabouts.

RIGHT TO CONFRONT AND CROSS-EXAMINE WITNESSES

The fourth due process right extended to juveniles from *In re Gault* is the right to confront and cross-examine hostile witnesses. This means that the state must produce the witnesses in the courtroom, and they must testify to the facts of the case so the juvenile and his or her lawyer can hear exactly how specific the testimony against the juvenile is. It's one thing to report misbehavior to the police, and an entirely different experience to testify under oath in the courtroom about the particulars of what you have seen and heard concerning the juvenile's alleged misconduct. The certainty of one's beliefs and opinions is scrutinized when testifying, and the state must rely on what is said in the courtroom, rather than interpret what is in the police report.

As the prosecutor builds the case by questioning witnesses, the defense lawyer has the opportunity to ask questions that can show inconsistencies in the testimony, devious motivations of the witnesses, or the incompetence of expert witnesses. For example, when someone testifies as an expert witness, the defense lawyer, who wants to demonstrate the witness's lack of qualifications, often challenges the witness's credentials. It's considered a matter of basic fairness to subject accusatory witnesses to cross-examination. When witnesses are instructed to directly answer the prosecutor's questions and not to volunteer additional insights, it matters what questions are asked, how the questions are asked, and what questions aren't asked. The defense lawyer can give the court a better picture of the witness's believability by asking questions that shed a more favorable light on the juvenile's activities.

PROTECTION AGAINST DOUBLE JEOPARDY

Protection against double jeopardy states that no one can be tried twice for the same offense. If a criminal defendant is accused of a serious offense and acquitted by a jury, then, even if further evidence is discovered, this person can't be brought to criminal trial again on the same charges. If this were the case, it would open the door for the state to keep trying the case until it won. The protection against double jeopardy doesn't mean the state can't appeal the case if there was some technical error or irregularity, but in doing so the state is limited to evidence and issues uncovered in the original case. This is why the prosecution must be careful that it has a strong case before filing charges.

In 1975, the Supreme Court extended the protection against double jeopardy to juveniles in *Breed v. Jones* (see Case in Point 13.3). In this case, a juvenile, Jones, was adjudicated delinquent in a juvenile court and detained. At his dispositional hearing, it was decided that Jones was not a good candidate for treatment as a juvenile, and the case was transferred to criminal court, where he was tried and found guilty of robbery.

Eventually, the Supreme Court found that the state had had its opportunity to contend the case and that sending him to criminal court to be tried as an adult violated the juvenile's Fifth Amendment protection against double jeopardy. The result of *Breed v. Jones* is that if the state wishes to prosecute a juvenile in criminal court, it must do so before the adjudicatory hearing.[38]

CONFIDENTIALITY AND ACCOUNTABILITY

As the juvenile justice system becomes more legalistic and adversarial, it's also becoming more open to public scrutiny. This is further evidence of the strain on the traditional juvenile justice philosophy of *parens patriae*. Before the 1990s, juvenile court proceedings were relatively closed and the circumstances of cases kept from the public and the press. The idea, based on labeling theory (see Chapter 5), was to involve only those who had an interest in the case, so the juvenile's reputation wasn't damaged. The danger of this stigma, it was believed, was that it would become a self-fulfilling prophecy: the youth would come to believe that the negative label accurately reflected his or her character.

13.3 CASE IN POINT

THE CASE

Breed v. Jones (1975)

THE POINT

Trying a juvenile as an adult for an offense that has already been adjudicated in juvenile court constitutes double jeopardy.

In February 1971, Jones, age 17, was accused of committing robbery armed with a deadly weapon. A juvenile court found that Jones had violated a criminal statute and should be detained pending a hearing. At a March hearing, the juvenile court took testimony from two witnesses for the prosecution, as well as from Jones, and determined that Jones had committed robbery with a deadly weapon.

At a subsequent hearing, the juvenile court determined that Jones was "unfit for treatment as a juvenile" and should be prosecuted as an adult. The superior court found Jones guilty of first-degree robbery and ordered him committed to the California Youth Authority. Jones, who had pled not guilty, argued that he had already been adjudicated in the juvenile court and that the criminal trial placed him in double jeopardy.

The case went to the Supreme Court, which ruled that Jones was indeed put in jeopardy at the juvenile court adjudicatory hearing, because the object of that hearing was to determine if Jones had committed acts that violated criminal law. The potential consequences of that finding included "the deprivation of liberty for many years."

The Supreme Court set forth that prosecution as an adult in criminal court after adjudication in the juvenile court for the same offense violates the Fifth Amendment double-jeopardy clause as applied to the states through the Fourteenth Amendment.

Under this philosophy, if an adult defendant had a juvenile record, this record wasn't available to the jury deciding the adult's case. So, on their first adult arrest, 18-year-olds with extensive juvenile delinquent histories were treated as first-time offenders. Many criminal justice administrators and citizens objected to ignoring juvenile delinquent histories and moved to make the juveniles' contact with authorities more open and transparent.

In addition to making juvenile records more available to criminal justice officials, such as law enforcement officers, some states also open large portions of juveniles' official files to the public and press, as well as to insurance companies that are asked to pay for juvenile delinquents' mental health or drug treatment. Similarly, hearings are increasingly opened to the public and press. At issue is a balancing of values. The protection of the delinquent's privacy is weighed against the public's right to know. Accountability is considered desirable all across society's institutions, and the juvenile justice system is evaluated on how well it meets the needs of its charges and how it responds to delinquent behavior. Privacy is sacrificed for accountability, which might not be a bad thing. Openness allows scrutiny, which allows for reform. This is a path that US society has taken for the past decade, and it's unlikely the juvenile court's secrecy and confidentiality will be reinstated at any time in the foreseeable future.[39]

Questions

1. Compare and contrast custody and arrest.

2. What are the three types of hearings?

3. What is the difference between "preponderance of evidence" and "beyond a reasonable doubt"?

4. What is plea bargaining? At what points does it occur?

Trying Juveniles as Adults

Some juveniles commit such serious offenses, they're tried in criminal court. This process exposes the youth to a more severe sanction but also allows for the full range of constitutional rights normally afforded to adult defendants. The process for sending juveniles to criminal court is different from state to state, so there is no nationwide, uniform procedure. Basically, the discretion to waive a case to criminal court is vested in one of three places: the judge, the prosecutor, or the legislature. All states try juveniles as adults. The three types of provisions for this are **judicial waiver**, **direct filing**, and **statutory exclusion**.

Judicial Waiver. A judge is responsible for sending the juvenile to criminal court. In 2007, juvenile courts handled 1.7 million delinquency cases, with 56 percent of those handled formally, meaning that a petition was filed requesting an adjudication or waiver hearing. Of those, less than 1 percent were waived to criminal court: for every 1,000 petitioned delinquency cases, 9 were waived to criminal court. Since 1994, the number of such cases declined 35 percent, to about 8,500 cases in 2007.[40] Cases involving males were more likely to be waived than those involving females.[41]

The drop in judicial waivers can be attributed to the decline in juvenile violent offending and to the increase in laws that send some cases directly to criminal court (see statutory exclusion, below).[42] It's estimated that between 20 and 25 percent of all suspects younger than 18 are prosecuted in adult court because they meet the criteria for their cases to be sent there directly, one of which is age.[43] In 2007, 16-year-olds were under the original jurisdiction of the criminal court in three states (Connecticut, New York, and North Carolina), as were 17-year-olds in ten states (Georgia, Illinois, Louisiana, Massachusetts, Michigan, Missouri, New Hampshire, South Carolina, Texas, and Wisconsin).[44]

Some juveniles commit such
serious offenses they're tried
in criminal court. Defendant
Nicholas Lindsey, 16, who was
accused of fatally shooting a
police officer in 2011 is being
tried as an adult on a first-
degree murder charge.

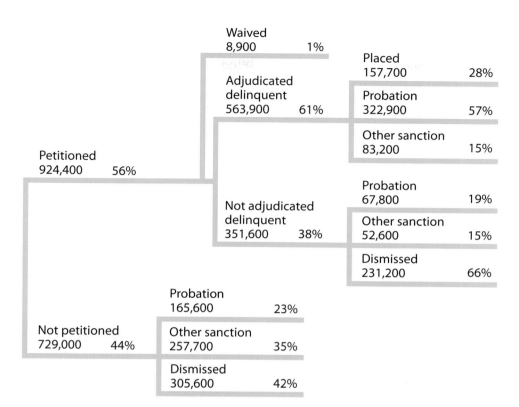

Waived
8,900   1%

Placed
157,700   28%

Adjudicated
delinquent
563,900   61%

Probation
322,900   57%

Other sanction
83,200   15%

Petitioned
924,400   56%

Probation
67,800   19%

Not adjudicated
delinquent
351,600   38%

Other sanction
52,600   15%

Dismissed
231,200   66%

Probation
165,600   23%

Not petitioned
729,000   44%

Other sanction
257,700   35%

Dismissed
305,600   42%

Figure 13.2 How Delinquency Cases Flow through the System

This figure tracks how 1,653, 300 delinquency cases moved through the juvenile justice system in 2008.

Think About It

1. What happened to most of the juveniles whose cases were petitioned but who weren't adjudicated delinquent?

2. What happened to most of the juveniles whose cases were petitioned and who were adjudicated delinquent?

3. Discuss reasons that a juvenile's case may not be petitioned, but the juvenile still receives a sanction.

Source: Crystal Knoll and Melissa Sickmund, Delinquency Cases in Juvenile Court, 2008 (Washington, DC: U.S. Department of Justice Office of Justice Programs Office of Juvenile Justice and Delinquency Prevention, 2011), 4. Online at www. ojjdp.gov/pubs/236479.pdf.

The three types of judicial waiver are mandatory, presumptive, and discretionary.

》 Discretionary waiver—Transfer of the juvenile to adult court is at the judge's discretion.

》 Mandatory waiver—The youth's age and the seriousness of the offense invokes automatic transfer to criminal court.

》 Presumptive waiver—The burden of proof shifts from the state to the juvenile, who must contest the transfer to criminal court.

Direct Filing. This is also called "concurrent jurisdiction." A prosecutor has the discretion to file charges in either juvenile or adult court.

Statutory Exclusion. This is also called "legislative waiver," because it comes from state legislatures and doesn't require a juvenile court hearing. Statutory exclusion automatically excludes juveniles who commit certain, serious offenses from juvenile court and sends them directly to criminal court. Offenses that may invoke statutory exclusion include murder and aggravated rape. Some states also use statutory exclusion for minor violations such as traffic, fish-and-game, and some local ordinances.

Because each state has its own mechanisms for **juvenile waiver**, blanket statements are difficult to make. However, some issues must be confronted. To give jurisdiction to the criminal court, the juvenile court's responsibility must be terminated. This is done in many courts with a waiver hearing. The waiver hearing is typically requested by the prosecutor to show good reasons for waiving the case to criminal court. Essentially, four issues must be decided:

1. **Age.** Most states have some lower age limit at which the juvenile cannot be waived to criminal court. For instance, in Virginia, the juvenile must be 14 or older. Those under 14, regardless of the offense, will remain under the jurisdiction of the juvenile court. It's fair to say that the older the juvenile is, the more likely the case will be considered for waiver.

2. **Seriousness of the offense.** Minor offenses are not sufficient reason to waive a juvenile's case. The offense must be something that would be a major offense if committed by an adult. For this reason, status offenses are never transferred to criminal court. Similar offenses that are considered misdemeanors start under the jurisdiction of the juvenile court. Offenses such as murder or rape may get waived to the criminal court, and usually these must have some aggravating factor. In sensational cases, the prosecutor is under public scrutiny to show that the justice system is sufficiently tough on crime, regardless of the offender's age.

3. **Probable cause.** The standard of proof needed to waive a juvenile to criminal court is low. There need not be proof beyond a reasonable doubt to waive the case to criminal court, although this standard is required to convict. Because a waiver hearing doesn't qualify as a trial in which the juvenile could lose his or her freedom, the standard of proof is lowered to "preponderance of evidence" or "clear and convincing." Further, illegally seized evidence can be admitted into the hearing to waive the case to the criminal court although that evidence might not be admissible in a criminal trial.

4. **Amenability to treatment.** In deciding whether to waive a serious case, the juvenile court judge will consider the likelihood that the juvenile would benefit from treatment in the juvenile justice setting. Because the youth's best interests are foremost in the juvenile court philosophy, a reasoned consideration as to whether the juvenile could benefit from one last chance at rehabilitation is appropriate. The judge must ask if all the resources of the juvenile justice system have been tried and whether there is good reason to suspect that the youth can be rehabilitated. However, amenability to treatment receives less serious consideration as the charge becomes more severe. For some particularly heinous offenses, waiver to the criminal system is a foregone conclusion even if the juvenile is a first-time defendant. In states without statutory exclusion, serious cases require a hearing. A prosecutor might examine the juvenile's delinquency record (if any), then make the argument that past treatment efforts have been unsuccessful and the only way to protect the public is to transfer the case to criminal court. If a juvenile has had extensive involvement with the juvenile justice system, treatment programs might no longer be willing to take the case.

A juvenile whose case goes to criminal court faces serious implications. On the positive side is the certainty of receiving all the constitutional rights generally afforded to adults. This means the juvenile will receive a trial by jury in which the prosecutor must prove beyond a reasonable doubt that the juvenile committed the offense. However, along with constitutional rights comes the prospect of long-term incarceration in adult facilities. Although juvenile delinquents are separated from adult offenders, adult institutions are more focused on punishment than on treatment and rehabilitation. Until recently, having a serious case waived to criminal court has exposed the juvenile to the death penalty. (This issue will be considered in greater detail in Chapter 14.) Also, most states have "once an adult, always an adult" requirements. In over half of the states, juveniles who are tried and convicted as adults will continue to be tried as adults for subsequent offenses.[45]

Is juvenile waiver effective at controlling delinquency and more serious offenses committed by juveniles? According to one study, juvenile lawbreaking is no lower in states that try more juveniles as adults, and juveniles who were tried as adults are no less likely to **recidivate** than youths who went through the juvenile court system. In fact, studies comparing juveniles released from adult facilities with those released from juvenile facilities find that those released from adult facilities are actually more likely to recidivate.[46]

Another concern is the treatment of juveniles in criminal court. A study found that juveniles tried in criminal court receive harsher dispositions than young adults tried for similar offenses. For example, juveniles in criminal court for drug offenses received sentences more than six times as severe as the ones young adults received for similar drug offenses. So, a 17-year-old drug offender would be 10 percent more likely than an 18-year-old drug offender to be not only incarcerated, but also incarcerated for about one year longer.[47]

INSTANT RECALL
FROM CHAPTER 3

recidivism

Continuing to commit delinquent or criminal offenses after being convicted and sentenced for prior offenses.

Blended Sentencing

A juvenile who is convicted in a criminal court is likely to receive an adult sentence, and a juvenile who receives a disposition in a juvenile court usually ends up with a juvenile sentence. However, in special cases, courts find it necessary to use **blended sentencing**, which has features of both. There are five types of blended sentences:

- » **Juvenile exclusive.** The case is adjudicated in a juvenile court, but the court may impose a disposition involving either the juvenile or criminal correctional system, but not both.

- » **Juvenile inclusive.** The case is adjudicated in a juvenile court, but the court has the authority to impose a disposition involving both the juvenile and criminal correctional systems. Usually, the criminal sentence is suspended pending the juvenile's successful completion of the juvenile disposition.

- » **Juvenile contiguous.** The case is adjudicated in a juvenile court, but delinquents must serve a juvenile sentence and then an adult sentence once they pass the age of the juvenile court's jurisdiction (usually age 17 or 18).

- » **Criminal exclusive.** The case is tried in a criminal court, but the court may impose a sentence involving either the juvenile or criminal correctional system, but not both.

- » **Criminal inclusive.** The case is tried in a criminal court, but the court may impose a sentence involving both the juvenile and criminal correctional systems. Usually, the criminal sentence is suspended pending the juvenile's successful completion of a juvenile disposition.

Who Gets Waived to the Criminal Court?

The most recent data available demonstrate some interesting sex and racial patterns. In 2007, more male cases than female cases in each of the four general offense categories (person, property, drugs, and public order) were waived to criminal court. For example, males charged with person offenses were four times as likely as similarly charged females to get their cases waived to criminal court. Black youths were more likely than white youths to be waived to criminal court regardless of the offense category. And regardless of race, person offenses were more likely to be waived than other types of cases.[48]

There is considerable variation across jurisdictions in the patterns of who gets waived to the criminal court. Because so many factors are considered and because each case is judged on its merits in states that require waiver hearings, an attitude has developed that it would be more appropriate to remove discretion from the decision.

State legislatures have done this by specifying that certain types of offenses are waived to the criminal court without a waiver hearing. This mechanism, statutory exclusion, represents a major departure from the juvenile justice philosophy. The legislators dictate that all offenses meeting certain conditions will be heard by the criminal court regardless of the defendant's age. They want offenders to be held accountable for serious and heinous offenses. Also, legislators, who want to be reelected, feel they must answer the public outcry when a juvenile commits a sensational offense. This public pressure introduces politics into the juvenile justice system and alters the ability of judges and prosecutors to decide what is in the best interests of the juvenile and society.

Questions

1. What are the five types of blended sentencing?
2. Which four issues must be decided to waive the case to criminal court?
3. What are the three provisions for moving a juvenile case to criminal court?

>> FOCUS ON ETHICS

Goodbye to Childhood

As a juvenile court judge, you've seen it all. Over the years you've managed to do a lot of good by crafting creative, individualized sentences that have rehabilitated juveniles headed in the wrong direction. You've won awards for your forward-looking approach to justice and delinquency, and as you near retirement you're proud of your reputation and accomplishments.

Now you are confronting the case of your career, and you're perplexed as to what to do. You have before you a 15-year-old boy, born in the United States of Syrian parents, who is accused of involvement in a terrorist plot. Samir has lived in the United States his entire life but has gotten mixed up in a suspicious venture involving his distant cousins who arrived from the Middle East six months ago.

Samir's cousins have been buying hundreds of cell phones from local stores, giving Samir the cash to make the purchases. Samir's cousins told him they could sell the phones overseas at a 200 percent profit and that he would earn enough money to pay for college. Now Samir and his cousins have been arrested by local police and charged with conspiracy to commit terrorist acts. The police think the phones will be used to construct bombs that will be used overseas against US citizens and troops. The government wants you to waive the case to federal court for Samir to stand trial along with his cousins. Before you do this, however, you have some questions:

» Is this simply a case of media and government hysteria over terrorism? Buying cell phones is perfectly legal, and you've seen no evidence that the phones are intended to be used to make bombs.

» Even if the cousins were planning to make bombs, did Samir know? It's possible that Samir's cousins lied to him and that he acted in good faith.

» Samir, unlike his cousins, is a US citizen, and linking his involvement to theirs might be unfair. He might fare better if you retained jurisdiction in juvenile court and monitored his activities for the next two years. Not only has Samir had no contact with the law before this, he's an excellent student and is involved in several extracurricular activities. You worry his promising life would be ruined if his case went to federal court.

You're under tremendous pressure to waive this case to federal court. The country is hungry for some news of a successful response to terrorism, and you're feeling the political heat.

WHAT DO YOU DO?

1. Should you waive the case to the federal court? You aren't an expert on international terrorism, and the juvenile court is no place to deal with this threat. If Samir is tried as an adult in the federal court, he will get all the due process rights guaranteed to US citizens.

2. Should you maintain jurisdiction of the case in state juvenile court? As a juvenile court judge whose responsibility is to look out for the best interests of the child, you're suspicious that Samir is being railroaded for political purposes.

Summary

Summary

Learning Objective 1. Discuss the problem of juvenile court fragmentation.	States vary in how they organize jurisdictional responsibilities. There are two possible solutions to this fragmentation of juvenile court structure. The first involves coordinating the activities of the various judges dealing with the same family. A second solution is to have one judge handle all issues of a case. Change in court structures is opposed for reasons of jobs, power, and court philosophy.
Learning Objective 2. Explain the relationship of the federal government to juvenile courts.	Juvenile courts are almost exclusively a state and county responsibility. The federal government has no juvenile court or juvenile correctional system. The federal government specifies some juvenile court rules and laws, especially those dealing with status offenders. For certain offenses, such as the killing of a federal officer, offenses on a military or American Indian reservation, and violation of a federal law, the federal government may become involved under the Federal Juvenile Delinquency Act. A "substantial federal interest" must be shown in order to try a juvenile in the federal court system.
Learning Objective 3. Tell why the players in the juvenile court aren't as adversarial as those in the criminal court.	The key players in the juvenile court must work together to achieve the goals of ensuring justice, providing for the best interests of juveniles, and moving a high volume of cases through the system. The players in the juvenile court have a greatly reduced adversarial relationship, but because of their elected or appointed positions, they still may have different ideas about how to proceed in specific cases.
Learning Objective 4. Describe the typical youth whose case goes to juvenile court.	White juveniles comprised 64 percent of the cases. Juveniles younger than 16 at the time of referral accounted for 54 percent of all cases. Although more females are involved in the juvenile court than ever, they still represent a relatively small proportion of the delinquency caseload.
Learning Objective 5. Understand why the prosecutor exercised important discretion in the juvenile court after the 1960s.	Historically, cases were presented directly by police officers, school officials, or caseworkers. After the due process revolution in the 1960s, the prosecutor became a fixture in the juvenile court and has evolved into a key player who exercises important discretion.

Summary

Learning Objective 6. Discuss the relationship between the concept of *parens patriae* and the juvenile court judge.	The juvenile court judge conducts the courtroom's business and sets the tone of the proceedings. The judge embodies the *parens patriae* principle, which requires the judge to act as a surrogate parent for the juvenile to ensure that his or her best interests are addressed. In cases in which a juvenile's parents have failed to care for, protect, and control their child, the judge must make decisions that provide for the juvenile's welfare, even if it means removal from the home or placement in secure detention.
Learning Objective 7. List and explain the two roles of juvenile probation officers.	One role is to craft supervised-treatment plans for juveniles on probation. The other role is to act as an officer of the court by investigating juveniles' social backgrounds and making recommendations to the judge on appropriate dispositions.
Learning Objective 8. Compare and contrast the taking of a juvenile into custody with the arrest of an adult.	Arrest is similar to custody in that the juvenile may be taken into custody if a police officer sees a law being broken, if there is a court order, or if a complaint has been filed. Juveniles, but not adults, also may be taken into custody for their own protection in cases of abuse, neglect, or dependency.
Learning Objective 9. List and discuss the three types of juvenile court hearings.	The preliminary hearing is the initial preadjudicatory hearing in which the judge explores the case and decides if it should be further processed. The adjudicatory hearing is similar to a criminal trial except that there is no jury. Juries are rarely used in juvenile court, and it's the judge who decides on the issue of culpability. In the dispositional hearing, the juvenile court specifies what should be done with the juvenile. This hearing can occur weeks after the adjudicatory hearing while the probation officer prepares the predispositional report.
Learning Objective 10. Compare the advantages and disadvantages of trying a juvenile in criminal court.	Trying a juvenile in criminal court exposes the youth to a more severe sanction but also allows for the full range of constitutional rights normally afforded to adult defendants. However, research has found that juveniles tried in criminal court receive harsher dispositions than young adults tried for similar offenses.
Learning Objective 11. List and discuss the three types of provisions for sending a juvenile to criminal court.	Under judicial waiver a judge is responsible for sending the juvenile to criminal court. Under direct filing a prosecutor has the discretion to file charges in either juvenile or adult court. Statutory exclusion comes from state legislatures and doesn't require a juvenile court hearing. Statutory exclusion automatically excludes juveniles who commit certain, serious offenses from juvenile court and sends them directly to criminal court.

Chapter Review Questions

1. Under what conditions will a juvenile be tried in federal court?

2. What are the advantages of a unified juvenile court structure?

3. What does it mean for a judge to act as a surrogate parent for the juvenile?

4. How have legislatures limited the prosecutor's discretion?

5. What factors do juvenile intake officers consider when deciding if a case should proceed?

6. What is the purpose of the preliminary hearing?

7. What factors tend to predict whether a juvenile will be committed to a secure facility?

8. What are the advantages of a criminal court trial for juveniles?

9. What aspect of the juvenile court philosophy is lost when plea bargaining occurs?

10. In cases involving offenses in which incarceration is unlikely, what process protections are denied juveniles?

Key Terms

adjudicatory hearing— The hearing in which a determination is made regarding whether the juvenile committed the offense with which he or she is charged.

beyond a reasonable doubt—The state of being as convinced as possible of a fact.

blended sentencing—A sentence that combines a juvenile disposition with the possibility of a criminal sentence, or a criminal conviction with a "last chance" at a juvenile disposition and treatment.

culpability—Blameworthiness. The moral state of being wrong, improper, or injurious.

direct filing—A process by which the prosecutor has the discretion to send a juvenile to criminal court.

dispositional hearing—The hearing in which the juvenile court renders judgment and specifies what should be done with the juvenile.

guardian *ad litem*—Someone appointed by the court to take legal action on behalf of a juvenile or an adult who, because of minor age or infirmity, is unable to manage his or her own affairs.

juvenile waiver—The process of sending a juvenile to be tried in criminal court.

plea bargain—A negotiation in which the defendant agrees to plead guilty or no contest to some offenses in return for some accession to the defendant.

predispositional report—A report prepared by a probation officer to assist the judge in designing an appropriate disposition.

preliminary hearing—The initial preadjudicatory hearing in which the judge explores the nature of the case and decides if it should be processed further.

preponderance of evidence— A standard of proof that is satisfied if it is determined that there is at least a 51 percent chance that a proposition is true.

public defender—An elected or appointed attorney who regularly defends those accused of criminal offenses who cannot afford a private attorney.

statutory exclusion—The legal requirement that certain offenses committed by juveniles automatically be waived to criminal court without a juvenile court hearing.

Endnotes

1 Barry Krisberg, *Juvenile Justice: Redeeming Our Children* (Thousand Oaks, CA: Sage, 2005). See especially Chapter 1Chapter, "Juvenile Justice: Myths and Realities."

2 Anthony Platt, *The Child Savers: The Invention of Delinquency* (Chicago: University of Chicago Press, 1969).

3 National Conference of State Legislatures, *A Legislator's Guide to Comprehensive Juvenile Justice, Juvenile Detention, and Corrections* (Denver, CO: National Conference of State Legislatures, 1996).

4 Amnesty International, Urgent Action Alert, October 8, 2003, web.amnesty.org/library/Index/ENGAMR511272003.

5 Rolando V. del Carmen and Chad R. Trulson, *Juvenile Justice: The System, Process, and Law* (Belmont, CA: Thomson Wadsworth, 2006), 224–225.

6 Leonard P. Edwards, "The Future of the Juvenile Court: Promising New Directions," *The Future of Children* 6 (1996): 143.

7 David S. Tanenhaus, *Juvenile Justice in the Making* (New York: Oxford University Press, 2004).

8 Benjamin Adams and Sean Addie, *Delinquency Cases Waived to Criminal Court, 2007* (Washington, DC: US Department of Justice, Office of Justice Programs, Office of Juvenile Justice and Delinquency Prevention,

2010), 2. Online at https://www.ncjrs.gov/pdffiles1/ojjdp/230167.pdf.

9 Ibid.

10 Ibid.

11 Leonard P. Edwards, "The Juvenile Court and the Role of the Juvenile Court Judge," *Juvenile and Family Court Journal* 43 (1992): 3–45.

12 Chester Harhut, "An Expanded Role for the Guardian 'ad Litem'," *Juvenile and Family Court Journal* 51 (2000): 31–35.

13 James Shine and Dwight Price, "Prosecutor and Juvenile Justice: New Roles and Perspectives," in Ira Schwartz, ed., *Juvenile Justice and Public Policy* (New York: Lexington Books, 1992), 101–133.

14 American Bar Association, *A Call for Justice: An Assessment of Access to Counsel and Quality of Representation in Delinquency Proceedings* (Washington, DC: ABA Juvenile Justice Center, 1995).

15 George W. Burruss and Kimberly Kempf-Leonard, "The Questionable Advantage of Defense Counsel in Juvenile Court," *Justice Quarterly* 19 (2002): 37–68.

16 Gus Martin, *Juvenile Justice: Process and Systems* (Thousand Oaks, CA: Sage, 2005), 207.

17 del Carmen and Trulson, *Juvenile Justice: The System, Process, and Law*, 181–183.

18 Adams and Addie, *Delinquency Cases Waived to Criminal Court, 2007*, 3.

19 Patrick Griffin and Patricia Torbert, eds., *Desktop Guide to Good Juvenile Probation Practice* (Pittsburgh, PA: National Center for Juvenile Justice, 2002).

20 Ira M. Schwartz and William H. Barton, *Reforming Juvenile Detention—No More Hidden Closets* (Columbus: Ohio State University Press, 1994).

21 Adams and Addie, *Delinquency Cases Waived to Criminal Court, 2007*, 3.

22 Roberto Hugh Potter and Suman Kakar, "The Diversion Decision-Making Process from the Juvenile Court Practitioners' Perspective," *Journal of Contemporary Criminal Justice* 18 (2002): 20–36.

23 Joseph W. Rogers, "The Predisposition Report: Maintaining the Promise of Individualized Justice," *Federal Probation* 54 (1990): 43–57.

24 Adams and Addie, *Delinquency Cases Waived to Criminal Court, 2007*, 3.

25 Jeffrey Fagan and Martin Guggenheim, "Preventive Detention for Juveniles: A Natural Experiment," *Journal of Criminal Law and Criminology* 86 (1996): 415–428.

26 Nancy Rodriguez, Hilary Smith, and Marjorie S. Zatz, "'Youth Is Enmeshed in a Highly Dysfunctional Family System': Exploring the Relationship among Dysfunctional Families, Parental Incarceration, and Juvenile Court Decision Making," *Criminology* 47, no. 1 (2009): 177–208.

27 Joseph B. Sanborn Jr., "The Right to a Public Jury Trial—A Need for Today's Juvenile Court," *Judicature* 76 (1993): 230–238.

28 *McKeiver v. Pennsylvania*, 403 U.S. 528 (1971).

29 Mary Clement, *The Juvenile Justice System: Law and Process* (Boston: Butterworth-Heinemann, 1997), 71.

30 Douglas Smith, "The Plea Bargaining Controversy," *Journal of Criminal Law and Criminology* 77 (1986): 949–957.

31 R. Barry Ruback and Paula J. Vardaman, "Decision Making in Delinquency Cases: The Role of Race and Juveniles' Admission/Denial of the Crime," *Law and Human Behavior* 21, no. 1 (1997): 47–69.

32 Joseph Sanborn, "Philosophical, Legal, and Systematic Aspects of Juvenile Court Plea Bargaining," *Crime and Delinquency* 39 (1993): 509–527.

33 Albert W. Alschuler, "The Prosecutor's Role in Plea Bargaining," *University of Chicago Law Review* 36 (1968): 50–112.

34 Tory Caeti, Craig Hemmens, and Velmer Burton, "Juvenile Right to Counsel: A National Comparison of State Legal Codes," *American Journal of Criminal Law* 23 (1996).

35 del Carmen and Trulson, *Juvenile Justice: The System, Process, and Law*, 254.

36 Barry Feld, "The Right to Counsel in Juvenile Court: An Empirical Study of When Lawyers Appear and the Difference They Make," *Journal of Criminal Law and Criminology* 79 (1989): 611–632.

37 del Carmen and Trulson, *Juvenile Justice: The System, Process, and Law*, 256–257.

38 *Breed v. Jones*, 421 U.S. 519 (1975).

39 Howard N. Snyder and Melissa Sickmund, *Juvenile Offenders and Victims: 2006 National Report* (Washington, DC: US Department of

Justice, Office of Justice Programs, Office of Juvenile Justice and Delinquency Prevention, 2006), 109.

40 Adams and Addie, *Delinquency Cases Waived to Criminal Court, 2007*, 3.

41 Ibid.

42 Ibid.

43 Jeffrey Fagan, "Juvenile Crime and Criminal Justice: Resolving Border Disputes," *The Future of Children* 18, no. 2 (Fall 2008): 81–118. Online at futureofchildren.org/ futureofchildren/publications/journals/ journal_details/index.xml?journalid=31.

44 Charles Puzzanchera, Benjamin Adams, and Melissa Sickmund, *Juvenile Court Statistics*

2006–2007 (Pittsburgh, PA: National Center for Juvenile Justice, 2010), 8, 105. Online at www.ojjdp.gov/ojstatbb/njcda/pdf/jcs2007 .pdf.

45 Snyder and Sickmund, *Juvenile Offenders and Victims: 2006 National Report*, 110.

46 Fagan, "Juvenile Crime and Criminal Justice: Resolving Border Disputes," 81–118.

47 Megan C. Kurlychek and Brian D. Johnson, "Juvenility and Punishment: Sentencing Juveniles in Adult Criminal Court," *Criminology* 48, no. 3 (2010): 725–757.

48 Adams and Addie, Delinquency Cases Waived to Criminal Court, 2007.

DON'T
THROW
AWAY
the KEY

www.DontThrowAwaytheKey.org

Juvenile Corrections

Once the juvenile court judge has determined that a juvenile is delinquent, the question becomes "What do we do about it?" Juvenile justice isn't a one-size-fits-all enterprise, and depending on the resources available, there are several options. The goal of the juvenile justice system is to craft a disposition that is in the juvenile's best interests while protecting society. But "the juvenile's best interests" isn't necessarily the least restrictive sentence. For a youth with drug or alcohol problems, anger-management problems, or gang affiliations, release to the community on standard probation might not be the best option. To put the youth back on the street to deal with the same social problems without equipping him or her with the educational background, interpersonal skills, and character to resist temptation is asking for trouble. To succeed, youngsters need a supportive environment and individual attention. This is the job of juvenile corrections.

Before we delve too deeply into juvenile corrections, it's worth noting that some issues are beyond the mandate and abilities of the juvenile justice system. The social conditions that lead to delinquency, such as poverty, a sagging economy, drugs, inadequate schools, and ineffective families, aren't things the juvenile justice system can fix. And yet, when these problems persist, they have a tremendous effect on the juvenile's chances of staying out of trouble. When families, the economy, schools, and communities fail to support youths in trouble, it's the juvenile justice system that gets blamed for high rates of **recidivism**. In previous chapters, we covered the issues and concerns of these other social institutions, so here we will simply acknowledge their importance and suggest ways the juvenile justice system can use them to develop an atmosphere in which delinquent juveniles can thrive.

The particular emphasis of this chapter is individual treatment. What can be done to prepare delinquents to return to society? What does it take to turn around a life that seems to be destined for a criminal career? And, finally, what mistakes have been made and continue to be made in treating delinquents? To

INSTANT RECALL FROM CHAPTER 3

recidivism

Continuing to commit delinquent or criminal offenses after being convicted and sentenced for prior offenses.

In this 1951 photo, four Burbank, California, youths are held in jail on suspicion of attempting to wreck a train.

address these questions, we will look at community-based efforts for dealing with delinquency, as well as institutional programs. We cover the philosophy of juvenile correctional treatment and the array of programs to assess the successes and limitations of the current response to juvenile delinquency.

Community Corrections

The traditional way to respond to juvenile delinquents is to provide the least restrictive treatment. The idea is to not harm the youth by placing him or her in a situation that doesn't allow for the positive growth envisioned by the court.[1] Placing juveniles in secure institutions is considered a last resort, and keeping them in the community so they can live with their parents and attend their own schools is the optimal goal. To keep the juvenile in the community, the juvenile justice system has devised some programs and agencies to ensure that society is protected and that the juvenile gets the treatment and supervision needed for successful reintegration.

Standard Probation

Probation, the conditional release of juveniles to the custody of parents or guardians, was developed in 1841 by John Augustus, a prosperous Boston shoemaker. Augustus bailed people out of jail, found work for them, allowed some to live temporarily in his home, and recommended dispositions to judges.[2] The concept of probation was attractive to those involved in the emerging criminal justice system. When the first juvenile court was introduced in Cook County, Illinois, in 1899, probation was instituted as one of its cornerstones.[3]

Currently, because of the large numbers of juveniles before contemporary juvenile courts, probation is necessary. Probation can be formal (court-ordered) as the result of being adjudicated delinquent, or informal (voluntary) as an alternative to formal processing. Property-offense cases are the most common type to receive either form of probation, followed by person offense, public-order offenses, and finally drug offenses (see Figure 14.1).[4]

In 2007, formal probation was the most severe disposition ordered in 56 percent of the cases in which the juvenile was adjudicated delinquent.[5] Of all cases placed on probation, 68 percent involved white juveniles, 29 percent involved

Learning Objective 1.

Discuss the many community corrections options for juvenile delinquents.

Learning Objective 2.

Understand that the juvenile justice system's goal is to craft a disposition that is in the best interests of the youth while protecting society.

Learning Objective 3.

Tell why placing juveniles in secure institutions is a last resort and keeping them in the community is the optimal goal.

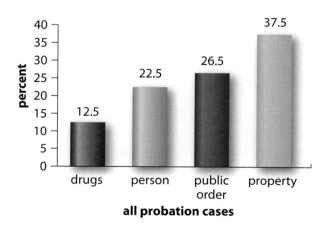

all probation cases

Figure 14.1 Cases on Formal and Informal Probation, 2007

Property cases are the most likely to receive some form of probation.

Think About It

1. Why would property cases be more likely to receive probation and drug-offense cases the least likely? Discuss your reasoning.

Source: Sarah Livsey, Juvenile Delinquency Probation Caseload, 2007 (Washington, DC: U.S. Department of Justice Office of Justice Programs Office of Juvenile Justice and Delinquency Prevention, 2010), 2. Online at www.ncjrs.gov/pdffiles1/ojjdp/230170.pdf.

black juveniles, and 3 percent involved juveniles of other races. Nearly all of these cases, 74 percent, involved males.[6]

Probation has several presumed advantages. First, it reduces stigma. By keeping youths out of secure detention facilities, it's hoped they won't adopt the self-image of a criminal. Staying at home and in the community allows youths to maintain their identities, for themselves and others, as good and decent people. The second advantage of probation is that it encourages rehabilitation by employing community resources. Almost always, schools in the community are better at helping children than schools in juvenile correctional facilities.[7] Additionally, other community resources, such as mental health centers, recreational facilities, and churches, can help treat the youth. It's believed that rehabilitation and reintegration are more easily accomplished by maintaining the youth's bonds to the community.[8] The final suggested advantage of probation over incarceration is cost. It's expensive to build and staff secure correctional facilities. Around-the-clock confinement means that the state must provide for three shifts of personnel, food, building costs, and therapy. On probation, most of these costs are the responsibility of the family, schools, and community. Detention space is a precious resource, and the juvenile justice system works hard to reserve it for only those delinquents who must be separated from society.[9]

The rules of probation require the youth to maintain contact with the probation officer. A variety of methods are used to maintain this contact, and these depend on the officer's caseload, the amount of trust in the youth, and technology. The youth may be required to report on a regular basis to the probation officer, the probation officer might visit the youth's home or school, or the youth might be required to submit monthly written reports attesting that he or she has met the conditions of probation.[10] Today, the officer must be wary of phone contact. Prior to cell phones, the officer could call the youth's home to check that curfews were being obeyed. Now, the officer has to be aware of the opportunities for evasion by the youth.

Youths on probation must adhere to certain conditions. **Standard conditions of probation** apply to all probationers. **Special conditions of probation** apply to the youth's particular needs. Probation often includes additional requirements, such as drug counseling, restitution, or community service. For instance, a youth with no history of drug or alcohol use isn't required by the standard conditions of probation to submit to drug tests, whereas a client with a history of drug use or whose delinquent adjudication involved drugs or alcohol may find drug testing to be part of the special conditions. The conditions of probation are extensive and greatly limit the youth's freedom and privacy, leading some scholars to question the ability of juveniles to fulfill all these requirements. For instance, Thomas Blomberg and Karol Lucken have compared the conditions of probation to a "stacked deck." So many demands are placed on the probationers, they are probably in some state of violation at any time.[11] This provides the probation officer with great latitude in supervising the case, because violations can be held against the youth.

Special conditions of probation are cause for further concern. The courts have ruled that these conditions can't be arbitrary and must relate to the juvenile's offense or a reasonable treatment intervention.[12] One condition of probation is that the youth waives certain rights, such as allowing the probation officer to search his or her person, car, or home without a warrant. Further, the probation officer can require the juvenile to maintain a curfew, refrain from driving an automobile, and demonstrate a respectful demeanor and tone of voice to parents, teachers, and police officers.

Sean Fitzpatrick is shown in 2004 after his sentencing in the Spokane (Washington) County Juvenile Justice Center. Fitzpatrick, then age 16, brought a gun to school hoping police would kill him. Instead, he was severely wounded. Fitzpatrick was sentenced to 45 days of electronic home monitoring and 400 hours of community service. Part of his sentence required him to talk to other teens about seeking help for depression. He was on probation until age 21.

How can the state restrict the freedom of those on probation to such a large extent? The reason is that probation isn't a right but a privilege, and it is contingent on the juvenile agreeing to the conditions. The juvenile signs for the conditions under which the probation is granted and virtually waives away rights. The alternative is to be placed in detention, where all these rights and privileges are also forfeited. For the youth committed to correcting his or her delinquent behavior, probation is a reasonable price to pay for being allowed to live a normal life at home. Youths who can't abide by the conditions of probation find that their lives become more transparent, which makes the detection of additional delinquent behavior more likely.

Intensive-Supervision Probation

Probation was designed to give offenders the benefit of having a probation officer to help them negotiate the justice system and to provide emotional support and employment counseling, along with firm accountability for deviant behavior. However, given the large numbers of juveniles on probation, the time and attention of probation officers are stretched so thin that many juveniles don't get the services they need. More importantly, many juveniles on probation aren't being supervised adequately and are committing additional offenses and abandoning their rehabilitative treatment plans.[13] Traditionally, probation officers practiced a kind of triage by informally dividing their caseloads into three categories:

1. **Cases who will do well no matter what the officer does.** Many juveniles on probation are good and decent people who got caught experimenting with relatively normal delinquent behavior. Juveniles go through a stage of testing the boundaries of appropriate behavior: they might drink alcohol, smoke marijuana, and drive fast and recklessly. Although these behaviors

are against the law and juveniles should be held accountable for them, many youngsters simply outgrow these things. Being taken into custody, processing through the juvenile court, and going on probation are a wake-up call for them. Aside from ensuring that juveniles are following the conditions of probation, the probation office spends little time and resources on supervision. In some jurisdictions, youths are placed on minimum-security caseloads and have little contact with the probation officer. Typically, these juveniles successfully complete their terms of probation and go on to live productive and law-abiding lives, not because of anything the probation officer has done, but because they're minor offenders who have adequate education, family support, and positive attitudes about life.

2. **Cases who will do poorly no matter what the officer does.** Some juveniles on probation should be sent to institutions where they can be adequately supervised and treated. Because many state juvenile corrections facilities are so crowded, the courts are forced to place some disturbed and even dangerous juveniles on probation. The probation officers realize that dealing with these serious delinquents requires extraordinary time and resources that simply aren't available. Probation officers do the best they can under the circumstances, but given the demands of the other juveniles on their caseload, they realize the best they can do is to keep a close eye on the serious delinquents and revoke probation at the first sign of trouble.

3. **Cases who can do well if the probation officer allocates time and resources.** This is the sweet spot that probation is designed to address. These juveniles are at a turning point in their lives, and if they receive the right guidance and support, they can succeed in getting on the right path. Probation officers who recognize these cases will work diligently to make sure these youths get every possible means of support, including firm supervision and the threat of probation revocation. These cases can take up a disproportionate amount of the probation officer's time and energy, but the payoff in terms of helping a young person and protecting society can be immense.

Intensive-supervision probation is designed to allow the probation department to provide extended services to the juveniles who fall into category 3. In some cases, if adequate resources are available, they can be targeted at those in category 2. It's a blunt reality that these are cases who, under better conditions, would go to a treatment center. Therefore, the probation department beefs up its supervision and tries to accomplish two goals. The first goal is to protect society by maintaining increased vigilance over these juveniles. The second goal is to provide treatment services that can affect the likelihood of turning these juveniles toward law-abiding behavior. Here the goal is to move the juvenile from a category 2 to a category 3 case. The risks are great, and the resources required are far beyond what standard probation has available, so intensive-supervision probation is designed to fill the gap between probation and incarceration in a secure facility.[14]

Intensive-supervision probation differs from standard probation in several ways. First, some jurisdictions don't use the normal caseload structure in which juveniles are assigned a single probation officer. Intensive-supervision probation programs often use a team approach in which a probation officer is supplemented by probation aides. By using teams, the probation department can be assured that someone is always available to respond to and monitor the juveniles' behavior. A second way in which intensive-supervision probation differs from standard probation is in the size of the caseloads. Instead of being responsible for over 100 cases, the intensive-supervision officer, often along with a team of aides, is responsible for 30 or fewer juveniles. Finally, intensive-supervision probation activities are more highly structured. There is more offender accountability and there are more frequent checks by officers and aides. For example, a typical program structure for an intensive-probation supervision in Peoria, Illinois, has four phases that target juvenile delinquents on probation for gang-related behavior or substance-abuse offenses:

>> **Phase 1: Planning and movement.** This phase is designed to stabilize participants through intensive monitoring and movement control while allowing time to assess treatment needs. During this phase, juveniles are assessed for substance abuse and mental health treatment.

>> **Phase 2: Counseling, treatment, and programming.** This phase occurs within one week of phase 1. Youths begin outpatient treatment, intensive outpatient treatment, residential substance-abuse treatment, or some combination of these three. Intensive-supervision juvenile probation program officers attend group sessions as frequently as possible. Youths are referred to aftercare following completion of a treatment program. An antigang program is also offered at this time.

>> **Phase 3: Community outreach.** This phase requires the completion of a community-service project or a report written and presented by the youth describing his or her experience in treatment.

>> **Phase 4: Reassignment.** This phase gradually reduces the frequency of contacts with the program officers to prepare youths for the transition to regular probation or probation termination. Throughout the first three phases, program officers make frequent contacts with program participants and their families, schools, and treatment providers. Parents are kept abreast of everything going on in their child's probation and are required to sign all case plans.[15]

As can be seen from this highly structured program, intensive-supervision probation includes many of the essential elements of standard probation but concentrates more on a few juveniles. For many of these youths, intensive-supervision probation is their "last, best hope" of turning their lives around before getting sent to a secure institution and losing daily contact with family members, friends, and schools, as well as their liberty. For those who can meet the requirements of intensive-supervision probation, the possibility of getting help to address treatment needs is high. For those who can't abide by the conditions and structure of intensive-supervision probation, the chance of getting caught in delinquent behavior again is virtually assured.

Electronic Monitoring

Another community-based corrections program often used in conjunction with probation, especially intensive-supervision probation, is **electronic monitoring**. Given the size of probation caseloads and the geographic mobility of youth today, it's extremely difficult for probation officers to be confident of the whereabouts of their caseloads. It's time consuming for probation officers to drive to the home of each probationer on a regular basis. Also, once a probation officer has confirmed that the juvenile has complied with curfew, it's always possible that the youth will slip out of the house after the probation officer has left and the parents have gone to bed.[16]

In an electronic-monitoring program, the probationer wears an electronic ankle bracelet or other device that is monitored by a computer. A number of technologies are used to provide this type of electronic surveillance, and it's changing all the time.[17] One early technique put a monitor on the offender's home telephone that would send a signal to the probation office if the wearer of the ankle bracelet strayed too far from the phone. Soon it might be legal to implant a tracking chip in offenders' bodies. Probation officers could then use a computer to set certain geographic areas off limits to the probationer and activate an alert when these locations are visited.

The advantages of electronic monitoring are obvious. A single probation officer can monitor many more clients with a minimum of effort or expense, meaning that electronic devices will eventually pay for themselves in terms of reduced personnel costs.[18] Electronic monitoring also allows probationers to avoid incarceration and live at home with minimal supervision and interference from the probation officer. However, some critics of electronic monitoring liken it to an Orwellian *1984* scenario in which Big Brother is invading everyone's privacy and watching every move.[19] The invasion of privacy is a serious concern in a society with surveillance cameras in public spaces, computer monitoring by employers in the workplace, and identity theft. Critics of electronic monitoring say it violates the Fourth Amendment protections concerning search and seizure. However, we must remember that, at least for now, no one is required to submit to an electronic-surveillance program. Probationers consent to be monitored to escape the more restrictive conditions of confinement in a secure detention facility. As the level of technology increases, however, legitimate privacy issues might arise in the future.

Another issue of electronic monitoring concerns tampering with technology. As our nation grows increasingly dependent on technology, it also grows increasingly vulnerable to hackers and system disruptions. For instance, a citywide electrical blackout can result in hundreds of probationers being "lost" for several hours. Similarly, people can hack into the probation office's monitoring system and manipulate the data. Some juveniles with sophisticated computer skills could introduce their own programs into the system to provide false information. So although this type of technology can be a useful supplement to probation, it can't completely replace a well-trained probation officer.

The public might also be concerned that those on electronic-monitoring programs aren't being punished enough. This criticism is especially pertinent to adult offenders but is less applicable to juveniles. Because the philosophy of the juvenile justice system is to act in the best interests of the youth, electronic monitoring can be regarded as a less restrictive and more supportive treatment option than incarceration. Finally, electronic monitoring is limited in what it can provide in terms of community security. Although knowing the exact geographic locations of juvenile probationers is useful, electronic monitoring can't tell the probation officer what the juvenile is doing. The juvenile could be selling stolen merchandise from home, using drugs, engaging in sexual activities, or playing illegal online poker.[20]

Home Confinement

Home confinement, or "house arrest," as it's sometimes called, restricts offenders and juvenile delinquents to their homes for large parts of the day. The idea behind home confinement for juveniles is to let them stay at home with their parents and attend school without disrupting their lives. It preserves the bond the youth has with family, school, and community while ensuring the juvenile isn't out causing trouble.

Home confinement is often used in conjunction with intensive-supervision probation and electronic monitoring.[21] The major advantage of home confinement is cost. Keeping the juvenile at home means the parents pay for room and board, not the state. The type of punishment inherent in home confinement depends entirely on the parents' social and economic status. For some juveniles, who can maintain access to their video games, big-screen television, family swimming pool, and refrigerator full of junk food, home confinement may not seem to be much of an inconvenience. For other children, who come from disadvantaged homes, being made to stay inside except when they have legitimate reasons, such as school, may seem like a major imposition. Probation officers must investigate the home to make sure it's a safe, positive environment in which to confine the youth.[22] Under some circumstances, the influence of a dysfunctional family might be the cause of the delinquency, and home confinement may be the wrong option.

Fines and Victim Compensation

Sometimes, the court orders juvenile delinquents to pay fines or make **restitution**. These sanctions are accomplished in a number of ways, and the philosophy behind each is slightly different. The overall idea of fines and restitution is to make the juvenile accountable for his or her actions.[23] The big drawback to these sanctions is that not every youth is equally able to pay for her or his actions in monetary terms. Therefore, judges have invented creative ways for youths to "pay for their crimes":

» **Fines.** Fines may be imposed for many behaviors, such as speeding or vandalism. The problem with fines is that, for the most part, juveniles don't have their own money. Consequently, the parents end up paying the fine, and the sanction's message is lost on the youth unless the parents require him or her to somehow work off the payment. Additionally, fines affect economically disadvantaged families more than those with financial resources. This means fines can give the impression that the wealthy can buy their way out of trouble.

» **Victim restitution.** Juveniles can be ordered to make monetary restitution to their victims, which can be accomplished in a number of ways. It can be as simple as paying the victim for damages. If a juvenile smashes the victim's car window and steals the stereo, it's relatively easy to determine the cost of replacement. If the amount is substantial, the court can order the payment to be made in installments. If the juvenile can't pay for the damages, the court may order the juvenile to provide victim-service restitution, whereby the juvenile mows the victim's lawn or washes the car. This service is negotiated with the juvenile, the victim, and the court or probation officer to ensure that it's proportionate to the damage and the juvenile's culpability.[24]

» **Community service.** Sometimes the victim doesn't want any further contact with the juvenile. It's understandable that victims wouldn't want delinquents anywhere near them or their property. Often, the juvenile damages schools, parks, or other public property, so there is no individual victim to make restitution to. Under these circumstances, the court may order the juvenile to perform community service. This might be cleaning the sidewalks in the park or helping supervise children in an after-school program (see Case in Point 14.1). Community-service programs have their drawbacks, however. To be effective, juveniles must be monitored to ensure they show up, work the required hours, and do a good job. This monitoring is done by either the probation officer or program staff. Either way, the cost of training and paying those who supervise the work may be as great as the value of the work that is performed.

Victim-compensation programs provide delinquents an opportunity to right the damage they do. Whether restitution is made directly to the victim or to the community at large, the idea of holding the juvenile accountable for delinquent acts is presumed to help develop character.[25] But trouble arises when the juvenile fails to make adequate restitution. If the fine or restitution was predicated on the youth having a job, getting fired or laid off can land the youth back before the court. At times, broad social forces, such as a downturn in the employment rate, can result in a juvenile losing the means to make restitution, even when he or she is willing to do so.

Restitution programs can be instituted at different stages in the juvenile justice system. Often, they're added as a special condition of probation, and sometimes they are applied before the juvenile is adjudged, as part of a diversion program. In this way, the juvenile can make restitution to the victim or community and avoid the stigma of being labeled a delinquent. However, restitution programs are susceptible to inequities in how they're administered. Juveniles who present the least threat to society, look clean-cut, have families who can provide transportation to community-service locations, and who have committed relatively minor offenses are more likely than others to succeed at restitution and community service. Without careful monitoring, it's likely that social class, race, and gender will become disproportionately important in who is selected for these programs and who receives a more severe penalty.

Residential Treatment Programs

For many youths, staying at home as part of a treatment plan isn't a good option, because the parents don't have the interest or competence to ensure a supportive environment. In this case, judges are forced to look elsewhere for a positive living situation. Judges generally have two options: secure and nonsecure facilities.

In 2007, 25 percent of the cases in which the juvenile was adjudicated delinquent were ordered into residential treatment.[26] As of 2008, 47 percent of juvenile facilities were publicly operated and held 69 percent of delinquents.[27] The reason a minority of available facilities (less than half) holds the majority of delinquents is because most private facilities are small; therefore, most delinquents

---

14.1 CASE IN POINT

THE CASE

M. J. W. v. State of Georgia (1974 Ga App.)

THE POINT

Community service for juveniles is considered to be "just restitution" and of rehabilitative value, not "involuntary servitude."

M. J. W. was accused of throwing a match into a trash can in the school restroom. The trash can contained dry paper, which burst into flame. The school's assistant principal testified the damage amounted to less than $25.

M. J. W. was placed on probation for one year and required to "contribute 100 hours to the Parks and Recreation Department of DeKalb County." The youth's attorney objected, stating that the community service amounted to a fine and that "no statutory authority exists for imposing a monetary fine on a minor adjudged to be delinquent," and also that the community service constituted "involuntary servitude," thus violating the juvenile's constitutional rights.

The court ruled that community-service work is restitution, not a monetary penalty, and is also a regular part of probation and a rehabilitative tool for "producing a good adult citizen."

Victim–compensation programs provide delinquents an opportunity to correct the damage they do. Here, a spectator wears a pin promoting juvenile justice during a press conference at the Capitol in Richmond, Virginia.

are held in the larger public facilities.[28] About 85 percent of all juveniles in residential placement are male, and most of them are 16 and 17 years old. One-third are white, one-third are black, and one-fourth are Hispanic.[29] The most common offense leading to residential placement is the status offense. More males than females are in placement for murder, rape, kidnapping, robbery, drug offenses, and public order offenses, whereas higher percentages of females are in placement for status offenses and assaults.[30] Fourteen percent of juveniles report that they have children, and nearly twice as many males have children as females.[31]

Secure facilities are the counterpart of adult prisons and will be discussed in greater detail later in this chapter. Nonsecure facilities allow the juvenile to stay in the community in some sort of alternative living arrangement that has the advantage of maintaining access to schools, recreational programs, religious activities, and other community-based services. Additionally, many of the previously discussed sanctions, such as electronic monitoring and restitution programs, can be used with **nonsecure detention**. Often, nonsecure detention is used in conjunction with probation as part of a blended-sentencing program.[32] The overall intent of these programs is to provide services to compensate for the deficiencies, both social and personal, that resulted in the behaviors that landed the youth in front of a judge in the first place. Three of the more common types of nonsecure juvenile treatment settings are foster care, group homes and halfway houses, and alternative-experience programs.

FOSTER CARE

Foster care is used when the court finds that a youth's parents are either unfit or unable to provide for his or her welfare. Social service agencies screen foster-care parents to weed out those who would exploit children. Foster-care parents may foster more than one youth in the home, and these children may come from different families. In addition, foster-care parents may have their own children in the home. The state pays these parents a stipend for the expenses of caring for the foster child, but it isn't a moneymaking proposition, and ideally, foster parents are motivated by a desire to help children in trouble, not to make money. Many of those placed in foster care are status offenders, and about half are delinquents.[33]

Foster care can last from a short period of weeks to a longer term of years. In some instances, the foster parents grow attached to the children and adopt them. Foster care can be an effective treatment strategy when all the youth needs is a stable and supportive environment. However, foster parents aren't trained social workers or psychologists and are usually ill-equipped to deal with children with serious emotional and behavioral problems.[34]

GROUP HOMES AND HALFWAY HOUSES

Group homes are different from foster care in that they accommodate more juveniles and are more structured. Although group homes vary widely, they typically hold 8 to 12 juveniles and have a professional staff that works shifts to ensure there is always a responsible adult at the home. Group homes are usually large, single-family homes in residential neighborhoods that are indistinguishable from other homes and tend to be privately run. They are intended to provide an as-normal-as-possible living environment so the youths can go to the same schools, recreational activities, and therapeutic services that are available to all children. Group homes also have strict rules. Juveniles are required to keep their rooms clean and orderly, maintain a curfew, attend school, and participate in therapeutic programs. Youths may be required to submit to drug testing or wear an electronic ankle bracelet.

Group homes and halfway houses are difficult to institutionalize because of high staff turnover, which diminishes the home's effectiveness. A well-trained and motivated staff is difficult to maintain. Because of low pay, the job is considered a stepping stone for many staff members, who find they need a more stable and better-paying job as they get older. Some group homes are run by a family, and as the family's circumstances change, the parents may find running a halfway house no longer desirable. Also, new staff members may not have developed a network with community and volunteer service agencies, or the trust of the juvenile court judges.

Staff members get little training, and most of what they learn is on the job, where mistakes in judgment can result in difficulties for themselves, the juveniles, and the halfway house. For instance, if a staff member gives a youth permission to stay out late, and the youth commits a serious offense, the publicity can severely harm the facility's reputation and bring calls to close it. Funding can also be problematic. Halfway houses are particularly vulnerable during times of scarce resources because they're easy to close. Often, the houses themselves are rented, so there isn't a costly building that is unused when the halfway house ceases to exist.

ALTERNATIVE-EXPERIENCE PROGRAMS

A number of programs seek to provide juveniles with experiences that can help change their work habits, self-concepts, and ability to get along with others. These programs are typically conducted on ranches, in camps, or out in the wilderness. The idea behind such programs is to take the youths out of their regular surroundings and subject them to physical and mental stress in a carefully controlled way that ensures that they pass tests of their character. Successful completion of a difficult task is sometimes the first time the youths have been able to feel truly proud of themselves. The youths are required to learn new skills, such as working with animals, learning to climb mountains, or surviving in the wilderness. Many of the skills won't be particularly useful to youths who return to cities, but the idea isn't having the skills, but the process of learning the skills.[35]

Pennsylvania Judge Kenneth Biehn hugs Kareem Watts at his last juvenile court hearing. Judge Biehn sentenced Watts, then 14, to a juvenile program called Alternative Rehabilitation Communities.

By learning to negotiate and work with others, persevere when extremely tired and uncomfortable, and follow directions in hazardous situations, it's believed the youths will learn that they have capabilities of their own and can compete in legitimate ways with others.

Often, these camps, ranches, or wilderness programs provide youths with life-changing experiences that can arm them with the positive self-image they need to resist the temptations they find when returning to their neighborhoods. If done correctly, these alternative-experience programs can be extremely beneficial. However, if done wrong, such programs verge on child abuse. Untrained or incompetent staff members can ignore warning signs of mental and physical breakdown and push the juveniles into unsafe situations that can have lasting negative effects.

ADVANTAGES OF RESIDENTIAL TREATMENT PROGRAMS

The first and most politically appealing advantage of residential treatment is that it's less expensive than placing the youth in secure confinement. The duration of residential treatment is much shorter than secure confinement. A residential treatment plan might last only 90 days, whereas incarceration often lasts longer than a year. So, each treatment opening in a wilderness program, halfway house, or foster home will typically accommodate three to five juveniles a year, whereas secure confinement can deal with only one youth per opening. It's also cheaper to staff, feed, and supervise youths in nonsecure residential programs than in secure facilities.[36]

The second major advantage of these programs is that they provide a less restrictive option—one that enables many juveniles to escape the negative consequences of being sent to a training school or other long-term correctional facility. To provide individualized treatment, residential programs are necessary. The more quality programs available, the better the judge can match a juvenile who has particular problems with a successful treatment option. But with fewer treatment programs, the judge is forced to send youths to programs that are neither appropriate nor effective.

Finally, these programs can limit the stigma placed on delinquents.[37] According to **labeling theory**, the further into the justice system juveniles go, the more difficult it becomes to reclaim them as productive citizens. Thus, only the most serious cases, who entail a danger to society, are considered for secure

INSTANT RECALL FROM CHAPTER 5

labeling theory
A theory that describes how a label applied by society can affect an individual's self-perception and behavior.

confinement. Nonsecure treatment programs, if there are available options, can deal more effectively with the rest.

Questions

1. What are the presumed advantages of probation for juveniles?
2. What are standard conditions of probation? What are special conditions of probation?
3. How is intensive-supervision probation different from standard probation?
4. What are the advantages and disadvantages of electronic monitoring? Home confinement?
5. How are fines, victim restitution, and community service different?

Secure Confinement

Learning Objective 4.

Reason why juveniles who have committed serious delinquent acts or who have demonstrated that they aren't amenable to community-based treatment options often go to secure institutions.

Learning Objective 5.

Discuss jails and detention centers as the two basic short-term confinement options.

Learning Objective 6.

Describe how juvenile correctional facilities provide for the extended, secure confinement of juvenile delinquents.

Juveniles who have committed serious offenses or who have demonstrated that they aren't amenable to community-based treatment options will often be sent to secure institutions. (They are no longer eligible for capital punishment; see Crosscurrents.) Larger facilities are more secure and more likely to be operated by the state. These facilities are also the most likely to be crowded.[38] Much like an adult prison, a secure institution restricts the youths to the institution. Most juveniles in secure institutions have committed non–status offenses, that is, offenses that would be criminal if committed by adults. The Juvenile Justice and Delinquency Prevention Act of 2002 prohibits status offenders from being placed in secure facilities, although federal regulations have interpreted that to mean that accused status offenders can be held in secure juvenile facilities for up to 24 hours following initial contact with the police or court.[39]

Secure confinement is a self-contained, closed environment that not only restricts freedom but also features other **pains of imprisonment**. To appreciate the conditions of secure confinement, it's useful to consider the daily life and routine of inmates. In his classic book, *The Society of Captives*, Gresham Sykes describes the five pains of imprisonment that adult offenders face. This concept is applicable to juveniles as well, because all secure institutions have these deprivations to some degree.[40]

» **Deprivation of liberty.** This is the most basic pain of imprisonment. Juveniles locked inside the institution can't leave to see friends and family. They may even be restricted to their cells. The deprivation of liberty entails having to ask a staff member to unlock a door or gate and means the freedom to come and go is no longer a choice.

» **Deprivation of goods and services.** Incarcerated juveniles aren't free to acquire the things that many youths take for granted. Television, video games, and other activities are no longer freely available. They don't have the family refrigerator to snack from, and they can't call their friends. They eat in an institutional dining room where there are no options and no menu. If the youth, for example, doesn't want to eat the liver and onions that are served, the alternative is to not eat. In most institutions, an underground economy of some sort develops in which some inmates will smuggle in cigarettes, drugs, or food and sell them for extravagant prices or trade them for services and favors.

» **Deprivation of autonomy.** Here the juvenile loses the opportunity to make decisions. The staff, who make all the important and most of the trivial

Juveniles who have committed serious offenses or who have demonstrated that they aren't amenable to community-based treatment options are often sent to secure institutions.

decisions, are concerned less about the inmates' comfort and happiness and more about institutional security. Long-term inmates may suffer **institutionalization**, meaning they lose the capacity to make decisions and often have a difficult time returning to society.[41]

》 **Deprivation of heterosexual relations.** For adult inmates, the deprivation of heterosexual relations means they're separated from their spouses or partners and no longer have normal releases for their sexual desires. One would hope the deprivation of heterosexual relations wouldn't be a major issue in juvenile institutions, but this isn't the case. Adolescents have a highly developed interest in sexual relations, and life in a single-sex institution can give their behavior yet another sexual dimension. When heterosexual persons are denied social contact with members of the opposite sex, they must find other ways of expressing their sexual identities. In adult male prisons, rape is so common it has become an expected part of the prison experience. In juvenile institutions, the inability to explore traditional sexual identities with members of the opposite sex can provide reasons for experimentation and exploitation. As of 2009, incarcerated juveniles with a sexual orientation other than heterosexual reported higher rates of sexual victimization by other youths (12.5 percent) as compared to heterosexual youths (1.3 percent).[42]

14.2   crosscurrents

No More Juvenile Executions

In *Stanford v. Kentucky* (1989), the US Supreme Court upheld laws that set the minimum age for capital punishment at 16. The Court had held that there was no national consensus on whether the death penalty for offenses committed at the ages of 16 and 17 constituted cruel and unusual punishment. In 2005, the Court overturned this ruling in *Roper v. Simmons*, setting forth that offenders who committed their capital offenses before age 17 could no longer be executed.

In 1993, Christopher Simmons, 17, planned to burglarize and murder Shirley Crook, with the help of two younger friends. The three met on the night of the offense, but one boy backed out. Simmons and the other boy broke into Crook's home, bound her hands and feet, and covered her eyes. They then drove her to a state park and threw her off a bridge into the Meramec River, where Crook drowned.

Simmons was convicted of first-degree murder and sentenced to death by a Missouri court. His appeals to state and federal courts on the grounds that he was 17 at the time of the murder, and that a death sentence constituted cruel and unusual punishment in violation of the Eighth Amendment, were rejected.

In 2002, the Missouri Supreme Court stayed Simmons's execution while the US Supreme Court decided *Atkins v. Virginia*, a case involving the execution of the mentally ill. The US Supreme Court ruled that executing the mentally ill violated the Eighth and Fourteenth Amendment prohibitions on cruel and unusual punishment because most Americans found it cruel and unusual. The Missouri Court then reconsidered Simmons's case.

Using the reasoning from *Atkins*, the Missouri Court held that a national consensus had developed since *Stanford*, and that society's standards of decency would no longer tolerate executions for offenses committed by defendants under the age of 18. The Missouri Court decided, 6–3, that *Stanford* was no longer valid and changed his sentence to life without parole. The US Supreme Court upheld the ruling.

THINK ABOUT IT

1. Compare the rulings in *Stanford v. Kentucky* and *Roper v. Simmons*. What changed, if anything, between 1989 and 2005?

» **Deprivation of security.** In any institution, the strong tend to take advantage of the weak, and those who are older, more experienced, and aggressive will attempt to dominate others through force. Juveniles might fashion homemade weapons to protect themselves, but there is little safety for anyone when juvenile gangs are active in an institution.[43]

These pains of imprisonment define life in an institution. They exist to varying degrees in every adult and juvenile institution and are an integral part of the incarceration experience. With the exception of deprivation of security, these pains of imprisonment are the foundation for making incarceration a deterrent. If they didn't exist, prison wouldn't be such a bad place. The deprivation of security, however, is unintended. Officials in adult and juvenile facilities are supposed to keep the inmates safe. The violence done behind bars is a direct result of the administration not having enough resources and options to keep inmates from fighting, raping, and killing each other.

Security problems are doubled when juveniles are incarcerated. Not only is the rehabilitation mandate of the juvenile justice system violated, but juveniles are more mentally and physically vulnerable than adults. Juveniles in adult facilities under criminal jurisdiction have the right to mental health and medical care, education, due process, and access to their families and the courts. These rights also apply to juveniles in juvenile detention centers, training schools, jails and prisons, and other secure facilities.[44]

Jails

Jails and detention centers (discussed later) are the two basic short-term confinement options. Jail is the most troubling option, because jails also hold adult offenders and detainees. However, when juveniles must be detained for short periods of time, they are generally sent to jails. Some youths who are confined in jails have actually been charged as adults and are waiting for criminal trials. Juveniles who are being held as juveniles are sent to jails because they require secure confinement until they can be seen by a judge.[45]

Federal law requires that jailed juveniles be held out of sight and sound of adults. Beyond that, the rules for young people in jail differ somewhat from state to state, with federal funding for each state depending on compliance with the "jail-removal" mandates of the Juvenile Justice and Delinquency Prevention Act. The act specifies that juveniles who are detained in jails for non–status offenses can remain there for only a maximum of six hours while awaiting processing or release, transfer to a juvenile facility, or a court appearance. The act further specifies that juveniles awaiting a court appearance must be separated from adults and have access to someone who has been trained to work with juveniles. States don't uniformly comply with the act, however, the most common reason being that they lack the resources and facilities to provide jail alternatives for juveniles.

For example, in one 2006 case, a 16-year-old girl charged as an adult with murder in the District of Columbia was held in the women's wing of the DC jail and locked in her cell for 23 hours a day to minimize her contact with adults. Boys charged under similar circumstances were kept in a special wing out of sight and sound of adult inmates, but there was no such special wing for girls because the situation was so rare. There simply weren't enough girls charged as adults with murder to warrant a special wing. In one of several hearings, the judge in the case admitted the city was probably violating federal law.[46]

Detention Centers

The use of detention varies by state, but most use secure detention facilities as sanctions, as well as to hold juveniles while their cases are processed. Some states use detention only for temporary holding, some use it to sanction probation violators, while others use it as a disposition. Some states use secure detention for all three

An aide at The Pat Andersen School monitors a language arts class at the Southwest Idaho Juvenile Detention Center. The school participates in the Cabin's Writers in the Schools program and recently secured a grant to create a garden that will provide tasks for the students and fresh vegetables for local community groups.

Figure 14.2 Juveniles were most likely to be sent to detention in 28 percent of person-offense cases, followed by public order, drug, and property offense cases.

Think About It

1. Discuss the order of the offenses. For example, why would juveniles be more likely to go to detention for person and public order offenses than for drug and property offenses?

Source: Crystal Knoll and Melissa Sickmund, *Delinquency Cases in Juvenile Court, 2007* (Washington, DC: U.S. Department of Justice Office of Justice Programs Office of Juvenile Justice and Delinquency Prevention, 2010), 3. Online at www.ncjrs.gov/pdffiles1/ojjdp/230168.pdf.

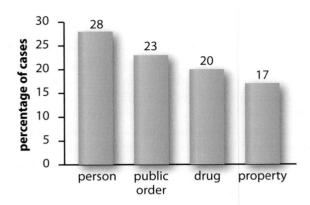

purposes. A judge sends a juvenile to detention if he or she thinks the youth presents a threat to the community, will be endangered by returning to the community, or will not show at a hearing. Juveniles also go to detention centers for diagnostic evaluation. However, the juvenile isn't detained in most delinquency cases, and the likelihood of detention varies by offense category (see Figure 14.2).[47]

All states require a detention hearing to be held within a few days of custody. The judge will review the decision to detain the juvenile and order either a release or continued detention. Some jurisdictions have juvenile detention centers in the same locations with jails or lockups. These facilities must ensure separate and distinct facilities for juveniles.[48] Generally, each state does detention a little bit differently and approaches it with a different philosophy.

Juvenile Correctional Facilities

Juvenile correctional facilities are called a variety of things depending on the state. In some states they are training schools, in others reform schools, and in still others industrial schools or youth facilities. Some states just call them juvenile correctional facilities. Regardless of the title, they all serve the same purpose: the extended, secure confinement of delinquents. So you can get a sense of the variety of titles, Table 14.1 lists a selection of states and what they call their long-term, secure juvenile facilities.

Whereas detention centers tend to be local, juvenile correctional facilities are run by the state. Some secure facilities have reception and diagnostic centers that assess newly committed juveniles to determine their mental health, educational needs, and appropriate treatment. Some large states, such as California, have reception and diagnostic centers that run special programs for juveniles needing treatment for mental health or sex-offender issues. Some also have schools structured like regular high schools. These facilities offer a variety of programs and education, as well as substance-abuse programs and public-service programs. Some states have separate facilities for older adolescents and younger children. Training schools are also the most likely type of facility to use restraints on juveniles, such as handcuffs, leg cuffs, waist bands, leather straps, restraining chairs,

TABLE 14.1

TITLE OF FACILITY	STATE
youth development campus	Georgia
youth services center	Colorado, DC, New Hampshire
training school	Connecticut, Michigan, Iowa, Mississippi, Nevada, Rhode Island, Texas, Wyoming, Delaware, New Mexico
youth center	Illinois
juvenile home (for girls)	Iowa
youth development center	Kentucky, Maine, North Carolina, Pennsylvania, Tennessee
industrial home	West Virginia

Think About It
1. If your state is not in the table, find out what your state calls its juvenile facilities.

or strait jackets, and most likely to lock juveniles into seclusion for four or more hours to control unruly behavior.[49]

Boot Camp Prisons

Sometimes an idea that falls outside the traditional treatment realm becomes so popular that it gets funded and introduced into the juvenile justice system. One such idea was the melding of treatment with punishment in what became known as **boot camp prison**. Sometimes it's difficult to distinguish between treatment and punishment. This is the case with shock incarceration programs such as juvenile boot camps, where inmates are considered not to need psychological services as much as they need to learn that deviant behavior can have negative consequences.

Zachary Neagle is shown during his sentencing in Caldwell, Idaho. Convicted of shooting and killing his father with a high-powered hunting rifle, Neagle was sentenced to at least seven years in the state juvenile corrections system.

Juvenile boot camps are patterned after military basic-training programs. In the 1990s, they became the new panacea for dealing with delinquents. The programs last anywhere from 30 to 180 days and include strict discipline, physical training, and hard labor.[50]

Juveniles are subjected to a highly regimented type of military structure that includes marching, being yelled at and insulted by correctional officers dressed as drill sergeants, and being forced to interact with military mannerisms, such as looking straight forward and standing at attention. However, the mandates of the military and juvenile corrections are considerably different.[51]

The military screens recruits to ensure that they are psychologically normal young men and women and then subjects them to physical and emotional stress in basic training to teach them military protocol and to follow orders without question. The goal of basic training is to ensure that these recruits are able to overcome their positive socialization and kill other human beings when ordered to do so. According to Gwynne Dyer, recruits come out of basic training a little bit crazy because it's such an artificial and stressful environment, and they are slightly traumatized by being treated in such a regimented and hostile manner. However, military boot camp is the beginning of military socialization, not the end. Recruits are sent for further training under more normal conditions, and the negative effects of boot camp are gradually overcome by the discipline and pride they develop as valued members of military units. Further, the recruits stay in the military for years, and the negative effects of boot camp have disappeared by the time they return to society.

The mission of juvenile corrections is different from that of the military. The task is to take youths who have violated the law and teach them to think for themselves, evaluate their behavior, and not hurt other people. The military-style boot camp prison isn't suited to these tasks. Military boot camps take some aspects of recruits' positive socialization and replace it with military-style socialization and training. Boot camp prisons take youths who have been negatively socialized and replace that with more negative socialization and little else. Also, there is no reintegration period for the juveniles once they're released. They're sent back into the same families, neighborhoods, and communities where they committed their offenses, armed not with new coping skills or educational experiences but rather with the effects of being degraded, dehumanized, dominated, and traumatized. Some scholars suggest that boot camp prisons are best suited to developing drug dealers and gang members, who benefit from seeing others as enemies who can be killed without remorse.[52]

State Prisons

Most youths in adult prisons are 17 years old, male and minority, and have committed offenses against the person.[53] These youths arrive in state prisons, which are populated mostly by adult offenders, after having been charged as an adult and given a criminal trial.

The conditions for the youths are the same as those for adults, except that, according to the Juvenile Justice and Delinquency Prevention Act, they must be kept out of sight and sound of adult inmates until they're of adult age themselves. The controversy regarding incarcerating such young people in state prison is closely connected to **juvenile waiver** and **statutory exclusion**. If these juveniles had not been tried as adults, they would not be in state prisons. See Case in Point 14.2 for *Graham v. Florida*, in which the US Supreme Court decided that sentencing juveniles to life without parole is unconstitutional.

INSTANT RECALL FROM CHAPTER 13

juvenile waiver

The process of sending a juvenile to be tried in criminal court.

INSTANT RECALL FROM CHAPTER 13

statutory exclusion

The legal requirement that certain offenses committed by juveniles automatically be waived to criminal court without a juvenile court hearing.

14.3 CASE IN POINT

THE CASE

Graham v. Florida (2010)

THE POINT

The imposition of a life sentence without parole on a juvenile convicted of a nonhomicidal offense violates the Eighth Amendment's prohibition of cruel and unusual punishment.

In 2003, Terrance Graham, 16, participated in a Jacksonville restaurant robbery, during which an accomplice beat the manager with a steel bar. A Florida trial court sentenced Graham to probation and withheld adjudication of guilt. The next year, Graham, now 17, and two 20-year-old accomplices invaded and robbed a home. The trial court adjudicated Graham guilty of the earlier robbery charges, revoked his probation, and sentenced him to life in prison. Because Florida has abolished parole, the life sentence left Graham no possibility of release.

The Supreme Court later agreed that the Eighth Amendment's ban on cruel and unusual punishment forbids such sentences as a categorical matter. The ruling marked the first time the Court excluded an entire class of offenders (nonhomicidal) from a given form of punishment (life without parole) outside the context of the death penalty.

Crowding

A 2008 survey of 2,860 public and private juvenile facilities found crowding to be a major shortcoming. Too many youths are housed in facilities that aren't designed to accommodate the population that is pressed into them. The result of crowding is "heightened stress, increased victimization and injury, more rapid spread of sickness and disease, and decreased security."[54] Twenty-five percent of facilities reported that the number of residents they held on the 2008 census date put them at or over their bed capacity or that they relied on makeshift beds. Public detention centers were more likely to be over bed capacity, and the largest facilities were the most likely to be crowded.[55]

Institutional crowding is a difficult problem for juvenile correctional administrators. Juvenile court judges decide who goes to a secure detention facility, and the administrators lack the discretion to refuse. In most states, the juvenile is sentenced for a fixed period of time, and the administrator can't grant an early release. Although building more juvenile facilities is possible, it's the legislature, not the juvenile justice bureau, that allocates the money and approves their construction. This places the administrators in a difficult position as more and more juveniles are crowded into facilities.

In *Rhodes v. Chapman*, an adult case, the Supreme Court ruled that crowding alone isn't unconstitutional. This ruling is considered to apply to juvenile institutions as well, except when the crowding leads to adverse conditions (see Case in Point 14.3). Consequently, as long as food is delivered, sanitation is adequate, inmates get medical care, and there is no increase in violence and victimization, crowding is something administrators and inmates must adjust to.[56]

Suicide Prevention

The adjustment to living in a secure detention facility is more than some juveniles can bear, but it's fair to say that suicide attempts are a relatively infrequent occurrence. Most institutions have developed screening procedures to identify those who might attempt to kill themselves. By being attuned to the warning signs of juveniles experiencing emotional stress when they're first brought to the institution, the staff can ensure they make an adequate transition during the first days of incarceration. Most institutions screen juveniles the day they arrive, because that is when they experience the greatest stress.

What types of institutions have the most suicide attempts? In general, the more restrictive the institution, the greater the threat of suicide. There are a few reasons for this:

》》 **Type of juvenile resident.** The residents of the most secure institutions are those who have committed the most serious offenses. A juvenile who has been adjudicated or convicted of homicide or rape and is looking at a long incarceration will probably experience high stress. In addition, juvenile residents who go to long-term, secure detention facilities are more likely than other delinquents to have significant drug or alcohol issues that add to their emotional instability.[57]

》》 **Isolation.** Secure facilities are more likely to have rooms where disturbed residents are isolated from the rest of the institution's population. Although this isolation is often considered a security measure, it also can make the

---

14.4 CASE IN POINT

THE CASE

Nami v. Fauver (1996)

THE POINT

Double-celling violates the Eighth Amendment under adverse conditions such as poor ventilation, exposure to tobacco smoke, lack of exercise, not enough beds, and abuse from violent or psychologically disturbed cellmates.

In December 1994, Robert Nami, Maurice Thompson, Bart Fernandez, and Kenneth Thompson, who were in protective custody at a New Jersey facility, claimed they were subjected to cruel and unusual punishment and denied access to the courts. Among other abuses, the plaintiffs alleged the following:

》》 Inmates in the protective-custody unit were housed two to a single, small, one-bed cell, so that one inmate had to sleep on the floor by the toilet. The cells' solid doors and small windows made it difficult to call for help. Inmates often had to share cells with violent or mentally disturbed inmates. Nonsmokers were paired with smokers, and the ventilation system shut down for long periods. Double-celling allegedly led to increased rapes and other assaults. Inmates who wouldn't share a cell were punished with solitary confinement.

》》 Recreation was limited to one two-and-a-half-hour period, two days per week. Inmates were denied bathroom access during outdoor recreation, resulting in unsanitary conditions in the exercise yard.

》》 Access to drug and alcohol programs and to jobs and educational programs was restricted for protective-custody inmates but not for the general population.

》》 When transported, protective-custody inmates had to wear a "black box," a device so uncomfortable that it deterred inmates from seeking medical care.

A district court ordered the complaints dismissed, referring to the Supreme Court decision *Rhodes v. Chapman*, which set forth that double-celling alone doesn't violate the Eighth Amendment. However, the circuit court concluded that the district court finding doesn't mean that double-celling *never* violates the Eighth Amendment.

troubled youth even more depressed and out of touch with reality.[58] When separation is necessary, it's recommended that the rooms or cells be made suicide-proof. By having padded rooms and ensuring that the youths don't have belts or sheets to fashion into nooses, the staff can better protect suicidal inmates.

» **Trained staff.** Often, security in an institution is inversely proportional to treatment. That is, the more secure an institution is, the less treatment is available. Security is paramount in facilities that house dangerous inmates. Because juvenile delinquents are also the most likely inmates to become violent, the staff must recognize that custody and treatment can be complementary.

Incarcerated Girls

Incarcerated girls haven't received a great deal of attention because their numbers are relatively modest when compared with those of incarcerated boys. However, the problems of girls in secure confinement are often more acute. This is because most programs are modeled for boys and not for the unique problems girls have when they are locked up.[59]

» Girls have higher rates of depression than boys throughout adolescence and are more likely to attempt suicide.

» The substance-abuse treatment needs of girls involved in the juvenile justice system are particularly acute.

» Adolescent girls who come into contact with the juvenile justice system report high levels of abuse and trauma.

» Adolescent female delinquents face significant challenges with parenting and other interpersonal relationships.[60]

These problems are even more serious for minority and impoverished girls. In a juvenile justice system based on middle-class values, those who come from disadvantaged circumstances aren't as successful in taking advantage of the limited opportunities that female institutions offer. Minority girls are victims of the double discrimination of their sex and racial or ethnic statuses and don't get services for "their unique developmental, physiological, and emotional needs."[61]

In Chapter 7, we discussed the special concerns of female delinquents. Here, it's important to remember some of these concerns, because they continue to play a part in how female juveniles are handled when incarcerated. The chivalry hypothesis stated that the system treats girls more leniently than boys because they are viewed sympathetically as being led into crime by their boyfriends. One indicator of the chivalry hypothesis at work is the vast disparity between the number of girls and boys who are arrested and processed. Although boys certainly commit more offenses than girls, girls get more consideration for diversion programs. The chivalry hypothesis has two exceptions, which shed some light on the difficulties of confined girls:[62]

1. **Status offenses.** Girls are more likely to be detained for status offenses, such as running away from home or engaging in sexual activities. Historically, juvenile justice officials have held the patriarchal attitude that girls' sexuality needs to be controlled more than that of boys. Because young girls can be physically victimized more readily than boys, who are stronger, and because adolescent girls risk becoming pregnant, the juvenile justice system has been more likely to lock the girls up "for their own protection."

This double standard, even though it's applied with good intentions, has resulted in greater penalties for girls who violate sexual norms. This disparity is most noticeable in secure detention.[63]

2. **Lost causes.** Secure confinement for girls is a problem for another reason. Because the system excludes many nonserious female delinquents, those who sink far enough into the system that they wind up in secure detention are viewed as lost causes and lose much of the sympathy usually reserved for girls. This gender disparity is compounded when race is considered, and just as minority boys are disproportionately incarcerated, so are minority girls.[64]

The experience for incarcerated girls is different than for boys. In the past, the treatment for girls has been to train them in the historically domestic roles of wife and homemaker. Boys received vocational education in subjects such as welding and small-engine repair, while girls were more likely to be schooled in cosmetology and food service. However, educational conditions are changing in some institutions because of personal computers. Most boys and girls are exposed to computers early in their schooling, and many training schools and detention centers provide access to them. One promising avenue of education for incarcerated youths that diminishes the geographic limitations of confinement is online education. An impressive range of subjects is available, and as states invest more resources, it's likely that being locked up in a training home or detention center will no longer be a barrier to getting a decent education. For some youths, the online education might be superior to what they were getting in their own school.

Another important difference in the custody of female and male delinquents concerns how each sex deals with the pains of imprisonment. Although males, to protect themselves, tend to develop extremely masculine roles that rely on strength, aggressiveness, and dominance, females tend to revert to traditionally feminine roles that emphasize family and connectedness. In both adult and juvenile female institutions, residents form **pseudofamilies** in which they act out the roles of father, mother, and children. The atmosphere is one of emotional involvement, companionship, and identity seeking. The females engage in courting behavior similar to that of traditional heterosexual relationships, and the intimacy is more emotional than sexual. They hold hands, touch, and kiss, but the homosexual relationships found in male institutions are largely absent. According to Coramae Mann, these pseudofamilies provide three functions for female inmates:[65]

1. **Affection and belonging.** Young female inmates tend to bond in emotional and economic ways to compensate for being removed from their families and loved ones. Rather than retreating into a protective shell, these young women turn to each other for intimacy, emotional support, and the sharing of what limited goods and services are available in the institution.

2. **Protection.** Pseudofamilies provide protection from attacks from other inmates. A resident who isn't connected to others is easy prey for those who would verbally harass or physically attack the weak. By belonging to a "family," the girl is insulated from being victimized by those who have mental problems or anger-management issues or are simply predatory.

3. **Social control.** Pseudofamilies provide a stable social structure for the resident population. This is useful, not only for the residents' well-being, but for maintaining overall social control in the institution. As long as the residents have a well-defined, informal social structure, they all know where they fit in and are comfortable there. This situation can be contrasted with one that has a constant turnover of inmates, frequent roommate changes, and uncertain rules and regulations.

Correctional Programs

The primary mission of secure correctional institutions is to confine the residents so they don't endanger society. Because virtually all delinquent inmates will eventually be released, institutions also have another extremely important mission. In an attempt to transform juvenile delinquents into self-sufficient, productive, and law-abiding citizens, juvenile detention facilities have instituted several programs to compensate for the social and vocational experiences society normally provides to youths. The four basic areas in which structured programs are available in juvenile institutions are education, vocational training, recreation, and counseling and treatment.

EDUCATION

Education in an institution presents many challenges that neighborhood schools normally don't have. Because so many juveniles who end up in secure detention facilities haven't had successful school experiences, detention facilities must offer the most basic remedial education. Many, if not most, of the juveniles are reading below their age and grade level, and some haven't attended school for a substantial period of time. In addition to lacking basic literacy, many of these juveniles have histories of absenteeism, expulsion, and suspension.

Educating juveniles in secure detention presents additional issues. Many of these youths have learning disabilities (often undiagnosed) that may have contributed to their delinquency. Educational programs in training schools usually don't have the specialized teachers who can help these youths overcome their problems. In addition, and not surprisingly, those who end up in secure detention often have severe behavioral issues that make education difficult.

The educational programs in a detention facility must provide a broad range of services from the most basic remedial reading programs to GED or high school diploma preparation. This is complicated by the fact that juveniles are in and out of the detention facility based on their legal issues, not educational ones. There is no semester or other school term to structure the instruction, so teachers must provide individualized instruction geared to each youth's specific needs and abilities.[66]

VOCATIONAL TRAINING

In addition to traditional education programs, many detention facilities offer vocational training aimed at providing youths with marketable skills that will enable them to get a job, support their future families, pay taxes, and, most important of all, stay out of trouble with the law. As the employment market changes, detention facilities must be flexible and forward looking in designing programs that can help youths find jobs.

This flexibility is especially important when gender is considered. The programs traditionally offered for females were food service, cosmetology, and secretarial training, while auto repair, carpentry, and drafting were aimed at males. Today, detention facilities don't attempt to track juveniles into these previously gender-related occupations but instead try to meet the needs and desires of youths in light of the limited resources that these training programs have.

RECREATIONAL PROGRAMS

Recreational activities can be an effective way to treat incarcerated juveniles. First, physical activity is a way for incarcerated youths to relieve stress. Playing basketball, running, or lifting weights can provide young people with beneficial exercise and relief from the tedium and boredom of institutional living.

Here, youths work in the carpentry shop at the Wisconsin Department of Corrections Ethan Allen School, which was slated to close in 2011. Several states are closing reformatories due to a falling crime rate, alternative treatment policies, and slashed budgets.

Engaging in competitive sports can give them team-building skills and teach them how to win and lose gracefully. However, there is also a negative side to relying too much on sports to mold character. This includes developing a win-at-all-costs attitude, the celebration of physical domination, and cheating. Recreational programs in detention facilities must be carefully planned and monitored to ensure they achieve their goals without negative unintended consequences.[67]

COUNSELING AND TREATMENT

Can we systematically change the behavior of juvenile delinquents by counseling and treating them? Given the high rates of recidivism, do our correctional systems actually prevent crime? Certainly, most individuals who break the law don't adopt a criminal lifestyle, but is this because they have been successfully rehabilitated, or could it be that they didn't like incarceration and are deterred from further offending by the threat of punishment?

Rehabilitation is a cornerstone of the correctional mission. Because nearly every inmate will eventually be released, it's considered essential to provide treatment and counseling so they can return to society. For a long time, no one argued with this ideal. However, in 1974 the rehabilitative philosophy came under attack because it was considered to be a practical failure. In his influential article "What Works? Questions and Answers about Prison Reform," Robert Martinson concluded that, although certain programs might work with certain offenders, no single approach would work for everyone.[68] This "what works" article was interpreted by politicians as "nothing works" and was used as a justification to dismantle rehabilitation programs and rely on punishment. Although prisons and youth detention centers have always maintained a treatment component, in many institutions it became only token treatment aimed at public relations and available to only a few offenders.[69]

Because juvenile justice system philosophy is more favorable to rehabilitation than the criminal justice system, more treatment programs are available. This is because society simply isn't ready to give up on delinquents, and detention is considered the last best chance that some of these youths have to turn around their lives. A vast number of counseling strategies have been used in correctional settings, ranging from the most traditional psychotherapies to New Age–style activities designed to provide inmates with greater insight. Let's review several types of treatments that have been used with adult offenders and delinquents.

Nondirective Counseling. Nondirective counseling techniques are the least effective treatment methodology used in the juvenile justice system because they rely too much on clients' ability to discover their capabilities and find their own direction in life. In nondirective counseling, the counselor is passive and tries to allow the clients to discover their own values and solutions to problems.

Although developing positive relationships with inmates is useful and important, there is always a conditional nature to the degree of acceptance the counselor can have with delinquents. Because counselors work for the institution, they must be concerned with the safety of society, the institution's rules and regulations, and the inmate's potential for dishonesty. The counselor must promote positive behavior and reject lawbreaking attitudes. For these reasons, nondirective counseling isn't well suited to dealing with delinquents.

Directive Counseling. Directive counseling techniques require the client and the counselor to be actively involved. Instead of passively trying to guide the inmate to develop insights into his or her reasons for breaking the law, the directive counselor challenges the inmate to identify and deal with problems quickly and to use reason rather than emotion to evaluate behavior. Transactional analysis and reality therapy place the burden of understanding on the inmate and, if done right, empower the inmate to understand and change his or her own behavior.

» **Transactional analysis.** Transactional analysis was developed by Eric Berne and is sometimes called the "poor man's Freud" because it splits the personality into three parts: child, adult, and parent. Transactional analysis focuses on the interaction between individuals and contends that people communicate best when they employ the "parent" part of the personality. The theory is relatively easy to understand, so the goal is to help offenders analyze how they communicate with others. Transactional analysis is useful for correctional counselors because it provides insight into inmates' manipulative behavior. However, the use of transactional analysis by inexperienced counselors can raise some problems. It's easy to get caught up in terminology (parent, child, adult, games, scripts) and treat counseling as an intellectual exercise. By focusing on the theory's analogies, it's easy to lose sight of the inmate as a person and to treat him or her as a puzzle to be solved or a game to be won. Also, many adult offenders and juvenile delinquents are verbally adept and can use transactional analysis not to reveal themselves, but to hide.[70]

» **Reality therapy.** William Glasser developed reality therapy from experiences dealing with troubled youths at the Ventura School for Delinquent Girls. Instead of analyzing feelings, reality therapy focuses on behavior. It doesn't have a fancy vocabulary like transactional analysis and is easier to teach the client. It's particularly useful with delinquents because it requires them to define their actions as either responsible or irresponsible. Reality therapy doesn't dwell on the past. Regardless of one's reasons or excuses for irresponsible behavior, reality therapy focuses on constructing a plan for responsible behavior. The plan is important, because it forces the inmate to take responsibility for his or her behavior. Clients aren't punished for failing to execute a plan; they're taught to analyze it to see where they went wrong and to make a new plan. For example, many clients make unrealistic or vague plans. If the goal is to get a job, the counselor helps the inmate identify specific steps that will lead to employment. A first step might be to write a résumé. If the inmate has trouble with this step, the counselor will break down the task and help the inmate decide what to put in the résumé, what format to use, and where to send it. The idea is to break the plan into parts that can be accomplished. To most college students, this seems like common sense, but Glasser argues that common sense isn't so common, especially for delinquents.[71]

>> **Rational-emotive behavioral therapy.** Albert Ellis developed rational-emotive behavioral therapy as a way to help inmates understand how the way they think about events can sometimes result in bad behavior. For instance, a youth might blame his behavior problems on his parents because they're divorced. Ellis would say it isn't the divorce that caused the problems, but the way the boy thinks about it. Because the marriage failed, he might harbor feelings of abandonment, misplaced guilt, or anger. In rational-emotive behavioral therapy, the counselor challenges the inmate's thinking patterns to uncover irrational reasoning.[72]

Directive-counseling techniques are best suited for the correctional setting. They provide inmates with expectations of appropriate behavior and expect them to evaluate the morality of their actions and make positive changes. Directive-counseling techniques are easy to understand and have the potential to allow delinquents to become emotionally self-sufficient, requiring no further contact with the counselor.[73]

Group Counseling. Group counseling is used in correctional settings out of necessity. There are simply too many inmates to provide one-on-one counseling services for everyone. Group counseling in a correctional setting takes advantage of having all the clients in one place, and incarcerated juveniles don't have the demands of family and jobs to hinder their treatment.[74] In fact, group therapy might be attractive as a way of breaking up the monotony of institutional living. Group therapy in juvenile detention facilities has a number of advantages and disadvantages:[75]

>> **Advantages.** Group therapy can provide a prosocial outlet for juveniles who want to improve their situation. In many institutions, cliques or gangs set an atmosphere of negativity and are counterproductive. An inmate code develops that works against those who understand why they're delinquent. Group counseling helps inmates learn alternative coping skills, leads to a sense of community, and teaches juveniles to work together to solve problems. Many of these youths have a difficult time relating to others, and learning to communicate respectfully within a group of delinquents is an effective way of learning to deal with others. Finally, group counseling doesn't have the authoritarian relationship present in individual counseling. There may be a trained leader who is a member of the institution's staff, but the real work is done by the juveniles, who are equal members of the group and can exert peer pressure or challenge irrational reasoning.

>> **Disadvantages.** Many juveniles aren't comfortable sharing their problems, concerns, and feelings with their peers. The group counseling session can intimidate those who are, for example, shy, physically small, or homosexual. To push these youths to reveal their vulnerabilities in front of more verbally

14.4 PREVENTION AND INTERVENTION

Crime Counseling

My first job after college was as a probation and parole officer for the Florida Probation and Parole Commission in Fort Lauderdale. We had 34 officers and supervisors who quickly taught me how to deal with offenders. After hearing many lies, I tried not to become cynical about the truthfulness, integrity, and honor of the 100-plus felons on my caseload.

One day my supervisor said to me, "John, why are you so surprised that murderers, rapists, and armed robbers turn out to be liars? They'll tell you what they think you want to hear. You have the power to send them back to prison, so don't think you can be their friend. Make sure you verify everything they tell you."

Although I understood what my supervisor said, I believed I was a great judge of character and could help some of my clients become productive citizens. Many of the department's old-timers told me I was kidding myself, but one other new hire, Paul, had the same goal as I: to help make people better.

Paul and I had over a dozen 18- and 19-year-old clients who were on probation for minor drug violations, breaking-and-entering, and motor vehicle theft. We thought they were basically good kids going through the transition from adolescence to adulthood and that, if properly guided, they would turn out fine. We entered them in GED and vocational training programs, and they seemed to be adjusting well to probation.

So Paul and I decided to form a group to meet with the young men twice a week. Without knowing what we were doing, we developed what we thought were dynamic, positive group-counseling sessions. About 8 to 12 clients showed up for each session, and the discussions were lively and interesting. Paul and I were delighted at how the group developed an instant cohesion in which everyone liked and respected one another. We bragged to the rest of the office about how successful we were in counseling these young men, and we decided that if we got graduate degrees, we could become professional counselors. We obviously had a knack for it.

After a year, I left the department and began my graduate education at Florida State University's School of Criminology. Paul stayed in Fort Lauderdale and continued the group. About four months later, he called to tell me that six of the group members had been caught sawing through the roof of a convenience store.

Our group, which we were so proud of, had formed a burglary ring and had been committing burglaries after each group session, which they had been doing since the third time the group had met. The reason they showed up so consistently and got along so well was that they indeed had something in common. They all loved burglary.

What did I learn? First, probation officers must ensure their perceptions of reality are corroborated by tangible evidence. Second, group counseling is difficult. Offenders must be carefully screened and monitored. Paul and I thought that all was well because the group was so successful. It was a classic case of putting rotten apples together and being surprised at the stink.

aggressive and judgmental peers can be damaging. It's easy to get off topic in group counseling sessions, and the group leader doesn't know where the discussion is going until it spins out of control. What may look like promising avenues of inquiry can waste time and divert the group from dealing with important rehabilitation issues. Also, the session's dynamics may have some unintended consequences. Despite the group leader's efforts, the group members may learn more negative attitudes from each other than positive attitudes. Selecting the right members for the group is important, as well as recognizing that some members can emerge as leaders with bad intentions. Finally, it's easy for the group to confuse activity with results. Although there may be a great deal of discussion about a topic, the time will be wasted if the group leader cannot connect the discussion to the goals of developing insights and positive attitudes, and reforming behavior. Group therapy shouldn't be a freewheeling discussion but should have structure, purpose, and realistic goals.

Treatment and rehabilitation are important goals in the juvenile justice system. Society can't afford to give up on all the youths who get into trouble with the law. According to the Department of Justice, longer sentences in juvenile institutions don't reduce recidivism, and some juveniles who had the lowest offending levels upon incarceration reported committing even more offenses after release.[76] By providing timely and effective interventions, the state can correct the wayward course of many delinquents. These interventions can occur in a variety of community-based or institutional settings and can include a wide array of services.

REENTRY

Once delinquents are released from detention, they must return to society. There are many barriers to successful reentry, not because the juveniles aren't motivated to succeed, but because the environment they're returning to and that likely fostered much of their deviant behavior in the first place hasn't changed. Think of it as being in a cold swimming pool. When you get out of the pool and dry off in the sun, you feel warm. But if you jump back into the pool you will immediately become cold again. Juveniles who have been placed in secure detention may have learned to function under the facility's rules, but, once returned to their dysfunctional families, deviant peers, blighted neighborhoods, and temptations of crime, they may quickly revert to their old activities.

This observation is nothing new. We have long understood that reentry for adult and juvenile offenders is precarious. Several ideas have been proposed to ease that transition. However, it isn't a lack of ideas that prevents successful reentry into conventional society, but a lack of resources. The juvenile justice system would be more successful if it had a range of reentry programs for juveniles with a variety of needs. Several factors are important in designing reentry programs. Four key findings from the *Pathways to Desistance Study* reveal the following:

» Most juveniles who commit felonies eventually reduce their offending regardless of intervention. In effect, they "age out" of crime. Those who have stability in living arrangements and work and school attendance do better at desisting from offending than those who don't.

» Longer stays in juvenile institutions don't reduce recidivism. Rather than deterring future deviant behavior, secure incarceration may actually influence it. The lesson here is to keep youths incarcerated for the shortest time possible. Whatever lessons they learn from incarceration are learned early, and the rest of their stay behind bars can be detrimental.

» Community-based supervision as a component of aftercare is effective for youths who have committed serious offenses. Those receiving community-based services are more likely to attend school, maintain a job, and reduce offending. The longer the aftercare program, the greater the reduction in future deviant behavior.

» Substance-abuse treatment reduces both substance use and lawbreaking. In the short term, it appears that drug treatment not only helps delinquents stay away from drugs, but also promotes prosocial attitudes that appear to result in less offending.[77]

The keys to successful reintegration of the delinquent into society center around providing a structured environment that allows youths to gradually learn to take responsibility for their actions. Halfway houses, electronic monitoring, home confinement, and aftercare programs allow youths to receive the community treatments while also earning increased freedoms and rewards based on good behavior. Rather than throwing young people out into society to fend for themselves, reentry programs provide treatment, structure, guidance, and the continuing threat of sanctions as ways of influencing their behavior.[78]

The biggest problem with juvenile reentry programs is that the required resources aren't always under control of the juvenile justice system. Many of the drug-treatment facilities, family counseling programs, and educational resources are administered by a variety of local, state, and federal agencies as well as private foundations, charities, and religious organizations. Not only is the coordination among all these resources problematic, but often it's unclear which agency or agencies should provide the services. Compounding the problem is the fact that when governmental agencies of all levels are hampered by an economic downturn, reentry programs often lack the funding priority that other aspects of the juvenile justice system enjoy. Citizens are more comfortable with locking up delinquents than with providing resources for their release and reentry.

Questions

1. What are the advantages of residential treatment?
2. Why is incarcerating youths in boot camp prisons and state prisons controversial?
3. Why is crowding in juvenile facilities a problem?
4. What are the four basic areas in which structured programs are available in juvenile institutions?

>> FOCUS ON ETHICS

To Bust or Not to Bust?

As a juvenile probation officer, you have been very successful working with troubled youths other probation officers have given up on. You are especially proud of your efforts with David, a tormented 14-year-old who has been adjudicated delinquent because his violent temper sometimes gets the better of him. He gets into fights at school, engages in shouting matches with his teachers, and acts surly and defiant toward police officers. He spray painted obscene graffiti on the courthouse steps and is suspected of being a drug user and dealer. However, repeated drug tests confirm that he doesn't use any type of drugs, and he contends that he only drinks an occasional beer.

After six months of working with David, you have found that he is a talented artist and have enrolled him in an after-school art program. According to his instructors, he has the potential for a career as a graphic artist. What David would really like to do is art for the video game industry. You have convinced him that, in order to do this, he needs to give up his antisocial behaviors, learn to take direction, work well with others, and develop a professional attitude toward his art.

Today, a police detective has asked you for a favor. David's foster parents are suspected of selling marijuana out of their home. David has been in this home for six weeks, and it's near the school where he takes his art classes. As far as you can tell, there was no problem with this home until the detective showed up at your office. The detective wants you to accompany him to the home because he can't make a search without probable cause. However, if he accompanies you and is invited into the home, he can claim that he smelled marijuana and make the search.

On one hand, you have no problems helping the detective make a case against foster parents who sell drugs. On the other hand, you think such subterfuge is morally questionable, and you're not sure if what the detective proposes is legal. David is doing well in this living situation, and you're afraid that if you help the detective bust his foster parents, David will no longer trust you and may revert to his bad behavior. You are making such good progress with David, you fear this could be a real turning point and that if he loses his confidence in you, he will give up on making something positive out of his life.

WHAT DO YOU DO?

1. Help the detective make a case against David's foster parents.
2. Tell the detective that you will investigate the home and if you see anything suspicious, you will alert him and cooperate in the case.
3. Get some advice from your supervisor on whether the detective's search is even legal.
4. Attempt to move David out of his home before any case is made.
5. Turn the detective down. David's future is too important to risk for what is probably a minor marijuana case.

Summary

Summary

| **Learning Objective 1.** Discuss the many community corrections options for juvenile delinquents. | Standard probation can be formal (court-ordered) as the result of being adjudicated delinquent, or informal (voluntary) as an alternative to formal processing.

Intensive-supervision probation is designed to allow the probation department to provide extended services to the juveniles who should go to institutions where they can be adequately supervised and treated.

In an electronic-monitoring program, the probationer wears an electronic ankle bracelet or other computer-monitored device.

Home confinement restricts offenders and delinquents to their homes for large parts of the day.

The idea of fines and restitution is to make the juvenile accountable for his or her actions.

For many youths, staying at home isn't a good option, because the parents might be unable to ensure a supportive environment. Judges generally have two options: secure and nonsecure residential treatment programs. |
|---|---|
| **Learning Objective 2.** Understand that the juvenile justice system's goal is to craft a disposition that is in the best interests of the youth while protecting society. | The traditional way to respond to juvenile delinquents is to provide the least restrictive treatment. The idea is to not harm the youth by placing him or her in a situation that doesn't allow for positive growth. |
| **Learning Objective 3.** Tell why placing juveniles in secure institutions is a last resort and keeping them in the community is the optimal goal. | Keeping youths in the community so they can live with their parents and attend their own schools is best. Juvenile justice system programs and agencies seek to ensure that society is protected and that the juvenile gets the treatment and supervision needed for successful reintegration. |

Learning Objective 4. Reason why juveniles who have committed serious delinquent acts or who have demonstrated that they aren't amenable to community-based treatment options often go to secure institutions.	Much like an adult prison, a secure institution restricts the movements of inmates to the institution. Most juveniles in secure institutions have committed offenses that would be criminal if committed by adults.
Learning Objective 5. Discuss jails and detention centers as the two basic short-term confinement options.	Juveniles who must be detained for short periods of time are generally sent to jails. Jails also hold adult offenders and detainees. Some youths confined in jails have been charged as adults and are waiting for criminal trials. Juveniles held as juveniles go to jails because they require secure confinement until they can be seen by a judge. The use of detention varies by state. Some states use detention only for temporary holding; some states use it to sanction probation violators, while others use it as a disposition. Some states use secure detention for all three purposes.
Learning Objective 6. Describe how juvenile correctional facilities provide for the extended, secure confinement of juvenile offenders.	The primary mission of secure correctional institutions is to confine the residents so they don't endanger society. Because virtually all delinquent inmates will eventually be released, institutions also attempt to transform juvenile delinquents into good citizens. To this end, they have instituted programs to compensate for the social and vocational experiences available in society. The four basic areas in which structured programs exist are education, vocational training, recreation, and counseling and treatment.

Chapter Review Questions

1. What kind of problems are beyond the mandate and abilities of the juvenile justice system?

2. What are the various approaches of community corrections?

3. What are the four phases a case goes through in intensive-supervision probation programs?

4. Who decides how much victim restitution a juvenile delinquent must pay?

5. What types of offenders are most likely to receive residential treatment?

6. What are the advantages of alternative treatment programs?

7. In what way do juveniles experience the "pains of imprisonment"?

8. What are the differences between jail and a juvenile detention center?

9. What are the advantages of boot camp prison?

10. What additional problems of incarceration are experienced by girls as compared to boys?

Key Terms

boot camp prison—A short-term prison, usually for young offenders, that uses military boot camp training and discipline techniques for rehabilitation.

electronic monitoring—The use of an electronic device, usually one that the offender wears, to monitor an offender's location and activities.

home confinement—A sentence that requires that the offender be confined in and around the area of the offender's home.

institutionalization—The loss of the ability to make decisions for oneself because of the long period of time spent in a secure facility.

intensive-supervision probation—Close, controlled tracking of a probationer's activities by a probation officer or a team of officers.

nonsecure detention—Placement of a juvenile in a group home, foster care, or other program in which the juvenile may come and go with permission.

pains of imprisonment—Deprivations that define the punishment aspect of incarceration.

probation—The conditional release of juveniles to the custody of parents or guardians.

pseudofamilies—The groups that females in adult and juvenile institutions form, as a response to the pains of imprisonment, in which they act out the roles of father, mother, and children.

restitution—Court-ordered compensation by the offender to the victim(s) for their psychological, physical, or financial losses resulting from an offense.

special conditions of probation—Requirements of a person on probation that apply specifically to that person.

standard conditions of probation—Requirements of a person on probation that apply to all probationers, regardless of individual needs or offense.

Endnotes

1   Anthony Platt, *The Child Savers: The Invention of Delinquency* (Chicago: University of Chicago Press, 1969).

2   Kären M. Hess and Robert W. Drowns, *Juvenile Justice* (Belmont, CA: Wadsworth, 2004), 369.

3   Platt, *The Child Savers: The Invention of Delinquency.*

4   Sarah Livsey, *Juvenile Delinquency Probation Caseload, 2007* (Washington, DC: US Department of Justice, Office of Justice Programs, Office of Juvenile Justice and Delinquency Prevention, 2010), 2. Online at www.ncjrs.gov/pdffiles1/ojjdp/230170.pdf.

5   Crystal Knoll and Melissa Sickmund, *Delinquency Cases in Juvenile Court, 2007* (Washington, DC: US Department of Justice, Office of Justice Programs, Office of Juvenile Justice and Delinquency Prevention, 2010), 2–3. Online at www.ncjrs.gov/pdffiles1/ojjdp/230168.pdf.

6   Livsey, *Juvenile Delinquency Probation Caseload, 2007*, 2.

7   Bruce I. Wolford, *Juvenile Justice Educating: "Who Is Educating the Youth,"* (Richmond, KY: Council for Educators of At-Risk Youth, 2000).

8   Randy Borum, "Managing At-Risk Offenders in the Community," *Journal of Contemporary Criminal Justice* (2003): 114–137.

9   Angela A. Robertson, Paul W. Grimes, and Kevin E. Rogers, "A Short-Run Cost-Benefit Analysis of Community-Based Interventions for Juvenile Offenders," *Crime and Delinquency* 47 (2001): 265–284.

10 Robert A. Shearer, "Probation Strategies of Juvenile and Adult Pre-Service Trainees," *Federal Probation* 66 (2002): 33–42.

11 Thomas G. Blomberg and Karol Lucken, "Stacking the Deck by Piling up Sanctions: Is Intermediate Punishment Designed to Fail?" *Howard Journal of Criminal Justice* 1 (1994): 62–80.

12 *In re J. G.* 692 N.E. 2d 1226 (Ill. App. 1998).

13 Richard G. Wiebush, "Juvenile Intensive Supervision: The Impact on Felony Offenders Diverted from Institutional Placement," *Crime and Delinquency* 39 (1993): 68–89.

14 Kim English, Suzanne Pullen, and Susan M. Chadwick, *Comparison of Intensive Supervision Probation and Community Corrections Clientele* (Denver: Colorado Division of Criminal Justice, 1996).

15 Intensive Supervision Juvenile Probation Program, www.findyouthinfo.org/program-details.aspx?pid=598. Accessed September 16, 2011.

16 Wendy Johnston, "An Innovative Solution to the Problem of Juvenile Offenders in Missouri," *Journal of Offender Monitoring* 13 (2000): 18–38.

17 Timothy P. Cadigan, "PACTS," *Federal Probation* 65 (2001): 25–30.

18 David Listug, "Wisconsin Sheriff's Office Saves Money and Resources," *American Jails* 10 (1996): 85–86.

19 Julie M. Houk, "Electronic Monitoring of Probationers: A Step toward Big Brother?" *Golden Gate University Law Review* 14 (1984): 431–446.

20 Alvin W. Cohn, "Electronic Monitoring and Graduated Sanctions," *Journal of Offender Monitoring* 13 (2000): 19–20.

21 Terry L. Baumer, Michael G. Maxfield, and Robert Mendelsohn, "A Comparative Analysis of Three Electronically Monitored Home Detention Programs," *Justice Quarterly* 10 (1993): 121–142.

22 Ronald Ball, Ronald Huff, and Robert Lilly, *House Arrest and Correctional Policy: Doing Time at Home* (Newbury Park, CA: Sage, 1988).

23 William Staples, "Restitution as a Sanction in Juvenile Court," *Crime and Delinquency* 32, no. 2 (1986): 177–185.

24 Sudpito Ray, "Juvenile Restitution and Recidivism in a Midwestern County," *Federal Probation* 59 (1995): 55–62.

25 Anthony Walsh, *Correctional Assessment, Casework, and Counseling*, 4th ed. (Alexandria, VA: American Correctional Association, 2006), 408.

26 Knoll and Sickmund, *Delinquency Cases in Juvenile Court, 2007*, 2–3.

27 Sarah Hockenberry, Melissa Sickmund, and Anthony Sladky, *Juvenile Residential Facility Census, 2008: Selected Findings* (Washington, DC: US Department of Justice, Office of Justice Programs, Office of Juvenile Justice and Delinquency Prevention, 2011), 2. Online at www.ncjrs.gov/pdffiles1/ojjdp/231683.pdf.

28 Ibid., 3.

29 Andrea J. Sedlak and Carol Bruce, *Youth's Characteristics and Backgrounds* (Washington, DC: US Department of Justice, Office of Justice Programs, Office of Juvenile Justice and Delinquency Prevention, 2010), 2. Online at www.ncjrs.gov/pdffiles1/ojjdp/227730.pdf.

30 Ibid., 4.

31 Ibid., 6

32 Patricia Torbet and Linda Szymanski, *State Legislative Responses to Violent Juvenile Crime* (Washington, DC: US Department of Justice, 1998).

33 Dean Champion, *The Juvenile Justice System: Delinquency, Processing, and the Law* (Upper Saddle River, NJ: Prentice Hall, 2004), 479.

34 Burt Galaway et al., "Specialist Foster Care for Delinquent Youth," *Federal Probation* 59 (1995): 19–27.

35 Thomas Castellano and Irina Soderstrom, "Therapeutic Wilderness Programs and Juvenile Recidivism: A Program Evaluation," *Journal of Offender Rehabilitation* 17 (1992): 19–46.

36 Angela R. Gover and Doris Layton MacKenzie, "Importation and Deprivation Explanations of Juveniles' Adjustment to Correctional Facilities," *International Journal of Offender Therapy and Comparative Criminology* 44 (2000): 450–467.

37 Jon Gunnar Bernburg and Marvin Krohn, "Labeling, Life Changes, and Adult Crime: The Direct and Indirect Effects of Official Intervention in Adolescence on Crime in Early Adulthood," *Criminology* 41 (2003): 1287–1318.

38 Hockenberry, Sickmund, and Sladky, *Juvenile Residential Facility Census, 2008*, 5–6.

39 Melissa Sickmund, *Juveniles in Corrections* (Washington, DC: US Department of Justice, Office of Justice Programs, Office of Juvenile Justice and Delinquency Prevention, 2004), 17. Online at www.ncjrs.gov/pdffiles1/ojjdp/202885.pdf.

40 Gresham M. Sykes, *The Society of Captives: A Study of a Maximum Security Prison* (Princeton, NJ: Princeton University Press, 1971).

41 Erving Goffman, *Asylums: Essays on the Social Situation of Mental Patients and Other Inmates* (Garden City, NY: Doubleday, 1961).

42 Allen J. Beck, Paige M. Harrison, and Paul Guerino, *Sexual Victimization in Juvenile Facilities Reported by Youth, 2008–09* (Washington, DC: US Department of Justice, Office of Justice Programs, Bureau of Justice

Statistics, 2010), 1. Online at bjs.ojp.usdoj.gov/content/pub/pdf/svjfry09.pdf.

43 Matthew Silberman, *A World of Violence: Corrections in America* (Belmont, CA: Wadsworth, 1995).

44 James Austin, Kelly Dedel Johnson, and Maria Gregoriou, *Juveniles in Adult Prisons and Jails: A National Assessment* (Washington, DC: US Department of Justice, Office of Justice Programs, Bureau of Justice Assistance, 2000). Online at www.ncjrs.gov/pdffiles1/bja/182503.pdf.

45 Paige M. Harrison and Allen J. Beck, *Prison and Jail Inmates at Midyear 2005* (Washington, DC: US Department of Justice, Office of Justice Programs, Bureau of Justice Statistics, 2006), 8.

46 Henri E. Cauvin, "Girl's Jailing Likely Breaks Federal Law, Judge Says," *Washington Post*, September 16, 2006, p. B4.

47 Knoll and Sickmund, *Delinquency Cases in Juvenile Court, 2007*, 2–3.

48 Sickmund, *Juveniles in Corrections*, 18.

49 Hockenberry, Sickmund, and Sladky, *Juvenile Residential Facility Census, 2008*, 5–6.

50 Roberta C. Cronin, *Boot Camp Prisons for Adult and Juvenile Offenders: Overview and Update* (Washington, DC: US Government Printing Office, 1994).

51 Margaret Bezer, "Juvenile Boot Camps Don't Make Sense," *American Bar Association Journal of Criminal Justice* 10 (1996): 20–21.

52 Malcolm Feeley and Jonathan Simon, "The New Penology: Notes on the Emerging Strategy of Corrections and Its Implications," *Criminology* 30 (1992): 449–474.

53 Sickmund, *Juveniles in Corrections*, 19.

54 Dale G. Parent et al., *Conditions of Confinement: Juvenile Detention and Corrections Facilities* (Washington, DC: US Department of Justice, Office of Juvenile Justice and Delinquency Prevention, 1994).

55 Hockenberry, Sickmund, and Sladky, *Juvenile Residential Facility Census, 2008*, 6.

56 *Rhodes v. Chapman*, 452 U.S. 337 (1981).

57 P. Rohde, J. R. Seeley, and D. E. Mace, "Correlates of Suicidal Behavior in a Juvenile Detention Population," *Suicide and Life-Threatening Behavior* 27 (1997): 164–175.

58 Craig Haney, "Infamous Punishment: The Psychological Consequences of Isolation,"

in Edward J. Latessa et al., eds. *Correctional Contexts: Contemporary and Classical Readings*, 2nd ed. (Los Angeles: Roxbury, 2005), 172.

59 American Bar Association and National Bar Association, *Justice by Gender: The Lack of Appropriate Prevention, Diversion and Treatment Alternatives for Girls in the Juvenile Justice System*, (Washington, DC: The Associations, 2001).

60 National Mental Health Association, *Mental Health and Adolescent Girls in the Justice System*, www.nmha.org/children/justjuv/girlsjj.cfm. Accessed September 16, 2011.

61 American Bar Association and National Bar Association, *Justice by Gender*.

62 E. A. Anderson, "The Chivalrous Treatment of the Female Offender in the Arms of the Criminal Justice System: A Review of the Literature," *Social Problems* 23 (1976): 350–357.

63 Meda Chesney-Lind, "Juvenile Delinquency: The Sexualization of Female Crime," *Psychology Today* 19 (1974): 43–46.

64 Michael J. Leiber, "Disproportionate Minority Confinement (DMC) of Youth: An Analysis of State and Federal Efforts to Address the Issue," in Everette B. Penn et al., eds., *Race and Juvenile Justice* (Durham, NC: Carolina Academic Press), 141–185.

65 Coramae Mann, *Female Crime and Delinquency* (Tuscaloosa: University of Alabama Press, 1984), 188–189.

66 Bruce I. Wolford, "Youth Education in the Juvenile Justice System," *Corrections Today* 62, no. 5 (2000): 128–130.

67 Brenda Robinson, "Leisure Education as a Rehabilitative Tool for Youth in Incarceration," *Journal of Leisurability* 27 (2000): 27–34.

68 Robert Martinson, "What Works? Questions and Answers about Prison Reform," *Public Interest* 35 (1974): 22–54.

69 James B. Jacobs, *Stateville: The Penitentiary in Mass Society* (Chicago: University of Chicago Press, 1977).

70 Walsh, *Correctional Assessment, Casework, and Counseling*, 193–200.

71 William Glasser, *Reality Therapy: A New Approach to Psychiatry* (New York: Harper, 1975).

72 Albert Ellis, *A New Guide to Rational Living* (Hollywood, CA: Wiltshire, 1975).

73 B. Sharp, *Changing Criminal Thinking: A Treatment Program* (Lanham, MD: American Correctional Association, 2006).

74 David Lester, "Group and Milieu Therapy," in P. Van Voorhis, M. Braswell, and D. Lester, eds., *Correctional Counseling and Rehabilitation* (Cincinnati, OH: Anderson, 2000).

75 For a comprehensive list of advantages and disadvantages of group counseling, see Walsh, *Correctional Assessment, Casework, and Counseling*, 253.

76 Edward P. Mulvey, *Highlights From Pathways to Desistance: A Longitudinal Study of Serious Adolescent Offenders* (Washington, DC: US Department of Justice, Office of Justice Programs, Office of Juvenile Justice and Delinquency Prevention, 2011), 2. Online at www.ncjrs.gov/pdffiles1/ojjdp/230971.pdf.

77 Ibid.

78 Shay Bilchik, "National Reentry Resource Center Addresses Juvenile Reentry," *Juvenile Justice News: Corrections Today* (October 2010): 100–101.

International and Comparative Delinquency

From health care to education to the control of juvenile delinquency, some nations appear to have developed superior responses to their youth problems. Although many of these solutions aren't feasible in the United States because of political, cultural, or societal reasons, it's worth considering how other nations' experiences might better inform some of the policies of the US juvenile justice system.

Before we consider other youth justice systems, we should discuss how a nation's particular culture affects not only how a government responds to youth crime, but also the reasons that young people break the law. To do this, we must consider the concept of culture.

Culture and the Discontented

If we're to appreciate why young people break the law, and learn how to effectively respond, we must look beyond our borders at how other societies handle youth justice. First, let's review the reasons why we seldom consider other cultures.

» **Cultural isolation.** To a large extent, the United States is culturally isolated from the rest of the world, primarily because of the size of the country. Because the United States is so large and can meet the needs of so much of its population, Americans tend to look inward. US isolation can also be observed in the relatively small number of Americans who speak a

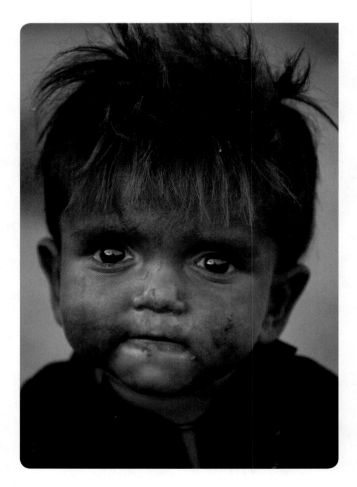

We must consider the concept of culture to understand how governments around the world respond to youth crime.

language other than English. In contrast, in a small European nation such as Switzerland, many people are multilingual because they have the opportunity to interact with individuals from many different cultures.[1]

)) **Ability to affect.** Another reason the delinquency experiences of other cultures are seldom considered is because as other nations do things differently, and perhaps even better, we often ignore them because we can't reproduce some of the underlying conditions that make their ways different. For example, because of cultural history, youths in other nations might have completely different experiences with alcohol. Nations that have embraced Islam have radically different laws, customs, and penalties for alcoholic consumption.[2] It's unlikely that the cultural and religious traditions of Islamic nations can be reproduced in the United States as a way to handle adolescent drinking.

)) **Ethnocentrism.** Sometimes there is a tendency to consider variations of behavior around the world and conclude that the way one's own culture does things is the best way. **Ethnocentrism** means that individuals believe that their own laws, religion, schools, and family practices are the right way, the natural way, or "God's chosen way."[3]

)) **Globalism. Globalism** refers to the shrinking of the world. Many cultures are losing their distinctiveness and are becoming homogenized. Because the United States is the world's only remaining traditional superpower, its culture is quickly spreading around the world. The English language has become the international language of trade, and with advances in satellite technology, American culture, including MTV and CNN, is available almost everywhere. Why learn about other cultures when they're becoming so much like our own?

Culture consists of art, technology, customs, laws, artifacts, and the bond that makes individuals believe they're connected and qualitatively different from others outside the culture.[4] Sometimes we're blind to culture and its effects. Like fish in water, we don't realize that a sea of culture surrounds us until we are plucked out and placed in a different culture. Then we flop around, trying to acclimate to a new environment and figure out how to communicate, find our way around the city, drive on the correct side of the road, and order a beer. We don't fit in because all our cultural reference points are gone, and we haven't deciphered the new cultural code.

To understand other cultures, we must first appreciate the limitations of our own perspective. We must use C. Wright Mills's **sociological imagination** to consider youth crime and understand what part of it is peculiar to a particular culture and what part applies to all cultures.[5] Do other societies raise their children in ways that avoid the problems of American delinquency? Are there better ways of socializing children? Our attempts to answer these questions won't be conclusive. The influence of culture, although pervasive, is difficult to pinpoint in rapidly changing societies. The goals of this chapter are more modest: we will highlight several of the pertinent and important issues of attempting cross-cultural comparisons and offer some examples of how other countries respond to delinquent behavior.

INSTANT RECALL
FROM CHAPTER 1

sociological imagination
The idea that one must look beyond the obvious to evaluate how social location influences how one considers society.

Comparative Delinquency

Before actually considering the problems of youth offending in other societies, we must consider how culture greatly determines what is acceptable behavior and what is unacceptable behavior. The cultural context in which behavior occurs dictates how a particular society will respond. For instance, premarital sex can be punished with death in some Islamic societies, but it's considered pretty normal in the United States, although it's frowned on by some segments of society. So, what components of culture determine whether behavior is rewarded or punished? At the most basic level, the list would include the following:

» **Religion.** Religion is a powerful social institution. It's the absolute social authority in some nations, while others marginalize it. In the United States, religion has an uneven history as an influencing force. Because of the constitutional provisions for the separation of church and state, religion doesn't play as important a part in the justice system as it does in other nations. Nevertheless, the proper place for religion in public life, especially in the justice system, continues to be contested.[6] From the controversy of displaying the Christian Ten Commandments in local courthouses, to the struggles to get federal judges who have specific views on abortion confirmed by the US Senate, to the federal funding of faith-based rehabilitation programs, religion has once again demanded a seat at the table of criminal justice policy. In societies dominated by a single religion, there's little or no controversy about religion playing a dominant role in the justice system. As we discuss later, other justice systems are tied much more directly to the prevailing religion in some nations.

» **Sex and gender.** Although the women's movement of the 20th century has made great strides in improving the level of sex equality in the United States, the struggle continues because of entrenched interests in maintaining distinct roles for women and men. Some other societies haven't been as progressive in breaking down gender barriers.[7] Therefore, any examination of the justice system must account for how women's issues are handled. In countries where women can't vote, enter into legal contracts, own property, or choose their husbands, it isn't surprising to see gender inequities encoded into the criminal law.

» **Economic development.** One of the most significant factors that make the social environment of nations different is the level of economic development. There is a great deal of difference between a fully developed, industrialized, Western nation like the United States and a developing nation such as Sudan. Comparing youth crime rates between these nations isn't only impossible, it is fruitless. The differences in what influences children's lives in each country are so great that it's pointless to even make such an attempt. In Sudan, where the daily concerns are genocide, famine, and political turmoil, the most pressing issue of youth is survival, not delinquency. Therefore, the stage of development can tell us more about the conditions of childhood in a country than can just the rate of youth crime.

With this understanding that culture is a determining force in how youth crime is defined, measured, and recognized, we can now consider youth crime and victimization throughout the world. Although this chapter can't cover all the circumstances that affect youths, we can highlight and compare certain youth issues, including laws, police treatment, rehabilitation, and detention. The United Nations has adopted a set of rules concerning juvenile detention. For a selection of these rules, see Programs for Children. As we skip around the globe in this section, our goal is simply to indicate patterns of youth crime and victimization and not to present a comprehensive view.

15.1 PROGRAMS FOR CHILDREN

Selected United Nations Rules for the Protection of Juveniles Deprived of Their Liberty

» The juvenile justice system should uphold the rights and safety and promote the physical and mental well-being of juveniles. Imprisonment should be used as a last resort.

» The Rules should be applied impartially, without discrimination of any kind as to race, colour, sex, age, language, religion, nationality, political or other opinion, cultural beliefs or practices, property, birth or family status, ethnic or social origin, and disability.

» A juvenile is every person under the age of 18. The age limit below which it should not be permitted to deprive a child of his or her liberty should be determined by law.

» Juveniles who are detained, under arrest, or awaiting trial ("untried") are presumed innocent and shall be treated as such.

» Juveniles should have the right of legal counsel and be enabled to apply for free legal aid, where such aid is available, and to communicate regularly with their legal advisers.

» No juvenile should be received in any detention facility without a valid commitment order of a judicial, administrative or other public authority.

» In all detention facilities juveniles should be separated from adults, unless they are members of the same family.

» The design of detention facilities for juveniles and the physical environment should be in keeping with the rehabilitative aim of residential treatment.

» Every detention facility shall ensure that every juvenile receives food that is suitably prepared and presented at normal meal times and of a quality and quantity to satisfy the standards of dietetics, hygiene and health and, as far as possible, religious and cultural requirements. Clean drinking water should be available to every juvenile at any time.

» Every juvenile of compulsory school age has the right to education suited to his or her needs and abilities and designed to prepare him or her for return to society.

» Every juvenile should have the right to a suitable amount of time for daily free exercise, in the open air whenever weather permits.

More than 200 young children live in Afghanistan's prisons because they must remain with their mothers who are incarcerated for various offenses. Here, Habiba, who has completed three years of a 10-year prison sentence for murder, holds her daughter who was born when Habiba entered prison but still can't walk.

» Every juvenile should be allowed to satisfy the needs of his or her religious and spiritual life, in particular by attending the services or meetings provided in the detention facility or by conducting his or her own services and having possession of the necessary books or items of religious observance and instruction of his or her denomination.

» The family or guardian of a juvenile and any other person designated by the juvenile have the right to be informed of the state of health of the juvenile on request and in the event of any important changes in the health of the juvenile.

» The carrying and use of weapons by personnel should be prohibited in any facility where juveniles are detained.

» All disciplinary measures constituting cruel, inhuman or degrading treatment shall be strictly prohibited, including corporal punishment, placement in a dark cell, closed or solitary confinement or any other punishment that may compromise the physical or mental health of the juvenile concerned.

Source: Abridged from United Nations Rules for the Protection of Juveniles Deprived of Their Liberty, adopted December 1990. Online at www.un.org/documents/ga/res/45/a45r113.htm.

Questions

1. Why are direct comparisons between international juvenile justice systems difficult and generally unproductive?
2. What are some of the major hurdles confronting comparative juvenile justice scholars?

Juvenile Delinquency and Juvenile Justice in Other Nations

Comparing foreign youth crime and youth justice systems to the United States' juvenile justice system is interesting because a variety of responses to problems can be seen, and it's always possible to find a better way. Remember, however, that major differences among cultures, justice systems, and data collection make direct comparisons difficult. We have already discussed how religion, gender roles, and level of development can affect the cultural conditions in which young people must negotiate their respective legal systems. Now let's turn to some features of youth justice systems to get a sense of why it's difficult to compare youth justice statistics. The first major hurdle that comparative researchers confront is language.[8]

Although some researchers may speak two or three languages fluently enough to do comparative research, few, if any, criminologists speak all the western European languages, much less those of the rest of the world. Therefore, one must either find a common language in which to communicate with officials from other nations or hire an interpreter. Luckily, many scholars study abroad, and the United States is the recipient of graduate students from around the globe who can provide a picture of their nations' justice systems.

In addition to the language barrier, there are certain definitional barriers. Offenses vary from nation to nation, and an activity that is considered a felony in one nation might be considered a misdemeanor in another and legal in a third. The terms "felony" and "misdemeanor" are problematic as well, because not all nations categorize seriousness of crime in this manner. Nations report and record crime data in a variety of ways. Resource constraints, political agendas, accuracy, and technology can make it difficult to compare criminal and youth justice data. For example, the nation of Oman collects delinquency statistics on males but not on females.[9]

It may be tempting to conclude that, with all the differences between nations in terms of culture and reporting procedures, attempting to do comparative analysis on crime and delinquency is a fruitless endeavor. If one wants a neat set of statistics that can easily be accurately coded into a data set and analyzed by a statistical computer program, this may be the case. However, even given the differences in culture, definitions of crime, and reporting practices, the comparative method can yield valuable information. In fact, by highlighting the differences, researchers can obtain insights, not only into how criminal and youth justice systems compare, but also into how these differences might provide ideas for improving the way juvenile justice is meted out in the United States.[10]

It's beyond the scope of this book to provide a comprehensive overview of youth justice around the world. Rather, the goal is to present some representative examples of the differences, not only in justice systems, but also in the cultures in which these systems operate. Because there is as much variation within regions of the world as between them, this material is organized based on the population size of the nation. As we move from the larger nations to the smaller ones, we will demonstrate, through the variety of systems of youth justice, the richness and ramifications of cultural differences.

China

China is a great place to start our investigation of other youth justice systems because it's so different from the United States and because it is undergoing extremely rapid social change. The cultural dynamics in China are so fluid that it's difficult to assume with any confidence what its future holds. It's quickly being transformed from a state-controlled economy to a market economy, and its people are demanding greater freedoms and more control over their lives. Here are some of the major issues pressing on China:

» **Population.** China has over 1.3 billion citizens.[11] When you consider that the United States has just over 300 million people, it becomes clear that the extra billion people China must support present immense challenges.[12] Family planning is a matter of government policy, and a one-child-per-couple rule is enforced. Because of its large population, there are restrictions on where people may live. China's citizens must obtain permission to move from one province to another because the government can't allow everyone to move to already-crowded urban areas. Population size is China's primary concern, and it influences not only government policy but also the entire range of China's cultural issues.

» **Government.** China is one of the few remaining communist nations in the world. It became communist in 1949 under the leadership of Mao Zedong, and, like the Soviet Union, it attempted centralized economic planning, which failed to provide for its people's needs. China's Cultural Revolution, in which all things Western were rejected, plunged the country into cultural isolation and poverty. China fell far behind the rest of the world in terms of industrialization and world trade and is now trying to modernize. Its economy is currently a changing mixture of capitalism and **communism** as its leaders compete on the world's economic stage without letting the marketplace dictate cultural and political change.

» **Religion.** China has no official religion. The government has a policy of atheism but is becoming somewhat tolerant of individual religious practices. Historically, the religion of China was Confucianism, with Buddhism and Taoism also practiced. Western missionaries introduced Christianity, and the northern Xinjiang Province is almost completely Muslim. After years of repressing all religions, China now has a more tolerant policy, but the government is far from supportive of religious freedoms.[13]

It's within this context of cultural change that China's youth justice system is emerging. In comparison to the United States, China doesn't have a formal juvenile justice system, so other social institutions handle the less significant cases.[14] Schools, families, and neighborhood organizations deal with many minor instances of deviant behavior, with the idea that these problems can best be solved without police involvement. When there are youth suspects in serious cases of homicide, rape, or robbery, the adult court and corrections programs handle them. In such cases, provisions are made to separate young children from adults, but the legal mechanisms are essentially the same.

The youth crime rate in China is difficult to measure because most available statistics are those of official agencies. China didn't even disclose its crime statistics to the public until 1986, and like the Uniform Crime Reports, China's official statistics can't reflect the vast dark figure of crime.[15] The differences in how crime is handled informally in China make comparisons with the United States even more inaccurate.

Although the age of criminal responsibility in China is 16, a youth between the ages of 14 and 16 who commits a serious offense, such as homicide, injurious assault, robbery, arson, or habitual theft, is considered to bear full criminal responsibility. Usually, however, the punishment is lighter than it would be for a person over the age of 16, and the death penalty isn't specified for youths under the age of 18. Youths under the age of 16 who aren't punished by the state are sent home, and the head of the family is ordered to discipline the youth.[16]

In 2003, authorities arrested 69,780 youths, which represented 9.1 percent of all suspects arrested that year, as well as an increase of 12.7 percent over the number of youths arrested in 2002. According to official statistics, 317,925 youths were arrested from 1998 to 2003, comprising 7.3 percent of the criminal suspects arrested during these five years.[17] A youth-delinquency-prevention-office survey reported that most young suspects were between the ages of 15 and 16, although an increasing number of youths under the age of 14 have been arrested in recent years.

According to the China Youth and Children Research Center, the main youth crimes were robbery, theft, assault, and rape. Gang crimes accounted for 70 percent of delinquency, and about 85 percent of the nation's drug addicts are youths.[18] Youth crime in China is almost exclusively male. Although females comprise only 2 percent of those arrested for youth offending, their numbers are rising.[19] As China continues to modernize, it can be anticipated that female delinquency will start to catch up with female delinquency in other nations while remaining only a small proportion of delinquency in China.

In 1984, Shanghai opened China's first youth courtroom, in which youths were differentiated from adult offenders. Although China still has no youth justice system, in 2004, the southern municipality of Guangzhou began the establishment of the nation's first dedicated youth court. Currently, China has more than 7,200 judges who hear delinquency cases.[20] As of 2004, about 19,000 youths were incarcerated in "education centers," which are separate from adult detention facilities. The adult system has provisions that specify how youths are to be processed, but there's no statutory authority to guide the development of a separate system as is found in the United States. As in the adult system, the primary dispositions available to young offenders who are sent to court are fines and incarceration. Although minor offenders are treated outside the system to a much greater extent than in the United States, once the offense is considered serious enough, the youth is inserted into a system that hasn't yet evolved well-defined processes and programs for prevention and rehabilitation.

This may be changing, however, as China has adopted an official policy of rehabilitation for young offenders, rather than punishment. In 2003, Shanghai and Beijing launched a program in which young offenders convicted of minor offenses worked in communities, instead of serving a jail term. This disposition may even be more critical in China than it is in the United States. Ding Shouxing, chief justice with Shanghai's Changning district court, has explained that, because most Chinese families have only one child, "Imprisonment would not only leave a scar that stains the young, but also makes their parents despair, and thus might change the life of a child and his family completely."[21]

Although one might be tempted to conclude that China has a long way to go before it catches up with the United States in its youth-offending response, this is a precarious conclusion, because so little is known about the comparative virtues of each system, given the wide gap in cultural conditions and quality of data.

Like Americans, the Chinese point to bad parenting as a cause of youth crime. In Shanghai, youths charged with minor offenses are urged to do volunteer work during their probationary periods, and both the youth and the youth's parents are counseled. In discussing the program, a district court official said, "Many juvenile crimes are related to the youngsters' parents, who are either too busy to take care of them or have spoiled them. We're hoping to help them better educate their kids."[22]

The one statement that can be made with certainty about China's delinquency issues and its response to youth offending is that these will certainly change in the years ahead. China is undergoing sweeping reforms in its economy and in the freedoms that its citizens expect. As Western culture via satellite television becomes available, China can expect more challenges to its society, which emphasizes conformity. Movement toward democracy will also bring more scrutiny of China's legal system.

India

With nearly a billion people, India is the world's largest democracy. Like China, it's an old country that has been plagued for centuries with overpopulation and poverty. Unlike China, India was exposed to Western-style government as a British colony. India gained its independence in 1947 and has been a self-governing democracy for as long as China has been a communist state. Part of the process of separation from Britain involved dividing traditional India into two nations, India and Pakistan, based on religion.[23] After a massive transfer of population, India is now 80 percent Hindu and 12 percent Muslim. By contrast, Pakistan is now a predominantly Muslim state.[24]

India has the world's highest number of users of opium products, including heroin, because of its proximity to Afghanistan and Myanmar, according to a United Nations survey. Here, a street child smokes a cigarette.

India was heavily influenced by British colonization. It based its legal institutions on the British model, and many of its lawyers and judges, such as Mohandas K. Gandhi, were educated in England. Once India gained independence, there was a relatively seamless transition in legal apparatus involving youths, because the British had already granted broad authority to India for a wide range of concerns.

The modern foundation of India's approach to juvenile delinquency was created in 1986 by the Juvenile Justice Act. The act's primary objective was to protect, care for, rehabilitate, educate, and give vocational training to delinquent children, as well as to make services available to neglected children. This program provides for a number of aftercare homes for children, many of them run by voluntary organizations. Formal introduction into the juvenile justice system occurs only after other alternatives have been explored. Additionally, the Juvenile Justice Act seeks to address the family's problems before employing detention. Prior to 2000, the age below which males were considered to be juveniles was set at age 16. Males over the age of 16 were considered to be adults. In 2000, the legislation was amended to raise the age to 18 (which is also the juvenile cutoff age for females). See Crosscurrents to learn why age is such a difficult juvenile justice issue in India.

In India, the age of criminal responsibility begins at 7. However, children between the ages of 7 and 12 aren't held responsible for criminal acts if it can be proved that the child doesn't understand what he or she has done. India has special courts to deal with young offenders.[25] Official statistics state that, in 2009, 33,642 youths were arrested and sent to court. At year's end, a large percentage were still awaiting trial, but of those who were adjudicated, most were placed under the care of their parents or guardians (see Figure 15.1).[26]

The proportion of offenses committed by youths, defined as those under the age of 18, was a little over 1.1 percent of all crimes committed in 2009.[27] This means that, statistically, about 99 percent of the crime in India is committed by those over 18 years of age (see Figure 15.2). Although it's important to remember that these data don't account for unreported crime, it's striking that India has such low levels of reported youth offenses compared to the United States. In 2009, there were 1,161,830 arrests in the United States in the 18-and-under age

Figure 15.1 Disposal of Juveniles in India Arrested during 2009

A total of 33,642 juveniles were arrested and sent to various courts during 2009.

Think About It

1. Aside from those pending disposal, what happens to most arrested juveniles in India?

Source: National Crime Records Bureau, *Crime in India 2009*, 137. Online at ncrb.nic.in/CII-2009-NEW/cii-2009/Chapter%2010.pdf.

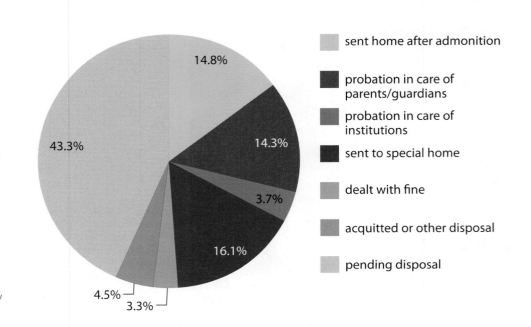

15.2 crosscurrents

In India: How Old Is Too Old?

In 1992, a civil engineer and his family were found murdered in their house in Assam, India. The family's young employee, Ramdeo Chauhan, was arrested soon after, but wasn't tried until 1998. The court found Chauhan guilty and sentenced him to death. His lawyers appealed several times, claiming that Chauhan was a juvenile at the time of the offense, but were rebuffed by the courts.

According to Indian law at the time, boys age 16 and over were adults. But in the case of Chauhan, chronological age was difficult to establish. Like thousands of other Indian youths, Chauhan not only had no birth records, he didn't even know how old he was. The law, then, does little good for youths like Chauhan who can't ascertain their age.

According to one Indian lawyer, "In my line of work I have met many children who look older than their age, they themselves don't know how old they are, and they don't have proper age proof since they belong to a family of migrant workers... These kids are then tried as adults and are thrown into prisons."

Chauhan remained in prison for five years before medical tests were done to determine his age. Finally, he was determined to be 15–16 years old at the time of the offense, right on the borderline between adult and child under Indian law. The court determined he was an adult and sentenced him to death. His lawyers continued to appeal, and in 2011, 19 years after his arrest, the Gauhati High Court ruled that Chauhan was indeed a juvenile at the time of the offense and should be treated as a juvenile.

THINK ABOUT IT

1. Why is chronological age important when determining whether a youth is a juvenile? Discuss your reasoning.

Sources: Vishwajoy Mukherjee, "A Long Wait for Freedom," *Tehelka*, September 12, 2011, www.tehelka.com/story_main50.asp?filename=Ws120911LAW.asp.

National Crime Records Bureau, *Crime in India 2009*, 131. Online at ncrb.nic.in/CII-2009-NEW/Home.htm.

group, comprising 14 percent of all US arrests.[28] Another interesting fact is that, of the youths arrested in India in 2009, 93 percent lived with parents or guardians; only 7 percent were homeless.[29]

Because of the large population living in poverty, India places a special emphasis on street children. The aim is to prevent the destitution of children and to help them off the streets. In addition to getting these children into alternative living situations, the program aims to ensure they have access to adequate nutrition, drinking water, education, and recreational facilities. Further, addressing abuse and exploitation of children is considered a primary objective. Street children are likely to fall victim to those who traffic in child slavery and prostitution.

Russia

Like China, Russia is a large, diverse nation that is undergoing rapid social change. As an emerging democracy, it's experiencing the growing pains of a free-market economy and the demands by its citizens for greater social freedoms. Geographically the largest country in the world, Russia has close to 150 million people spread out over 21 republics, 6 territories, and 49 provinces.[30]

Russia is a very old country, but its present government is very new. For centuries, it was ruled by monarchs who were part of the royal families of Europe. In 1917, a workers' revolt led by Vladimir Lenin overthrew the czar and instituted a communist government that lasted for approximately 70 years.[31] Everything changed in Russia in 1989 when the Soviet state collapsed, and many of the nations under its control claimed independence. Russia struggled with the new market economy and plunged into economic turmoil as numerous assets of the

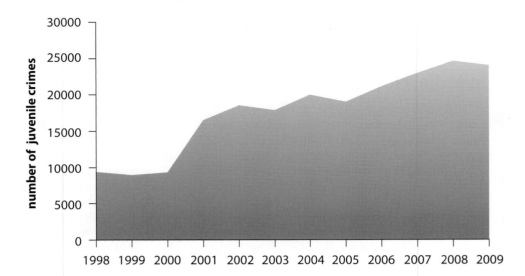

Figure 15.2 Juvenile Crimes in India, 1998-2009

The rise in crime from 2001 on is attributed to a revision of the juvenile age of responsibility for males from under age 16 to include those under age 18.

Think About It

1. Why did juvenile crime in India rise after 2000?

Source: National Crime Records Bureau, *Crime in India 2009,* 133. Online at ncrb.nic.in/CII-2009-NEW/cii-2009/Chapter%2010.pdf

old Soviet state were acquired by capitalists, many of them former high-ranking members of the Soviet Party.[32] The economy quickly changed from one controlled by the government to one in which private citizens controlled the major industries. Conditions in Russia are slowly changing as it develops democratic institutions and a capitalist economy. However, it's a rocky road, and this can be readily seen in the problems of crime, especially organized crime.[33]

Along with a new and problematic capitalist economic system, Russia is struggling with introducing democratic institutions. Accompanying its newfound freedoms is a growing youth delinquency problem. The former Soviet government controlled street crime with its repressive criminal justice system. Now, with democratic institutions struggling to develop interdisciplinary and interagency approaches to crime, Russia must address the causes of youth crime that stem from social upheaval, poverty, and individuals' rising expectations.

In 1994, Russia adopted a new criminal code that defines criminal responsibility and other legal aspects that pertain to young offenders. The code specifies that youths be afforded both punishment and compulsory measures for reeducation. Reeducation in Russia is roughly equivalent to rehabilitation and is used when young offenders are deemed likely to benefit from further training, treatment, or schooling. Punishment options include a range of possibilities that are alternatives to imprisonment. Age is considered a mitigating factor, and those who recruit others into criminal activity can expect to be treated more harshly than those who are recruited.[34]

Russia's criminal code divides youths into three groups of responsibility based on age. The age of criminal responsibility is 16, and youths age 14 and over are considered responsible only for offenses such as murder, major bodily injury, rape, kidnapping, larceny, robbery, burglary, and the theft of firearms and drugs.[35]

Thefts and robberies comprise more than half of youth offenses, with the most common offense being the theft of mobile telephones.[36] In 2005, Sergey Manakhov of the Interior Ministry's Investigation Commission gave a news conference in which he outlined a number of facts about rising youth crime in Russia:

» One in eight known offenders in 2004 was a minor.

» Youth crime was 6 percent higher in 2004 than in 2003.

» In 2004, the total known number of youth offenses was over 154,000, with 1,500 homicides.

Grisha, left, and Denis smoke outside a shelter for homeless children in Moscow, Russia. The youths are among scores of children who face abuse and neglect because of the poverty, moral drift, and alcoholism caused by the 1991 collapse of the Soviet Union. Despite Russia's economic recovery, a human rights report stated that violations of children's rights remain "systematic," and the number of children victimized by their parents has been rising.

>> In 2004, one in six young offenders was intoxicated at the time of the offense.

>> In 2004, young offenders were the subject of 79,000 criminal investigations, 72,000 of which went to court. Cases might be dropped if victims were compensated, if all parties agreed to drop the case, or if the offender was remorseful.[37]

Like many other nations, Russia attempts to use informal or alternative dispositions in its youth justice system whenever possible. The law allows youth justice administrators to consider the circumstances of each case when fashioning a disposition. This individualized justice is consistent with efforts in the United States and recognizes that the effective treatment or education of the offender must be imposed with an appreciation of the youth's personal limitations as well as the resources available for changing the behavior. Two other facets of the Russian youth criminal code deserve mentioning at this point. First, capital punishment can't be applied to those under the age of 18. Second, a minor can't be incarcerated for more than 10 years.

In an effort to develop alternative means of handling young offenders, Russia instituted a number of educational-labor colonies. Some are similar to American boot camp programs in which the offenders undergo an intensive regimen of work and discipline in an effort to develop conforming behavior. Some of these colonies have more mild regimens and are geared toward providing youths with workplace skills they can use upon release.[38]

South Africa

South Africa has unique youth-offending issues that are a direct result of its tumultuous history. Few Western-style nations have experienced the kind of social turmoil and disruption that South Africa has, and few nations have as many natural resources that can ultimately be brought to bear on its issues of economic inequality.

Originally colonized by the Dutch in 1652, South Africa has had a history of suppressing black Africans. The Dutch and the British fought the Boer War to establish dominance in the region, and black South Africans were seldom considered as having claims of their own to the land and natural resources.[39] After World War II, the British granted independence to South Africa, and the white British and Dutch descendants established an **apartheid** system of government that disenfranchised all the black citizens. Rigid racial segregation relegated black Africans to shantytowns from which they commuted back and forth to work as low-paid laborers.[40]

The plight of children in the shantytowns was harsh. Children were caught up in the struggle for equality, and many were incarcerated along with adults. Adults who had committed common offenses and children who were being held for political purposes were incarcerated together, and little was done to separate these children from each other or from adult inmates.[41]

South Africa was transformed, relatively peacefully, into a constitutional republic in 1996. The South African legal system is still being developed, and at this point, young offenders have no separate statute. The laws that govern the treatment of youths in the criminal justice system are distributed throughout a variety of other laws, including the country's constitution. These laws specify that the government must consider the age of the child and that detention should be used only as a last resort.

South Africa has no courts specifically designed for young offenders. Their cases are heard by the same judges who preside over adult cases, and court personnel aren't specially trained to deal with youth cases. Some court personnel have a great deal of experience dealing with youths, but they end up spending most of their time dealing with adult cases. Although a youth has a right to legal counsel when substantial injustice is possible, such as incarceration, many families can't afford it. Many youths decline the offer of representation by court-appointed attorneys. Less than 50 percent of those who appear before the court are represented by counsel.

South Africa is undergoing rapid social change as a result of its move from apartheid to democracy. In addition, there's the problem of vast income inequality between whites, who are losing political control, and blacks, who are gaining it. The country is in such flux it's difficult to forecast how the legal system will eventually handle young offenders. Until some of the underlying problems of crime, such as poverty, illiteracy, and gangsterism, are successfully addressed, South Africa's legal system will continue to struggle with issues such as due process. The new government has yet to establish laws that create a separate system for youths, but as the entire relationship between citizens and the state is newly specified, one can expect that South Africa will address the issue of justice for children.

Japan

Japan is an ancient country with a fascinating history. Its first constitution was written in 604 CE and has undergone many changes since. The most recent change happened after World War II when the Allied nations forced Japan to institute a democracy. Its criminal code was patterned after the US system to guarantee due process, whereas its fundamental framework was similar to the legal models found in most of western Europe.[42]

Japan's juvenile law might best be described as following the welfare and rehabilitation models. However, there has been strong pressure from the ministry of justice and prosecutors to amend the law to give them more power to be tougher on young offenders. In the 1990s, there were some sensational cases in which children murdered other children and, in one case, a youth put the severed head of a classmate on the gate at school. These cases, along with a growing victims' rights movement, led the media to advocate harsher sentences for youths who committed heinous crimes.[43] In 2004, police arrested 219 children younger than 14 for serious offenses such as murder, robbery, and arson. Up 3.3 percent from 2003, this was the highest such figure in the last decade, according to Japan's National Police Agency.[44]

Generally, Japanese tradition favors avoiding disputes. Although the number of lawsuits has increased, informal resolutions, such as mediation and arbitration, are still preferred. People younger than 20 are considered juveniles, and juvenile cases go to the district's family court. Adjudications include probation and commitment to a training home or training school. Juveniles might be prosecuted in the criminal court when the offense is very serious. The death penalty is prohibited for anyone under age 18.[45] Offenders under age 14 are typically not held criminally responsible and are subject instead to Japan's Child Welfare Law.[46] In 2000, the nation's youth law was revised to reflect the following concerns:

» At the hearing, the youth should reflect on his or her offense and, along with the parents, take responsibility for the deviant behavior.

» The input of the victim is considered in the case. However, the victim isn't allowed to be present at the hearing. The court makes the name of the offender known to the victim and provides reasons for his or her disposition.

» In serious cases, the prosecutor can appear in court to provide judges with the pertinent facts as long as there is a legal representative also appearing for the young offender.

» The law is concerned with accountability. Offenders as young as 14 can face charges for homicide or other serious offenses. However, offenders as old as 19 who haven't committed heinous crimes will be kept in family court, which hears their cases.[47]

One interesting feature of Japan's efforts to deal with potential juvenile delinquents is the resources it puts into prevention activities. These activities take many forms and are found in various parts of Japan's culture. For instance, one prevention activity not found in the United States is the company-police conference. In the 1960s, corporations brought many teenagers from rural areas to the cities to work in factories after they graduated from junior high school. Police officers were assigned to specific companies to counsel and direct these young people as they adjusted to living away from home and learned to negotiate the challenges and temptations of living in the city. Today, Japan's companies do not employ as many young teenagers, but there are still 300 company-police conferences each year.

Another prevention activity is the school-police conference, which is aimed at the high delinquency rate in high schools that began to appear right after World War II. By 1998, there were about 2,400 school-police conferences that reached 90 percent of all students in elementary, junior high, and senior high schools. A police officer is placed in the school to learn the concerns of students and present a positive role model. It's somewhat similar to the Officer Friendly programs that have been tried in some US jurisdictions.

The police also participate in community prevention efforts. They have developed police boxes (*koban*) in urban areas and police houses (*chuzaishos*) in rural areas to facilitate prevention activities. Of special concern for officers are the amusement areas where juveniles gather and are most likely to break the law. These prevention efforts are very similar to the community-policing movement in the United States.

The police in Japan also actively engage volunteers in organized prevention efforts. In 1998, approximately 51,000 guidance volunteers assisted the police in

A police officer talks to a lost three-year-old boy at one of Tokyo's busiest *kobans*. The *koban* system, which is the backbone of Japan's police patrols, consists of booths equipped with a kitchen and sleeping area.

preventing youth crime. There are three types of police volunteers: the guidance volunteer, the police helper for juveniles, and the instructor for juveniles. Each specializes in a different kind of prevention activity, and each is credited with helping to provide an environment where juveniles are under constant control and surveillance by families, schools, the police, and community volunteers.

Although Japan is a densely populated country, it isn't overwhelmed with young people, as is the case in some of the developing countries of Africa and Asia. In fact, the proportion of teenagers to the rest of the population has been declining for a number of years. So much attention is being paid to the children that some fear they are becoming excessively protected, guided, and supervised.

England and Wales

The juvenile justice system in England and Wales is separate from those in other parts of the United Kingdom. The countries were united by the 1536 and 1542 Acts of Union, and their common legal systems are adversarial in all courts, including the juvenile courts.[48] Northern Ireland and Scotland have juvenile justice systems that operate under different laws and circumstances, so it would be confusing and misleading to lump them together. What makes England and Wales so interesting is the long history of attempts to deal with delinquency and the declining status of the nation as a world power.

England was once the world's foremost industrial and economic power. Now the nation struggles with immigration, economic stagnation, and unemployment. Consequently, it has fashioned a juvenile justice system that has been subject to wide fluctuations in philosophy as it tries to respond to changing political conditions and the new challenges of racial animosity and ethnic tensions.[49] The age of criminal responsibility in England and Wales is 10, and offenders between the ages of 10 and 17 appear before a youth court. Youth court sanctions are more restricted than those for adult courts; also, the court might impose fines that parents must pay, and youths might receive supervision or attendance-center orders.[50] The youth crime culture of England and Wales is distinctive in three ways. The use of drugs is pronounced, the stealing of cars for joyriding is of concern, and the existence of the "yob" culture is unique. Each of these issues is worth further exploration.

DRUGS

As in the United States, illegal drug use in England and Wales is a major social issue. It's estimated that half of young males and a third of young females have used illegal drugs at one time.[51] Further, there's a growing trend for younger children to experiment with drugs. Much of the drug use is restricted to marijuana, but other drugs are readily available. There is a clear link between drug use and crime among young people. Those who use drugs are more likely to engage in other types of deviant behavior. Many of those who use drugs become addicted, require substantial financial resources to pay for their habit, and turn to stealing or selling drugs.

JOYRIDING

Car crime accounts for about a quarter of the offenses committed by young males in England and Wales. Breaking into cars and stealing radios or personal effects, as well as the car itself, are perceived as problems committed by young urban males. The taking of the car for a joyride is a popular youth offense. The car isn't stolen to be kept as personal property or broken down and sold for parts. Rather, the car is driven, often at high speeds, and later abandoned, sometimes with considerable damage. The purpose of the offense is excitement. For working-class young men who are unemployed and lacking in ways to demonstrate their masculinity and bravado, joyriding represents an opportunity to don the mantle of manhood.

YOB CULTURE

The growing public concern over the yobs is a facet of youth crime that isn't familiar to observers in the United States. The term "yob," which is usually used to describe a young, male hooligan, comes from the backward spelling of "boy."[52] These young urban males, typically age 16 to 24, are typical perpetrators of delinquency, especially victimizing the elderly and those who live in low-income areas. Rosalind Coward gives us one way of considering yobs:

> Yobs is a species of young white working class male which, if the British public is to be believed, is more common than ever before. The yob is foul-mouthed, irresponsible, probably unemployed and violent. The yob hangs around council estates where he terrorizes the local inhabitants, possibly in the company of his pit-bull terrier. He fathers children rather than caring for them. He is often drunk, probably uses drugs and is likely to be involved in crime, including domestic violence. He is the ultimate expression of macho values: mad, bad and dangerous to know.[53]

It's difficult to estimate how much the yob culture contributes to the delinquency problem in England and Wales. In 2005, after a group of about 20 youths beat and severely injured a man who had chased them after a rock was thrown at his car, local legislators instituted a crackdown, vowing punishments of up to three months' detention or a £5,000 fine.[54] Business owners have also complained about yob crowds making shopping areas unsafe. In 2003, the Anti-Social Behaviour Act was created to address the problem, with many of its provisions aimed directly at yob activities (see Prevention and Intervention).

It's tempting to speculate that if the economy in England and Wales were to improve drastically, especially in the industrial sectors, yob behavior would diminish. However, economic conditions are only one factor that contributes to yob culture. In 2005, there were reports of well-to-do undergraduate students

15.5 PREVENTION AND INTERVENTION

England's Anti-Social Behaviour Act

The Anti-Social Behaviour Act was passed in 2003 as part of the government's "Together" campaign, which gave local councils, police, environmental health officers, housing officers, and officials new powers to address antisocial behavior. The act's provisions include the following:

» Powers to disperse groups in designated areas suffering persistent and serious antisocial behavior

» Extended powers to deal with aggravated trespass

» Restrictions on the use of air weapons and replica guns and bans on air-cartridge weapons that can be converted to firearms

» New mechanisms for enforcing parental responsibility for children who behave in an antisocial way in school or in the community

» Banning the sale of spray paints to youths under 16

» Powers for landlords to take action against antisocial tenants, including faster evictions

» Improved powers to deal with public assemblies and aggravated trespass

» Penalty notices for parents in truancy cases[1]

[1]Home Office, Anti-Social Behavior Act, June 2005, www.homeoffice.gov.uk/crime/antisocialbehaviour/legislation/asbact.html.

engaging in yob-style behavior at Oxford University. School officials even worried publicly that the bad behavior of the rich students would discourage impoverished ones from attending the university.[55]

Whatever its prevalence and real harm, media reports make yob behavior appear to be epidemic. In 2009–2010, England's government reported that crime was continuing to fall, dropping by 9 percent since 2008.[56] The public's perception of antisocial behavior fell, also. And despite the public's reported fear of yob behavior, the most likely victims of violent crime were also most likely to be yobs.[57]

What are the processes for dealing with young offenders? The English system of juvenile justice is very similar to that of the United States, making for some interesting comparisons and contrasts. Before 2000, one of the first steps was the "police caution," which was a formal warning from a senior police officer to someone who admitted an offense that could have led to prosecution. Cautioning was intended to give minor offenders, traditionally juveniles and first-time offenders, a chance to reform and avoid a criminal record. The offender had to admit guilt and agree to a caution in order for one to be given. However, in 2000, the Crime and Disorder Act replaced the use of cautions for offenders under 18 with reprimands and final warnings.

Reprimands are also given to first-time offenders for minor offenses, except that any further offenses lead to either a final warning or a charge. A youth who receives a final warning is referred to a local youth-offending team, which assesses the youth and prepares a rehabilitation program to address his or her behavior. This assessment usually involves contacting the victim to determine whether victim-offender mediation or reparation to the victim or community is appropriate. Older youths are more likely than younger ones to receive final warnings rather than reprimands.[58]

Young offenders between 10 and 17 are sent to youth courts. The youth court, introduced in 1992, replaced the juvenile court, which was established in 1908 and handled young offenders only up to age 16. Youth courts have specially trained judges, and no one is allowed in youth courts except for court officers, the parties to the case, parents or guardians, the youth's legal representatives, witnesses, and specified media representatives. The press can report on proceedings but can't identify the offender. The following are circumstances in which a youth is tried in the adult criminal court (the Crown Court) instead of youth court:

» A youth is charged with homicide (either murder or manslaughter).

» An offender between the ages of 10 and 18 is charged with indecent assault, dangerous driving, or a "grave crime," an offense for which an adult could be incarcerated for at least 14 years. Such a case may go to the Crown Court if a judge decides that the appropriate sentence would be more than the youth court is allowed to give.

» A youth is charged jointly with another person age 18 or over. Both offenders are sent to the Crown Court.[59]

As for detention, some young offenders are held outside the government's Prison Service. Secure Training Centres hold young offenders up to age 17 and are run by private contractors. Local Authority Secure Children's Homes generally accommodate offenders ages 12 to 14, girls under age 16, and boys ages 15 to 16 who are considered to be vulnerable.[60]

RIOTS

The August 2011 riots in London, England, were called "criminality, pure and simple" by Prime Minister David Cameron. At the end of seven days of violence, police arrested 1,715 people in connection with the burning and looting, most of whom were under age 24: 364 of the arrestees were age 10–17, 525 were age 18–20, and 365 were age 21–24. Although the riots began in connection with protests against the police shooting of a 29-year-old man, many say what eventually happened had nothing to do with justice.

On August 4, 2011, Mark Duggan was shot dead by police in Tottenham, an area in North London. The death occurred while police officers were attempting to make an arrest. The next day, about 300 marchers gathered outside Tottenham police station demanding justice for the man and his family. Witnesses said the protest was peaceful. Later, however, crowds threw bottles at two police cars and then set them on fire. Riot officers and mounted police who attempted to disperse the crowds were attacked with bottles and fireworks. The violence continued to spread throughout London over the next few days as rioters looted and burned shops and homes and fought with police. The violence was finally quelled on August 10.[61]

As authorities sorted through the arrests and charges, it turned out that the main offense was burglary. According to a BBC reporter, "Many of those out on the streets were out shopping with a crowbar."[62] Judges have handed down longer-than-usual incarcerations to rioters. The average sentence for violent disorder has been 10 months, compared with 5 months in 2010. The average sentence for theft has been over 7 months rather than 2 or 3. Not only were more offenders being incarcerated, they were locked up for longer periods.[63]

Given these statistics, the riots seemed to be a youth phenomenon, as well as a recidivist phenomenon. Apparently, the average rioter had 15 previous offenses, and more than half of juveniles had one or more prior offenses.[64] The English criminal and juvenile justice systems will likely continue to endure criticism and scrutiny as the riots, and the role of youths in them, are examined.

Many of the rioters in the 2011 London riots turned out to be youths with prior offenses. Numerous businesses, such as this looted supermarket, were almost completely destroyed.

Hong Kong

The final place in which we examine juvenile delinquency is Hong Kong. Although not a nation (in 1997 it reverted to China after 155 years of British control), Hong Kong has such a fascinating history and is such a unique city that it's worth considering.

Hong Kong has always been very much a Chinese city. Although the British ruled for a century and a half, the culture was predominantly Chinese. The administrative governing procedures and the capitalist economy were patterned after England's, but many cultural aspects were unaffected by British control. Most importantly, for the purpose of discussing youth crime, we must appreciate the strong emphasis on family that exists in China and Hong Kong. Traditionally, Chinese society was organized on the Confucian principle that individuals were to act according to the duties imposed on them by their social status. A person was bound to obey all forms of authority, and most issues of youth lawbreaking were handled within the family. However, other influences within Hong Kong upset the traditional social structure that emphasized social control within the family. Since World War II, industrialization and urbanization have changed how families control their children. With both parents working away from home and youths in school with their peers, the socialization functions of the past have shifted.[65]

In the 1960s, Hong Kong experienced many incidents that raised the profile of youth crime. With youths staying out late at night and disobeying parents, the media began to report on young offenders at a greater rate. The result was public concern about a perceived growing youth crime rate. In truth, the rate wasn't much different.

In 1964, the media reported on the *ah fei* (teddy boy) problem. In Hong Kong, *ah fei* referred to young hooligans, usually under the age of 23, who engaged in petty offenses and were visible on the streets in the form of loose-knit gangs. Further, organized crime groups called *triads* were highlighted in the press, and there was widespread concern that young people with no jobs and little parental control would end up being recruited into organized crime. In the years since the triads first concerned law enforcement officials, they have grown into Hong Kong's most troubling problem for young people. What used to be considered normal schoolyard bullying is now suspected to be triad activities.[66]

Hong Kong has some features that give it a different relationship with its young people. First, Hong Kong is a culturally and linguistically homogeneous city, at 96 percent Chinese. Hong Kong has virtually no racial or ethnic minorities. Because of widespread economic development, Hong Kong has had a powerful surge in building and wealth. Hong Kong has virtually no ethnic ghettos and no underclass. All this presents an environment in which youth crime is a concern but, in terms of frequency, isn't as severe as in many other nations.

The youth crime that does exist in Hong Kong might be overstated. Hong Kong is basically one of the safest cities in the world. In 2005, the overall crime rate in the first quarter fell 6.6 percent over the same period in 2004, and the number of young offenders was down 32 percent compared to the same period.[67] The minimum age of criminal responsibility is 10. In 2000 and 2001, 721 children age 10 to 13 were prosecuted for offenses such as wounding, serious assault, and robbery.[68] Because of the media's amplification of the problem, the government instituted a number of diversion programs to identify and prevent youth crime. This brought an increased number of adolescents under the control of authorities and led to **net-widening,** in which youths who, under normal circumstances, would be released are now introduced into a diversion program. Although this type of intervention might preclude future offending, it makes the situation appear more serious because so many youths are under state control.

What is the future of youth justice in Hong Kong? There will be more changes in the government structure. Even though the city reverted to China in 1997, it retained much of its independence and administrative structure. It's now considered a special administrative region and continues to enjoy a high degree of autonomy. As part of the agreement to return Hong Kong to China, the law provides for the existing justice system to be maintained for the next 50 years. This means that the rule of law and existing policies of treatment and rehabilitation will be preserved.

Fifty years from now, China will be a much different place also. Given China's move toward capitalism, it might be that when the time comes for Hong Kong and China to fully integrate, the differences between the two will be much less than they are today. Already, Hong Kong is showing the rest of China the benefits and principles of capitalism, and in a sort of tail-wagging-the-dog scenario, Hong Kong may show China the way to other Western features of culture such as democracy.

INSTANT RECALL
FROM CHAPTER 12

net-widening
Measures that bring more offenders and individuals into the justice system or cause those already in the system to become more involved.

Questions

1. What are some of the major issues pressing on China? How do these affect its methods for handling young offenders?

2. What is India's foremost youth concern? Does India have a serious youth crime problem?

3. How is the youth crime culture of England and Wales distinctive?

4. What unique political issues in South Africa affect its youth crime policy?

5. What is the status of juvenile capital punishment in Russia?

6. What models does Japan's juvenile law follow?

7. Does Hong Kong have a youth crime problem? What is the government doing about it?

International Victimization of Children

Other aspects of youth justice require a broader scope than the study of individual nations can provide. Two of these are the use of children as soldiers and as prostitutes. Although these international problems have more to do with youth victimization than youth crime, they illustrate the context of childhood in some nations. These two pressing issues also emphasize the mutable definitions of youth crime. In the United States, a child who shoots and kills a person is considered a juvenile delinquent. In Afghanistan, this child may be valued as a soldier. In the United States, children who are forced into prostitution are considered victims and taken under the wing of the state, and their parents or guardians are prosecuted. In some Asian nations, child prostitution is common and sometimes has the tacit approval of the authorities because of the thriving sex-tourism trade.

The use of children as soldiers and prostitutes in some nations sheds some light on the United States' status offender laws. Regardless of the society, children don't control their place in it. Children don't get a say in how laws are made, how their status as children is considered, and how their societies restrict, enable, or use them as children. If a society requires a child under age 16 to attend school, then the child attends school. If another society requires a child to be a soldier as soon as he or she is physically able, then that child becomes a soldier. This is a power that practically every nation uses, regardless of its modernity or style of government. As mentioned earlier in the chapter, in the 1960s, young men in the United States could be forced into military service at age 18, although they could neither drink alcohol nor vote. Although legally considered to be adults, they were still subject to juvenile status laws. The US government, at that time, used the status of young people to serve its needs.

The status of youth is subject to a society's dictates like no other status. This is one reason status is such an important concept in the study of delinquency. Children, and most adolescents, are physically, intellectually, and psychologically inferior to adults. This is fundamental to their status. Children are vulnerable and can be both nurtured and controlled. The issue is control that becomes abuse.

Americans generally believe it's society's responsibility to nurture and protect children and to keep them from harming themselves and others. In the United States, when a child strays too far from control, he or she is considered delinquent. Both the control and the delinquency are circumscribed by laws. Most of these laws are the same ones that govern adults, but some are created especially for juveniles. In the United States, the laws that apply to everyone protect society, and status offender laws exist mainly to protect children from themselves and predatory adults.

It can be argued that delinquency doesn't exist in many developing nations. Just as there's no crime without laws, there's also no juvenile delinquency, only varying degrees of child victimization and victimizers, abuse, and neglect. To be fair, the United States has taken a hundred years to develop its juvenile justice system and specify the rights of youths. Some juvenile rights are still under contention. Only relatively recently, in 2005, did the US Supreme Court exempt juveniles from capital punishment.[69] Ideally, rights accompany laws. This is one reason the framers of the US Constitution attached the Bill of Rights. However, none of the world's governments or constitutions has a children's bill of rights to balance the laws it uses to control them.

Children at War

Traditionally, the role of warrior was reserved for only the strongest men. Women and children were not only excluded from the ranks of soldiers but, in many societies, also considered off-limits in terms of inflicting casualties.[70] In some ancient societies, it was considered wrong to kill an enemy's animals or destroy crops. War was strictly an affair between soldiers.

This has changed in modern times. Now it's common to wage war on civilian populations. Children are targeted as victims and used as warriors: in Afghanistan, children as young as 5 have fought in battles, and a 14-year-old killed the first US soldier there.[71] Modern wars with high-altitude bombing have ravaged civilian populations since World War II, and the introduction of "smart bombs" has encouraged governments to place schools and hospitals next to military targets in the vain hope that the military targets will be spared. Being a civilian is no longer a guarantee that one won't be sought out for killing. In fact, it can make one an even more attractive target when military organizations desire to break their enemies' will.

Children used to be excluded from war for several reasons. Aside from their being considered too valuable to risk losing, children were also considered too fragile to wield arms. It was considered a man's work to engage in warfare, and children were relegated to minor supporting roles, such as herding cattle, blowing bugles, or carrying supplies, if they were allowed on the battlefield at all. Boys who longed to prove their manhood on the battlefield were told to wait their turn.[72]

Today, these rules are being violated in underdeveloped nations around the world. As traditional societies break down in the wake of rapid social change,

Child soldiers of the rebel Sudan People's Liberation Army (SPLA) wait for their commander at a demobilization ceremony in 2001. Under an agreement with United Nations Children's Fund, the SPLA demobilized 2,500 child soldiers.

breaking the rules against targeting civilians and children or using children as soldiers has become commonplace. For example, in the aftermath of the demise of communism in the former Yugoslavia, a civil war broke out involving several ethnic groups. In an effort to destroy the enemy's will to fight or to avenge past atrocities, Serbian snipers targeted children walking between parents.[73]

In other parts of the world, children are recruited as soldiers and forced to kill wounded or captured prisoners in order to harden them to the realities of being on the battlefield. For example,

> Children's presence as fighters also affects the norms of good behavior in war. The protections typically afforded to wounded soldiers and prisoners of war are often ignored in lieu of indoctrination needs. Rebel groups with child soldiers tend not to take prisoners. Instead, they typically kill the POWs on the spot or bring them back to camp to kill as instructive victims. Likewise, even the force's own wounded children are subject to being executed by their fellow fighters, as leaders see them as needless drains on the organization and easily replaced. One survey in Colombia found that more than a third of former child soldiers admitted to having directly participated in out-of-combat killings.[74]

Child Prostitution

There is a well-known worldwide scandal involving the sexual exploitation of children. Citizens from some of the world's wealthiest nations, including the United States, travel to other nations to have sex with children.[75] Child prostitution laws are overlooked because of the money brought in by sex tourism. (For a look at organizations that work to save children from sex tourism, see Programs for Children.) Although many of these sex tourists consider themselves to be stellar citizens of their own nations, they adopt different attitudes when visiting Thailand, the Philippines, Cambodia, Indonesia, Sri Lanka, or Vietnam.

Prostitution is often considered a victimless crime. When two people agree on a transaction that includes a specific service for a specific price, it's considered

A Chinese police officer takes notes about prostitution suspects during a raid on a bath center in Hunan province. Thousands of suspects were arrested in a crackdown on prostitution in more than 26 Chinese cities.

15.6 PROGRAMS FOR CHILDREN

Preventing Prostitution

The problem of child prostitution in Southeast Asia is pervasive. In addition to Thailand, Cambodia is a nation that hasn't been able (or willing) to control the sexual exploitation of children. However, some privately funded nongovernment organizations (NGOs) try to ease the circumstances that propel children into exploitation. One such NGO is M'lop Tapang, which is located in the seaside community of Sihanoukville, a favorite destination of pedophiles from many nations.[1]

Established in June 2003, M'lop Tapang operates on an annual budget of about $60,000 and has a staff of 23 workers, including a full-time nurse. The program identifies young children who are on the street, using drugs, and in danger of falling victim to crime, disease, and exploitation. Each morning, the program takes the children to a center where they are fed breakfast, given medical care, and entered into education programs. The program has helped more than 250 children and even provides services to older sisters and mothers who are likely to be recruited by the sex industry.

Removing children from life on the street in Cambodia can be difficult. The M'lop Tapang centers won't allow children to attend if they're carrying knives or are inebriated. An inexpensive amphetamine in the form of crystal methedrine, known as *Yaba*, or "crazy medicine," sells for less than a dollar. A tube of glue that can keep the child intoxicated for a day costs about 12 cents.

An important part of the program is attempting to reintegrate the children into their families. Poverty can make difficult demands on families, and the children who are left to fend for themselves on the street are often denied support and family bonding. By educating the parents through the children on issues such as health care, sanitation, and AIDS, the centers are able to help maintain some the connections between children and parents.

Thousands of NGOs serve children around the world, filling in the gaps where government services are lacking. In some nations, they are major providers of youth services. Funded by churches, charities, anonymous benefactors, or foundations, nonprofit, nongovernment organizations are sometimes the only resource that stands between poor children and a brutal life.[2]

THINK ABOUT IT

1. Why would removing children from life on the street be so challenging? Discuss.

[1]Cynara Vetch, "Coming In Off the Streets," *The Guardian*, November 21, 2009, 8.

[2]Lisa Smith, "Suffer the Children," *Weekly Standard*, June 18–19, 2005, www.Thestandard.com.hk/stdn/std/Weekend/GF18Jp03.html.

to be consensual sex. Prostitution is legal in some nations and, if well regulated, isn't a social problem.[76] However, some forms of prostitution are considered social problems and are grounds for arrest, prosecution, and incarceration. The most obvious form considered a problem is the use of children as sexual partners. Few people (although there are some) would argue that it's appropriate for adults to engage in sexual relations with children. Even some who engage in the sexual exploitation of children in other nations wouldn't deem it permissible in their home nations. Although children in Western, industrialized nations may be regarded as innocent and out-of-bounds, those in impoverished developing nations are often considered to be legitimate sex partners because the authorities of these nations often welcome this type of commerce.

Thailand is ground zero for the sex-tourism industry. Although accurate numbers of child prostitutes are impossible to find, trade has long been aimed at foreigners. In the 1960s and early 1970s, thousands of US servicemen were stationed in Thailand. The airmen, along with thousands of soldiers who went to Thailand on R&R (rest and recreation), provided a ready market for prostitution, a market that has survived and prospered. Young Thai women are pictured in advertising brochures as smiling and compliant. Typically, they are from the poorer northern provinces and are sent to Bangkok to earn money for their families. Sometimes their parents sell them to a brothel, where they are forced to work off the price of their room and board, as well as the money paid to their parents. However, the young women are never able to earn their freedom. The very young ones service foreigners in grand hotels, but as they age, they slip down the hierarchy of prostitutes until they have to work on the street.[77] Because of rural Thailand's poverty, even poorly paid prostitutes earn more than a typical police officer, so corruption within law enforcement is prevalent.[78]

Questions

1. Why can it be argued that delinquency doesn't exist in many developing nations?

2. Why was it customary to exclude children from war? Why do some cultures include them now?

3. Why does child prostitution thrive in some nations?

>> FOCUS ON ETHICS

No Way to Treat a Lady

As a manager of your university's basketball program, you have befriended an international student who was recruited because he's a 6'10" power forward with a great three-point shot. You introduced him to a friend of yours, and they moved in together. Your friend has been showing up for classes with bruises on her arms, and today one of her girlfriends has come to you and told you she has a cut over her eye and a swollen lip.

After going to your friend's apartment, you confirm that she has injuries, and you also observe that your basketball-playing international student has scratches on his neck. You demand an explanation but the ballplayer tells you to mind your own business.

"You Americans don't know how to make your women behave. They have to learn that the man is the boss and to do what I say."

You turn to your friend, and she says, "Please stay out of this. We will work this all out. I love him and plan to go back with him to his homeland, so we will have to establish our own way of dealing with problems. I can't expect him to suddenly adopt American culture. I'm sure I can educate him on how to have a mutually supportive relationship, but it's going to take some time."

You aren't sure what to do. Over the next several weeks, you notice even more evidence of physical abuse, and your friend's girlfriends are pressuring you to confront the basketball player, tell the coach about the problem, or somehow solve the problem before something really bad happens. In the meantime, the basketball player is lighting up the court and leading the team to a conference championship.

WHAT DO YOU DO?

1. Stay out of this essentially domestic dispute. It's none of your business, and you can only lose two friends by butting in.

2. Tell the coach. You have a responsibility to the team, and this is a potential problem that could blow up and force the coach to suspend the player.

3. Tell your friend's parents. You have known them for years, and you feel an obligation to them because they are neighbors of your family.

4. Get some of your friends, confront the basketball player, and tell him that in the United States, we don't beat women. Threaten to rough him up if he doesn't stop physically abusing his girlfriend.

Summary

Summary

Learning Objective 1. Review the reasons why Americans seldom consider other cultures.	Cultural isolation. The United States is culturally isolated from the rest of the world, primarily because of its geographic size. Ability to affect. We have little opportunity to make changes in other nations. Other nations may do things differently, and perhaps even better, but we often ignore them because we can't reproduce the conditions that make their ways different.
Learning Objective 2. Tell why cultural components determine whether behavior is rewarded or punished.	Religion is a powerful social institution. It's the absolute social authority in some nations, while others marginalize it. Some societies haven't been as progressive in breaking down the barriers between the rights of women and men. One of the most significant factors that affect the social environment of nations is the level of economic development.
Learning Objective 3. Reason how major differences among cultures, justice systems, and data collection make direct comparisons among nations difficult.	Researchers must either find a common language in which to communicate with officials from other nations or hire an interpreter. Definitional barriers mean that offenses vary. An activity that is considered a felony in one nation might be considered a misdemeanor in another and legal in a third.
Learning Objective 4. Compare and contrast the effects of social change on dealing with youth crime in China, Russia, and South Africa.	China is quickly being transformed from a state-controlled economy to a market economy. China doesn't have a formal juvenile justice system, so other social institutions handle the less significant cases. Schools, families, and neighborhood organizations deal with minor deviance, with the idea that these problems can be solved without police involvement. Russia is a large and diverse country that is undergoing rapid social change. Geographically the largest country in the world, Russia has close to 150 million people in 21 republics, 6 territories, and 49 provinces. Along with a new and problematic capitalist economic system, Russia is struggling with democratic institutions. The former Soviet government controlled street crime with its repressive criminal justice system. Now, Russia must address the causes of youth crime that stem from social upheaval, poverty, and individuals' rising expectations.
Learning Objective 5. Describe India's Juvenile Justice Act.	India's Juvenile Justice Act is designed to protect, care for, rehabilitate, educate, and give vocational training to delinquent and neglected children.
Learning Objective 6. Compare Japan's philosophy for handling juveniles with that of England.	Japan's juvenile law follows the welfare and rehabilitation models. The common legal systems of England and Wales are adversarial in all courts, including the juvenile courts.
Learning Objective 7. Discuss how the use of children as soldiers and prostitutes may be considered differently in some developing nations.	In the United States, a child who shoots and kills a person is considered delinquent. In Afghanistan, this child might be valued as a soldier. In the United States, children who are forced into prostitution are considered victims, and their parents or guardians are prosecuted. In some Asian countries, child prostitution is common and sometimes has the tacit approval of the authorities because of the thriving sex-tourism trade.

Learning Objective 8. Understand how the use of children as soldiers and prostitutes in some nations compares to US status offender laws.	The status of youth is subject to a society's dictates. Children can be both nurtured and controlled. The issue is control that becomes abuse. Children don't get a say in how a nation's laws are made, how their status as children is considered, and how their societies restrict, enable, or use them as children. This is a power that practically every nation uses, regardless of its modernity or style of government. Americans believe it's society's responsibility to nurture and protect children and to keep them from harming themselves and others.
Learning Objective 9. Why could it be argued that delinquency doesn't exist in many developing nations?	Without laws, there's no crime or juvenile delinquency, only varying degrees of child victimization and victimizers, abuse, and neglect. The United States has taken a hundred years to develop its juvenile justice system and specify the rights of youths.

Chapter Review Questions

1. Why do we neglect to consider other cultures when we think about the problems of delinquency?

2. Is it fair to judge how other nations deal with juvenile delinquents by US standards and laws?

3. Given the language barriers between nations, is it possible to have a uniform data-collection effort on juvenile delinquency?

4. In what ways does China's juvenile delinquency problem differ from that of the United States?

5. In 1947, India was divided into what two nations?

6. How has the move to democracy affected Russia's attempts to deal with delinquency?

7. In what ways have the lingering effects of apartheid complicated the problems of dealing with delinquency in South Africa?

8. How do police in Japan use crime-prevention activities to address delinquency?

9. Why are the riots of England in the summer of 2011 considered a youth phenomenon?

10. In what ways are children around the globe considered victims of crime?

Key Terms

apartheid—An official policy of racial segregation involving political, legal, and economic discrimination against nonwhites.

communism—A system of social organization in which the ownership of property is ascribed to the community or to the state.

ethnocentrism—The belief in the natural superiority of one's particular ethnic group or culture.

globalism—The philosophy or act of placing the interests of the world above those of individual nations.

Endnotes

1 For a classic example of a work that speaks to the cultural isolation of the United States, see *A Nation of Sheep* by William J. Lederer (New York: Norton, 1961).

2 Nagaty Sanad, *The Theory of Crime and Criminal Responsibility in Islamic Law*

(Chicago: University of Illinois at Chicago, 1991).

3 Martha Crenshaw, "Why Is America the Primary Target? Terrorism as Globalized Civil War," in Charles W. Kegley Jr., ed., *The New Global Terrorism: Characteristics,*

Causes, and Controls (Upper Saddle River, NJ: Prentice Hall, 2003), 160–172.

4 Ruth Benedict, *The Chrysanthemum and the Sword: Patterns of Japanese Culture* (Rutland, VT: Charles E. Tuttle, 1946). Although dated now, this book is considered a classic on how culture affects a society. Of particular interest to students of juvenile delinquency is Chapter 11 on self-discipline.

5 C. Wright Mills, *The Sociological Imagination* (New York: Oxford University Press, 1959).

6 Michael Braswell, John Fuller, and Bo Lozoff, *Corrections, Peacemaking, and Restorative Justice: Transforming Individuals and Institutions* (Cincinnati, OH: Anderson, 2001). See especially Chapter 8, "Toward Restorative and Community Justice," 141–153.

7 Alice Walker and Pratibha Parmar, *Warrior Marks: Female Genital Mutilation and the Sexual Blinding of Women* (New York: Harcourt Brace, 1993). This remarkable book includes interviews with young women who have undergone painful surgery that alters their genitals. The reasons are varied but are bound up in the cultures that practice this procedure.

8 Graeme Newman, "Problems of Method in Comparative Criminology," *International Journal of Comparative and Applied Criminal Justice* 1, no. 1 (1977): 17–31.

9 United Nations (1990), *Prevention of Delinquency, Juvenile Justice and the Protection of the Young: Policy Approaches and Directions* (A/CONF.144/16). Vienna: UN Crime Prevention and Criminal Justice Branch.

10 Piers Beirne and Joan Hill, *Comparative Criminology: An Annotated Bibliography* (New York: Greenwood Press, 1991).

11 *CIA World Factbook: China*, www.cia.gov/library/publications/the-world-factbook/geos/ch.html. Accessed September 16, 2011.

12 *CIA World Factbook: United States*, www.cia.gov/library/publications/the-world-factbook/geos/us.html. Accessed September 16, 2011.

13 Liling Yue, "Youth Justice in China," in John A. Winterdyk, ed., *Juvenile Justice Systems: International Perspectives* (Toronto: Canadian Scholar's Press, 2002), 103–126.

14 Lening Zhang et al., "Crime Prevention in a Communitarian Society: Bang-Jiao and Tiao-Jie in the People's Republic of China," *Justice Quarterly* 13, no. 2 (1996): 199–222.

15 Jianan Guo et al., *World Factbook of Criminal Justice Systems: China*, 1993. Online at www.ojp.usdoj.gov/bjs/pub/ascii/wfbcjchi.txt.

16 Ibid.

17 Stacy Mosher, "Juvenile Crime Fact Sheet," *China Rights Forum: Growing Up in China* 4 (December 18, 2004): 39. Online at www.hrichina.org/fs/view/down-loadables/pdf/downloadable-resources/JuvenileCrime4.2004.pdf.

18 Ibid.

19 *CIA World Factbook: China*, 110–111.

20 Xinhua, "China's First Juvenile Court to Open in Guangzhou," January 28, 2004.

21 Xinhua, "Community Service Gets Offending Minors Back on Track," July 25, 2003.

22 "Youth Offenders Get Voluntary Service," *China Daily*, April 16, 2005, 2.

23 Robert Payne, *The Life and Death of Mahatma Gandhi* (New York: Smithmark, 1994), 517–580.

24 Tapan Chakreborty, "Juvenile Delinquency and Juvenile Justice in India," in John A. Winterdyk, ed., *Juvenile Justice Systems: International Perspectives* (Toronto: Canadian Scholar's Press, 2002), 265–296.

25 R. K. Raghavan, *World Factbook of Criminal Justice Systems: India*, 1993, www.ojp.usdoj.gov/bjs/pub/ascii/wfbcjind.txt.

26 National Crime Records Bureau, *Crime in India 2009*, 131, 136. Online at ncrb.nic.in/CII-2009-NEW/Home.htm.

27 Ibid.

28 Federal Bureau of Investigation, Uniform Crime Reports, *Crime in the United States*, Table 32: Ten-Year Arrest Trends, www2.fbi.gov/ucr/cius2009/data/table_32.html.

29 National Crime Records Bureau, *Crime in India 2009*, 138.

30 Dmitry A. Shestakov and Natalia D. Shestakova, "An Overview of Juvenile Justice and Juvenile Crime in Russia," in John A. Winterdyk, ed., *Juvenile Justice Systems: International Perspectives* (Toronto: Canadian Scholar's Press, 2002), 127–151, 411–440.

31 Aleksandr I. Solzhenitsyn, *The Gulag Archipelago 1918–1956* (New York: Harper and Row, 1973), 3–73.

32 Seymour M. Hersh, "The Wild East," *Atlantic Monthly* (June 1994): 61–86.

33 Joseph Serio, "Organized Crime in the Soviet Union and Beyond," *Low Intensity Conflict and Law Enforcement* 1, no. 2 (Fall 1992): 127–151.

34 Shestakov and Shestakova, "An Overview of Juvenile Justice and Juvenile Crime in Russia," 418.

35 Ilya V. Nikiforov, *World Factbook of Criminal Justice Systems: Russia*, 1993, www.ojp.usdoj.gov/bjs/pub/ascii/wfbcjrus.txt.

36 Ivan Novikov, "Juvenile Crime Rate on Rise in Russia," ITAR-TASS, April 18, 2005.

37 Interfax/BBC, "Russian Police Spokesman Reports Rise in Juvenile Crime," March 15, 2005.

38 Shestakov and Shestakova, "An Overview of Juvenile Justice and Juvenile Crime in Russia," 435.

39 Thomas Pakenham, *The Boer War* (New York: Random House, 1979).

40 Nelson Mandela, *Long Walk to Freedom: The Autobiography of Nelson Mandela* (Boston: Little, Brown, 1994). See especially Part Three, "Birth of a Freedom Fighter," 93–140.

41 Ann Skelton and Hennie Potgieter, "Juvenile Justice in South Africa," in John A. Winterdyk, ed., *Juvenile Justice Systems: International Perspectives* (Toronto: Canadian Scholar's Press, 2002), 477–501.

42 Geoffery Perret, *Old Soldiers Never Die: The Life of Douglas MacArthur* (New York: Random House, 1996). Perret credits MacArthur with writing the Japanese constitution. "It was the most important single achievement of the occupation. The new constitution put Japan on the path to becoming a truly free and democratic country in a part of the world where freedom and democracy had never existed before. It helped make Japan a country that was the envy, not the scourge of East Asia," 506–507.

43 Minoru Yokoyama, "Juvenile Justice and Juvenile Crime: An Overview of Japan," in John A. Winterdyk, ed., *Juvenile Justice Systems: International Perspectives* (Toronto: Canadian Scholar's Press, 2002), 322–352.

44 Kyodo News Service/Japan Economic Newswire, "Serious Crimes by Juveniles under 14 on Rise," February 3, 2005.

45 Tadashi Moriyama, *World Factbook of Criminal Justice Systems: Japan 1993*, www.ojp.usdoj.gov/bjs/pub/ascii/wfbcjjap.txt.

46 Skelton and Potgieter, "Juvenile Justice in South Africa," 477–501.

47 Yokoyama, "Juvenile Justice and Juvenile Crime: An Overview of Japan," 327–328.

48 Corretta Phillips, Gemma Cox, and Ken Pease, *World Factbook of Criminal Justice Systems: England and Wales*, 1993, www.ojp.usdoj.gov/bjs/pub/ascii/wfbcjeng.txt.

49 Loraine Gelsthorpe and Vicky Kemp, "Comparative Juvenile Justice: England and Wales," in John A. Winterdyk, ed., *Juvenile Justice Systems: International Perspectives* (Toronto: Canadian Scholar's Press, 2002), 127–169.

50 Ibid.

51 Helene Raskin White, Robert Padina, and Randy LaGrange, "Longitudinal Predictors of Serious Substance Use and Delinquency," *Criminology* 25 (1987): 715–740.

52 BBC, "'Yobs' Not a Banned Police Word," October 2, 2006, news.bbc.co.uk/2/hi/uk_news/england/london/5400184.stm.

53 Rosalind Coward, "Whipping Boys," *Guardian Weekend*, September 2, 1994, p. 5, as quoted in Gelsthorpe and Kemp, "Comparative Juvenile Justice: England and Wales," 161.

54 Mark Blacklock, "Being Soft on Yobs Just Doesn't Work," *The Express*, May 19, 2005, UK first edition, p. 9.

55 Sarah Cassidy and Richard Garner, "Public School Yobs Deter Bright Pupils from Applying to Oxford, Says Patten," *The (London) Independent*, February 4, 2005, first edition, 16.

56 Home Office Statistical Bulletin, *Crime in England and Wales 2009/10*, July 2010, 2. Online at webarchive.nationalarchives.gov.uk/20110218135832/rds.homeoffice.gov.uk/rds/pdfs10/hosb1210.pdf.

57 Tricia Dodd, Sian Nicholas, David Povey, and Alison Walker, *Crime in England and Wales 2003/2004* (London: Communication and Development Unit, July 2004), 67. Online at www.homeoffice.gov.uk/rds/pdfs04/hosb1004.pdf.

58 *Criminal Statistics England and Wales 2003* (London: The Stationery Office, 2004), 23, 91. Online at www.archive2.official-documents.co.uk/document/cm63/6361/6361.pdf.

59 Ibid., 95.

60 Ibid., 54.

61 BBC, England Riots: Maps and Timeline, August 15, 2011, www.bbc.co.uk/news/uk-14436499.

62 Dominic Casciani, "Analysis: The Riots Data So Far," BBC, September 15, 2011, www.bbc.co.uk/news/uk-14931987.

63 Ibid.

64 Tom Whitehead, "London Rioters Had Average 15 Previous Offences, Figures Show," *The Telegraph*, September 18, 2011, www.telegraph.co.uk/news/uknews/crime/8764809/London-rioters-had-average-15-previous-offences-figures-show.html.

65 Harold Traver, "Juvenile Delinquency in Hong Kong," in John A. Winterdyk, ed., *Juvenile Justice Systems: International Perspectives* (Toronto: Canadian Scholar's Press, 2002), 208–234.

66 Ibid., 213.

67 Financial Times Information, "Hong Kong: First Quarter Crime Down 6.6%," May 1, 2005.

68 Polly Hui, "Groups Urge Change in Criminal-Age Law," *South China Morning Post*, February 6, 2004, 3.

69 Warren Richey, "Juvenile Death Penalty Abolished," *Christian Science Monitor*, March 2, 2005, sec. USA, 1.

70 P. W. Singer, *Children at War* (New York: Pantheon Books, 2005), 3–8.

71 Paul J. Nyden, "Modern Warfare Lighter Weapons, Non-State Armies Have Led to a Limber and Teachable Worldwide Pool of Killer Recruits: Children at War," *Charleston Gazette* (West Virginia), March 20, 2005, p. P1E.

72 Singer, *Children at War*, 9.

73 Ibid., 5.

74 Ibid., 102.

75 Sarah Shannon, "The Global Sex Trade: Humans as the Ultimate Commodity," *Crime and Justice International* 17 (2001): 5–7.

76 Robert Meier and Gilbert Geis, *Victimless Crime? Prostitution, Drugs, Homosexuality, Abortion* (Los Angeles: Roxbury, 1997).

77 Alex Renton, "Learning the Thai Sex Trade," *Prospect* 110 (May 2005). Online at www.prospect-magazine.co.uk/article_details.php?id=6889.

78 Ibid.

Glossary

A

adjudicate To arrive at a judicial decision. To pass judgment.

adjudicatory hearing The hearing in which a determination is made regarding whether the juvenile committed the offense with which he or she is charged.

adolescence The period between puberty and adulthood in human development that typically falls between the ages of 13 and 19.

adolescence-limited offender In life-course criminological theory, youths who engage in antisocial and deviant behavior for only a short period of time and only in certain situations.

adolescent egocentrism The belief common to many adolescents that they are the focus of attention in social situations.

aging out In juvenile justice, reaching the age at which the system no longer serves a person, usually age 18.

androgen A general term for male hormones.

anomie A condition in which people or society undergo a breakdown of social norms and values. Also, personal anxiety and isolation produced by rapidly shifting moral and cultural values.

apartheid An official policy of racial segregation involving political, legal, and economic discrimination against nonwhites.

arrest rate The number of arrests made in a given year divided by population, to produce a measure that can be compared to other jurisdictions.

ascertainable criteria In peacemaking criminology, the concept that the language and procedures used to pursue justice must be made clear to all.

atavism The appearance in a person of features thought to be from earlier stages of human evolution.

B

behaviorism A field of psychology that focuses on the study of behavior that is observed.

beyond a reasonable doubt The state of being as convinced as possible of a fact.

biosocial theory The study of the effects of Darwinian evolution on brain structure and human behavior.

binge drinking A pattern of consuming alcohol that brings a person's blood alcohol concentration to 0.08 gram percent or above.[1]

blended sentencing A sentence that combines a juvenile disposition with the possibility of a criminal sentence, or a criminal conviction with a "last chance" at a juvenile disposition and treatment.

boot camp prison A short-term prison, usually for young offenders, that employs military boot camp training and discipline techniques for rehabilitation.

bourgeoisie In Marxist theory, those who own property and the means of production.

broken-windows This perspective states that aggressively pursuing minor offenses and offenders prevents neighborhoods from deteriorating into major crime.

bullying The psychological or physical victimization of youths by other youths.

C

capitalism An economic system characterized by the private or corporate ownership of production and distribution; the prices and production of goods are determined by competition in a market.

categorical imperative In peacemaking criminology, the concept that a system of justice must treat cases with similar characteristics consistently if the system is to be perceived as fair and impartial.

causality The relationship between an event and a following event.

Cesare Lombroso An Italian physician who developed a theory of criminal behavior based on offenders' physical characteristics.

child neglect According to criminologist Harvey Wallace: "The negligent treatment or maltreatment of a child by a parent or caretaker under circumstances indicating harm or threatened harm to the child's health or welfare."

child savers People at the end of the 19th century who were instrumental in creating special justice institutions to deal with juvenile delinquents and troubled youths.

classical school of criminology A school of thought that employs the idea of free will to explain criminal behavior.

clearance by exceptional means A special condition used by law enforcement to generate a clearance in the case of an offender who cannot be formally charged and prosecuted.

clearance rate The number of offenses cleared or "solved" by at least one offender being arrested, charged, and prosecuted.

---

[1]National Institute on Alcohol Abuse and Alcoholism, "NIAAA Council Approves Definition of Binge Drinking," *NIAAA Newsletter* no. 3 (2004): 3. Online at pubs.niaaa.nih.gov/publications/Newsletter/winter2004/Newsletter_Number3.pdf.

clique Any small, exclusive group of people that controls how and if others may join.

cohort A set of people who share a particular statistical or demographic characteristic.

collective efficacy A group's shared belief of the extent to which the group can successfully complete a task.

communism A system of social organization in which the ownership of property is ascribed to the community or to the state.

consent The voluntary agreement by a person of age or with requisite intelligence who is not under duress or coercion and who understands the proposition to which he or she is agreeing.

corporal punishment The infliction of physical harm on a person who has broken a rule or committed an offense.

correct means In peacemaking criminology, the concept that the process of arriving at justice must be done in a just manner.

crack cocaine A highly addictive form of cocaine that is processed into a crystal that can be smoked.

crime A violation of a law in which a person or persons are harmed.

critical race theory A theory that asserts that race is central to law and social justice issues.

culpability Blameworthiness. The moral state of being wrong, improper, or injurious.

cultural criminology A theory that explores the relationships among culture, media institutions, crime, and social control.

D

dark figure of crime A term used to describe crime that goes unreported to police and criminal justice officials and is never quantified.

decriminalize To remove the legal penalties from a prohibited activity.

death penalty A punishment in which the offender is sentenced to death. Also called *capital punishment.*

decriminalize To remove the legal penalties from a prohibited activity.

defensible space The philosophy of creating living and working spaces that are secure by design.

delinquent See *juvenile delinquent.*

demographics The study of the characteristics of human populations.

dependent A term describing the status of a child who needs court protection and assistance because his or her health or welfare is endangered due to the parent's or guardian's inability to provide proper care and supervision.

detention The temporary care of a child alleged to be delinquent who requires secure custody in physically restricting facilities pending court disposition or execution of a court order.

determinism The philosophical doctrine that human action is determined by external forces and is not a result of free will.

deterrence The control of behavior through the fear of consequences.

deviant Differing from a norm or from the standards of a society.

deviant Differing from a norm or from the standards of a society.

differential association theory A theory by Edwin Sutherland that states that crime is learned.

differential reinforcement The rewarding of one behavior and not another, or the rewarding of one behavior and punishment of another.

direct filing A process by which the prosecutor has the discretion to send a juvenile to criminal court.

direct filing A process by which the prosecutor has the discretion to send a juvenile to criminal court.

discretion The power of a legal authority to decide what to do at any given point in the justice process.

disposition The final determination of a case or other matter by a court or other judicial entity.

dispositional hearing The hearing in which the juvenile court renders judgment and specifies what should be done with the juvenile.

DNA (deoxyribonucleic acid) The substance inside a cell nucleus that carries the instructions for making living organisms.

E

ego In Sigmund Freud's theory of the human psyche, the ego is the conscious part of the personality which one typically identifies as "self," and which mediates between the pleasurable drives of the id and the moral demands of the superego.

electronic monitoring The use of an electronic device, usually one that the offender wears, to monitor an offender's location and activities.

emotional neglect From criminologist Harvey Wallace: "Acts or omissions of acts that are judged by community standards and professional expertise to be psychologically damaging to the child."

ethnocentrism The belief in the natural superiority of one's particular ethnic group or culture.

eugenics The idea that humans can be improved by controlled breeding.

evolution A gradual process in which the genetic composition of a population changes over many generations as natural selection acts on the genes of individuals.

F

false consciousness In Marxist theory, the belief that the arrangement of the bourgeoisie owning the means of production and the proletariat working for the interests of the bourgeoisie is legitimate.

fetal alcohol syndrome (FAS) The National Institutes of Health defines this condition as a pattern of mental and physical birth abnormalities found in some children of mothers who drank excessively during pregnancy.

fraternal twins Siblings produced by the simultaneous fertilization of two egg cells; the twins are only as genetically similar as regular siblings.

free will The ability or discretion to make choices that are unaffected by agencies such as fate or divine will.

G

gateway drug A term to describe less-harmful substances that are believed to lead to abuse of more-harmful substances.

gateway drug A term to describe less-harmful substances that are believed to lead to abuse of more-harmful substances.

GED (general education diploma) A document that certifies that a student has passed a high school equivalency test.

gender The characteristics attributed and accorded to males and females by society and/or culture on the basis of sex.

general deterrence A method of control in which the punishment of a single offender sets an example for the rest of society.

generalizability The degree to which the results of an individual study or investigation sample can be applied to other studies and samples.

generation All of the children in a society who are at about the same stage in their lives. Generations are about 20 years apart.

genes Short lengths of DNA that determine the inherited characteristics that distinguish individuals.

globalism The philosophy or act of placing the interests of the world above those of individual nations.

globalization Extensive economic relationships among nations.

greedy institution A formal or informal group or organization that demands undivided loyalty from its members.

guardian *ad litem* A person appointed by the court to take legal action on behalf of a juvenile or an adult who, because of minor age or infirmity, is unable to manage his or her own affairs.

H

Hawthorne effect The tendency of research subjects to act differently than they normally would as a result of their awareness of being studied.

hearing A session that takes place without a jury before a judge or magistrate in which evidence and/or argument is presented to determine some factual or legal issue.

hedonistic calculus The idea that potential offenders plan their actions in order to maximize pleasure and minimize pain.

heredity The handing down of traits from parents to their offspring.

heterogeneity The quality of consisting of dissimilar elements or parts.

home confinement A sentence that requires that the offender be confined in and around the area of his or her home.

house of refuge An early form of the reformatory during the mid- to late 19th century that housed impoverished children, juvenile delinquents, and status offenders.

hypothesis An untested idea set forth to explain a given fact or phenomenon. An educated guess.

I

id In Sigmund Freud's theory of the human psyche, the id represents the most primitive, irrational instincts and is controlled by the pleasure principle.

identical twins Siblings produced by the division of a single fertilized egg cell and who are genetically identical.

impulsivity The tendency to act quickly without considering the consequences.

incorrigible Unruly. Resisting correction, rehabilitation, or punishment.

indictment A formal written statement that charges a person or persons with a serious offense, usually a felony.

institutionalization The loss of the ability to make decisions for oneself because of the long period of time spent in a secure facility.

intelligence quotient (IQ) A measure of intelligence as indicated by an intelligence test, usually the ratio of mental age to chronological age.

intensive-supervision probation Close, controlled tracking of a probationer's activities by a probation officer or team of officers.

J

juvenile An age-related status that has legal ramifications. The United States legal system generally considers anyone under 18 years of age a juvenile.

juvenile boot camp A short-term prison for juvenile delinquents and young offenders that uses military boot-camp techniques for rehabilitation.

juvenile delinquency A legal term describing the behavior of a youth that is marked by violation of the law and anti-social behavior.

juvenile delinquent A person, usually under the age of 18, who is determined to have broken the law or committed a status offense in states in which a minor is declared to lack responsibility and who may not be sentenced as an adult.

juvenile waiver The process of sending a juvenile to be tried in criminal court.

K

knowledge model of drug-use prevention The idea that educating individuals about the potential harms of substance use will stop them from using substances.

L

labeling theory A theory that describes how a label applied by society can affect an individual's self-perception and behavior.

larceny-theft The completed or attempted taking of property or cash without the owner's consent.

left realism A theory suggesting that mainstream criminology underestimates the victimization of the poor and women; it is concerned with why the poor commit offenses mainly against one another.

legalize To make an illegal activity legal.

lex talionis A law of retribution and/or retaliation in which an item is taken to make up for an item that has been wrongfully taken or destroyed.

life-course-persistent offender In life-course criminological theory, an offender who begins inappropriate behavior at an early age and continues to commit antisocial and deviant acts.

longitudinal study A type of study or survey in which the same subjects are observed over a long period of time.

M

metacognition The act of thinking about one's processes and means of thinking.

methamphetamine A white, odorless, crystalline powder that stimulates the central nervous system.

Miranda rights The rules concerning arrest and police interrogation that stem from the 1966 criminal case *Miranda v. Arizona.*

N

National Incident-Based Reporting System A crime reporting system in which each separate offense in a crime is described, including data describing the offender(s), victim(s), and property.

negative reinforcement Avoidance of painful or stressful conditions or events.

net-widening Measures that bring more offenders and individuals into the justice system or cause those already in the system to become more involved.

neurotransmitter A chemical that transmits information between neurons.

No Child Left Behind Act of 2001 A federal law passed in January 2002 that seeks to improve the performance of K–12 schools.

nonorganic failure-to-thrive (NFTT) A medical term that describes an infant or child who has a measurable lag in height, head size, and/or development caused by environmental factors rather than an illness or disorder.

nonsecure detention Placement of a juvenile in a group home, foster care, or other program in which the juvenile may come and go with permission.

O

operant conditioning A form of learning based on the positive or negative consequences of an action.

orphan trains A term that encompasses the practice of 19th- and early 20th-century child-welfare societies of placing orphans, impoverished children, and young adults on trains to less populated parts of the United States, primarily the West.

P

pains of imprisonment Deprivations that define the punishment aspect of incarceration.

parens patriae Latin for "father of his country." Refers to the philosophy that the government is the ultimate guardian of all children and disabled adults.

patriarchy A social system in which males have authority and fathers are considered the absolute head of the family.

peacemaking criminology An idea that considers the social and personal effect of crime as a whole: not only the offender and victim, but also the social structure that accepts, enables, or encourages the offense.

peer relationships The connections among those of equal standing within a group.

performance-enhancing drugs Substances typically taken by athletes to increase power, endurance, or strength.

performance-enhancing drugs Substances typically taken by athletes to increase power, endurance, or strength.

per se requirement The legal requirement that an arrested juvenile consult with a parent, guardian, or other "interested adult," before or during interrogation, in order to waive Miranda rights.

petition In juvenile court, a document that alleges that a juvenile is delinquent and that asks the court to assume jurisdiction over the juvenile or asks that an alleged delinquent be waived to criminal court to be prosecuted as an adult.

phrenology The outdated study of the skull as an indicator of personality.

physical child abuse According to criminologist Harvey Wallace: "Any act that results in a nonaccidental physical injury by a person who has care, custody, or control of a child."

plea bargain A negotiation in which the defendant agrees to plead guilty or no contest to some offenses in return for some accession to the defendant.

positivist school of criminology A school of thought that considers the causes of crime and delinquency to be external to the offender and uses scientific techniques to study crime.

postmodern criminology In criminology, a theory that considers justice, law, fairness, responsibility, and authority not to be absolute, but to be mediated by personal contexts.

predispositional report A report prepared by a probation officer to assist the judge in designing an appropriate disposition.

preliminary hearing The initial preadjudicatory hearing in which the judge explores the nature of the case and decides if it should be processed further.

preponderance of evidence A standard of proof that is satisfied if it is determined that there is at least a 51 percent chance that a proposition is true.

presentism A belief that people of an earlier time should be accountable to the standards of the present time.

primary deviance A term from labeling theory that describes the label that society places on the offender.

primary group A small social group whose members share personal, enduring relationships.

primogeniture A system of inheritance in which the oldest son receives the entire estate.

probable cause Sufficient reason for a police officer to believe an offense has been committed; probable cause must exist for an officer to arrest (or take into custody) without a warrant, search without a warrant, or seize property.

probation The conditional release of juveniles to the custody of parents or guardians.

proletariat In Marxist theory, the working class.

pseudofamilies The groups that females in adult and juvenile institutions form in response to the pains of imprisonment; they act out the roles of father, mother, and children.

psychopath A person with a personality disorder who behaves without remorse or caring for others.

public defender An elected or appointed attorney who regularly defends those accused of criminal offenses who cannot afford a private attorney.

R

rational choice theory A perspective that holds that people consciously choose to break the law.

reasonable suspicion Doubt that is based on specific facts or circumstances and that justifies stopping and sometimes searching an adult or juvenile thought to be involved in criminal activity or, in the case of a juvenile, a status offense.

recidivism Continuing to commit delinquent or criminal offenses after being convicted and sentenced for prior offenses.

reintegrative shaming A form of justice in which an offender is confronted and dealt with by those in his or her social network.

restitution Court-ordered compensation by the offender to the victim(s) for their psychological, physical, or financial losses resulting from an offense.

restorative justice An alternative justice model that uses community programs to repair the harm done by crime and attempts to craft long-lasting and satisfying solutions to the problems of crime.

routine activities theory A theory that states that three conditions must be addressed in order to eliminate crime: motivated offenders, targets of opportunity, and ineffective guardianship.

S

school bonding The connection that students have to school and their academic work.

school-to-prison pipeline A phenomenon in which children leave school or are expelled be-cause of inappropriate behavior and poor academic performance and turn to law-breaking which eventually leads to incarceration.

scientific method The rules for the systematic pursuit of knowledge, typically the recognition and formulation of a problem; the collection of data through observation and experimentation; the formulation and testing of hypotheses; and the formulation of a conclusion.

secondary deviance A term from labeling theory that describes the labels that individuals internalize and come to believe as accurate.

sex The biological designation of male or female.

shaming The act of applying a mark or stigma on disgraced individuals.

shock deterrence The practice of subjecting minor offenders, often juveniles, to an alarming experience with the justice system in order to convince them to obey the law.

shock incarceration The practice of sentencing offenders to a long period of incarceration and then granting them probation after a short time without their prior knowledge.

snowball sample A method of field research in which information is gathered by asking each person interviewed to suggest additional people for interviewing.

social cohesion A condition in which the majority of a given society's citizens respect the law and are committed to social order.

social control The framework of rules and customs that a society collectively applies to the individuals within it to maintain order.

social ecology The study of the relationships among people, their behavior, their social groups, and their environment.

socialization The process by which people learn the norms, values, and culture of their society.

social learning theory The idea that people learn behaviors by watching other people and mimicking interactions that are rewarded and avoiding those that are punished.

social location An individual's class, race, sex, and age.

sociological imagination The idea that one must look beyond the obvious to evaluate how social location influences how one considers society.

special conditions of probation Requirements of a person on probation that apply specifically to that person.

specific deterrence A method of control in which an offender is prevented from committing additional offenses by either incarceration or death.

spiritual explanations Explanations for crime and deviance that stem from religious belief.

standard conditions of probation Requirements of a person on probation that apply to all probationers, regardless of individual needs or offense.

station adjustment Handling and release of a juvenile delinquent within a police department.

status offense An act considered to be a legal offense only when committed by a juvenile; it can be adjudicated only in a juvenile court.

statutory exclusion The legal requirement that certain offenses committed by juveniles automatically be waived to criminal court without a juvenile court hearing.

strain theory The idea that juvenile delinquency is at least partially a result of being excluded from economic rewards.

street crime Common violent and property offenses.

superego In Sigmund Freud's theory of the human psyche, the superego internalizes the values and standards of society and represents morality.

symbolic assailant The mental picture that many people have of criminal offenders.

T

target-hardening Making a focus of crime or delinquency as difficult as possible for potential offenders to access.

techniques of neutralization A theory that describes how some youths who break the law use rationalizations to explain away their deviant behavior.

theory A set of interconnected statements or propositions that explain how two or more events or factors are related to one another. (Daniel J. Curran and Claire M. Renzetti, *Theories of Crime,* 2nd ed., Boston: Allyn and Bacon, 2001, p. 2.)

totality of circumstances The consideration by the court of all the conditions surrounding an issue, such as police interrogation or juvenile consent to a search or interrogation.

tracking Educational paths that schools use to group students into classes with other students who have similar needs.

typology A systematic classification of types.

U–Z

Uniform Crime Reports An annual publication by the Federal Bureau of Investigation that uses data from all participating US law enforcement agencies to summarize the incidence and rate of reported crime.

war on crime The philosophy that the prevention of crime and treatment of offenders should be fought as a nation would fight a war, with similar tactics and strategies, and the idea of an enemy.

zero-tolerance policies School regulations that give teachers and administrators little to no discretion in dealing with rule infractions.